ORACLE®

Oracle Press™

Advanced Tuning for JD Edwards EnterpriseOne Implementations

This book is dedicated to our friends and family, whose support made this effort possible.

About the Authors

Michael Jacot (Senior Principal Consultant, Oracle Consulting) has more than 13 years of experience working with JD Edwards clients all over the world. Michael is currently a Senior Principal Consultant for Oracle Consulting Services. In this role, he assists clients in the design, setup, and tuning of advanced technical architectures. These efforts have provided him with experience on multiple platforms (Windows, HP, Sun, AIX, Linux) and databases. Michael has had the unique opportunity to assist Oracle clients with specialized tuning to meet their JD Edwards business requirements.

Allen Jacot (Director of Technology, Capscient) has more than a decade of JD Edwards EnterpriseOne implementation experience and worked with the product since its original base release in 1996. Allen currently serves as the Directory of Technology at Capscient. During his career, he has had the opportunity to design, implement, and tune implementations for small to very large/complex projects. This experience has provided Allen with a unique view into what it takes to design, configure, and maintain a system over the life span of an implementation. This holistic view has assisted Allen in provided unmatched support to his client base.

Frank Jordan (Director JD Edwards Technology Consulting, ERP Suites) has more than 30 years of experience in technology, ranging from implementing JD Edwards EnterpriseOne client/server systems, IBM iSeries and mainframe application systems, to software installation, performance tuning, database installation/administration, technology assessments, and project management. He has worked with the JD Edwards EnterpriseOne CNC technology since 1996 from the first release. He has been involved in all technology phases of a project life cycle from a customer and consulting perspective. He has experience working with all supported JD Edwards EnterpriseOne operating systems and databases. Frank has assisted more than 250 small to large customer accounts in a variety of technology engagements. Frank currently works for ERP Suites as a Director of JD Edwards Technology Consulting. He previously worked for Oracle Corporation as a Consulting Technical manager for more than 12 years. He enjoys spending time with his wife, Angela, and two daughters, Hally and Hunter, with their various activities. One of his hobbies involves creating computerized animated lighting shows at his home for the Halloween and Christmas seasons.

Gurbinder Bali (Senior Manager, Oracle Development) currently serves as the Senior Manager of the Foundation Tools Development Team at Oracle in Denver, Colorado. Gurbinder is an industry-leading developer with more than 11 years of experiences with the JD Edwards application set and was one of the founding team members that built the web-based architecture utilized in the JD Edwards application today. During the course of his career, Gurbinder has accumulated extensive performance-tuning expertise. Gurbinder and his team assist large customers with problem diagnosis and isolation in complex computing environments. This has provided Gurbinder a unique multifaceted view of performance issues from the operating system level, the database level, and the JD Edwards kernel/application level. It is this experience that has made Gurbinder Bali an industry leader.

Patrick Scott (Senior Developer, Oracle Development) has experienced a wide and varied career that has exposed him to many of the components required for effective performance tuning. In his career, Pat has been a Unix administrator, a JD Edwards field consultant, and a developer. This wide breadth of experience and Pat's 12 years of experience with the JD Edwards product line has given him a unique set of skills to assist clients in performance tuning in a multilevel approach. Pat brings his expertise with Unix operating systems and the Oracle database to bear to assist clients in meeting their performance requirements.

Kyle Kinder (Software Engineer, Oracle Development) has worked in the computer software industry for more than 15 years. His jobs have included customer support, training, documentation, management, and software engineering. Currently he works as a support software engineer for the Oracle JD Edwards EnterpriseOne product line. He specializes in backend technologies for web-based applications.

About the Technical Editor

Scott Watson has more than 14 years of information technology experience with ERP systems and financial software. For more than 11 of those years, he has provided CNC support for JD Edwards EnterpriseOne. During this time, Scott has been involved with a variety of projects, including installations, upgrades, disaster recovery configurations, architecting high availability solutions, and general support for a number of clients in a variety of industries. These projects have included all releases from Xe to 9.1 on Unix, AS/400, and Windows platforms. To complement his experience, Scott has a Masters degree in Computer Information Systems from the University of Denver and a B.S. in Financial Accounting from Colorado State University.

ORACLE®

Oracle Press™

Advanced Tuning for JD Edwards EnterpriseOne Implementations

Michael Jacot
Allen Jacot
Frank Jordan
Gurbinder Bali
Patrick Scott
Kyle Kinder

Mc Graw Hill Education

New York   Chicago   San Francisco   Athens
London   Madrid   Mexico City   Milan
New Delhi   Singapore   Sydney   Toronto

Cataloging-in-Publication Data is on file with the Library of Congress

McGraw-Hill Education books are available at special quantity discounts to use as premiums and sales promotions, or for use in corporate training programs. To contact a representative, please visit the Contact Us pages at www.mhprofessional.com.

Advanced Tuning for JD Edwards EnterpriseOne Implementations

1234567890   DOC DOC   109876543

ISBN   978-0-07-179854-9
MHID   0-07-179854-4

Sponsoring Editor Paul Carlstroem	**Technical Editor** Scott Watson	**Composition** Cenveo Publisher Services
Editorial Supervisor Janet Walden	**Copy Editor** Lisa Theobald	**Illustration** Cenveo Publisher Services
Project Manager Harleen Chopra, Cenveo® Publisher Services	**Proofreader** Paul Tyler	**Art Director, Cover** Jeff Weeks
Acquisitions Coordinator Amanda Russell	**Indexer** Jack Lewis	**Cover Designer** Pattie Lee
	Production Supervisor James Kussow	

Contents

Foreword

For more than 25 years, JD Edwards ERP software has set the standard for quality enterprise software from its home deep in the Colorado Front Range. Applications Release 9.1 and its foundation Tools Release 9.1 are the latest exciting releases that continue this tradition. Of course, there are plenty of new technical- and business-level features, but what is capturing the imagination of the market is a revolutionary user interface that's key in delivering new levels of user experience and performance. New customers are amazed by the innovation found inside an Enterprise Resource Planning (ERP) solution, while existing customers are not only seeing their customary high expectations being met, but are surprised that the current release exceeds those expectations beyond what they believed possible only a few years ago.

Customers who implement JD Edwards Application Release 9.1 along with its Tools release counterpart will find that the wealth of cutting-edge features are well harmonized to improve customers' overall business experience and performance. The new user interaction patterns are designed to make business processes faster and information easier to access. For example, the One View Reporting feature, powered by Oracle BI Publisher technology, puts new reporting options in the hands of end users, making the analysis of your business data easy and useful. Also, JD Edwards Application Release 9.1 continues to provide more detailed vertical functionality for key industries such as consumer goods, real estate management, manufacturing, and distribution.

Business keeps changing, and JD Edwards changes with it. The software you know will always be there to make your business life easier. New features will continue to be included to allow you to do more with less. More technologies will be supported to allow you to adapt to the needs of the future. JD Edwards will continue to make the business of your business better.

Over the life of the JD Edwards product, several books and papers have been written covering a number of topics in the software; however, a reference dedicated to performance tuning for JD Edwards has been missing. This book fills that void in covering performance strategies and techniques for tuning the different layers of the JD Edwards system and allowing them to perform at the highest level. Within the pages of this book, you will find a wealth of information to improve your JD Edwards experience. Whether you want to tune your database, optimize your enterprise server, or implement clustered web servers, you'll find the information you need here. For example, if you want to use JD Edwards EnterpriseOne software to seize the initiative on the forefront of the mobile device revolution, start with this book. I encourage you to read on, whether you are looking to explore the art of the possible or you are just seeking to understand best practices in JD Edwards EnterpriseOne performance tuning. In the end, of course, it is about moving at the speed of business, and you'll find this reference an incredible beginning to the process of improving the speed and success of your business.

Lyle Ekdahl
Group Vice President, Oracle JD Edwards

Acknowledgments

Without the amazing efforts of the following people we would have been unable to complete this book effort: Michael Guerra, Mike Malone, Dave Anderson, Paul Reynolds, Brian Lundberg, Charles Barber, Mike Herandez, and Duncan Mills.

Introduction

This book will provide tools to leverage a structured methodology to measure the performance of implementations and deliver on key service level agreements. It has been written with the following readers in mind:

- Technical managers or consultants responsible for JD Edwards implementations
- Database administrators who want to gain a better understanding of the components used to tune an ERP solution

Chapter 1: Outline of a Structured Tuning Methodology

This chapter provides a glimpse into a structured tuning methodology for ERP implementations. We will acquaint you with the high-level components of the tuning process and outline the bones of the overall performance practices. We provide a view of how you can apply these concepts to the layers of an ERP implementation. This chapter identifies and presents an overview of the major components/layers and strategies that affect performance.

Chapter 2: Understanding the Components of Performance Tuning

Ask an experienced JD Edwards system administrator what worries him or her, and the answer you will most likely get is "the small things." When things really go wrong, it seems to be traceable back to one small item. Keep this in mind when you approach tuning. The system needs to behave like an orchestra. If one instrument is out of tune, it can ruin a masterpiece.

Of course, people have different listening ability. The same is true with performance tuning. This chapter continues to provide more in-depth detail about the components of the methodology and how to tune your implementation effectively.

Chapter 3: Building Blocks of an EnterpriseOne Implementation

Oracle JD Edwards EnterpriseOne supports a wide range of database and hardware platforms. The fundamental building blocks needed to use EnterpriseOne are fairly consistent across implementations. You must have certain servers and services in place to provide the needed functionality to support the EnterpriseOne applications along with other software in the ecosystem. This chapter gives you a view into these key building blocks.

Chapter 4: Implementing a Performance Tuning Methodology

The proper tuning of an ERP system is a complex, ongoing process that can be affected by myriad factors. This chapter takes a detailed look into a structured methodology, or "playbook," for system administrators looking to tune their implementations.

Chapter 5: Understanding Base EnterpriseOne Technical Architecture

This chapter presents an overview of the EnterpriseOne architecture design and functional components. The EnterpriseOne process flow is discussed and key network and kernel processes are defined. The chapter then presents a number of points regarding how to improve the processes, procedures, tuning, and configuration of your EnterpriseOne implementation.

Chapter 6: Tuning by Tier: The Web Tier

In this chapter, we go in depth with performance tuning of the web tier for JD Edwards EnterpriseOne. We look at tuning the different layers in the web tier, such as HTTP Server, WebLogic- and WebSphere-specific settings, as well as a few of the critical jas.ini, jdbj.ini, and jdelog.properties settings.

Chapter 7: Tuning by Tier: The Foundation Tier

This chapter covers the JD Edwards EnterpriseOne Foundation tier, which includes database connections, SQL Packages, JDENET, and JD Edwards kernels. Understanding the underlying technology of these components is the key to tuning them. Advanced troubleshooting techniques are explored, which will assist you in performance tuning.

Chapter 8: Tuning by Tier: The Database Tier (Oracle)

Oracle JD Edwards EnterpriseOne supports a wide range of database and hardware platforms. The database is the fundamental building block needed to utilize JD Edwards EnterpriseOne and a critical element of the infrastructure. We liken it to the heart of the system, which if it beats strong and regular, the body works well. If not, you have a number of other areas of the body that become negatively affected or even die. Without an effectively performing and sized database server the majority of the JD Edwards EnterpriseOne application operations will be negatively affected. This chapter focuses on providing a detailed technique to assist you with performance tuning the Oracle database component of your implementation.

Chapter 9: Tuning by Tier: The Database Tier (Microsoft SQL Server and IMB System i)

The proper tuning of the database layer can dramatically affect the success of an implementation. This chapter provides a view into the tuning of a SQL or IBM System i database in an EnterpriseOne implementation. It addresses key points such as reviewing SQL logs, database configuration, and performance monitoring. Items like these will help to ensure that your database layer continues to runs efficiently.

Chapter 10: Tuning by Tier: The Interface Tier

The BSSV (Business Services Server) software solution gives clients the ability to extend business applications into a Services Oriented Architecture (SOA). BSSV provides the ability to expose native EnterpriseOne business services through web service standards. It delivers the capability to develop, publish, consume, and administer web services directly for JD Edwards EnterpriseOne tools. As you can imagine, this represents a powerful tool in a successful ERP implementation, and another component for the administrator to tune. This chapter covers the intricacies of tuning the interface tier. It reviews clustering the Business Services Server and transaction server and some of the new functionality associated with mobile applications

Chapter 11: Virtualization

This chapter concentrates on full hardware virtualization, which allows you to provide a standardize platform on which to deploy your architecture. Full virtualization completely separates the OS from the hardware layer, while paravirtualization is more hardware dependent. Virtualization can be used to deploy a fully configured workstation or server within just a few hours. Both solutions allow you to provide a standardized platform on which to deploy your architecture.

Chapter 12: Oracle Exadata Database Machine and Exalogic Elastic Cloud

The "Exa" revolution, as it has been dubbed by many in the computer industry, refers to a set of engineering solutions that couples software enhancements with the hardware to achieve a more integrated architecture. Exadata Database Machine and the Exalogic Elastic Cloud integrate hardware and software technologies together with EnterpriseOne and demonstrate what good scaling and performance can look like if many of the traditional limitations in IT technology are removed. This chapter discusses the technologies of Exadata Database Machine and the Exalogic Elastic Cloud.

Chapter 13: Load Balancing/Scalability Opportunities for EnterpriseOne

Oracle JD Edwards EnterpriseOne supports a wide range of database and hardware platforms that can scale both horizontally and vertically. If you scale horizontally, it typically means you are dividing the users or processes across several discrete servers or logical machines. This chapter provides a view into how you can leverage software or hardware load balancing solutions in your architecture to meet the availability goals of your business.

CHAPTER
1

Outline of a Structured
Tuning Methodology

To a technical person, it is truly an incredible feeling when a system performs flawlessly; this is especially true with an Enterprise Resource Planning (ERP) system. You might compare the feeling to listening to a symphony or the roar of a high-performance sports car thundering down the highway—the simple fact is that things are better when they work and work well.

As ERP systems continue to evolve, CEOs, CIOs, and system administrators will continue to push to get as much out of their implementations as they possibly can. Similar to a coach training professional athletes, a system administrator must have a solid execution plan to build, grow, and tune his or her implementations. Just as any athlete has to adapt to win, ERP implementations need to be able to meet ever-changing business requirements.

Tuning an ERP system is a complex process that can be affected by a myriad of factors. It can feel like a giant game of Jenga—modify one part of the system, and you can adversely affect other parts. Change the wrong part at the wrong time, and the whole system comes crashing down.

This book will provide a detailed methodology, or "playbook," for system administrators. The main thrust of this methodology is a structured way to break down performance problems into smaller parts, identify key bottleneck(s), implement change, and measure the performance effects of these changes. Once we have addressed the primary performance issues, we will expand the methodology to assist system administrators with benchmarking and boilerplating their systems.

NOTE
This chapter will review the major components involved in performance tuning an ERP implementation. It will provide a base outline of the low-level concepts that will be reviewed in detail in later chapters.

This chapter provides a glimpse into a structured tuning methodology. It will acquaint you with the high-level components of the tuning process and outline basic overall performance practices. It offers a view of how you can apply these concepts to the layers of an ERP implementation and provides an overview of the major components and technical pillars that can affect performance. Once the basics of the strategy have been detailed, you will learn more in-depth details about the components of the methodology and how they can be utilized to tune your implementation effectively.

Overview

That all sounds great, but how do you take full advantage of your system and ensure that it not only meets the needs of your business but grows with it?

As with any complex problem, it helps to break down an issue into smaller parts:

1. The first step is to define the performance problem adequately. Without first identifying your performance problem, you are basically flying blind.

2. Next, define the scope of your problem. Does the identified problem occur for one user or multiple users? Does the problem occur only under load? Can the problem be reproduced? By identifying the scope of the problem, you can start to define what it will take to resolve the issue.

3. Determine where the majority of the processing time is being spent. This will allow you to focus on the proper components of the implementation. You can think of these components as pillars of a Roman building. Performance bottlenecks can occur at any pillar, but by understanding how each interacts and applying a structured methodology, you can identify and resolve performance issues.

The high-level components, that is pillars, of an ERP system are:

- User interface

- EnterpriseOne foundation

- Interface

- Database

- Network

- Operating system/server

- Disk

Once you have established an awareness of the major components of the system, you can leverage this knowledge to isolate a performance issue. Think of this as first dividing an issue into major groups, then subgroups, and so on. Each of these components can have a major impact on the overall performance and stability of an implementation.

A performance bottleneck can exist in any of the major components. An administrator's primary goal is to identify where that bottleneck exists and remove it.

This process involves not only removing the bottleneck, but ensuring that the problem is not just moved from one part of the implementation to another. To identify and correct a performance issue, you must look at the problems at each pillar of the implementation. When a performance issue is encountered, you evaluate what pillar of the implementation needs your attention. To do this, a structured plan comes in handy.

After defining a performance problem, identifying the scope, and determining what components are causing performance issues, you need to be able to measure your successes or failures. To do this, you need to establish a *performance baseline* which determines what is considered acceptable versus unacceptable performance. If, for example, a process takes ten minutes, a 20 percent improvement might sound great, but it might not mean much if the true goal is to have the process run in less than a minute. Depending on the problem, you might have to leverage different measures: A long-running SQL query that needs to be tuned may take minutes, or a very quick part of the code that gets called thousands of times can be improved by reducing the number of calls to eliminate a bottleneck.

Next, you can take a first cut at tuning efforts at a high level; macro changes get the system into the ballpark of your performance goals. These changes are implemented at the layer of the implementation where the problem is occurring (such as database, disk, and so on) and are generally larger component changes. Of course, after each change, the system administrator(s) need to measure the impact of the change.

Once the major changes have been made, you can start moving into more micro tuning efforts. These types of efforts will allow you to identify and address reported performance issues. Micro changes are more directly focused on the identified issue rather than on general performance tuning settings. An example might be adding an index to a table to address a specific query that the business requires. Once applied, the identified business process can be benchmarked with the changes in place to provide an accurate measure of the change.

The application of a structured performance tuning methodology not only allows you to identify and address performance issues at the macro and micro levels, but it provides the structure to help you benchmark the process and start "boilerplating" major setting changes. This gives you more tools to address not only performance issues, but also common business drivers in your implementation.

Benchmarks

Now that we have provided an outline of the performance tuning methodology and some general examples of how to apply the methodology, you can begin to develop system benchmarks. This information will allow you to adjust your system to meet your changing business requirements. An example of this might be adding users to your implementation to meet increased business needs. If you apply the methodology, you will be able to identify an average number of users to leverage per Java Virtual Machine (JVM). Once you reach this number, you will know to increase the number of JVMs and/or adjust your kernel processes and other processes to allow for the additional users.

Along with identifying these general performance methods, you can encourage administrators to continue monitoring their systems. This helps create benchmarks for "good" versus "bad" performance. Benchmarking provides you with a feel for the system and helps you understand how changes affect the implementation. In addition, it provides a view of system utilization by the business over time. All of these items are essential to maintaining the performance and stability of your implementation.

Merits of Continuous Performance Tuning

Savvy clients invest large amounts of capital, time, and tears executing performance testing prior to moving into production. This is an important part of the successful rollout of any ERP implementation. But what happens after you go-live? Does that mean the performance of the system is assured and there is no more work to be done? Not likely—just as a professional athlete needs to continue to train, an effective system needs ongoing performance tuning efforts.

These types of efforts may encompass the following:

- Use of automated testing scripts: LoadRunner and Oracle Application Testing Suites (OATS). Identification of key business processes: order to cash, general ledger, and so on

- The ability to apply and measure load

- The ability to identify benchmarks for good/acceptable performance: database, CPU, memory and disk I/O

So what does all this buy?

- You know how much load your system can take.

- You can show the effects of changes to the system not only through general testing but also under load/stress conditions.

- You can effectively automate your testing processes to meet your business needs.

Business Drivers

Let's take a look at what types of business drivers can affect the performance of your implementation:

- Addition of new divisions

- Acquisition of new companies

- Increased business growth

- Migration of old systems to a new ERP solution

- New functionality rollout

Any of these items can affect how a system operates; it is a good practice and a recommended part of our performance methodology to develop general performance benchmarks to address these and other common issues. For example, you should know how many users access each JVM. After you exceed the threshold (around 85 users per JVM), you might need to add JVMs if you add new users to your system. This, in turn, will require more CPUs and memory. General performance benchmarks help you stay ahead of such requirements and ensure that you have sufficient resources to meet your systems' needs. This might mean simply knowing when to acquire more disks, or knowing when you need to ask the CIO for another server to accommodate the increased load on the system.

Automated Scripting/Server Manager

So with the new methodology and EnterpriseOne, everything comes ready to go out of the box, right? Not quite. Although you have the base functionality, you need to put your stamp on your implementation. A useful tool to help accomplish this is *scripting*. Different operating systems support different types of scripting, but the results are the same, improving the stability and performance of your system.

In EnterpriseOne, you can leverage scripting to perform a number of tasks:

- Manage temporary files.

- Clear log files.

- Capture key performance indicators (KPIs) such as disk I/O, CPU, and memory indicators.

- Produce alert messages to operations/support staff.

- Automate support tasks.

In addition to scripting, you can take advantage of the EnterpriseOne Server Manager application that is delivered as part of the standard code line. Server Manager can help to effectively identify areas in your implementation and monitor performance areas in your implementation such as the following:

■ Number of users attached to specific kernels (call object)

■ Number of outstanding requests on a kernel

■ Number of kernels defined

■ CPU

■ Memory

Conclusion

This chapter provided a high-level overview of a structured performance methodology to assist you not only in identifying and addressing performance issues, but also in allowing for the development and implementation of key industry practices and benchmarks. As you continue your journey through this book, we will provide more detail about each of the implementation pillars. It is our hope that you are able to leverage the information presented here to tune and maintain your ERP implementation effectively. May your system run flawlessly.

CHAPTER
2

Understanding the
Components of
Performance Tuning

Ask an experienced JD Edwards system administrator what worries him or her, and the answer you will most likely hear is, "the small things." When things go very wrong, it seems that the problem can often be traced back to one small item. Keep this in mind when you approach tuning. The system needs to behave like an orchestra: If one instrument is out of tune, it can ruin the entire symphony.

Of course, as with music, people have different listening abilities, and the same is true with performance tuning. You may be able to get the system to run even faster, but to do so, you might have to dedicate more time and resources than is reasonable for the return on your investment. As you review the components of performance tuning, ask yourself, "What does my organization really require?" This will help you avoid spending too much time and money without seeing an equitable return.

In this chapter, we cover many important concepts that can help you realize an equitable return on your investment of time, money, sweat, and tears:

- You'll learn how to create a performance tuning strategy, a plan to help you implement your performance tuning approach.

- You'll set the system boundaries, where you'll decide where, exactly, you declare success.

- You'll learn about the different operating systems that you may encounter. This information will help you to lock tasks into your strategy.

- You'll read about disk layout, which can directly affect system performance of the system. EnterpriseOne allows you to use multiple databases, so these must also tie into your performance strategy.

- General tuning levers are covered next. These "big" levers can influence performance across your system.

- You'll learn about setting up your network to help achieve the best performance with your EnterpriseOne system.

- You'll learn about direct application tuning, including changes that are common during performance tuning engagements.

Creating a Performance Tuning Strategy

An old friend of mine used to say, "Plan to plan or you plan to fail." This adage holds true for ensuring system performance as well as life in general. The first step is to understand that you need a performance tuning strategy. The next step is the actual planning of that strategy. To do this, you must ensure that you dedicate enough time to accomplish the required tasks and that you involve the appropriate people. You need to look at the pillars of your system to determine who needs to be in the room for any strategy session.

Here are the tiers of the implementation:

- System boundaries
- Operating system
- Operating system levels
- Patches for the operating system
- Disk considerations
- Database components
- General tuning levers
- Network
- Direct JD Edwards application tuning

A strategy session should occur during your implementation, but it can occur anytime, so don't panic if you don't have a formal strategy yet. Based on the tiers of the implementation just listed, you will need to include people with the appropriate skill sets in this session to help you produce a formal performance tuning strategy document.

Here are the required roles:

- JD Edwards system administrator/Configurable Network Computing (CNC)
- Database administrator
- Operating system engineer (infrastructure)
- Virtual machine administrator (such as VMware or Oracle VM)
- Network administrator
- Application server administrator (IBM WebSphere or Oracle WebLogic)
- Key business unit representatives
- Executive sponsor

Unless you define what constitutes acceptable performance, you can't really create a strategy for achieving it. You need metrics to measure what performance means to your business. These metrics will be different for each business, and all areas of the business are not equal.

We are sure some of you are wondering about including business unit representatives in a technical discussion. If you do not first identify what your organization's requirements are, you are wasting your time. These business unit representatives are usually the only ones who can give you the true detail of what is happening at the end user level for performance. We cannot tell you how many times we have been called when problems occur and a CIO or an IT director says the system is "slow." Our response is, "The sky is blue."

Performance metrics are real and can be measured by taking samples; this helps you to truly know how your system is performing, day-to-day and month-to-month. This type of information is extremely useful. It allows you to chart the impact of specific business cycles. For example, you can measure what performance looks like during open enrollment, at a quarter close, or at a year-end close.

If you are the IT director, performance metrics are critical when you need to justify the purchase of additional hardware to meet the business requirements. You can also establish a Service Level Agreement (SLA) with the business, so you can spend time tuning the system instead of trying to agree about what "slow" really means. If you cannot reach agreement on what this metric is up front, you are in for a difficult fight. Without defining what constitutes acceptable performance, you will never be able to say whether the system is fast or slow—everything will be subjective to each area.

How do you determine what to include in these metrics? A better question might be, What are the top five to eight reports and applications required for your business? Start with these and work from there. Find your top reports and applications, then determine which of these are not performing up to what the business expects. Reports are fairly simple: they normally need to be completed with a certain amount of data within a certain period of time. You'll need to take a closer look at the applications.

Consider a sales order entry application, for example. How do you determine the time it takes to complete a sales order? You start by breaking the process apart. First, determine what an average order is. Then break down the process so you can see where a slowdown in the process might occur. For example, measure how long it takes to open the application, then how long it takes for the add screen to come up, and then how long it takes to calculate everything on the line of an order, such as advanced pricing. This provides a baseline of details you'll need to determine whether a performance decrease or increase has occurred. It offers real data points, and quite a bit of data must be looked at. Later in this chapter, in the section, "Common Performance Tools," we'll discuss some of the tools you can use to collect this type of information.

System Boundaries

As systems have become more complex, the integrations have become real time, and bolt-on applications have become critical to the performance of the system. The business does not care that a specific screen affects another application that is maintained by a different team. But you should care, and it is critical that you determine the true boundaries of your system and create the metrics to measure it. This is also where having an executive sponsor for your tuning strategy comes in very handy.

To determine your system boundaries, examine your system architecture diagram and interface diagram (such as Figure 2-1). Identify where transactions "leave" the EnterpriseOne system. Say, for example, you are using EnterpriseOne Business Services to make a web services call to a third-party system. This call occurs at the end of a sales order process: a customer is on the phone or waiting at your company's web page for a customer self-service application to process an order.

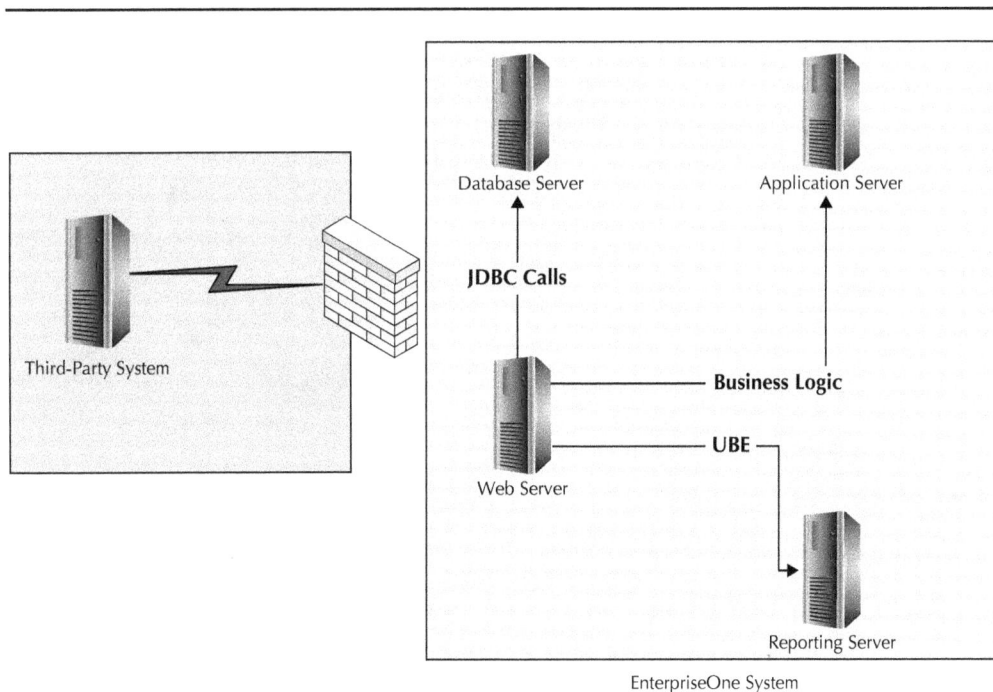

FIGURE 2-1.   *Example systems boundary diagram*

When determining the system boundaries in this scenario, you need to work with the other team that manages the third-party system as well, to track the metrics of how long it takes to send data to the system and receive the return. You'll also need to calculate how long it takes to handle erroneous data. Multiple performance issues can be tracked to bad error handling. Even though you do not own or manage the third-party system, the team that does manage it is smack-dab in the middle of a critical process for your business. So you need to create a metric for both systems—JD Edwards EnterpriseOne and the third-party system. This will let you know whether a performance problem is due to your EnterpriseOne system or whether you need to involve the other team.

Operating System

When it comes to performance tuning, our first stop is the operating system. One of the great strengths of JD Edwards EnterpriseOne is that it is platform-independent. Several different operating systems can be included in your architecture and the software can handle it without issue. This also means that from a performance tuning perspective, you need to be familiar with multiple operating systems.

All implementations will have two operating systems in their architecture: the development clients require one level of a Microsoft operating system and the servers require a different level, even if you are solely a Microsoft shop. If you are an i-Series (AS/400) or Linux shop, you have a few more operating systems to contend with.

Let's start this discussion by considering the different types of operating systems that you may have in your architecture:

- OS/400
- Linux
- Microsoft Windows
- Solaris
- IBM AIX
- HP-UX (Hewlett-Packard UniX)

NOTE
HP-UX support is not in place for version 9.1 currently. You should reference the Oracle Platform Statement of Direction, as Oracle has said it plans to support HP-UX Itanium. We mention this as there are customers running HP-UX.

OS/400

The OS/400 operating system ships with the I-Series. There are many different levels of this operating system. V5R4 has been around for a long time but is being deprecated with EnterpriseOne Tools 9.1, so customers will need to be using V6R1 or higher. The OS/400 has its own unique requirements to tune with regard to JD Edwards EnterpriseOne and requires an experienced system administrator.

Linux

Oracle has announced its Unbreakable Enterprise Kernel for Linux. To run Oracle virtual machines in your architecture, you'll need to be running this operating system. If you want to drop your support costs, Linux may be an operating system worth considering, because Oracle does not charge a large amount for support.

Microsoft Windows

Oracle supports several versions of Microsoft Windows. With Tools 9.1, you should be running 64-bit operating systems, which will help to ensure performance on the system. Your servers should be running Windows 2008 and your development workstations running Windows 7. You will need to be aware of the patches that come from Microsoft and ensure that you test against these patches.

Solaris is an operating system developed by Sun Microsystems. This operating system is very scalable and reliable. Oracle has continued support of this operating system after purchasing Sun.

AIX

AIX is the operating system for IBM's RS/6000. This operating system is a form of Unix. To ensure success, make sure that a member of your team is deeply familiar with this operating system.

HP-UX

Because of changes in its strategic direction, Oracle is discontinuing support of Hewlett-Packard UniX. As of Tools 9.1, Oracle was no longer testing, validating, or supporting HP-UX on HP PA RISC. If your system is currently running HP-UX, you should attempt to find a partner to help migrate your enterprise to one of the supported operating systems. Oracle has indicated its plans to support HP-UX on Itanium, but currently this is not validated for EnterpriseOne 9.1.

Operating System Levels

You can choose from among several different levels of operating systems and still be supported. As OS vendors move forward with new releases, Oracle will certify these releases against different tools releases and software releases. Oracle's product strategy team communicates which operating system levels they support and which will be decremented in the JD Edwards EnterpriseOne Platform "Statement of Direction."

This document can be found on Oracle's metalink site, at http://metalink3.oracle.com. It is important for your team to know which direction Oracle is going with regard to your OS.

NOTE
The JD Edwards EnterpriseOne Tools releases contain the code that handles the operating systems and databases. A developer in EnterpriseOne does not have to worry about what type of OS or database their report will be used against; the Tools release handles all of this. Each Tools release is aligned or certified with specific releases of the JD Edwards software. These applications and business logic deliver functionality to the end users. For example, you can run EnterpriseOne release 9.0 with Tools 9.1, or you can run EnterpriseOne release 9.1 with Tools 9.1, but you cannot run EnterpriseOne release 8.12 or below with Tools release 9.1.

You may be wondering how to choose which OS level you should run. This is a very valid and important consideration. The answer depends upon how you answer questions about several components: Where are you at in your implementation? Are you just planning now, in testing, or are you about to go live? It also depends upon how easily your organization can absorb testing and change.

If you are just starting your implementation, you should always try to aim for the latest version of the operating system, which will help to keep your system up-to-date and functioning correctly. Ensure that your third-party and bolt-on software can handle the new operating system as well; sometimes these vendors may lag behind on the certification of a new operating system.

Suppose, for example, that your system has been live for a while, and you are running V6R1 on an iSeries. How do you decide when it is time to move to V7? Although it's not as large as an implementation, the upgrade of an OS level in your JD Edwards EnterpriseOne architecture needs to be taken seriously. Before you undertake such a change, you need to plan for the change and dedicate the proper resources to the endeavor.

As for when you should do this, our advice is that you should always strive to keep your operating system and your EnterpriseOne software up-to-date. One way to accomplish this is to set aside some time and money biannually or annually to perform updates. This will ensure that you are using current software and will already have the resources set aside to help with the testing. When you are scoping out your project, don't forget to inform the CIO and CFO that you have set aside time and resources to keep your system up-to-date.

TIP
An automated testing tool such as the Oracle Automated Testing Suite (OATS) will help you test and reduce the level of effort required by your business to test new systems.

Patching the Operating System

When reviewing performance tuning, the operating system is a key component of your approach. If you do not maintain your operating system, your chances of experiencing performance issues in EnterpriseOne will increase significantly. No matter which supported operating system you are using with EnterpriseOne, it needs to be maintained.

Many operating systems are supported, including the following:

- iSeries

- Linux

- Solaris

- Windows 2008

We recommend that you patch your operating systems in a controlled manner and that you schedule time to install these patches. You can coordinate patch installations with the application of EnterpriseOne Tools releases, as support for new operating system levels come from these releases. This works well if the patch is significant.

You should develop a test script to be executed when applying operating system patches. The patches should be applied in a separate area that does not affect production—that is, your architecture should allow you to have production separated from development and prototyping to allow for isolated testing (see Figure 2-2). As a best practice, your architecture should support testing of operating system patches without affecting production.

Often, organizations with this type of separation can take a month to apply system patches to production after the patches have been installed in development and prototyping systems. This practice ensures that they run the system after patch installation for a full month. This helps to isolate issues and ensure production uptime.

If the customer has defined metrics to track performance, you can also gather data points on the effect, if any, of the operating system patch. This type of information can help to show where performance improves or drops off. To ensure accuracy, do not change too many variables at the same time.

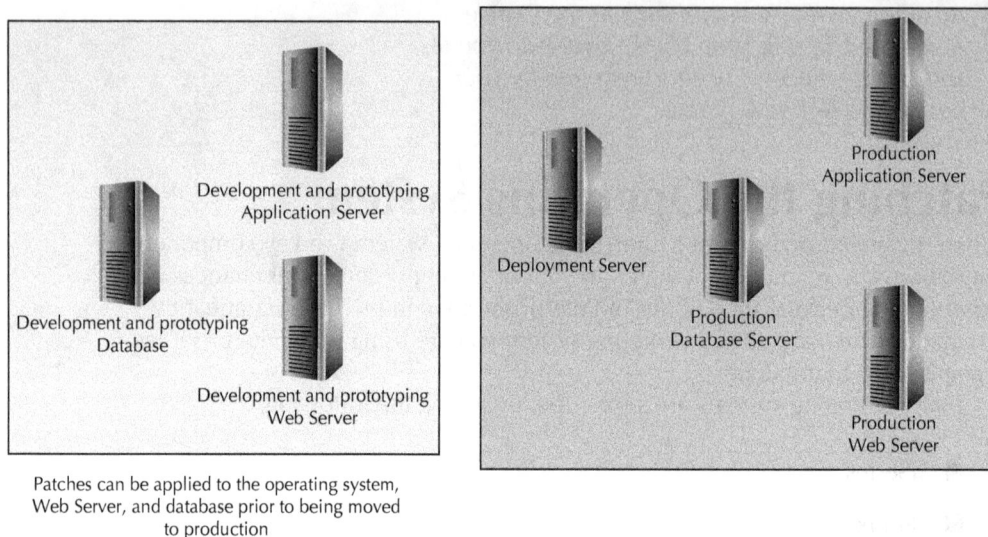

Patches can be applied to the operating system,
Web Server, and database prior to being moved
to production

FIGURE 2-2. *Architecture showing separation of development and prototyping from production*

TIP
Although, as an administrator, you may sometimes feel alone, you are not. You can take advantage of many message boards to gather information about how patches have affected other sites. You'll find such message boards on Oracle's web site www.oracle.com, the Quest user group web site www.questdirect.org, and the famous JDE List www.jdelist.com. Use these tools to help you; if others are having consistent issues on either operating system levels or patches, you can get support.

Disk Considerations

You don't expect a monster truck to go fast; you expect it to be powerful and have the ability to crush other cars. But when you look at a smaller racecar or sports car, you do expect it to be quick. In some ways, you can think of your disk in the same manner. For example, a slower disk is less expensive, but it can directly affect system performance.

When thinking about disk performance, you should consider the following:

- Disk speeds

- Disk layout

- Storage area network (SAN) versus network area storage (NAS) options

Disk Speeds

Most of your users will always feel the need for speed. To help your system perform, you must first analyze your disk speed requirements. You need to look at not only the speed of the disk, but the seek time on the arm. If you have fast disks with fast seek times, you should have very little disk latency in your system. This will allow for a faster overall system.

As with everything in life, there are compromises. The faster the disk, the more expensive it is. However, there is nothing to say you have to use the same disk across your entire system architecture. You can use a slower disk for the development and prototyping servers, for example.

Disk Layout

The layout of your disk also can greatly affect your performance. Layout means how many disk arms you have included in the architecture, as well as what kind of Redundant Array of Independent Disks (RAID) system you use in your system (see Figure 2-3). There are several different types of RAID:

- RAID 0

- RAID 1

- RAID 2

- RAID 3

- RAID 4

- RAID 5

The following information was gathered from professional experience as well as referencing Wikipedia (http://en.wikipedia.org/wiki/RAID).

RAID 0

RAID 0 is commonly *striped*, which means that the data is written across both disks, so there is no parity and thus no redundancy. So you may be asking yourself, Why on Earth would I ever use this type of configuration? The answer is speed.

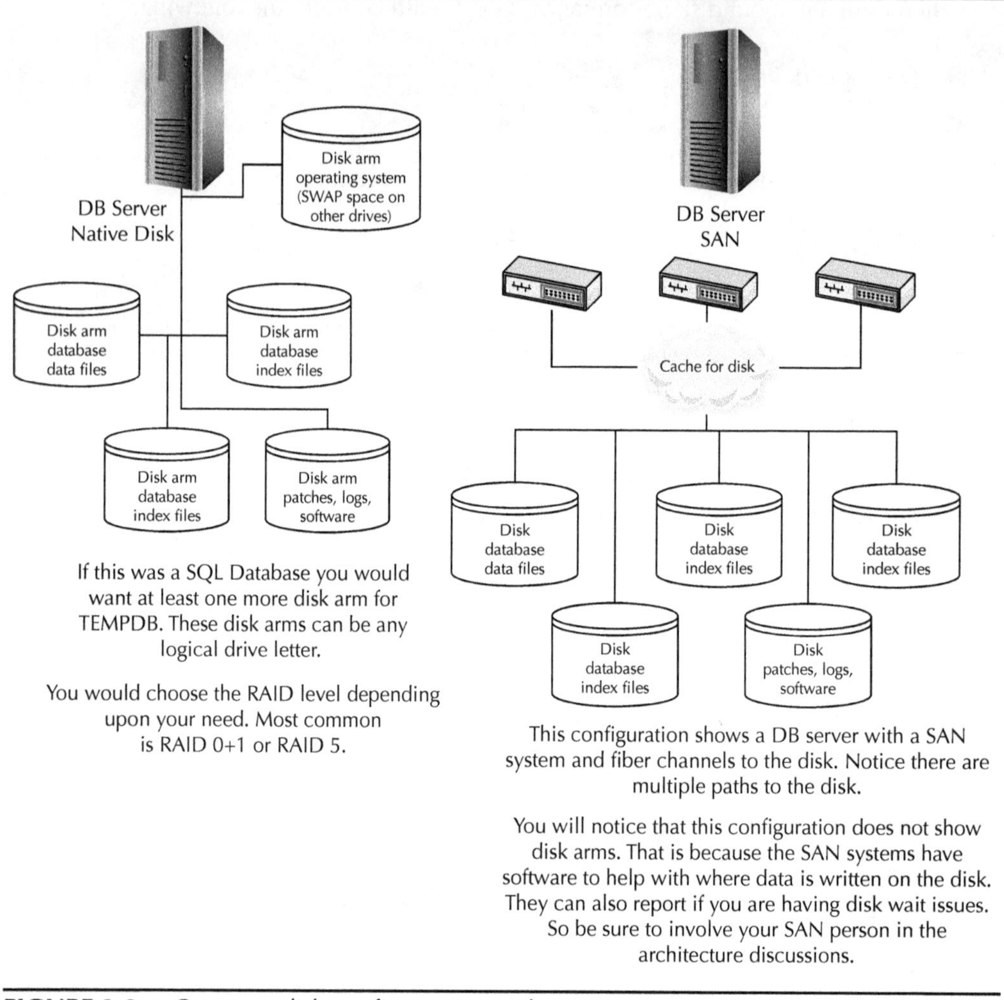

FIGURE 2-3. *Common disk configurations with EnterpriseOne*

When speed is more important than data integrity, RAID 0 is an option. An example is a drive that you use for temporary files only.

RAID 1

RAID 1 is a very common and simple configuration. In this case, the data is written to two disks identically. So the exact same data that is written to one disk will be written to the second disk, unlike RAID 0, where the data is striped and all the data is split across the disks. RAID 1 gives you some redundancy, meaning you can lose a disk and not lose all your data.

Because the same data is written to both disks at the same time, it takes longer in this configuration to write data to the disks. However, reading data is quick with this configuration. If you have operations that are read-specific, without lot writing, then RAID 1 may be the configuration for you. For example, RAID 1 may be appropriate if you have a database that is used only for reporting and is read-only.

RAID 2
RAID 2 is not really relevant anymore with the advance of disk technology. This configuration consisted of striping data at the bit rather than block level. It used Hamming code for error correction, which allowed for single-bit corruption recovery. However, as disk technology advanced, the Hamming code was implemented directly onto the hard disks.

RAID 3
This technology has striping with parity on a dedicated disk. We have not really experienced RAID 3 in use in the real world. This is probably because all activity on the disks need synchronized disk arms. This obviously has an effect on performance of the disk and thus the system.

RAID 4
RAID 4 is a little different from the others because it also uses striping across the disks with a separate parity disk. However, unlike RAID 3, which uses bit striping, RAID 4 stripes in blocks. This makes it act more like RAID 5. However, like RAID 3, RAID 4 has only one parity disk. This technology, like RAID 3, has become obsolete. It was replaced by RAID 5.

RAID 5
This is the RAID configuration most of you are probably familiar with. Almost everyone is familiar with RAID 5 on some level, because it is one of the most common configurations (see Figure 2-4). We see this type of configuration a lot in the industry with servers that use native disks.

Storage Area Network (SAN)
A disk is a disk is a disk, right? Well, not quite. You'll find many different vendors of SAN systems, such as EMC, IBM, and HP. Each offers its own solutions to the disk storage issues. Which one is best will depend upon your needs, budget, and preference.

EnterpriseOne will likely be only one of the systems utilizing the disk storage solution. Although those of us who work on software sometimes think everything should revolve around our system, this is not always the case.

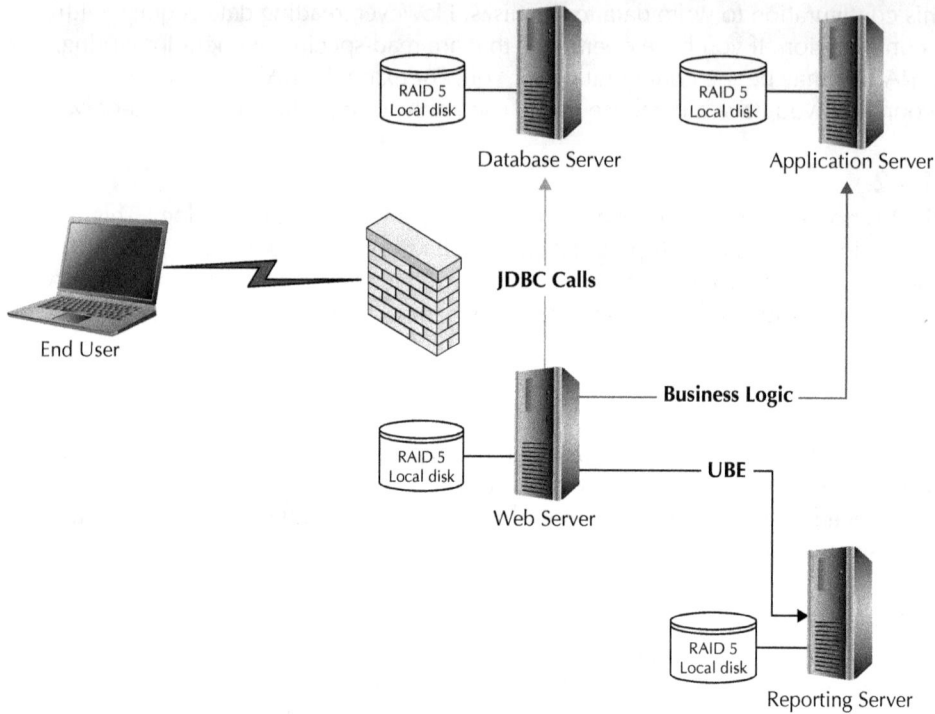

FIGURE 2-4. *Example of RAID 5 with EnterpriseOne*

Does EnterpriseOne care about which solution you choose? To answer this question, you need to think about what is actually required. From a technical perspective, EnterpriseOne does not care which product you choose for storage. As long as you can get a drive letter or volume recognized by the operating system, EnterpriseOne does not know or care whether you've opted for a native disk or a SAN solution. Does that mean all of the solutions will perform the same? No, of course not; almost any technology has pros and cons.

Although you are probably getting tired of hearing this—yep, you guessed it—to ensure success, you must plan, plan, and plan some more. With SAN solutions today, you must choose among a variety of options, such as how much cache capability is built into the solution. This capability will keep data that is accessed frequently in memory so that the access speed is much faster.

The SAN solutions also allow for your database administrator not to have to worry so much about what data is stored on what disk. With a native disk, this is a necessary exercise to ensure that there is no disk arm contention. A common mistake for SQL Server databases, for example, is for people to put their TEMPDB on the same disk as their database. Because TEMPDB is accessed all the time, this slows down access to the database due to contention. With current SAN technology, this is not an issue. The SAN takes care of what disks are written to and where the data is stored. To the database and to EnterpriseOne, the data is simply on a volume or drive letter.

So what do you need to plan for? What could possibly go wrong with all this useful technology? A lot can still go wrong, even with all this useful technology. Consider a real-world example: We had a system up and running that experienced great performance. All of the machines used a SAN solution. Development used a machine with an older disk and production used one with a faster disk. Both of these SAN solutions were shared with other systems in the company's IT portfolio.

One day, everything came to an absolute crawl. We looked everywhere. The network team proved that the network was performing correctly and data was being sent back and forth. The database administrator saw a slowdown on some SQL statements, but he couldn't identify any kind of pattern in the performance. We were finally able to track this down to a problem with the switch that EnterpriseOne was assigned to access the disks. Even with a cache and high-speed disks, we still needed a path to the data. Someone had put EnterpriseOne in the same data path as another system that was using a lot of bandwidth to the disk. So EnterpriseOne got strangled, and thus slowed down and then sped back up randomly as the other system used the SAN.

Here's the moral of this story: Don't assume everything will be fine because you have a SAN system in place and it offers lots of great technology. Bring your SAN engineer into the discussion. Have him or her sit down with you and discuss the path to the data. Ask the following questions:

- How many other systems share this path?

- Once you start testing the EnterpriseOne system, what sort of reporting can you expect?

- If you have a cache, how often will you get your data out of cache versus getting it from the disk?

- Are too many systems or requests coming down the same path?

Disk performance is a key metric to keeping your system running effectively. Insist on regular reports you can compare with your other data to show your system's performance.

TIP
SAN systems usually use fairly inexpensive disks, but the cabinets that contain the disks are not quite so inexpensive. You should always know how much disk space is available before a new cabinet is required to house additional disk drives. Also ensure that you communicate your projected disk growth to your infrastructure team so they can help plan accordingly. This will save you a lot of budgetary and time headaches down the road.

Figure 2-5 shows an example of a SAN system with EnterpriseOne. EnterpriseOne sees this disk as simply a logical disk volume—drive F: or G: or mount point /u01. The system is not aware that this disk is actually a SAN system. As long as the system can access the disk, the system will function. As discussed previously, you cannot forget about disk speed as you undergo performance tuning. This one component can kill your entire system performance. So be sure to have a person available to your EnterpriseOne support team who knows this system and can monitor its performance.

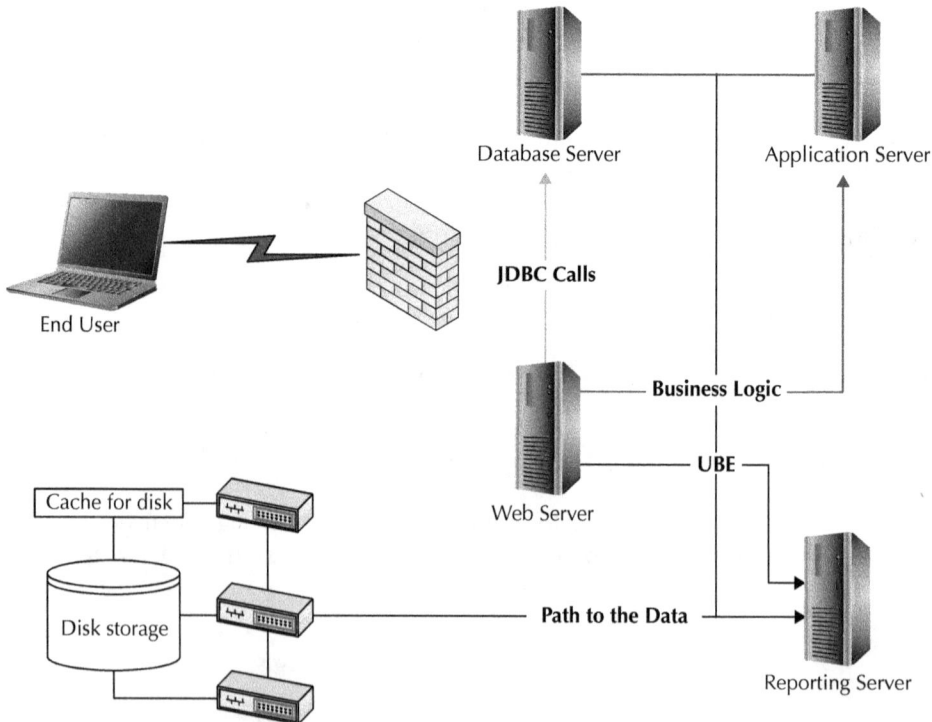

FIGURE 2-5. *Example of EnterpriseOne using a SAN system*

Network Area Storage (NAS)

Another system that is not really used that often with EnterpriseOne is network area storage (NAS). A NAS system is slightly different from a SAN system. (Some of you are probably asking, Does this industry have enough acronyms?)

Let's take a minute to talk about the differences between a SAN and a NAS. The main thing to keep in mind is that on a SAN system, your machine's operating system handles the file system. This means that the disk will show up as a mount point or a drive letter. However, with a NAS system, the NAS handles the file system. It's similar to mapping a drive to a file server. This is why you normally do not see a NAS used in an EnterpriseOne architecture.

A NAS is usually appropriate for media objects. The EnterpriseOne software, upon install of clients, platform pack, and deployment server, will look for a true drive letter, not a mapped drive to another machine. However, as you probably know, EnterpriseOne uses the Universal Naming Convention (UNC) to find data, such as check-in locations and media object files, so these types of files could be placed on a NAS.

Database Components

The database knows all and sees all. Let's pull back the curtain a little bit and see how this component can affect your system performance. But before we do this, we need to cover a few items.

First, we'll discuss several types of databases you can use with EnterpriseOne software. Because EnterpriseOne is platform-independent, you have a variety of choices when it comes to the type of database you want to use. Your database layout is another important consideration. We will briefly cover this here, and you'll learn a lot more about this topic in later chapters. Finally, we will touch on general tuning levers, including some high-level items that you need to be aware of for your database.

Types of Databases

One of the true powers of the EnterpriseOne system is that it supports a variety of database types. This gives customers who use the software a lot of flexibility when architecting their system. Oracle's Minimum Technical Requirements documents for database servers 9.1 can be found on Oracle's support web site at http://myoraclesupport .com. Currently, the EnterpriseOne 9.1 release supports the following databases:

- Oracle
- SQL Server

- DB/400

- DB2

These database types run on different supported platforms. Currently Oracle supports the following platforms for EnterpriseOne 9.1:

- Linux

- Solaris

- AIX

- Windows

NOTE
Some of you are probably wondering why HP 9000 is not in this list. It used to be a supported platform, but Oracle no longer offers support for HP 9000. How do you know which direction Oracle is going? Well, we are glad you asked. Oracle provides a "JD Edwards EnterpriseOne Platform Statement of Direction" for EnterpriseOne clients that will let you know what platforms and operating systems are supported and when support of some operating systems will be deprecated. This document can be found on http://myoraclesupport.com. We recommend that you review this document at least once a quarter to ensure that you are working with supported platforms, operating systems, and databases. Obviously, if you are not using a supported architecture, the chances of good performance are significantly reduced.

Oracle Database
When selecting a database, you will at least want to consider Oracle Database. Currently, the EnterpriseOne Tools release 9.1.0.x is compatible with EnterpriseOne releases 9.0 and 9.1. At this Tools release level, you need to run an Oracle 11g database.

SQL Server
SQL Server is a very popular database type. Currently Oracle supports SQL Server 2008 and 2008 R2. This database is a very good choice for shops that already have the skill set in-house for other applications. The database also scales and performs quite nicely when configured properly.

DB2 for iSeries

If you have been working in the industry a long time, you probably still call the platform database runs on an AS/400 instead of IBM iSeries. DB2 i-series is a popular midrange system with an integrated database. Currently Oracle supports versions 6.1 and 7.1. The advantage here is that you don't need a separate DBA; you simply need a system administrator. This is an advantage, but also it requires that the administrator have a specialized skill set. A DBA will know the details of the database only, and not the operating system necessarily. In SQL Server and Oracle, there are very specialized skill sets to handle this. An iSeries administrator does need to know the database details, but simply the operating system. Most of the details are masked from the administrator.

DB2

With Tools 9.1.0.x, Oracle supports DB2 releases 9.7.0.1 and 9.7.0.5. We do not see this database in use as often as others with regard to EnterpriseOne. Like the others, however, it is a solid and viable database option.

Database Layout

When you are working with different databases, you'll need to consider the layout of each. There are many different examples of layouts, but in this chapter, we are going to keep it at a fairly high level because we go into much greater detail in Chapter 8.

Oracle Database

When you architect the database, it's important that you consider the database layout and involve your DBA. And remember that just because your CNC knows about Oracle Database does not mean he or she is a DBA. Be sure that you involve the DBA early in this process. The DBA should help plan the layout of the disk for your database as well as the System Global Area (SGA) and Program Global Area (PGA).

SQL Server

With SQL Server, you also need to ensure that a DBA is involved up front. Some of the issues you need to look at, other than disks, are where you are going to store different databases, because EnterpriseOne installs multiple databases. In addition, if you are a large company, you may need to divide the data from specific tables, such as the general ledger F0911, across different disks. You also need to ensure the TEMPDB, which is active constantly, is on its own disk with the correct RAID configuration. In addition, when you work with SQL Server, you must know how many CPUs and how much memory you are going to dedicate to the database. This will help to ensure a good foundation for building your tuning approach.

DB2 iSeries

The DB2 iSeries database is unique, because it is integrated into the platform itself. In this case, you need to involve your iSeries administrator. Several parameters need to be set, including disk and memory pools. Also, if you have a large iSeries server system, you may be using a logical machine or logical partition (LPAR). How you configure and set up this system will affect the performance of your EnterpriseOne system.

DB2

With DB2, you also need to ensure that disks are laid out correctly and that the memory is allocated correctly. Work with an experienced DBA.

General Tuning Levers

It is important at this point to discuss a few general tuning levers. These levers are items that can change performance across the entire system, instead of just one small part, such as sales order entry. To help you understand the framework for starting with a system or starting to look at tuning your database, we'll cover the following:

- SGA

- PGA

- TEMPDB

System Global Area (SGA)

Related to Oracle Database, the SGA is a group of shared memory areas that are dedicated to the database. SGA is one of the important large tuning levers, so you must be sure to allocate enough memory to your database to accommodate SGA. You might, for example, start with only 150 concurrent users and expand later to 500. As your user base grows, you need to ensure that you allocate enough memory to accommodate this. You may also need more SGA, depending on how you are using the database—that is, are you doing mostly reads or a lot more writing to the database?

Program Global Area (PGA)

The PGA stores the control data for your database. How you set up PGA depends on the size of your database, the number of users, and what the database is being used for. The PGA setup can affect the speed of your database. The PGA holds the sort area, among other things: The sort area in memory handles different types of sorting for your database, such as hash joins. If insufficient memory is allocated to the PGA and you are doing lots of sorting, you will experience slower performance. Worse, the performance will vary for the users. Most EnterpriseOne users do not understand or care whether their application or report is producing a large sort that requires more memory. They simply want their report or application to perform in a quick and efficient manner.

TEMPDB

With SQL Server, the TEMPDB is the temporary workspace for storing temporary tables, storing intermediate results, and processing sorting and queries. This workspace is constantly active. If TEMPDB shares a disk arm with another database, it can slow down your database. Some people use solid memory for their TEMPDB; a solid state drive is simply circuitry and does not have the moving parts like a "normal" drive. This means that it can be very fast for finding data.

If you research "tuning SQL Server" on Microsoft's web site you will find many articles related to the use of the TEMPDB. This type of tuning occurs at a base database level, so it can apply to systems other than JD Edwards EnterpriseOne. Therefore, any other items you are running from your SQL Server database can also benefit.

NOTE
Be sure that TEMPDB has its own disk arm!

Network

If you have implemented JD Edwards EnterpriseOne within a large company, you've probably dealt with sites over a wide area network (WAN). Sometimes these sites are located across town, and sometimes they are across the globe. Following are some real-world examples of network issues across a WAN.

At a client's corporate headquarters, everything was working great on the system, but operations in Finland were not going so well. The users were constantly complaining that the system took too long to navigate and enter data onto screens. The batch performance seemed fine once the job was submitted, but the interactive parts were performing unacceptably.

You can guess the first place that was suspected as the problem: It must be the network! Break out the tar and feathers. When you look at these types of performance issues, take the network into account, but realize that it might not be the whole problem. Let's examine what we did in this case.

We tested timings from multiple sites. We started by sending simple pings from the client machine to the web server—we started at a DOS command line and typed **ping *WEBSERVERNAME***. This gave us information on the trace route over the network that the client machine was taking to get to our web server. (Sometimes, you'll find interesting things when doing this exercise.)

We found a serious latency issue. The pings from Finland where taking 120 milliseconds, and when we pinged from the corporate office we experienced times of less than 8 milliseconds. Even when we pinged across the WAN in the United States, it took 40 to 80 milliseconds.

So why is this information important? Isn't some latency just a fact of life with a WAN? Yes, it is. Latency will always be an issue in any system—to a point. The trick is to minimize the latency whenever possible. Now, that does not mean we stormed into the network manager's office and demanded less latency. Because, as with all things in life, nothing is free!

NOTE
It is rare that a network administrator gets to start from scratch and design the perfect network. Most administrators inherit history from someone else and must work with systems that are not always the best, but that were what the company could manage when the network was created. So sometimes you find networks that take "the long way" around. Such problems, however, can be fairly simple to fix with correct resources and plan.

Our WAN example was further complicated by the fact that the company did not technically own the network it was using. They had paid another company for office space, and thus the actual wiring and switches did not belong to them. They asked for the hardware to be upgraded and got a polite "no" for an answer.

Users were suffering due to this network issue, but the company had no control over the network. But, even so, all was not lost. We identified the problem—the latency was caused by all the turns. Perhaps performance would improve if all those requests were placed closer to the web server. So this is exactly what we did.

A multitude of software packages will compress some of your web traffic requests and help reduce latency. However, we took an easier approach. We decided that, instead of sending all of these requests across the WAN, the network would simply send screen scrapes, that is, pictures of the browser results rather than all information on the browser. This meant a lot fewer turns and less information would be flowing back and forth. Even though EnterpriseOne uses only about 5 to 6 KBps of bandwidth, it sends a lot of requests. We used a Citrix solution to publish our browser. The company had already been using Citrix to publish other applications, so this solution did not require a lot of investment or training.

Citrix was perhaps not our only choice, but it was a simple choice for us. Using Citrix made a huge difference in network performance. It also really helped the IT team by reducing the number of tickets. The browser was set at a standard level, with no extra software or toolbars, such as Yahoo! toolbar or other items. This greatly helped to reduce the number of complaints about an application's performance on one machine versus another.

NOTE
Oracle does not test against Citrix. Oracle looks to Citrix to validate Citrix software against different solutions. You can refer to the minimum technical requirements documentation at www .myoraclesupport.com.

You can always reduce latency on your network, but the question is, is it worth the cost? Let's return to the base problem. Why is latency such an issue for the EnterpriseOne software? JD Edwards EnterpriseOne software is very chatty across the network. In order for the software to be user friendly and to validate data as it is entered, the software takes a lot of turns. This means it communicates with the server and then an answer is returned to the client.

An easy example of this is when you tab out of a user-defined field (UDC). The EnterpriseOne software will instantly validate the entry. This is a turn, because it sends a request to the web server, and then information is sent back to the client. The EnterpriseOne software did not always require this process, however. In the infancy of the HTML solution for EnterpriseOne, the software waited until all the data was entered and then the user submitted it. This might sound great on paper, but when you are a sales order entry clerk and you just typed in more than 100 lines of data, only to find out you have an error on every line, it is not very user friendly. Thus, the software was changed to be more interactive with the user.

TIP
As with other components for performance tuning, you need to plan your approach and ensure that you have a repeatable process. This is not really a one-size-fits-all solution. Different sized companies have different network configurations. Involve your network administrator up front. He or she can often also provide information from third-party monitoring. It should be rare that you actually have to get to the packet-sniffing level, but it can happen. If you have already mapped out our requirements and monitoring with your network team, you will be able to identify quickly whether the network is really part of the issue.

Network Cards

Network cards are simple, right? You have gigabyte cards in the data center and a lot of bandwidth in the data center. So it's all good—right? Well, not so much. Although EnterpriseOne has gotten a lot better, sometimes it will experience an issue with network interface card (NIC) teaming. You should be aware of how NICs are configured on the EnterpriseOne Servers. If addition, you should not have auto-detect turned on for these cards, if possible, because this is a waste of time. As long as you have configured your network so that you know the connection speed no matter what, auto-detect is not required.

Packet Priority

Another issue when dealing with WAN issues is packet priority. By working with your network administrator, you can give specific information a higher priority on the network (although this is not always the best thing to do). This is sometimes a good solution for remote offices, and not just with regard to EnterpriseOne performance. Sometimes, certain traffic to your web servers gets higher priority than general e-mail and other network traffic. Adjusting priority can help to ensure that requests to your web server get a higher priority. Again, nothing is free, so work with the network engineer to determine whether this is necessary and/or beneficial.

Generate Server Layout

Suppose you are starting from scratch and installing a new EnterpriseOne system or servers for the next release. You know that these servers talk to each other a lot. They constantly send traffic saying they are on the network, through JDENet. They also send traffic through the server manager agents, which monitor and help administer each of these machines.

Keeping all this in mind, do you really want the servers located on different subnets? Do you want them to have to go through a switch every time they need to communicate with each other? The answer is, as usual, it depends. For some companies, putting everything together is the best option. Others have strict controls and need to isolate all their productions servers from the rest of the network. (For example, a life sciences customer is required to meet specific guidelines for how it handles IT processes.) This is an area where you need to do a little up-front planning.

You also need to consider whether you are going to use a network appliance to help load balance for your EnterpriseOne configuration. You can use a content switch to help balance the load across your web servers. You can also use this solution to help load balance your business logic and Universal Batch Engines (UBEs). This would mean EnterpriseOne would see an alias instead of the actual application server names.

NOTE
You can read one of several white papers on how to do this at www.myoraclesupport.com. One that might be a useful start is "Configure JD Edwards EnterpriseOne Servers on IBM WebSphere Application Server with F5 Big IP." This is a more complex configuration, so if you are going to take this on, be sure you allocate enough resources and time to configure and test the solution.

Direct Application Tuning

In this final section, we will discuss some things that directly affect your tuning of the EnterpriseOne application. We will cover the following areas:

- User interface

- Application tier

- Batch tier

- Interfaces

- Common performance tools

- Reporting

User Interface

You might be wondering how the user interface (UI) can affect performance. EnterpriseOne gives you a lot of flexibility, including the user interfaces you choose. However, as you know, nothing is free, and the UI you choose can impact performance. Often this impact is very small, but sometimes it can make a huge difference.

When you log into EnterpriseOne 9.1, you will see a screen similar to the one shown in Figure 2-6. This screen includes a lot of information, but it's not normally where you can see hits to your performance. You need to look a little deeper for that.

To see performance hits, you need to look at an application screen; you'll often see some performance impacts on application screens with grids. For example, consider a sales order entry application; this screen is commonly used and also has a large grid. The number of columns in the grid will need to be rendered on the workstation, and this can sometimes cause performance slowdowns.

Oracle has taken steps to help resolve this. For example, the newer tools release will render only what is shown on the screen, so unless you scroll all the way

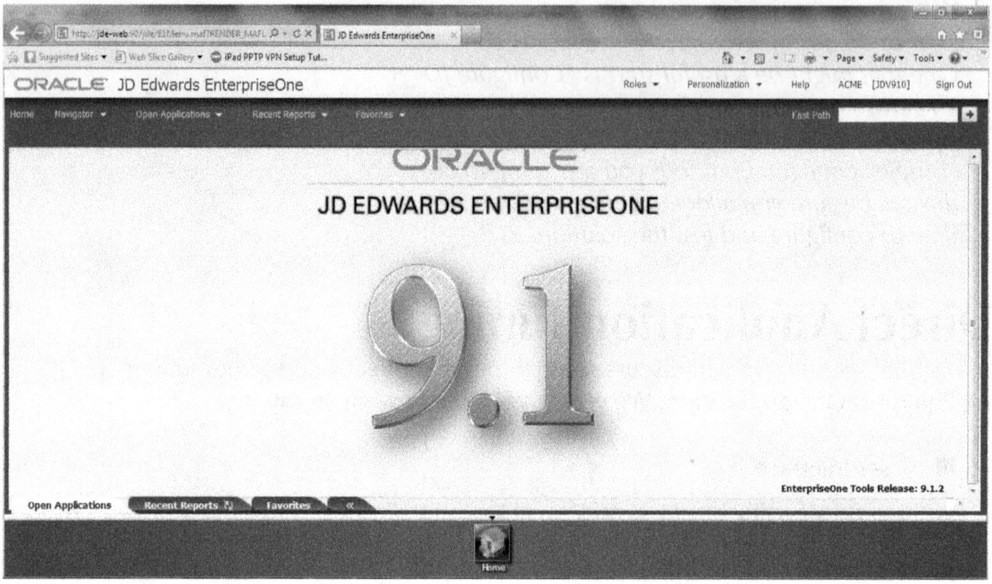

FIGURE 2-6. *Example of EnterpriseOne 9.1 screen after login*

over you don't have as much of an impact. Still, it may be worth limiting the number of columns in your applications that appear on screen, not only to help with performance, but to get them out of the user's way if they are not useful. You can use user overrides to change the appearance of the application so that specific groups, or everyone, can view only the information that's necessary for the work to be done. These overrides can also be promoted to higher path codes using Object Management Workbench (OMW).

Application Tier

The application tier handles all of the business logic in the EnterpriseOne architecture. This should be separated from report handling for performance reasons, because UBEs and reports use a lot of CPU and memory, which "steals" memory from the business logic or call object kernels that perform work for the interactive piece of the software. Thus, performance can fluctuate as UBEs grab CPU and memory.

To avoid this issue, you can change your architecture to dedicate machines to handle only business logic or only reports/UBEs. You can also combine your database server with your logic or UBE server, but again this is not recommended because of performance issues. Figure 2-7 shows how you can effectively divide up your architecture to handle the load on your system.

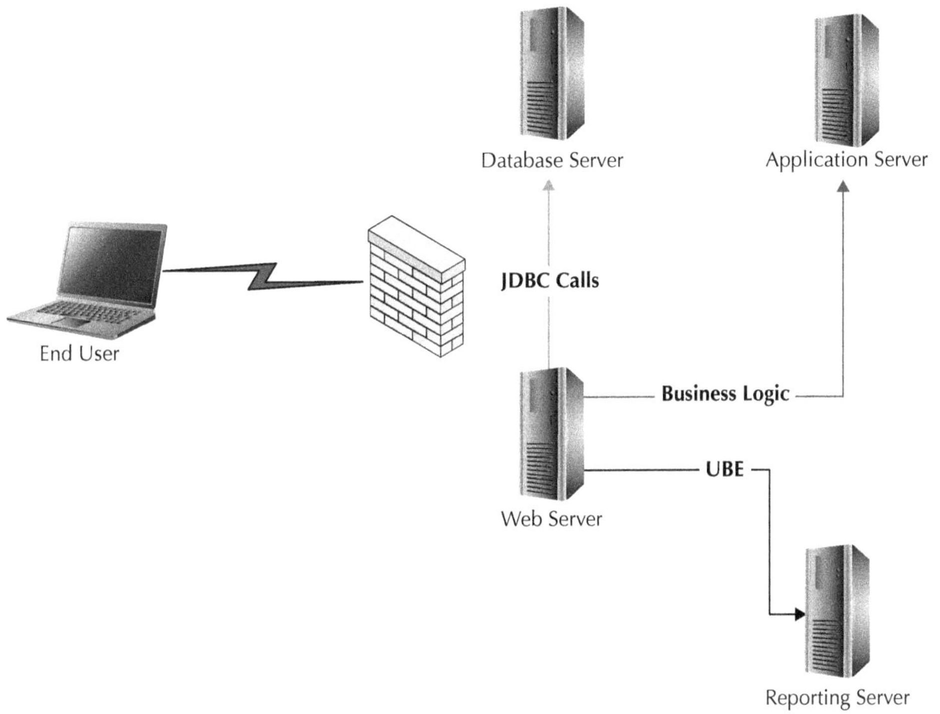

FIGURE 2-7.   *Example architecture to maximize impact of the application tier*

Batch Tier

The batch tier handles your reports or UBEs. These reports can be somewhat CPU and memory intensive. Sometimes they are long-running. So when looking at performance, you need to consider whether your system has enough computing power to handle all of the reports that you require.

To determine whether your system can handle the reports, you need to estimate your reporting requirements. If you've not used EnterpriseOne in the past, this may be difficult, but it's still very manageable. Work with an experienced applications consultant by describing your processes to determine the standard reporting load you will need. The module you are running also affects the load. If your system is performing manufacturing resource planning (MRP), for example, this will have a much larger impact on the system than accounts receivable. If you know how much your estimated reporting load is going to be, this will help you correctly size the machines for the batch tier.

Next, consider your job queues. You can have the biggest machine on the block, but it won't help you much if you are sending your jobs through a tiny pipeline, one at a time to the machine to process. An experienced applications consultant can help you with your job stream. The job queues should be set up in a logical way. Many jobs in EnterpriseOne are *single-threaded jobs*, which means they can run only one at a time through a job queue. That being said, if you design your system in the appropriate way, you can set up multiple single-threaded job queues. This requires that the data selection for these jobs be set correctly so that double-posting does not occur.

When setting up job queues, you can specify a default job queue within the UBE version itself, so that a specific version of the report will always go to a specific job queue. However, be aware that this information is stored in a binary large object (BLOB) field, so unless you are using special software or you write your own program to update this field, once you set all your versions to be overridden to specific job queues it can be difficult to change them. So, for example, if your business analysts are going to copy a version, make sure you verify the job queue prior to promoting it. Also, be sure to publish the job queues and the approach to the business. This may sound simple and obvious, but we can tell you that we've experienced people who are in a rush to get started fail to pay attention to this detail; it is more difficult, then, to get the reports aligned to it later.

The JDE.INI settings must also be addressed on your batch tier. JDE.INI settings are covered in detail in Chapter 7. For now, you should know that these INI settings control your system's kernels. When you tune your batch server INI file, make sure you have enough JDENet kernels as well as UBE and call object kernels. The JDENet kernels are often forgotten. These kernels are like the system's postal workers. Their job is to open messages and route them to the correct kernels for work. If your system has too many packages and too few workers, your system will slow down, even though your CPU and memory may look fine on your batch server. Be sure to use Server Manager to monitor the system. This will show you are having a slowdown due to too few JDENet kernels.

Interfaces

It's important that you map out the system interfaces and the processes that use them. While planning for interface use, you need to account for growth as well as actual performance requirements. Then you need to ask, How am I going to monitor the performance on these interfaces? Often, a different team, and sometimes a different company, handles the "other side of the interface." You must ensure that you can measure your system performance up to the point of porting the data over to the other system.

You also need to ensure that you have an agreement with the team that maintains the system into which your system interfaces. If performance issues are noticed, how are you going to approach the problem? Can the other team gather metrics on their side and report them to you, and vice versa, so that issues can be identified early and before users complain?

Metrics is an area that is sometimes tricky and neglected. The end users don't care that the data goes "over the wall" of the EnterpriseOne system. All they know is that they need to get through a business process, and if it is not performing to expectations, they can't get their work done. Metrics help you establish what is acceptable performance and help ensure that everyone's expectations of the system are the same.

NOTE
Many third-party tools on the market can help you establish system metrics. One example is Oracle's plug-in to their Enterprise Manager. They have a plug-in for JD Edwards as well as other systems to help monitor performance.

Common Performance Tools

One of the first questions you should ask when looking for performance tools is, What am I trying to measure specifically? Sometimes you want to get lots of detail about your database. Other times you want to monitor the server's operating system or storage system. Of course, you also want to see what is going on inside the EnterpriseOne system.

To do all this, you need to use different tools. A variety of network, database, and operating system tools are on the market—way too many for us to cover in this book. As you're considering which tools you need, consider which tools best handle what you want to monitor. Consult your network team, your DBA, and your infrastructure team to select the appropriate performance tools, and ensure that the reporting can be pulled in and combined with information gathered from other tools to give you a complete view of your system.

Several tools can assist you in monitoring, tracking, and troubleshooting performance issues in EnterpriseOne, particularly the following:

■ Server Manager

■ Performance Workbench

■ JD Edwards EnterpriseOne Application Pack for Oracle Enterprise Manager Cloud Control

Server Manager

Server Manager will be covered in multiple chapters later in the book. Server Manager allows you to monitor and administer your EnterpriseOne system. The software is generally installed on the deployment server, and agents are installed on each of the different types of EnterpriseOne servers. These agents communicate with the Server Manager software, telling it about what is occurring on each of the servers. The agents also work with the installed software to allow the administrator to administer the machines through an HTML user interface. This means you can start and stop your web servers, check log files, or check to see what activities are occurring on the system from pretty much anywhere on your network. Figure 2-8 shows how Server Manager works.

Performance Workbench

Performance Workbench is often an unsung hero when it comes to troubleshooting performance issues with EnterpriseOne. It has been around for a while and is kind of like the crescent wrench of EnterpriseOne performance tuning. As we have discussed, when you're approaching performance tuning, you need to know where to look for the performance issues. This tool can actually help you with that. It quickly runs through your logs and tells you where the system is spending its time during a process and if it spots any errors.

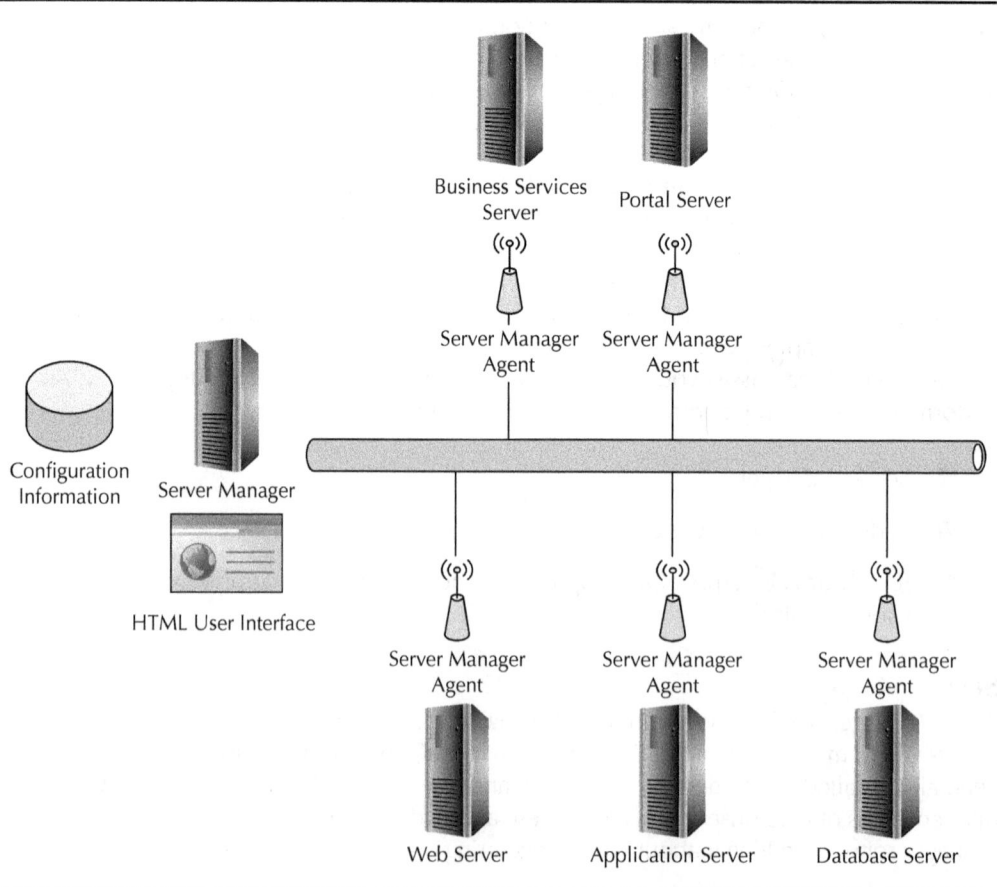

FIGURE 2-8. *Server Manager overview*

If you have been working with EnterpriseOne for a while, you know that if you turn on the debug logs they can get large very quickly. Running through these by hand is not a fun process. This is where Performance Workbench, as shown in Figure 2-9, really helps out.

As you can see in Figure 2-9, this tool offers many options. You can use it to parse a JDEDEBUG log from a client workstation or an enterprise server. It allows you to look for different levels of detail, including business function, open table and close table counts, or you can look at everything—that is, counts of business functions, selects, inserts, deletes, updates, and all information related to business functions. It can also generate a call stack file, which is useful when you're debugging an application error. This parse functionality can also be used with a JAS debug log.

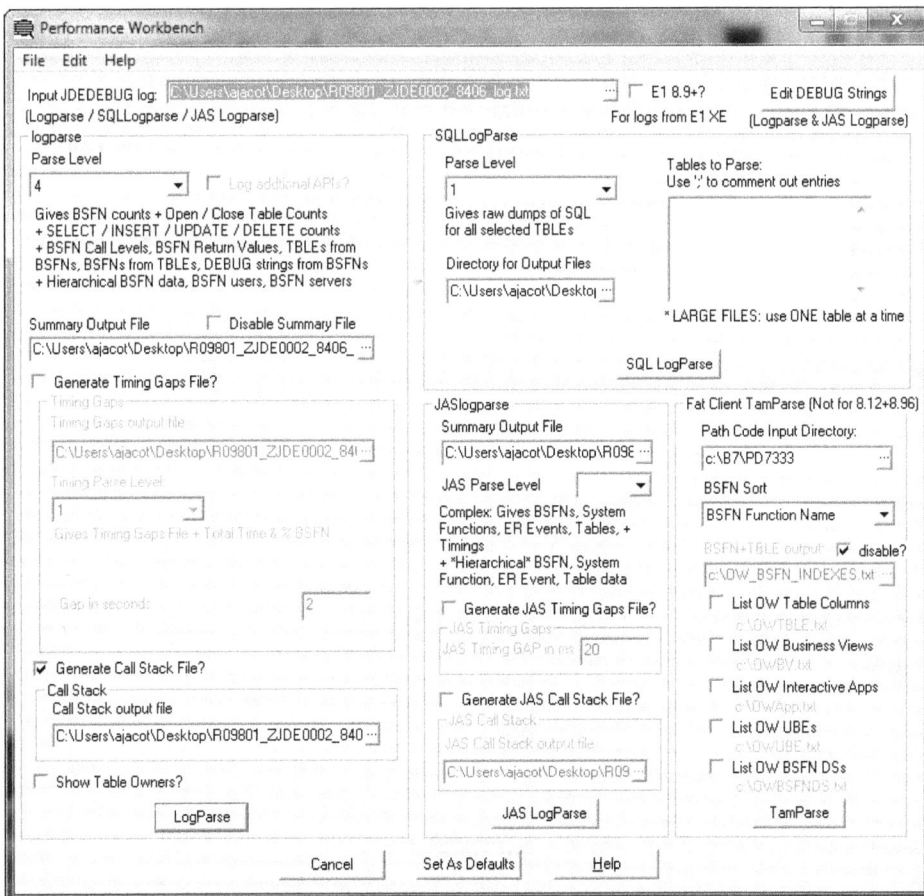

FIGURE 2-9. *Performance Workbench*

This means that you can trace a process, such as entering a sales order, all the way through to see what is happening. You can gather logs for issues on both the HTML server and Enterprise server to see if an error occurred on either server. Thus you can see what is happening at a specific point in time during a process.

This tool is useful not only for finding errors, but it includes a setting to generate a timing gap file that shows how much time various processes on your system are taking, down to the millisecond in releases 8.9 and later. So, for example, you can see if SQL selects are using up the majority of the time when you perform your trace or if a business function is taking more time during a transaction.

JD Edwards EnterpriseOne Application Pack for Oracle Enterprise Manager Cloud Control

We haven't seen this tool in use as often as we'd like. It is a very neat tool. It's actually a plug-in for Enterprise Manager, the console that you use to manage Oracle databases. The Cloud Control plug-in allows you to do a lot of performance monitoring with your EnterpriseOne servers. You can use it to gather metrics and even monitor the system for an SLA. It requires that you obtain an additional license fee from Oracle, but depending upon your enterprise size and requirements, this tool might be worth the cost.

Figure 2-10 shows an example of using the Enterprise Manager to see JD Edwards EnterpriseOne servers. You can see the types of servers as well as their status. You can

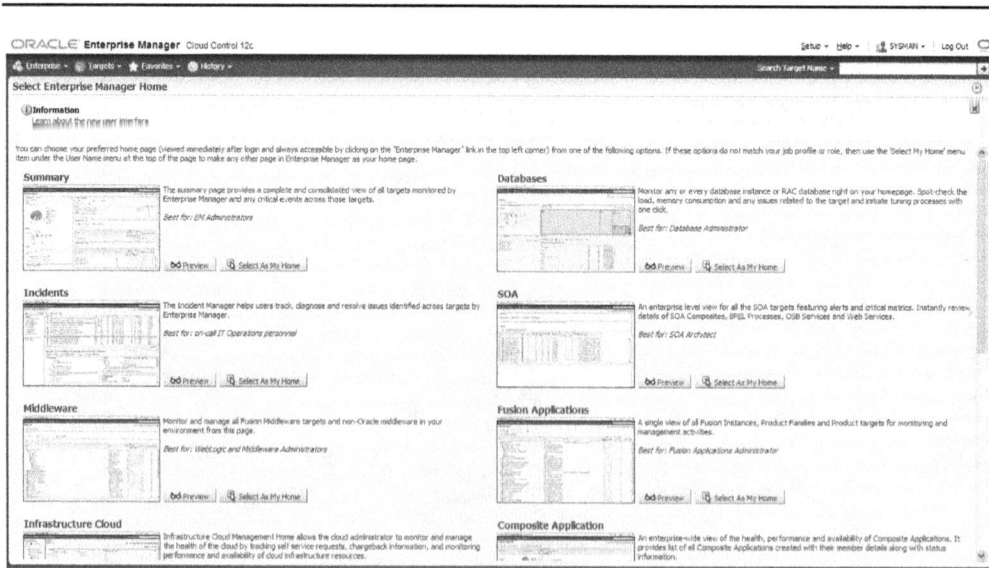

FIGURE 2-10. *Enterprise Manager E1 Application Pack*

also use this software to set up specific monitoring of your EnterpriseOne system, including web servers and enterprise servers.

Let's start with the web server, because this is where a lot of really good information can be gathered using the Cloud Control plug-in. You can gather the following metrics using this tool:

- Average execution time
- Cache group
- Call object statistics
- Number of applications that are open
- Database data source information
- General system uptime
- JDENet connection manager
- JDENet connection pool socket
- Java heap memory used
- Response
- Number of system errors
- Time-out errors
- Total number of users logged onto the system
- User sessions

This type of information can tell you what is happening at any moment on your HTML server. This software also allows you to collect information for reports. This means you can see whether you are within an SLA. So, for example, if a user complains that the user interface—the HTML server—is slow, you can see the actual performance of the particular server itself.

You can also use this software to monitor and gather information on your enterprise servers. This is very useful because it can tell you how each machine is performing. Following are some of the important metrics that you can gather:

- Average CPU
- Monitor kernel processes

- Response from server
- Number of database connections
- Number of incoming network connections
- Number of outstanding requests
- Number of users for server

Reporting Using the Cloud Control Plug-in   One of the main advantages of the plug-in is the reporting you can get on the actual performance of your system. Having this information at your fingertips allows you to see quickly where the problems exist in the system. With performance tuning, you sometimes have to sort through a lot of data to determine where problems reside. This tool allows you to see all of the data in an easily digestible format—in other words, you get quality information instead of just quantity.

You can configure and set up dashboards to show what is happening on your system. All areas of your business are not equal, so, for example, if part of your EnterpriseOne system is customer-facing, you'll give this a much higher priority than back-office functions. (After all, it takes only a few seconds to lose a customer.) Figure 2-11 shows an example of how you can view the data gathered. This data shows how your HTML server is performing at a particular point in time.

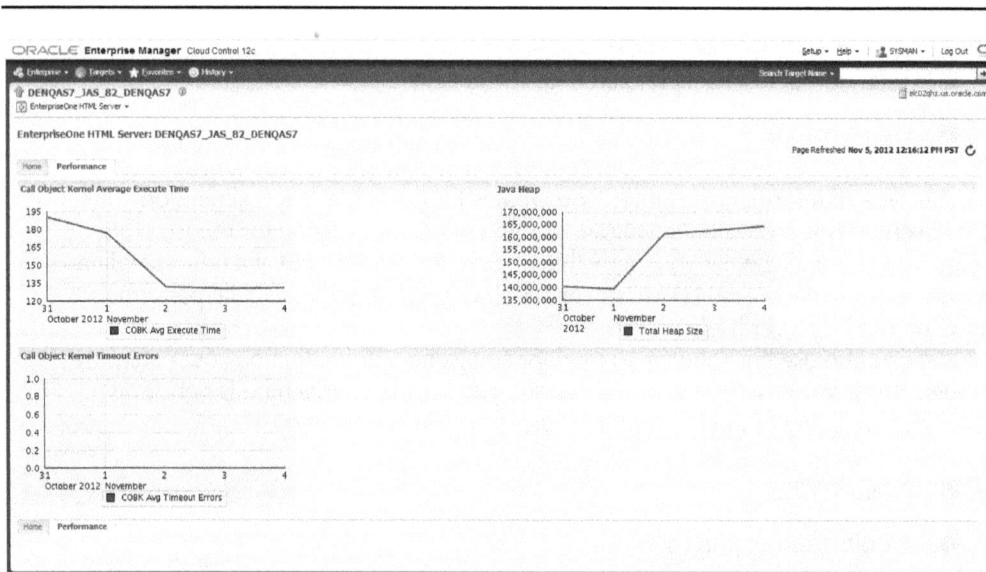

FIGURE 2-11.   *Browse performance data*

You can also use the tool's dashboard functionality to enable a view in which individual business units or divisions may be interested. This functionality makes it very easy for executives to see and evaluate performance in their areas of the business. You can also restrict the dashboard view to show only areas that are of particular interest, at a system level, to you. Figure 2-12 shows an issues overview as well as the availability of the different servers.

This plug-in offers even more, but here we've given you a high-level overview so that you can consider using this type of solution in your JD Edwards EnterpriseOne architecture. Performance issues become more manageable when you can actually show baseline measurements and thus get the business to agree on a specific service level agreement on performance. This will allow you to see any performance changes, for example, after you apply new patches to your system.

TIP
The JD Edwards EnterpriseOne Application Management Suite also allows you to monitor an iSeries. So do not think that just because you are using a blue stack architecture that you cannot take advantage of this tool.

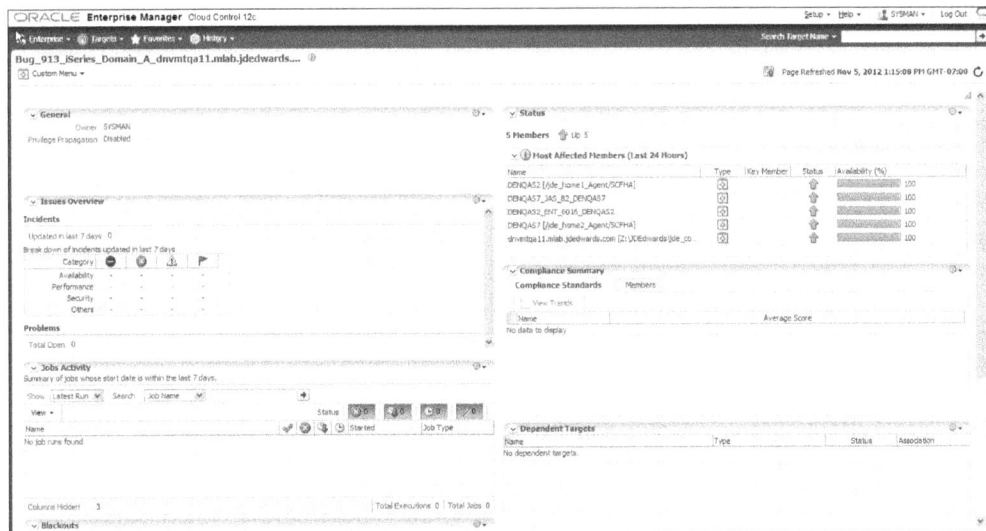

FIGURE 2-12. *Issues overview and availability*

Handy Third-Party Tools

Over the course of working on the JD Edwards software package, the authors have found several handy third-party tools that you can leverage to help you in performance tuning. These tools are fairly specific to circumstances. They can make the difference between an issue that takes a few hours to resolve and one that takes a few weeks to resolve.

IBM Pattern Modeling and Analysis Tool (PMAT) for Java Garbage Collector can be downloaded from the Internet. It allows you to analyze verbose garbage collection. This will help you quickly to identify any issues in garbage collection. The tool also provides a graph view that can help you quickly identify issues.

Another tool, SunSpider JavaScript Benchmark, can also be downloaded from the Web. This tool lets you benchmark a browser's performance, which can be handy if you are trying to determine whether performance issues are directly related to the browser or are within EnterpriseOne. If a problem occurs with a browser, support staff or your CNC consultant may ask you to try performing the same task using a different browser to see if the problem persists. If, for example, Firefox seems to be fast and Internet Explorer is slow, you can determine whether the slowness is really a speed issue or the browser.

Wireshark is helpful if you suspect that the trouble may be at the network level. This tool is basically a package analyzer that lets you see what is happening with the traffic from the web server to the database server or from client to web server. This is a fairly technical tool, and you should always have permission from the network team to employ this type of tool before using it. Wireshark can help to pinpoint an issue or prove that the issue is not at the network level.

Summary

In this chapter, we covered a lot of topics. The idea was not to go into too much detail here, but to help provide the basics of the components of performance tuning. We covered each of the different tiers, dove into the supported platforms and their operating systems, and talked about considerations while patching these operating systems.

We also spent some time on disk considerations for system performance. We talked about the different disk types as well as disk layouts. We covered how you could use a SAN system with your software as well. We then moved on to the database component of the system and covered several database types that are supported by EnterpriseOne. You learned about different layouts and the general tuning levers for databases.

We discussed some real-world examples of how a WAN can affect your EnterpriseOne system. This chapter wrapped up with a discussion of direct application tuning, including a discussion on the user interface, the application tier, batch tier, database tier, interfaces, and performance-tuning tools.

CHAPTER
3

Building Blocks of an EnterpriseOne Implementation

Oracle JD Edwards EnterpriseOne supports a wide range of database and hardware platforms, and the fundamental building blocks you need to use EnterpriseOne are fairly consistent across implementations. You must have certain servers and services in place to provide the necessary functionality to support the EnterpriseOne applications along with other software in the ecosystem. For example, you must have a database to store the information needed and a server to run EnterpriseOne logic and batch (reports), along with some type of presentation services such as a web server. A deployment server is also used for the initial installation and provides a repository for software updates and code changes. You can extend the implementation with additional servers, which we will discuss throughout this book. You also have options such as BI Publisher for documents or One View Reporting, Business Services (BSSV) for integrations, portals for collaboration, and several other important options.

The technical infrastructure that you create is the foundation for the entire EnterpriseOne implementation. It is critical that all areas are sized and configured to provide the performance, availability, and scalability that your enterprise needs. Undersize the equipment in any of the areas, and you potentially create bottlenecks that can become a challenge for performance tuning to remedy. Oversizing the hardware provides more headroom in case the capacity is underestimated or inefficiencies occur in the processes or code. However, this can sometimes lead to additional costs, such as in the number of processors or servers required, depending on how the software operates on the platform. Oversizing can influence areas such as licensing charges or support maintenance depending on the vendors' methods of tracking the usage or number of users.

The bottom line is that correct hardware sizing and ensuring that performance and scaling exercises are conducted will allow the EnterpriseOne implementation to support the business processes in use now and in the future. Fail to invest in your infrastructure, and you increase the risk that the system will not support the business processes it was designed for. Over the years, we have seen a number of implementations in which the hardware was undersized or the business processes were not tested for production loads, which can lead to "tuning under pressure." Generally this ends up costing the customer more in potential time, effort, and resources to correct after the fact.

Let's delve into the various types of EnterpriseOne servers and how they are utilized in the implementation from a tuning perspective.

TIP
It is usually beneficial to obtain an EnterpriseOne sizing estimate from your hardware vendor and then, once the majority of business processes have been configured, to examine the sizing again to ensure that your system meets the requirements, before moving on to a production system. This is common sense, but it seems to be ignored by some customers we have worked with over the years. If sizing is ignored, it usually becomes a consulting opportunity that typically occurs near or shortly after a go-live, which creates grief and frustration for the business.

Types of EnterpriseOne Servers

The JD Edwards Configurable Network Computing (CNC) model gives you quite a bit of flexibility regarding how the system is architected. The EnterpriseOne applications are generally separated from the technology areas, providing a robust number of options. With the large number of choices, you can also get yourself into some trouble from a performance and complexity perspective if you don't understand the pitfalls that can occur. As you read this book, we will provide additional details about a number of architectures and some common configurations for various sized operations.

Separating various workloads offers a key advantage in performance tuning. For example, it is a good practice to leverage dedicated equipment for the development/ prototype architecture and use other equipment for production. Within such architectures, you may also have servers dedicated to specific functions, such as database and enterprise servers, or these functions could be running within one physical server or complex. Each configuration has advantages and disadvantages, along with complexity and support factors that you should consider. The servers used typically are influenced by the datacenter IT staff's skill sets. When your company has its own IT staff, these individuals usually have experience and skills with a specific infrastructure that has been used over the years. It is possible to change platforms, but depending on the change, a significant investment might be required to help staff obtain the skills required to operate and maintain the new platform.

For example, if you migrate from an IBM System i platform to a commodity-based Linux platform, you will need to be familiar with commodity hardware and the Linux operating system (OS). The database would also change from DB2/400 to Oracle or IBM DB2/UDB, which runs on a Linux platform. If you outsource or use a hosting service, it will most likely be a platform on which you have skills and experience. Business users, on the other hand, usually don't know and perhaps even don't care what infrastructure you are using, as long as they can do their work.

Enterprise (All-in-One)

An all-in-one (AIO) enterprise server allows multiple services/functions to run on the same physical machine. Multiple path codes/environments can run in the same EnterpriseOne instance along with the database and web services. For some customers, an AIO configuration may make sense, because it allows everything to stay together in one place.

IBM System i is an excellent example of an AIO configuration in which the database DB2/400 is part of the OS. It can make sense to have the web and EnterpriseOne services such as security, call objects, and batch running where the database is located. This can offer improved performance, because data and logic are within the same partition running at memory speeds instead of using network communication.

System i AIO Customer Case Study

We visited a customer that was upgrading to EnterpriseOne from World Software on the System i platform. The partner they used had architected the World Software and EnterpriseOne data libraries to be in one logical partition (LPAR), and the EnterpriseOne services ran in another partition and also on a Windows server. This architecture was similar to that used for Windows servers, but it was not ideal for batch jobs or heavy call-object processes.

They experienced performance concerns with their payroll batch when compared to World Software runtimes. (Not a good apple-to-apple comparison to begin with, but that is another story.) The World Software payroll would run in about 5–10 minutes, and the EnterpriseOne batch running on Windows took about 40–50 minutes. Tuning System i reduced this to 30 minutes for the jobs running from Windows. We provided some background about the advantages of ensuring that the larger batch I/Os be as close to the data as possible. We recommended that they install EnterpriseOne services in the same partition where the data libraries resided.

In this particular situation, using Windows, the connections were coming across the local network through the QZDASOINIT jobs used for Open Database Connectivity (ODBC) connections. While relatively fast, the remote connections would not be nearly as efficient as local queries running in the same partition. The client also tried to run the payroll Universal Batch Engines (UBEs) from a separate LPAR where the original EnterpriseOne services were located; those ran in about 20 minutes. In several instances, the hardware sizing was understated quite a bit, and once the hardware was resized accordingly, the batch runtime was under the 10-minute goal. With the improved hardware, the Windows executions were still in the 20–25 minute range. The key point in this example is that running the batch from a Windows server to the System i for longer running jobs was not an advantage from a performance perspective; instead, keeping the UBEs closer to the data provided the optimal configuration once the needed hardware and tuning were in place.

Generally, AIO machines use IBM System i and larger Unix configurations, because, in the past, these operating systems had 64-bit address spaces or greater. However, with the use of 64-bit computing on Windows and Linux, this particular strategy could be used on Windows and Linux platforms.

With the releases of EnterpriseOne, the enterprise database requirement is for a 64-bit platform, which assists the scalability and, in a number of situations, the performance of the database. Even though the EnterpriseOne kernel processes are 32-bit, you gain more headroom with a 64-bit OS, which provides more memory space to the processes, and you can have more processes that in total surpass the 4GB address limit of a 32-bit OS. With a 64-bit OS, you can keep more objects and data in memory, which is where the best performance gains occur. If you have to go to a disk or network system, you typically experience a wait time, which contributes to potential performance concerns.

Certain customers prefer an architecture that scales *up*, which can include the AIO strategy, while others prefer specialization of services that allows them to scale *out* instead. There is no right answer to the combination of building blocks, but certain strategies work better in certain customer environments. Table 3-1 provides some potential advantages and disadvantages for each hardware platform.

Application Logic

An EnterpriseOne application logic server is usually a dedicated server that runs the JD Edwards kernel processes. Example kernel processes include security and call objects that are used by the web or BSSV servers. The batch kernels and UBEs may or may not be running on an application logic server. Some customer configurations run all three major services together (security, call object, and UBE), while others are even more specialized and dedicate a subset of the services, such as security and call objects for logic services.

A typical configuration used by the Oracle VM templates and a number of different platforms use the EnterpriseOne services on one server, with the database and web services on separate machines/partitions (see Figure 3-1). This type of configuration leverages the hardware resources that can be dedicated to specific services, while maintaining a relatively low number of servers.

With the use of 64-bit operating systems at all levels, the scalability on a single machine has improved significantly. The capability has been present on System i and Unix platforms for years, but it has become more recently available on the commodity-type Windows and Linux platforms. You have more flexibility to mix and match the services you need now or those that will allow for growth if the organization's workload changes significantly. Again, the flexibility to scale up or scale out can help you meet various business and availability objectives along with the performance goals of the system.

The use of the EnterpriseOne services on a separate server allows you to isolate and tune functions from the database and presentation layers. With a single machine,

Hardware	Advantages	Disadvantages
IBM System i	– Web, EnterpriseOne services, and database in one partition are well integrated – One partition to manage instead of multiple machines – Workload management tuning by subsystem and memory pools – Usually observe the best performance if EnterpriseOne services and data are in same partition	– Potential increased cost for memory and/or processor when Web is utilized – Licensing costs may be in a higher class – Fewer System i administrative resources may be available
Unix/Linux 64-bit edition	– Unix systems have been in use for years, and Linux support has been present since 8.10 release – Very scalable from a single-server perspective	Unix/Linux skill sets not as pervasive as Windows
Windows 2008 64-bit edition	– Widely adopted platform from a client and server perspective – Commodity hardware provides additional choice – Skill sets are more widely available for Windows	– 64-bit support is relatively new compared to other platforms, so potential exists for maturity issues, but they seem to have been addressed, such as SQL Server database – Tuning/grouping workload processes is not as granular as System i

TABLE 3-1. *AIO Advantages and Disadvantages of Various Platforms*

if you need more capacity in one service area, it generally involves the entire machine—adding memory, processors, or disks. Separating the server functions allows you to have redundancy of services, such as the database in a cluster or Oracle Real Application Clusters (RAC) and multiple enterprise and/or web servers. This provides a potentially granular approach to capacity and performance tuning, where, if needed, you can update individual servers or add them at the layer desired with incremental costs, compared to the monolithic/single machine costs. Again, there is no right or wrong approach here—just what makes sense for your organization's infrastructure objectives.

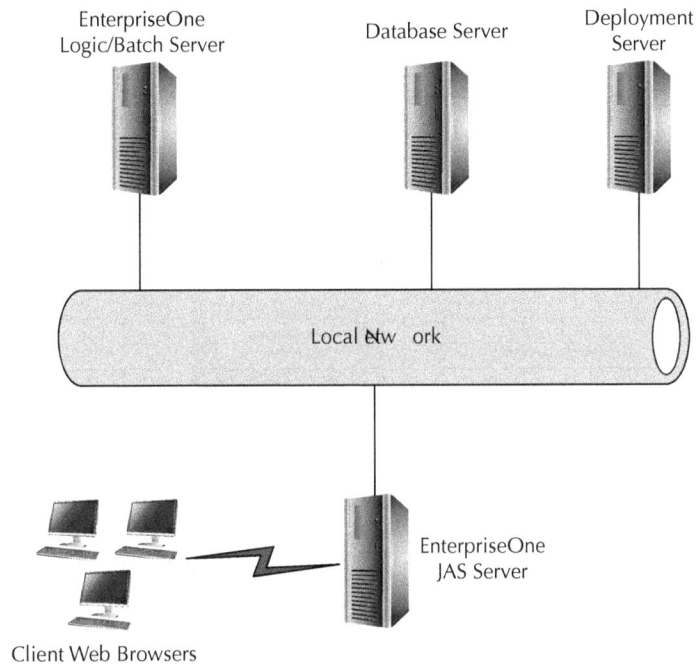

FIGURE 3-1. *Common EnterpriseOne configuration*

This configuration also allows you to start small, such as with a development or proof of concept (POC) architecture, and then scale/break it out to the more demanding environments, such as production, where most users would be working. It is also very common to have a separate set of application/logic servers for change-management and testing purposes, in which one is used for development/prototype and the other for production, as shown in Figure 3-2.

Separating workloads in this way offers potential performance advantages and disadvantages (see Table 3-2); for example, if you have high usage testing processes, they have less chance of affecting your production environment if they are performed on a separate system.

Within CNC architectures the application/logic server is considered one of the fundamental building blocks of an Oracle JD Edwards EnterpriseOne system. Without this server, there won't be much talking to the database and the web presentation layer can't run the logic needed for most applications. Note that BSSV also runs in the web presentation layer with similar requirements for the application logic.

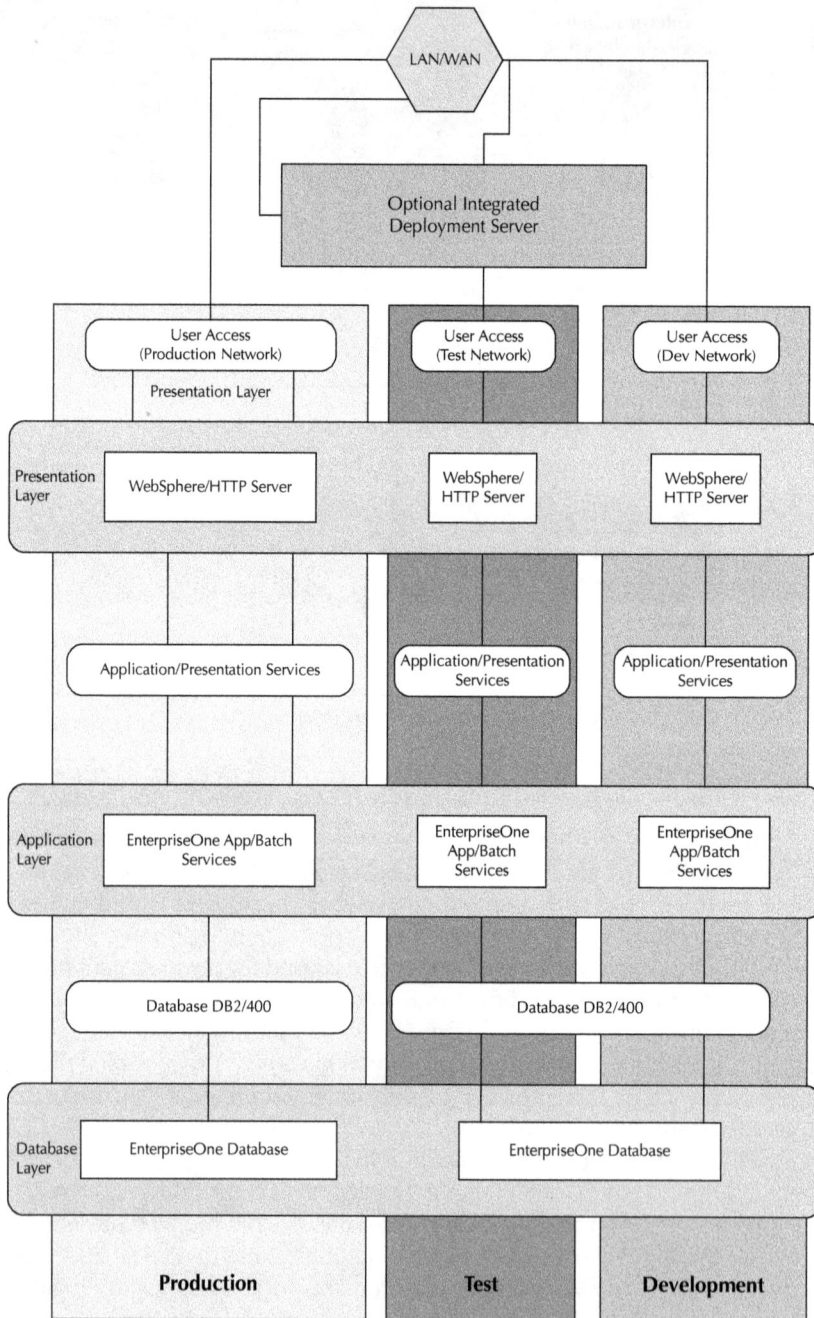

FIGURE 3-2. *Example AIO configuration*

Advantages	Disadvantages
– Can be tuned and scaled separately from other servers such as the database or web. – Incremental capacity and performance can occur at the individual server level or by adding servers. – Commodity hardware/software can be used. – Helps you isolate different environments such as development and production, both from a data/code perspective and the hardware/operating system.	– Additional servers may incur more operating and licensing costs. – Adds to the complexity of the architecture to monitor, maintain, and operate (more care and feeding).

TABLE 3-2. *EnterpriseOne Application/Logic Advantages and Disadvantages*

Batch/Universal Batch Engine

A batch/Universal Batch Engine (UBE) server is dedicated primarily to batch tasks that are submitted by the user, a scheduler, or perhaps some type of integration. A UBE is a collection of various JD Edwards functions that can be a report or that can actually modify the data. Larger database I/O tends to be in C business functions (BSFNs), and smaller selects/changes are in named event rules (NERs). UBE servers have several advantages and disadvantages, as shown in Table 3-3. Usually, the main reason to use a separate batch server is to isolate heavier workloads, which can be the equivalent of tens or hundreds of web users, depending on the job. This can help separate the web interactive users that usually require subsecond responses with much smaller transactions from the UBE that tends to retrieve thousands to millions of rows of data. As noted, you can have both call objects and batches running on the same server, but some architectures favor separating the workloads depending on the business requirements. One size definitely does not fit all situations.

Advantages	Disadvantages
– Incremental capacity and performance can occur at the individual server level. – Specific tuning of kernels for batch or other processes can occur where needed. – Batch workload is less likely to affect the interactive workload. – Helps you isolate different environments such as development and production, both from a data/code perspective and the hardware/OS.	– Additional servers may incur more operating and licensing costs. – Adds to the complexity of the architecture to monitor, maintain, and operate.

TABLE 3-3. *Batch/UBE Server Advantages/Disadvantages*

Customer Example Separating the Servers

One of our customers had recently upgraded from Enterprise Resource Planning (ERP) 8.0 to EnterpriseOne 9.0. The business processes had changed over the years, and during the upgrade, some of those processes were revisited and changed. The production system was running an Oracle database on a Unix server, EnterpriseOne services on another Unix server, and Unix WebSphere for the web presentation layer on a third server. The enterprise server had about 400–450 users on the system, and the workload was divided among about 200–225 web users and various warehouse management system (WMS) sites that had large batch-level interfaces and bar coding taking the other 200 sessions. They experienced some performance issues in the past on ERP 8.0 and with the change to EnterpriseOne had experienced some improvement, but not at the desired level.

After some analysis, the various tuning recommendations included some web changes that stabilized how they used the memory and separated the interactive call objects from the batch workload. The batch workload remained on the original Unix enterprise server and the web call object processes went to a new Unix enterprise server. This effectively doubled the capacity and split the workloads almost right down the middle from a user perspective. The WMS and interface jobs ran faster and more consistently, and the web users saw a marked reduction in "response time pauses," as they liked to call them. The customer had significantly improved stability from tuning, and the system response was viewed very favorably in this situation. We did have other options that were considered, but this was the one they liked, and for their particular situation it was the best.

HTML/Java Application Server

The HTML/Java Application Server (JAS) operates at the presentation layer for EnterpriseOne web users in addition to Java applications for BSSV or the transaction server. The current application servers supported by EnterpriseOne are Oracle WebLogic, IBM WebSphere, and Oracle Application Server (OAS, which is being phased out in favor of WebLogic as of EnterpriseOne Tools 9.1). Within these application servers, the Java bytecode is operated in a container or instance. For example, you can create a production web instance for the PD900 path code and another web instance for prototype (PY900). If you're authorized to run the particular instance, you would be running the serialized objects (Java bytecode), which are generated from XML specifications that describe the various application objects, such as a web form. Since you could have different code and data in an environment, a dedicated web instance is used to prevent mixing the information in the various web caches used for performance. This also helps you classify or group various users according to the environment they need.

NOTE
Because OAS is no longer supported as of EnterpriseOne Tools 9.1, we don't include much about it in this book, but since a large number of customers on earlier releases utilize OAS, we've chosen to cover the topic briefly in a section later in this chapter.

Both Oracle WebLogic and IBM WebSphere allow you to create single instances or use a cluster to scale the web instances vertically on one server and/or horizontally across multiple servers. Clustering is typically used in larger configurations that serve several hundred or thousands of users, and that desire higher availability. Starting with EnterpriseOne Tools 8.98.3.x, Server Manager allows you to manage the cluster capabilities, which eases some of the administration and installation tasks. The cluster capability in Server Manager lets you manage one set of configuration settings that can be propagated to any other web instances/nodes defined in that cluster. Clustering also lets you add capacity incrementally if the workload or business requirements change over time.

Individual web instances can be used for larger installations as well, if you want to maintain individual configuration INI settings. Most EnterpriseOne web instances serve from 1 to 100 users. With a 64-bit Java Virtual Machine (JVM), you can configure instances to facilitate higher numbers of users, but as with most situations in life, there is no free lunch. The larger the memory allocation you use, the longer it can take to perform a full garbage collection (GC), which can temporarily halt the JVM or, from the user's perspective, the web application "pauses." If you can keep the GCs in the millisecond range with a maximum of less than 1 second, you generally don't upset the user community.

NOTE
Newer releases of Java do help reduce the likelihood for full GCs but may not eliminate them. For most customers, we use a JVM that is in the 768–1520MB range with the sweet spot typically being 1024–1280MB. For the 64-bit JDK, you can consider memory allocations in the 2048–4096MB range, but load testing is strongly recommended to determine whether the performance will meet your objectives or to determine the optimum web instance configuration for your infrastructure.

Web Server Configuration	Advantages	Disadvantages
Dedicated web server	– Can be tuned for the specific web workloads – Very common configuration used for EnterpriseOne – An option if you do not want web applications running on System i	Software and licensing costs may be higher
Web/application server (Web and EnterpriseOne logic on same server)	– Web and EnterpriseOne call objects running on same machine (fewer servers) – Used mainly in virtualized or "grid" architectures where web and logic layers are located together for high availability and redundancy	Additional resources such as memory/processor needed since you combine services
All-in-one (AIO) (Web, EnterpriseOne services, and database together)	All services on one server	If more capacity needed for any layer, it may be more costly than individual server architectures

TABLE 3-4. *Potential Web Server Configurations*

As noted, the flexibility of the servers provides a number of advantages and disadvantages, some of which are listed in Table 3-4.

If, for example, you have four web instances of EnterpriseOne HTML running on different servers, or on the same server, you'll likely need to supply some method for the user to access those web instances transparently (unless you like challenging users to type unfriendly port numbers in their web browser URL). A popular method is to use some type of hardware or software load balancer that manages a user's connection to a virtual IP (VIP) address and then, once it is distributed, the user's session "sticks" to that web instance. (Chapter 13 provides various load balancer configurations that can be used.) The individual instance is the relatively easiest to install and configure with less complexity than using a WebLogic or WebSphere cluster.

By using the flexible combinations, you can influence the application server according to your business requirements and operational goals:

- If you like to have all the services running on one machine, the AIO configuration lends itself well and is generally how the System i is used. In some situations, customers run the EnterpriseOne services and database on System i and use Windows or Linux for the web servers to reduce the resources on the System i.

■ The web/application server allows you to use a model that was common in the OneWorld Xe days with terminal servers, where the client and logic ran together. With EnterpriseOne, multiple web servers can use a common application server, or the web/application server allows you to group the servers, such as the terminal servers. Using a load balancer, you can then put various servers in service and have others offline for various reasons, such as package deployment or maintenance.

■ The dedicated web server is the most commonly used configuration. In some cases, it is used in front of a System i machine to reduce the complexity and potential cost on that server. Or it can be used to standardize the server configuration, which is Oracle's installation/upgrade guide perspective.

As we've mentioned, there is no "right" answer for all customers. You must determine which configuration, or perhaps a combination, works best for your particular environment. The beauty of EnterpriseOne CNC is that with the flexibility it offers, you are not always locked into one specific method or infrastructure. You can choose from many options. In fact, what is interesting about CNC is that its strength is in the large number of choices available for creating an architecture; however, that can also mean that if you go too far with those choices, you can create an architecture that does not perform well. (Too much of a good thing can become bad for you, so consider using moderation.)

Database Server

The database is another critical service that is essential to EnterpriseOne. If the database is the heart and lungs of the system, the enterprise server is the brains, and the web server is the skin that everyone sees. Without the heart and lungs, the rest of the body just doesn't work well, and so it is with the database server. It is critical for a production configuration that the database server has enough resources to perform well. If you short-change the hardware, it negatively impacts the other servers in the ecosystem.

The database server tends to be one of the larger machines in a configuration, since we normally scale up rather than scale out with multiple servers. Oracle's RAC database option does provide the ability to scale up or out with the proper hardware in place.

Here's a rule of thumb (or an "experienced estimate"): If you can estimate the size of the database on disk, you can roughly determine the hardware, such as the processors and memory, that you'll need. Your mileage can vary greatly depending on the business processes being used, but if your processes do not repeatedly go through entire large tables, a memory estimate can be 10–20 percent of your database on disk if it is not compressed and you are using Unicode. For example, if you think the database will be 1000GB (1 terabyte) in size, a good amount of memory would be 96–192GB. You could certainly operate with less memory, and in some customer situations you might even need more, but that would be an exception.

NOTE
We've seen some well-tuned databases in which full table scans were limited and run with a much lower percentage of memory—quite nicely, in fact. With no tuning performed on older database releases, we've seen customers use what we call "forklift" upgrades, who replaced entire machines because the database usage continued to grow without monitoring/tuning occurring. In such a situation, we helped them migrate to a different database, provided education about the value of indexes, and helped with strategic custom code changes. We removed a day's worth of processing from the company's month-end cycle.

Processors are a bit trickier, since you need to know how many users and concurrent batch type processes you would have. That is why we suggest working with the hardware vendor, especially for large machine configurations, where you want to get the number of processors needed as close as possible. Using commodity hardware can give you a little more leeway, since it tends to be lower cost, from the purchase price perspective at least. Total cost of ownership, however, is an area of debate that we leave to the customer to decide, since many differing opinions and studies are available to consider.

One key to an effective database is ensuring that you have the best disk subsystem that you can reasonably afford. This can be a storage area network (SAN), network file system (NFS), an integrated solution with various levels of caching, such as the Oracle Exadata database server or IBM System i; or you can just ensure that the disk architecture provides optimum response for the various demands presented. Performance for most systems regards four major areas: processor, memory, disk I/O, and the network. Whichever element is the slowest tends to be a potential bottleneck until a good balance is reached while running the EnterpriseOne applications. A particular area being slower is not necessarily bad, but you need to recognize where the limitations may exist and account for them in the architecture.

WebCenter/Portal Server

EnterpriseOne currently supports two portals. The Oracle Portal was used by older Tools releases and has transitioned to the Oracle WebCenter Portal for various collaboration tasks in Tools 8.98 and 9.1. The IBM WebSphere Portal collaborative features are also used by EnterpriseOne. These portals provide a very rich set of functionality that allows you to bring together a number of different applications that adhere to a set of standards. A number of collaboration tools can be implemented as well, in addition to several infrastructure elements such as directory and authentication/identification services that are used in portals.

The portals are usually implemented when the customer wants to consolidate a number of different web applications to provide a single point of entry for the user. Other examples are the EnterpriseOne self service applications for which the end user account can be enrolled/created automatically with a specific set of applications. Employee and supplier self service are commonly used examples of EnterpriseOne applications created for this purpose.

Business Services/Transaction Server

If you have integrations/interfaces to other systems, the EnterpriseOne BSSV and Real Time Events (RTE) or transaction server may be for you. For larger and more complex integrations, you can examine the Oracle Fusion Middleware products or the IBM Message Queuing (MQ) series products as well. BSSV utilizes HTTP responses, so the potential for custom applications to involve mobile devices with specialized forms is another option. EnterpriseOne also offers options for mobile devices beyond the specific custom integrations you might want to create, as discussed in Chapter 10.

Deployment Server

The EnterpriseOne deployment server is a required part of the infrastructure to begin the initial installation of the software. Depending on your requirements, the deployment server provides a multitude of potential services for the installation. Table 3-5 lists the services you can install on the deployment server.

The deployment server is another critical part of the infrastructure that is needed for the Electronic Software Updates (ESUs), Tools releases, package builds, and usually Server Manager. You could technically operate the production environment without the deployment server running if some of the services are loaded to another server, but we have not found that to be common for the majority of customers. The deployment server generally should have a minimum of two processors, at least 4GB of memory to provide room for the local Oracle or Microsoft SQL Server Express (SSE) database, and other services. The minimum technical requirements (MTRs) on the Oracle Metalink site are considered minimum levels to operate the software. If you can ensure that your hardware levels are sufficiently above the MTR levels, you should experience good performance on this server.

Now that we have reviewed the different types of servers in a typical EnterpriseOne architecture, let's examine each area in more depth.

Deployment Server Function	Usage	Required/Optional
Installation planner/ software maintenance	Basic installation of EnterpriseOne software with a code repository for the C objects and package builds.	Required on a Windows deployment server.
Server Manager	Allows you to monitor and install tools and configure the various EnterpriseOne services.	Required for Tools 8.97 and above but can be installed to a different Windows server. In Tools 9.1.2 and later, Linux, Windows, and Unix platforms are supported.
Media objects	Default file storage for various media object attachments such as MS Word or text files.	Optional, but almost always used by customers with development or media object attachments; this Windows file share can be installed on a different server.
EnterpriseOne Help system	Help files on the Web or on Windows client.	In prior releases was based on PeopleSoft Books format, but newer releases let you point to an Oracle Internet site that has the help files. If using the PeopleSoft Books format, this service can be on a Windows machine.

TABLE 3-5. *Services That Can Reside on the Deployment Server*

Enterprise/Application/Batch Servers

Overall, the EnterpriseOne enterprise server provides multiple services, or kernels, with each kernel serving a specific purpose. Examples include security, package build, UBE, workflow, and call object kernels. As EnterpriseOne has evolved over the years, several kernel types have been added and some are no longer in use. From a building block perspective, the following sections provide general tuning guidelines for certain kernels. If you have an enterprise server, most likely a majority of the kernel types are in use. When using a batch server, the kernels are likely configured toward batch activities and fewer call objects may be started. An application server would tend to have more call object kernels allocated, for example.

Kernels

The EnterpriseOne kernels use certain values for the number of processes, and other kernels can have *only* one process running or they will function incorrectly. Table 3-6 lists a sample of various kernels in the later Tools releases. Keep in mind that, over time, these will change.

Kernel Index	Kernel Type	Starting Point MaxNumberofProcesses	Comments
1	JDENET RESERVED KERNEL	1	*Never* start more than one JDENET master kernel in this stanza; do *not* autostart this kernel
2	UBE KERNEL	1	1 per 50 users
3	REPLICATION KERNEL	1	Deprecated after EnterpriseOne application release 8.9 and later
4	SECURITY KERNEL	1	1 per 100 users
5	LOCK MANAGER KERNEL	1	Typically no longer used; provides timestamp processing, but introduces additional overhead/complexity
6	CALL OBJECT KERNEL	10	Single thread, 1 per 3–6 users; multithread, 1 per 5–20 users
7	JDBNET KERNEL	1	Generally JDBNET is not utilized so a kernel should not be autostarted
8	PACKAGE INSTALL KERNEL	0	Deprecated after EnterpriseOne application release 8.12 and later

(continues)

TABLE 3-6. *Kernel Types*

Kernel Index	Kernel Type	Starting Point MaxNumberofProcesses	Comments
9	SAW KERNEL	1	Provides information to management kernel
10	SCHEDULER KERNEL	1	Autostart *only* if EnterpriseOne scheduler is in use on this server
11	PACKAGE BUILD KERNEL	1	Normally one kernel started for server package builds
12	UBE SUBSYSTEM KERNEL	1	Manages F986113 subsystem table entries; max 1 kernel should be started to prevent issues
13	WORK FLOW KERNEL	5	1 per 40 users Default of 5 kernels and 1 autostarted; can consume significant memory and processor if tables not maintained or monitored
14	QUEUE KERNEL	1	Handles jobs queues and monitors UBE's status Allow *only* 1 kernel or batch submission; stability issues may occur if greater than 1 kernel
15	XML TRANS KERNEL	1	XML transactions interoperability
16	XML LIST KERNEL	1	XML list requests

TABLE 3-6. *Kernel Types* (continued)

Kernel Index	Kernel Type	Starting Point MaxNumberofProcesses	Comments
17	MQSI KERNEL	1	IBM MQ-Series interface: varies on concurrent workload
18	MSMQ KERNEL	1	Microsoft MQ interface: varies on concurrent workload
19	EVN KERNEL	1	Event notifications: used in older interfaces before the transaction server was introduced
20	IEO KERNEL	1	Interoperability event observer: converts events from database to XML
21	OPE KERNEL	0	Order Promising Engine Integration kernel rarely used
22	XML DISPATCH KERNEL	1	XML request dispatcher: used by interfaces and certain bar code solutions to route requests to the proper kernel
23	XTS KERNEL	1	XML translation service: transforms XML from one format to another
24	XML SERVICE KERNEL	1	Handles older XAPI messages and callback business functions

(continues)

TABLE 3-6. *Kernel Types*

Kernel Index	Kernel Type	Starting Point MaxNumberofProcesses	Comments
25	QE RESERVED 1	0	Reserved for future
26	QE RESERVED 2	0	Reserved for future
27	CLIENT KERNEL	0	Reserved for future
28	QE RESERVED 3	0	Reserved for future
29	APP SERVER KERNEL	0	App Server Kernel May be invoked for Transaction Server messages, but typically not started
30	METADATA KERNEL	1	Converts XML to C structures for call objects. UBE runtime cache entries
			Generally 1 per 300 users unless high batch activity
31	XMLPUBLISHER KERNEL	5	BI/XML Publisher workload depends on embedded BIP UBEs
32	MANAGEMENT KERNEL	1	Server Manager Enterprise server metrics; Max 1 kernel
33	SBF JAVA KERNEL	1	
34	TEXTSEARCH KERNEL	1	Secure Enterprise Search (SES) that replaces the former Verity search engine; launches a JVM if used

TABLE 3-6. *Kernel Types* (continued)

Here are some general kernel sizing rules for EnterpriseOne kernels:

- **MaxNetProcess**   10-to-1 of total kernel processes, or one JDENet process for every 10 call object kernels (consider the 10-to-1 ratio unless you want to run more network processes)

- **UBE Kernels**   1 per 50 users (may be higher if concurrent batch is greater than 20 jobs)

- **Security Kernels**   1 per 100 users to available processes

- **Call Object Kernels**   1 per 6–10 users (lower for single thread and higher for multithread kernel)

- **JDBNet Kernels**   1 per 90 users (do not autostart and don't use unless you need different enterprise servers to access a different platform database— example, System i UBE to work with SQL Server database on Windows)

- **Workflow Kernels**   1 per 40 users

- **Metadata Kernel**   1 per server unless high concurrent batch (generally 1 kernel, but in some cases you may need 2 or 3 if timeouts occur)

Batch Processes

Within EnterpriseOne, UBEs provide a significant amount of flexibility for reporting and modifying the data. Literally thousands of UBEs are provided in EnterpriseOne. They can be submitted by users or scheduled or invoked from other applications. If you need to process hundreds of rows or more of data, UBE is the preferred method to operate on the data. It is better to batch the requests than have the user wait for an interactive application to take several minutes to process.

You can streamline batch processing by adding multiple job queues via the P986130 Job Queue Definition application. This will allow you to partition or divide various batch jobs based on their requirements. Most batch jobs can operate concurrently as long as they do not have overlapping data selection that causes unexpected database locks and contention. Some do, however, require that all data be selected to ensure that it processes consistently. With the batch queues, you can define single-process job queues where only one particular UBE can execute at a time. The main consideration is reviewing the data and particular UBE processing requirements. Some UBEs can be easily divided into multiple versions with roughly equal data selection, and others do not lend themselves to concurrent jobs because they must total all the data, for example.

NOTE
You can review a number of Oracle Metalink articles and papers for specific UBEs and general batch performance suggestions. Some Oracle Metalink documents are Article IDs 1301768.1 and 748333.1. We strongly suggest that you take advantage of this information or consult with experienced application and CNC consultants who are familiar with the functional areas. An application consultant provides the data and configuration knowledge along with the CNC, which helps you configure the architecture and monitor the performance/scaling tests.

It is a good industry practice to divide up your job queues by speed rather than by functional area. For example, you might have a fast concurrent job queue for quick jobs and a long concurrent job queue for longer running jobs. This type of strategy keeps the number of job queues manageable while providing the throughput that the business requires.

For example, when placing jobs in certain queues, you should ensure that you don't place high-priority, short-running UBEs in queues that may have long-running jobs. If you do not recognize or identify these types of jobs, the batch turnaround times may be skewed by long wait times in the queue that the user views as a slow batch, when in fact the job was just waiting in line to run. A good tool for critical path batch analysis in EnterpriseOne is R986114A. Oracle Metalink document ID 965569.1 provides more details on how to execute and interpret the results, which lets you see where in a large-batch schedule your system may experience delays.

Business Functions

EnterpriseOne utilizes business functions (BSFNs) and named event rules (NERs) to execute the majority of the logic functions. The BSFNs are ANSI C code that is compiled on the platform(s) on which it executes, such as a Linux server. The NERs are generated from the EnterpriseOne tools and become ANSI C code. The NERs are easier for developers to create using the EnterpriseOne tools, and the BSFNs generally are coded to obtain additional performance and flexibility. For example, for sales orders, the master BSFN B4200310/B4200311 contains the major logic for the database to create or change sales orders. If this was attempted as an NER, a number of the programming constructs would not be available and the performance would not be as efficient. BSFNs tend to be more complex and require additional expertise to create and maintain than the NERs generated from EnterpriseOne.

On the enterprise server, the call objects house the logic and are called from interactive or interface JD Edwards APIs that are published. In the later releases since 8.11 SP1, the BSFNs have been engineered to be multithreaded, and this provides additional concurrency within a call object process via threads. Previously, if you

UBE Subsystem Case Study

On the subject of short-running jobs, a number of our customers have designed entire batch printing/processing in which hundreds to thousands of the same UBE were executed each day. This can lead to batch processing of thousands of UBEs per day, with the UBE itself being mainly a pick slip or invoice pack slip print. When a UBE is executed hundreds or thousands of times per day, you should consider a batch subsystem version. You can reduce the number of jobs and the execution runtime can be significantly reduced. (In some cases, the runtime can decrease by 5 to 10 times.)

Years ago, a customer was using several packing stations and a custom UBE that was based on a couple of standard UBEs. They would submit hundreds of jobs per day, with the critical time during the peak activity in the afternoon, when the boxes of orders would be packed and labels printed. The process using submitted UBEs from an interactive application took 5–60 seconds and caused significant resource usage on the batch server. Even with multiple queues and a dedicated server, the reliability and turnaround did not meet the customer's expectations.

The interactive application was modified to call a custom business function that created a subsystem job record that contained the pertinent data selection information the UBE needed. The custom UBE was modified to use a subsystem version that polled the F986113 subsystem master table every 500 milliseconds, or twice a second. With the UBE launched as a subsystem job, only one specific job was required, and enough information was available to determine to which packing station to direct the print job. The overall design change improved the reliability to one or two print issues per month, and the printing time was reduced to 1–5 seconds during peak activity. In addition to the number of batch UBE submissions being reduced, the overall batch server utilization was significantly lower.

Batch subsystems are an option that is frequently not considered by higher volume configurations, in our experience. It is a strategic opportunity, and, with experienced developers and CNC, you can reap several benefits under the right circumstances. There are some Oracle Metalink documents regarding how to create a custom UBE subsystem, such as Article ID 649658.1, that you can read to gain additional insights into this EnterpriseOne feature.

had multiple users on one call object kernel and the request would take several seconds to process, the other users on that kernel would have to wait in line since it was a single-threaded process similar to a UBE job queue. With multithreaded call objects, each user has his or her own thread and can operate independently of other users' requests within that process. This basically eliminates the queuing, which to the user appears to be a better response even though the actual time to process the request is the same.

Call objects are controlled by the kernel definition in the JDE.INI of the enterprise server. The main control is the number of processes that can be started, which does require some planning and thought, depending on the workload requirements. If you allocate too many kernels, you can overcommit the memory and slow the overall system. Too few kernels can result in resource and thread shortages that impact the response time as well. The physical resources of the server greatly influence the performance of the kernels, since, as with most processes, you do *not* want to overcommit the memory or processors.

TIP
Initially, in EnterpriseOne 8.11 and later releases, the call object MaxNumberofProcesses was set to 100 in the JDENET_KERNEL_DEF6 stanza. On a Windows server with, say, 4GB of memory, you could overcommit the memory once the user workloads had started all 100 processes. A call object, depending on the platform, can use between 40 and 300MB of memory per process/job. Using a conservative number of 100MB per call object, multiplied by 100 processes, you could have a virtual memory commit of 10,000MB, or 10GB. This would be much greater than the physical memory, so the page file would hold these processes addressing requests. If you had 100 users accessing the system, this would mean only 1 user per call object kernel, and the overall response would be constrained by the paging rate and activity of your system. (This is sometimes called system "thrashing.") In this example, assuming you were using multithreaded call objects, the sweet spot would most likely be 10–20 call object processes (5–10 users per call object), which would consume 1 to 2GB of memory and would place much less stress on your server. As always, before you make any changes, you should monitor and verify the best settings for your configuration.

After reading the tip, you can see that one single change based on your hardware capabilities could dramatically influence the performance of your system. (In fact, over the years, it has been our experience that a small number of changes usually result in the largest effect on the system.) You must focus on specific areas once the overall architecture has been matched to the infrastructure/business process requirements that have been defined and are in use. Normally, the business requirements cause hardware and resource changes to be needed because a balance is desired for performance.

Java

Several EnterpriseOne kernels beginning with application release 8.12 use Java processes for services such as the metadata, BI Publisher (formerly XML Publisher), and management kernels. The metadata kernel helps convert XML to C structures for the call object kernels and creates runtime cache entries for UBEs. Other kernels, such as management and BI Publisher, have an embedded JVM that performs specific functions such as the enterprise server runtime metrics via the management kernel. The BI Publisher kernel handles XML report requests to format them from UBEs that use the embedded BI Publisher. Java, of course, is also used for the web application servers, with various flavors depending on the platform used. Later versions generally offer improved performance when supported on your platform.

TIP

If you are using Tools 9.1 or later, consider the 32-bit JRockit R28 version or later JVM, which can improve the performance of the embedded BI Publisher and, in some situations, the metadata kernel. You can explicitly point to your JVM under the [JDE JVM] stanza using the InProcessJVMHome *setting.*

Configuration Settings

The enterprise server's main configuration files are the JDE.INI and jdelog.properties files. These settings are maintained and managed by the EnterpriseOne Server Manager web-based application and sometimes optionally directly in the files themselves. Whenever possible, the Server Manager should be used, since it is updated with each Tools release to be current with various functionalities, with information windows for each parameter.

NOTE

You'll also find a number of documents about the JDE.INI settings on the Oracle JD Edwards Metalink site. A good example is the EnterpriseOne Kernels White Paper *that provides background information and references regarding the kernels. This can be found on Oracle Metalink, document ID 961823.1.*

JDE.INI

Because there are multiple kernel types, you tune them according to the functionality you want for a particular enterprise server. Each enterprise server should use its own security server, for example, which can reduce cross-server traffic. A minimum of five JDENet processes should be present to direct the incoming network requests to the appropriate kernels. As shown in Table 3-6, various kernel types and some potential values should be considered. For most customers, the default settings work, but a review is definitely suggested.

The debug logging section can be used for application or performance logs that are controlled in the JDE.INI. With later Tools releases, you can dynamically enable UBE debug logs through P986116/execution details, and if debug level 0 or 1 is invoked with `DumpLPDS=0`, it can provide performance debug logs useful in the Performance Workbench log analyzer. The Performance Workbench is an excellent log-parsing tool to profile where a UBE or specific Java Application Server (JAS) session is spending time. The help file and several supporting documents/ presentations are available regarding the Performance Workbench tool at the Metalink web site (https://support.oracle.com).

Kernel recycling for the call object kernels can provide performance benefits by reclaiming resources that may slow down the enterprise server. This also allows the enterprise processes to remain up longer for customers that prefer to run the services for weeks between recycles. Call object kernel recycling can be set for daily or weekly intervals, as required by the business. The default setting is weekly recycling, on Sunday mornings at 3 A.M. This capability is also potentially planned for other kernel types in later EnterpriseOne tools releases, such as security and metadata, to help provide additional options for system flexibility and uptime.

Jdelog.properties

The jdelog.properties file is usually located in the system\classes folder. It controls the logging from various embedded JVMs. Server Manager is used to configure this file, but normally these logs would not contain any information unless unexpected issues occur. Note that you would need to change the logging configuration if you were debugging a performance problem in the embedded JVMs.

HTML/JAS Servers

The web application server provides the presentation layer to the client browser. EnterpriseOne applications are generated from the central objects specifications to the serialized objects tables as Java bytecode. This code is executed within the application server to render the various elements you interact with on the browser. Myriad files are sent to the HTML browser, such as Internet Explorer or Firefox. Each JVM allocates a set of heaps that consume a certain amount of memory on the server. The trick is to ensure that you have enough memory without paging and a processor available for the JVM(s).

With the advent of Windows 2008 x64, all of the EnterpriseOne web server platforms have 64-bit addressing. This reduces the potential resource and performance constraints that sometimes occurred under 32-bit operating systems. The JVMs can be 32- or 64-bit, depending on your application server choice. WebLogic, for example, is generally a 64-bit JDK, and Oracle application server uses a 32-bit JDK for EnterpriseOne. Even though a 64-bit JVM can address much more memory, you might not want to create large heaps above 2 or 3GB since you may observe longer garbage collection times that affect the web users' response during a full collection.

TIP
In JRockit R28, you can consider a command-line parameter argument of `-Xgc:pausetime` for the garbage collection instead of the throughput default. This requires a slight performance overhead, but garbage collections work concurrently with the Java application threads instead of pausing them. For EnterpriseOne web sessions, you may find this more appropriate, but generally the default throughput option works well in most situations.

Your mileage will vary due to the application mix and amount of data and queries, along with system configuration combinations. From a processor standpoint, most customers tend to allocate one JVM per processor, but depending on the hardware, you can have more JVMs per processor in certain situations with very good response. It is a good practice to remember to allocate one processor for the operating system outside of your processor allocations for the JVMs.

TIP
A number of customers ask how many JVMs should be used in a configuration. As with most options, there is no cut-and-dry answer. Generally, for the later EnterpriseOne releases, you can get somewhere between 50–150 users per JVM. That said, it is a good industry practice to plan for a maximum of 85 users per JVM so that a JVM can take on the load if another JVM process goes offline.

A point to remember about an EnterpriseOne JAS is that it is a shared JVM of resources. If you bump up certain settings to allow sessions to remain longer, to allow larger import/exports of spreadsheets, or to increase query result set timeouts, you increase the resources consumed for longer periods of time. Most of the default settings for the JAS provide a fairly good balance for a typical 50–100 user workload. Several settings can change the features of the web instance, which can impact the number of users due to increased resource usage. Some of those will be discussed later in the EnterpriseOne Web/JAS Server Configuration Settings section. For this reason, measuring, monitoring, and tuning are sometimes needed because of the wide variations of hardware and configurations present.

Application Server–specific Settings

The web application servers do have a variety of settings at the JVM, Apache, and EnterpriseOne JAS.INI/JDBJ.INI levels that can influence performance. Most of the out-of-the-box settings work well for a workload of 50–100 users, for example. However, each customer configuration and hardware is unique, with a number of various business process requirements. User behaviors can be very different between environments, depending on how the applications are used. Some customers want the grid sizes increased from 10 rows to 50, for example, which seems pretty innocent—but that means the data result set retrieved will need to be increased substantially, consuming more memory, network transfer time, and so on. Oracle development has done an excellent job of minimizing areas that consume significant resources, but when you ratchet up some of those defaults, you increase the risk for an issue occurring in JVM. The trick, as with most tuning, is to find a balance in your configuration that meets your business needs when possible but does not compromise the performance/stability of the system.

WebLogic

Oracle WebLogic for EnterpriseOne is a very robust application server with many available options. (Sometimes we think that, like IBM WebSphere, the amount of flexibility is actually too much for our EnterpriseOne needs. However, if some of the features were missing, it would most likely be those that benefit our applications, so we're not complaining.)

The EnterpriseOne Technology Foundation (aka "Red Stack") provides a WebLogic Standard Edition that does not license the clustering component. The WebLogic Enterprise Edition offers licensing for clustering that certain customers may desire. Server Manager (EnterpriseOne Tools 8.98.3.x) supports these types of clustering solutions and provides the ability to manage them. A number of configurations can use the Standard Edition, but if you want clustering capabilities, you may want to check on your licensing. The various minimum technical requirements (MTR) documents discuss the differences.

The main key to clustering is that instead of managing individual web instances vertically and/or horizontally, you have one set of configuration files that are propagated to the cluster members. This allows you to scale your configuration with additional cluster members to meet your needs. You should also consider load balancers to direct requests to individual ports of a web instance on WebLogic Standard to scale your solution. However, you end up with multiple INI files to maintain for each instance since it is not clustered. Again, because your needs are unique, there is no "right" choice—just the best fit for your particular situation.

WebLogic also includes an embedded HTTP server, or some customers will need an Oracle HTTP server to handle these requests. For the majority of customer situations, the embedded HTTP server will work well, but if you desire additional scale/control or need to put an HTTP server into a demilitarized zone (DMZ) behind a firewall, other options are available. The advantage with a dedicated HTTP server is that, as a dedicated server, it can provide finer controls in the httpd.conf file and some additional flexibility.

Your main control for WebLogic from an EnterpriseOne perspective is the Java heap size. Currently, WebLogic uses multiple JDKs, depending on the platform you are running. On the 64-bit platforms, which are primarily used, 64-bit JDK will usually be required. You should always refer to the EnterpriseOne MTR regarding the various web servers to ensure that you have the appropriate heap size for your application/ Tools levels.

Previous WebLogic releases that used the 32-bit JDK will normally have a smaller heap size, in the 768–1280MB range, with the general "sweet spot" being 1024 or possibly 1280MB. You normally wouldn't go above the 1280MB level, because the heap allocation within a 32-bit address space will usually have other heaps that need some memory as well. If you go too far above 1280MB, you decrease available memory to those other heaps to the point that they may be exhausted under certain loads.

NOTE
These are not absolute limits by any means, but if you see out-of-memory errors, heap size might be the cause. Also, on the 32-bit platforms such as Windows, we would sometimes see customers operate eight or more JVMs with the Physical Address Extension (PAE) option enabled. A misunderstanding can occur even though Windows could address the memory above 4GB—that does mean it was executing code above 4GB since the 32-bit address is still a limit. What would sometimes occur is that with so many large processes using memory, you would exhaust portions of the Windows OS, which would cause performance issues. The usage of 64-bit OSs now removes this limitation, but you might consider this in case you have older Windows 2003 boxes with a large number of JVMs.

The 64-bit JDKs provide much more potential address space for the memory, but, as mentioned, you need to balance that with the potential garbage collection pause times. Depending on the JDK version in use, the Java heaps are created and allocated differently. The Sun and IBM JDKs have multiple heaps, while the JRockit JDK generally has two heaps by default or sometimes just one, depending on command arguments. In the EnterpriseOne MTRs for web servers, Oracle recommends for Linux, Solaris, and Windows that you consider using the JRockit JDK, and we strongly agree with that recommendation. The production mode JRockit appears to operate very well with WebLogic, with noticeable performance improvements. This doesn't mean that the others are bad or run slowly, but it helps demonstrate how important it can be to match the JDK to your platform.

The 64-bit JVM heap sizes that we recommend are in the 768–3072MB range for JRockit with most instances using 1024 or 2048MB. If you're using the Sun or IBM JDK, you might want to stay in the 1024–2048MB range as well. Also of note for the later JDKs of 1.6 and higher, opinions/documents differ about whether the –Xms and –Xmx (min and max heap) values should be equal or different. Table 3-7 shows some basic settings for JDK vendors' products, but you can, of course, experiment yourself and your results may be different.

NOTE
For the JRockit R27 JDK, a performance case study document on Metalink, document ID 1199775.1, has sometimes been misunderstood by customers for later releases such as R28. The –XXcallProfiling -XXaggressive:opt applied to R27 only and the syntax changed in R28 so that they would not work. There are equivalent values (–XX:+UseCallProfiling –XXaggressive), but the application of these recommendations does not appear to be needed in R28 and later. This means you shouldn't consider using these settings, even though they did provide value in a previous JDK. This example shows that changes in the software don't always have the same effect in later releases, so you should not generalize a practice across releases. Just because it worked before doesn't always mean it will behave that way in the future.

JDK Vendor	–Xms (min) –Xmx (max) Settings
JRockit R27 or R28	Should be equal. Example: –Xms=1024m –Xmx=1024m
Sun JDK 1.6 or later	Should be equal. Example: –Xms=1024m –Xmx=1024m
IBM JDK 1.5 or later	Min should be lower to ramp up heap. Example: –Xms=64m –Xmx=1024m

TABLE 3-7. *JVM Heap Argument Observations*

WebSphere

IBM WebSphere is another option with a deep and vast array of features. You can cluster web instances using Server Manager, similar to WebLogic, to scale and manage a large configuration with WebSphere Network Deployment (ND). Generally, the installed JVM command-line arguments will work well; you just need to adjust the min and max heap sizes for that JVM.

The IBM JDK should be used for best performance on WebSphere, and for most platforms you can select either a 32- or 64-bit JDK. With newer hardware and EnterpriseOne Tools releases such as 9.1, you may want to consider using a 64-bit JDK for additional memory addressing. As noted, for the minimum and maximum Java heap, you can consider a minimum value of 64MB for the 64-bit IBM JDK and the maximum heap in the 1024 to 2048MB range. If you're using a 32-bit IBM JDK, the maximum value should be lower, since you have a lower address ceiling. Older WebSphere releases and operating systems should use the 32-bit JDK, and you have the option for 64-bit JDK on newer hardware/operating systems. You can generally switch between them for evaluation in your configuration if desired.

Smaller web instances can benefit from 32-bit JDK, and larger numbers of users and heaps benefit from the 64-bit JDK in most situations. The key point for the 64-bit JDK is that it is not always a better performer, since you double the memory pointer sizes and the various heap sizes do increase. IBM has performed a number of optimizations in IBM JDK 1.6 and WebSphere V7.x and later, but each customer situation is different. If you can run the JVMs in 1024MB, a 32-bit JDK may be the best bet, but if you have the hardware and operating support, a 64-bit JDK may be a valid consideration. Table 3-8 shows some basic settings for IBM JDK versions.

Oracle Application Server (OAS)

The Oracle Application Server (OAS) is in "sunset" for EnterpriseOne, meaning that WebLogic Server is the direction for the future. Remember that OAS is no longer supported as of EnterpriseOne Tools 9.1, but we will cover this topic briefly since it is still widely used on older releases.

JDK Vendor	–Xms (min) –Xmx (max) Setting
IBM JDK 1.6 or later 64-bit	Min should be lower to ramp up heap. Example: `–Xms=64m –Xmx=2048m`
IBM JDK 1.5 or later 32-bit	Min should be lower to ramp up heap. Example: `–Xms=64m –Xmx=1024m`

TABLE 3-8. *IBM 32- and 64-bit JDK Min/Max Heap Suggestions*

One of the key features we will miss about OAS that WebLogic and WebSphere do not offer is the multiple JVM option. For smaller EnterpriseOne customers, this was a nice vertical scaling option on a server to expand your JVMs easily by just "changing the number" in the OAS console or Server Manager. It essentially used the same INI files for that web instance and would launch an additional java.exe process that was internally load balanced. So if your server had the capacity and the HTTP server was set correctly, you could double or triple the users on a server. For those customers that desired a simple feature to increase their web instance capacity on a server without going to clusters or load balancers, this was ideal. OAS offers clustering features as well, but they are not managed from the Server Manager application.

OAS uses Sun JDK 1.5 or 1.6 in the 32-bit version. As noted, the min/max heap is generally equal and usually should be at 1024MB or 1280MB at the highest. Also, another key JVM argument for OAS is the `-XX:MaxPermSize=128m`. In some cases, if this is not present for an OAS JVM, it will not start or will experience out-of-memory errors relatively quickly. This setting increases the permanent generation heap (remember that Sun and IBM JDKs have several heaps created). Here's an example statement:

```
-XX:MaxPermSize=128m -Xms1024m -Xmx1024m
```

One item to note about these settings for production is that you can allocate lower values down to about 50 percent for test instances if you have low numbers of users. So for a development web instance, you might have the settings at

```
-XX:MaxPermSize=128m -Xms512m -Xmx512m
```

Apache HTTPD

The Apache HTTP server can be used by any of the aforementioned application servers. WebLogic contains an embedded HTTP server, but it can use the Oracle HTTP server as well. The main advantage to this open source–based server is the flexibility of the httpd.conf directives you can use, depending on your configuration. Three main settings provide improved performance and stability in an EnterpriseOne configuration.

`ThreadsPerChild` (Windows) or `MaxClients` (Unix/Linux) can be set for the number of HTTP requests that can be handled. This is the main setting for an HTTP server that must be tuned for the workload coming in. You'll usually set this to be at a minimum equal to the total number of users that all JVMs running on that server can handle. For example, if three JVMs are running with a JAS.INI `MaxUsers=100` on each, the `ThreadsPerChild=300` or `MaxClients=300` should be the minimum specified. If these values are not the minimum and lower values are used, users will probably report unexpected timeouts and errors in the various JAS logs as the sessions are denied.

HTTP compression reduces the size of objects moving across the network. With Server Manager, these settings can now be applied from the application server; see the example directives listed next. (Generally, only the IBM HTTP server uses these directives if you don't want to use Server Manager.)

```
# Compression module for HTTP

LoadModule deflate_module modules/mod_deflate.so

SetOutputFilter DEFLATE

AddOutputFilterByType DEFLATE text/html text/plain text/xml

AddOutputFilterByType DEFLATE application/ms* application/postscript

SetEnvIfNoCase Request_URI \.(?:gif|jpe?g|png|js) no-gzip dont-vary

SetEnvIfNoCase Request_URI \.(?:exe|t?gz|zip|bz2|sit|rar)$ no-gzip
dont-vary

SetEnvIfNoCase Request_URI \.(?:pdf|ube|csv)$ no-gzip dont-vary
```

It's important to note that you must ensure that you enable compression *only* at either the HTTP server or in the Server Manager Web runtime settings under Enable Compression. You'll find several documents on the Oracle Metalink site regarding HTTP server compression, but the recommend method is to use the Server Manager option.

Expiration headers such as the following are also extremely beneficial to cache static content on the local browser to speed up the web page loads. As with HTTP compression, you can set this option in Server Manager web runtime settings under Static Cache Expiration to 31 days, which in pre-9.1 Tools was set in seconds at 2592000, or now 31 days. If you want to use the HTTP server, an example appears next, but the key again is to ensure that you do NOT set this feature in both Server Manager and httpd.conf. If you do enable in both it can result in incorrect web pages at the client browser since you are "double expiring" the files.

```
LoadModule expires_module modules/mod_expires.so

LoadModule expires_module modules/mod_expires.so

# HTTP header expirations Directives

ExpiresActive on

ExpiresByType image/gif "access plus 30 days"

ExpiresByType image/jpeg "access plus 30 days"

ExpiresByType text/css "access plus 30 days"

ExpiresByType application/x-javascript "access plus 30 days"
```

EnterpriseOne Web/JAS Server Configuration Settings

The JAS.INI for the HTML web server contains a large number of settings that allow you to tailor the EnterpriseOne web server to your requirements. The JDBJ.INI is used to configure the database and web cache settings used to access the database. The web.xml file is important because it includes many areas for the HTML web server configuration, such as the compression, expiration headers, and the ability to change the application server timeout manually, which influences the resources held for a user's session.

NOTE
The following suggestions concern the major settings that influence the overall HTML server resource usage and capacity. They are by no means a definitive recap of all the settings that can be changed. You can review individual settings via the Server Manager Help icons for more information, or consult installation guides and Metalink documents.

JAS.INI

The JAS.INI controls the HTML server in areas such as the web runtime, logging, security, and network settings. The defaults, listed in Table 3-9, do work well for the majority of customer configurations, but you will most likely want to review them for your specific implementation.

The main control is for the number of users, session timeouts, and the size of the grid. Other areas such as the grid row import option can increase memory usage if you change the default number of rows allowed. These settings involve a balancing act between the amount of heap memory available, the number of users, and the actions they perform. If you have 100 or more users opening 10 applications each, that will consume more resources than 100 users opening 3 applications each. The main point is that settings can influence the amount of data retrieved or the number of users in the web instance. The defaults give you a good starting point, but you'll have to monitor/evaluate the system over time to determine how well it performs.

JDBJ.INI

The JDBJ.INI controls the database access and cache settings. The defaults (see Table 3-10) will normally work well, but in some cases you'll need to modify them based on your EnterpriseOne configuration. For example, if you don't use a shared database proxy user, but have either a one-to-one or a few users–to-one database user proxy, the database connection pooling will need to be adjusted to reduce the minimum connections, so that you do not create a large number of JDBC connection pools utilizing the memory.

INI Setting	Usual Value	Comment
`MaxUsers`	100	Maximum number of users in the web instance. The applications in use influence whether this can be reached. Generally leave this at 100, but if changed, make sure the corresponding JDBC connections are adjusted.
`UserSession`	1200000 ms or 20 minutes	The user session timeout. When increased, resources are held in memory longer. Try to keep under 75 minutes or reduce the number of users in the web instance. Remember to adjust the timeout settings in httpd.conf and web application console to minimize unexpected issues. Several reference Metalink documents are available.
`EnableCompression`	True	HTTP compression helps the browser response time. It's recommended to enable at this level instead of HTTP server.
`CacheStaticContentSeconds`	2592000	Expiration headers for the web browser save static content in temporary Internet files folder.
`CacheStaticContentDays` (Tools 9.1 and later)	31	Replaces `CacheStaticContentSeconds` in prior tools release using days instead of seconds. Use 31 days since the default of 30 may not enable the expiration headers.

TABLE 3-9. *Suggested JAS.INI Settings*

INI Setting	Usual Value	Comment
[JDBj-CONNECTION POOL] minConnection	5	The minimum number of JDBC connections in a pool. If using a shared proxy, this can work well. With multiple proxy users, it's usually best to set this to 0 connections so you don't reserve connections that may not be used.
[JDBj-CONNECTION POOL] maxConnection	105	The JDBC maximum connection setting. Generally, must be greater than the JAS.INI MaxUsers. It's an artificial ceiling and doesn't allocate the connections until needed. Always set to at least MaxUsers + 5 or higher.
[JDBj-CONNECTION POOL] initialConnection	5	The JDBC connection pool initial connections. Default of 5 works with a shared proxy, but with several proxy users, set this to 1 to reduce the potential connections.
[JDBj-RUNTIME PROPERTIES] resultSetTimeout	60000	Result set data held in memory. Do *not* increase this beyond 3 to 5 minutes, since the longer the data is in memory, the increased risk for potential "out-of-memory" errors exists if a user retrieves a large set of data.

TABLE 3-10. *Default JDBJ.INI Settings*

Web.xml

The main item that can be added to the web.xml is a session timeout for OAS or WebLogic. For IBM WebSphere, this is done from the console under Server/Session Management/Session Timeout. The JAS.INI UserSession default is 20 minutes and controls when JAS cleans up an idle session. The application servers should generally be set for the timeout you desire, and the UserSession should be slightly longer in case the application server cleanup does not work for some reason.

For example, if you want a 60-minute timeout, the web.xml or WebSphere session timeout would be 60 minutes. The JAS.INI setting UserSession=4200000 or

70 minutes, which is slightly greater than the 60-minute timeout to allow web.xml or WebSphere to timeout first. If you reverse these, you run the risk of unexpected timeouts while the application server session is still present. You'll find several Oracle Metalink documents by searching for "session timeout" or document IDs 1266793.1, 647799.1, and 635265.1.

NOTE
Some Oracle documents suggest making this setting double the desired timeout value to allow the application server to perform the timeout first; if that does not occur for some reason, the JAS UserSession *will clean up after the fact. We have found that in later releases, you can keep these values closer, but make sure the* UserSession *timeout is still greater than the application server timeout.*

Database Server

The EnterpriseOne database server is the heart of the system. Without this key server you have no way to search or change the data. Whatever database platform(s) you choose for EnterpriseOne, try to choose the best combination of hardware/software to go with it. If you anticipate a lot of batch activities, you typically may need more database memory and better performing disk rates to retrieve large amounts of data quickly.

The batch requirements for customers tend to be understated in a number of situations, or how the data selection is created may be inefficient. Some have an erroneous perception that most tuning should occur at the database level to speed up the performance. Although it is true that an index can help a key query in most situations, the application design and business process are usually sending a multitude of requests to the database. The main purpose of a database server within an EnterpriseOne infrastructure is to respond to requests for data. We don't place logic/procedures or triggers on the database because the CNC architecture insulates the applications from the underlying technology. To do this would bend that base rule, and you would become dependent on specific features of that database platform.

Purpose

EnterpriseOne database server is a critical building block of the implementation and should be sized to meet or exceed your projected workloads. Working with the hardware vendor for sizing can be very useful, and input from an experienced technology/CNC consultant offers additional benefits. The main goal of sizing is to ensure that the database infrastructure can meet the demands of the business processes executed against it.

With new installations, the sizing may not be quite right if some of your assumptions do not hold true during the implementation. This is a frequent occurrence, which is why it is so important to include performance and scaling tests once the business processes and code development have been completed. You then have an opportunity to ensure that the infrastructure can satisfy the desired business goals.

Configuration Aspects

In Chapters 8 and 9, we will discuss various tuning scenarios for the EnterpriseOne database platforms. With regard to the infrastructure design, you should consider the following high-level elements:

- The database server(s) from the processor, memory, network speed, and disk configuration that it uses.

- The disk subsystem upon which the database is highly dependent:

  - If you're working with System i, you can leverage the IBM hardware sizing that has JD Edwards' statistics and benchmarks to provide very good disk performance configurations.

  - If a SAN or network appliance is used, the overall disk read and write response under various loads is critical. Typically, a SAN may be shared with other servers, and you may need to consider those workloads.

  - For a production configuration, if possible, try to separate the EnterpriseOne system from other workloads to minimize contention for disk resources.

WebCenter/Portal Server

The Oracle WebCenter and IBM WebSphere Portal are very robust environments that help you bring together a number of different systems. Implementing these configurations generally requires expertise and experience with a number of infrastructure items in place, such as a database for the metadata, directory services, application servers for the portal code, and content servers to provide the information. EnterpriseOne may be the only application used for the portal, but most customers usually encompass in the portal project scope a number of areas or websites for the company. For most customers, portal configuration is a project comprising a number of objectives and scope.

Due to this potential complexity, we suggest that, unless you have experience implementing a portal configuration, you enlist assistance. Planning, tuning, and implementing a portal may be a challenge for a number of IT organizations with a large number of disciplines required to pull it all together.

Portal Configuration Settings

The following is by no means a comprehensive list of performance recommendations, but it provides some considerations when you're implementing and tuning your portal configuration from an EnterpriseOne perspective:

- Review and ensure that the MTR levels are present, because EnterpriseOne usually supports very specific release and patch levels.

- Consider load balancing and cache accelerator functionality since most portals tend to have high-availability requirements and user workloads. If some of the content is cached, that can reduce the internal traffic needed to request pages continuously from a content server.

- Ensure that you have HTTP compression and expiration headers in use to reduce the client browser and network traffic requirements.

- Review the various timeout settings through the multiple servers in the portal configuration to ensure a good experience for the customer. You can set timeouts at a number of places, such as the load balancer, HTTP server, content servers, and portal servers. If any of the timeout settings are significantly different, you can observe session issues or resources being consumed unexpectedly.

- Ensure that the various middleware infrastructures, such as database repositories and directory and identity/authentication services, can handle the workloads being introduced. These infrastructures also usually have levels of redundancy that provide higher availability in case of failures.

Business Services/Transaction Server

BSSV and the EnterpriseOne Transaction Server (Real Time Events, or RTE) are typically used when you want to interface with other systems. The BSSV server exposes the EnterpriseOne business functions from either predefined or custom functions created through the Object Management Workbench (OMW) toolset accessed via web standards. Using these services allows you to expose certain functions with EnterpriseOne security and insulate your system from underlying changes that can occur to the ERP system. These services have evolved from previous architectures, such as XPI (XPInstall) and webMethods. Some example services delivered in BSSV by Oracle are address book inquiries and sales and purchase order lookup. Oracle Metalink document ID 967281.1 provides reference information regarding getting started and running EnterpriseOne BSSV.

One item essential for tuning your BSSV server is to know the various sizes of SOAP (Simple Object Access Protocol) messages arriving at the server. If these are smaller messages, under 10–12K, you can use transaction rates that are higher than you'd use for much larger messages in the 100–150K range. (This makes sense, since the workload is similar to an interactive web user.)

The transaction server allows you to trigger real-time events as they occur in the business functions for another system. The transaction server utilizes real-time events from EnterpriseOne that can be placed on different queue types using Java-based messages. A couple of examples are a JMSQueue and JMSTopic queue, in which you publish the event and a subscriber (or subscribers) retrieves the information. These events are placed in tables and queues with communication mechanisms to help guarantee delivery between the systems.

Both servers operate within web containers on application servers similar to the HTML instances used for the web client. You can tune for performance with JVM heap settings, and various INI settings can change the concurrency and sessions.

Configuration Settings

Below in Tables 3-11 and 3-12 we provide some useful settings for the BSSV and EnterpriseOne Transaction server to consider.

Setting	Usual Value	Comment
Enterprise server call objects	6–10 users per Call Object kernel (COK)	Generally place 6–10 BSSV users per COK.
[NETWORK QUEUE SETTINGS] JDENETTimeout	60	JDENet timeout may need to be increased if SOAP messages are large; large messages consume more call object thread memory and hold a connection longer. Consider a timeout in the 120 to 300 second range.
JVM heap size	-Xmx768m	You can set the JVM max heap between 768MB to 1500MB for 32-bit and 768MB to 4096MB for 64-bit. The main influence is the memory on the server and how you want to break out the JVMs.
httpd.conf	ThreadsPerChild (Windows) or MaxClients (System i, Unix/ Linux)	Similar tuning to an HTML server; ensure you have enough sessions for the concurrent BSSV workload coming in. Generally 250 is a good number for 1 to 2 JVMs, assuming 100 users/JVM.

TABLE 3-11. *BSSV Potential Settings*

JAS.INI Setting	Potential Value	Comment
[EVENTS] `processingConcurrency`	1–4	Number of threads that can be used. For additional throughput can be set to 4.
[EVENTS] `triggerListenerDelay`	10000–5000	Default is 10 seconds; you can reduce this to 5 seconds if you have higher workloads. The value is in milliseconds.
[EVENTS] `maxTransferSessionSize`	5000–10000	Event transfer session size can be increased to 10,000 bytes for each transmission.
JVM heap size	`-Xmx1024m`	Set the JVM max heap between 512MB to 1500MB for 32-bit and 768MB to 4096MB for 64-bit. Main influence is the memory on the server.

TABLE 3-12. *Transaction Server Potential Settings*

Deployment Server

The deployment server typically does not have much tuning needed as long as the EnterpriseOne MTRs have been met or exceeded. The only time we find performance or tuning opportunities is when full package builds are executed on the deployment server. The full package build process involves significant disk, memory, processor, and network activity, which can bring to light limitations in those server resources. The resolution to any performance concern is to increase the server resource such as network speed or the memory if paging is observed.

We listed in the above deployment server section the generally recommended resources that may be required above the EnterpriseOne MTRs for good performance. The one caveat to remember is that you should NOT add other Windows services to the deployment server such as DNS, DHCP, WINS, or other third-party software. The reason is that we want to minimize contention of the deployment server resources and reduce the risk of potential software conflicts.

Summary

In this chapter, we reviewed the major building blocks required to implement the EnterpriseOne system. In later chapters, we'll provide information regarding a number of tuning areas. The base services required for EnterpriseOne are the database, EnterpriseOne services, web/HTML services, and a deployment server. You can consider a number of architecture choices, depending on the platform(s) chosen for the implementation. The key point is that if you can keep the architecture streamlined and consistent, this typically provides a stable infrastructure upon which to operate the configuration. If you take CNC architecture to the extreme, such as mixing/matching all the various platform choices in one configuration, you will have a much more complex environment that requires many different skill sets to operate, manage, and maintain.

The ideal CNC architecture has the three main layers—presentation, logic, and database—placed as close together as possible. We reference layers in different contexts throughout this book because the CNC architecture can separate or blend them as needed. At least the logic and database layers should be on the same server, or the servers should be on the same high-speed network switch to minimize latencies. The database should have the fastest disk subsystem that can be procured, since disk I/O tends to be the bottleneck in most implementations. The web server(s) should be within the same local network as well if possible for optimum performance.

Whenever possible, if you have significant change in the architecture, work with the hardware vendor and experienced consultants to assist with the EnterpriseOne sizing. Remember to execute performance and scaling exercises if you have untested business processes with response or runtime expectations. If you don't test and evaluate how your particular configuration works, you may be in for a number of surprises and heartaches when you move into production. The only true way to know whether your configuration can support a specific load is to test the system with that load on it prior to go-live.

CHAPTER
4

Implementing a
Performance Tuning
Methodology

As technical solutions continue to evolve, companies will push boundaries to squeeze as much out of their implementations as they possibly can. Many companies ask the basic question, How do we get the most out of our system? To meet this type of challenge, system administrators must have a solid execution plan, be armed with tools to meet ever-changing business requirements, address expanding system growth, and ensure that their implementations operate as efficiently as possible. The proper tuning of an Enterprise Resource Planning (ERP) system is a complex, ongoing process that can be affected by a myriad of factors.

Chapter 1 of this book provided an overview of our performance tuning methodology and the major components (pillars) that affect performance of an ERP solution. This chapter takes a closer look at these concepts and provides an in-depth view of how they can help you get the most out of your implementation. We'll cover in depth the details of the methodology components and how to leverage them to tune your implementation effectively.

The primary tenant of the tuning methodology is a structured way to break down a performance problem into smaller parts. (It's like the old joke: How do you eat an elephant? One bite at a time!) To do this, we must identify the key bottleneck(s), examine the different layers of the system, implement system change(s), and measure the performance effects of these changes. After all, if we don't have a way to measure, how do we know whether we had any effect?

By applying the tuning practices associated with this methodology, administrators will not only be able to solve existing performance issues, but by extending these practices into continuous tuning efforts, they will be able to benchmark their implementations to show historical performance data. This type of data can be crucial, especially if your company has acquired another company and you need to determine whether you can absorb a new set of users using your existing hardware.

NOTE
This actually happened to one of our customers. The IT manager later told me how good it felt to tell his IT VP that they had plenty of room to add all the users from the new acquisition and had the data to back it up. This helped ensure that the acquisition went smoothly, which was a major part of the company's business plan that year.

Our review of the major components of the methodology will start with the concept of tuning by pillars (see Figure 4-1). This concept is designed to help an administrator define where to focus their efforts in addressing a performance problem. To do this, we divide an EnterpriseOne implementation into multiple pillars, which

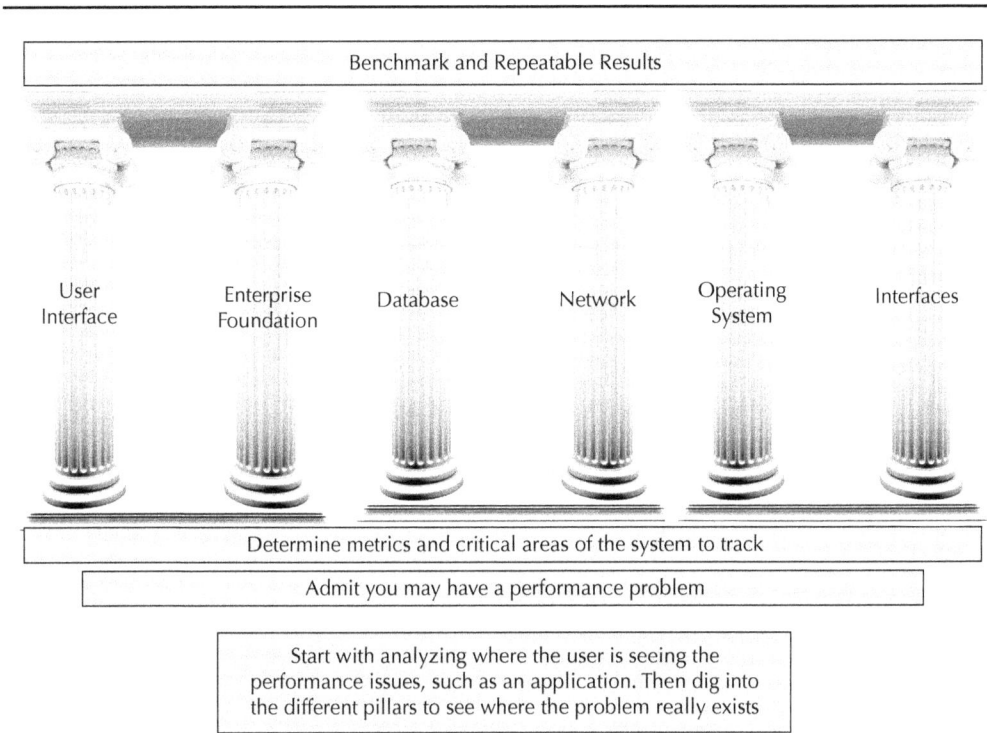

FIGURE 4-1. *Tuning methodology pillars*

will support your approach and success, just like the Greeks used pillars to support some their greatest architectural marvels.

The next step of the methodology is to drill into the components identified as containing the performance issue. In this part of the process, we move from the general view to the more detailed view; we start by identifying the problem in general terms. For example, suppose a user identified an issue in the application, and you have identified a very long SQL select statement. Next, by looking at the application, you can drill into the issue at the identified pillar. In this example, you have isolated your issue to the database pillar. Suppose the performance problem is limited to the database and revolves around specific SQL statements:

- Do you need to tune this statement to meet your performance goal? (Remember always to set a goal to achieve, or you will never know when you are done tuning.)

- Does this mean you'll need to add an index, change the SQL statement, purge unneeded data, or change database-specific settings?

These are the type of detailed performance questions that should be considered during the second step of the methodology. Once you've identified the changes that need to be made, you can implement them one at a time and measure the effects to ensure that the changes being made are heading in the direction you want. Your objective here is to provide the user community and management with specifics. (For example, you have made a 10 percent improvement in performance by adding index A.) In addition to having a solid metric in place (to measure your improvements), you need to define your goal clearly so you not only know when you are successful but can prove it.

As you complete more and more detailed changes and keep knocking reported performance issues off your list, you might think that you are close to completing your tuning journey. Truth is, however, that you have just started your travels. Making your user community and management happy is a good first step; the true key is to keep them happy.

To keep them happy and your implementation running efficiently, the final part of the methodology is designed to provide continuous improvements. This part deals with setting a baseline for the system. This effort allows you to know what level of performance is in the "sweet spot" and when the system is operating outside of that performance window. The second part of this concept is to use this type of information as a boilerplate to help you know exactly what change need to be made when more users are added, a new company is acquired, data requirements increase, and so on.

Performance Tuning Methodology Basics

A wise man once said, "Don't try to swallow a whale in one bite." This sage advice can be applied successfully regarding performance tuning as well as seafood. As with anything complex, it is a good practice to be able to break down an issue into smaller parts. This represents one of the main pillars of a solid tuning methodology.

In the context of tuning an EnterpriseOne implementation, one of your first requirements is to be aware of the key components of your system. Next, you'll need to identify groups of subcomponents.

The next major step in the process is to leverage a structured way to help identify where the performance issue is occurring. IT professionals always hate to hear the general feedback, "the system is slow," and although this is truly an issue, it does not really help in your efforts to identify or resolve the problem for your user community. Like many things, the devil is in the details. So part of a solid methodology is to continue your efforts by having some structured questions/procedures in place to help users identify where a problem is occurring. These will help identify where the system administrator needs to start looking for a performance issue and will help isolate issues quickly.

Let's assume, then, that the administrator has already looked through some of the components (or pillars). The general questions you ask and procedures followed at this point can provide a first cut at tuning efforts at the "big-knob" level—the macro-level changes that get you into the ballpark. These changes are implemented at the pillar of the implementation where the problem is occurring (such as the database, disk, and so on) and are generally larger component changes. After each change, the system administrator(s) would measure the performance impact of the change.

NOTE
You must have agreed-upon metrics regarding what you are measuring in order to show that your changes have affected the system. Do not depend on user perception only, because different users will have different perceptions. By using solid data points and metrics to show the effects to the system, you will be able to achieve your performance tuning goals.

Once you have made the major changes, you can start moving into the "small-knob," or micro-tuning, efforts. These efforts will allow you to identify and address very specific reported performance issues to make changes that are directly focused on the identified issue rather than on general performance issues. An example of this might be adding a specific index to a table to address a specific query that the business requires. Another possible example would be changing the logic of a program that executes thousands of quick SQL statements to leverage the database to gather this information (a join). Once changes are applied, the identified business process can be benchmarked with the changes in place to establish the performance.

The application of a structured performance tuning methodology not only allows you to identify and address performance issues at the macro and micro levels (big knob/small knob), but it also provides the structure to benchmark the process so you can start "boilerplating" major settings. You'll have the tools in your belt to address not only performance issues but to address common business drivers in your implementation.

TIP
Don't reinvent the wheel every time you are trying to resolve performance issues. Keep a log of the changes made to your system for performance tuning. This historical data often helps you to identify future issues more quickly.

Parts of the Methodology

Let's take a closer look at the individual concepts. As we mentioned, one of the first steps in the methodology is to be aware of all of the major technical components that can affect your implementation's performance and stability. Let's take a moment to break these down a little more, and then we can discuss how to leverage them effectively in your performance tuning efforts.

The User/Web Interface Pillar

This pillar may seem like a little bit of a misnomer, because it covers a lot more than just how the application or report looks and feels. However, this is an easy way to discuss what the user is directly experiencing when trying to perform their job duties. The user interface pillar comprises several different parts.

- Applications: Specific programs reported/identified as underperforming

- Batch reports/UBEs (Universal Batch Engines)

    - Reports running longer than acceptable

    - Reports that interfere with others (locking/blocking issues)

    - Reports with poor data selection

- HTML/Java Application Server

    - Application server settings that affect overall session performance

        - Pool settings

        - Threads

        - Heap size

        - Garbage collection settings

    - EnterpriseOne JAS settings: JAS.INI settings that can help you tune performance

First, you identify the business process that is slow. What is the user doing when the problem occurs? Is he entering sales orders or receiving large purchase orders? This type of information allows you to identify the applications and reports that are considered slow. Remember that, at this point, you want to have or set metrics to measure what acceptable performance truly is.

After you identify the application and reports that are slow, you can use tools such as Performance Workbench to identify where the application is spending most of its time. This type of tool can help you quickly isolate where a process is spending its time in a large debug log file. Is the slowdown due to a database call, or is the time spent in a business function? The answer to this question will help you identify what pillar you need to focus on next.

NOTE
Performance Workbench can be downloaded from support.oracle.com.

The next part of the user interface pillar comprises the HTML/JAS components that present or serve up the application to the user community. This is where you can do some analysis and improve performance across multiple application suites within EnterpriseOne. For example, you can evaluate whether your users are having problems with specific applications (such as sales orders or purchase orders) or if the issues are limited to a certain subset of users (maybe you need to look into security settings).

TIP
It is a good practice to test with and without security.

As you collect a solid list of problematic applications, you can continue to isolate the problems by collecting and reviewing the JAS logs. These logs will help you identify whether any base-level errors are occurring. Use the information gathered from these logs with information from the Call Object kernel (COK) logs on the server, and you can quickly identify what the problematic applications are actually doing. As you further examine the HTML/JAS pillar, you can focus on items such as load balancing to determine whether this is being handled correctly. (For example, is one server over-stressing more than another, or do the reported problems only occur on one server only?) In addition to these issues, the JAS logs will generally indicate whether you need to adjust heap size (java.lang.out.of.memory errors). It is a good practice to set your heap size from 1GB to 3GB. It is also a good practice to keep an eye on your garbage collection by setting verbose garbage collection on the JVM. You can also look at database connections to ensure that they are set correctly for each HTML server (JVM). As you can see, the user interface/web pillar has a lot of subcomponents.

TIP
You should perform stress tests on your system— with both production users and in a controlled manner. What will your approach be? The authors recommend that you use an automated testing tool if possible. These tools can help to identify performance issues when volume is the only way to isolate them.

At this point, even if it appears to the user that the application is running locally, you know that the majority of the EnterpriseOne application executes on back office servers. With this in mind, let's talk about the EnterpriseOne foundation pillar.

The Enterprise Foundation Pillar

The following EnterpriseOne services are part of the foundation pillar:

- EnterpriseOne Kernel processes

- JDE.INI configuration

The EnterpriseOne foundation pillar is composed of the Enterprise, Logic, Batch, and Application servers:

- The Enterprise server includes the database as well as the EnterpriseOne host code. The host code runs the business logic (BSFNs) and batch applications or reports.

- A Logic server runs the EnterpriseOne host code and service business function (BSFN) calls. These calls are from the interactive (user) front end.

- A Batch server runs the EnterpriseOne host code and handles batch or UBE processes.

- An Application server runs the EnterpriseOne host code but services BSFN or batch processes.

When thinking about this pillar, think not only horizontally, but vertically. This means you can tune an individual server or you can add servers to help handle load if you need more horsepower.

A real-world example would be dividing up your business logic and your batch application or reporting. This allows you to dedicate each server to one function, such as an intensive report, so will not take CPU and memory away from business logic. Many of our clients leverage this type of strategy so that they can focus specific resources on their solution (servers for interactive and different servers for batch, for example).

Regardless of the type of server you're leveraging, a number of settings in the JDE.INI file can affect the server's overall performance. To determine where in this pillar you need to look, you should determine what the purpose of the server is. For example, if the server is configured to service interactive users (a logic server), then you should have a number of call objects configured. A good rule of thumb is to have five users per COK; this will prevent too many users being placed on any one COK, and it's a large enough setting to avoid consuming more resources to start the kernel than you get out of it. If you are configuring a batch server, you do not need any COKs. If the system has a large number of users, you might need to increase the number of security kernels—a good rule of thumb is 80 users per security kernel.

In this pillar you can also adjust things like the number of job queues (multithreaded or single threaded). While it is common to leverage multithreaded queues to allow batch processes to run in parallel, an effective practice is to set up queues for short- and long-running jobs. This type of strategy prevents short-running jobs from being stuck behind long-running jobs (which provides users the impression that the system is performing poorly). By dividing your single threaded and multithreaded job queues by the speed of the job, it is also possible to limit the number of job queues you need to manage. As you can see, the foundation pillar provides a number of ways to tune the system, not only to address existing performance issues but also to allow your system to grow with your business.

The Database Pillar

The database pillar of an EnterpriseOne implementation is the backend relational database solution component of the system.

This pillar stores business data/information as well as code components. The EnterpriseOne solution offers a great advantage, because it supports a number of different database solutions: SQL Server, UDB, or DB/400 can be used as a database with EnterpriseOne. So if staff is trained on one of these database types or a corporate standard requires a type, you can leverage that database in your implementation.

Regardless of the database solution you choose for your implementation, however, you need to ensure that the database is tuned to accommodate how the EnterpriseOne system will be used. Unfortunately, there is no one-solution-fits-all scenario here (no silver bullets). You will configure your database one way if you are performing more updates, for example, versus doing more reads of large files. Do not shortchange your implementation—to be successful, the correct database resources must be part of your implementation team.

That being said, you can look at performance issues by reviewing a number of high-level items, such as the size of your redo logs and temporary database, and the location of your database files. Because the database has a large effect on overall performance, this is generally one of the pillars you will examine closely. If you are examining log files, you will be able to determine whether any SQL statements are taking an extended amount of time. This will help you determine whether you might tune these items to improve statements generated from the applications run by users. (We'll go into this in more detail in Chapters 8 and 9.)

The Network Pillar

The network pillar is like the mail service: it moves information between servers in the implementation. Some key items of the network pillar are

- Bandwidth
- Packet priority
- Latency

EnterpriseOne does a lot of talking between its different servers and the user interface. This is why the network pillar can have a direct impact on system performance, especially if you are working on a global implementation of EnterpriseOne. In such instances, you need to be very aware of what bandwidth is available to each office and the latency. EnterpriseOne does a lot of turns, so if high latency is an issue, users will experience slower performance due to the amount of traffic going back and forth. This latency adds up for the user. (This is why some clients leverage a solution such as Citrix to publish their Internet Explorer application for sites with limited bandwidth.)

You can also look into packet priority—which packets get a higher priority on the network. This can sometimes help ensure that you won't get "stuck behind traffic" for standard Internet access or even e-mail when you attempt to access the system.

NOTE
Be sure to set aside time to work with your network team as you work through your implementation.

The Operating System Pillar

A great strength of JD Edwards EnterpriseOne is that it is platform-independent. Different operating systems can be included in your architecture and the software can handle them without missing a beat. Although EnterpriseOne supports a number of different operating systems (AS/400, HP-Unix, Linux, Windows), it is important that you are aware that how these OSs are configured can affect performance.

We will focus on the Windows and Unix platforms, starting with the Windows operating system. In Windows, it is a good practice to validate some general settings, including the page file setting. The rule of thumb is to set it to 1.5 times the size of memory. As with other operating systems, it is a good idea to verify whether disk I/O issues exist. We would recommend using the Performance Monitor to validate items such as CPU, memory utilization, disk I/O, and other key performance indicators (KPIs). This will allow you to monitor the overall performance of your windows platform. This will help you to understand how your EnterpriseOne components (UBEs/BSFNs) are executing on your Windows operating system and let you head off potential performance bottlenecks.

Let's now move on to Oracle JD Edwards EnterpriseOne Enterprise Servers for UNIX operating systems (HP-UX, IBM RS/6000 AIX, and Sun SPARC platforms). EnterpriseOne is shipped with a standard directory structure for Unix and Linux Enterprise Servers. As most CNC administrators know, these directories are loaded off the platform pack and are installed to a base directory, such as /u01/JDEdwards/E900.

- The path code directory (under the base directory) holds information on business function (BSFN) shared libraries, object files, source files, and some limited spec files.

■ Under the path code directory are the bin32 (BSFN shared libraries) and spec directories.

■ The system directory holds system-wide executables, shared libraries, and source files. These are held in the subdirectories bin32, include, includev, lib, and libv32. System is shared across all of the path codes.

■ While the ini subdirectory holds the JDE.INI configuration file, the PrintQueue directory holds the PDF and UBE log information.

■ The log directory holds information on the jde.log/jdedebug.log information.

■ The package directory holds information on the server package processes.

Several aspects of the directory layout can be beneficial to the performance of your system. A key component here can be the performance of the disks for some of these key directories. If your system is I/O bound, this can have a dramatic effect on the overall performance of your system. It is a good practice to ensure that you do not have any wait queues.

As you start digging into disk performance, you'll find the `iostat` command particularly helpful. It reports asynchronous input/output (AIO), and I/O statistics for the entire system. Although it will provide you a view into the performance, you might have to go deeper, because it is common for clients to leverage SANs or NAS solutions. Work with your administrator to leverage the tools available on your solution to determine whether you have a disk issue. (Starting your examination with `iostat` can help determine where you might need look closer with your NAS/SAN specific tools.)

Another important part of the configuration of Unix systems is how interprocess communication (IPC) parameters are handled. (Note that the EnterpriseOne Server and Workstation Administration guide discuss these types of settings.) When you're starting the JD Edwards EnterpriseOne software on the server, the jdenet_n process will create a semaphore array containing the number of elements indicated by the maxNumberOfSemaphores parameter in the JDE.INI file. By default, Solaris 10 will allow a semaphore array with a maximum of 512 elements. If the semaphore setting in the JDE.INI file is greater than 512, the OS system default will need to be adjusted. This can be changed in Solaris 10 through the following command:

```
projmod -K 'process.max-sem-nsems=(privileged,2048,deny)' default
```

The command adjusts the default project to allow semaphore arrays with up to 2048 elements.

Kernels for HP-UX include a long list of configurable parameters that control the quantity of various resources available within the kernels. The EnterpriseOne Server software, IPC facilities, is sensitive to numerous kernel parameters. These settings differ across various vendor implementations of Unix. You can use the System

Administration Management (SAM) tool to adjust these parameters (this could require a reboot). On HP-UX systems, you can leverage the kmtune command. One of the types of parameters to keep an eye on is Message Queue:

- **mesg**   This value should be set at 1 (System-V style message queues are valid).

- **msgmni**   This setting represents the number of message queue identifiers. These determine the number of message queues that can exist in the system. You can use the following equation to estimate the number of message queues required:

  1 + jdenet_n + 2 × jdenet_k + (maximum number of concurrent runbatch, runube, and runprint processes)

- **msgtql**   Represents the number of message headers, the total number of messages that can be included in all the message queues at the same time. A good rule of thumb is to set the value equal to 10 times the message queue parameter (msgmni).

- **msgmap**   The value of this setting is the number of entries in the map of free message segments. The default value of msgtql + 2 should be used. (Note that this parameter is no longer used in Solaris 8.)

- **msgmnb**   This parameter is the maximum number of bytes that can reside on a single message queue at any one time. A rule of thumb is to set msgmnb at only a fraction of msgseg × msgssz.

- **msgmax**   Maximum size of a single message. Do not set msgmax with a larger value than the value of msgmnb. A rule of thumb is msgmax = msgmnb.

Here are a few more settings that can be used to verify semaphores:

- **sema**   This should be set at 1.

- **semmni**   The maximum number of semaphore identifiers that can exist throughout the system. The default value supplied with HP-UX and Solaris should be okay.

- **semmap**   Entries in the map of free semaphores. The default value of semmni + 2 is generally acceptable.

- **semmns**   The maximum number of semaphores that exist throughout the system. EnterpriseOne allocates 1000 semaphores by default, but this value can be modified in the JDE.INI file. The maxNumberOfSemaphores would then need to be adjusted.

■ semmnu   The number of semaphore undo structures for the entire system. Represents the maximum number of semaphores that can be locked at the same time. You can use the following rule of thumb for this setting:

1 + jdenet_n + jdenet_k + maximum number of runbatch processes + maximum number of runprint processes + maximum number of runube processes

■ semume   The maximum number of semaphore undo structures per process. Represents the number of semaphores that a process can lock. EnterpriseOne needs at least a value of 4 for semume.

■ semmsl   Applies to Solaris and newer versions of HP-UX and represents the maximum number of semaphores per unique identifier. This value should be equal to or higher than the maxNumberOfSemaphores in the JDE.INI file.

Shared memory settings can also be important:

■ shmem   This value must be 1 to allow shared memory.

■ shmmax   The value of maximum size of a single shared memory segment. Default value should be fine.

■ shmmni   The number of shared memory segments in the system. A good rule of thumb is to have 20 per instance of EnterpriseOne.

■ shmseg   The maximum number of memory segments that any process can attach. Default value is generally acceptable.

File descriptors can also have an effect:

■ nfile   The number of open files (sockets) in the system. This value needs to be set large enough to address EnterpriseOne's requirements. Ensure that this value at least matches the maxNetConnections parameter in the JDE.INI file.

■ maxfiles   The limit on the number of file descriptors that a process can have. This setting should equal a least the largest of maxNetConnection values in every JDE.INI files in use + 10.

■ maxfiles_lim   Represents the hard limit of file descriptors. The minimum value should be equal to at least the largest of all maxNetConnections + 10.

It is a good practice to verify the maxuprc (process setting), which represents the maximum number of processes that can run under a single user ID. Make sure you are not limiting the setting when starting your services to the point at which it cannot take advantage of your hardware.

The Interfaces Pillar

The interfaces pillar of an EnterpriseOne implementation comprises servers or services that move information in or out of the EnterpriseOne implementation. This can include EnterpriseOne Business Services or any other third-party applications.

- EnterpriseOne Business Services

- Z file loads

- Electronic Data Interchange (EDI)

- Application programming interface (API)

- Third-party interfaces: Bottomline Technologies Create!form, DCLINK

- Vertex

Business Services (BSSV) are web services for EnterpriseOne; they allow you to provide integrations using industry standards. This means this code can be reused, so it doesn't lock you into point-to-point integrations. The big piece here is that you have the correct number of BSSV JVMs and the correct number of servers to support the business logic that will be executed from your BSSV integrations.

Some other common integrations that can play into your tuning strategy are JD Edwards Z files (both custom and standard processes) and EDI. Depending on what you are loading through the Z files, you may need to change some logic and/or add some indexes. Both integrations should be examined to determine performance bottlenecks.

An API is a direct program call to the EnterpriseOne COK. This is normally done through an XMI call object API. Sometimes the call will use functionality that it really does not need, and/or that can be improved from a process perspective.

A final category for the interfaces pillar is kind of a catch-all, because it changes from implementation to implementation: third-party bolt-on applications. Some common applications are Create!form, DCLINK, and Vertex. To end users, it doesn't matter whether the performance issue they are experiencing is an interface or is driven from an external system; they simply view the issue as a problem that prevents them from doing their jobs. Because such interfaces can slow your system down, it is a good practice to ensure that you have identified performance bottlenecks both in and out of the EnterpriseOne implementation.

Having a Structured Plan

Each EnterpriseOne component can have a major impact on the overall performance and stability of the implementation. A performance bottleneck can exist in any of the major component pillars. The primary goal is to identify where that bottleneck exists and remove it. This process involves not only removing the bottleneck, but ensuring that you don't simply move it from one part of the implementation to another. To avoid that, when a performance issue is encountered, you need to evaluate the system to determine what layer of the implementation to examine. This is where having a structured plan comes in handy.

When performance issues are reported, you may hear general complaints, such as "It is just slow," that do you little good in resolving the overall issue. IT professionals need to focus on resolving the underlying issue(s) by asking users structured questions that help to isolate and identify issues. The following list provides examples of some structured questions that generally help get the ball rolling:

- Does the problem occur for only this user or for all users? This question allows you to isolate whether security might play a part in the issue.

- Does the problem occur in a batch application? This type of question helps you isolate where the problem is occurring.

- Does the problem occur in an interactive application? Is the user waiting for a response from a select? (This could be an issue at the database layer.) Is the delay moving between screens? Is the delay between lines? (This could be a code-related issue.)

- Can the performance issue be re-created?

Ideally, you can capture logs on the performance issue while it is happening, so you can focus in on the nature of the performance issue. Of course, in a lab environment you can do this easily, but in the real world this is not always possible.

TIP
When you're attempting to log an issue, it can be very painful to sort through a lot of clutter in your JAS/HTML logs. Instead of doing this, you can use Server Manager to set up logging for a specific user. You can then use the information to duplicate the performance issues and thus avoid having to sort through lots of data.

This discussion will review the application of the base methodology regarding a general performance issue when we are able to collect logs and when we are not able to collect logs. Let's assume that a user reports a performance issue. When our general performance questions are applied, we learn the following information:

When a select is performed in an interactive application, performance is not acceptable. The user is able to reproduce the issue, and every time she performs the select, performance is unacceptable. In addition, this problem occurs for multiple users.

How would we apply the methodology?

1. We have already isolated the issue by asking some specific questions. We have identified that the problem occurs in an interactive application, occurs for multiple users, and can be reproduced.

2. We break the issue down into smaller parts. Because this issue centers around a select statement, we'll start by examining the following:

   ■ **Security** Does the same issue occur for a user with no row security applied? Our row security may need to be changed from exclusive to inclusive, or vice versa. We may also have inefficient row security.

   ■ **Database** What does the select statement look like on the back end?

3. Next, we should try to reproduce this issue in a test environment with and without security applied. First, we'll capture a log on the issue:

   a. Identify the SQL statement in question in the log.

   b. Execute the statement outside of the ERP application directly against the database.

   c. Run processes such as explain plan to show how effective this statement performs on the database level. Then ask the following questions:

      ■ Are we scanning over the entire contents of a large table?

      ■ Are we leveraging indexed fields effectively?

4. At this point, we isolate this issue to a poorly performing SQL statement at the database level. But why is that statement performing poorly?

   In the case of our example, the statement is performing a full scan over a large table that contains sales information. To be most effective, this select should be performed over keyed or indexed fields. The user says she did leverage an index field. The logs we were able to capture show that this field is not to be utilized due to the user's row security.

5. At this point, it is essential that the users in this security role leverage another indexed field to ensure that their select statements perform effectively against the database.

NOTE
Savvy clients invest large amounts of capital, time, and tears executing performance testing prior to cutting their systems over to production. This is an important part of the performance tuning approach.

As you can see, applying a structured logical process can help you quickly identify problems in your implementation. Let's continue with our example, assuming this time that the user is unable to reproduce the issue at will. But even when you get into the annoying issue of sporadic problems occurring at seemly random times, you can still apply the logic of the structured methodology.

1. As in the first example, we have already isolated the issue quickly by asking specific questions. We determine that the problem occurs in an interactive application and occurs for multiple users. However, this time, the issue cannot be reproduced.

2. We continue to break the issue down into smaller parts: Because this issue centers around a select statement, we'll start by looking at the following:

   ■ **Security** Does the same issue occur for a user with no row security applied?

   ■ **Database** What does the select statement look like on the back end?

3. At this point, we try to reproduce this issue in a lower-level environment. Then we test this process with and without security applied.

4. Because the issue occurs at random times, we know it will be difficult to capture a log. However, we can still do the following:

   a. Identify the SQL statement in question by applying a different database user and tracing the session at the database level.

   b. Execute the statement outside of the ERP application directly against the database.

   c. Run processes such as explain plan to show how effective this statement performs at the database level.

      ■ Are we scanning over the entire contents of a large table?

      ■ Are we leveraging indexed fields effectively?

5. At this point, we've isolated this issue to a poorly performing SQL statement at the database level. But why is that statement performing poorly?

   The process occurred randomly, and when the user searched for a current order, the process went quickly. However, when the user performed a search on an order that was entered in the past, the application performed a join over the current and historical tables. This join was not properly indexed, so for each record it pulled from the current sales table, it would scan the complete contents of the historical table. As you can imagine, this placed quite an overhead on this type of inquiry (especially over time).

6. To be most effective, we should perform this select over keyed or indexed fields. In this case, the issue was easily resolved by matching the indexes between the sales and sales history tables.

TIP
Sometimes the where clause can impact performance. Examine where clauses to make sure they are properly formed.

In these two examples, we demonstrated how a bottleneck might appear at the database level and affect the performance of your system. These types of issues might be reproducible, or they might occur at seemingly random times. But what about the other parts of the implementation? Bottlenecks could appear at any of the identified layers of the implementation. If your system experiences slow network response times, application performance will suffer. If your system experiences slow I/O responses on your disks, you will experience performance lag. If your system is CPU or memory bound, you will find that your implementation will not meet your expectations. Regardless of the issue, following a structured process will allow you to identify and address performance problems.

Applying the Methodology with Benchmarks

So now that we have provided the outlines of the performance tuning methodology and some general examples of how to apply this type of methodology, we can expand on this information to discuss development of system benchmarks. The information you gather can be leveraged as "rules of thumb" that allow you to adjust your system to meet changing business requirements. This is essential to maintaining the performance and stability of your implementation. For example, you can make adjustments to your implementation to accommodate additional users required to meet increased business. The methodology will allow you to identify an average number of users to leverage per JVM. Once this number is reached, you will be able to trigger adding JVMs or adjusting kernel processes and other processes to allow for the additional users.

After you've identified these rules of thumb, you can encourage users to continue monitoring their systems. This will help you create benchmarks for "good" and "bad" performance. Benchmarking helps you understand how changes affect the implementation. In addition, it provides a view of system utilization by the business over time.

Conclusion

This chapter provided a detailed view of a structured performance methodology to assist you not only in identifying and addressing performance issues but to allow for the development and implementation of key industry practices and benchmarks. It is our hope that you are able to leverage the information presented here to tune and maintain your ERP implementation effectively. May your system run and run flawlessly.

CHAPTER
5

Understanding Base EnterpriseOne Technical Architecture

A s an administrator or as an end user of JD Edwards EnterpriseOne software, you'll need to keep up with the growing enhancements, features, and functionality of the evolving technology, and this can be a daunting challenge. You can spend 90 percent of your time to achieve a 10 percent benefit, or you can spend 10 percent of your time in key areas of the architecture to address 90 percent of the issues surrounding performance, scaling, and stability within the JD Edwards EnterpriseOne architecture. This chapter intends to show you how to achieve the latter.

The following discussion provides an overview of the EnterpriseOne technical flexible architecture. The chapter provides a foundation that will help you understand how the software is defined and a framework to help you answer the challenges of administration and performance characterization of the software. This chapter will also help you understand the capabilities of the software and why tuning these component areas will provide the best benefits.

Basic Principles of Performance Tuning

The goal of performance tuning is to achieve an EnterpriseOne application configuration that meets the needs of the business. Performance tuning can be required to accommodate EnterpriseOne batch applications, end user experiences of slowness, consumption of system resources such as processors and memory, scalability concerns, and future business plans.

Performance tuning is a disciplined approach to problem-solving that involves the following:

- Assessment of the area that requires tuning

- Identification and measurements of performance metrics

- Performance scope, goals, and problem definition where performance tuning is to be performed

- Design and planning of performance enhancements or changes to the system to achieve these goals, which should include a level of risk analysis, back-out procedures if the goal is not met, and timeframe or maintenance window in which the change can be implemented

- Metric measurements that are made to assess the level of post-change performance and to determine whether the goals of performance tuning have been met; also, an assessment of whether these changes have impacted other areas of the EnterpriseOne application needs to be made

- Final approval of the permanent change to the EnterpriseOne architecture

Performance tuning using these as guidelines can be very beneficial; however, it is often not practical in the real world. Customer experience has taught us that good performance can be accomplished in the EnterpriseOne architecture in the areas of the application code, database configuration, EnterpriseOne architecture design, and adjustments to the EnterpriseOne configuration files. The problem is, however, that performance tuning is often accomplished through modifications of the wrong area of the EnterpriseOne application architecture, and the resulting benefits are minimal. The following principle and analogies are presented to illustrate this point. What you're ultimately trying to determine is where the application is spending its time. If we address the performance issues in which the performance is the worst, then we can achieve the best benefit with the best chance at increasing a measurable performance metric goal.

Principle of Gears and Cogs

A *gear* is a rotating machine part with teeth, or cogs, that mesh together with other machine parts to provide torque. The most common example of a gear is used on a bicycle—the pedal gear assembly is used to provide torque to the bicycle chain, to transfer the power the bicyclist is providing to the pedals in a circular motion to the bicycle wheels, to generate forward momentum. When you're tuning gears and cogs, there are large gears for gross tuning and small gears for finer tuning.

As with a bicycle, the approach to tuning the EnterpriseOne architecture is to first adjust the larger "cogs" and then fine-tune the application by adjusting the smaller "gears." I like to call this adjusting the "big knobs" and adjusting the "small knobs." The big knobs dramatically change the functionality and performance of the EnterpriseOne software, and the small knobs have an important but lesser performance effect.

This top-down performance tuning method is most effective when you're defining the architecture of the EnterpriseOne hardware design. Turning the knobs too far in either direction can create hardware resource bottlenecks or an environment in which the CPU, memory, or disk resources of the hardware are underutilized. Furthermore, you need to consider designing the architecture for scaling the EnterpriseOne application and future business needs as you're working on the initial design and implementation.

You'll use the small knobs to fine-tune specific areas of the EnterpriseOne architecture. Such precision performance tuning is reserved for specific processes, process flows, or applications. The goal is to achieve a specific metric (execution time, transaction rate, level of performance, consumption of resources, and so on) and still meet the business requirements.

Principle of Peeling the Onion

You can also look at tuning as analogous to peeling an onion, which involves pulling back each layer to eventually expose the inner core. Each layer represents changes in the architecture and evaluation of the new level of performance.

Increasing performance is the goal, but often, changes in one specific area of the EnterpriseOne application can result in a decrease in performance in another area. For example, adding an index to optimize the performance of a specific batch job may benefit that batch job time execution, but it may decrease the performance of another batch process that relies on another index that is not chosen by the database optimizer because of the newly added index.

The other aspect of peeling the onion, for anyone who has worked in the kitchen, is that it can bring about a little discomfort in the form of crying or watering of the eyes. The analogy here is that the process of tuning is laborious and involves planning, trial and error, frustration, and anxiety—and, sometimes, tears.

Consider, for example, the addition of a new component to the JD Edwards EnterpriseOne architecture—say, a new batch process. The process introduction may be known to a few individuals in the company but not to the general user population. After the component is added, a flood of calls comes into the call center complaining of performance issues with interactive users: "It is slow," is the complaint. The call is made to the Oracle support staff with the entry in the problem description, "Performance is bad."

Your understanding of the basic components of the EnterpriseOne technical architecture will help you identify where best to address tuning the software application, tuning the database, or tuning the Java Application Server (JAS) and will help you provide Oracle support with a better problem description.

Understanding the EnterpriseOne Technical Flexible Architecture

Many resources, including the Oracle support web site for EnterpriseOne and the EnterpriseOne installation and administrative guides, are available to help you understand the basic components of the EnterpriseOne architecture. Although these guides are useful, they do not provide enough tuning and configuration information for the identification of the key parts of the EnterpriseOne architecture related most to performance. These guides and web sites can also be difficult to navigate when you're looking for information specific to scaling interactive application users and adjusting for high batch throughput to provide high stability in the EnterpriseOne architecture.

The EnterpriseOne administrator must also adjust for the ever-changing hardware resource fluctuation needs of the dynamic JD Edwards EnterpriseOne software. Interactive processes tend to be light on requests to the database but must provide quick response times while initiating business logic on the EnterpriseOne logic server. Batch processes are typically much heavier, in terms of database requests as well as logic execution, than normal interactive processes. The times of day that these processes are initiated must also be considered. Daytime processes are normally dominated by interactive application users, and the nightly processes are predominantly batch processes.

Complexity and Implementation Types

Two important points regarding the EnterpriseOne architecture are presented in this chapter:

- The complexity that can exist with an EnterpriseOne implementation

- The types of Enterprise Resource Planning (ERP) implementations—including the basic EnterpriseOne installation, the EnterpriseOne components, and the EnterpriseOne process flows

Each component will describe what areas of the technical components are best modified to handle each individual design scenario for performance tuning.

For the purpose of this discussion, size and complexity of the implementation are not simply defined by the traditional small, medium, and large categories. Traditional models historically base the EnterpriseOne design, architecture, installation, configuration, and implementation only on the basic requirements, including the number of interactive users and batch processes initiated on the system. A more accurate approach would be to define the EnterpriseOne implementations based on the *complexity* of the implementation.

Complexity can be viewed in terms of the amount of work required to achieve the technical and business goals of the company. It starts from a base installation of the EnterpriseOne software and is further defined by the amount of work that is involved to produce an environment in which the business continuance meets EnterpriseOne consumer needs, meets requirements from an IT support perspective, and provides for an acceptable level of business goals of the company. During the implementation, you must be careful to anticipate how each stage of the complexity will affect the overall performance of the architecture as it scales, grows, and evolves with the changing technical and business requirements of the company. You must provide for the maximum amount of flexibility while maintaining the most efficient environment for business continuity.

The levels of complexity are not a progression like a simple set of building blocks, but are aspects of the architecture that can impact performance and thus require a greater understanding of how these complexities must be managed as the architecture evolves.

EnterpriseOne Environments

The EnterpriseOne environments have specific roles and functions, from a pristine non-modified code set, through environments that support development of custom code, application of known code fixes, and staging areas for testing that comprise the EnterpriseOne software architecture design. Brief descriptions of the four main environments are provided here:

- **Production (PD)** This environment is the "live" or "go-live" user environment where tested code has been promoted and is available to the general user of the EnterpriseOne community. This environment is where "real" and actual users and processes are initiated. Little to no tolerance is accepted by the business, end users, or administrators of the system when things do not flow in a streamlined and efficient manner. There is a reason why "production environment" is two words: it is the environment that is the most important for a company's survival and business continuance, and it is what the company "produces" that brings services and a process flow for managing its business.

- **Staging (CRP)** This environment is the preproduction staging area, where final testing and validation of the environment is performed before customized code changes are applied and promoted to the production environment.

- **Development (DV)** The DV environment is where you develop customized code, apply EnterpriseOne bug fixes and security enhancements, and install performance and memory changes to existing software code to meet ongoing technical and business requirements. The DV environment is normally in a constant state of fluctuation and requires the greatest amount of software changes to control processes, procedures, and updates.

- **Pristine (PS)** The PS environment is commonly used for training, demonstration, and staging for upgrades and table conversions. The PS environment is also used for support issues to compare unmodified code, or out-of-the-box installed code, with modified code in other environments to help troubleshoot functional and performance problems with the EnterpriseOne software.

NOTE
A customer can implement multiple versions of any of these environments for use in quality assurance, training, development, and production on different servers. They are not limited to the specific function that the names may imply.

Complexity Categories

The complexities of the EnterpriseOne architecture are presented in Table 5-1 as categories 1 to 4. The use of the word "standard" in the context of complexity applies to the out-of-the-box EnterpriseOne software modules, programs, and processes that are delivered as part of the EnterpriseOne installation and application of Electronic Software Updates (ESUs) and versions of the EnterpriseOne Tools release. Table 5-1 presents the levels of complexity in increasing value: the higher the level of complexity, the more complex the EnterpriseOne architecture.

Complexity Level 1

Complexity level 1 is characterized by the following:

- Standard JDE modules

- Standard batch processing

- No third-party integrations

Standard JDE Modules   The standard JD Edwards EnterpriseOne modules include the complement of ERP software modules. The most common of these are the manufacturing, distribution, and finance modules.

Level of Complexity	Characteristic of Complexity
1	Standard JDE Module Standard batch processing No third-party integration
2	Custom and interactive processing Adding and configuring pathcodes
3	External integrations
4	High availability Redundancy Load balancing Fault tolerance Scalability Disaster recovery

TABLE 5-1.   *Levels of Complexity*

Standard Batch Processes Batch processes are the EnterpriseOne jobs that are initiated and that require no manual intervention to complete. All data input to these batch processes are in the form of batch processing options and predefined data selection; this gives the EnterpriseOne software the parameters it needs to initiate and run the batch process without manual intervention.

No Third-party Integrations Software integration involves processes that provide add-on functionality to the base EnterpriseOne feature set to enhance the overall ability and usefulness of the software. For the purpose of discussing complexity level 1, no integrations are yet implemented in the EnterpriseOne architecture.

Complexity Level 2

Complexity level 2 is characterized by the following:

- Custom interactive and batch processes
- Adding and configuring pathcodes

Custom Interactive and Batch Processes One of the greatest advantages that EnterpriseOne software has over its competitors is its flexibility. Much of the code that runs the EnterpriseOne software is available for the customer to view to help them understand its business logic, integrate its externally facing functions with other software, and modify it for their specific information technology and business needs. Customization is required to enhance the current software by changing the base logic component of the EnterpriseOne software. Normally, these enhancements would take the form of ESUs provided by EnterpriseOne software support; however, customers might need to make these modifications manually apart from this process or when immediate changes to the code are required.

Adding and Configuring Pathcodes Additional pathcodes may have been implemented as part of the EnterpriseOne installation, or they can be added and configured as the need arises. Level 2 complexity involves integrating existing pathcodes processes, procedures, and maintenance of the code base they represent into the current working customer environment.

Complexity Level 3

Complexity level 3 is characterized by the following:

- External integrations of third-party software

External Integrations of Third-party Software   External products brought into the EnterpriseOne architecture are considered a third level of complexity when describing the EnterpriseOne implementation. Integrations bring together other vendors' software into the EnterpriseOne architecture to enhance or replace current functionality.

Integration is performed for a number of reasons:

- Replace current functionality of the EnterpriseOne software with an integration that is either provided by other software already in use or intended to replace the current available module in EnterpriseOne.

- Many customers must integrate their current legacy systems along with the implementation of EnterpriseOne to meet their business needs. Bringing together current online and live software functions and integrating them with the EnterpriseOne software is, in the end, a common practice to achieve a coherent working ERP system environment for the company.

- Integrations of EnterpriseOne software may include Oracle Enterprise, E-Business Suite, and other Fusion Middleware components as well as other third-party ERP solutions.

- Integrations provide new functionality that is not currently available with the release of EnterpriseOne software that is desired by the information technology or business process requirements of the company. Examples of such products may include Cisco Tidal Enterprise Scheduler, Create!form Report generation, and Data Systems International's dcLINK interfaces used in hand scanners in a manufacturing warehouse.

It is common to find the first three levels of complexity in just about every implementation of JD Edwards EnterpriseOne software. The challenge of understanding complexity level 4 is the topic of the next discussion.

Complexity Level 4

Complexity level 4 is characterized by the addition of hardware and software infrastructure components to provide the following:

- High availability

- Redundancy

- Load balancing

- Fault tolerance

- Scalability

- Disaster recovery

High Availability   An EnterpriseOne architecture approach intended to provide availability to the EnterpriseOne application at a prearranged service level is considered highly available. Highly available solutions to an EnterpriseOne end user means that the user can perform typical actions such as login and interactive application queries, running batch jobs and accessing the underlying EnterpriseOne processes at all times. Table 5-2 presents uptime service availability in terms of percentage of available time per year, month, and week. Discussion of availability on a per-day level is not a normal practice but can be extrapolated further.

Table 5-2 represents uptime calculations that are a result of *unscheduled* downtime. Scheduled downtimes, as opposed to unscheduled downtime, are maintenance windows that are necessary for code updates, operating system patches, and other updates to the EnterpriseOne architecture. Scheduled downtimes are also communicated to the end user community when the system is going to be down and unavailable for use. Scheduled downtime is not normally included in the high availability matrix downtime calculations.

Providing an EnterpriseOne highly available architecture is the most costly of all of the options at complexity level 4 (excluding disaster recovery) and can include the components of redundancy, load balancing, and fault tolerance in its design and implementation.

Redundancy   Redundancies are additional software or hardware components of an EnterpriseOne architecture in which parts of the architecture are replicated to provide service in the event that one of these components is unavailable due to failure or planned downtime. Redundancy provides a means of maintaining availability by duplicating hardware and software EnterpriseOne components that provide redundant paths to the EnterpriseOne application. The end user is not aware of this redundancy and accesses the system in the same way they would in a nonredundant architecture.

Common redundancy components include multiple Java Virtual Machine (JVM) managed server instances in a WebLogic cluster, multiple batch and logic servers for processing business logic, and multiple database nodes in an Oracle Real Application

Percent Available	Downtime (per Year)	Downtime (per Month)	Downtime (per Week)
90	36.5 days	72 hours	16.8 hours
95	18.25 days	36 hours	84 hours
99	3.65 days	7.20 hours	1.68 hours
99.99	52.56 minutes	4.32 minutes	1.01 minutes

TABLE 5-2.   *High Availability Uptime Matrix*

Clusters (RAC) configuration. Immediate manual intervention is also not required in a redundant environment in maintaining the service level agreement for EnterpriseOne architecture.

The main two types of redundancies are *passive* and *active* redundancy. With active redundant components, processes actively service EnterpriseOne requests. Passive components are not currently servicing EnterpriseOne requests but are ready to receive those requests if traffic is directed toward them.

Load Balancing   Load balancing is a form of redundancy in the software and hardware components of the EnterpriseOne architecture, in which each of the components is in an active mode of providing service to EnterpriseOne requests. Load balancing can be implemented through hardware or software solutions.

Typical load balancing algorithms, shown next, depend on the availability of the EnterpriseOne component upon which they are based. Check the load-balancing solution specifications for the algorithms that are available on the hardware or software that are implemented in the EnterpriseOne architecture.

- **Round robin (RR)**   One of the most basic and simplest algorithms for load balancing, round robin involves servicing EnterpriseOne requests in a time slice and circular order of available redundant components.

- **Operating system load**   This algorithm will direct EnterpriseOne traffic based upon the current metrics of possible operating system variables, such as CPU, memory, and disk utilization. The lower the measured metric of the operating system, the more likely the traffic will be directed to that component of the architecture.

- **Source of the EnterpriseOne traffic**   The load balancing of EnterpriseOne traffic may be directed based upon the source of the traffic. EnterpriseOne requests initiated from internal users may be given a higher priority than vendor requests. This may occur at the source network at which the request is initiated.

The most common forms of load balancing are multiple nodes that are configured in a WebLogic Server for clustering and the F5 BIG-IP network traffic hardware switches for directing requests to a bank of EnterpriseOne business logic or web servers. An F5 BIG-IP switch may also support multiple instances of web services controlled by the Oracle HTTP Server (OHS) software.

Fault Tolerance   EnterpriseOne fault tolerance describes an architecture of redundant components in which the failure of a redundant component will result in a reduced level of performance, instead of losing availability to the EnterpriseOne functionality altogether. The higher the fault tolerance, the less susceptible the architecture is to performance degradation.

Typical degradations will be observed in the throughput of the EnterpriseOne application and are more commonly seen as slowdowns in end user response times and increase processing times of batch applications in a fault-tolerant architecture.

A fault tolerant example is the implementation of multiple EnterpriseOne security server processes. When one redundant server is down and no longer accepts security server requests, a secondary security server can be provided on another EnterpriseOne server. The load is no longer split between these two redundant EnterpriseOne servers, but all new security server requests are now being fulfilled, notably in a degraded mode, on the remaining active EnterpriseOne server.

Scalability   Scalability refers to the EnterpriseOne architecture's ability to handle an increased amount of work. Scalability in the EnterpriseOne architecture is normally an increased amount of work in the following areas:

- Interactive end users

- Increased batch load

- Increased external requests

- Level of integration component load

Scalability also refers to the ability of the EnterpriseOne architecture to handle this growth in a capable manner, where minor adjustments can be made to the EnterpriseOne architecture to handle the increased load within the margins of acceptable performance.

Two concepts closely tied to scaling of the EnterpriseOne architecture are horizontal and vertical scaling. Each of these scaling methodologies is described in greater detail further on in this chapter.

Disaster Recovery   Disaster recovery involves not just hardware, but a whole set of processes, policies, and procedures that will ensure business continuance. Business continuance involves keeping all components, software, and hardware functioning in the event of various failure conditions. Common conditions that might interrupt business continuance include failures in the following areas:

- **Power**   A power loss occurs for the data center or machine servers supporting EnterpriseOne. EnterpriseOne services must then be rerouted to the disaster recovery site until a stable power condition can be reestablished.

- **Server**   An extensive list of failures can occur at a server level. Although building redundancy at the server level can avoid the need for a disaster recovery event for server failures, the IT staff must be prepared in the event that a cascade of server failures would constitute the need for transitioning all traffic to the DR location.

Common failures can occur in the following areas:

- **Hardware**   CPU, memory, network, and more commonly in the disk subsystem.

- **Operating system**   Operating system limits are reached within the operating system subsystem processes, creating bottlenecks in the server that can hang server processes. Active processes consuming server resources beyond normal limits commonly create these problems.

- **Software**   Corruption, EnterpriseOne software process failures, and web HTTP processes not responding to service requests are example occurrences that can cause server outages on a software level. Normally, restarting these services can resolve these outages and return processes to responding to EnterpriseOne requests. Although this would be the best scenario in the event of a software failure, recovery might not be as easy as this, and a disaster recovery site would be the best architectural solution for maintaining business continuance where high service level agreements must be maintained and recovery from a failure would take an extended period of time.

- **Data center**   The events of the disaster of 9/11 brought new meaning to the need of a disaster recovery site and to have that site located a significant distance from the main data center. There are well-documented cases of companies that had their operations, including their data center disaster recovery site, within the two New York City twin tower buildings that were brought down by the terrorist attack. In most of those cases, the companies no longer exist, and they lost all of their information in that disaster.

Complexity Level Examples

Complexity is not a progression that is achieved over time, but a way of describing how the EnterpriseOne architecture is designed. For example, development EnterpriseOne architectures might implement only complexity levels 1 and 2, whereas the production environment will implement all four levels of complexity as part of its architecture. The need for redundancy, load balancing, and providing a service level agreement just does not make good economic sense when the target support group needing these services is for QA, development, training, and demonstration purposes.

Two simple EnterpriseOne architectural designs will be presented here, including their basic requirements and a brief discussion of the initial network diagram solution.

Company A

- Small company (100 employees)
- Less than 10 EnterpriseOne direct employee concurrent users on the system
- Large community of business partners that access the system (500 users)
- Large batch processing requirements
- No integrations: EnterpriseOne is the only ERP software
- Fault tolerance implemented on the JAS level

Figure 5-1 for Company A illustrates what can be implemented to fulfill the business requirements of the customer.

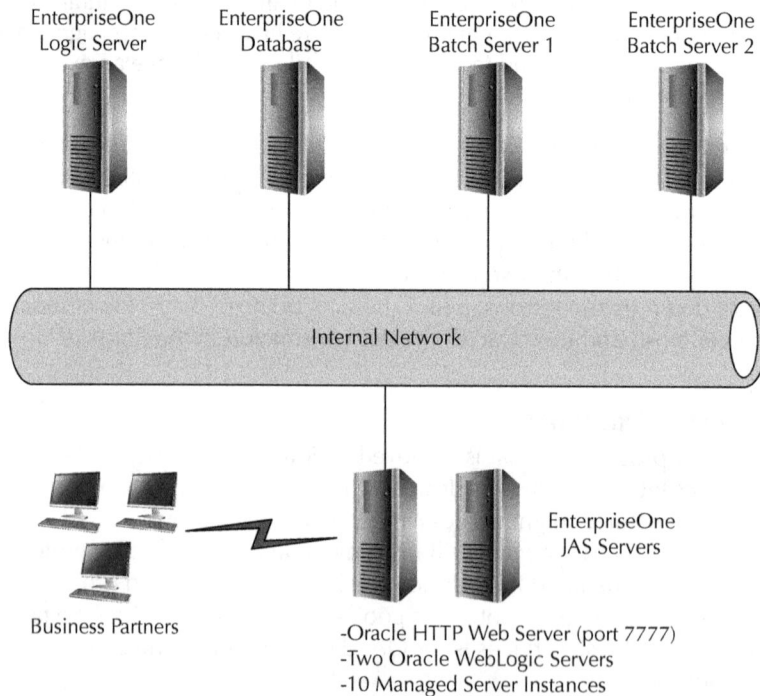

FIGURE 5-1. *Company A EnterpriseOne network diagram*

Here is a list of the Company A components:

■ Two JAS servers support fault tolerance and redundancy into the EnterpriseOne architecture.

■ A single Oracle HTTP server services EnterpriseOne requests from both external and internal end users on the same port of 7777 (default OHS port).

■ Ten managed server instances on the Oracle WebLogic Server can handle the HTTP requests. This is both a fault-tolerant and highly available environment configuration. Fault tolerance in the managed instances on each WebLogic Server was achieved by having 10 managed instances. If any one of the managed instances was inoperable, then the other instances could handle the end-user requests. The JAS servers themselves are highly available in the two JAS servers that were employed in the EnterpriseOne architecture.

■ Multiple batch servers are defined in this architecture to offload any high-batch processing load from the main EnterpriseOne logic server.

Company B

■ Large company (tens of thousands of employees)

■ EnterpriseOne used for internal human capital management (HCM) purposes, also known as the human resources (HR) interface

■ No high availability requirements

■ Small amount of batch processing

■ Only two of the four EnterpriseOne environments are implemented

Figure 5-2 for Company B illustrates what can be implemented to fulfill the business requirements of the customer.

Here is a list of the Company B components:

■ All main logical functions of the EnterpriseOne architecture are on their own servers; no consolidation has been done. EnterpriseOne business logic, EnterpriseOne batch processing, and EnterpriseOne JAS have all of their processes running on their own servers.

■ Batch and EnterpriseOne logic are still separated onto their own servers because of the anticipated load on the EnterpriseOne logic server.

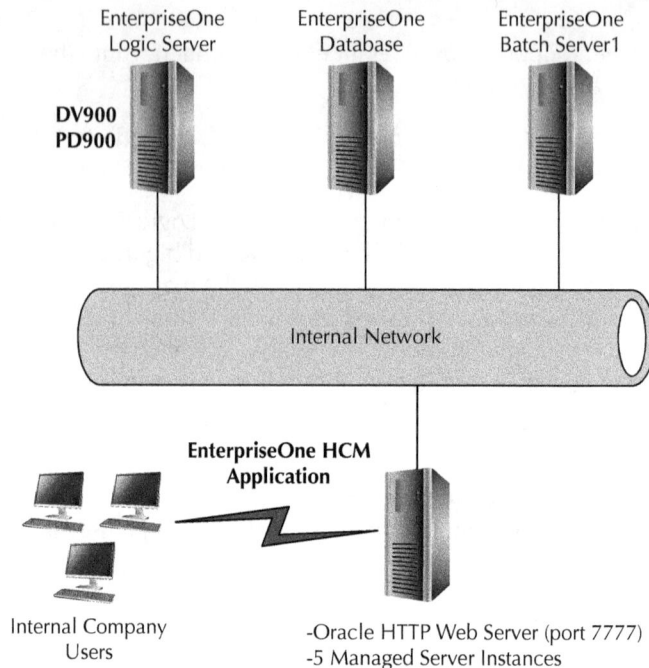

FIGURE 5-2. *Company B EnterpriseOne network diagram*

■ Internal end users, the employees, and staff of the company access the EnterpriseOne services through the default OHS web server port 7777 and on the internal network.

■ In this environment, both Production (PD) and Development (DV) pathcodes have been implemented. They are on the same server but possibly on a different logical partition.

EnterpriseOne Technical Components

Every EnterpriseOne implementation has four basic functional components. Each of the following components can exist on one or more hardware servers, or they can be combined to coexist on the same server.

■ JAS server

■ EnterpriseOne logic server

■ EnterpriseOne batch server

■ Database server

JAS Server

The JAS server processes interactive application user requests (HTTP) from the web interface browser and forwards them for processing to the EnterpriseOne logic and batch servers. Java and JavaScript processing as well as database requests can be generated from the JAS server. A basic JAS server process encompasses the following:

- The process that accepts the HTTP requests (web HTTP server) and the JAS framework: An example of the web HTTP server is OHS. An example of the JAS framework is WebLogic Server node services and WebLogic Server administrative console.

- The EnterpriseOne Tools code and JAS configuration files: The EnterpriseOne Tools code and JAS server configuration directs the traffic to the EnterpriseOne logic server using the EnterpriseOne Tools code installed on the JAS framework and information from properly configured JAS configuration files.

Configuration and tuning is necessary at the HTTP server level and through the JAS server configuration files from the default installation if interactive users are expected to handle scaling, the server is expected to handle a high load, and under a variety of stress conditions. Initial default configurations for the JAS server are sufficient for approximately 50 to 100 EnterpriseOne interactive users for a single managed server instance.

EnterpriseOne Logic Server

The EnterpriseOne logic server processes business logic—mainly the compiled C-based source code of the EnterpriseOne software, though some of the processing is performed through Java processing. The functional calls are C-based in nature and form the basis of the EnterpriseOne compiled libraries, which are commonly known as the business function (BSFN) libraries.

EnterpriseOne Batch Server

The EnterpriseOne batch server is an identical duplication of the software that is installed on the EnterpriseOne logic server, except the EnterpriseOne batch software is specifically configured (through the Object Configuration Manager, or OCM) to initiate selected batch processes on a different server than that of the EnterpriseOne logic server. EnterpriseOne batch process initiation, in smaller batch process requirement implementations, is typically done on the same server as the EnterpriseOne logic.

Database Server

The database server is where all of the Structured Query Language (SQL) database requests are serviced. Although the database server may be an IBM/DB2, a SQL Server, or an Oracle database server, this section will describe the database in terms of an Oracle database.

Figure 5-3 illustrates a basic EnterpriseOne architecture diagram. Some notable aspects of the diagram in Figure 5-3 should be highlighted:

- All components of the EnterpriseOne architecture—the EnterpriseOne logic server, EnterpriseOne batch server, EnterpriseOne database server, and EnterpriseOne JAS server processes—are located on individual servers; no combining of services is designed.

- All EnterpriseOne servers are on the same internal network. This is a common recommended implementation, in which the servers all communicate on the same network segment (that is, the same virtual LAN, or VLAN).

- Access into the EnterpriseOne environment is through the JAS server (more specifically the web HTTP server).

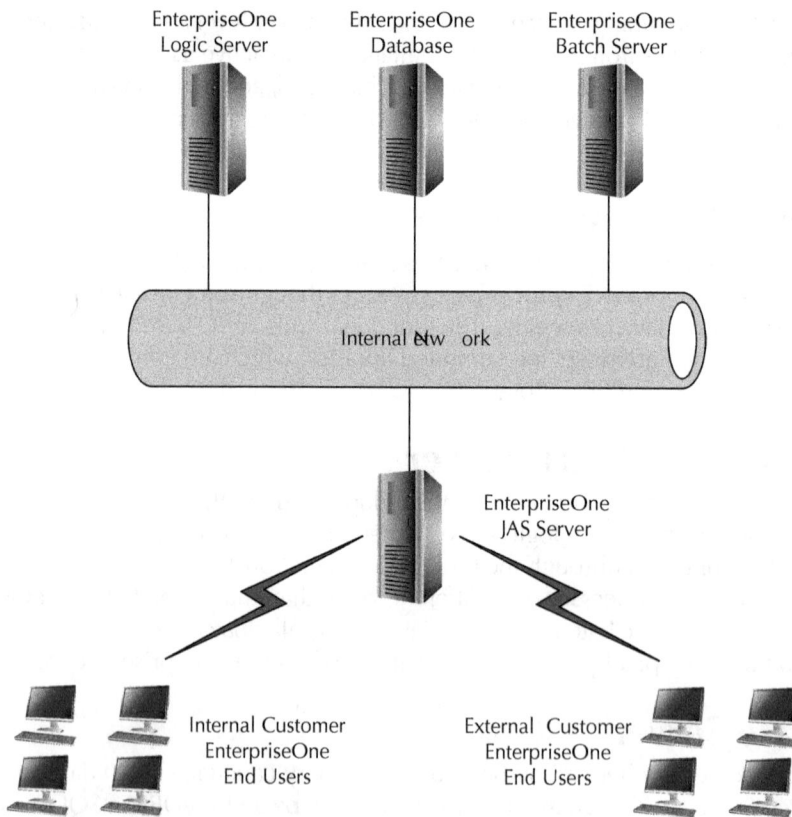

FIGURE 5-3. *Basic EnterpriseOne diagram*

■ The community of EnterpriseOne users has been divided into two categories: internal and external users. The EnterpriseOne access may be defined by two separate networks or by different ports:

■ **Internal EnterpriseOne end users**   Normally, these are the direct employees of the company using EnterpriseOne as an internal resource to perform their daily tasks. Tasks can include taking sales orders through the Sales Order module of EnterpriseOne. EnterpriseOne may also be an internal software support for a customer's human resources application or the processing of employee requests and information.

■ **External EnterpriseOne end users**   These end users may include business partners who are granted access into the EnterpriseOne application. Functions such as generating vendor reports for manufacturing and distribution and gathering inventory information from the customer are common application access rights defined by EnterpriseOne that might be granted.

EnterpriseOne Process Flow

In this section, we'll highlight the important areas in the architecture and discuss them in detail. The EnterpriseOne processes shown in Figure 5-4 communicate with the database and JAS server. Server-to-server communications are performed using operating system network sockets. All communications between the jdenet_n and jdenet_k processes are performed using interprocess communication (IPC) operating system calls that reside in shared memory.

The jdenet_n processes form the communications framework between all external server and other internal server processes. Internal server processes are other jdenet_n system processes, jdenet_k kernel processes, batch and other integration processes (such as XML Protocol or XMLP kernel), and BI Publisher services. These processes are the traffic cops that direct the processing of internal and external requests to the EnterpriseOne software to the internal jdenet_n and jdenet_k kernel processes, where the actual business logic and processing is performed by the software.

JDENet kernel processes (jdenet_k) are individual and self-contained processes with specific functions:

■ **Call object kernel**   EnterpriseOne business logic

■ **Security kernel**   EnterpriseOne authentication

■ **Metadata kernel**   Code specification requests

■ **UBE/Queue kernel**   Used to process batch requests

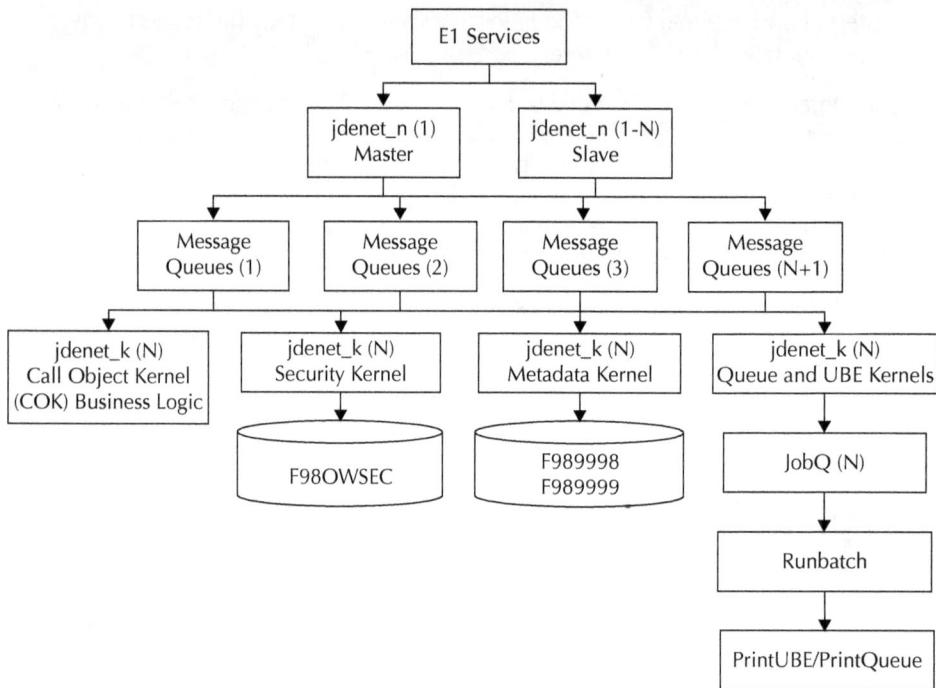

FIGURE 5-4. *EnterpriseOne process flow*

Starting EnterpriseOne Services

EnterpriseOne services can be started in different ways, depending on the operating system. Table 5-3 provides a list of startup commands. All EnterpriseOne services can be initiated through the Server Manager console

Operating System	Command
AS/400	STRNET—Command line interface
Windows	JDE E1 Services—Start and stop the JDE E1 application processes using the Windows Services Interface (Control Panel)
Unix	RunOneWorld.sh—Shell script for manual starting or by using the EnterpriseOne interactive application Server Manager

TABLE 5-3. *EnterpriseOne Manual Startup Commands*

EnterpriseOne Requests

Once EnterpriseOne receives a request on its listening port from the main jdenet_n process (master), it will pass these requests to other jdenet_n processes (slave), which will maintain these socket connections for the duration of the EnterpriseOne request. The jdenet_n processes can also initiate jdenet_k, or kernel, processes, as necessary for the functioning of the EnterpriseOne services. The main function of the message queues, also an IPC shared memory operating system resource, is to relay the EnterpriseOne requests from the jdenet_n network processes to the jdenet_k kernel processes for fulfilling the request.

EnterpriseOne Call Object Kernel

The primary jdenet_k kernel process is the Call Object Kernel (COK). It is the job of the COK process to initiate all of the business logic that is performed through the EnterpriseOne application. All integrations and external c-API function calls use these COK processes for executing EnterpriseOne business logic.

EnterpriseOne Security Kernel

It is the job of the EnterpriseOne security kernel to read EnterpriseOne profiles stored in the database in the table F98OWSEC to validate and authenticate the user to use specific functionality of the EnterpriseOne application and to pass a security token for the life of the process to maintain security.

EnterpriseOne Metadata Kernel

The EnterpriseOne metadata kernel process, introduced in EnterpriseOne Tools release 8.96, is responsible for managing the new XML format code specifications that used to reside in the earlier table access management (TAM) format. The XML code specs are stored in the database in the tables F989998 and F989999 in the Central Objects data source. Batch and call object kernel processes often request specifications from the metadata kernel process, and so the metadata kernel process plays a key role in performance and stability of the EnterpriseOne architecture. (See Oracle document ID 820367.1 for tuning tips with the Metadata kernel: https://support.us.oracle.com/oip/faces/secure/km/DocumentDisplay .jspx?id=820367.1&h=Y.)

EnterpriseOne Queue and UBE Kernels

EnterpriseOne batch processing makes use of two of the EnterpriseOne kernel processes: the UBE and Queue kernel processes. These kernel processes will update the server map data source table F986110 (Job Control Status Master) when submitting and updating the status of the batch process. These kernel processes are also responsible for directing the output of any PDF or resulting log file.

NOTE
Other kernel processes can be a part of the EnterpriseOne process flow, but those described here are the key processes involved with normal operations. Specific tuning recommendations for these kernel processes will be covered in later chapters.

Defining the Size of an EnterpriseOne Implementation

Technological improvements occur frequently and provide newer and faster hardware and software enhancements that are available for download and implementation at an almost constant pace. Given the dynamic nature of the IT industry and rapidly changing performance characteristics of hardware and software, attempting to define the size of an EnterpriseOne implementation is not a simple task.

The first task in defining the size of an implementation is defining the workload. Following are the main sources of workload and consideration for the EnterpriseOne architecture:

- Interactive and batch processing

- EDI and other mass upload/download processing

- Common and additional modules of integration

- Horizontal and vertical scaling of the architecture

Interactive and Batch Processing

The central processing use of the base EnterpriseOne software is the interactive processing (direct access by an end user into the JD Edwards software) and the batch processing. *Batch processing* is the automation of certain actions within the software in batch form where no manual intervention is required.

EDI Processing

The transferring of data in and out of the JD Edwards environment is called *Electronic Data Interchange (EDI)*. EDI is the process whereby data is either moved from one software location repository to another or from one computer to another through a specified mechanism. EDI was developed to replace any manual re-entry of data and provide a quicker means of transferring data between disparate systems.

EnterpriseOne has a number of EDI implementation methodologies available; you can consult support information for the specific module and processes for which the EDI process is targeted.

Modules of Integration

BI Publisher and Business Services (BSSV) are common modules, or components, that integrate with the EnterpriseOne architecture.

BI Publisher

This EnterpriseOne reporting tool helps extend the base EnterpriseOne software functionality by providing end users the ability to create and maintain custom reports formats based on output from the EnterpriseOne standard reports. BI Publisher can support common formats for customization including PDF, XML, EDI, and RTF documents. End users can also use BI Publisher to design these reports with common desktop utilities such as Microsoft Word, Microsoft Excel, or Adobe Acrobat. (For more information, see www.oracle.com/us/products/applications/057092.pdf.)

BSSV

EnterpriseOne Business Services has been supported by Oracle since EnterpriseOne Tools release 8.97. BSSV is an interoperability solution that exposes the C-based functions of many of the EnterpriseOne modules for external use. Most commonly, BSSV utilizes HTTP and SOAP protocols as part of the Java framework to perform its functions.

Additional Integration Components

Additional access points into the EnterpriseOne application have emerged along with the standing EDI processes and up the JD Edwards C-API functionality to third-party applications. The JD Edwards EnterpriseOne software allows third-party software to communicate with it through its externally facing application program interface (API) calls. The EnterpriseOne software has exposed a collection of predefined functions and tasks that can be performed from external C-based, third-party software products to allow a more seamless integration into the EnterpriseOne software.

NOTE
For more information, see the "EnterpriseOne Tools API Reference Guide" on the Oracle Support web site: https://support.oracle.com/, *(Document ID: 705446.1).*

Horizontal and Vertical Scaling of the Architecture

Many discussions focus on whether the EnterpriseOne architecture should be scaled in a horizontal or vertical manner.

Horizontal Scaling

EnterpriseOne horizontal scaling adds physical servers to the EnterpriseOne architecture. Each additional server provides a redundant component to that area of the EnterpriseOne functionality and provides an increase in the fault-tolerance, performance, and overall redundancy of the EnterpriseOne architecture.

Horizontal EnterpriseOne architecture scaling has an impact on network traffic. Since all the services no longer exist on the same box, the server must communicate externally on a common network segment to service EnterpriseOne requests. EnterpriseOne requests are then subject to network constraints such as latency and bandwidth, possibly traversing routers and switches within the network framework of the company. All of these factors can play a significant role in performance.

Horizontal scaling can include the following:

- Web HTTP servers

- JAS application servers

- EnterpriseOne logic servers

- EnterpriseOne batch servers

- EnterpriseOne database server nodes (RAC environment)

Additional software and/or hardware may be required to direct the EnterpriseOne traffic to the newly introduced physical server EnterpriseOne component of the architecture.

Two common horizontal scaling examples are shown in Figure 5-5.

In the first example, a third Oracle RAC node is added to the Oracle database component of the EnterpriseOne architecture. The Oracle RAC database software handles the EnterpriseOne database requests and distributes them to the respective server nodes, distributing the load among three servers.

In the second example, a third JAS server is added to the EnterpriseOne architecture. After the JAS server is added, only a minor change to the Oracle HTTP server is required to bring online the new JAS server functionality.

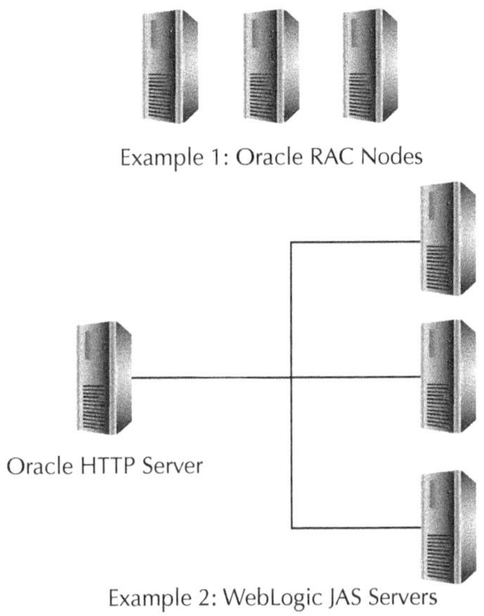

Example 1: Oracle RAC Nodes

Oracle HTTP Server

Example 2: WebLogic JAS Servers

FIGURE 5-5. *Horizontal scaling of Oracle RAC nodes and WebLogic JAS servers*

Vertical Scaling

Vertically scaling in the EnterpriseOne architecture involves adding components and resources to the current physical servers defined in the IT infrastructure. It may include the addition of the following components on the same server:

- **Operating system components**   CPU, memory, disk, and network cards are typical vertical scaling techniques used to allow for larger loads of EnterpriseOne traffic by increasing the amount of available resources on the same server.

- **Additional managed server instances on the JAS server**   A WebLogic cluster allows the addition of multiple managed server instances (JVM processes) to be defined within the same WebLogic domain.

- **Multiple Oracle Database listener processes on the EnterpriseOne database server**   Multiple servers can distribute database requests to multiple database listener processes.

- **Additional web HTTP server instances on the same EnterpriseOne server**   Multiple processes for servicing HTTP requests can overcome operating system limitations that a single process might encounter under high load. This includes the maximum number of open files for a single process or the amount of memory a single process can handle efficiently.

NOTE
As in horizontal scaling, with vertical scaling, additional software and hardware components may be required. Licensing of certain features such as clustering is available only in the Enterprise Edition release of the software. (Contact the minimum technical requirements pages and sales consultants for the specific edition versions of the software that are licensed for the installation and implemented with EnterpriseOne.) Additionally, hardware switches, such as the F5 BIG-IP switch, are not part of the standard EnterpriseOne installation and may require additional consulting services to install and configure for EnterpriseOne.

A JAS server managed instance is defined as an individual JVM process for processing EnterpriseOne HTTP traffic directed to it by a web server. In the example shown in Figure 5-6, the number of managed server instances that can be vertically created on a single JAS server is limited only by the operating system resources—namely CPU, memory, and other operating system parameters such as user process limitations and threading capabilities. As stated, proper licensing of the software for a cluster configuration may require uplift in support services for the software.

Increasing the number of EnterpriseOne logic server network and kernel processes is a common practice to vertically scale the EnterpriseOne logic server, increasing user load by adding more processes in the configuration (see Figure 5-7). Network processes are increased to handle higher volumes of traffic; kernel processes are normally increased to distribute the load of business logic, security authentication, and batch processing requests.

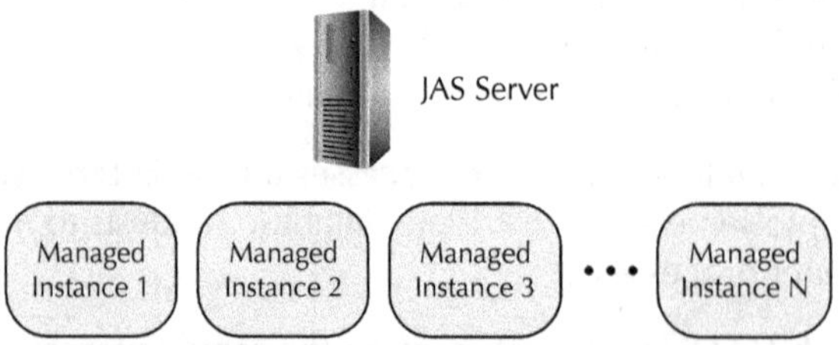

JAS Server

Managed Instance 1   Managed Instance 2   Managed Instance 3   • • •   Managed Instance N

FIGURE 5-6. *Vertical scaling of JAS server managed instances*

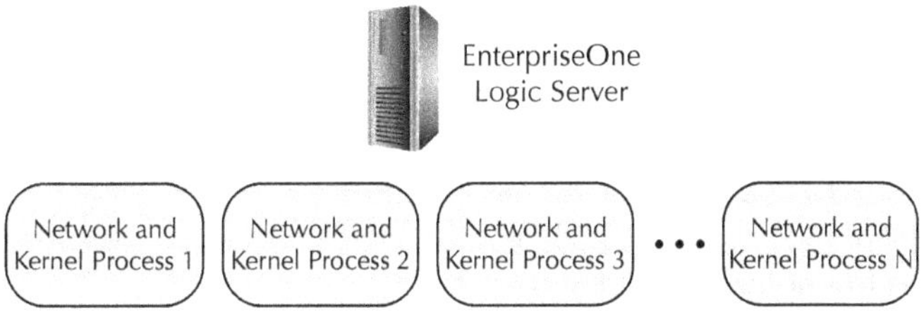

FIGURE 5-7. *EnterpriseOne logic server vertical scaling*

Horizontal and Vertical Scaling Considerations

Following are a few things to consider regarding horizontal and vertical scaling:

- **Management complexity** Simply put, the more server and node additions to the EnterpriseOne architecture, the more operational management will be involved to monitor, maintain, and service these components.

- **Increased load to operating system resources** Increased load to the operating system components of CPU, memory, disk, and network bandwidth and throughput should be considered before adding components to the EnterpriseOne architecture.

- **Effects to performance and increased overhead** The main purpose of adding a horizontal or vertical component to the EnterpriseOne architecture is to increase performance. Beware of the consequence of increasing the performance in one area of the application, only to directly shift that previous area of contention for another. Bottlenecks are always shifting, and some shifts in performance have unintentional consequences (good and bad).

- **Additional hardware and software components** Hardware and software must be added for directing EnterpriseOne traffic to these additional components, such as the Oracle HTTP Server (OHS) and Oracle web HTTP solution software, that can direct traffic to multiple URL targets. The OHS is more functional and can handle higher loads than some default web server installations.

Implementation Stages of EnterpriseOne Architecture

EnterpriseOne architectures in the past have been relatively simple in their approach: Either every component of the EnterpriseOne architecture resided on the same server, or each component of the architecture—namely, JAS server, logic server, and database server—was contained in its own server. The increasing need for redundancy, integration of greater functionality (that is, BSSV services and transactional servers), and implementation of more complex architectures using load balancing, high availability, and fault tolerance have driven the architectural designs of EnterpriseOne to greater depths of management, implementation, and planning.

This section provides some ideas and thoughts on various concerns regarding the EnterpriseOne architecture given the increased scope and complexity driven by the advances in technology and the business requirements of the customer. You have made the decision to implement JD Edwards EnterpriseOne architecture. You have already participated in planning for the design and technical/business requirements. It is now time to start the planning, purchase, and implementation of the conceptual ideas. If properly planned, the EnterpriseOne components installation should be an easy and smooth transition, from the planning phase to the implementation phase.

Designing the Architecture

Although most customers will engage a team of highly qualified professional information technologists to accomplish the actual design of the architecture, following are some high-level approaches that might assist in conveying the desired end product.

Conceptual Design

This is the first and most basic part of planning the design. In this phase, the main components of the architecture are listed. Since this is the early phase of the design, these components will not yet be assigned to a specific machine.

Some assumptions and questions will be initially addressed:

- Assumption: EnterpriseOne will provide a logic and batch component in the base installation.

- Assumption: Approximate size, power, and number of servers available to be assigned in the architecture will be driven by budget considerations.

- Question: Do I need to integrate a BSSV service?

- Question: Do I need to integrate an RTE server or other transactional component for integration?

- Question: Do I need to configure redundancy, load balancing, and/or fault tolerance?

- Question: Do I build this architecture with scaling in mind, or should I grow the architecture along the way?

- Question: Do I need any redundancy in my architecture, such as high availability, fault tolerance, or disaster recovery?

Network Architecture Design

In this phase, you'll construct the most basic high-level network architecture diagrams. It involves your first attempts at assigning server designations to the components you listed in the conceptual design phase. In essence, the conceptual design is translated and depicted as a network design of server machines.

The following activities are associated with the network design:

- Ideas for the location of servers

- Basic network connectivity requirements for each of the servers

- Initial size of each server

- The initial review of the technical and business requirements

Detailed Network Architecture Design

In this phase, high-level network design is detailed. In this planning phase, the following actions are normally taken:

- Detailed review of minimum technical requirements of hardware and software

- Final assignment of each EnterpriseOne component to a specific server

- Design of any redundancy components, such as additional servers for high availability, load balancing, and fault tolerance

- Detailed layout of each of the installed components of the EnterpriseOne architecture

- Review of the CPU, memory, and disk requirements to support each of the components in the EnterpriseOne architecture

- Review of the customer and technical requirements in terms of performance and service level agreements with this architectural design

Installing the Components

At this point, the EnterpriseOne architectural components are installed, tested, and reviewed for proper configuration. This section lays out a number of useful tips and techniques that have proven to pay dividends in the later stages of the EnterpriseOne lifecycle.

Note that if you use the advice in this section, your installation will take a little longer than normal to complete. A minimum of an additional 30 minutes per EnterpriseOne architecture component is normally required to implement these changes. The small cost of proceeding carefully and methodically in the installation has numerous benefits, including:

- Documents the installation process

- Provide a central repository for future review

- Provide a repository of information for support and technical calls

- Provide a central place for IT and other consultants to review for validation and accuracy

Normally, the installation of the EnterpriseOne architecture components will be in the form of a GUI installation. Many times the information entered through this installation will be lost in log files or retained by the installation engineer, and it will be available only while performing the installation and not available for further inquiries at a future time.

Creating a Central Repository for Installation Information

The first recommendation is to create a central area for a repository for installation information. The most reasonable location of this repository is on the deployment server. In this location, it is recommended that you create a specific directory for all installation information and include the following:

- Details of the network design and network architecture of the EnterpriseOne environment.

- All minimum technical requirements for each of the components of the EnterpriseOne architecture design as they exist at the time of installation.

- All EnterpriseOne architecture component installation, administration, and tuning guides used to install the software on each of the servers. Tuning guides followed should be saved for future reference. These documents may be difficult to find later in the implementation cycle of JD Edwards EnterpriseOne.

- If the installation is through a GUI, a screenshot of all of the actions, answers, and grid field values should be recorded. This information is often lost after the installation process but can prove useful in the future. Furthermore, the installation may differ from the provided installation documentation of the EnterpriseOne component because of specific version and choices made during installation.

Initial Configuration and Testing

The second recommendation involves the log files and initial configuration files that result from the initial installation. It is not likely that any of the EnterpriseOne installation components failed to produce a series of installation log entries and create initial configuration files and parameters. Initial configurations can be stored in simple text files and/or are available through the EnterpriseOne component administrative console.

Make a copy of the following initial configuration files for the few specific components of the EnterpriseOne architecture, along with any installation logs:

- EnterpriseOne logic/batch servers

    - JDE.INI configuration file

- EnterpriseOne WebLogic Server (WLS) components

    - JAS.INI

    - JDBJ.INI

    - jdelog.properties

    - httpd.conf

    - mod_wl_ohs.conf

- Oracle Database component

    - init.ora or output of Oracle's SQLPlus `show parameters` command

Configuring and Validating the Installation

Depending on the EnterpriseOne component installation, minor configuration changes may be required for the validation of the component to be completed. Any changes to the initial configuration should be documented and recorded in the central installation repository.

Following is a list of simple validations of selected EnterpriseOne components in the architecture. These validations can also be used to test the health of the EnterpriseOne component. This is commonly known as "unit testing" the EnterpriseOne component architecture; the validations typically show the health of various views of the EnterpriseOne logic and batch servers.

- EnterpriseOne logic/batch server test

    - Porttest

- URL tests

    - Login test

    - RUNUBE test

    - Server Manager

    - NETWM

- Web server tests

  - URL test

  - Snoop test

Customizing the Implementation

Customizing the EnterpriseOne architecture design refers to the architecture, not the EnterpriseOne application code. Customization is related to the considerations necessary to implement a more complex ERP system for customer support. This discussion of customization will include the following topics:

- EnterpriseOne batch and logic servers

- EnterpriseOne WebLogic and web servers

- EnterpriseOne database servers

Customizing EnterpriseOne Batch and Logic Servers

Setting the configuration values in the JDE.INI file either manually or through the recommended method of using Server Manager is the first step in EnterpriseOne customization.

As discussed in the "Principle of Gears and Cogs" and "Principle of Peeling the Onion," at the beginning of the chapter, the following "large knobs" or "cogs" in the EnterpriseOne JDE.INI configuration file are largely responsible for performance:

- **UBE Kernel, KDEF2**   Handles batch requests

- **Security Kernel, KDEF4**   EnterpriseOne authentication

- **Call Object Kernel, KDEF6**   EnterpriseOne business logic execution

Customizing EnterpriseOne WebLogic and Web Services

WLS and OHS, which have replaced the Oracle Application Server, comprise two components:

- **Web HTTP server**   The configuration file of httpd.conf

- **JAS**   Using the administrative console, the following are the most common performance tuning options:

  - Turning off access logging

  - Increasing the default heap size

■   Increasing the maximum allowed connections (MaxConnections)

■   Increasing the maximum number of users (MaxUsers)

Customizing EnterpriseOne Database Server

The EnterpriseOne database server can be Oracle, DB2, or SQL Server. Refer to Chapters 8 for the specific performance tuning recommendations.

Extending Nodes/Resources

Extending the nodes and resources on an EnterpriseOne architecture, depending on the EnterpriseOne component, may involve the following steps:

1. Creating the additional EnterpriseOne Resource (logic or batch server)

2. Using Object Configuration Manager (OCM) to redirect the specific traffic to the new EnterpriseOne node

For the JAS component, extending nodes and resources is performed through cloning a current JVM process into a new container and adding the container to a web server cluster configuration.

Extending EnterpriseOne Batch and Logic Servers

Normally all that is required for adding EnterpriseOne batch and logic servers is a method for redirecting the traffic to the newly introduced servers. This can be done in the following ways:

■   Load balancing hardware or software

■   OCM mappings

Extending EnterpriseOne WebLogic and Oracle HTTP Web Services

WebLogic Servers extend their resources vertically by adding managed instances to a WebLogic cluster definition in WebLogic Server. Additional web servers can be added through the Oracle HTTP command-line interface.

Extending EnterpriseOne Database Server

Additional nodes are handled by Oracle RAC; additional resources (CPU, memory, disk) will require modification to the database server configuration file for allocation of resources and more extensive work.

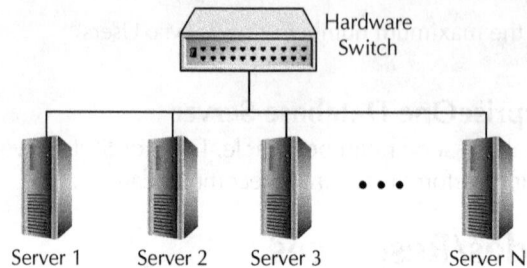

FIGURE 5-8. *Implementing a hardware switch*

Directing Traffic by Implementing Hardware Switches

Hardware and/or software load balancers are an effective means of redirecting traffic.

Hardware switches in the context of EnterpriseOne are devices that redirect EnterpriseOne network traffic to a set of EnterpriseOne component servers (see Figure 5-8).

Hardware switches in the EnterpriseOne environment are commonly used for the following:

- JAS servers

- Web HTTP servers

- EnterpriseOne logic and batch servers

Hardware switches offer the following advantages:

- They offer additional network security, preventing unwanted source network traffic.

- They can load balance network traffic to specific EnterpriseOne servers based on source location of the network traffic or on availability of the EnterpriseOne servers.

- Network switches can provide additional software that allows for easy manageability and performance characterization of the network traffic.

Setting Up Security

A major area for performance concerns is adhering to federal and local government regulations such as the Sarbanes-Oxley Act. The overhead of these regulations will impact performance for the EnterpriseOne application by requiring more security to be applied to the architecture. Performance is impacted by the following:

■ Adding overhead in EnterpriseOne business logic processing.

■ Adding entries in the EnterpriseOne database requests "where" clause, making them less efficient, and changing the database index optimization choices within the database to those that are not as efficient.

■ Increasing the complexity of EnterpriseOne software security. This may mean adding security for row, column, page, application access, and data filtering. In general, the more complex the security, the more detrimental its impact to performance. Drivers that increase the requirement for security complexity are normally related to the industry that EnterpriseOne supports. Financial and health services–based industries have higher application software security restrictions than other implementations.

For simple security implementations, there is normally no observable impact for interactive and batch applications for EnterpriseOne. However, with greater complexity in the security implementation, selected applications' interactive performance might seem slightly "slower."

Further Testing and Validation

Further testing, other than the unit testing, is recommended before production go-live and may take the form of unit, performance, stress, load, and reliability testing projects. Descriptions of additional testing methodologies and definitions are provided here.

Unit Testing   In unit testing, a single interactive application user, batch process, or transactional event is initiated and tested for proper functionality. All production-level EnterpriseOne functions should have a properly documented unit test.

Performance Baseline   A performance baseline process helps to locate bottlenecks and server configuration limitations by establishing a known set of metrics for comparison. Projects that involve establishing performance baselines can assist in evaluating trends in EnterpriseOne efficiencies and business process flow limitations.

Load Testing   Increasing the number of users, batch processes, and transaction load onto the EnterpriseOne architecture can identify any architectural limitations in the EnterpriseOne installation. Load testing is useful in a controlled environment as opposed to finding limitations in a production environment, where testing of solutions will be greatly restricted.

Stress Testing Stress testing is the process of creating an increasing performance load on the EnterpriseOne software or hardware configuration to intentionally create a bottleneck. Loading users and transactions onto a system and measuring the effects given a limitation in the environment can be a useful tool in understanding how and why bottlenecks shift in an EnterpriseOne architecture when changes are made or when a resource limitation is encountered.

Reliability Testing Reliability testing is defined by initiating EnterpriseOne processes and load over a long period of time, and measuring a large set of metrics, with the goal of understanding how the application, operating system resource, and network are affected over the long term. Reliability testing is key to identifying issues such as memory leaks, timeout conditions, and long-term database query impacts.

Validation The types of validation vary, but should include the following:

- **SQL** Processes that insert, update, delete, and transform the database in any way should be checked for proper functionality.

- **Log review** Any errors (warning, informational, and severe) should always be documented and researched for impacts to performance and code deficiencies.

- **Metrics review** A minimum number of metrics should be reviewed on a periodic basis. These include CPU, memory consumption, disk utilization, and network throughput. Many of these are now available through the EnterpriseOne Server Manager. Documentation of these metrics can assist with future planning and scaling.

Training

Performance would not be complete if end user training was neglected. A major source of performance bottlenecks is users who were not properly trained to use the environment. The EnterpriseOne application end user might be a real person or might be an automated process by an end user that is used by EnterpriseOne. For example, an end user sets up a process to generate a report by calling the batch process to generate that report; however, the report gets called every minute. The typical EnterpriseOne administrator can try to handle such situations by training the end user in how to generate a report properly.

Typical observation of end user training performance issues are

- Open-ended database queries, either through poor grid search criteria within EnterpriseOne or direct queries to the EnterpriseOne database

- End users running large reports or running reports too frequently

Bringing It All Together

In this chapter, the discussion has covered a variety of topics, from a simple implementation of EnterpriseOne, to the complexities and challenging technologies of implementing high availability in an EnterpriseOne environment.

An overview of the EnterpriseOne architecture design and functional components of EnterpriseOne was presented. The EnterpriseOne process flow was discussed, and the key network and kernel processes were defined. In the end, a number of discussions and points were made regarding how best to improve the processes, procedures, tuning, and configuration of EnterpriseOne.

CHAPTER
6

Tuning by Tier:
The Web Tier

I n this chapter we'll take an in-depth look at performance tuning of the web tier for JD Edwards EnterpriseOne. We look at tuning the different layers in the web tier, such as the HTTP server, WebLogic, and WebSphere-specific settings as well as a few of the critical jas.ini, jdbj.ini, and jdelog.properties settings. As stated in previous chapters, the only supported web servers are Oracle's WebLogic and IBM's WebSphere, so we will address those web application servers in this chapter. This chapter will elucidate techniques that have been devised and improved over several years to dive into the heart of web performance issues.

Isolating Performance Issues to a JAS Server

When you're facing ambiguous, "random" performance issues with the Java Application Server (JAS), the first thing you must do is try to isolate the source of the problem. Most incidents of ambiguous performance issues are somewhat confusing to both end users and administrators alike. They range from "white screens of death" to unexpected disconnects from the web server, random or progressive slowness in web interaction, to long-running interactions on the web applications. Because the web or HTML pillar is the application's front end, it seems as if all the problems originate there, so that's a standard place to start looking.

You'll need to determine whether your performance issue originates from the web pillar, Enterprise Server pillar, database pillar, or some combination of these. If it indeed originates at the web pillar, you must determine where exactly within the pillar needs your focus. Following is a step-by-step overview of the diagnosis process.

Step 1: Isolate the JAS Layer The first step in the process of determining where the performance issue is originating from is to isolate the JAS layer. The most efficient way to do this is to create an alternate JAS instance that is a *clone* of the affected JAS production server. You can do this quite easily by leveraging a web dev client, or more preferably by installing a new production JAS port via Server Manager. Figure 6-1 shows an example for this.

The key element in this step is that your test server should be identical to the one that's affected by performance issues, with the same set of INI files, the same login environment, and the same user actions.

Step 2: Partner with End Users Once you have a test server (Web Dev Client or a separate JVM), you must find a few reliable end users who have experienced performance issues and make them partners in your efforts to isolate the problem. Whenever these users experience performance issues on the main server, they will be asked to switch to the test server and replicate the same or similar actions that caused the performance issues on the main server.

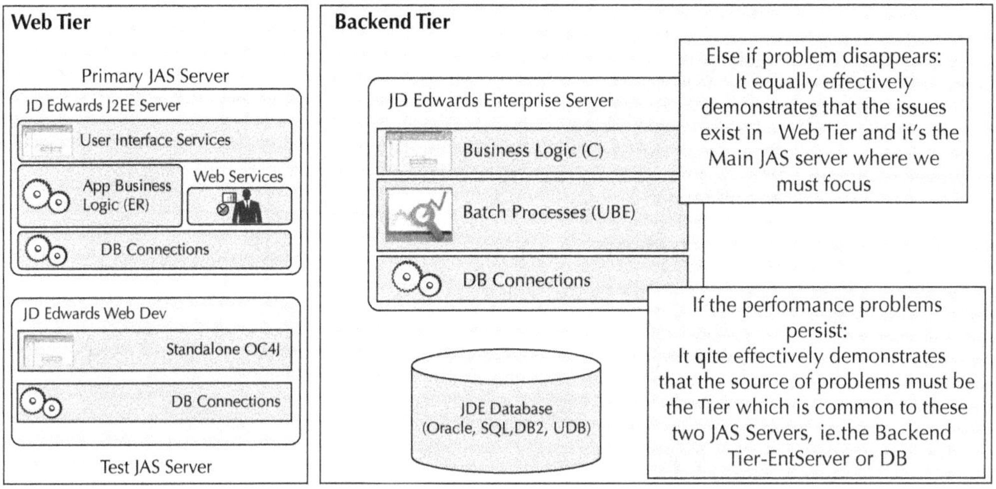

Web Tier	Backend Tier

FIGURE 6-1. *Isolating web tier performance issues by creating a control test server*

Step 3: Determine Problem Timing   After communicating your results to the Configurable Network Computing (CNC) administrator, you can deduce whether the performance problems persist or occur at similar time intervals on both the main and test servers. If so, you know the source of these issues must be common to both the main and test servers—that is, the backend servers that include the enterprise or database pillar. Alternatively, if the performance issues are not reproducible on the test server during the same time interval for the same environment and activities for which they occur on the production web server, logic dictates that the issue is limited to the production JAS server.

Step 4: Isolate the Issue   If you determine that the problem is in the web pillar, you must decompose various components of the pillar, and by using logical measurements and analysis, isolate the issue(s). The good news is that, when diagnosed, web pillar performance problems are simple to fix.

Components of the JAS Architecture

Let's back up and talk about the components of the JAS architecture web pillar:

- Java 2 Platform, Enterprise Edition (J2EE) server on which the JD Edwards HTML Web Server runs—either Oracle WebLogic or IBM WebSphere

- The HTTP server

- The JD Edwards Web Server application, also known as the Java Application Server (JAS)

  - The JAS Event Rules (ER) Interpreter Engine

  - The JAS Database Connections

Figure 6-2 provides an overview of the components of the JD Edwards web pillar.

Tuning the J2EE Server

The J2EE server is most susceptible to the scale of users or the activity of those users. Anything that can cause high memory growth will cause performance issues with the J2EE server. Most common performance issues with a J2EE server are a result of the following:

- Large number of users on the server

- Large number of applications in use

- Amounts of data with which each application is interacting

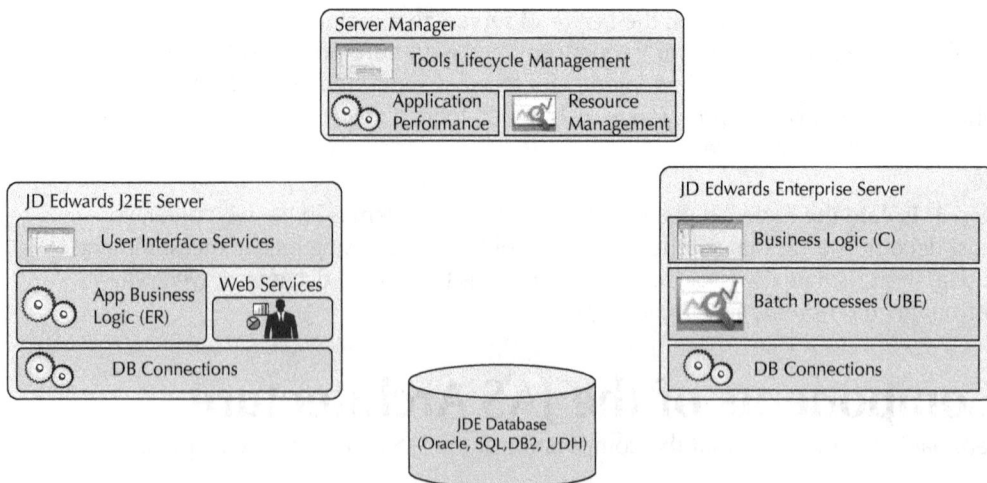

FIGURE 6-2. *Components of the JD Edwards web pillar*

All 32-bit Java Virtual Machines (JVMs) have a mathematical limit of 2GB of memory; however, in reality, this is closer to 1.5GB. Whenever the memory that's required for end users approaches 70 percent of the maximum JVM memory threshold, the JVM will trigger a "stop-the-world" garbage collection cycle that tries to clean and defragment Java heap memory. This causes all threads to pause and is perceived by end users as a performance issue. The frequency and duration of these garbage collections is a severe root cause of performance issues in the web pillar. *Compact GCs* for an IBM JDK and *tenured GCs* for an Oracle JDK are accompanied by high CPU consumption as the JDK tries to complete this phase as aggressively as possible. In some respects, many people consider reduction of compact GC or tenured GC as the whole art of J2EE server tuning. Common sense would tell you to provide as much memory as possible, but several subtleties must be considered.

Setting Adequate Heap Memory

A WebSphere or WebLogic server as a Java application has its memory managed by the JVM. When the application server running JAS is started through either WebSphere or WebLogic, the JVM allocates memory and manages it on behalf of JAS.

Setting the initial heap size for the JVM helps manage the amount of memory used by the J2EE server. Because Java objects are cleaned up by the JVM, the system JVM also uses the initial heap size as the indicator for when to perform a garbage collection. Therefore, setting the initial heap size to an appropriate value for the workload is very important. Setting the heap size too small causes frequent garbage collections, which consume CPU resources. Setting the heap size too large causes excessive memory usage and paging, and can result in a higher cache miss ratio because the heap is so large.

Setting Xms and Xmx Parameters

The most important parameters you can set for a J2EE server would be the initial and maximum memory allocation for the JVM. Xms is the initial memory to be allocated and Xmx is the maximum memory to be allocated. Debate on whether or not to set Xms equal to Xmx has been raging for several years, with proponents on both sides. However, with extensive real-world experience, we conclude that the answer is Java Runtime Environment (JRE)–specific: for IBM JDK, set Xms and Xmx as far apart as possible; for Oracle JRockit or Sun, set these values equal to each other.

Following are the recommended minimum heap sizes:

- **IBM JDK**   Set Xms = 32m

- **Oracle JDK (JRockit or Sun)**   Set Xms = Xmx

And the recommended maximum heap sizes:

- **32-bit JVM**   Set the Xmx value close to 2GB (in most cases, 1536m)

- **64-bit JVM**   Set the Xmx value close to 8GB

   For 32-bit JVMs we want to provide as close to a 2GB limit memory as we can allocate to provide ample working space. For 64-bit JVMs, based on our testing a 8GB Heap will provide enough headroom for 100–150 users on a given JVM including sudden burst of activities. However, like any Java Heap Setting, this needs to be fine tuned to accommodate for a given number of users and the activities they are performing.

Enabling Verbose Garbage Collection

Verbose garbage collection can be enabled easily on a WebSphere or WebLogic server; it usually involves checking a box in the Administration Console or adding generic JVM arguments. Enabling verbose garbage collection causes each garbage collection cycle to be written out to a file. These garbage collection files can then be interpreted to see historic and immediate trends in memory usage patterns. The output produced is usually quite cryptic and is best analyzed by utilities written to parse and make sense of garbage collection log records. You can use the following utilities to analyze the output produced by each JRE:

- **Sun JDK**   GCViewer

- **JRockit**   Mission Control

- **IBM JDK**   IBM Pattern Molding and Analysis Tool (PMAT)

   As shown in Figure 6-3, the garbage collection logs have captured points in this JAS instance that are in the "Slow Performance Region," and they also show a crash. This information can be used to help you determine the maximum load along with the appropriate heap settings.

Changing the JVM Options on a WebLogic Application Server

The following denotes the general steps for changing JVM options on the WebLogic Application server:

1. Log onto the WebLogic Server Administration Console (for example, at http://host:7001/console). You can see that port 7001 is the default port.

2. Figure 6-4 shows how you can select the server you want to change (in this case, JAS910DV at port 8082, at the bottom of the console screen).

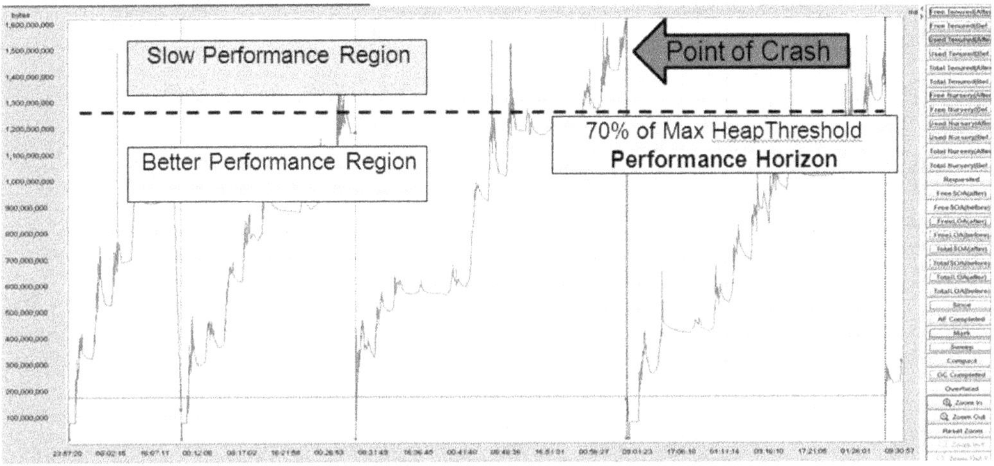

FIGURE 6-3. *Garbage collection logs*

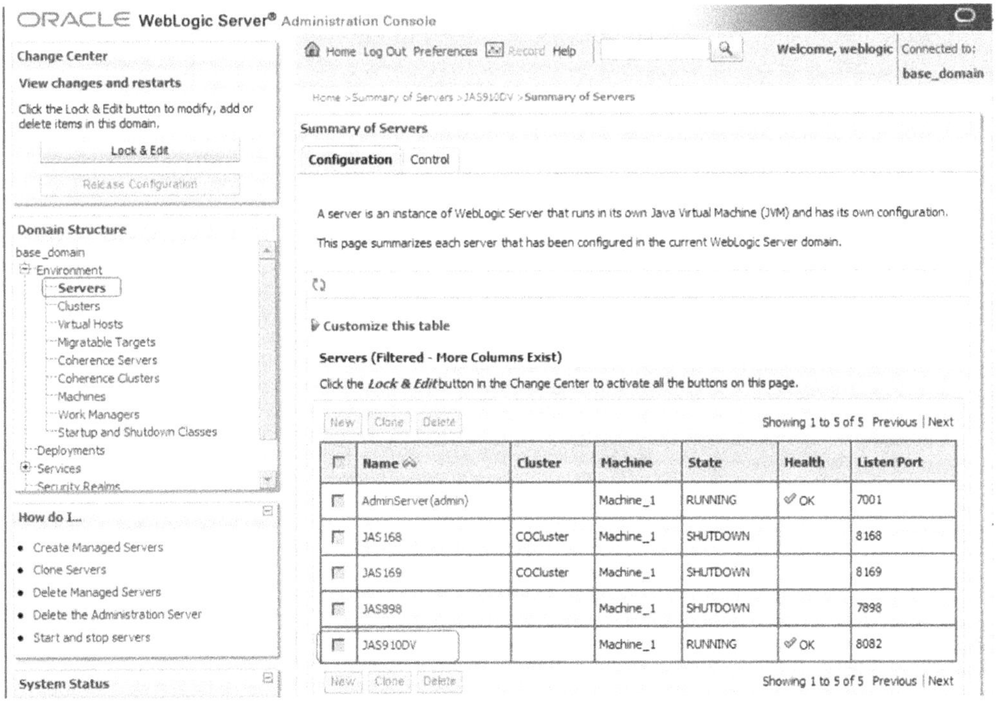

FIGURE 6-4. *WebLogic Administrator Console showing where to set JVM-specific arguments*

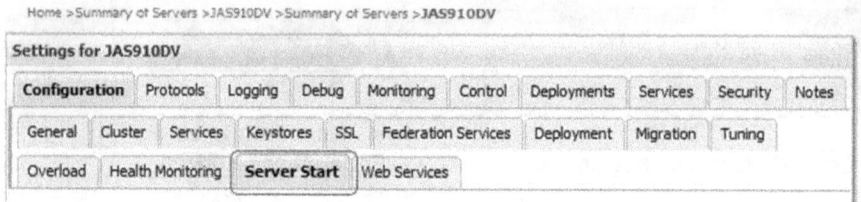

FIGURE 6-5. *WebLogic Administrator Console*

3. Select the Server Start tab, shown in Figure 6-5.

4. The Class Path and Java Arguments options will show as Read Only. Click the Lock & Edit button at the upper-left of the console to switch to Edit mode.

5. Then you would enter your arguments as shown in Figure 6-6.

6. Click Activate Changes when you are done.

7. Bounce the server.

   The class path and java arguments are stored in the config.xml file, which is located at MW_HOME/user_projects/domains/*<your domain>*/config/.

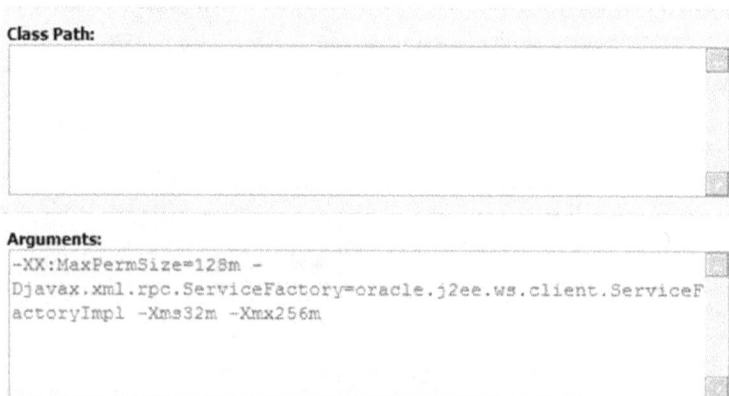

FIGURE 6-6. *JVM Arguments in Weblogic Console*

8. Open the config.xml file and search for your server name.

```
<server>
  <name>JAS910DV</name>
  <machine>Machine_1</machine>
  <listen-port>8082</listen-port>
  <cluster xsi:nil="true"></cluster>
  <listen-address></listen-address>
  <server-start>
    <name>JAS910DV</name>
    <arguments>-XX:MaxPermSize=128m -
javax.xml.rpc.ServiceFactory=oracle.j2ee.ws.client.
ServiceFactoryImpl -Xms32m -Xmx256m</arguments>
  </server-start>
</server>
```

NOTE
If you start your managed server (JAS) from a command line or your own script, you must include the class path and Java argument in your script. WebLogic Server will not pick those up unless you are starting the server using Node Manager.

Changing the JVM Options on a WebSphere Application Server

The following is an example of how you might change the JVM options on the WebSphere Application server.

1. Log on to WebSphere Administration Console (for example, at http://host:9060/ibm/console).

2. Select your server. Figure 6-7 provides an example of the WebSphere Administrator Console.

3. In the Java and Process Management area on the right side of the console window, select Process Definition, as shown in Figure 6-8.

4. In the Additional Properties area, select Java Virtual Machine, as shown in Figure 6-9.

5. Adjust the Xmx, Xms, or verbose GC parameters, as shown in Figure 6-10.

FIGURE 6-7. *WebSphere Administrator Console*

The following information is stored in a configuration file located at WAS_HOME/AppServer/profiles/AppSrv01/config/cells/<*Your*>Node01Cell/ nodes/<*Your*>Node01/servers/<*Your Server*>:

```
<jvmEntries xmi:id="JavaVirtualMachine_1288813020659"
verboseModeClass="false" verboseModeGarbageCollection="false"
verboseModeJNI="false" initialHeapSize="32" maximumHeapSize="768"
runHProf="false" hprofArguments="" debugMode="false" debugArgs="-
agentlib:jdwp=transport=dt_socket,server=y,suspend=n,address=7777"
genericJvmArguments="">
```

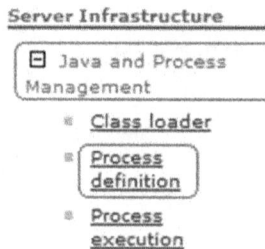

FIGURE 6-8. *WebSphere Administrator Console: Java Process Definition's JVM properties*

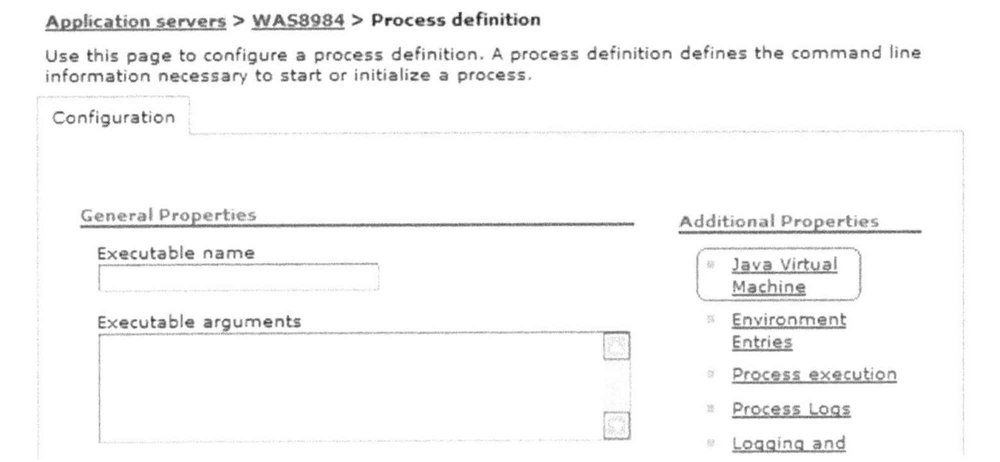

FIGURE 6-9.   *WebSphere Administrator console: Java virtual machine properties*

Tuning the HTTP Server

The HTTP server is one of the most stable but easily forgotten components in the web pillar. When it becomes necessary to tune the HTTP server, the access and error logs can be of great assistance. The httpd.conf file contains the tuning parameters for the HTTP server, and it is highly recommended that you create a backup of this file before making any changes to it.

As discussed, a key part of J2EE server tuning involves allocating adequate memory. Tuning of the HTTP server primarily includes determining the simultaneous connections that the HTTP server needs to provide at peak load. The maximum load is usually equal to the number of maximum concurrent users; if the HTTP server has not been configured to support the peak load, the end users will usually see a white screen or a nonresponsive browser intermittently as the HTTP server tries to swap connection threads among different users. This problem is notoriously difficult to reproduce, because it depends on the timing of availability of HTTP connections, or the lack thereof. Remember to ensure that you have configured HTTP to take into account the users for all JVMs on the server. It is a common mistake to allocate only for a single JVM.

Tuning the HTTP server is usually required when a customer upgrades from an old release to a new one and also changes the underlying HTTP server. For example, HTTP server tuning often occurs with the installation of a new HTTP server; since the default values for the number of simultaneous connections in the new HTTP server are usually lower than the peak loads, the end users experience intermittent performance issues. This problem, however, is easy to confirm by reviewing the HTTP logs for the following errors:

■ **Windows [warn]**   Server ran out of threads to serve requests; consider raising the ThreadsPerChild setting.

■ **Linux and Unix [error]**   Server reached MaxClients setting; consider raising the MaxClients setting.

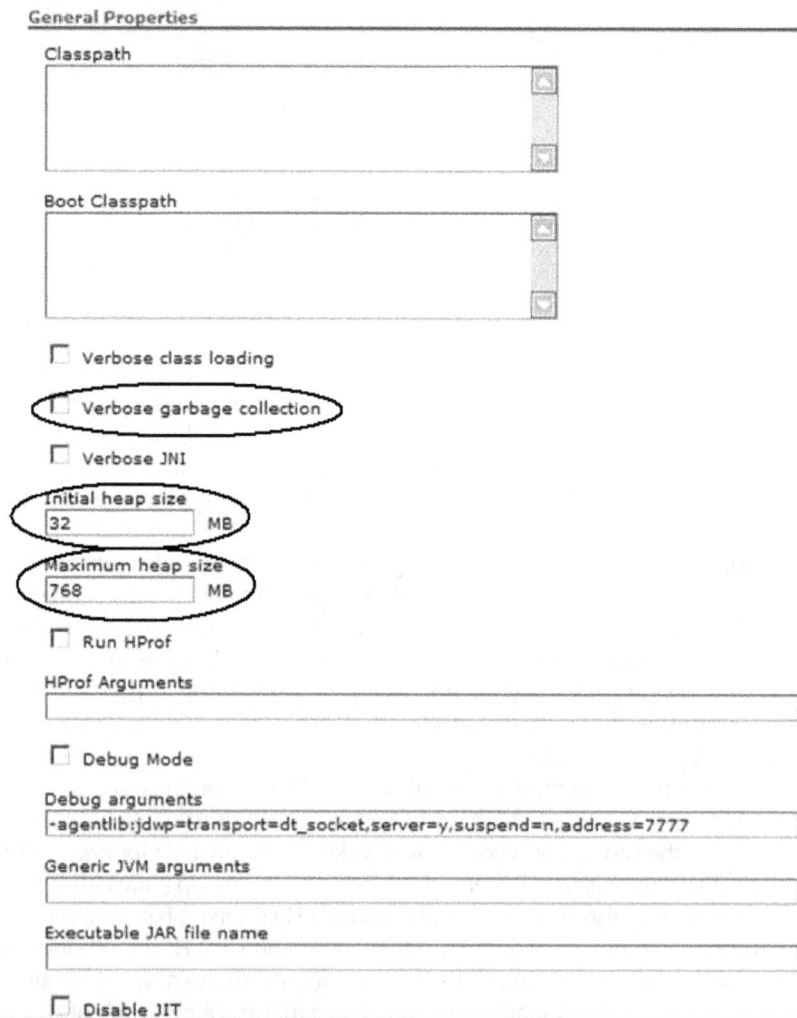

General Properties

Classpath

Boot Classpath

☐ Verbose class loading

☐ Verbose garbage collection

☐ Verbose JNI

Initial heap size
32   MB

Maximum heap size
768   MB

☐ Run HProf

HProf Arguments

☐ Debug Mode

Debug arguments
-agentlib:jdwp=transport=dt_socket,server=y,suspend=n,address=7777

Generic JVM arguments

Executable JAR file name

☐ Disable JIT

FIGURE 6-10.   *WebSphere Administrator: adjust minimum and maximum heap size and enable verbose garbage collection*

The solution is quite simple: Adjust the httpd.conf setting for the number of users: MaxClients (Unix) or ThreadsPerChild (Windows), which represents the maximum simultaneous connections.

HTTP Server Key Parameters

As our example demonstrated, the following two settings often need to be changed from their default values:

- **ThreadsPerChild** Set equal to maximum concurrent incoming connections for Windows (for example, MaxClients 200).

- **MaxClients** Set equal to maximum concurrent incoming connections for Linux (for example, MaxClients 200 [default is 50]).

Some other settings in the httpd.conf file influence the performance of the HTTP server:

- **HostNameLookups** Disable. When HostNameLookups is set to On, the server queries the DNS system on the Internet to find the host name associated with the IP address of each request. Depending on the server load and the network connectivity to your DNS server, the performance impact of the DNS HostNameLookups may be high. Set the following parameter:

  HostNameLookups Off

- **Access Logging** Disable. Modify the LogFormat and CustomLog directives in httpd.conf (for example, logFormat "%hxx" combine and Customlog /dev/ null combined).

- **KeepAlive** Set to improve serving of static content. The KeepAlive extension to HTTP/1.0 and the persistent connection feature of HTTP/1.1 provide long-lived HTTP sessions that allow multiple requests to be sent over the same TCP connection. In some cases, this has been shown to result in an almost 50 percent improvement in latency times for HTML documents with many images. Set the following parameter:

  KeepAlive On

Advanced and Sensitive Settings

These settings can be beneficial to fine-tune for a given end user load; however, it's easy to tune them incorrectly, so you'll need a thorough understanding of these parameters before making any changes.

Timeout   Amount of time the server will wait for certain events before failing a request.

- Total amount of time it takes to receive a GET request.

- Amount of time between receipt of TCP packets on a POST or PUT request.

- Amount of time between ACKs on transmissions of TCP packets in responses.

  - Reducing it from the default value of 300 (seconds) will cause long requests to be terminated abruptly—for example, downloading a large UBE may be interrupted because of this timeout interval.

  - Surprisingly, increasing it can have the same effect as reducing it, so it's best to leave this parameter alone to its predefined default value.

KeepAliveTimeout   Amount of time the server will wait for subsequent requests on a persistent connection.

- Increasing KeepAliveTimeout effectively reduces the number of threads available to service new inbound requests and will result in a higher maximum number of simultaneous connections that must be supported by the web server.

- Decreasing KeepAliveTimeout can drive extra load on the server from handling overhead from unnecessary TCP connection setup.

MaxKeepAliveRequests   Limits the number of requests allowed per connection when KeepAlive is On. If it is set to 0, unlimited requests will be allowed.

KeepAlive directives provide the benefits of the persistent connections, while minimizing the drawbacks. However, if your user base is large and makes short-term requests, the KeepAlive directives work against you by keeping the HTTP connections open longer than desired; in such cases, you may want to reduce the KeepAlive directive default settings or even set KeepAlive to Off.

Determining the Number of Connections to the HTTP Server

To determine the accurate number of connections inbound to a HTTP server, you can use an HTTP directive: `mod_status`.

Add these directives to httpd.conf, or uncomment those already there:

```
Loadmodule status_module modules/mod_status.so
<Location /server-status>
SetHandler server-status
Order deny,allow
```

```
Deny from all
Allow from serverfarm.com      <--- replace with your domain name
</Location>
```

Request the /server-status page (http://serverfarm:8082/server-status/) from the web server at busy times of the day and look for a line similar to the following:

```
51 requests currently being processed, 149 idle workers
```

The number of requests currently being processed is the number of simultaneous connections at this time. You can take this reading at different times of the day to determine the maximum number of connections that must be handled.

Tuning the JAS Layer

Let's take a look at some of the areas that can be leveraged when tuning the JAS layer. Each of these areas can help you isolate and address performance issues in your implementation.

Application ER Loops

In some applications, there have been instances of long-running ER (Event Rule) loops. Because Application ER is an interpreted language in the Web Runtime Engine, its execution takes an inordinate amount of time compared to a similar loop running as a C business function. In any case, long-running logic loops should be written in C business functions, because even a loop of 1000 iterations in ER can cause high CPU spikes and memory consumption.

If you are experiencing high CPU spikes on the JAS Server that do not correspond with periods of high garbage collection, you can use Server Manager to set the loop iteration warning to a low value, such as 1000. This setting will provide a warning message in the logs that indicate you have an Event Rule issue.

Check the JAS logs for this message:

```
*** INFINITE LOOP DETECTION WITHIN APPLICATION ER:****
```

This message will provide additional information on which application, event, and ER line number this long loop originates from. To fix this, if it's an Oracle application, ask Oracle Support for a fix; or, if it's a custom application, remove or reduce the number of loop iterations in the application's ER logic. These types of efforts can have a significant effect on performance.

Tuning of INI Files for JAS

The INI files contain numerous tuning parameters; however, you should always evaluate a few, including the following, because they can have a dramatic effect on the performance of the web tier.

jdelog.properties   Make sure in jdelog.properties that the debug or application level logging is disabled. Debug or application level logging causes severe performance degradation. The proper setting is WARN or ERROR.

jas.ini   For the following, ensure that the `UserSession` timeout value is not greater than 1 hour.

```
[CACHE]
UserSession=3600000 (or less) (default is 1200000)
```

NOTE
Any change to the `UserSession` *timeout value must also be matched in the Application Server session timeout value.*

For the following, ensure that the maximum number of browsers that users can open is limited to less than or equal to seven.

```
[ERPINTERACTIVITY]
MaxOpenBrowsers=7 (default is 10)
Ensure that TimeWaitBeforeAutoResume is set to 0
Ensure FetchAllPageSize >=500
```

For the following, ensure that `MAXUser`, the maximum number of simultaneous user sessions (both active and inactive) within the web instance, is large enough. Denied logon requests will be experienced when this value is too small.

```
[OWWEB]
TimeWaitBeforeAutoResume=0
FetchAllPageSize=500
MAXUser=70 (default is 100)
```

Under heavy load, JAS timeouts often occur, and increasing the `enterpriseServerTimeout` value will help avoid these issues. However, be careful that you do not increase these timeouts by too much. When set too high, a timeout value could mask issues on Enterprise Server. The timeouts will be encountered in the JAS logs under normal warning and error settings. It might take a little time to get the feel of what is a timeout value issue and what is truly an issue on the Enterprise server

```
[JDENET]
enterpriseServerTimeout=150000 (default is 90000)
```

This serves to cache the .js and .img content on the local PC of the web user. Setting the following value to several months or more is preferred:

```
[OWWEB]
CacheStaticContentDays=30
```

jdbj.ini   Ensure that the `connectionTimeout` value is set to a value of less than 20 minutes:

```
[JDBj-CONNECTION POOL]
connectionTimeout=1200000 (default)
```

For an environment in which all users connect to the database using only a few proxy users (low cardinality), the following settings are recommended. Note that these are on a per-JVM basis.

For an environment in which all of the users connect to the database using only a few proxy users (low cardinality), these settings should be used:

```
[CONNECTION POOL]
minConnection=5 (default)
maxConnection=num of max Concurrent Users (default is 50)
initialConnection=5 (default)
poolGrowth=10 (default is 5)
```

For an environment in which each user is mapped to a unique proxy profile (high cardinality), the following settings should be used:

```
[CONNECTION POOL]
minConnection=0
maxConnection= 10
initialConnection=1
poolGrowth=1
```

Set the JDBj cache timeout values to 20 minutes or less:

```
[JDBj-RUNTIME PROPERTIES]
securityCachePurge=1200000
serviceCachePurge=1200000
specCachePurge=1200000
e1MenuCachePurge=1200000
ocmCachePurge=1200000
```

Set `ResultSetTimeout` to a low value of less than 2 minutes, or, ideally, 1 minute:

```
[JDBj-RUNTIME PROPERTIES]
updateableResultSetTimeout=60000
resultSetTimeout=60000
```

Using Server Manager to Detect Issues in the JAS Server

Server Manager can be a very effective tool in determining whether excessive or long-running queries originate at the web pillar.

Excessive DB Connections from JAS

To evaluate the number of database connections emerging from a JAS instance, look in Server Manager for the desired web server; under Runtime Metrics, click the Database Connections link, as shown in Figure 6-11.

The JDBC connections are keyed off *<DB_ProxyUserID>*; the only time you will have high number of connections is if either of these two variables has a high level of uniqueness.

Understanding JDBC Connection Pool Keys

To understand the effect of increasing the number of JDBC connection pools, you need to understand how JDBC connection pools are created. JDBC connection pools depend on the underlying database and the number of proxy users.

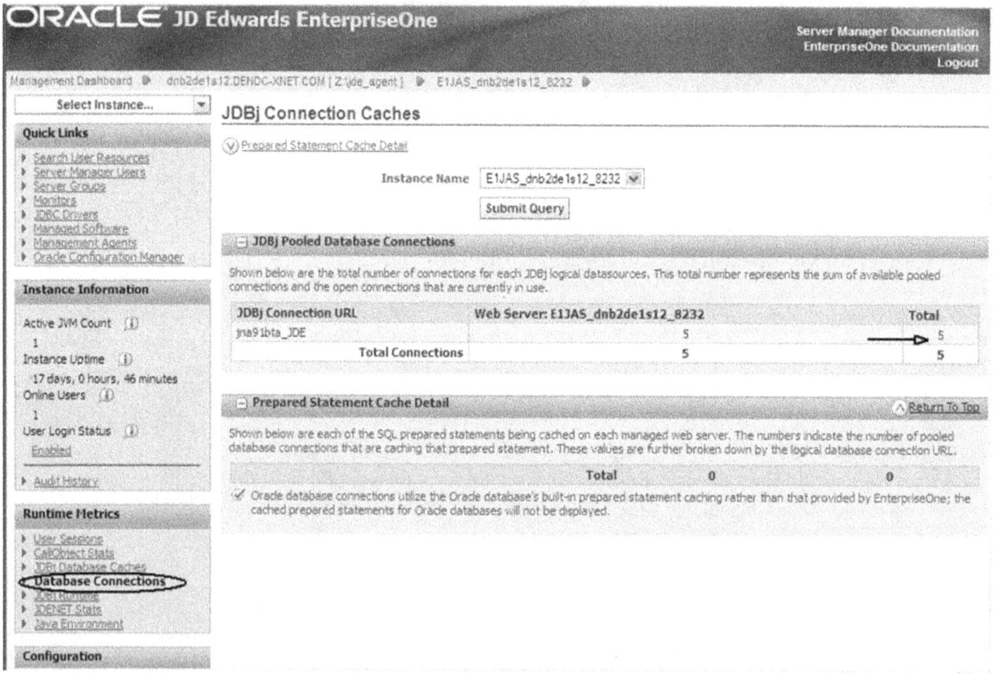

FIGURE 6-11.   *Server Manager Console displaying DB Connections from JAS Server*

System i   The pool key is one of the following:

- ServerName_*DBUser_DBPwd*

- ServerName_*DBUser_DNT_DBPwd* (based on "Do not translate" flag)

This server name is the column OMSRVR in F98611. This is the actual server name.
Example: JDEV_jdeow_bfree4me

Oracle   The pool key is Database_DBUser. The database is OMDATB in F98611, which is TNSNAMES.ORA.
Example: e1aix3orcl_jdeow

SQL Server   The pool key is ConnectURL_PhysicalDBName_IsUnicodeFlag_DBUser. The PhysicalDBName is OMDATB2 in F98611. This is the actual physical database name, not the ODBC DSN or OW DS name.
Example: jdbc:sqlserver://DENMLPS22:1433_PS8111_true_jdeow

UDB   The pool key is Database_DBUser. The Database is the ODBC DSN name. It is OMDATB in F98611.
Example: RS2u_jdeow

Conclusions   Based on this understanding, we can infer that the pool of JDBC connections makes sense only if multiple end users are mapped to a single JDBC proxy user. This would allow multiple users to take advantage of shared JDBC pooled connections. However, if you have a lot of one-to-one mapping between end users and database proxy users, there is no pooling of connections, and instead we end up spawning multiple connections to the database, which wastes memory on the database and ends up causing performance issues on both the web and database tiers. Therefore, for an environment with a limited set of proxy user profiles serving end users for connecting to the database, we should create a JDBC pool with shared resources, like so:

```
[CONNECTION POOL]
minConnection=5
maxConnection=num of max Concurrent Users
initialConnection=5
poolGrowth=10
```

But for an environment in which each user is mapped to a unique proxy profile for connecting to a database, we'd create a pool like this:

```
[CONNECTION POOL]
minConnection=0
maxConnection=num of max Concurrent Users( again its no harm in keeping
this a high value)
initialConnection=1
poolGrowth=1
```

Long-Running Queries from JAS

When you need to isolate long-running queries that are running from a JAS Server, you can find them quite easily by creating a user-level log and setting a threshold for query execution. Figure 6-11 provides an example of how to see the database connections to the JVM instance.

1. Open Server Manager for the JAS instance. In the Configuration section, click jdelog.properties Logging.

2. Click Create a User Specific Log in Server Manager (as illustrated in Figure 6-12):

    a. Enter the user ID you would like to log for.

    b. Set your log level threshold (Application Level Activity).

    c. Click Apply.

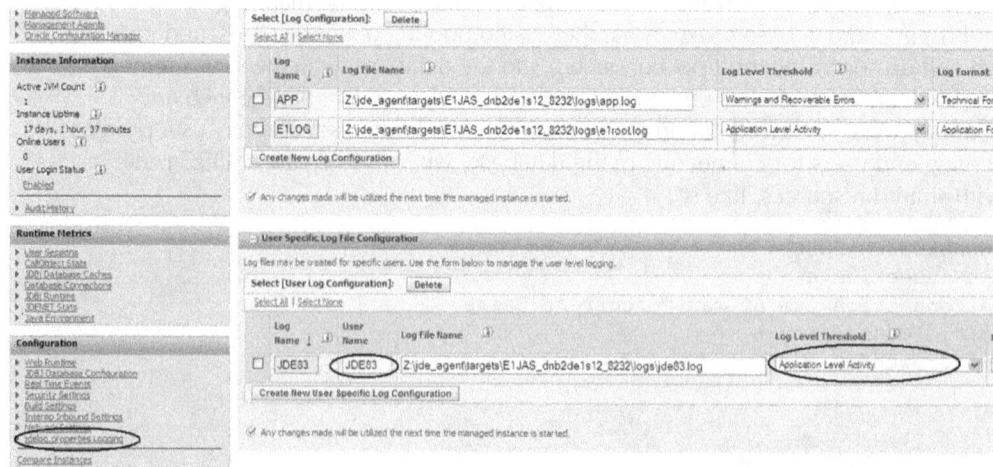

FIGURE 6-12. *Setting and enabling the Query Usage Execution Threshold*

   3. Now you'll need to enable JDBC Query Usage Tracking:

   a. Open Server Manager for the JAS instance. In the Configuration Section, click JDBJ Database Configurations.

   b. Check the box for Enable Usage Tracking, and then, in the Usage Execution Threshold field, set a threshold in milliseconds for the query execution, as shown in Figure 6-13.

Any query which takes about 5 seconds to execute will be captured in the user's log:

```
28 Mar 2012 14:25:25,594 [APP   ]  - [JDBJ]            SELECT
LMLL,LMRLS,LMPATHCD,LMENHV01 FROM SY811.F00941 WHERE (LMLL = ? )
28 Mar 2012 14:25:25,594 [APP   ]  - [JDBJ]            SQL statement
parameter marker values are :
28 Mar 2012 14:25:25,594 [APP   ]  - [JDBJ]            Param1 :
PY8111C1_Types.VARCHAR,
28 Mar 2012 14:25:25,594 [APP   ]  - [JDBJ]            Usage Tracking:
Usage tracking: Statement execution took 5469 ms: select.
28 Mar 2012 14:25:25,609 [APP   ]  - [JDBJ]            Usage Tracking:
Usage tracking: Field F00941.ENHV01 was fetched but not used.
28 Mar 2012 14:25:25,609 [APP   ]  - [JDBJ]            Usage Tracking:
Usage tracking: Field F00941.PATHCD was fetched but not used.
28 Mar 2012 14:25:25,609 [APP   ]  - [JDBJ]            Usage Tracking:
Usage tracking: Field F00941.LL was fetched but not used.
28 Mar 2012 14:25:25,609 [APP   ]  - [JDBJ]            Usage Tracking:
Usage tracking: Field F00941.RLS was fetched but not used
```

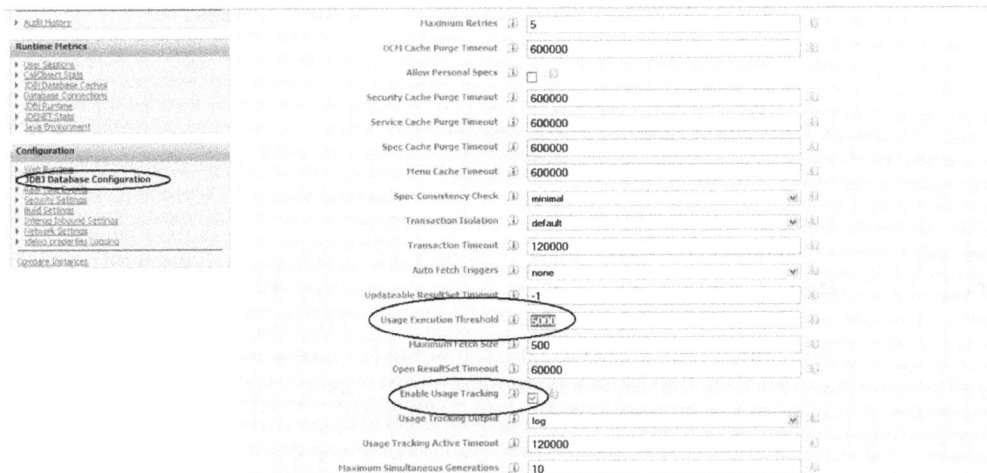

FIGURE 6-13. *Usage Execution Threshold/Usage Tracking*

Other usage thresholds can be considered as well. The following is a summary of all the query usage thresholds that can be enabled; these can be found in the [JDBj-RUNTIME PROPERTIES] section of the ini file:

- **usageTracking = true** Enables or disables usage tracking. This setting provides additional tracking and logging to use during testing. Usage tracking does incur a performance penalty, so it should be disabled for production code. Values are `true` and `false`.

- **usageExecutionThreshold = 20000** Maximum time (in milliseconds) for a single database operation to execute. If a single database operation takes longer than this threshold, then the statement and time will be logged as part of usage tracking. Values are 0 or greater.

- **usageFetchSizeThreshold = 500** Expected maximum fetch size (in rows) for a single fetch to return. If a single fetch returns more than this threshold, then the actual fetch size will be logged as part of usage tracking. Values are –1 or greater. The value –1 indicates that any fetch size is valid.

- **usageResultSetOpenThreshold = 60000** Maximum time (in milliseconds) for a result set to remain open. If a result set is left open longer than this threshold, then the result set and time will be logged as part of usage tracking. When this setting is reached, the system does not automatically close the result set. Values are –1 or greater. A usage result set open threshold value of –1 indicates that no such usage tracking will occur.

- **usageTrackingOutput = log** Specifies the destination of usage tracking output. Values are log and exception.

- **usageTransactionActiveThreshold = 120000** Values are –1 or greater.

Preventing Wide-Open Queries on the JAS Server

Allowing end users to run wide-open queries from an application or data browser affects the performance of both the JAS Server and backend database. In some cases, a certain subset of users may need the functionality of unrestricted query access. However, indiscriminate use of wide-open, unbound query results that fetch a lot of data back to the JAS Server will consume excessive memory (JVM Heap) in a short time period. If this type of activity is repeated by several users, it can cause performance issues. Since Tools 8.98 Update 2, there exists a very useful feature of Application Query Security that allows system administrators to fine-tune the ability to encourage end users to use the more discerning filter criteria to limit the amount of data fetched on queries. A wide-open query would produce a message as seen in Figure 6-14. Oracle document ID 884562.1 explains this feature.

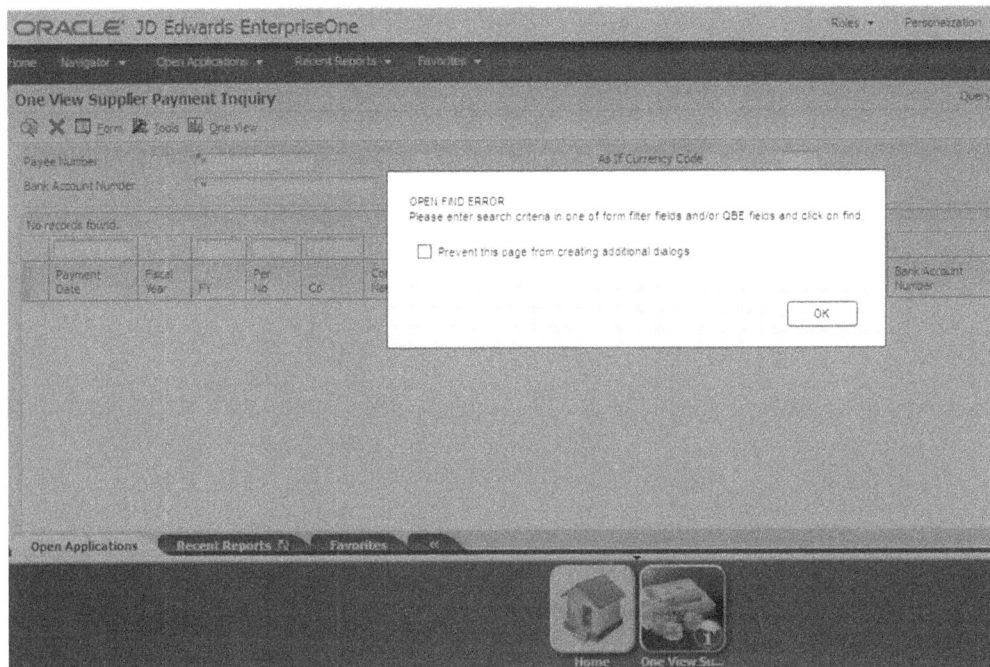

FIGURE 6-14. *Screenshot of Application Query Security in action*

Using the Correct Database JDBC Driver
Using the appropriate JDBC driver will tremendously improve the performance of the database queries from the JAS Server. The rule of thumb is to use the highest supported JDBC driver for the backend database; the only caveat is that you need to ensure that the JDBC driver is supported on the Java Runtime Environment (JRE) that your J2EE Server is running on.

A simple search for "Oracle JDBC Driver" using your favorite search engine will take you to the JDBC page on Oracle's web site. From this search you can determine the latest drivers at this point are 11.2.0.3:

- ojdbc5.jar for JRE 1.5

- ojdbc6.jar for JRE 1.6

Often, however, a web server will have several JDBC drivers in its CLASSPATH, and more often than not, an older version of JDBC driver is being used. So how can you find which driver is being used and which JDBC drivers are present? This is explained in the next section.

Am I Using the Correct Database JDBC Driver? The simplest way to ensure that the JDBC driver you think is being used is in fact being used is to check the CLASSPATH on the desired JAS Server by going to Server Manager, and under Runtime Metrics, choosing Java Environment, as shown in Figure 6-15.

Make sure that you see the desired JDBC driver in the CLASSPATH or the directory in which you have supplied the JDBC driver. It's noteworthy if you find several JDBC drivers: the one that's referred to first either directly or as being contained in a folder will be used. Hence, the order of referral in Java CLASSPATH is essential if the correct driver is to be used.

Analyzing the Impact of Business Functions on JAS Server Performance

Business Functions are the interface between JAS and the Enterprise Server. All the complex logic for an application is written in Enterprise Server business functions. If a business function crashes or takes longer than the jas.ini parameter [JDENET] `enterpriseServerTimeout` timeout value, the end user will see a WebClient Exception error. Server Manager provides a simple intuitive chart in which to observe business function runtimes, timeouts, and errors. By recording the CallObject Stats (business function runtime) on an hourly interval in the day, and resetting stats, you can get a very good idea whether the "random" performance problems correlate to when a long-running business function is being executed.

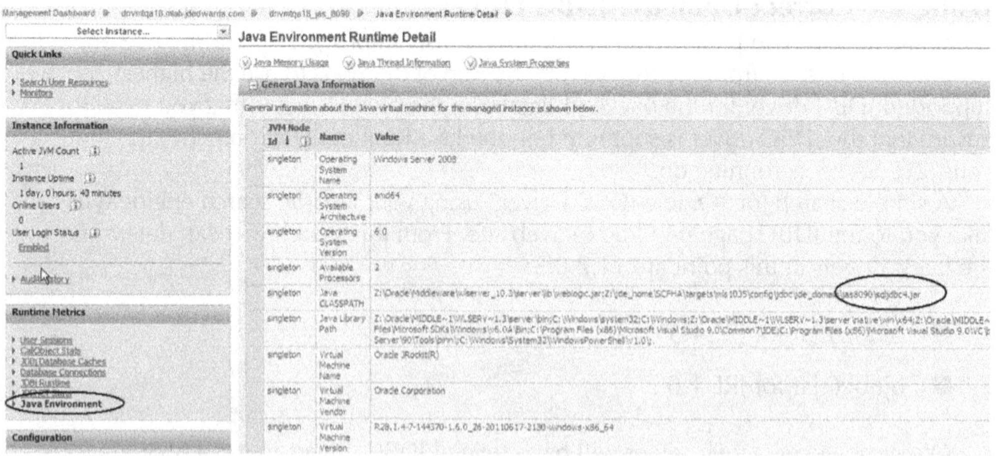

FIGURE 6-15. *JAS Server CLASSPATH*

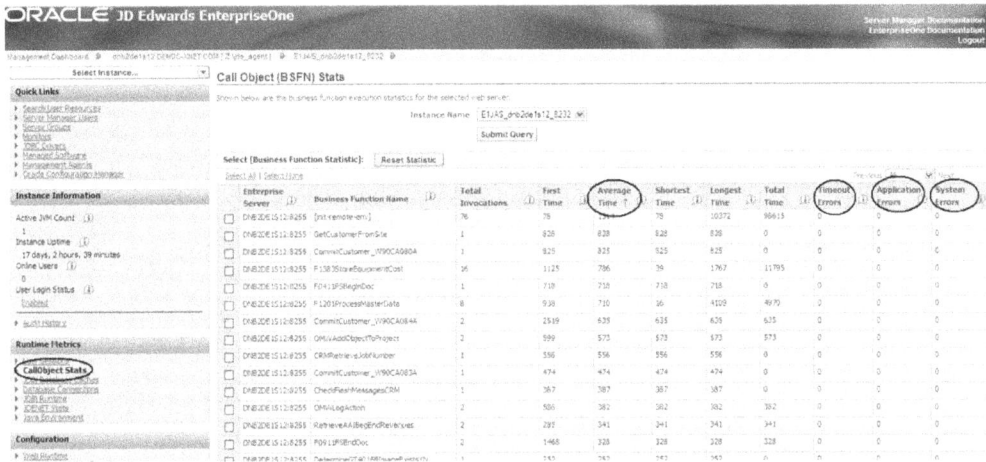

FIGURE 6-16.   *Server Manager for HTML server showing business function runtimes and possible timeouts*

It's quite easy to check if any of the business functions are timing out or taking an excessively long time to execute. Access Server Manager for the desired JAS Server and navigate to Runtime Metrics, and then click CallObject Stats, as shown in Figure 6-16.

WebLogic Application Server–specific Tuning

We will now look at specific tuning that can be done at the application server level. We will start with WebLogic.

WebLogic Console and JRockit Command-Line Arguments

Although most administration functions for WebLogic and JRockit can be performed through EnterpriseOne Server Manager, changing JRockit command-line arguments requires the WebLogic Administration Console. The default port and page for the console is 7001/console—for example, http://MyServer:7001/console. From the

WebLogic Administration Console home page, the following navigation will allow changes to the JRockit command line arguments:

1. Using Server Manager, stop the Managed Server whose command-line arguments are to be changed.

2. Under the Domain Structure box on the left, locate the domain name established during the installation process.

3. Open the Environment tree.

4. Click the Servers option under the Environment tree.

5. In the Servers list, click the managed server name created during the installation process. (The AdminServer will also be visible in the Servers list.)

6. On the Server Settings page, click the Server Start tab at the top.

7. Locate the Arguments box. This is where you can enter JRockit arguments.

8. If your WebLogic installation is in Production mode, click the button in the upper-left corner labeled Lock & Edit. This will open the Arguments box for editing.

9. After you've made changes, click the Save button near the top of the screen.

10. A message should appear near the top of the screen: "Settings Updated Successfully."

11. Click the Activate Changes button near the upper-left corner of the screen.

12. A message should be displayed stating that all changes have been activated.

13. At this point, the Managed Server can be restarted through Server Manager. When it starts successfully, the changes will be in effect.

If the JRockit arguments are edited incorrectly, such as with misspelled argument entries, a "Failed" status will be displayed in Server Manager. Errors must be corrected until the server comes up successfully.

Memory Considerations

WebLogic and JRockit provide a number of memory handling and garbage collection options. By default, the generational parallel (GENPAR) garbage collection mode is used. This method involves the division of the heap into a nursery memory block as well as an old generation section. Newly encountered objects are placed in the nursery section where garbage collection passes happen more frequently. This generational design is intended to clear memory used by short-lived objects quickly so that the memory can be reused by newly encountered objects without performing a full garbage collection across the entire heap memory. The default size of the nursery heap section is one half the total heap size in GENPAR mode.

Longer living objects will be moved (promoted) to the old generation where garbage collection happens less frequently. This generational heap design has been found to be more efficient with many types of applications and has become a standard with most JVM designs.

Some Java Development Kits (JDKs) (including Sun HotSpot) use a three-generational design—that is, a nursery, and old generation area as well as a permanent generation section used to hold objects. JRockit does not use a permanent area. If a default argument for the permanent area (such as `-XX:MaxPermSize=128m`) is found among the JRockit command-line arguments, it can be removed since it will never be used.

Recommendations from the JRockit development team state that the minimum heap size and the maximum heap size should be set to the same value. Figure 6-17 shows the minimum and maximum sizes set to 2GB of memory. This setting is appropriate for a dedicated web server with 4GB of total physical memory. Obviously, this setting may not be appropriate for machines with less than 4GB of physical memory or for machines with larger amounts of physical memory.

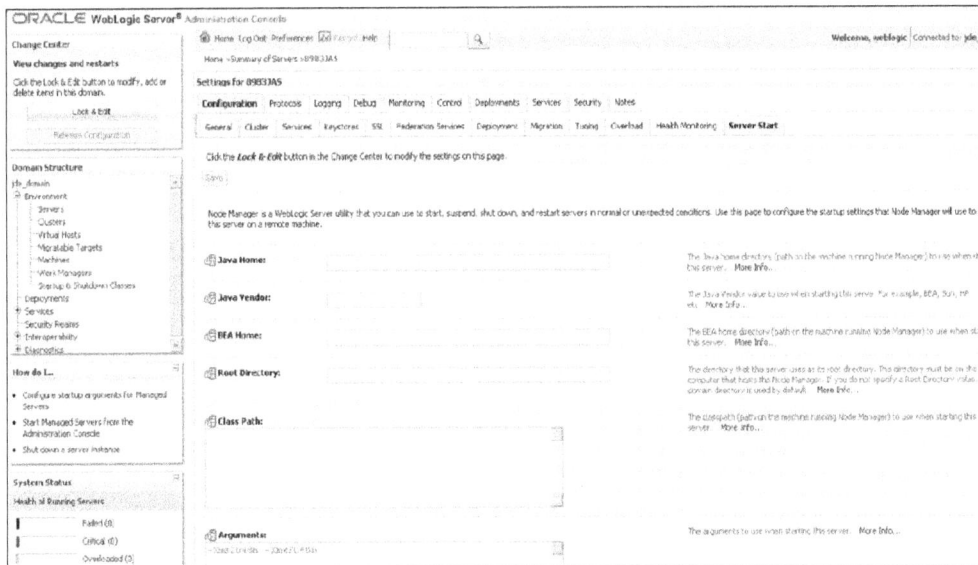

FIGURE 6-17. *Weblogic Admin Console showing where Heap Memory Allocation is defined*

The 64-bit version of WebLogic and JRockit are required on the EnterpriseOne web server. These 64-bit machines can address huge amounts of memory, so performance testing will be required to find the optimal heap size per managed server, as well as the optimal number of managed servers per machine. Machines that are not dedicated web servers (those that are running other applications as well) will require performance testing to determine appropriate heap sizes.

Verbose Garbage Collection and Other Information

There are times when understanding the web server performance problems requires that you examine a verbose garbage collection log. The verbose garbage collection setup in JRockit is different from that of other JDKs in several ways. First, the setup requires command-line arguments as opposed to a check box on the console like other JDKs. The following command-line argument will turn on verbose garbage collection, place it in a log named gc.log, and record memory and garbage collection activity with a time stamp. (Heap size parameters are not shown in this example.)

```
-Xverboselog:gc.log -Xverbose:memory,gc -Xverbosetimestamp
```

The gc.log will contain the verbose garbage collection information, which will be located under the domain folder of the JRockit directory structure created during installation. Second, much more data can be displayed, if requested, including optimization, pauses, and compaction. Here is an example of a command-line argument to record other types of JRockit activity:

```
-Xverboselog:gc.log -Xverbose:opt,memory,gcpause,memdbg,compaction,gc,
license -Xverbosetimestamp
```

Also, upon request, a Memory Usage Report will be added to the end of the log during shutdown. The Memory Usage Report can be useful in understanding where JRockit is spending its garbage collection time and minimizes the need for a verbose garbage collection viewer. The following is an example of the command-line argument to generate a Memory Usage Report at the time the server is shut down:

```
-Xverboselog:gc.log -Xverbose:memory,gc -Xverbosetimestamp -Xgcreport - 7 -
```

Figure 6-18 shows an example of a Memory Usage Report. Notice that separate report sections and counters are being kept for young (nursery) collections as opposed to the old collections. During the time that 59 collections were performed on the young part of the heap, only 4 collections were performed on the old part of the heap.

Based on extensive testing, we found that no specific settings, such as -XXcallProfiling or -XXaggressive:opt, should be used—in fact, they reduce the performance throughput and, in some cases, cause the JVM to freeze or crash. The only optimization settings we can recommend for WebLogic are the heap parameters -Xms2048m -Xmx2048m.

```
[memory ][Mon Jun 21 14:50:54 2010][10713]
[memory ][Mon Jun 21 14:50:54 2010][10713] Memory usage report
[memory ][Mon Jun 21 14:50:54 2010][10713]
[memory ][Mon Jun 21 14:50:54 2010][10713] young collections
[memory ][Mon Jun 21 14:50:54 2010][10713]     number of collections = 59
[memory ][Mon Jun 21 14:50:54 2010][10713]     total promoted =        55779677 (size 1817781344)
[memory ][Mon Jun 21 14:50:54 2010][10713]     max promoted =          1539629 (size 64372992)
[memory ][Mon Jun 21 14:50:54 2010][10713]     total GC time =         21.829 s
[memory ][Mon Jun 21 14:50:54 2010][10713]     mean GC time =          369.983 ms
[memory ][Mon Jun 21 14:50:54 2010][10713]     maximum GC Pauses =      464.419 , 475.873, 534.422 ms
[memory ][Mon Jun 21 14:50:54 2010][10713]
[memory ][Mon Jun 21 14:50:54 2010][10713] old collections
[memory ][Mon Jun 21 14:50:54 2010][10713]     number of collections = 4
[memory ][Mon Jun 21 14:50:54 2010][10713]     total promoted =        0 (size 0)
[memory ][Mon Jun 21 14:50:54 2010][10713]     max promoted =          0 (size 0)
[memory ][Mon Jun 21 14:50:54 2010][10713]     total GC time =         3.735 s (pause 3.735 s)
[memory ][Mon Jun 21 14:50:54 2010][10713]     mean GC time =          933.720 ms (pause 933.714 ms)
[memory ][Mon Jun 21 14:50:54 2010][10713]     maximum GC Pauses =      930.100 , 942.731, 1152.473 ms
[memory ][Mon Jun 21 14:50:54 2010][10713]
[memory ][Mon Jun 21 14:50:54 2010][10713]     number of parallel mark phases  = 4

[memory ][Mon Jun 21 14:50:54 2010][10713]     number of parallel sweep phases  = 4
```

FIGURE 6-18.   *Memory Usage Report for Verbose Garbage Collection from Weblogic Server*

WebSphere Application Server–specific Tuning

We will now look at some of the performance tuning measures that can be done with WebSphere.

WebSphere Class Sharing Option

In an effort to minimize storage requirements, WebSphere Application Server uses a shareclasses cache so that the class information can be shared by multiple JVMs within the WebSphere version and release. In some cases, contention for access to this cache can result in severe performance problems. There are two possible solutions to this problem:

- Specify a generic JVM option of `-Xshareclasses:none`.

- Specify the JVM configuration to ensure that each JVM uses its own shareclasses cache. You do this by specifying generic JVM options as part of the WebSphere Application Server configuration. For example, this line

  `-Xshareclasses:name=jde1cache,groupAccess,nonFatal -Xscmx50M`

  indicates that this JVM should use a cache named jde1cache with a maximum size of 50MB.

NOTE
A unique cache name must be specified for each JVM to avoid conflict. The name itself can be anything convenient—for example, it could be the name of the JVM.

WebSphere Heap Fragmentation

Usually WebSphere heap dumping is caused by an Out of Memory signal brought on by large object allocation. WebSphere Application Server cannot handle these repeated large object requests and will likely heap dump. An error message in the logs will appear, such as the following:

```
Too large object request.  Could not locate 10,629,024 bytes of contiguous
Space with 213,859,392 bytes available  [Mon May 7 09:33:25 2012]
```

In this example, WebSphere Application Server could not allocate 10MB of contiguous space out of 200MB free memory.

Here is what you can do to mitigate these errors:

1. Separate the minimum heap and maximum heaps as much as possible: you can use the IBM 32-bit heap recommendations of Xms = 32m, Xmx = 1536m.

2. Increase the Xmx parameter. In some cases, this setting needs to be increased to Xmx = 1856m; the only concern is hitting the 2GB limit imposed by 32-bit architecture.

3. Turn on verbose garbage collection for further analysis.

    ■ You can do this in the IBM WebSphere Application Server Administration Console by selecting Servers, then Process Definition, and then JVM Properties.

    ■ You can also add the parameter `xtgc2` to the generic JVM command-line settings and send the native_stderr.log to the development server.

4. Add the class `kCluster` parameters.

The JD Edwards EnterpriseOne Web solution has about 9,000 to 12,000 class objects resident in the memory. To store them properly and cause overflow to `pCluster`, you need to set these to their own `kCluster`.

How to Calculate -Xk and -Xp

Consider the following native_stderr log, which is obtained by enabling verbose garbage collection and -Xtgc2.

```
GC(VFY-SUM): pinned=8093(classes=7338/freeclasses=0) dosed=6439 movable=18370573
free=266805>
<GC(VFY-SUM): freeblocks: max=9453576 ave=1673 (446547760/266805)>
<GC(VFYAC-SUM): freeblocks: max=16796464 ave=309446 (446531184/1443)>
```

Here is how to read the previous log entries:

- Total pinned = 8093

- Max number of classes = 7338

- -Xk = 7338 × 1.1 = 8071; let's say -Xk10000

- Pinned = 8093 − 7338 = 755

So how much space would 755 objects take? If, on average, an object is 5KB, it would be 3.7MB, rounded up to 4MB. And overflow to five times an averaged sized object (25KB). So finally we get to the correct setting of -Xk10000 -Xp4096k,25k. This calculation is done based on the previous logs and cannot be used blindly everywhere.

IBM WebSphere Application Server Large Object Allocation

On IBM 1.3.1 Sovereign SDK Service Release 10 and later (build date of June 5, 2006, and later) and IBM 1.4.2 Sovereign SDK Service Release 4 and later, the environment variable ALLOCATION_THRESHOLD enables a user to identify the Java stack of a thread making an allocation request larger than the value of this environment variable. You can set the ALLOCATION_THRESHOLD environment variable on IBM WebSphere Application Server V5.1.1 and V6.0 with 1.4.2 Service Release 4 and later SDKs.

This is useful when you need to find where a specific thread is allocating large objects, and tracking that activity is very elusive. This variable will output the following information when the threshold is exceeded and allow for finding the location of the offending class:

- Allocation request for <allocation request> bytes <java stack>.

- If there is no Java stack, <java stack> becomes No Java Stack.

- If you set this option to a value nnn (bytes), whenever an allocation request is made for an object size >= nnn (bytes), the Java stack trace corresponding to the thread requesting the allocation is printed into the standard error log.

NOTE
Refer to the following links from IBM for more information: www-01.ibm.com/support/docview .wss?uid=swg21236523 and www.ibm.com/ developerworks/mydeveloperworks/blogs/ troubleshootingjava/entry/profiling_large_objects

IBM WebSphere Application Server "Break/Native" Memory

Users viewing large PDF files via a JAS client running on IBM WebSphere Application Server have encountered some problems. Customers running iSeries with i9 JVM are running out of "native memory" or "break memory" when large PDF files are viewed. It seems that the native memory used by IBM WebSphere Application Server is equivalent to the size of the PDF file. Because there is a hard limit on the amount of native memory allowed, viewing several large PDF files may crash the Application Server. The solution provided by IBM is to change one configuration setting.

1. In the Admin Console, navigate to Servers | Application Servers | *serverName* | Web Container Settings | Web Container | Custom Properties.

2. Click New.

3. Add the following information:

   ■ Name: com.ibm.ws.webcontainer.channelwritetype

   ■ Value: sync

4. Click OK, and then save the configuration.

5. The Application Server must be recycled to pick up the property.

NOTE
For more details see instructions at www-01.ibm .com/support/docview.wss?uid=swg21317658.

Tuning WebSphere on System i

Running IBM WebSphere on System i requires special considerations for peak web performance.

Memory Pool

Make sure that WebSphere is running in its own separate memory pool that has been set to four times the Xmx—that is, to the maximum memory for the JVM. Check in IBM Performance Manager to ensure that this memory pool and its jobs are not paging.

J9 JVM

Use the newer J9 JVM as opposed to the Classic JVM; the J9 JVM performs better. Additional considerations include the following:

- Reserve space for `kClusters` and large object allocation. To do this, add following parameters to generic JVM arguments: `-Xk9000 -Xloratio0.15`

- Break memory: Create a new custom property, com.ibm.ws.webcontainer. channelwritetype, and set it to sync.

- Class sharing: Set the JVM argument `-Xshareclasses:none`.

Prestart System i Jobs

The JD Edwards system uses QSQSRVR and QZDASOINIT jobs for DB operations. Use Display Active Prestart Jobs (DSPACTPJ) and Change Prestart Job Entry (CHGPJE) to monitor and adjust the prestarted job settings to the maximum observed number of QSQSRVR and QZDASOINIT.

jdbj.ini Parameters

Use the following jdbj.ini parameters to disable the native AS/400 JDBC driver. Use a common library for SQL packages.

```
[JDBj-RUNTIME PROPERTIES]
as400NativeJDBCDriver=false
as400PackageLibrary=QRECOVERY #not QTEMP
```

Garbage Collection and Its Interpretation

One of the most powerful features of Java is its platform-agnostic memory management. This makes programs written in Java quite robust, especially in matters of memory corruption. However, this automatic support for allocating and deleting memory on the JVM heap needs to be orchestrated by the JVM itself on behalf of the user.

When the JVM cannot allocate an object from the current heap because of lack of space, a memory allocation fault occurs, and the garbage collector is invoked. The first task of the garbage collector is to collect all the garbage that is in the heap. This process starts when any thread calls the garbage collector either indirectly as a result of allocation failure or directly by a specific call to `System.gc()`.

The first step is to get all the locks needed by the garbage collection process. This step ensures that other threads are not suspended while they are holding critical locks. All other threads are then suspended, and garbage collection can begin. It occurs in three phases: mark, sweep, and compaction (optional).

Verbose GC is a command-line option that you can supply to the JVM at startup. The format is `-verbose:gc`, `-verbosegc`, or `-Xverbose:memory,gc`.

This option switches on a substantial trace of every garbage collection cycle. The format for the generated information varies among various platforms and releases.

This trace should allow you to see the gross heap usage in every garbage collection cycle. For example, you could monitor the output to see the changes in the free heap space and the total heap space. This information can be used to determine whether garbage collections are taking too long to run, whether too many garbage collections are occurring, and whether the JVM crashed during garbage collection.

The three major JVMs handle the implementation of garbage collection differently, and although this is a complex and rapidly evolving topic, we can discuss the high-level concepts that are essential in understanding the memory management details.

Oracle Sun HotSpot JVM

The Sun HotSpot JVM uses a generational heap. A heap memory model of HotSpot is shown in Figure 6-19.

In HotSpot, young objects are allocated in Eden Space. When Eden Space gets filled with these young objects, a young generation garbage collection is triggered. The survivors of this garbage collection are moved to Survivor Space. Any survivor objects are moved to Survivor Space 2. Any object that survives garbage collections in Eden, then Survivor Space 1, and then Survivor Space 2 is promoted to Tenured Space.

Garbage collection in the Young Heap space is always fast. Garbage collection of objects in Tenured Heap space is more time-consuming because the objects are numerous with more references, which makes tracking them difficult. In addition, the Tenured Heap space gets fragmented due to repeated garbage collection and often there is no more contiguous space on heap for an object allocation—this triggers a major garbage collection, which pauses all threads until the Tenured Heap space is defragmented and compacted.

In addition to Eden, Survivor, and Tenured Spaces, HotSpot has a Perm Space that contains class objects and string constants.

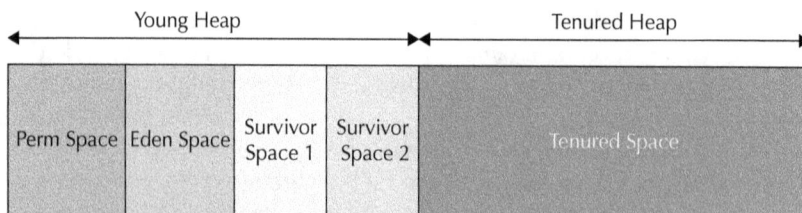

FIGURE 6-19. *Heap memory model of Oracle Sun Hotspot VM*

Key Ideas

- Since Tenured Space garbage collections always take longer, it's essential that you tune the size of the Eden and Survivor spaces so that objects are promoted to the Tenured Space only when they are truly permanent and are not prematurely promoted.

- Fragmented heaps cause the longest garbage collection cycles; therefore, based on the application's behavior, you'll need to choose garbage collection policies that would offer the highest throughput. In our experience, the `-XX:+UseParallelGC` policy offers a high throughput and a good baseline to tune further.

- Perm Space is often forgotten and must be accounted for and explicitly allocated: `-XX:MaxPermSize=128M`.

- To enable verbose garbage collection reports, use one of the following JVM arguments:

  `-verbose:gc`
  `-Xloggc:<file>` to log GC status to a file with time stamps

The verbose garbage collection log may be interpreted by using the GCViewer tool. It provides excellent summary on overall heap usage. Figure 6-20 shows a

```
90219.796: [GC 90219.796: [DefNew: 1023K->4K(1024K), 0.0004903 secs] 7665K->6708K(9264K), 0.0005109 secs]
90219.843: [GC 90219.843: [DefNew: 964K->9K(1024K), 0.0004286 secs] 7668K->6713K(9264K), 0.0004512 secs]
90239.849: [GC 90239.849: [DefNew: 715K->22K(1024K), 0.0005597 secs] 7420K->6861K(9264K), 0.0005840 secs]
90239.853: [GC 90239.853: [DefNew: 981K->64K(1024K), 0.0007507 secs] 7821K->7020K(9264K), 0.0007765 secs]
90239.876: [GC 90239.876: [DefNew: 1023K->45K(1024K), 0.0005975 secs] 7980K->7062K(9264K), 0.0006183 secs]
90239.921: [GC 90239.921: [DefNew: 1005K->6K(1024K), 0.0003706 secs] 8022K->7066K(9264K), 0.0003897 secs]
90259.935: [GC 90259.935: [DefNew: 966K->19K(1024K), 0.0005015 secs] 8026K->7079K(9264K), 0.0005247 secs]
90259.944: [GC 90259.944: [DefNew: 978K->63K(1024K), 0.0006777 secs] 8038K->7332K(9264K), 0.0006973 secs]
90259.953: [GC 90259.953: [DefNew: 1023K->63K(1024K), 0.0007462 secs] 8292K->7417K(9264K), 0.0007693 secs]
90259.998: [GC 90259.998: [DefNew: 1023K->8K(1024K), 0.0004591 secs] 8377K->7422K(9264K), 0.0004788 secs]
90260.017: [GC 90260.017: [DefNew: 967K->13K(1024K), 0.0004283 secs] 8382K->7427K(9264K), 0.0004496 secs]
90280.021: [GC 90280.021: [DefNew: 973K->64K(1024K), 0.0007398 secs] 8387K->7641K(9264K), 0.0007639 secs]
90280.029: [GC 90280.029: [DefNew: 1023K->63K(1024K), 0.0007202 secs] 8601K->7774K(9264K), 0.0007388 secs]
90280.060: [GC 90280.060: [DefNew: 1023K->8K(1024K), 0.0005305 secs] 8734K->7777K(9264K), 0.0005528 secs]
90280.093: [GC 90280.093: [DefNew: 968K->11K(1024K), 0.0003490 secs] 8737K->7780K(9264K), 0.0003684 secs]
90300.099: [GC 90300.099: [DefNew: 971K->38K(1024K), 0.0005564 secs] 8740K->7943K(9264K), 0.0005784 secs]
90300.104: [GC 90300.104: [DefNew: 998K->64K(1024K), 0.0007931 secs] 8903K->8126K(9264K), 0.0008113 secs]
90300.139: [GC 90300.139: [DefNew: 1023K->4K(1024K), 0.0004812 secs] 9086K->8129K(9264K), 0.0005002 secs]
90300.185: [GC 90300.185: [DefNew: 964K->9K(1024K), 0.0004321 secs] 9088K->8133K(9264K), 0.0004536 secs]
90320.189: [GC 90320.189: [DefNew: 702K->22K(1024K), 0.0005926 secs]90320.190: [Tenured: 8259K->3637K(8376K),
0.0322219 secs] 8826K->3637K(9400K), 0.0329039 secs]
90320.226: [GC 90320.226: [DefNew: 959K->63K(1024K), 0.0007889 secs] 4596K->3933K(9264K), 0.0008068 secs]
90320.234: [GC 90320.234: [DefNew: 1023K->45K(1024K), 0.0005284 secs] 4893K->3978K(9264K), 0.0005479 secs]
90320.279: [GC 90320.279: [DefNew: 1005K->6K(1024K), 0.0004787 secs] 4938K->3982K(9264K), 0.0005007 secs]
90340.293: [GC 90340.293: [DefNew: 966K->20K(1024K), 0.0005192 secs] 4942K->3996K(9264K), 0.0005421 secs]
90340.302: [GC 90340.302: [DefNew: 980K->64K(1024K), 0.0006801 secs] 4956K->4245K(9264K), 0.0007002 secs]
90340.311: [GC 90340.311: [DefNew: 1023K->63K(1024K), 0.0007354 secs] 5205K->4334K(9264K), 0.0007577 secs]
90340.356: [GC 90340.356: [DefNew: 1023K->7K(1024K), 0.0004499 secs] 5294K->4338K(9264K), 0.0004695 secs]
90340.375: [GC 90340.375: [DefNew: 967K->12K(1024K), 0.0004238 secs] 5298K->4344K(9264K), 0.0004456 secs]
90360.381: [GC 90360.381: [DefNew: 971K->64K(1024K), 0.0007174 secs] 5303K->4555K(9264K), 0.0007413 secs]
```

FIGURE 6-20. *A sample verbose garbage collection logs from Hotspot JVM*

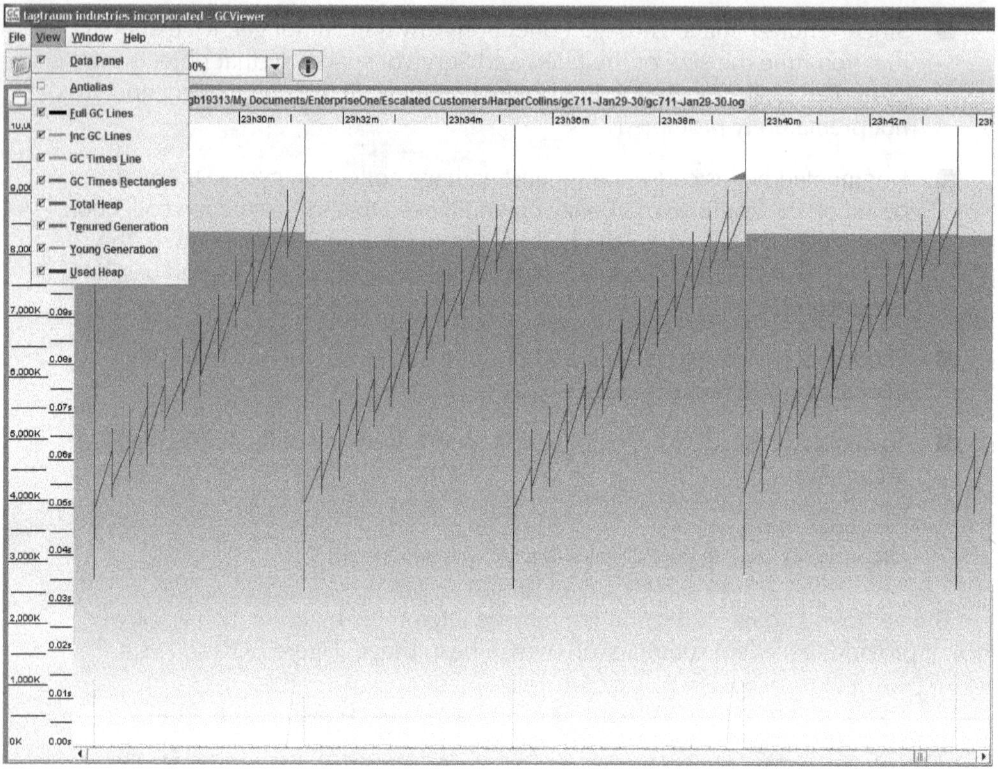

FIGURE 6-21. *GC Log viewed in GCViewer tool*

sample verbose garbage collection log from HotSpot. Figure 6-21 shows the same log views in GCViewer: observe the Young Generation, Tenured Generation, Used Heap, and garbage collection timelines.

Oracle JRockit JVM

Oracle JRockit JVM also uses a heap generational model, as shown in Figure 6-22. The young objects' space is called the Nursery Heap and the mature objects reside in Tenured Heap. Objects, when first allocated, are kept in the Keep Area of Nursery Heap, and garbage collection does not touch them on the first collection cycle. After the first garbage collection, the objects are promoted to the Tenured Space.

The biggest difference between JRockit and Sun HotSpot is that JRockit offers continuous heap, which means that garbage collection does not distinguish between young and tenured objects. JRockit uses several sophisticated garbage collection strategies to offer high throughput and low pause garbage collections. Also, JRockit does not have a Permanent Generation Space.

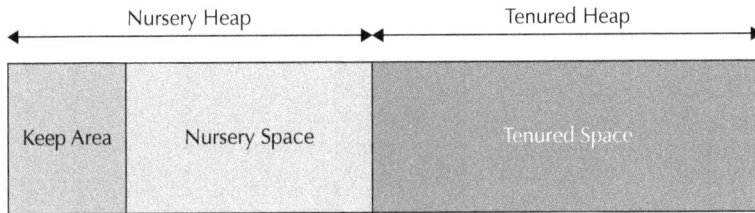

FIGURE 6-22. *Generational heap memory model of JRockit JVM*

JRockit also uses an elegant method of allocating objects in Thread Local Area Space—this leads to faster allocation of objects, because heap does not have be locked between different threads. Large objects, which are larger than 128KB, are allocated directly onto the Tenured Space.

Key Ideas

- Based on extensive research, we conclude that JRockit performs best with no explicit suggestion on which garbage collection policy to use. Hence it's recommended that you not provide any suggestions, such as `-Xgc:Gencon` or `-XXaggressive:opt`.

- JRockit uses innovative garbage collection schemes to reduce the overall pause time and achieves high throughput times.

- JRockit does not tune for Permanent Generation Space as is required by HotSpot.

- The biggest advantage of JRockit is that it can allocate noncontiguous heaps; this is an enormous advantage over other JVMs, because often Java Out of Memory conditions occur due to lack of contiguous space on heap.

- Verbose garbage collection reports may be triggered by using this JVM argument: `-Xverboselog:gc.log -Xverbose:memory`

- Verbose garbage collection logs may be best interpreted by using the JRockit Mission Control utility.

IBM JVM

The IBM heap model is also generational and resembles the HotSpot heap model, as shown in Figure 6-23: the Allocate Area is similar to Sun's Eden Space and the Survivor Space corresponds to the same space in the HotSpot model. New objects are created on the Allocate Area and, based on various sizing inputs, are promoted

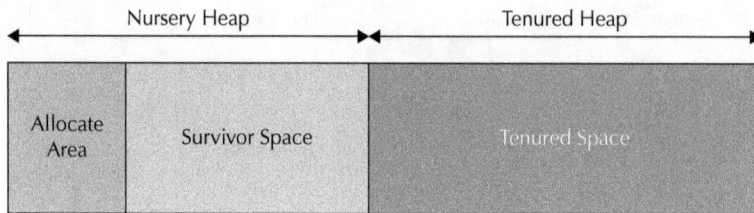

FIGURE 6-23. *Generational heap memory model of IBM JVM*

to the Survivor and finally to the Tenured Areas. IBM has also dedicated an area for large object allocation in its Tenured Space.

IBM JVM offers four different garbage collection policies:

- **-Xgcpolicy:optthruput** Throughput is more important than a short pause

- **-Xgcpolicy:optavgpause** Shorter GC pause; more important than overall throughput

- **-Xgcpolicy:gencon** Optimizes the garbage collection of short-lived objects

- **-Xgcpolicy:subpool** Is same as optthruput but tries to utilize a strategy more suited for multiprocessor machines

Key Ideas

- The IBM heap, like HotSpot, tends to fragment, so it's necessary to plan for large object allocation by using the parameter Xloratio—for example, -Xloratio0.15 reserves 15 percent of the heap for large objects.

- IBM recommends -Xgcpolicy:gencon, with Nursery Heap between 256 and 1024m. This, of course, needs to be tested at each customer site; however, it provides a new way to optimize the HTML Server.

- To enable verbose garbage collection reports, use the JVM argument -verbose:gc or simply check the box in the WebSphere Administration Console, resulting output can be found in the native_stderr.log.

- The verbose garbage collection log may be interpreted by using the IBM Pattern Modeling and Analysis Tool (PMAT).

```
<af type="tenured" id="179" timestamp="Mar 23 08:31:53 2012" intervalms="57074.293">
  <minimum requested_bytes="96" />
  <time exclusiveaccessms="0.067" />
  <tenured freebytes="0" totalbytes="169043968" percent="0" >
    <soa freebytes="0" totalbytes="169043968" percent="0" />
    <loa freebytes="0" totalbytes="0" percent="0" />
  </tenured>
  <gc type="global" id="179" totalid="179" intervalms="57074.523">
    <expansion type="tenured" amount="4709376" newsize="173753344" timetaken="1.323" reason="insufficient free space following gc" />
    <refs_cleared soft="261" threshold="32" weak="31" phantom="5" />
    <finalization objectsqueued="272" />
    <timesms mark="26.233" sweep="1.333" compact="0.000" total="29.073" />
    <tenured freebytes="52126512" totalbytes="173753344" percent="30" >
      <soa freebytes="52126512" totalbytes="173753344" percent="30" />
      <loa freebytes="0" totalbytes="0" percent="0" />
    </tenured>
  </gc>
  <tenured freebytes="52125224" totalbytes="173753344" percent="29" >
    <soa freebytes="52125224" totalbytes="173753344" percent="29" />
    <loa freebytes="0" totalbytes="0" percent="0" />
  </tenured>
  <time totalms="29.352" />
</af>

<af type="tenured" id="180" timestamp="Mar 23 08:36:41 2012" intervalms="288293.256">
  <minimum requested_bytes="16696" />
  <time exclusiveaccessms="0.051" />
  <tenured freebytes="13856" totalbytes="173753344" percent="0" >
    <soa freebytes="13856" totalbytes="173753344" percent="0" />
    <loa freebytes="0" totalbytes="0" percent="0" />
  </tenured>
  <gc type="global" id="180" totalid="180" intervalms="288293.458">
    <expansion type="tenured" amount="5458944" newsize="179212288" timetaken="1.155" reason="insufficient free space following gc" />
    <refs_cleared soft="162" threshold="32" weak="13" phantom="16" />
    <finalization objectsqueued="650" />
    <timesms mark="25.532" sweep="1.430" compact="0.000" total="28.291" />
    <tenured freebytes="53781024" totalbytes="179212288" percent="30" >
      <soa freebytes="53781024" totalbytes="179212288" percent="30" />
      <loa freebytes="0" totalbytes="0" percent="0" />
    </tenured>
  </gc>
  <tenured freebytes="53764328" totalbytes="179212288" percent="30" >
    <soa freebytes="53764328" totalbytes="179212288" percent="30" />
```

FIGURE 6-24. *IBM verbose garbage collection log*

Figure 6-24 shows a sample output from an IBM verbose garbage collection log. Figure 6-25 shows the IBM PMAT chart view: Observe the memory utilization, mark, sweep, and compact garbage collection times. Notice the steadily increasing memory consumption results in complete heap exhaustion on May 6, along with 3 seconds of compact garbage collection times.

Enabling Verbose Garbage Collection on Application Servers

To enable verbose garbage collection, you can check an explicit check box on the Administration Console or add JVM level arguments. The following instructions cover how to enable verbose garbage collection on IBM WebSphere and Oracle WebLogic application servers.

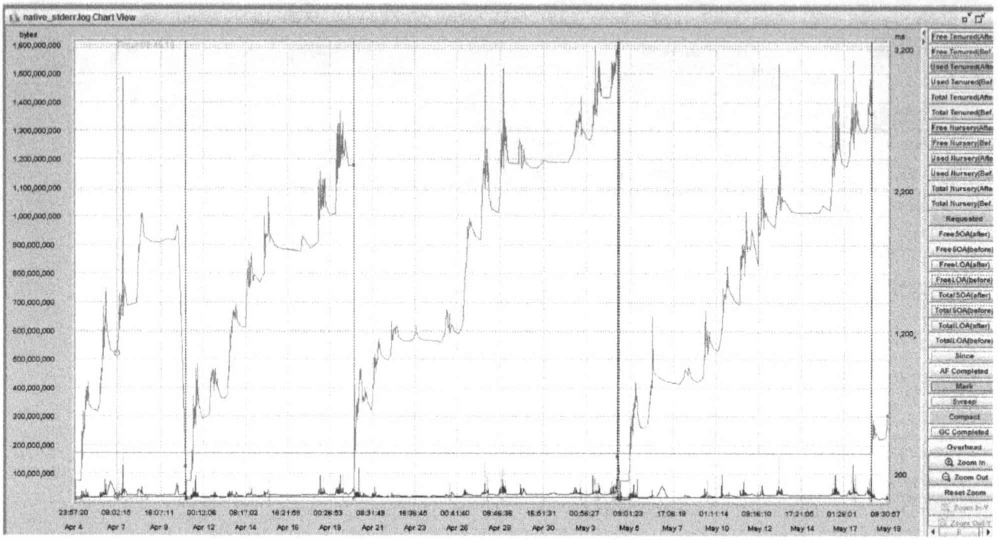

FIGURE 6-25. *IBM PMAT providing analysis of verbose garbage collection log*

For IBM WebSphere Server Here's how to enable verbose garbage collection on an IBM WebSphere server:

1. Go to the Administration Console, and then choose Application Servers | *<Server Name>* | Process Definition | Java Virtual Machine, as shown in Figure 6-26.

2. Check the Verbose Garbage Collection check box.

This will produce verbose garbage collection in the file native_stderr.log.

For Oracle WebLogic Server Here's how to enable verbose garbage collection on an Oracle WebLogic server:

1. Go to WebLogic Console | *<Server Name>* | Server Start | Arguments.

2. Add the following JVM arguments to enable verbose garbage collection:

```
-Xverboselog:gc.log -Xverbose:memory,gc -Xverbosetimestamp
```

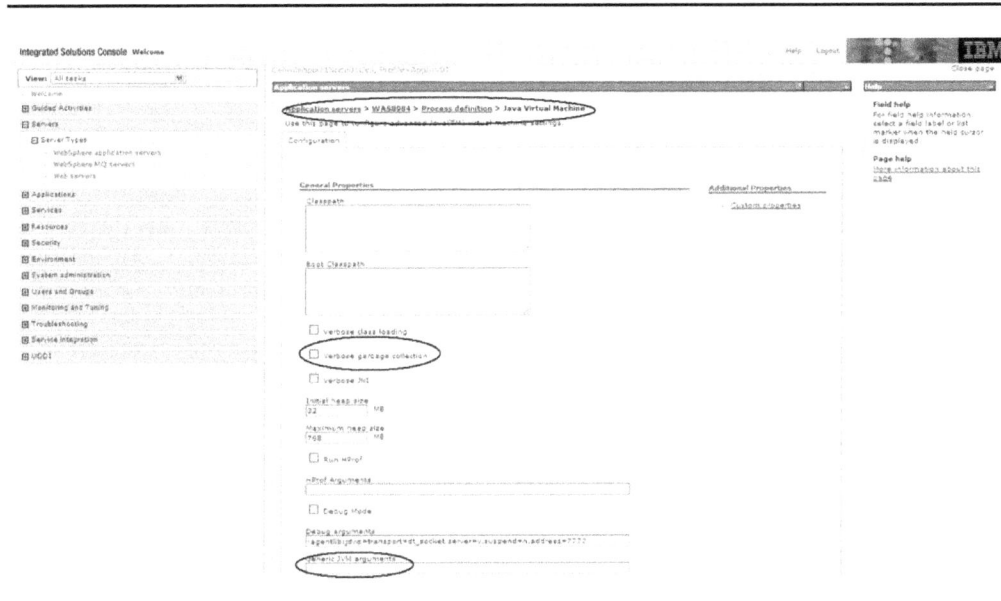

FIGURE 6-26. *IBM WebSphere Admin Console showing how to enable verbose GC logs*

Analysis of Verbose Garbage Collection

As mentioned, garbage collection is cryptic to analyze by simply eyeballing it. Therefore, you should use the appropriate tool to help you understand it. Three tools are helpful for analysis:

- **Oracle Sun HotSpot JDK**   GCViewer
- **Oracle JRockit JDK**   Mission Control
- **IBM JDK**   Pattern Modeling and Analysis Tool (PMAT)

For demonstration purposes, here's how to perform a use case analysis using IBM PMAT:

1. Download the PMAT tool by searching for "IBM PMAT" in your favorite web browser search engine. (Here is a good demonstration of how to use IBM PMAT Tool: www-01.ibm.com/support/docview.wss?uid=swg27007240&aid=1.)

2. Extract the contents of PMAT—essentially a JAR file—into a folder of your choice.

3. From a batch file, launch PMAT as shown:

```
"C:\Program Files\Java\jre6\bin\java" -Xmx512m -jar ga401.jar
pause
```

4. Click File, and Open Verbosegc Files (IBM SDK).

5. Path to *X:\WebSphere\AppServer\logs\Your_Server_Name* and open native_
stderr.log. You will see output similar to that shown in Figure 6-24.

6. Look for the recommendations that it provides:

```
Tue Jan 9 15:52:33 2007       Too large object request. Could
not locate 9,437,192 bytes of contiguous space with 350,713,352
bytes available.
[Mon Jan 8 16:03:54 2007]      Java heap critical shortage
0.037709374 % free.
[Wed May 18 12:44:20 2011]     Increase maximum Java heap size
using -Xmx option. If it does not work, review Java heap dump
with IBM HeapAnalyzer (http://www.alphaworks.ibm.com/tech/
heapanalyzer).
```

7. From the menu at the top of the screen, choose Analysis | Graph View All to
see the graph shown in Figure 6-27.

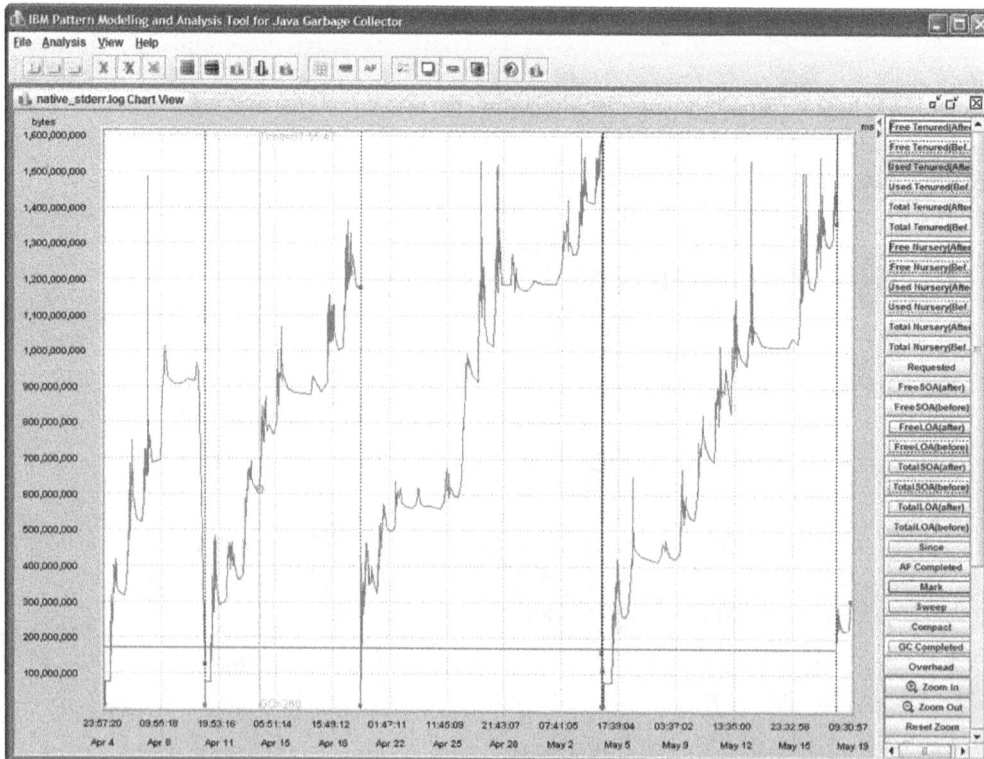

FIGURE 6-27.   *PMAT graphical explanation of a heap dump caused by lack of memory*

In Figure 6-27, observe the upward-moving lines that denote the Java heap memory growth. On later analysis, you would see that this was due to the use of an out-of-date JDBC driver holding onto memory, as shown in Figure 6-28.

The WebServer java core dumped due to a heap-fragmentation that occurred because of large object allocation. This was caused by an end user performing a large number of import grid rows, as shown in Figure 6-29.

In Figure 6-30, notice the sudden/abrupt rise in memory consumption from 14:05 to 19:03 on January 15th. Also notice the abrupt drop in memory use. Another interesting thing to notice is that this huge jump in memory consumption is not due to large object requests (shown as the line at the very bottom of the graph).

This abnormal behavior occurred because of long-running loops in Application ER Logic, which created a lot of short-lived objects that were garbage collected as soon as they were created. Figure 6-30 shows the same set of logs shown in Figure 6-29, but with added Compact GC times.

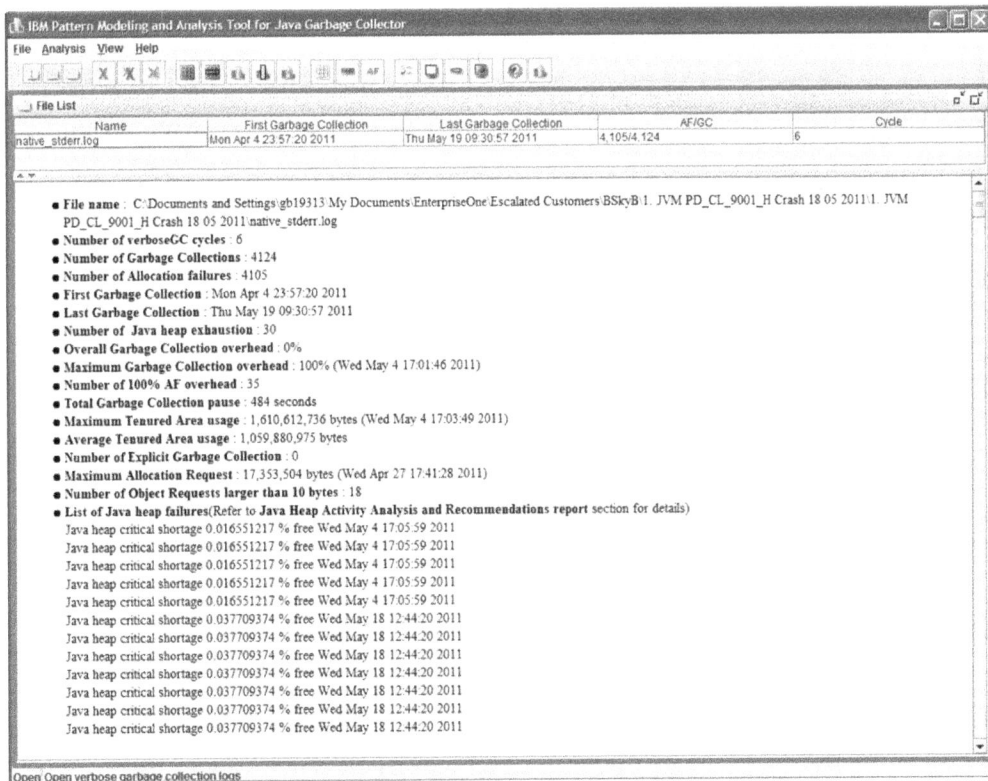

FIGURE 6-28. *Summary screen of Verbose Garbage Collection Logs in IBM PMAT tool*

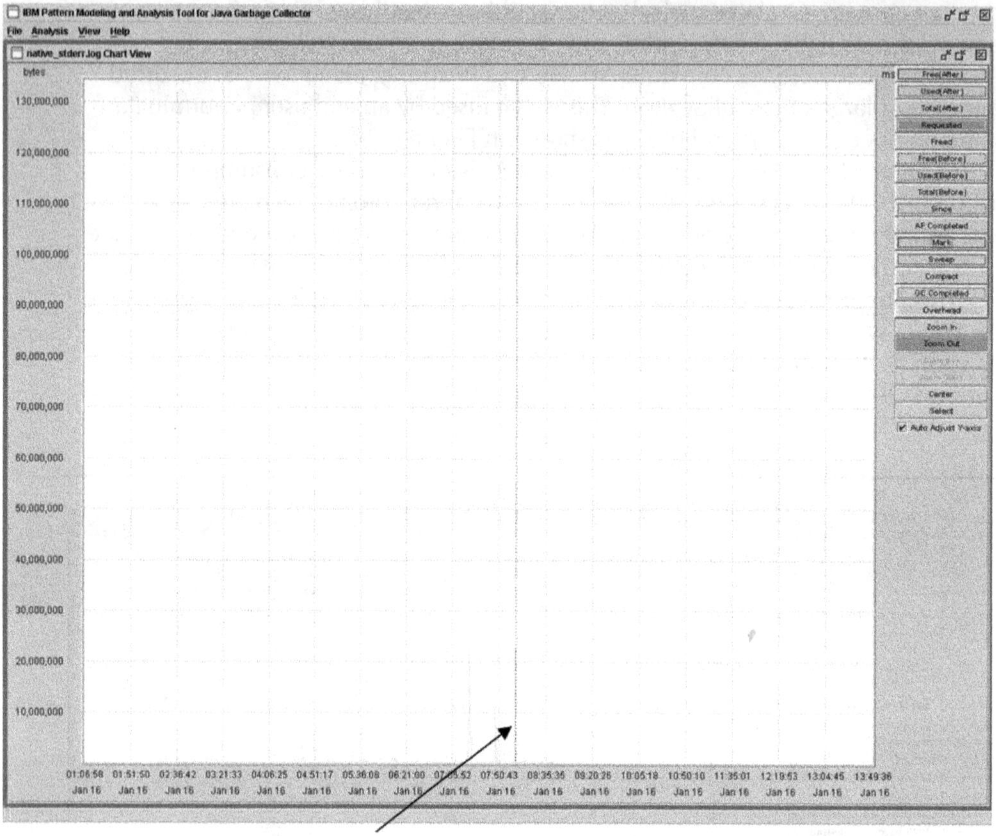

FIGURE 6-29. *PMAT graphical explanation of high CPU and memory consumption*

In Figure 6-30, notice the excessive Compact GC that occurs during this time period of high memory usage—the Compact GC duration shown in green (the lower section of the graph). This would lead to high CPU consumption on the web server and nonresponsive behavior to the end user.

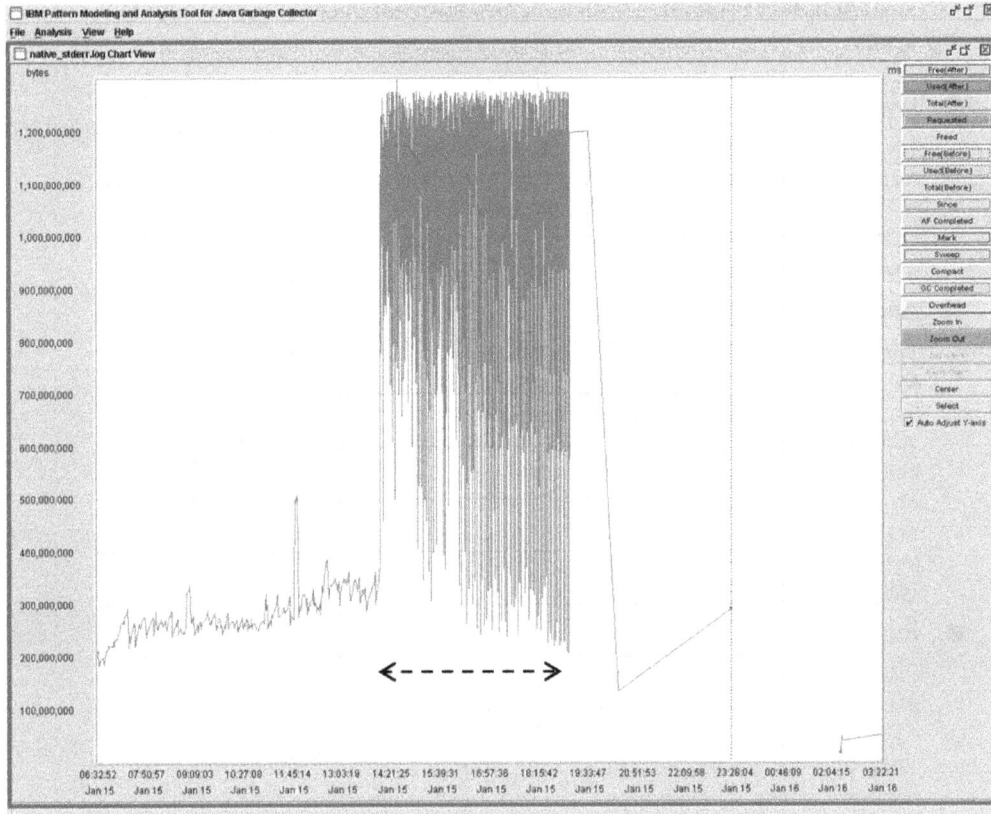

FIGURE 6-30. *PMAT memory usage and compact garbage collection*

End User Browser Tuning

Sometimes web users experience applications that get "stuck"—the processing indicator bar just keeps spinning—forever. Users have to close the browser and reopen another to continue. This can happen during find and form/interconnect (row and form exit) operations. There is no way to reproduce the problem because it is intermittent, and it happens to all users in multiple applications while users are performing multiple tasks.

In Internet Explorer, for example, some, but not all, users see a pop-up error: "HTTP error: 400: Bad Request." In such a case, errors in the logs could include the following.

- **systemout.log**

  ```
  [6/19/08 12:09:11:696 EDT] 00000030 SRTServletReq E SRVE0133E:
  An error occurred while parsing parameters. java.io.IOException:
  SRVE0216E: post body contains less bytes than specified by
  content-length at com.ibm.ws.webcontainer.servlet.RequestUtils.
  parsePostData(RequestUtils.java:538)
  ```

- **Another systemout log error**

  ```
  [2/27/08 14:33:59:479 CET] 0000001d SRTServletReq E SRVE0133E:
  An error occurred while parsing parameters. java.net.
  SocketTimeoutException: Async operation timed out at com.
  ibm.ws.tcp.channel.impl.AioTCPReadRequestContextImpl.proc
  essSyncReadRequest(AioTCPReadRequestContextImpl.java:157)
  at com.ibm.ws.tcp.channel.impl.TCPReadRequestContextImpl.
  read(TCPReadRequestContextImpl.java:109) at com.ibm.
  ws.http.channel.impl.HttpServiceContextImpl.fillABuffer
  (HttpServiceContextImpl.java:4136)
  ```

- **http_plugin.log**

  ```
  [Thu Jun 19 12:20:02 2008] 0000117c 00001e1c - ERROR: ws_common:
  websphereGetStream: Failed to connect to app server on host
  'jdewas1.herrs.com', OS err=10061
  [Thu Jun 19 12:20:02 2008] 0000117c 00001e1c - ERROR: ws_
  common: websphereExecute: Failed to create the stream [Thu
  Jun 19 12:20:02 2008] 0000117c 00001e1c - ERROR: ws_common:
  websphereHandleRequest: Failed to execute the transaction to
  'jdewas1Node01_AS_JS_81'on host 'jdewas1.herrs.com'; will try
  another one[Thu Jun 19 12:20:02 2008] 0000117c 00001e1c - ERROR:
  ws_common: websphereWriteRequestReadResponse: Failed to find an
  app server to handle this request
  ```

The following guidelines can help you with tuning your Internet Explorer or Firefox browser.

Internet Explorer

The HTTP 1.1 specification states that two connections should be available to a server from a client browser. This is a requirement to meet HTTP 1.1 standards, but it is not a restriction. Internet Explorer sets this limit by default to a minimum specification of two. Each of these connections is synchronous, so the effect of this limitation is that Internet Explorer can download only two resources at the same time. When a menu is launched, approximately 20 static resources are downloaded (JavaScripts and images), while approximately 35 to 40 static resources are downloaded for a typical EnterpriseOne form.

You can change the default amount of connections to the server to ten, and customers should observe significant improvements in EnterpriseOne menu and form rendering. To change this value for Internet Explorer, do the following:

1. Open regedit.exe.

2. Navigate to [HKEY_CURRENT_USER\Software\Microsoft\Windows\ CurrentVersion\Internet Settings].

3. Add a new DWORD entry named MaxConnectionsPerServer.

4. Set the value of this new key to Decimal 10 or Hexadecimal a.

5. Add a new DWORD entry named MaxConnectionsPer1_0Server.

6. Set the value of this new key to Decimal 10 or Hexadecimal a.

7. Close regedit.exe and restart your browser.

NOTE
Because this registry setting changes HKEY_ CURRENT_USER (HKCU), make sure it is set for the user that will be running EnterpriseOne on this particular machine.

If the clients are using a proxy to access their EnterpriseOne system, Internet Explorer defaults to using the HTTP 1.0 specification. HTTP 1.1 far outperforms HTTP 1.0, so this default behavior should also be altered. Firefox always defaults to using HTTP 1.1.

Here's how to change this behavior in Internet Explorer:

1. Open Internet Explorer.

2. Choose Tools | Internet Options.

3. Navigate to the Advanced tab.

4. Find the entry for Use HTTP 1.1 Through Proxy Connections and ensure that it is checked.

5. Click OK.

The final fix should be implemented in Internet Explorer. In IE 8, the default connections allowed per browser/server pair is set to six when Asynchronous JavaScript and XML (AJAX) is enabled. (See the web site http://msdn.microsoft.com/en-us/library/cc197013(VS.85).aspx.)

Firefox Browser

The Firefox browser has set the max-persistent-connections-per-server limit default to six, so Firefox can simultaneously download six resources. Fewer customers are experiencing issues with this higher default setting in Firefox, but some issues do occur.

The about:config preference network.http.max-persistent-connections-per-server sets the limit for the number of connections. You can find out more about this setting at http://developer.mozilla.org/en/docs/XMLHttpRequest#Limited_Number_Of_Simultaneous_xmlHttpRequest_Connections.

> **NOTE**
> *Internet Explorer and Firefox browsers can be affected by antivirus software running on end-user client machines.*

Wide Area Network Tuning

Tuning for wide area networks (WANs) comes down to tuning for two aspects:

- **Excessive round-trips—latency of the network**   Rendering the web page takes a lot of roundtrips to the web server.

- **Voluminous data transferred—bandwidth of the network**   Large amounts of bytes being transferred back and forth from the web server to the browser accessing it can produce lag.

Both of these issues can be fixed by enabling HTTP compression and expiry headers. These HTTP compression or expiry header settings can be done in either the HTTP server or the jas.ini—but not in both.

Cache Expiration Settings

Cache Expiration can be enabled either in HTTP Server or jas.ini.

HTTP Server

1. Remove the comment from this line in the httpd.conf. This allows for the manual control of object cache expiration.

    ```
    LoadModule expires_module modules/ApacheModuleExpires.dll
    ```

2. Add the following lines to the end of the httpd.conf. This will not expire cached objects unless they have not been accessed for 30 days. The time can obviously be changed to suit your requirements. Loading a new browser window or pressing F5 will check the images regardless.

```
ExpiresActive on ExpiresByType image/gif "access plus 30 days"
ExpiresByType text/css "access plus 30 days" ExpiresByType
application/x-javascript "access plus 30 days"
```

jas.ini   The following jas.ini setting can also be set to expire cached objects; this should only be done at the HTTP layer or in the jas.ini.

```
[OWWEB]
CacheStaticContentDay= number of days to set the expiry headers
```

Compression

Compression can also provide a performance benefit. This is configured as shown next. Again, this should only be done at the HTTP layer or in the jas.ini, but not both.

HTTP Server

1. Remove the comment from this line in the httpd.conf (this loads the compression module):

```
LoadModule deflate_module modules/mod_deflate.so
```

2. Add the following lines to the end of the httpd.conf (this specifies the type of requests to deflate, or compress):

```
SetOutputFilter DEFLATE
AddOutputFilterByType DEFLATE text/html text/plain text/xml
AddOutputFilterByType DEFLATE application/ms* application/
postscript
DeflateFilterNote Input instream DeflateFilterNote Output
outstream DeflateFilterNote Ratio ratio
LogFormat '"%r" %{outstream}n/%{instream}n (%{ratio}n%%)'
deflate CustomLog logs/deflate.log deflate
DeflateCompressionLevel 9
SetEnvIfNoCase Request_URI \.(?:gif|jpe?g|png|js)$ no-gzip dont-
vary SetEnvIfNoCase Request_URI \.(?:exe|t?gz|zip|bz2|sit|rar)$
no-gzip dont-vary SetEnvIfNoCase Request_URI \.(?:pdf|ube)$ no-
gzip dont-vary
```

jas.ini   The following jas.ini setting can also be set to enable compression. This should only be done at the HTTP layer or in the jas.ini.

```
[OWWEB]
EnableCompression= true
```

After these changes are made, restart the HTTP or JAS server.

Web Timeouts and Their Interrelationships

There are several timeouts in the jas.ini and jdbj.ini files, and they have a cascading effect on each other. We've often observed that a customer would tune a lower level timeout too narrowly, which inadvertently affects the higher layers.

Table 6-1 lays out the various timeouts and their impact on the system as a whole in hierarchical fashion.

Server	Setting	File	Details	Preferred Value	User Impact

J2EE	Web Session Timeout	web.xml (WAS) or opmn .xml (OAS)	Amount of idle inactivity before a web session to a J2EE container will timeout:
			`<session-config>`
			`<session-timeout>60</`
			`session-timeout>`
			`</session-config>`
			OR in J2EE Administration Visual Console
				< 1hour	High

HTTP	HTTP TimeOut	httpd .conf	TimeOut directive currently defines the amount of time Apache will wait for –total amount of time to receive a `GET` request –time between receipt of TCP packets on a `POST` or `PUT` request –time between ACKs on transmissions of TCP packets in responses	300 (5 min) Do not change unless viewing large PDFs or a transaction takes > 5 minutes in a single post	Low

JAS	`UserSession` timeout	jas.ini	Implementation of J2EE timeouts prior to J2EE servers. Now these two timeouts co-exist:
			`[CACHE]`
			`UserSession=3600000`
				< 1 hour and greater than the J2EE server timeout value	High

JAS	`LogoutProcessTimeout`	jas.ini	Maximum time the JAS will wait for AychBusinessFunctions to finish when user logs out.
			`[OWWEB]`
			`LogoutProcessTimeout=720000`
				+/– 12 min.	Low

(Continued)

TABLE 6-1.   *Timeouts and Their Impact on the System*

Server	Setting	File	Details	Preferred Value	User Impact
BSSV	`manual_timeout`	interop .ini	User session on Enterprise Server initialized from Java Connector will be cleared if session is idle for longer than the timeout value (in msec). `[INTEROP]` `manual_timeout=30000000`	10 min	Low
JAS	`jargonCacheTimeout`	jas.ini	Time that Jargon is cached in EnterpriseOne if enabled. `[SERVER]` `jargonCacheTimeout=360000`	10 min	Low
JAS	Connection timeout	jdbj.ini	Inactivity time period after which JDBC connection will timeout. Critical for a 1 to 1 end user to DataBaseUSER configuration as pooling effect is minimal. `[JDBj-CONNECTION POOL]` `connectionTimeout=1800000`	< 30 min (1800000)	Medium
JAS	`resultSetTimeout`	jdbj.ini	Inactivity time period after which result set, or page fetch, times out. Will cause connection to be dedicated to single user. High values will cause excessive DB connections to build up. `[JDBj-RUNTIME PROPERTIES]` `resultSetTimeout=60000`	< 3 min (180000)	Medium
JAS	JDBJ caches	jdbj.ini	Inactivity time period after which JDBJ caches timeout; these caches cache data from following tables: JDBJ_CACHES `[JDBj-RUNTIME PROPERTIES]` `ocmCachePurge=600000` `securityCachePurge=600000` `serviceCachePurge=600000` `specCachePurge=600000` `e1MenuCachePurge=600000`	< 10 min (600000)	Medium
JAS	SQL Server `Querytimeout`	jdbj.ini	Inactivity time period after which JDBC query to SQL Server will retry; after three retries will issue the query in NOLOCK mode. `[JDBj-RUNTIME PROPERTIES]` `msSQLQueryTimeout=10`	+/– 10 sec (10000)	Medium

TABLE 6-1. *Timeouts and Their Impact on the System*

WebServer Caches

Here are the recommended cache values and detailed explanations for HTML Server:

```
[JDBj-RUNTIME PROPERTIES]
securityCachePurge=1200000
serviceCachePurge=1200000
specCachePurge=1200000
e1MenuCachePurge=1200000
ocmCachePurge=1200000
```

These caches contain DB Table values as they are fetched from underlying tables, and the timeout values indicate the amount of time after which the value is removed from the web cache. Table 6-2 provides greater detail on EnterpriseOne caches.

Cache Setting	Description	Table(s)
E1 Menu Cache	Explorer/menu cache	F9000X
Service Cache	Lookup service that looks up table F9500001	F9500001
ABFullName	Table F0092 and Table F0111 for address book number and full name for a JDE user.	F0092/F0111
CompanyLookup	Database lookup service that looks up identifiers in the company master table and returns corresponding company information objects (mCurrencyCode/mCurrencyEnvironmentValue/mCurrencyEnvironment/mBookToTax/mAddressBookInterface)	F0010
Currency	Queries currency information	F0013
Ledger	Data returned from the ledger type master table	F0013
OMW (Object Management Workbench)	Database lookup service that looks up Object Librarian (OL) detail and returns corresponding OLDetailInformation objects	F9861
Pathcode	Database lookup service that looks up environment name (strings) in Table F00941 and returns corresponding path code information objects	F00941
Role	Database lookup service that looks up portal role information in the portal role tables	F0092

(Continued)

TABLE 6-2. *EnterpriseOne Caches*

Cache Setting	Description	Table(s)
Role Relationship	Database lookup service that looks up role information in the role tables	F95921
User Defined Codes (UDC)	Retrieve UDC information; UDC data is different for different environments, so UDC tables are not system tables. Users should therefore perform UDC lookups with the full connection and not the bootstrap logical connection. The lookup service must also cache UDC data based on the data source name, so it needs the user, role, and environment information to do a OCM lookup on the UDC tables internally.	F0004, F0005, F0005D
Daylight Savings Time (DST) Rule	Lookup service that looks up DST Rule information in the DST Rules tables and returns corresponding DST Rule	F00085
SpecCache	Caches the specs for Apps, NERs, Views, Tables, DDs, and Report Selection /Sequencing	F989999 F989998
OCM Cache	Caches the data source master and OCM tables	F98611 F986101
Security Cache	Caches EnterpriseOne security information. It is a good practice to clear this cache (via Server Manager after security changes).	F00950
BusinessUnitSecurity Cache	Caches user role business unit relationship information	F95300 F95302

TABLE 6-2. *EnterpriseOne Caches*

TCP/IP Level Tuning and Its Impact on Web Tier Performance

The TCP/IP layer should not be overlooked when undergoing a performance tuning exercise.

TCP Tuning with Selective Acknowledgment (SACK)

Relying purely on the cumulative acknowledgment scheme employed by the original TCP can lead to inefficiencies when packets are lost. Suppose, for example, that 10,000 bytes are sent in ten different TCP packets, and the first packet is lost during transmission. In a pure cumulative acknowledgment protocol, the receiver cannot say that it received bytes 1000 to 9999 successfully, but failed to receive the first packet, containing bytes 0 to 999. Thus, the sender may then have to resend all 10,000 bytes. SACK allows the receiver to acknowledge discontinuous blocks of packets that were received correctly, in addition to the sequence number of the last contiguous byte received successively. Internal lab tests using SACK showed performance improvements of around 35 percent.

TCP Tuning with TCP Window

TCP SEND (congestion window) and RECV windows are the sizes of data that can be sent without waiting for ACK. Suppose, for example, that a sender receives an ACK that acknowledges byte 5000 and specifies a receive window of 10,000 (bytes). The sender will not send packets after byte 15,000, even if the congestion window allows it. The defaults on most operating systems are very low compared to modern network bandwidth—anywhere from 14K to 64K.

- **The optimal TCP window** equals bandwidth (Mb/s) × round-trip time (RTT) (or ping). A transmission line of 1.5 Mb/s was used over a satellite link with a 513 millisecond RTT.

- **TCP window** equals 1,500,000 × 0.513 = 769,500 bits, or 769,500 / 8 = 96,188 bytes. Compared to default 64K window—we can improve performance by 70 percent.

TCP Settings: Nagle's Algorithm and MTU Size

We have observed very interesting performance behavior between Windows and Linux servers with respect to JAS performance. This is by no means an indictment of Linux servers relative to Windows servers, but is something quite esoteric that is worth discussing. However, at times, the difference is quite profound: *Windows offers a 20-times better runtime of business functions than Linux;* thus, the topic deserves a closer look.

On deeper analysis, we've found that the performance difference is found in the business function runtime only.

So what are the differences between Linux and Windows servers that cause a difference in the interaction between the JAS Web Server and the backend Enterprise Server? These differences are due to two TCP parameters: Nagle's algorithm and loopback MTU.

Nagle's Algorithm   *Nagle's algorithm* is an optimization on the TCP frame that reduces the number of packets that need to be sent over the network. The algorithm works by combining numerous small packets into one larger packet and sending it as a single packet, thereby overcoming the overhead involved in TCP handshakes for each packet transmission. For network devices, this is determined by the Ethernet card; for all-in-one JAS, enterprise boxes, its value is set by the operating system simulating a virtual network card—loopback MTU.

Loopback MTU   *MTU, or Maximum Transmission Unit,* defines the size of the largest data packet that can be sent across the network. The default value of the loopback MTU on Linux is 16,436 packets. Generally, a larger MTU is more efficient because it allows larger payloads of user data to be sent without the overhead of packet management; however, if the network has high latency, the larger-sized packets occupy the network link layer and tie up the routers.

How Nagle and MTU Influence the JAS Business Function Performance   Business functions runtime, as we know, has a direct impact on a JAS server's ability to process requests. So as business function, data is passed between the JAS server and the Enterprise Server. The Nagle algorithm aggregates all small running business function data structure packets up to the MTU size. Therefore, it is sometimes possible that the Nagle algorithm combined with a large MTU can throttle the performance of small and fast-running business functions. These small business functions, by definition, are chatty, and by aggregating those into a larger packet to MTU size, we can slow them by several hundred milliseconds—however, over thousands of runs, these differences start to add up, reducing the throughput capacity. In one use case, for example, we found that up to 20 seconds were added to a 500-line sales order application processing time.

The reason we have not observed this behavior in Windows server is that Windows disables the Nagle algorithm automatically on loopback TCP connections for better performance. Therefore, reducing the MTU on Linux servers in low latency, especially loopback conditions where JAS and Enterprise Server exist on the same server, helps the JAS–Enterprise Server communication:

- Loopback MTU size: 1642 – BSFN runtime – 42ms

- Loopback MTU size: 1500 – BSFN runtime – 2ms

Conclusion

This chapter provided a view into tuning the web pillar of the Oracle JD Edwards EnterpriseOne software. Steps to isolate JAS performance issues and the effects of garbage collection and EnterpriseOne caches were discussed in detail. Finally, TCP/IP tuning was covered. We hope that you will find the items covered in this chapter valuable in your efforts to continue performance tuning your implementation.

CHAPTER
7

Tuning by Tier: The Foundation Tier

T his chapter covers the JD Edwards EnterpriseOne Foundation tier, which includes database connections, JDENet, and EnterpriseOne kernels. Understanding the underlying technologies of these components is your key to tuning them. Advanced troubleshooting techniques are also explored, which will assist you in performance tuning as well as in finding the cause of zombie kernels.

EnterpriseOne JDB Infrastructure

You can use two parallel methods to access EnterpriseOne databases: JDB and JDBj. For C/C++ code, access is through the JDB interface, and for Java code, access is through the JDBj interface. The tables in an EnterpriseOne database are referenced by table name in the specs; to determine which table is to be referenced, the Object Configuration Manager (OCM) uses environment, path code, user, and role information to associate the table name with one specific table in one specific database. The column names consist of a base name, from the data dictionary definition of that column, along with a two-letter prefix from the tables specs.

Access to these tables is provided through the JDB API and the JDBj class/ method interface. Both interfaces support most data manipulation language (DML) functionality, and the JDB interface provides basic data definition language (DDL) functionality. Both interfaces support the basic database data manipulation operations such as data retrieval, insertion, modification, and removal. These correspond to the SQL operators of SELECT/FETCH, INSERT, UPDATE, and DELETE, respectively. Direct use of user-defined SQL statements is not allowed, however.

The basic table description operations are supported by JDB. These include creating tables and indexes, updating tables (adding and dropping columns), and dropping tables and indexes.

The databases that are supported with EnterpriseOne are Oracle databases on Windows and Unix platforms, SQL Server databases on Windows platforms, Universal Database (UDB) databases on UNIX platforms, and DB2 databases on System i platforms.

JDBj uses JDBC driver jar/zip files (from database vendors) as its route to the actual database. The JDBC drivers generally allow access across platform types. JDB uses native database drivers as the route to the actual database. These drivers are usually available only on the database-specific supported platforms.

From Windows platforms, the JDB/ODBC combination is used to access all supported database types. For other cross-platform database access, JDB can use the JDBNet interface. For example, JDB/JDBNet is required to access SQL Server data from a System i enterprise server and to access DB2 data from a Unix enterprise server. Only a few customers use the cross-platform database access, which are usually non-production or low workload circumstances.

The JDB and JDBj database connections can be either manual-commit (for transactions) or auto-commit (for single-statement SQL operations). The sequence of Select-for-Update and Update-Current is supported on the auto-commit connections, even though they make up a transaction sequence.

JDB and JDBj automatically provide the appropriate data conversions between EnterpriseOne data and database data. The EnterpriseOne applications use data in the defined EnterpriseOne data formats. In many cases, the database data requires a database-specific format, depending on the native database (Oracle, SQL Server, UDB, or DB2).

EnterpriseOne Database Middleware Features

The EnterpriseOne database middleware supports the basic database features. Within the middleware are many feature extensions, such as EnterpriseOne authentication, row security, and currency conversions. At the lowest level, the EnterpriseOne middleware functions as a wrapper around the supported types of databases. It supports applications written in C and C++ through the JDB API. The JDB interface is used by EnterpriseOne enterprise servers, EnterpriseOne Windows full clients, and most business functions (BSFNs).

The EnterpriseOne middleware supports applications written in Java through the JDBj group of classes and methods. The JDBj interface is used by the JAS servers, which support web clients. A limited number of BSFNs are supported on the JAS servers.

User Sign-on

The EnterpriseOne database middleware is the starting point for getting authentication to access the entire EnterpriseOne system. Authentication consists of a user name, a password, an environment name, and an optional role. These authentication parameters are sent to a running EnterpriseOne security server process, which will then set up an authentication token that can be used throughout the running EnterpriseOne system.

Database data sources are defined in EnterpriseOne as specifications pointing to an actual database location. For a user to access a specific database table, the OCM data is used to map that table to a specific data source. The OCM mappings, which indicate which data source to use, can vary by user, environment, and role. In other words, if a user signs on with a different environment, the same table name could be located using a different data source. The different tables could be in the same database with a different owner/schema name, or they could be in different databases.

Users are given authority to access specific databases, based on proxy user values returned from the security server. The database access is derived through the OCM association between the user/role and a data source. The database proxy values are set up by a security administrator and are generally not known to the

EnterpriseOne users. EnterpriseOne users can access database tables within EnterpriseOne, while not having the authentication parameters to access those tables outside of EnterpriseOne.

A bootstrap user, password, and environment must be provided when the EnterpriseOne enterprise server starts. This is because some database tables must be accessed in order to initialize some server kernel processes (such as the security kernel), which must be running before any EnterpriseOne users can be authenticated.

Database Connections

There are two modes of connecting to the databases: auto-commit and manual-commit. Auto-commit connections are generally used for single operations, and manual-commit connections are used for a sequence of operations that must be grouped to be valid such as transaction processing boundaries. The exception is the support of auto-commit connections for Select-For-Update / Update-Current sequences.

Auto-Commit Connections

There is typically one auto-commit connection for each proxy user per database. This connection is reused for all users within a process when those users possess the same database proxy user credentials. The reuse of the auto-commit connections minimizes the total required number of database connections.

The Select-For-Update (SFU) / Update-Current sequence is supported from the application level on auto-commit connections, but in most cases it requires a separate database connection to perform correctly. For most databases, the SFU connections are checked in and out of a pool of connections. The connection pooling for SFU operations allows faster processing for those applications that use SFU operations in a loop.

Manual-Commit Connections

The manual-commit connections are provided to support transactions within the EnterpriseOne applications. A separate database connection must exist for every concurrent transaction. The manual-commit connections are usually checked in and out of a connection pool. The pool allows a high level of transactions to be performed quickly, without requiring a large number of connections to be opened and closed. The opening of database connections is a relatively expensive process, for both time and resource usage.

Connection Pooling

Connection pools are used to minimize the overhead generated when opening database connections. For JDB, each type of database has a database driver, and these database drivers maintain their own connection pools. In most cases, one new connection will be added to the connection pool when a connection is requested and the entire pool has been checked out.

SQL DML Statements

The applications request database operations through the JDB and JDBj interfaces and reference EnterpriseOne tables and columns as stored in the tables spec. These are the names used to open the tables and to set up column data for input, output, or selection criteria.

The database table names will match the table names in the specs, except when special characters must be substituted. For example, @ in the table spec table name becomes an underscore (_) in the database table name. The table spec column names consist of a base name that is found in the EnterpriseOne data dictionary. The database column name consists of a two-letter prefix followed by the data dictionary name for the column. The two-letter prefix is associated with the table, so the same two-letter prefix is assigned to all columns within one table.

There is a mapping from the data used by the applications and the data stored in the database. All of the necessary data conversion is done within the JDB and JDBj interfaces. Some basic data type conversions occur. For example, the applications' `MathNumeric` data type will be mapped to a supported numeric data type within each type of database.

More elaborate conversions are also supported, such as row security and currency conversions. The data conversion includes row-level security to prevent access to unauthorized data rows. EnterpriseOne administrators specify the row-level security to apply to various users and roles. The data conversion also includes currency conversions based on specific columns and data-dependent criteria. The currency conversions are very flexible and can be modified by changing BSFNs.

Select

Select requests parallel the SQL select statements for the databases. The parameters set by the applications include column lists, WHERE clause values, ORDER by values, and so on. Those parameters define which columns and rows will be returned from the database, and in what order. The applications must follow the select requests with fetch requests in order to get any actual database data. The fetch requests may be called many times, until data runs out and a "no more data" return code is passed back. With JDB, the numeric return code for "error" matches the return code for "no more data," so an additional function call is required if an application needs to differentiate between no more data available for fetching and an actual database error. For JDB, the function `JDB_GetLastDBError` can be called to identify a specific type of error, with one of the return values indicating "no more data."

At the application level, the data is always fetched one row at a time. Within JDB, at the database driver level, the fetched data is frequently returned as an array of fetched data. That improves fetching performance significantly. After the first fetched row, subsequent fetches will only move the data in memory from the driver's buffer to the application, without going back to the database. The actual database will be accessed again only when the driver's buffer of fetched data is empty.

Update

Update requests parallel the SQL update statements for the databases. The parameter conversions are similar to those previously described for select requests.

Insert

Insert requests parallel the SQL insert statements for the databases. The parameter conversions are similar to those previously described for select requests.

Buffered Inserts

Buffered inserts provide a performance improvement by lowering the number of round trips to the actual database. The application must select to do buffered inserts. By default, database inserts will be done one row at a time.

When the application sends a request to insert data, that row is added to a buffer in the JDB drivers. The buffers may hold up to 100 rows of data, depending on the size of the data columns for the table. When the buffer becomes full, all of the data rows in the buffer are inserted into the database as an array. The application can also request that the buffered inserts be "flushed." That will cause all current rows in the buffer to be sent to the actual database.

Delete

Delete requests parallel the SQL delete statements for the databases. The parameter conversions are similar to those previously described for select requests.

Transactions

Transactions are a sequence of database operations that must be processed as a group. We will discuss how Select-For-Update and manual-commits are performed within EnterpriseOne. In the context of the database these operations are the fundamental methods used to process or manipulate the tables.

Select-For-Update / Update-Current Sequence

As mentioned earlier in the chapter, the Select-For-Update (SFU) / Update-Current sequence can be performed on either auto-commit connections or manual-commit connections.

When SFUs are performed on auto-commit connections, they are actually being performed on a separate connection behind the scenes. A separate connection is required to prevent interference from other operations that might occur on the auto-commit connection. The SFU will hold a lock on the selected rows, and the locks will be released when the application closes the table. At that point, the behind-the-scenes connection can be committed or rolled back, and then put back into the available connection pool.

When SFU sequences are performed on manual-commit connections, they become part of the larger transaction that is being performed on that connection. The SFU data will be committed or rolled back along with the rest of the database operations that were performed on that connection.

SFU sequences usually have a fetch following the SFU request. That fetched row is usually updated using the Update-Current request. Common usage in applications is to have one SFU fetch, followed by an Update-Current. Although less common, it is possible to do multiple fetches following the SFU request, with the option of doing an Update-Current operation for any, all, or none of those fetched rows. The database system typically sets a lock on all rows that match the "where" clause of the SFU request.

SFU sequences usually involve Update-Current operations. Although rarely used, Delete-Current operations perform similarly.

NOTE
Sometimes we see this error in the jde.logs:
```
checkoutSFUConnection:No available
SFU connection! Increase OS400RV009 -
DBInitRequest:DBInitConnection failed.
```

To temporarily relieve it add these settings in jde.ini:
```
maxAUTOConnection=20 maxSFUConnection=20
```

However special care must be taken in not setting these too high in System i Enterprise Servers where there are a total of 60 connections per process. In this example, we are increasing the limit of SFU to 20, auto connections to 20, and then remaining manual connections to 20 (60–20–20=20).

Operations Within Manual-Commit Connections

Transactions are a sequence of database operations that must be processed as a group. In other words, the entire group of operations is applied to the database, or none of the group is applied to the database. Manual-commit connections provide the mechanism to support transactions in both JDB and JDBj interfaces. An application requests the start of a transaction by opening a manual-commit connection. Within JDB and JDBj, this may create a new database connection, or it may involve checking a connection out of the appropriate connection pool.

All subsequent database operations using the manual-commit connections are considered temporary. When the application completes the group of database operations, it can then request a commit operation on that connection, which makes those database operations permanent. If some of the database operations resulted in errors, the application has the option to request a rollback, which reverses the temporary database operations, with the database state returning to what it was before the transaction started.

In most cases, when data is modified during the transaction, the database system will create locks on the database data. The locks prevent other connections from changing data that could affect the first transaction. Those other connections may be put in a waiting state until the first transaction gives up its database locks.

The application can end a transaction by requesting a commit or a rollback, or by closing the manual-commit connection. When an application closes the connection, an implied rollback occurs. After a commit or rollback, the database should release all of the locks that were required when the transaction operations were in a temporary state.

The scope of the database locks may be at the data row level, at the table level, or even at the database schema level. The scope of the locking is determined by the native database system. The JDB and JDBj interfaces rarely request locks directly.

Each database uses settings for locking levels, called "isolation levels," to determine when to apply database locks. A trade-off occurs between data integrity (maximum locking) and performance (minimal locking). The available locking levels depend on the type of database. EnterpriseOne data usually requires an isolation level of "read-consistency." That setting is usually the best trade-off between data integrity and performance.

To minimize waiting for locks (improve performance), the SQL Server database allows timeouts when requesting data that has been changed by a different connection. After the timeout, the JDB and JDBj interface will retry the read while ignoring the lock. This is called a "dirty read." The fetched data may not be correct, based on whether the connection holding the lock does a commit or rollback. The performance of the SQL Server database appears to be impacted by locks more than the other database types, so the shortcut of using dirty reads is limited to SQL Server databases. In Chapter 8 we will discuss an alternative option for Microsoft SQL Server using read committed snapshot isolation (RCSI) that eliminates the potential "dirty read" situation.

JDB Connection Pooling

Java Database (JDB) connection pooling is used to efficiently allocate and share the Java database connections. Similar database connections are grouped into a pool so that we don't have a large number of unused connections sitting idle and consuming resources.

JDB Connection

We maintain a list (linked list) for auto-commit and manual-commit connections. When a request comes for a new connection, we first traverse this linked list to determine whether any of the existing available connections satisfy the request.

The database user ID and Transparent Network Substrate (TNS) service name (server) should be the same in order to reuse the existing connection. If a connection is available, we reuse the connection. If not, we create a new connection and put it in the pool. We share a single connection for multiple requests as long as it is an auto-commit connection.

As in ODBC, we can use the same handle database connection (HDBC) to create multiple handle statements (HSTMT), but we do not share a manual-commit connection. We maintain a reference count to keep track of the number of shared requests on a single connection. This reference count is incremented when a new request is satisfied (for example, select/insert/update/delete). When the operation is completed (for example, a record set is closed for a select), we decrement the reference count. This reference count is used to clean unused connections after a certain interval.

Whenever a request arrives for opening/sharing a connection, we first traverse through the existing connections in the pool to see whether any existing connection with a reference count of 0 can be cleared or closed. The default value for expired connection timeout is 5 minutes. So if we find any connections (both manual and auto) that have been idle for more than 5 minutes, we remove them from the pool and then close the connection.

Database Request Timeout

For the enterprise server, the default timeout for an unused database connection is 5 minutes; however, you can influence the timeout by modifying the JDE.INI setting:

```
[NETWORK QUEUE SETTINGS]
JDENETTimeout = 60
```

This value is in seconds, and we always multiply it inside our code by 5 to get 300 seconds, which is 5 minutes.

NOTE
When you change the JDENETTimeout *value, remember that the value will be multiplied by 5 to get the final timeout in seconds.* JDENETTimeout *is also used by other modules such as kernels and UBEs, so changing this value will also change the timeout behavior of these kernels; therefore, it's not recommended if the sole reason is for the database request timeout.*

SQL DDL Statements

DDL SQL statements are available from the JDB interface only, not the JDBj interface. They are generally called from install programs, EnterpriseOne full clients, or enterprise servers. These programs are all C/C++ programs, so there has been no need to include that functionality in the Java code to date.

Tables

The operations supported by JDB for tables are "create table," "drop table," and "alter table," which is used to add or drop columns. These operations are used only in applications that are run by administrators or developers. They are not normally called by the BSFNs and UBEs that are run by the business users.

Specific parameters for different database types can be defined for specific tables—for example, a specific tablespace name for a table in an Oracle database. These parameters are set up using an administrative application and the values are stored in the database. For example, if a table is re-created in Oracle, it will be placed in the specified tablespace.

Indexes

The operations supported by JDB for indexes are "create index," "create primary key," and "drop index." These operations are usually used in conjunction with table creation and drop operations. Most indexes are created initially, and are those specified in the table specs. As long as primary key indexes remain, most other indexes can be added or dropped, based on the performance optimums for the database.

Auditing

Auditing can be set up to record changes to a table. The data saved for each row that is changed includes the user's name, the time stamp, and the before and after values. Administrators can run an application to view and generate reports of the auditing activities.

The setup for auditing is performed at the table level. To prepare for auditing, the table is renamed and additional columns are added. Then, a view is created with the same column descriptions as the original table. The new view maps to the corresponding original columns of the renamed table. Native-database stored procedures perform the capture of the auditing data. Those stored procedures run automatically whenever the table is being modified. An audit table is also created, where the before and after audited column values are saved. Applications access the table through this new view, which resembles the original table at the application level, and the original columns are accessed through the view. The new table columns are filled in by native-database stored procedures and include the user name and time stamp. The stored procedures also save the changed data (before and after) in the audit table.

Incoming Database Connections

One of the most common causes of concern in database tuning is the number of incoming connections from JD Edwards EnterpriseOne. The first step is to ascertain where these incoming connections are originating; use the following queries to determine the number of incoming queries into a database:

Oracle Database

```
select s.username, s.osuser, s.machine, s.program, s.process, count(*) from v$session
s, v$process p where s.paddr = p.addr and s.type != 'BACKGROUND' group by s.username,
s.osuser, s.machine, s.program, s.process
```

SQL Server

```
select count(*),loginame,nt_username,hostname,program_name,cmd
from master.dbo.sysprocesses
where rtrim(cmd) not in ('TASK MANAGER','CHECKPOINT SLEEP', 'CHECKPOINT','LOCK
MONITOR','SIGNAL HANDLER','LOG WRITER','LAZY WRITER','GHOST CLEANUP','BACKUP LOG')and
(rtrim(hostname) not in ('denmlsp44.mlab.jdedwards.com'))
group by loginame,nt_username,hostname,program_name,cmd
order by count(*) desc
```

Excessive Oracle Database Connections

Some performance issues can be related to an excessive amount of database connections. You can check the following areas to determine the cause.

Different Server Names Used for the Same Database TNS Name

Using a different server name will cause additional, unnecessary connections. The server name and TNS names must match, in a case-sensitive compare, before JDB will reuse an existing connection.

Within the P986115 "Work With Data Sources" application, if the "Data Source Use" is "DB" (not "SVR"), and the "Data Source Type" is "O" (for Oracle), then each occurrence of a specific "TNS/ODBC/JDBNet Data Source" value should repeat the same "Server Name" value. The easiest way to accomplish this during setup is to use the name of the server on which the Oracle database is located. If multiple server pathways are used to reach the same database, you should arbitrarily pick one and use it consistently. The EnterpriseOne code passes the TNS name to Oracle, but not the server name, so Oracle will use the server path that is configured in the Oracle TNSNAMES.ORA file (or Oracle Names Server, if used).

In the JDE.INI files, the same TNS name and server names that are shown in the P986115 "Work With Data Sources" application should be used. Under "[DB SYSTEM SETTINGS]," the enterprise server JDE.INI "Database=" is the same value as the "TNS/ODBC/JDBNet Data Source" value in the app, and the enterprise server JDE.INI "Server=" is the same value as the "Server Name" value in the app.

OracleServerHandleReuse—JDE.INI Setting

This JDE.INI setting is no longer used, because the Oracle server handles are no longer used for multiple connections. Although it is supposed to be a performance benefit to reuse the server handles, the Oracle Database does not enable sufficient locking internally to prevent conflicts between connections on the same server handle. The conflicts show up only under very high database usage, and only from a few applications. So, originally, that JDE.INI setting allowed a customer to choose not to reuse handles if they encountered problems during peak usage. Customers that did not experience the problem could continue with server handle reuse and had faster performance.

Originally, only two or three customers experienced these peak high usage problems, and the JDE.INI setting worked for them. Over a couple of years, many more customers began reporting database problems at peak usage, so the JDE.INI setting and the reuse of server handles were dropped. SAR 5871016, "Oracle Table Locking Issues," was created to remove the hidden JDE.INI setting and make it the default.

Oracle DB—Timer Initiated Disconnect or Dead Connection Detection

Dead connection detection is a feature that allows SQL*Net to identify connections that have been left hanging by the abnormal termination of a client. On a connection with Dead Connection Detection enabled, a small probe packet is sent from server to client at a user-defined interval (usually several minutes). If the connection is invalid (usually due to the client process or machine being unreachable), the connection will be closed when an error is generated by the send operation and the server process will exit. This feature minimizes the waste of resources by connections that are no longer valid. It also automatically forces a database rollback of uncommitted transactions and locks held by the user of the broken connection.

Specify the `SQLNET.EXPIRE_TIME=n` parameter in your SQLNET.ORA file (usually in $ORACLE_HOME/network/admin). This parameter will instruct SQL*Net to send a probe through the network to the client every *n* minutes; if the client doesn't respond it will be killed.

NOTE
*This parameter is useful only on the database server side. Specifying it on a client workstation will have no effect. Also, this is applicable only for SQL*Net releases 2.1 and later.*

SQL Packages for iSeries DB2 Databases

SQL packages are System i objects that contain both the control structures and the access plans that are necessary to process SQL statements on the application server when running a distributed program such as EnterpriseOne. Since SQL packages are shared resources, the information built when a statement is prepared is available to all the users of the package. This saves time, especially in an EnterpriseOne web client environment where many of the users execute the same or similar queries.

SQL packages can be used by the IBM Access for Windows ODBC driver and the IBM JDBC driver. They are also used by applications that use the QSQPRCED (SQL Process Extended Dynamic) API. The SQL packages created by ODBC and QSQPRCED are called "extended dynamic SQL packages" and are the subject of the following questions and answers. IBM Distributed Relational Database Architecture (DRDA) also uses SQL package objects, but they are considerably different in behavior and are not covered here. SQL packages are also used by the Xtended Design Architecture (XDA) API.

When Do SQL Packages Get Created?

In the case of ODBC and JDBC, the existence of the package is checked when the client application issues the first prepare of a SQL statement. If the package does not exist, it is created at that time (even though it may not yet contain any SQL statements). In the case of QSQPRCED, creation of the package occurs when the application calls QSQPRCED specifying function '1'.

How Are SQL Packages Named?

The name of the System i SQL package is partially determined by the connection type for which it is used. EnterpriseOne uses three main types of connections: ODBC, DBDR QSQPRCED, and JDBC.

ODBC

SQL packages for ODBC are named by taking the application name specified in the data source configuration and appending three letters, which are an encoded set of the package configuration attributes. So, for EnterpriseOne, the ODBC packages will be named JDSHRDATA/ACTIVCO.

DBDR QSQPRCED

The name of the DBDR SQL package is provided by the application. For example, these are the usual packages in EnterpriseOne:

EnterpriseOne Process	SQL Package Name
OW Kernels	OW_JobNum
OW Kernels Manual Transaction	OW_MJobNum
Table Conversions (TCs)	TJobNum
Reports	ReportName or TJobNum

JDBC

The SQL package for JDB connections will begin with a *J*, such as J*xxx* (where *xxx* is a system-generated suffix, typically BBA or BAA).

Examples of these packages are

- JAVAMIGxxx
- JDBCxxx

What CNC Activities Are Required?

All the types of database interfaces used by EnterpriseOne make use of SQL packages, with the exception of the native JDBC driver (used with All-in-One [AIO] environments). Consider the following three points when using SQL packages in an EnterpriseOne web client environment:

- Ensure that SQL packages are being used effectively.
- Know when to delete SQL packages.
- Delete SQL packages.

JD Edwards EnterpriseOne uses SQL packages in three ways:

- **JAS server** JDBC connections via jt400.jar driver
- **Fat client** ODBC connections
- **Enterprise server** DBDR

JDBC Connections The JDBj code creates a separate SQL package in each library it accesses with JDBC. It is more efficient to use only one SQL package for all JDBC access. This setting is in the JDBj.ini file in the [JDBj-RUNTIME PROPERTIES] section. Add a new setting to force all JDBC access to use a single library for storing SQL packages:

```
[JDBj-RUNTIME PROPERTIES]
as400PackageLibrary=QRECOVERY
```

This setting adds the JAS SQL packages to the same library already used by the EnterpriseOne kernel jobs. The SQL package JDBJxxx (where xxx is a system-generated suffix, typically BBA or BAA) is initially created during the Java serialized object generation. Once the installation is completed, delete this SQL package, because it contains installation-specific information that is not necessary for normal web client sessions.

ODBC Connections ODBC connections may or may not use SQL packages, depending on how they are configured. In the ODBC administrator, under Control Panel, select an iSeries ODBC data source, then select Configure, and then select the Packages tab. The enabled extended dynamic support indicates whether you want to use packages or not. Under Customize Settings Per Application, you can specify a particular name and library for an application. (We usually leave it in the library where the data files for that data source reside.) This is how EnterpriseOne does the configuration during the install.

The packages created for ODBC are per data source; there should not be a lot of them created because they can be reused if another connection is made for the same data source. If they are deleted, all the statements prepared via ODBC will be prepared again instead of being reused. So unless the ODBC packages are getting really big and using a lot of space, they should be left alone and you can simply monitor their size.

DBDR Connections   EnterpriseOne kernel jobs use SQL packages created in the QRECOVERY library. Each time the enterprise server is stopped and restarted, new SQL packages are built and associated with the new kernel jobs. Old SQL packages associated with kernel jobs that have ended are never used again and can be deleted to save disk space.

What JDE.ini Settings Are Used to Change How SQL Packages Are Created and Used?

Since release 8.9, the following EnterpriseOne server JDE.INI settings can be used to change the behavior of how SQL packages are created and used:

```
[DB System Settings]
SQL Package Library =
```

The `SQL Package Library` value can be set to 2, 1, or 0. The behavior of these values is described here:

- **2**   Create packages in QRECOVERY. UBEs and TCs will have a unique (job number) name (for example, T123456). Kernels will use package names starting with *OW* or *OW_M*.

- **1**   Create packages in QRECOVERY. UBE packages will receive names of R*xxxx*. Kernels will have package names starting with *OW* or *OW_M*. You will need to delete any old UBE SQL packages in QRECOVERY. Note that no UBEs can be running on the server while you are deleting these packages.

- **0**   Create packages in the system library (for example, E910SYS) based on the following server JDE.INI setting. This can be helpful if you are running multiple instances of EnterpriseOne on one iSeries. If the `DefaultSystem` parameter is not set, the SQL packages will be created in the QGPL (General Purpose Library).

  ```
  [INSTALL]
  DefaultSystem =
  ```

The JDE.INI settings for SQL Package Library will *only* change the library location of SQL packages for UBEs and TCs. You cannot change the location of kernel SQL packages; they will always be created in the QRECOVERY library.

NOTE
You can leave SQL Package Library = 2 *for upgrade operations; however, it will make the startup for your frequently run UBEs a little slower, because they will not be able to use existing SQL packages. Changing this setting to a 1 or 0 is recommended during normal operations to take advantage of the benefits of SQL packages. Remember, if upgrade TCs need to be run, you need to leave this set to 2 during the upgrade conversions, but be aware that normal UBEs will run slower and SQL packages will need to be deleted when recycling EnterpriseOne services.*

When Should a SQL Package Be Deleted?

Packages should be deleted in the following circumstances:

- When the underlying metadata for statements stored in the package has been changed.

- If a table, view, stored procedure, or other SQL object is altered, information in the package is not updated. Therefore, EnterpriseOne SQL packages should be deleted whenever significant changes have been made to the database, operating system, or hardware

Examples of significant changes are those that may cause a large amount of access plan rebuilds, such as the following:

- Applying a database group program temporary fix (PTF) or upgrading the operating system

- Applying an Electronic Software Update (ESU) that contains table changes

- Making changes to the characteristics of all logical files and indexes—such as access path size

- Making changes to and the creation of logical files and/or indexes

- Making changes in client access release levels

Here are a few tips to remember about deleting SQL packages:

- Do not delete IBM-supplied packages; these usually start with letter "Q."

- Before deleting SQL packages, all applications using the package must first be ended.

- To delete a specific SQL package, use the `DLTSQLPKG` command.

- To locate and delete SQL packages, use the `WRKOBJ` command and select Option 4 to delete them. The command syntax is as follows:

```
WRKOBJ OBJ(*ALL/*ALL)  OBJTYPE(*SQLPKG)
```

- When enterprise services are down, the following commands can also be used to delete SQL packages in mass:

```
DLTSQLPKG SQLPKG(QRECOVERY/OW*)
DLTSQLPKG SQLPKG(QRECOVERY/T*)
DLTSQLPKG SQLPKG(QRECOVERY/R*).
```

Only extended dynamic SQL packages are automatically re-created by the application.

CAUTION
Do not delete IBM-supplied SQL packages, packages in QSYS, packages whose names start with Q, and DRDA packages. If you are unsure about whether a specific SQL package is used by DRDA, use the `PRTSQLINF` *command and look at the first page of the report. DRDA packages will contain an RDB keyword entry identifying the relational database for DRDA.*

What Are the Negative Performance Considerations for Using Large Packages?
The IBM i OS Version 4 Release 3 (V4R3) enhancements for larger packages also include support for hash tables, which improves performance of searches either by statement name or by statement text. There are no significant performance impacts for using relatively large packages. There are, however, performance impacts associated with a large number of concurrent users (1000 or more) adding new statements to a package. This includes a large number of users running statements already in the package but whose SQL statements require new access plans.

What Happens When SQL Packages Get Full?

In the case of the database host server (QZDASOINIT jobs), the database server attempts to detect the package full condition (SQL0904, reason code 7). When a database server job detects the package full condition, it sends one PWS0018 message to the job log but no warning or error to the client (ODBC or JDBC). The database server job transparently switches over to dynamic SQL for the newly prepared statements. Statements that were previously prepared in the SQL package continue to be used. This is equivalent to switching to the ODBC/JDBC package use setting as opposed to use/add.

The package full condition is detected based on remaining space in the package versus an estimate of the amount of space the new statement requires. In rare cases, this estimate may be incorrect or a new plan for a statement previously prepared in the package may require more space than is available. In these rare cases, the application may receive an error message. The only recovery is to delete the package.

In the case of QSQPRCED, a SQL code of -904 is returned in the SQLCA data structure and the application must decide how to proceed.

When Else Can a SQL Package Become Unusable?

SQL packages have some attributes that are stored at the package level and must be compatible with the application. For example, ODBC SQL packages allow specification of a default collection for unqualified table names. If the SQL package already exists and its default collection does not match that of the client application, the package will not be used and the user will use dynamic SQL. The same issue can occur if the job CCSID changes.

What Are the QSQLPKG2 and QSQXDPKG Packages Used For?

The QSQLPKG2 and QSQXDPKG packages in QSYS are system packages used as models to create application packages. *Do not delete these packages.* If they are accidentally deleted, they must be restored from backup. There may also be several system SQL packages in library QGPL that start with a Q. If these are deleted, they will be re-created when the jobs using them are restarted.

EnterpriseOne Kernel Infrastructure

The EnterpriseOne kernel can sometimes encounter certain complex issues that have proved intractable to resolve. Following are some of these issues:

- Kernel crashes, aka zombie kernels

- High or low CPU kernels

- High memory–consuming kernels

Each process has its own level of impact on the system, and the cumulative effect of all processes currently running will impact performance. Appropriate data can be captured and used with measurement tools to evaluate overall performance as well as the impact of individual processes. When utilization or performance exceeds certain thresholds, it is critical that you use tools that can diagnose which process is creating the resource overload in order to correct the problem and restore the performance to normal levels before the system crashes.

Crashed Processes, or Zombie Kernels

These processes are called *zombies* because of a technical term in Unix Process State, wherein a process has completed execution or crashed but still has an entry in the process table. It is similar to the fiction concept of the "undead" zombie who behaves like the living, but is a reanimated body. When an EnterpriseOne server process crashes due to a programming error in running code, the kernel stops from the perspective of the OS. The process is flagged as a zombie kernel within the EnterpriseOne Enterprise Server, where some of the process interprocess communication (IPC) data is saved in shared memory. The process is listed in Server Manager as a zombie process. There are many potential causes of a zombie process, including but not limited to null or invalid pointer references, heap memory corruption, stack memory corruption, and race conditions.

A Call Object kernel (COK), or runbatch process, will "go zombie" or go into a crashed state when it encounters bad memory in the business function or underlying foundation code. This crash will produce an extra log file with .dmp.log as its extension, as shown in Figure 7-1. Viewing the .dmp.log file for a crashed COK will show all the threads that were running at the time of the crash. The thread that

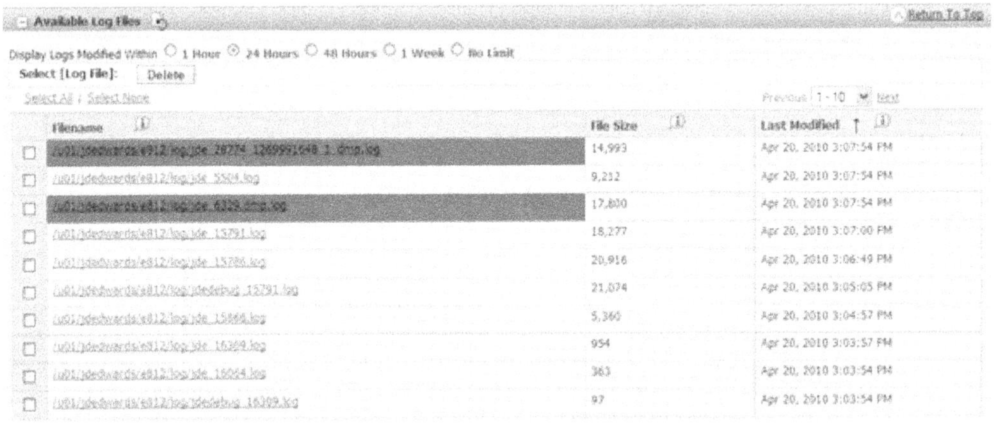

FIGURE 7-1.   *EnterpriseOne .dmp log files*

encountered the bad memory and crashed will be highlighted in red and often will serve as a good starting point for investigation of the bug.

When analyzing the .dmp log file, begin by looking for the thread that contains the `jdeLogCallStack` function, as this is the thread that initiated the crash. It is usually necessary to analyze a few .dmp log files to determine a pattern of which business function is crashing. This pattern analysis is required since the crashed business function is equally likely to be a victim or culprit of the crash.

Analyzing Crashed .dmp.log Files

Two kinds of patterns will emerge when you analyze the crashed .dmp log files— either victim or culprit business functions, as shown in the following list:

- **Victim business function**   The business function may be a victim of memory that has been corrupted by another process or thread within the same process. If this is the case, the pattern that emerges will show a random distribution of business functions that crashed.

- **Culprit business function, point of crash**   The business function would be the culprit that caused the memory corruption and caused the crash. In this case, the same business function will show up.

- **Culprit business function, threaded/timing issue**   Pay close attention, because there may be a random distribution of crashed business functions, but it would be accompanied by the same functions in the call stacks. An example would be a function that clears all caches, which causes another business function to crash that was using that cache.

To begin your analysis, open the .dmp.log file that was highlighted in red in the Log Files list. Search for "jdeLogCallStack()," and then look for the closest business function in that thread stack.

Following are some examples of crashed business functions in .dmp.log files. The boldfaced lines would appear in red (color not available in this book):

Example 1:

```
---------- tid# 41092007 (pthread ID:    1029) ----------
0xd0504eb0  _p_nsleep(??, ??) + 0x10
0xd0136ea4  nsleep(??, ??) + 0xe4
0xd026c288  sleep(??) + 0x88
0x20f42498  logCallStackOnUnixSigSafe() + 0xe0
0x20f42a6c  jdeLogCallStack() + 0x88
0x2004971c  krnlSignalHandler() + 0x468
<signal>
0x20e90d7c  jdeStrcpy() + 0x4
```

```
0xd0504eac   _p_nsleep(??, ??) + 0xc
0x200c9cac   jdeCallObjectV2() + 0x1ae0
0x200cd400   jdeCallObject() + 0x40
0xda72671c   IB4500542_CallAdvancedPricingServer() + 0x19c
0xda72e290   IB4500542_ProcessSummaryGroups() + 0x7d0
0xda731ee4   ProcessRepriceAdjustments() + 0x244
0x200c9cac   jdeCallObjectV2() + 0x1ae0
0x200cd400   jdeCallObject() + 0x40
0x203f4524   JDEK_ProcessCallRequest() + 0xa40
0x203f5e0c   JDEK_StartCallRequest() + 0x350
0x203e43d0   runBusinessFunction() + 0xbc
0x203e4244   runCallObjectJob() + 0x18
0x20c83b74   psthread_pool_job_execute() + 0x2c
0x20c82810   psthread_pool_worker_function() + 0x15c
0x20c8d370   threadFunctionWrapper() + 0xa4
0xd04edc4c   _pthread_body(??) + 0xec
```

Example 2:

```
---------- tid# 66388019 (pthread ID:    1286) ----------
0xd0504eb0   _p_nsleep(??, ??) + 0x10
0xd0136ea4   nsleep(??, ??) + 0xe4
0xd026c288   sleep(??) + 0x88
0x20f42498   logCallStackOnUnixSigSafe() + 0xe0
0x20f42a6c   jdeLogCallStack() + 0x88
0x2004971c   krnlSignalHandler() + 0x468
<signal>
0x200c8674   jdeCallObjectV2() + 0x4a8
0x200cd400   jdeCallObject() + 0x40
0xd654638c   I4200310_CallConfiguratorEndDoc() + 0x24c
```

Example 3:

```
---------------- lwp# 2 / thread# 2 --------------------
fc340408 lwp_park (0, 0, 0)
f6667034 kpuexec (f8e9d800, f1aa34, f14ce0, 0, 0, 18814c) + 2b8
f65c5e50 OCIStmtExecute (188118, f1aa34, 0, 0, 0, 0) + 2c
f657e348 BFOCIStmtExecute (188118, f1aa34, f14ce0, 0, 0, 0) + 28
f656eacc performRequestInternal (116d930, 0, 116d938, 116ca98, ff0ed1c0, 0) + 4f8
f656e46c dballPerformRequest (116d930, 116e920, 0, 116e920, 116e923, 1000) + 3e4
feb937a4 JDB_DBPerformRequest (93bc18, 116d930, 116ca98, 181240, 181318, 181240) + e4
fe13a894 TM_DBPerformRequest (17d050, 1, 116ca98, a6f318, 1b3ab8, 5) + 41c
feba75b4 SelectKeyed (a6f318, 17d050, f635eecc, 1, 1, 1) + 1ec8
febb3c00 FetchKeyed (0, 1, a7cb68, 116ca98, feddd4dc, 0) + 286c
febb114c JDB_FetchKeyed (a6f318, 1, a7cb68, ff338dfc, f636128c, 0) + 214
ee688ab4 EditSystemExistenceF99410 (a7cb68, 689800, f6367910, 3, ff976770, 110c6e0) +
30c
fefb88f8 jdeCallObjectV2 (f1f3d5ec, d38030, a73c40, 3, ff0c36fc, 20) + a3d0
fefae518 jdeCallObject (f1f3d5ec, 0, d38030, 0, 0, 0) + 38
f0b6b804 I4500250_GetGrowerSystemConstant (d38030, a9be40, f6367a80, f6367912,
```

```
ff990790, 0) + e8
 f0b65e50 CalculatePurchasePrice (d38030, a9be40, f6370b3c, f6367a84, ff98bfa8,
f6370bda) + 220
 fefb88f8 jdeCallObjectV2 (f1ff38fc, d38030, e1af50, 2, ff0c36fc, 20) + a3d0
 fefae518 jdeCallObject (f1ff38fc, 0, d38030, 0, 0, 0) + 38
 f0f500cc IXTF4311Z1_CalcPurchasePrice (a9be40, f63765ce, 1243948, 1243688, f6376ce8,
f63756f0) + 15d8
 f0f39fd0 IXT4311Z1_F4311EditLineInternalFunctions (d38030, a9be40, 1243688, f6376f38,
0, f63756f0) + 23b8
 fefb88f8 jdeCallObjectV2 (6f7a20, d38030, d28008, 1, ff0c36fc, 20) + a3d0
 fefae518 jdeCallObject (6f7a20, 0, d38030, 0, fe963658, f637eea4) + 38
 fe79f4dc JDEK_ProcessCallRequest (f637ef58, f076b0, 7d9d08, a80f90, d38030, 20) +
3d30
 fe79a5e8 JDEK_StartCallRequest (f637fc40, f076b0, 0, a80f90, 7d9d08, 0) + f74
 fe77db24 runBusinessFunction (c44eb8, 0, 0, 7174, ff338dff, fe93c6ec) + 32
 fe77dea8 runCallObjectJob (c44eb8, 0, c44ec8, c44ec8, c44ec8, 20) + 5c
 fe354394 psthread_pool_worker_function (0, 0, 74, d5cc8, fe10d7b8, fe367de8) + 628
 fe0f48fc threadFunctionWrapper (c3548, 204, 0, c4, c354b, fe353d6c) + f4
 fc340368 _lwp_start (0, 0, 0, 0, 0, 0)
```

Analyzing Parent Process Files

If the .dmp log file cannot be obtained in a thread-safe way, the file will not be created. In that case, you'll need to analyze the logs from the parent process. For a crashed COK, the Parent Process Number will refer to a JDENET_N process. The details of the crashed process will be found in this JDENET_N process log file.

For a crashed runbatch process, the details will be found in the Queue kernel. There is only one Queue kernel process per server.

Once the parent process has been identified, search for the word "died" and you will have the business function call stack along with the application and user at the point of the crash. It is often necessary to collect statistics on the number of crashes and their details, which include the business functions, applications, and users; eventually, a pattern will emerge.

Example 1:

```
3670280/1 MAIN_THREAD                       Wed May 23 02:58:50.850156
      netsig.c417
      Kernel Process 4522316 has died

3670280/1 MAIN_THREAD                       Wed May 23 02:58:50.850407
      netsig.c184
      net process: process 4522316 set to Zombie

3670280/1 MAIN_THREAD                       Wed May 23 02:58:50.853306
      ipcmisc.c299
      State information for process 4522316, User=CROSSJ, Role=*ALL,
Environment=JPD900, Profile=NONE, Application=P4210, Client Machine=aix122,
Version=HRC0055, Thread ID=258, Thread Name=WRK:CROSSJ_301AC018_P4210.

3670280/1 MAIN_THREAD                       Wed May 23 02:58:50.853438
      ipcmisc.c299
```

```
        Call stack for process 4522316, thread 258:
libCSALES.so/UNKNOWN/F4211FSEndDoc
```

Example 2:

```
7077998/1 MAIN_THREAD                     Wed May 23 08:57:12.125911
      netsig.c417
      Kernel Process 3211750 has died

7077998/1 MAIN_THREAD                     Wed May 23 08:57:12.126380
      netsig.c184
      net process: process 3211750 set to Zombie

7077998/1 MAIN_THREAD                     Wed May 23 08:57:12.132105
      ipcmisc.c299
      State information for process 3211750, User=LIONI, Role=*ALL,
Environment=JPD900, Profile=NONE, Application=P4210, Client Machine=aix120,
Version=HRC0055, Thread ID=2314, Thread Name=WRK:LIONI_30188548_P4210.

7077998/1 MAIN_THREAD                     Wed May 23 08:57:12.132326
      ipcmisc.c299
      Call stack for process 3211750, thread 2314:
libCSALES.so/UNKNOWN/F4211FSEndDoc:
```

Example 3:

```
6161064/1 MAIN_THREAD                     Thu May 24 14:48:34.042028
      netsig.c417
      Kernel Process 5374824 has died

6161064/1 MAIN_THREAD                     Thu May 24 14:48:34.042376
      netqueue.c3035
      Kernel 5374824 does not exist, return eAssociateKernelNotExist to msgId=1777
hostIP=10.100.153.117 hostKrnl=4980982 msgType=920

6161064/1 MAIN_THREAD                     Thu May 24 14:48:34.042955
      netsig.c184
      net process: process 5374824 set to Zombie

6161064/1 MAIN_THREAD                     Thu May 24 14:48:34.046729
      ipcmisc.c299
      State information for process 5374824, User=LUERSM, Role=*ALL,
Environment=JPD900, Profile=NONE, Application=P3210, Client Machine=aix121,
Version=HRC0001, Thread ID=2314, Thread Name=WRK:LUERSM_32EA8738_P3210.

6161064/1 MAIN_THREAD                     Thu May 24 14:48:34.046894
      ipcmisc.c299
      Call stack for process 5374824, thread 2314:
libCMFG.so/UNKNOWN/InitConfiguratorData_D3202300A
```

Obtaining a Fix via Change Assistant

Based on the pattern that emerges on the crashed business function, the most obvious step to fix the crashed function would be to apply an ESU. This can be done through Change Assistant (Figure 7-2) and by checking whether a "memory" fix exists for the crashed business function.

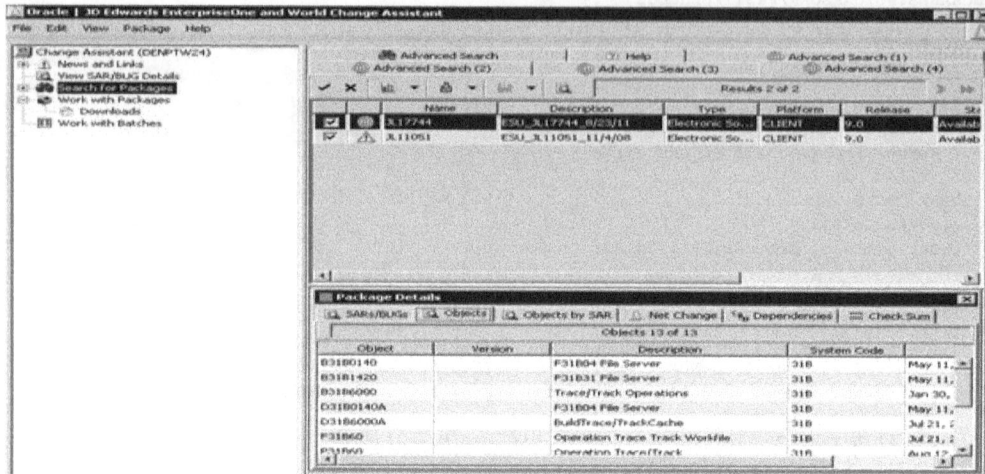

FIGURE 7-2. *Change Assistant*

Engaging a Profiler for Finding the Exact Point of Crash

If the ESU for the crashed business function does not help, a more direct action may be necessary. Engaging Oracle Support at this time would be prudent, but you can find the point of corruption without too much difficulty if a profiler is engaged. To engage a profiler is quite complicated, but we'll explain one very effective profile here: Microsoft Global Flags Editor (GFlags). GFlags can help to find heap corruption only (not stack corruption), but only on Windows servers.

Engaging GFlags to Find Heap Corruption on a Windows Server　Here are the steps that you might take on a non-production server. Keep in mind that it does not matter that the issue is not reproduced; this profiler will extract it! Start by doing one of the following:

- Download and install GFlags (32-bit) from http://msdn.microsoft.com/en-us/windows/hardware/gg463016 on the Windows server where the EnterpriseOne server is running.

- When Tools is upgraded to 64-bit, download and install GFlags (32-bit) from http://msdn.microsoft.com/en-us/windows/hardware/gg463012 on the Windows server where the EnterpriseOne server is running.

Typically, the JDE.INI will be set up to run multiple COKs. It needs to be changed to run a single COK; this will make it easier to debug the kernel.

1. Go to the JDE.INI (the path would be \\jdedwards\E910\ddp\system\ bin32\jde.ini).

2. Go to the [JDENET_KERNEL_DEF6] section.

3. Change `maxNumberOfProcesses=1`. Note the previous value, because we'll need to restore it after we are done.

4. Change `numberOfAutoStartProcesses=1`. Note the previous value, because we'll need to restore it after we are done.

NOTE
You might also want to reduce the other kernel types to a maximum of 1. This is because of the increased memory usage involved with this process. If the EnterpriseOne Server is starting up several security, UBE, and/or workflow kernels with the GFlags turned on, the memory on the machine might be fully consumed.

5. Save the JDE.INI file and close it.

6. Go to the Server Manager to stop the Enterprise Server. If Server Manager is not set up, you can stop the services (using JDE 910 Network, or something similar).

7. Clean the log files in the log folder (the path would be \\jdedwards\E910\ ddp\log).

8. Go to Start | All Programs | Debugging Tools for Windows | Global Flags.

9. Go to the Image File tab.

10. In the Image File Name, type jdenet_k.exe.

11. Enter the executable name jdenet_k.exe and press TAB to exit—*do not press* ENTER—and then check the options, as shown in Figure 7-3.

12. Once all the options are set as in Figure 7-3, click OK.

13. Start Microsoft Visual Studio (if prompted, select VC++ Development settings).

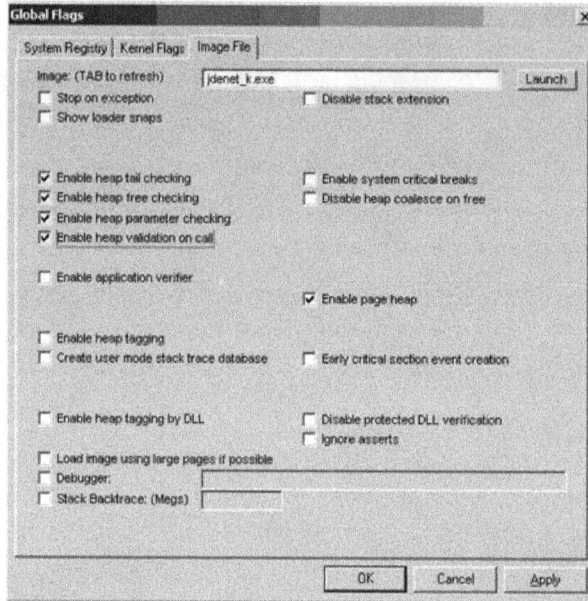

FIGURE 7-3. *Global Flags*

14. Now start the Enterprise Server using Server Manager or Windows Services.

15. After the server is started, go to the logs folder and determine the process ID for the COK.

16. You might see multiple JDE logs. Open them all until you find a log that says INITIALIZING CALL OBJECT KERNEL. That's the log we are interested in.

```
8484/9844 SYS:Dispatch                    Thu Mar 01 11:47:31.991000
    Jdekdisp.c2197
    INITIALIZING CALL OBJECT KERNEL
```

17. Note the number 8484; it is the process ID we need to debug.

18. In Microsoft Visual Studio, go to Tools | Attach To Processes.

19. Look for the process with the ID found from the JDE logs (in this case, 8484).

20. If the ID is not shown, make sure the two check boxes Show Processes From All Users and Show Processes In All Sessions are checked, as shown in Figure 7-4.

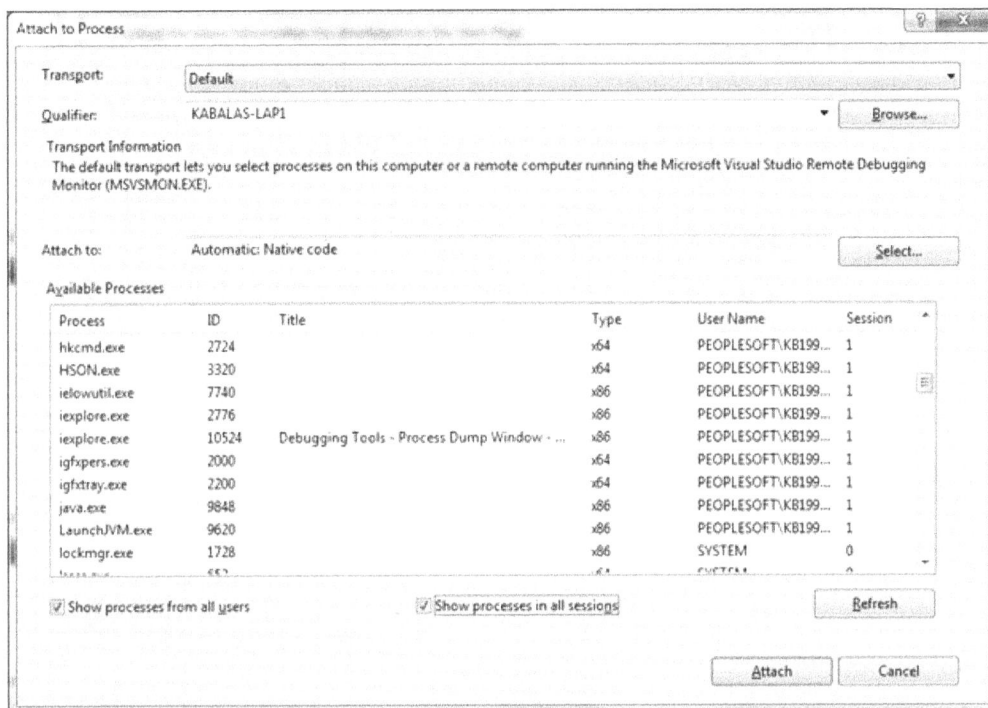

FIGURE 7-4.   *Attach to Process check boxes*

21. After finding the process, select it and click Attach.

22. Now perform the process to duplicate the issue.

If this is a heap overwrite issue, the debugger will bring up the BSFN and stop at the line of code that is causing the issue. Now you can analyze the code.

After this GFlags analysis is complete, make sure to change the INI setting back to what it was and restart the server. Also, make sure to remove the GFlags setting once the test is over.

1. Go to GFlags.

2. Uncheck all check boxes.

3. Remove the Image Name but *DO NOT tab out*.

4. Click OK.

Call Object Kernels or Runbatch with High CPU or Deadlocked Processes

A "hung kernel with high CPU" refers to a kernel that has stopped functioning correctly but whose process continues to run with significant CPU activity or zero CPU activity. Generally, these symptoms points to a root cause related to an infinite loop (high CPU) or a deadlock (low CPU).

Using Server Manager to Obtain Call Stacks

To obtain details on why a call object or run batch is behaving abnormally with respect to CPU processing, you can access the process details via Server Manager's Diagnostics section, shown in Figure 7-5.

Click the CPU Diagnostics button, and the system will write the in-memory business function call stack(s) to the EnterpriseOne server process JDEDEBUG log (whether or not debug logging has been enabled). You can use this to debug hanging (low CPU) or looping (high CPU) EnterpriseOne processes. The OS call stacks of all threads are then available, and the following data will be displayed in the CPU diagnostics:

- Process OS data

  - Memory (megabytes)

  - CPU (percent)

  - Threads (number of threads)

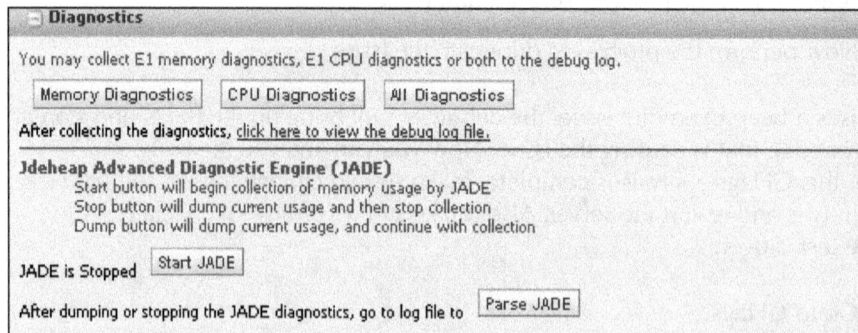

FIGURE 7-5. *Diagnostics in Server Manager*

- CPU diagnostics

  - BSFN call stacks

  - BSFN call stack for thread 1

  - BSFN call stack for thread 2 (thread BSFN call stacks beyond the first thread are applicable only to COK processes)

One .dmp file will not reveal much because it's a snapshot of the process at a given time. You can click the CPU Diagnostics button several times quickly for a complete insight into the fluid process. Here is an example:

```
********** Begin OS Data **********
Memory Usage = 257MB
CPU Usage = 1%
Number of Threads = 7
********** End OS Data **********
********** Begin Detailed CPU Data **********
********** Begin BSFN Call Stacks **********
CALLSTACK,5,WRK:JDE_000BDB60_P4310,JDE,*ALL,JPD812,NONE,P4310,denicsn5,ZJDE0001
libCDIST.so/UNKNOWN/F4311EndDoc
********** End BSFN Call Stacks **********
********** Begin OS Call Stacks **********
5504: jdenet_k 6014
---------------- lwp# 1 / thread# 1 --------------------
fc342d74 msgsys (2, 39000021, 3e6018, 200c, 0, 0)
fc333b84 msgrcv (39000021, 3e6018, 200c, 0, 0, 0) + 68
ff23e7b4 receiveMessage (5, 39000021, 200c, 0, 0, 0) + 1dc
ff21d73c ipcGetQueueEntry (92d60, ffbfc0c4, ffbfc0c8, ffbfe0d4, 5, 3e6018) + 334
ff139a24 getExternalQueueEntry (0, 5, 1, ffbff28c, fb3a00ab, ff1d1b58) + 35c
ff195c60 getKernelQueueEntry (0, 8fd68, ffbff28c, 92d60, 8fd54, 8fd58) + 49c
ff19606c processKernelQueue (ffbff28c, fb3a0000, 0, 0, 0, ff1cd2c8) + 300
ff16e250 JDENET_RunKernel (20, 8fd68, 1, ff1cd2c8, 0, 5) + 428
00011cc0 main (0, 0, 4c, 0, 2218c, 0) + 6bc
000111d4 _start (0, 0, 0, 0, 0, 0) + 108
---------------- lwp# 2 / thread# 2 --------------------
fc340408 lwp_park (0, 0, 0)
fc33a49c cond_wait_queue (24e8d0, bd298, 0, 0, 0, 0) + 28
fc33aa1c cond_wait (24e8d0, bd298, 0, 0, 20, 0) + 10
fc33aa58 pthread_cond_wait (24e8d0, bd298, 0, 0, 20, 1) + 8
fe0f3db8 psthread_cond_wait (24e6c8, bd088, 1, 1, 1, fe10d810) + 274
fe352da4 ps_blocking_queue_dequeue (24e4a0, f637ff24, bd088, 0, fe10d7d8, 20) + 224
fe354214 psthread_pool_worker_function (24e4a0, 0, d5cd4, d5cc8, fe10d7b8, fe367de8) +
4a8
fe0f48fc threadFunctionWrapper (c3548, 204, 0, c4, c354b, fe353d6c) + f4
fc340368 _lwp_start (0, 0, 0, 0, 0, 0)
---------------- lwp# 5 / thread# 3 --------------------
fc341850 waitid (0, 15c9, f58e6ab0, 3)
fc334758 waitpid (15c9, f58e6c04, 0, 0, f58e6c5c, faa82740) + 60
fc327eec system (1b3360, fc36ff74, 20000, 1, fc368288, f58e6c5c) + 2ec
fd9e6350 jdeSystem (f58e6db8, 6a, 0, 1b3360, 4b, f58e6db8) + 50
ff30f6bc logCallStackOnUnix (1580, 0, f58e7694, f58e74b1, 24fc, 2500) + 130
ff30fb0c allocCallStackUnix (0, f58e81e4, ff316d56, 0, 2518, 2400) + 88
```

```
ff30fd7c jdeAllocCallStack (1580, f58e81e4, f58e83ec, 8c00, 50e598, f58e83ec) + 20
fed27dd8 logProcessDumpData (2, 0, 0, ffffffff, 810060, 8c00) + e04
f6571310 doQueryDiagnostics (238, 810060, 0, f74bb544, 234, 0) + 3d8
f656eaf0 performRequestInternal (82f3e0, 1, 0, ae6f88, ff0ed1c0, 0) + 51c
f656e46c dballPerformRequest (82f3e0, 8303d0, 0, 8303d0, 8303d3, 3) + 3e4
feb937a4 JDB_DBPerformRequest (aeaad8, 82f3e0, ae6f88, 18a268, 18a340, 18a268) + e4
fe13a894 TM_DBPerformRequest (65be18, 0, ae6f88, 8ab250, 7d70c0, 5) + 41c
fec083fc InsertTable (8ab250, 7d70c0, 0, ae6f88, f58eb1f0, 0) + 392c
fec0bf74 JDB_InsertTable (8ab250, f32d3854, 0, f58ed714, 0, ff338dfc) + 208
f214177c IXT4311Z1_EndDocWriteNewOrderDetail_2 (f32d3818, 7d0868, 675720, a53750,
f58f4c28, f58f6bfc) + dd4
f213efbc IXT4311Z1_EndDocProcessCurrentDetailLine (3e5d48, 7d0868, 675720, f58f770c,
a53750, f58f62e0) + 1338
f2139694 F4311EndDoc (7d0868, 675720, a53750, 31, 0, 1) + 16d4
fefb88f8 jdeCallObjectV2 (1b8df8, 7d0868, 506be0, 1, ff0c36fc, 20) + a3d0
fefae518 jdeCallObject (1b8df8, 0, 7d0868, 0, fe963658, f58feea4) + 38
fe79f4dc JDEK_ProcessCallRequest (f58fef58, 6e1018, bdb60, 3e5d48, 7d0868, 20) + 3d30
fe79a5e8 JDEK_StartCallRequest (f58ffc40, 6e1018, 0, 3e5d48, bdb60, 0) + f74
fe77db24 runBusinessFunction (94ef0, 0, 0, 7174, ff338dff, fe93c6ec) + 328
fe77dea8 runCallObjectJob (94ef0, 0, 94f00, 94f00, 94f00, 20) + 5c
fe354394 psthread_pool_worker_function (0, 0, 74, d5cc8, fe10d7b8, fe367de8) + 628
fe0f48fc threadFunctionWrapper (c34c8, 204, 0, c4, c34cb, fe353d6c) + f4
fc340368 _lwp_start (0, 0, 0, 0, 0, 0)

********** End OS Call Stacks **********
********** End Detailed CPU Data **********
```

When Server Manager Does Not Obtain a Call Stack

Sometimes, when you're using Server Manager, CPU Diagnostics will not yield call stacks in the .dmp files. In this case, the main thread is deadlocked and cannot respond to the dump of a call stack request. The OS features can be used instead. The following sections demonstrate how to obtain call stacks using various OS commands.

Unix   Run the following on the respective various Unix OS to dump call stacks:

- **HP-UX**   /usr/ccs/bin/pstack <pid>

- **AIX**   /usr/bin/procstack <pid>

- **Sun**   /usr/bin/pstack <pid>

- **Linux**   /usr/bin/pstack <pid>

Windows   To obtain information from a nonresponsive process on the Windows OS, follow the description found on this Microsoft document: http://support.microsoft .com/kb/286350.

System i   The following creates a spool file containing the program stack (call stack):

```
Cmd: DSPJOB JOB(072347/ONEWORLD/JDENET K) OUTPUT(*PRINT)
OPTION(*PGMSTK)
```

Corrective Process for High CPU–Consuming Process

Cache or recycling actions are available in the Corrective Actions section of the Server Manager process detail page, shown in Figure 7-6.

- **Clear Cache**   Click the Clear Cache button to clear internal tools caches for the process that has been selected. This should reduce the memory footprint of the process and may cause some performance impact while the caches are being rebuilt.

- **Recycle Kernel**   Click the Recycle Kernel button to begin recycling an individual COK process on demand. This button allows administrators to "gracefully" shut down a process that appears to have problems to reclaim the resources and prevent a single process from impacting or bringing down the entire system. It also prevents new users from being associated with the kernel and possibly being impacted if the kernel zombies.

Before these two buttons were available, the only options for an administrator were to allow the process to continue running or to kill the process from the OS. If the process were allowed to continue, it could become attached to new user sessions, which could be detrimental to those sessions, and which could make the perceived problems within the kernel process even worse than what they might have been. On the other hand, if the process were killed manually, the applications that were currently running would be ungracefully stopped, which would prevent the applications from completing and would force any open transactions to be rolled back.

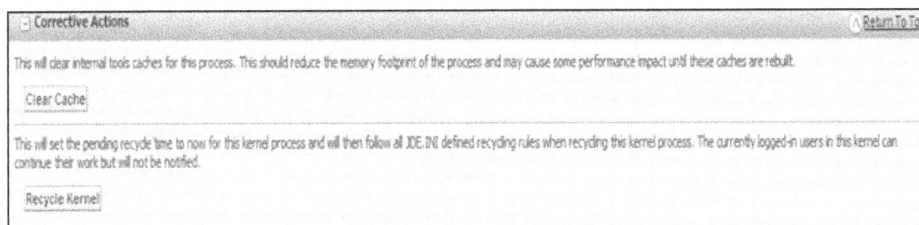

FIGURE 7-6.   *Server Manager's Corrective Actions section*

The recycling option tries to avoid both of those issues. When a kernel process begins recycling, no additional user sessions are attached to it. But the kernel is not stopped immediately, which allows the current users to complete their processing. When all users have completed their processing, that kernel will be shut down.

Call Object Kernels or Runbatch Crash Due to Out of Memory

COKs, or runbatch processes, can also crash when they are unable to allocate memory. This can happen for two reasons:

- If the process hits the per-process memory limit for the given OS, possibly due to the process leaking memory or consuming excessive memory. The limit could be anywhere from 700MB to 1.5GB, but the theoretical limit for most processes is close to 2GB.

- A general lack of memory is available in the machine environment where it is running. This is usually due to an undersized box or a side effect of leaking processes on other sibling processes.

Similar to memory corruption, the out-of-memory issue also produces a .dmp log file. In this case, it produces a memory dump that contains the list of all EnterpriseOne objects in the process memory at the time of the crash. If the crash is due to raw allocation of memory or a third-party leak, this memory diagnostic dump will not show any large quantities of EnterpriseOne objects.

Here is a .dmplog for a crash due to out of memory: The bold type indicates the key lines of information to recognize which in this case is a very large cache memory allocation of 948,722 rows which contributed to the "Memory Allocation Failure" message.

```
Apr  5 17:31:27.459991  DEBUG INIT0 - 6329   ****   jdeDebugInit -- output disabled in
INI file.
Apr  5 17:31:27.461443  jdemem.c131 - 6329   BMD OFF - Not running BSFN MEMORY DIAG-
NOSTICS v8.98.2.0 level 0
Apr  5 17:59:03.229258    jdb_util1.c13485 - 6329/2  MEMORY ALLOCATION FAILURE
Apr  5 17:59:03.229365  jdb_util1.c13485 - 6329/2  File: jdb_rq1.c   Line: 192


********** Begin OS Data **********
  Memory Usage = 4281MB
  CPU Usage = 0%
  Number of Threads = 7
********** End OS Data **********
********** Begin Detailed Memory Data **********
  ********** Begin Process Data **********
    ENVIRONMENT,Ptr=00652d78,Env=JPD812,PathCode=PD812
    JDBTABLECACHE,Ptr=007ccec8,Name=JDB_BV_1270510706JPD812F4009,#Records=1
```

```
    JDBTABLECACHE,Ptr=003e6f38,Name=JDB_BV_1270510706JPD812F40203,#Records=2
    JDBTABLECACHE,Ptr=003ed418,Name=JDB_BV_1270510706JPD812F40205,#Records=1
    JDBTABLECACHE,Ptr=004fb430,Name=JDB_BV_1270510706JPD812F41001,#Records=2
    JDBTABLECACHE,Ptr=00501078,Name=JDB_BV_1270510706JPD812F41002,#Records=3294
    JDBTABLECACHE,Ptr=0051ead0,Name=JDB_BV_1270510706JPD812F7306,#Records=1
    JDBTABLECACHE,Ptr=00319358,Name=JDB_BV_1270510706JPD812F99410,#Records=2
    JDBTABLECACHE,Ptr=00338690,Name=JDB_BV_1270510706JPD812F0004,#Records=25
    JDBTABLECACHE,Ptr=00342d40,Name=JDB_BV_1270510706JPD812F0005,#Records=27
    JDBTABLECACHE,Ptr=00346cf8,Name=JDB_BV_1270510706JPD812F0006,#Records=1
    JDBTABLECACHE,Ptr=00378de1,Name=JDB_BV_1270510706JPD812F0901,#Records=948722
    JDBTABLECACHE,Ptr=00349ca0,Name=JDB_BV_1270510706JPD812F0008,#Records=1
    JDBTABLECACHE,Ptr=0034e6a8,Name=JDB_BV_1270510706JPD812F0010,#Records=2
    JDBTABLECACHE,Ptr=00358420,Name=JDB_BV_1270510706JPD812F0013,#Records=1
    JDBTABLECACHE,Ptr=0035d780,Name=JDB_BV_1270510706JPD812F0014,#Records=1
    JDBTABLECACHE,Ptr=006454d8,Name=JDB_BV_1270510707JPD812F1609,#Records=1
    OCIDBCONN,Ptr=0012e530,DBServer=densun28,DBUser=JDE,TNSDB=orcl,ConnState=AutoInUse
,CommitMode=A,RefCount=196
OCIDBCONN,Ptr=0082ee18,DBServer=densun28,DBUser=JDE,TNSDB=orcl,ConnState=ManualInUse,C
ommitMode=M,RefCount=1
OCIDBCONN,Ptr=006aca68,DBServer=densun28,DBUser=JDE,TNSDB=orcl,ConnState=ManualInUse,C
ommitMode=M,RefCount=1
    OCIDBCONN,Ptr=00a46d08,DBServer=densun28,DBUser=JDE,TNSDB=orcl,ConnState=ManualInU
se,CommitMode=M,RefCount=1
OCIDBCONN,Ptr=00880b98,DBServer=densun28,DBUser=JDE,TNSDB=orcl,ConnState=ManualInUse,C
ommitMode=M,RefCount=1
OCIDBCONN,Ptr=015f64c0,DBServer=densun28,DBUser=JDE,TNSDB=orcl,ConnState=ManualAvailab
le,CommitMode=M,RefCount=0
OCIDBCONN,Ptr=01b150c8,DBServer=densun28,DBUser=JDE,TNSDB=orcl,ConnState=ManualAvailab
le,CommitMode=M,RefCount=0
OCIDBCONN,Ptr=01546400,DBServer=densun28,DBUser=JDE,TNSDB=orcl,ConnState=ManualInUse,C
ommitMode=M,RefCount=1
OCIDBCONN,Ptr=015e0808,DBServer=densun28,DBUser=JDE,TNSDB=orcl,ConnState=ManualAvailab
le,CommitMode=M,RefCount=0
OCIDBCONN,Ptr=01632938,DBServer=densun28,DBUser=JDE,TNSDB=orcl,ConnState=ManualAvailab
le,CommitMode=M,RefCount=0
OCIDBCONN,Ptr=01240ac0,DBServer=densun28,DBUser=JDE,TNSDB=orcl,ConnState=ManualInUse,C
ommitMode=M,RefCount=1
OCIDBCONN,Ptr=01242d48,DBServer=densun28,DBUser=JDE,TNSDB=orcl,ConnState=ManualInUse,C
ommitMode=M,RefCount=1
OCIDBCONN,Ptr=01465c00,DBServer=densun28,DBUser=JDE,TNSDB=orcl,ConnState=ManualAvailab
le,CommitMode=M,RefCount=0
OCIDBCONN,Ptr=00eee538,DBServer=densun28,DBUser=JDE,TNSDB=orcl,ConnState=ManualAvailab
le,CommitMode=M,RefCount=0
OCIDBCONN,Ptr=0165e2e8,DBServer=densun28,DBUser=JDE,TNSDB=orcl,ConnState=ManualInUse,C
ommitMode=M,RefCount=1
OCIDBCONN,Ptr=00bf3318,DBServer=densun28,DBUser=JDE,TNSDB=orcl,ConnState=ManualAvailab
le,CommitMode=M,RefCount=0
OCIDBCONN,Ptr=00e369e0,DBServer=densun28,DBUser=JDE,TNSDB=orcl,ConnState=ManualAvailab
le,CommitMode=M,RefCount=0
    ********** End Process Data **********
    ********** Begin Session Data **********
    SESSION,Ptr=000bdb60,User=JDE,Env=JPD812,Role=*ALL,Machine=denicsn5,SignOnTime= 4/
5/2010 17:38:27,LastActiveTime= 4/ 5/2010 17:58:55
OPENJDBTRANSACTION,Ptr=0014eb28,CommitMode=Auto,Owner=InitUser,AppName=(UNKNOWN),File=
jdb_ctl.c,Function=JDB_LoadEnv,Line=5829
TABLE,Ptr=00a2bac0,Name=F0013,CommitStatus=Active,File=jdb_curr.c,Function=JDB_Retriev
eF0013RowUsingCurrencyCode,Line=73
```

```
TABLE,Ptr=013f0830,Name=F0010,CommitStatus=Active,File=jdb_curr.c,Function=JDB_Retriev
eF0010RowUsingCompanyNumber,Line=246
OPENJDBTRANSACTION,Ptr=007f4538,CommitMode=Auto,Owner=InitUser,AppName=(UNKNOWN),File=
jdb_ctl.c,Function=CallStartupBusinessFunction,Line=8551
OPENJDBTRANSACTION,Ptr=004299c0,CommitMode=Auto,Owner=InitUser,AppName=(UNKNOWN),File=
jdekinit.c,Function=JDEK_ProcessInitUserRequest,Line=356
OPENJDBTRANSACTION,Ptr=00783a08,CommitMode=Auto,Owner=InitUser,AppName=(UNKNOWN),File=
jdekinit.c,Function=JDEK_ProcessInitUserRequest,Line=356
JDECACHE,Ptr=000fabe8,Name=2XT4311Z1A,#Cursors=1,#Records=0,#Indices=1,#References=1,F
ile=xt4311z1.c,Function=F4311InitializeCaching,Line=23018
JDECACHE,Ptr=005ce150,Name=2XT4311Z1B,#Cursors=1,#Records=0,#Indices=2,#References=1,F
ile=xt4311z1.c,Function=F4311InitializeCaching,Line=23027
JDECACHE,Ptr=00ef3390,Name=2XT4311Z1C,#Cursors=1,#Records=1,#Indices=1,#References=5,F
ile=xt4311z1.c,Function=IXT4311Z1_InitiateOrderCache,Line=5758
JDECACHE,Ptr=014397a8,Name=2B4302570Cache,#Cursors=1,#Records=0,#Indices=1,#References
=2,File=b4302570.c,Function=ApprovalsFieldConstants,Line=158
JDECACHE,Ptr=014f8000,Name=2F45UI73,#Cursors=1,#Records=0,#Indices=2,#References=4,Fil
e=b4500200.c,Function=F4573GetNextFreeGood,Line=100
JDECACHE,Ptr=00beae30,Name=2B3201470213107,#Cursors=1,#Records=0,#Indices=7,#Reference
s=3,File=b3201470.c,Function=I3201470_CreateInitCache,Line=732
JDECACHE,Ptr=00b65350,Name=2B3201470213144,#Cursors=1,#Records=0,#Indices=7,#Reference
s=3,File=b3201470.c,Function=I3201470_CreateInitCache,Line=732
JDECACHE,Ptr=004d1438,Name=2B4302180F632910,#Cursors=1,#Records=1,#Indices=1,#Referenc
es=19,File=b4302180.c,Function=CacheProcessPOHeaderCache,Line=1173
JDECACHE,Ptr=01876570,Name=2213190PricingDecimals,#Cursors=2,#Records=2,#Indices=1,#Re
ferences=1,File=b4504500.c,Function=CreateDataMapCDIST,Line=229
JDECACHE,Ptr=006d05d0,Name=2213190DataMapCDISTCache,#Cursors=1,#Records=3,#Indices=1,#
References=1,File=b4504500.c,Function=InitDataMapCacheCDIST,Line=2108
JDECACHE,Ptr=01765910,Name=2213190PricingHistory,#Cursors=2,#Records=1,#Indices=1,#Ref
erences=1,File=b4504500.c,Function=CreateDataMapCDIST,Line=229
JDECACHE,Ptr=017ed260,Name=2213190PricingCatCodes,#Cursors=2,#Records=1,#Indices=1,#Re
ferences=1,File=b4504500.c,Function=CreateDataMapCDIST,Line=229
JDECACHE,Ptr=0104aaf0,Name=2B4302180G632910,#Cursors=1,#Records=6,#Indices=2,#Referenc
es=12,File=b4302180.c,Function=CacheProcessPODetailCache,Line=1510
JDECACHE,Ptr=015b0138,Name=2B4302180H632910,#Cursors=1,#Records=0,#Indices=3,#Referenc
es=6,File=b4302180.c,Function=CacheProcessBlanketCache,Line=1848
JDECACHE,Ptr=013c0960,Name=2F40UI74_213190,#Cursors=1,#Records=6,#Indices=3,#Reference
s=1,File=b4504610.c,Function=F40UI74_Init,Line=719
    JDECACHE,Ptr=013b0f80,Name=2F40UI70-213190,#Cursors=1,#Records=0,#Indices=5,#Ref
erences=18,File=b4500720.c,Function=ProcessPriceAdjustmentListCache,Line=335
    SESSION,Ptr=00811f78,User=JDE,Env=JPD812,Role=*ALL,Machine=denicsn5,SignOnTime= 4/
5/2010 17:38:44,LastActiveTime= 4/ 5/2010 17:58:56
OPENJDBTRANSACTION,Ptr=0084a660,CommitMode=Auto,Owner=InitUser,AppName=(UNKNOWN),File=
jdb_ctl.c,Function=JDB_LoadEnv,Line=5829
TABLE,Ptr=00d4a3b8,Name=F0013,CommitStatus=Active,File=jdb_curr.c,Function=JDB_Retriev
eF0013RowUsingCurrencyCode,Line=73
TABLE,Ptr=0142e000,Name=F0010,CommitStatus=Active,File=jdb_curr.c,Function=JDB_Retriev
eF0010RowUsingCompanyNumber,Line=246
OPENJDBTRANSACTION,Ptr=0084a968,CommitMode=Auto,Owner=InitUser,AppName=(UNKNOWN),File=
jdb_ctl.c,Function=CallStartupBusinessFunction,Line=8551
OPENJDBTRANSACTION,Ptr=00822b00,CommitMode=Auto,Owner=InitUser,AppName=(UNKNOWN),File=
jdekinit.c,Function=JDEK_ProcessInitUserRequest,Line=356
OPENJDBTRANSACTION,Ptr=00878840,CommitMode=Auto,Owner=InitUser,AppName=(UNKNOWN),File=
jdekinit.c,Function=JDEK_ProcessInitUserRequest,Line=356
JDECACHE,Ptr=0085a448,Name=5XT4311Z1A,#Cursors=1,#Records=0,#Indices=1,#References=1,F
ile=xt4311z1.c,Function=F4311InitializeCaching,Line=23018
```

```
JDECACHE,Ptr=00a3a360,Name=5XT4311Z1B,#Cursors=1,#Records=0,#Indices=2,#References=1,F
ile=xt4311z1.c,Function=F4311InitializeCaching,Line=23027
JDECACHE,Ptr=0104ea50,Name=5XT4311Z1C,#Cursors=1,#Records=1,#Indices=1,#References=5,F
ile=xt4311z1.c,Function=IXT4311Z1_InitiateOrderCache,Line=5758
JDECACHE,Ptr=00e868a8,Name=5B4302570Cache,#Cursors=1,#Records=0,#Indices=1,#References
=2,File=b4302570.c,Function=ApprovalsFieldConstants,Line=158
JDECACHE,Ptr=00fe2170,Name=5F45UI73,#Cursors=1,#Records=0,#Indices=2,#References=4,Fil
e=b4500200.c,Function=F4573GetNextFreeGood,Line=100
JDECACHE,Ptr=01add638,Name=5B3201470213118,#Cursors=1,#Records=0,#Indices=7,#Reference
s=3,File=b3201470.c,Function=I3201470_CreateInitCache,Line=732
JDECACHE,Ptr=01aca2b8,Name=5B3201470213155,#Cursors=1,#Records=0,#Indices=7,#Reference
s=3,File=b3201470.c,Function=I3201470_CreateInitCache,Line=732
JDECACHE,Ptr=00c27ed0,Name=5B4302180F632911,#Cursors=1,#Records=1,#Indices=1,#Referenc
es=19,File=b4302180.c,Function=CacheProcessPOHeaderCache,Line=1173
JDECACHE,Ptr=0080e4e0,Name=5213191PricingDecimals,#Cursors=2,#Records=2,#Indices=1,#Re
ferences=1,File=b4504500.c,Function=CreateDataMapCDIST,Line=229
JDECACHE,Ptr=00ed3570,Name=5213191DataMapCDISTCache,#Cursors=1,#Records=3,#Indices=1,#
References=1,File=b4504500.c,Function=InitDataMapCacheCDIST,Line=2108
JDECACHE,Ptr=01afd6e8,Name=5213191PricingHistory,#Cursors=2,#Records=1,#Indices=1,#Ref
erences=1,File=b4504500.c,Function=CreateDataMapCDIST,Line=229
JDECACHE,Ptr=018a5ae8,Name=5213191PricingCatCodes,#Cursors=2,#Records=1,#Indices=1,#Re
ferences=1,File=b4504500.c,Function=CreateDataMapCDIST,Line=229
JDECACHE,Ptr=012ea670,Name=5B4302180G632911,#Cursors=1,#Records=6,#Indices=2,#Referenc
es=12,File=b4302180.c,Function=CacheProcessPODetailCache,Line=1510
JDECACHE,Ptr=01a4ef80,Name=5B4302180H632911,#Cursors=1,#Records=0,#Indices=3,#Referenc
es=6,File=b4302180.c,Function=CacheProcessBlanketCache,Line=1848
JDECACHE,Ptr=01054bb8,Name=5F40UI74_213191,#Cursors=1,#Records=6,#Indices=3,#Reference
s=1,File=b4504610.c,Function=F40UI74_Init,Line=719
    JDECACHE,Ptr=01913c10,Name=5F40UI70-213191,#Cursors=1,#Records=0,#Indices=5,#Ref
erences=18,File=b4500720.c,Function=ProcessPriceAdjustmentListCache,Line=335
    SESSION,Ptr=006922b0,User=JDE,Env=JPD812,Role=*ALL,Machine=denicsn5,SignOnTime= 4/
5/2010 17:38:37,LastActiveTime= 4/ 5/2010 17:58:58
OPENJDBTRANSACTION,Ptr=00640a90,CommitMode=Auto,Owner=InitUser,AppName=(UNKNOWN),File=
jdb_ctl.c,Function=JDB_LoadEnv,Line=5829
TABLE,Ptr=00ad7720,Name=F0013,CommitStatus=Active,File=jdb_curr.c,Function=JDB_Retriev
eF0013RowUsingCurrencyCode,Line=73
TABLE,Ptr=01420ac0,Name=F0010,CommitStatus=Active,File=jdb_curr.c,Function=JDB_Retriev
eF0010RowUsingCompanyNumber,Line=246
OPENJDBTRANSACTION,Ptr=00640e48,CommitMode=Auto,Owner=InitUser,AppName=(UNKNOWN),File=
jdb_ctl.c,Function=CallStartupBusinessFunction,Line=8551
OPENJDBTRANSACTION,Ptr=00870d28,CommitMode=Auto,Owner=InitUser,AppName=(UNKNOWN),File=
jdekinit.c,Function=JDEK_ProcessInitUserRequest,Line=356
OPENJDBTRANSACTION,Ptr=009610e0,CommitMode=Auto,Owner=InitUser,AppName=(UNKNOWN),File=
jdekinit.c,Function=JDEK_ProcessInitUserRequest,Line=356
JDECACHE,Ptr=00923838,Name=4XT4311Z1A,#Cursors=1,#Records=0,#Indices=1,#References=1,F
ile=xt4311z1.c,Function=F4311InitializeCaching,Line=23018
JDECACHE,Ptr=0088b7a0,Name=4XT4311Z1B,#Cursors=1,#Records=0,#Indices=2,#References=1,F
ile=xt4311z1.c,Function=F4311InitializeCaching,Line=23027
JDECACHE,Ptr=00efa2c0,Name=4XT4311Z1C,#Cursors=1,#Records=1,#Indices=1,#References=5,F
ile=xt4311z1.c,Function=IXT4311Z1_InitiateOrderCache,Line=5758
JDECACHE,Ptr=01466478,Name=4B4302570Cache,#Cursors=1,#Records=0,#Indices=1,#References
=2,File=b4302570.c,Function=ApprovalsFieldConstants,Line=158
JDECACHE,Ptr=01b73728,Name=4F45UI73,#Cursors=1,#Records=0,#Indices=2,#References=4,Fil
e=b4500200.c,Function=F4573GetNextFreeGood,Line=100
JDECACHE,Ptr=006d0498,Name=4B3201470213115,#Cursors=1,#Records=0,#Indices=7,#Reference
s=3,File=b3201470.c,Function=I3201470_CreateInitCache,Line=732
```

```
JDECACHE,Ptr=01672288,Name=4B3201470213145,#Cursors=1,#Records=0,#Indices=7,#Reference
s=3,File=b3201470.c,Function=I3201470_CreateInitCache,Line=732
JDECACHE,Ptr=005c10a0,Name=4B4302180F63299,#Cursors=1,#Records=1,#Indices=1,#Reference
s=22,File=b4302180.c,Function=CacheProcessPOHeaderCache,Line=1173
JDECACHE,Ptr=013db780,Name=4213184PricingDecimals,#Cursors=2,#Records=2,#Indices=1,#Re
ferences=1,File=b4504500.c,Function=CreateDataMapCDIST,Line=229
JDECACHE,Ptr=00b58770,Name=4213184DataMapCDISTCache,#Cursors=1,#Records=3,#Indices=1,#
References=1,File=b4504500.c,Function=InitDataMapCacheCDIST,Line=2108
JDECACHE,Ptr=018e3658,Name=4213184PricingHistory,#Cursors=2,#Records=1,#Indices=1,#Ref
erences=1,File=b4504500.c,Function=CreateDataMapCDIST,Line=229
JDECACHE,Ptr=019e56d0,Name=4213184PricingCatCodes,#Cursors=2,#Records=1,#Indices=1,#Re
ferences=1,File=b4504500.c,Function=CreateDataMapCDIST,Line=229
JDECACHE,Ptr=016c6e90,Name=4B4302180G63299,#Cursors=1,#Records=7,#Indices=2,#Reference
s=14,File=b4302180.c,Function=CacheProcessPODetailCache,Line=1510
JDECACHE,Ptr=013a6d88,Name=4B4302180H63299,#Cursors=1,#Records=0,#Indices=3,#Reference
s=7,File=b4302180.c,Function=CacheProcessBlanketCache,Line=1848
JDECACHE,Ptr=013b0bc8,Name=4F40UI74_213184,#Cursors=1,#Records=7,#Indices=3,#Reference
s=1,File=b4504610.c,Function=F40UI74_Init,Line=719
 JDECACHE,Ptr=00b54138,Name=4F40UI70-213184,#Cursors=1,#Records=0,#Indices=5,#Referenc
es=21,File=b4500720.c,Function=ProcessPriceAdjustmentListCache,Line=335
    SESSION,Ptr=005051b8,User=JDE,Env=JPD812,Role=*ALL,Machine=denicsn5,SignOnTime= 4/
5/2010 17:38:28,LastActiveTime= 4/ 5/2010 17:59:01
OPENJDBTRANSACTION,Ptr=00341fc8,CommitMode=Auto,Owner=InitUser,AppName=(UNKNOWN),File=
jdb_ctl.c,Function=JDB_LoadEnv,Line=5829
TABLE,Ptr=00974bb0,Name=F0013,CommitStatus=Active,File=jdb_curr.c,Function=JDB_Retriev
eF0013RowUsingCurrencyCode,Line=73
TABLE,Ptr=01442d30,Name=F0010,CommitStatus=Active,File=jdb_curr.c,Function=JDB_Retriev
eF0010RowUsingCompanyNumber,Line=246
OPENJDBTRANSACTION,Ptr=001a4e48,CommitMode=Auto,Owner=InitUser,AppName=(UNKNOWN),File=
jdb_ctl.c,Function=CallStartupBusinessFunction,Line=8551
OPENJDBTRANSACTION,Ptr=00331720,CommitMode=Auto,Owner=InitUser,AppName=(UNKNOWN),File=
jdekinit.c,Function=JDEK_ProcessInitUserRequest,Line=356
OPENJDBTRANSACTION,Ptr=0035dcb8,CommitMode=Auto,Owner=InitUser,AppName=(UNKNOWN),File=
jdekinit.c,Function=JDEK_ProcessInitUserRequest,Line=356
JDECACHE,Ptr=0034d490,Name=3XT4311Z1A,#Cursors=1,#Records=0,#Indices=1,#References=1,F
ile=xt4311z1.c,Function=F4311InitializeCaching,Line=23018
JDECACHE,Ptr=005da0f0,Name=3XT4311Z1B,#Cursors=1,#Records=0,#Indices=2,#References=1,F
ile=xt4311z1.c,Function=F4311InitializeCaching,Line=23027
JDECACHE,Ptr=00ceef28,Name=3XT4311Z1C,#Cursors=1,#Records=1,#Indices=1,#References=5,F
ile=xt4311z1.c,Function=IXT4311Z1_InitiateOrderCache,Line=5758
JDECACHE,Ptr=00e47ab8,Name=3B4302570Cache,#Cursors=1,#Records=0,#Indices=1,#References
=2,File=b4302570.c,Function=ApprovalsFieldConstants,Line=158
JDECACHE,Ptr=011050f0,Name=3F45UI73,#Cursors=1,#Records=0,#Indices=2,#References=4,Fil
e=b4500200.c,Function=F4573GetNextFreeGood,Line=100
JDECACHE,Ptr=004044e0,Name=3B3201470213104,#Cursors=1,#Records=0,#Indices=7,#Reference
s=3,File=b3201470.c,Function=I3201470_CreateInitCache,Line=732
JDECACHE,Ptr=00e187b0,Name=3B3201470213163,#Cursors=1,#Records=0,#Indices=7,#Reference
s=3,File=b3201470.c,Function=I3201470_CreateInitCache,Line=732
JDECACHE,Ptr=00ef0248,Name=3B4302180F632912,#Cursors=1,#Records=1,#Indices=1,#Referenc
es=16,File=b4302180.c,Function=CacheProcessPOHeaderCache,Line=1173
JDECACHE,Ptr=00cddec0,Name=3213203PricingDecimals,#Cursors=2,#Records=2,#Indices=1,#Re
ferences=1,File=b4504500.c,Function=CreateDataMapCDIST,Line=229
JDECACHE,Ptr=00eaedd0,Name=3213203DataMapCDISTCache,#Cursors=1,#Records=3,#Indices=1,#
References=1,File=b4504500.c,Function=InitDataMapCacheCDIST,Line=2108
JDECACHE,Ptr=00859440,Name=3213203PricingHistory,#Cursors=2,#Records=1,#Indices=1,#Ref
erences=1,File=b4504500.c,Function=CreateDataMapCDIST,Line=229
```

```
JDECACHE,Ptr=019f8360,Name=3213203PricingCatCodes,#Cursors=2,#Records=1,#Indices=1,#Re
ferences=1,File=b4504500.c,Function=CreateDataMapCDIST,Line=229
JDECACHE,Ptr=017737c8,Name=3B4302180G632912,#Cursors=1,#Records=5,#Indices=2,#Referenc
es=10,File=b4302180.c,Function=CacheProcessPODetailCache,Line=1510
JDECACHE,Ptr=00c338f0,Name=3B4302180H632912,#Cursors=1,#Records=0,#Indices=3,#Referenc
es=5,File=b4302180.c,Function=CacheProcessBlanketCache,Line=1848
JDECACHE,Ptr=01bee1b0,Name=3F40UI74_213203,#Cursors=1,#Records=5,#Indices=3,#Reference
s=1,File=b4504610.c,Function=F40UI74_Init,Line=719
      JDECACHE,Ptr=01ab54b0,Name=3F40UI70-213203,#Cursors=1,#Records=0,#Indices=5,#Ref
erences=15,File=b4500720.c,Function=ProcessPriceAdjustmentListCache,Line=335
   ********** End Session Data **********
********** End Detailed Memory Data **********
```

Analysis of Memory Dumps for the .dmp log File   Use the following guidelines to aid you in analyzing the memory dump files just shown. We created these guidelines after spending long hours troubleshooting and resolving issues. Hopefully, they will assist you whenever you next need to diagnose and fix a problem.

1. Look for the memory usage at the point of the crash. If this number is much lower than the per-process memory limit, as previously determined in the Server Manager Console, it means that the system as a whole is running low on memory and this process is also being affected.

2. If the process crashed at a memory utilization close to the per-process memory limit, evaluate the likely suspects that may be excessively consuming memory in the process.

3. Look at the global process level objects such as JDBTABLECACHE or database connections for any extreme numbers.

4. Analyze the per-session objects such as JDBTRANSACTIONS (manual), JDECACHEs, or DATAPOINTERs in each session.

In the dump file example, the culprit is the JDB caching of F0901 table, which has led to caching of close to a million (948,722) data rows in memory, leading to a "memory exhaustion" condition. This is easily solved either by dynamically clearing the cache from Server Manager or by removing this table from JDB cache in P98613 application.

Advanced Memory Leak Diagnostics: JADE and BMD

JADE and BMD are two advanced profiling tools that work cross-platform with production-level builds to diagnose memory leak issues. These profilers are used when the normal memory diagnostics do not yield adequate information. When the memory dumps do not reveal any of the traditional objects, it's possible to discern where the memory is being leaked by using these advanced memory diagnostics tools:

- **JADE** JDEHEAP Advanced Diagnostics Engine is a more sophisticated tool that can be engaged at runtime without bouncing the server. It tracks the memory consumed within the parameters of the JD Edwards API.

- **BMD** Business Function Memory Diagnostics is more appropriate for finding usable memory on the OS level; it has multiple levels.

BMD and JADE are both used to find the source of memory consumption or leaks within EnterpriseOne kernel space. However, they specialize in different use cases:

- **BMD level 1** offers an overall idea of memory consumption.
- **BMD levels 2 and 3** offer growth of memory as a function of business functions.

BMD helps isolate the business functions that are likely candidates for a memory consumption or leak. On the other hand, JADE is a finer diagnostic tool that works by collecting all memory allocations from the given enterprise server kernel. All memory that is unallocated at the end of the run can be considered a memory leak or excessive consumption—if start and stop points are chosen judiciously.

JADE Standard Mode JADE is delivered with EnterpriseOne and can be accessed through Server Manager. JADE allows you to identify the location of JDEHEAP memory leaks. This tool can be helpful in diagnosing memory issues. Figure 7-7 shows an example using porttest to create 10 threads that utilize a large amount of memory.

Configuration settings for JADE are accessed by selecting Logging and Diagnostics in the Configuration section of Server Manager (Figure 7-8). The tool can be easily turned on and off.

CAUTION
Do not use these settings unless investigating a tools-level problem, because system performance may be affected.

For memory investigations within the scope of business functions, use the buttons on the Server Manager process screen instead of these INI settings. JADE tracks memory usage of all JDEHEAP functions (`jdeAlloc`, `jdeCalloc`, `jdeRealloc`, and `jdeFree`). The JADE JDE.INI settings take effect whenever a process starts, but you can deactivate the settings by clicking the Start/Stop JADE button on the Server Manager process screen.

```
> porttest JDE JDE PD812 MEMORY 10
Start memory leak simulation test in 10 child threads
Begin simulation in thread 1, OS thread 4
Begin simulation in thread 2, OS thread 5
Begin simulation in thread 5, OS thread 8
Begin simulation in thread 7, OS thread 10
Begin simulation in thread 9, OS thread 12
Begin simulation in thread 3, OS thread 6
Begin simulation in thread 4, OS thread 7
Begin simulation in thread 10, OS thread 13
Begin simulation in thread 8, OS thread 11
Begin simulation in thread 6, OS thread 9
The test may take a while to run...

Porttest failed to allocate 1000 bytes of memory after process memory reached 4086184000 bytes
Porttest failed to allocate 1000 bytes of memory after process memory reached 4086208000 bytes
Porttest failed to allocate 1000 bytes of memory after process memory reached 4086208000 bytes
Porttest failed to allocate 1000 bytes of memory after process memory reached 4086208000 bytes
Porttest failed to allocate 1000 bytes of memory after process memory reached 4086120000 bytes
End simulation in thread 2, OS thread 5
Porttest failed to allocate 1000 bytes of memory after process memory reached 4086208000 bytes
Porttest failed to allocate 1000 bytes of memory after process memory reached 4086208000 bytes
End simulation in thread 4, OS thread 7
End simulation in thread 8, OS thread 11
End simulation in thread 6, OS thread 9
End simulation in thread 3, OS thread 6
Porttest failed to allocate 1000 bytes of memory after process memory reached 4086208000 bytes
End simulation in thread 5, OS thread 8
End simulation in thread 10, OS thread 13
Porttest failed to allocate 1000 bytes of memory after process memory reached 4085864000 bytes
End simulation in thread 1, OS thread 4
End simulation in thread 7, OS thread 10
Porttest failed to allocate 1000 bytes of memory after process memory reached 4086208000 bytes
End simulation in thread 9, OS thread 12
Stop memory leak simulation test in 10 child threads.

Congratulations!  Porttest completed successfully.

All Done!
Bye!
```

FIGURE 7-7. *JADE example using porttest*

All JADE logging is placed in the JDEDEBUG log files, even if JDEDEBUG logging is turned off in the JDE.INI.

Following are two use case examples.

Use Case 1

In this use case we can determine, at the end of an application's run, whether any unallocated memory exists. If so, JADE can determined where it is being allocated.

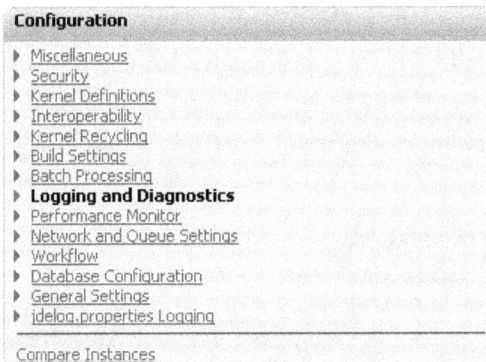

FIGURE 7-8. *Configuration section of Server Manager*

If an application is known to have a memory leak, follow these steps:

1. Launch the EnterpriseOne application to the application entry point.

2. Associate the application to a given call object by correlating them using Server Manager "Search for User Resources" or the enterprise server processes list for the Call Object Kernel or within the HTML Instance Remote Env column of HTML Web Sessions.

3. Drill into the Call Object Kernel and click the Start JADE button.

4. Execute the predefined transactions on the application.

5. When done, click the Dump JADE button.

6. Exit the application and click on Stop JADE.

7. Click Parse JADE to see the possible leak locations.

Use Case 2
If a running process, such as runbatch, has a runaway memory leak, follow these steps:

1. Go into Server Manager for the enterprise server instance and you can see if a process is using a large amount of memory as shown in the graph in Figure 7-9. The legend and sorted memory column will show you which process is using a large amount of memory. Drill into the known process.

2. Enable JADE by clicking Start JADE in the Diagnostics section as shown in Figure 7-10.

3. Let the process run for the representative period of the leak.

4. Press the Stop JADE button.

5. Click Parse JADE to see the possible leak locations.

6. Click the Download JADE Parse of Log File link (Figure 7-11).

7. Open the downloaded parse file in your favorite CSV reader (Figure 7-12) and analyze the memory allocation patterns that may suggest the location of the leaks.

JADE Advanced Mode   JADE Advanced Mode provides a deeper level of information for analysis of situations when Standard Mode is not able to resolve the issue. For example, if you are working to resolve an issue of high memory usage, but you don't see any corresponding rise in memory of any known EnterpriseOne objects, either in analyzing the graphs or using the diagnostic buttons, you'll need to use Advanced Mode.

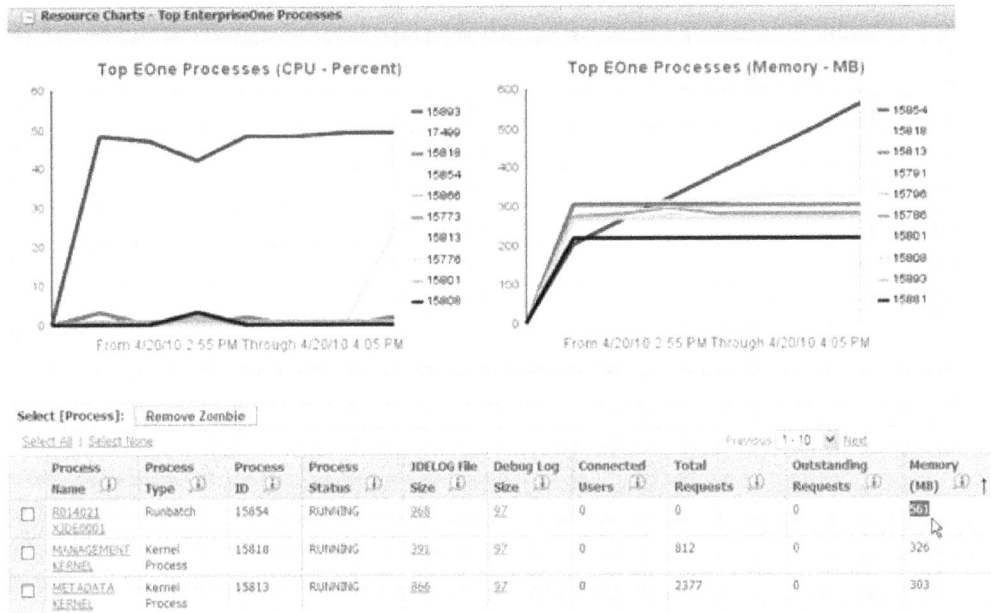

FIGURE 7-9.   *Top memory usage identified by graph and by sorting on Memory column*

Three levels of JADE logging are available:

■   **JADE level 1** logs a summary of memory usage.

■   **JADE level 2** logs the summary, plus detail lines for each BSFN-scoped memory pointer.

■   **JADE level 3** logs the summary, plus detail lines for all JDEHEAP memory pointers.

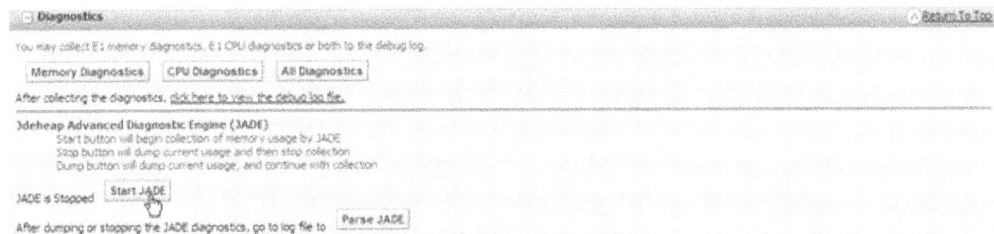

FIGURE 7-10.   *Click the Start JADE button.*

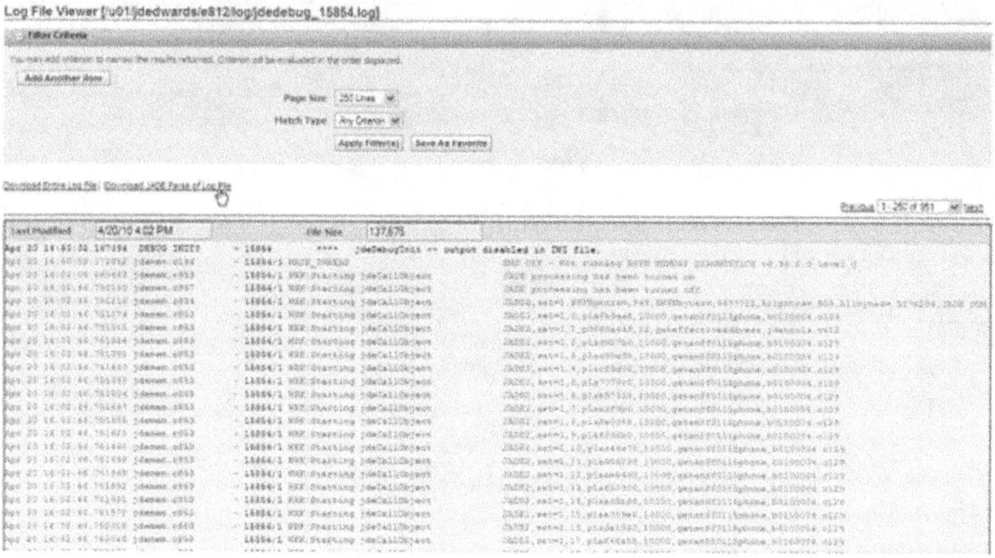

FIGURE 7-11. *Click the Download JADE Parse of Log File link*

	A	B	C	D	E	F	G	H
1	seqnum	month/dat	setNumbe		BSFNpntrs		BSFNbytes	
2	1	02:46.8	set=1	BSFNpntrs	946	BSFNbytes=	9377722	Allpntrs=
3	seqnum	month/dat	setNumber	indexInSet	pointer	memSize	bsfnName	fileNameLineNumber
4	2	02:46.8	set=1	0	p1afe9ee8	10000	getan8f0115phone	b0100004.c129
5	3	02:46.8	set=1	1	p0060a648	12	geteffectiveaddress	jdetools.c412
6	4	02:46.8	set=1	2	p1ad927b0	10000	getan8f0115phone	b0100004.c129
7	5	02:46.8	set=1	3	p1ac35e08	10000	getan8f0115phone	b0100004.c129
8	6	02:46.8	set=1	4	p1acf3d00	10000	getan8f0115phone	b0100004.c129
9	7	02:46.8	set=1	5	p1a7070c0	10000	getan8f0115phone	b0100004.c129
10	8	02:46.8	set=1	6	p1ab97358	10000	getan8f0115phone	b01000[illegible]129
11	9	02:46.8	set=1	7	p1aa3f9b0	10000	getan8f0115phone	b0100004.c129
12	10	02:46.8	set=1	8	p1a9e0058	10000	getan8f0115phone	b0100004.c129
13	11	02:46.8	set=1	9	p1a8836b0	10000	getan8f0115phone	b0100004.c129
14	12	02:46.8	set=1	10	p1ac44e78	10000	getan8f0115phone	b0100004.c129
15	13	02:46.8	set=1	11	p1a656238	10000	getan8f0115phone	b0100004.c129
16	14	02:46.8	set=1	12	p1aaeb4d0	10000	getan8f0115phone	b0100004.c129
17	15	02:46.8	set=1	13	p1a630900	10000	getan8f0115phone	b0100004.c129
18	16	02:46.8	set=1	14	p1aac5b98	10000	getan8f0115phone	b0100004.c129
19	17	02:46.8	set=1	15	p1ae089e8	10000	getan8f0115phone	b0100004.c129
20	18	02:46.8	set=1	16	p1ada1330	10000	getan8f0115phone	b0100004.c129
21	19	02:46.8	set=1	17	p1af4fa58	10000	getan8f0115phone	b0100004.c129
22	20	02:46.8	set=1	18	p1a7c3450	10000	getan8f0115phone	b0100004.c129
23	21	02:46.8	set=1	19	p1ac54ee8	10000	getan8f0115phone	b0100004.c129
24	22	02:46.8	set=1	20	p1a666aa8	10000	getan8f0115phone	b0100004.c129
25	23	02:46.8	set=1	21	p1aafbd40	10000	getan8f0115phone	b0100004.c129
26	24	02:46.8	set=1	22	p1a67a008	10000	getan8f0115phone	b0100004.c129
27	25	02:46.8	set=1	23	p1ae8ece8	10000	getan8f0115phone	b0100004.c129
28	26	02:46.8	set=1	24	p1ad05080	10000	getan8f0115phone	b0100004.c129
29	27	02:46.8	set=1	25	p1ab0f2a0	10000	getan8f0115phone	b0100004.c129
30	28	02:46.8	set=1	26	p1ae9f248	10000	getan8f0115phone	b0100004.c129
31	29	02:46.8	set=1	27	p1aba86d8	10000	getan8f0115phone	b0100004.c129
32	30	02:46.8	set=1	28	p1a892230	10000	getan8f0115phone	b0100004.c129

FIGURE 7-12. *Parsed JADE log file*

You can start JADE memory tracking based on specified BSFN triggers, and you can turn on debug logging when the BSFN trigger is met. JADE data is dumped to the log file based on a minimum time interval. The INI-initiated JADE tracking is terminated whenever you click the Stop JADE button on the Server Manager process detail screen for the call object process being reviewed.

JADE Configuration   JADE can be configured by accessing the JADE Configuration section in Server Manager. To access this section, do the following:

1. In Server Manager, select the EnterpriseOne server.

2. Select Logging and Diagnostics in the Configuration section (Figure 7-13).

The fields used to configure JADE are explained in Table 7-1.

Troubleshooting with BMD   The BMD tool can also be used to troubleshoot memory issues, and it can be accessed from Server Manager like JADE. This memory profiler can track and isolate memory leaks to a particular business function and provides output of memory in .csv format. The BMD is considered a last resort to identify the cause of memory problems.

There are three levels of BMD:

- **BMD level 1** provides memory usage through the lifetime of all processes to help narrow down where the problem is occurring.

- **BMD level 2** provides information about BSFNs (for BSFN levels 1 and 2) after the kernel memory exceeds a given threshold.

- **BMD level 3** provides information about BSFNs (all BSFN levels) after the kernel memory exceeds a given threshold within a specified BSFN running at a specified level.

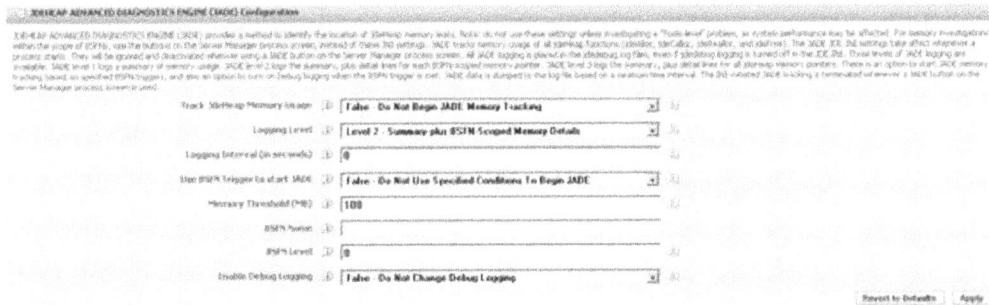

FIGURE 7-13. *JADE configuration section*

Field	Description
Track JDEHEAP Memory Usage	INI Filename: /u01/jdedwards/e812/ini/JDE.INI INI Section Name: JADE INI Entry: trackMemUsage Default Value: 0 Allowed Values: False: Do Not Begin JADE Memory Tracking (0) True: Begin JADE Memory Tracking At Process Start (1) Track JDEHEAP memory usage by JADE. The tracking will start with the first JDEHEAP usage of the process. It will terminate when the process shuts down and when any of the JADE buttons on the Server Manager process screen are used.
Logging Level	INI Filename: /u01/jdedwards/e812/ini/JDE.INI INI Section Name: JADE INI Entry: logLevel Default Value: 2 Allowed Values: Level 1: Summary of JDEHEAP Memory Usage (1) Level 2: Summary plus BSFN-Scoped Memory Details (2) Level 3: Summary plus All JDEHEAP Memory Details (3) Level of logging the JADE diagnostics. Level 1 logs a summary of BSFN-scoped pointers and of all pointers. Level 2 logs the summary, plus detail lines for each BSFN-scoped JDEHEAP usage. Level 3 logs the summary, plus detail lines for all JDEHEAP usage.
Logging Interval (In Seconds)	INI Filename: /u01/jdedwards/e812/ini/JDE.INI INI Section Name: JADE INI Entry: logInterval Default Value: 0 Logging interval (in seconds) between dumping of JADE data to the debug log file. This is a minimum interval, not an exact interval. No dumping will occur if there has been no JDEHEAP activity since the last dumped data. This interval-based dumping will be terminated if any of the JADE buttons on the Server Manager process screen are clicked.

(continues)

TABLE 7-1. *JADE Configuration Values*

Field	Description
Use BSFN Trigger To Start JADE	INI Filename: /u01/jdedwards/e812/ini/JDE.INI INI Section Name: JADE INI Entry: bsfnTriggerUseTrigger Default Value: 0 Allowed Values: False: Do Not Use Specified Conditions To Begin JADE (0) True: Use Specified Conditions To Begin JADE (1) Use BSFN Trigger to begin JADE memory tracking. The BSFN-related trigger conditions are given in this section of the INI file. When the trigger conditions are met, JADE memory tracking begins. The trigger does not cause any JADE data to be dumped to the log files.
Memory Threshold (MB)	INI Filename: /u01/jdedwards/e812/ini/JDE.INI INI Section Name: JADE INI Entry: bsfnTriggerMemThresholdMB Default Value: 100 Memory threshold (in MB) to begin JADE tracking of JDEHEAP memory usage. Can be combined with a specified BSFN name and level to trigger when tracking starts.
BSFN Name	INI Filename: /u01/jdedwards/e812/ini/JDE.INI INI Section Name: JADE INI Entry: bsfnTriggerBsfnName Business Function name. When combined with the BSFN level and memory threshold, triggers JADE tracking.
BSFN Level	INI Filename: /u01/jdedwards/e812/ini/JDE.INI INI Section Name: JADE INI Entry: bsfnTriggerBsfnLevel Default Value: 0 Business Function level. When combined with the BSFN name and memory threshold, triggers JADE tracking. Not used when set to zero.
Enable Debug Logging	INI Filename: /u01/jdedwards/e812/ini/JDE.INI INI Section Name: JADE INI Entry: bsfnTriggerEnableDebug Default Value: 0 Allowed Values: False: Do Not Change Debug Logging (0) True: Turn On Debug Logging When JADE Is Triggered (1) Option to turn on debug logging. If selected, debug logging will be dynamically turned on when trigger conditions for JADE are met. This does not change the debug logging settings of JDE.INI.

TABLE 7-1. *JADE Configuration Values*

The first level is sampled memory logging that can be used for all types of kernel processes. The second and third levels are BSFN-specific memory logging. The types of kernel processes that run BSFNs are COKs, UBEs, and subsystems.

The BMD data is written to the debug log file, even if debug logging is not turned on. The trigger for the third BMD level can also be used to activate full debug logging, to provide a detailed context around the memory problems.

NOTE
Waiting to turn on debug logging until after the trigger conditions are met can eliminate huge debug log files, which might take a lot of analysis to identify the portion of the log file that is related to the actual problem.

Following are the BMD logged values:

- **BMD level 1** Collected at the allocation frequency specified in the BMD configuration—Allocation frequency:
  - Current CPU percent
  - Current total process memory being used
- **BMD level 2** Collected at the exit point of each BSFN after the specified memory threshold is hit for BSFNs at levels 1 and 2 only:
  - Current CPU percent
  - Current total process memory being used
  - Change in the memory during the BSFN (delta-memory)
  - BSFN name
  - BSFN level
- **BMD level 3** Collected at the exit point of each BSFN after the specified threshold of memory *and* business function name *and* business function level (any level) is hit:
  - Current CPU percent
  - Current total process memory being used
  - Change in the memory during the BSFN (delta-memory)
  - BSFN name

- BSFN level
- Debug logging (optional)

BMD Configuration   Follow these steps to configure BMD:

1. Select the enterprise server instance in Server Manager.

2. You should see the *<EnterpriseOne Enterprise Server>* instance.

3. Make sure that the server is up and running.

4. Go to the Configuration section.

5. Click the Logging And Diagnostics link.

6. Find the BSFN Memory Diagnostics (BMD) Configuration section.

The BMD JDE.INI settings specify the BMD level, and then the trigger conditions within each level. The settings are found in the JDE.INI in a block called [BSFN MEMORY DIAGNOSTICS]. They can be accessed from Server Manager by clicking the link called Logging And Diagnostics.

The primary BMD setting is the BMD level, called bmdLevel. That can be 0 (BMD off), or 1, 2, or 3 (BMD level).

For BMD level 1 (Figure 7-14), the trigger condition is based on the allocation frequency (allocFrequency). That is a count of all calls to the system-level

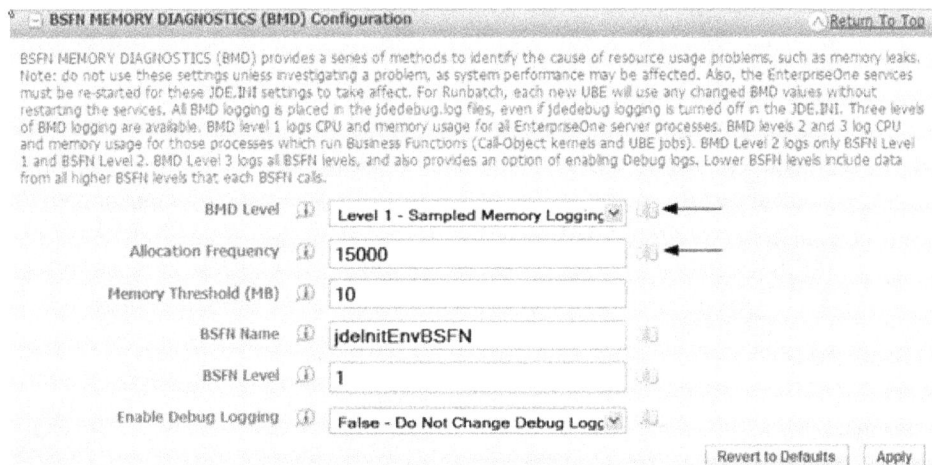

FIGURE 7-14. *BSFN Memory Diagnostics (BMD) Configuration section – Level 1*

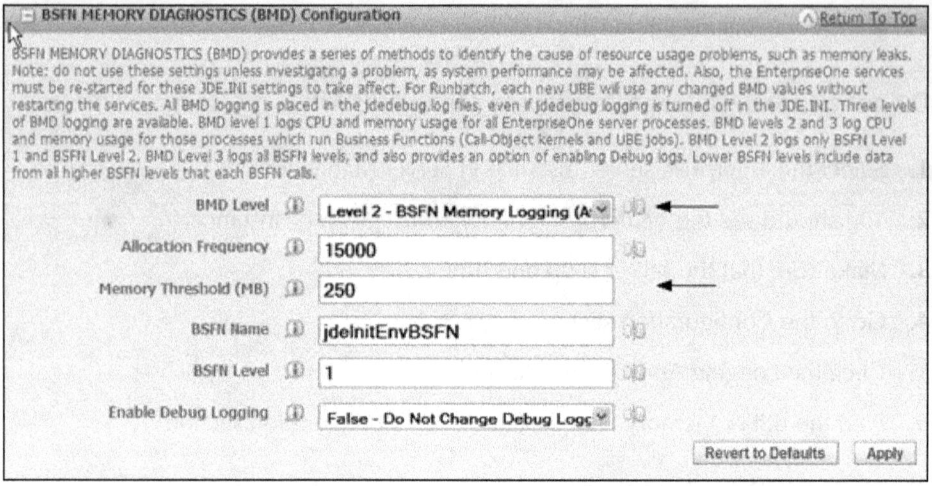

FIGURE 7-15. *BSFN Memory Diagnostics (BMD) Configuration section – Level 2*

allocation functions (`malloc`, `calloc`, and `realloc`). The default setting is 15000, with a minimum of 7000. At 15000, for active COKs, this can result in memory-level logging several times per minute.

For BMD level 2 (Figure 7-15), the trigger condition is passing a specified memory threshold (`memThresholdMB`). After that memory threshold is first passed, there will be BMD logging each time a BSFN level 1 or 2 exits.

For BMD level 3 (Figures 7-16 and 7-17), the trigger is based on a combination of three conditions: a specified memory threshold (`memThresholdMB`, same as BMD level 2), a specified BSFN name (`bsfnName`), and a specified BSFN level (`bsfnLevel`). After those three conditions are met, there will be BMD logging each time a BSFN (all BSFN levels) exits. At BMD level 3, you have the option of turning on full debug logging that starts when the trigger conditions are met. The optional setting is called `enableDebug`, with possible values of 0 (debug logging unchanged) or 1 (debug logging turned on if it had been off).

The EnterpriseOne services must be restarted for any changed BMD settings to take effect. For runbatch processes, each new UBE will use any BMD values that are changed before that UBE starts.

BMD Parsing   The BMD feature also includes an easy parsing system that is set up through links on the Server Manager Log File Viewer (Figure 7-18), which can be accessed through the Server Manager console.

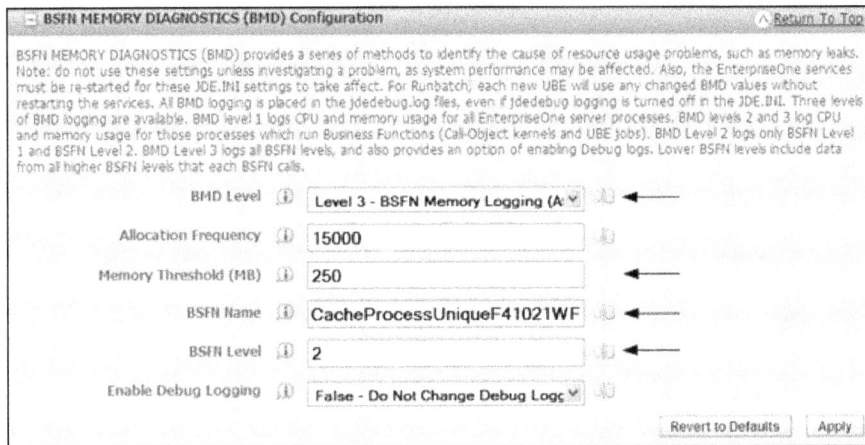

FIGURE 7-16. *BMD Configuration section – Level 3, Enable Debug Logging = False*

Following are the steps required to access BMD parsing:

1. Select the enterprise server instance in Server Manager.

2. You should see the *<EnterpriseOne Enterprise Server>* instance.

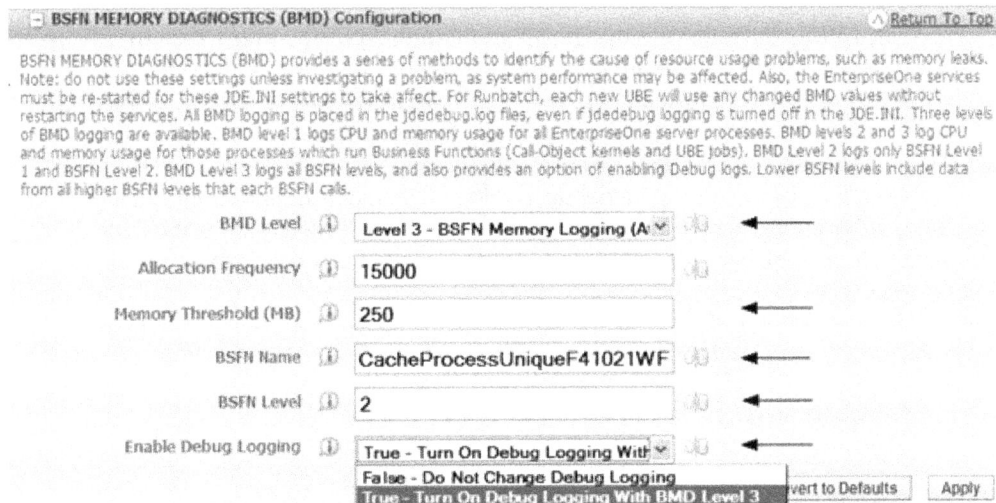

FIGURE 7-17. *BMD Configuration section – Level 3, Enable Debug Logging = True*

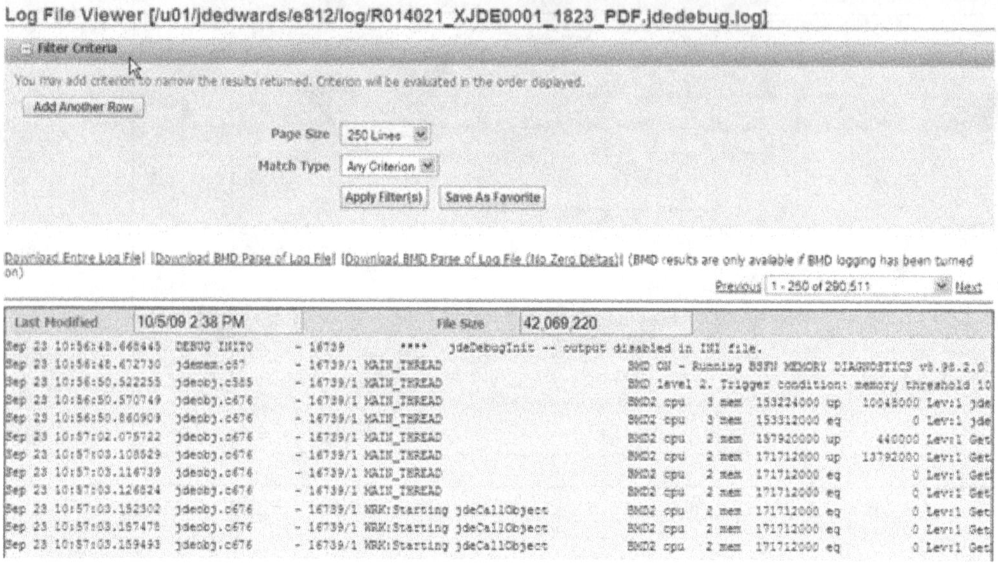

FIGURE 7-18. *Log File Viewer*

3. Make sure that the server is up and running.

4. Go to the *<Available Log Files>* section.

5. Select a BMD parsing option link (Figure 7-19).

For level 1 BMD data, there is one parsing option that puts all of the data in CSV format. For levels 2 and 3, there are two parsing options. One brings all BMD data for the BSFNs into the CSV format. The other excludes those BMD data rows which have a zero delta. The second option presumably keeps the most interesting BMD data, while reducing the CSV file size substantially.

For COKs, the corresponding jdedebug_pid.log file contains the BMD information. If a UBE is still running, the corresponding jdedebug_pid.log file contains the BMD information. If the UBE has completed, the log file is moved to the /printqueue folder.

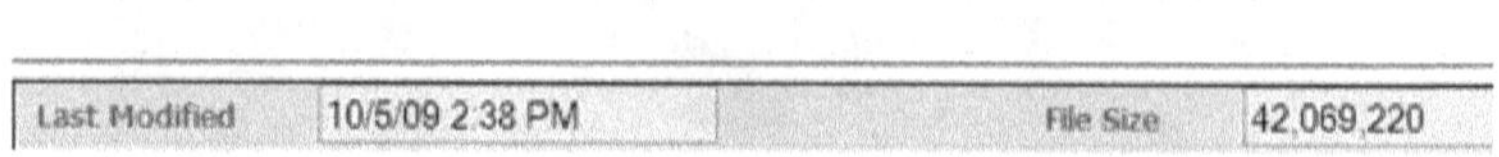

FIGURE 7-19. *BMD parsing option links*

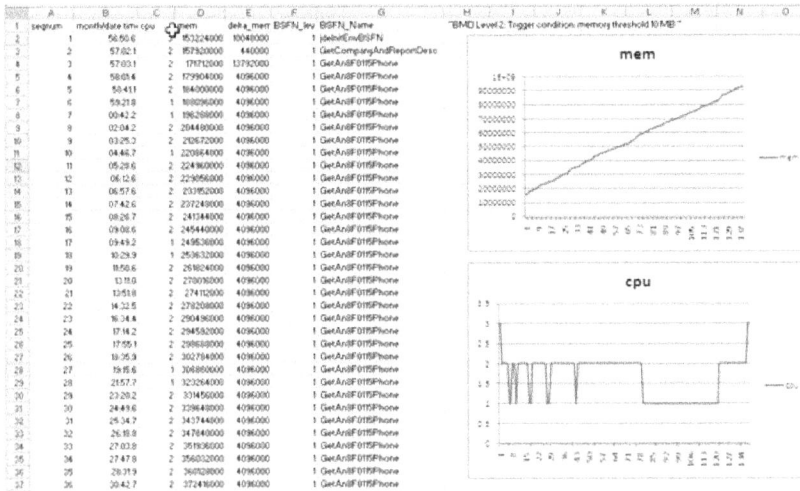

FIGURE 7-20. *BMD data parsed and retrieved in CSV format*

Copy the UBE-BMD log manually from the /printqueue folder to the /log folder so that the log file can be processed by BMD parsing within Server Manager.

The BMD data is parsed and retrieved in a CSV format (Figure 7-20). That parsed data can be saved to a file on the local machine, or it can be entered directly into a spreadsheet application, such as Microsoft Excel or OpenOffice Calc. Within Excel, the BMD data is easily searched and graphed.

Kernel Processes and Common Tuning Recommendations

The following sections cover JD Edwards kernel processes and tuning recommendations. A wide range of both commonly tuned (UBE kernel) and rarely tuned (XTS kernel) processes are covered. We'll start with a discussion of JDENET.

When EnterpriseOne Services are started on Enterprise Server, a parent (JDENET_n) process is initiated. Requests from a client or server to a server are handled through JDENET_n processes to communicate the request between different types of kernels.

This parent process initiates other child processes called *kernel processes* (JDENET_k). Any of these JDENET processes can also start new kernel processes as new requests are received. JDENET_k processes can be configured in the JDE.INI file. A minimum setting for JDNET_n is 2: one is the parent process and another is the child process. It is best to have at least two child JDENET_n (JDENET_k) process plus one parent JDENET_n.

A single JDENET_n process can handle a maximum of 1024 connections. The JDENET process or the parent process that is started when you start JDE services can launch the required kernels as and when request messages arrive from clients. When a request is made from an EnterpriseOne client or server, the message queues, which are interprocess communication (IPC) resources, are generated by calls to the operating system from EnterpriseOne processes. The packets are routed to the JDENET_n job from a client or another server and are placed in a message queue based on the type of process. This architecture also allows BSFNs and UBEs to execute remotely.

Based on the message identifier, the JDENET will decide which kernel would handle this message, and if this kernel is not available, it will be started automatically. The only kernels that we usually set to autostart are the Scheduler kernel (this is one kernel that has to be set to autostart due to design complications) and the COK (set to autostart only for performance purposes, and they are not mandatory).

JDENET Reserved Kernel

This kernel is used for internal purposes and testing. The value for this kernel process in INI should not be changed.

UBE Kernel

The UBE kernel receives requests from clients and schedules batch jobs in the job queue. A UBE kernel inserts a record in the job table. The value of the job queue name field of the inserted record indicates the job queue assigned to the new batch job.

Whenever a UBE kernel inserts a record in the job table, the batch job status field of the inserted record is always set to W (wait status). After inserting, for OneWorld queues, UBE kernel sends a message to the Queue kernel to schedule the job. For iSeries native queues, the UBE kernel does an SBMJOB to the native queue.

UBE kernels are also responsible for retrieving all non-BI Publisher UBE output to clients, whether those outputs are PDF, CSV, logs, or other kinds of output.

Recommendations

Turn to the following for more information about UBE kernel tuning:

- Performance and Tuning: UBE Performance and Tuning (Doc ID 748333.1)

- EnterpriseOne UBE Performance Tips (Doc ID 825373.1)

- E1: UBE: New utilities for Batch Monitoring Tools release 8.98 (Doc ID 803246.1)

- ■ E1: UBE: How to turn on logging for UBE submitted on server from fat client/web (Doc ID 662087.1)

- ■ E1: SCHED: How to cause the UBE scheduler server to not catch up after being down (Doc ID 657826.1)

- ■ E1: SEC: Errors in Call Object and UBE Kernel Logs for User Profiles (Doc ID 815013.1)

- ■ E1: OS: UBE Kernel zombie upon submission to AS400 (Doc ID 796014.1)

- ■ E1: UBE: UBEs die after printqueue filled up (Doc ID 636233.1)

- ■ E1: UBE: Unable to Submit UBEs to AS/400 Enterprise Server (Doc ID 646270.1)

- ■ E1: UBE: What Is the Process ID value specified in Work With Submitted Jobs? (Doc ID 639086.1)

- ■ E1: UBE: Unable to run UBES on AS400 Enterprise Server (Doc ID 664626.1)

- ■ E1: UBE: Failed to validate auth token error when submitting UBES to server (Doc ID 638685.1)

- ■ E1: UBE: Configuring Multiple Job Queues for Use by OneWorld (Doc ID 644511.1)

Replication Kernel

This kernel processes data replication requests. It has been deprecated starting with version 8.9 and is mainly a throwback to previous releases.

Security Kernel

The Security kernel processes security server requests. It also handles all user profile- and security-related table updates via messaging from the COK (or Win32 client) when the appropriate BSFNs are called. The Security kernel provides security tokens to all EnterpriseOne server processes such as JDENET_K, runube, runbatch, and porttest, and also EnterpriseOne client processes such as fat client, JAS client, Interop Connector clients, and Real Time Events (RTE). Upon initialization, the security kernel is contacted by all kernels.

The Security kernel will be notified by appropriate BSFNs whenever modifications are made to user profile/security record/security tables. The Security kernel is not multithreaded.

Recommendations

Turn to the following for more information about Security kernel tuning:

- E1: SEC: How To Avoid LDAP Related Messages In Security Kernel Log When Not Configured? (Doc ID 827956.1)

- E1: SEC: Changing the JDE User Password (Doc ID 626139.1)

Lock Manager Kernel

Designed to process Transaction Manager and Lock Manager requests, Lock Manager is used to monitor time/date stamp changes to records.

Call Object Kernel

The Call Object kernel (COK) runs the business functions on the server based on the message received from clients through JDENET. When an application calls the BSFN for the first time, JDENET will determine the type of message received and will route the request over to the COK based on the BSFN message type. If the user has already established the COK process, the JDENET will route the BSFN to the same COK process. If a UBE triggers the BSFN, it will run the BSFN within the UBE process. The only time the BSFN will run on the different COK process is when the BSFN is OCM-mapped to a different server. Currently, only the COK supports multithread processing. All other kernels are meant to handle data/cache one at a time.

Recommendations

The following three settings are merely a good starting point for tuning. Every customer's environment and user case is different, and they may achieve better performance by tweaking these settings based on user response time and outstanding requests by running netwm. You can turn to the documents listed here for more information about COB kernel tuning:

- 1 kernel for 6–10 interactive users

- ThreadPoolSize = 30

- ThreadPoolSizeIncrement = 10

- E1: KER: Troubleshooting Call Object Kernel Zombie Issues and Gathering Information for Oracle Support (Doc ID 837800.1)

- E1: SAW: How to use web SAW to turn on JDEDEBUG for a user's call object kernel (Doc ID 662290.1)

NOTE
*Set one kernel for every 10–15 users if you are
not running Vertex. Use one kernel for every 5–10
users if you are running Vertex. If you are on an
IBM i platform, increase these numbers by 10 (for
example, one kernel for every 20–25 users if you are
not running Vertex on an IBM i platform).*

JDBNet Kernel

The JDBNet kernel processes database requests using a client and server. It can also
be configured to process server-to-server requests: one server functions as a JDBNet
client and the other functions as a JDBNet server. JDBNet eliminates the need for
database-specific network software. All database requests are transported to the
JDBNet server, processed in a local database, and the results are transported back to
the JDBNet client. Note that typically, database drivers such as SQLNET, ODBC, and
DBDR are the preferred methods. JDBNet is used if a driver for that platform is not
available. JDBNet, when used, is normally from a non-production server where the
workload is much lower. For example, Linux Enterprise server could be used to
access an IBM iserver for a test configuration, but you would normally not want to
operate production level volumes using this combination.

Recommendations

- One kernel is recommended for every 50 to 60 users.

- You need not have this kernel running if users are not using JDBNet drivers.

Package Install Kernel

As the name suggests, the Package Install kernel processes package installation
requests to the server. It is used when packages are deployed to the Enterprise Server.
The Package Install kernel is valid only for releases prior to 8.12, and as of 8.12, this
kernel is no longer used.

Management Kernel

The Management kernel is the process type used to instantiate the embedded
management agent. The embedded management agent reports runtime information
between the Enterprise Server and the Server Manager console. This kernel setting
should not be set larger than 1.

Recommendations

Turn to the following for more information about Management kernel tuning:

- E1:SVM: Missing Enterprise Server Runtime Metrics on Server Manager Console Troubleshooting Steps (Doc ID 867232.1)

- E1: SVM: Runtime Metrics is Unavailable When Firewall is Enabled (Doc ID 876702.1)

- JD Edwards EnterpriseOne Tools 8.98 Server Manager Guide, Update (Doc ID 705509.1)

- E1: SVM: How to turn on logging for interactive apps in Server Manager (Doc ID 658887.1)

Scheduler Kernel

The Scheduler kernel handles Scheduler application requests. The Scheduler kernel launches batch processes in a server/environment/user combination, based on the information in the Job Master table (F91300). After Scheduler is started, JDENET keeps it in a wait state by calling the Scheduler dispatch function every minute with an idle message. This idle message allows the Scheduler process to check whether it should launch a job or monitor the jobs that are running. In addition, JDENET also sends the Scheduler any message sent from the workstation (for example, messages that new job schedules have been added).

Recommendations

Turn to the following for more information about Scheduler kernel tuning:

- E1: SCHED: How Scheduler Server Works When Daylight Saving Is In Effect (Doc ID 833253.1)

- E1: SCHED: Commonly Asked Questions About EnterpriseOne (JDE) Scheduler (Doc ID 849457.1)

- E1: SCHED: Setup Scheduler on multiple servers (Doc ID 659655.1)

Package Build Kernel

The Package Build kernel is responsible for processing package build requests.

UBE Subsystem Kernel

The UBE Subsystem kernel controls the submission of UBE subsystem requests. The This kernel should be set to one process, because the role/functionality of this kernel is to add/update/delete records from table F986113. If this kernel is set to more than one subsystem kernel, it will cause problems when adding/updating/deleting data against F986113.

Workflow Kernel

The Workflow kernel is responsible for handling workflow requests. The kernel's parameters are rarely changed, except as noted in the "Recommendation" section (or to turn the kernel off and on). The same set of parameters applies for all applications using the Workflow kernel.

Recommendation

■ One kernel is recommended for every 30 users.

Queue Kernel

The Queue kernel handles the job queues. It launches jobs based on the Queue configuration in F986130, which is configured by the application – P986130 (Work with Job Queues). After launching jobs, the Queue kernel monitors the jobs that run on the system, catching those that crash, dumping the crashed child processes' call stacks to the Queue kernel log, and then moving crashed jobs to the E status and their logs to the PrintQueue directory.

XML Transaction Kernel

The XML Transaction kernel process handles XML requests. This kernel has XML-based interoperability that runs as an Enterprise Resource Planning (ERP) kernel process. You can also use XML Transaction with a messaging adapter. The kernel interacts with interface tables (Z tables) to update the ERP database or to retrieve ERP data. You can create one XML document that includes both updates to ERP and retrieval of data from ERP.

Event Notification Kernel

The Event Notification (EVN) kernel, also known as the event distributor, is an ERP kernel process. The EVN kernel manages the subscribers and notifies them when an event occurs. The EVN kernel is shared by Z events, Real Time Events (RTEs), and XAPI events. This kernel processes real-time events and XML documents generated by the Interoperability Event Observer, as well as Z file events. It publishes all E1 events to subscribers.

The Enterprise Server jde.ini file must be properly configured to support Z, real-time, and XAPI event generation. Use a text editor to edit and verify specific settings in the Enterprise Server jde.ini file.

Interoperability Event Observer Kernel

The Interoperability Event Observer kernel processes information from business functions calling real-time APIs and uses that information to create an XML or a Z file that is publishable to subscribers by the Event Notification kernel.

XML Dispatch Kernel

The XML Dispatch kernel sends XML messages to their proper kernel. XML Dispatch is XML-based interoperability that runs as an ERP kernel process. This kernel is the ERP central entry point for all XML documents.

For incoming XML documents, XML Dispatch identifies what kind of document is arriving to ERP and sends the document to the appropriate kernel for processing. If XML Dispatch does not recognize the document, it sends the document to the XML Transformation Service (XTS) kernel to recognize and transform into native ERP format. After XTS transforms the document, the document is sent back to XML Dispatch to be sent to the appropriate kernel for processing.

For outgoing documents, XML Dispatch is able to remember whether the request document was transformed into ERP native format. If the incoming request was transformed, then the outgoing response document is sent to XTS for transformation from native ERP format back into the format of the original request. After XTS transforms the document, the document is sent to XML Dispatch to distribute to the originator.

The XML Dispatch kernel is able to route and load-balance the XML documents. For example, if many XML CallObject message types are arriving at once, XML Dispatch will try to instantiate a new COK. You can set up the number of instances that a kernel can have in the jde.ini file. For example, if you set the number of instances for the COK to 5, if more than one CallObject document comes into ERP, XML Dispatch sees that a particular kernel is busy and instantiates another one (up to five). XML Dispatch is able to recognize new kernel definitions (such as XAPI) if the kernel is defined in the jde.ini file.

XTS Kernel

This kernel transforms XML messages from one type to another. The XTS kernel must be defined in the server jde.ini file. The name of the configuration file is retrieved from the config_file system variable in the JVM, and these property settings are part of a configuration file other than jde.ini. The jde.ini file does not require any special configurations, other than defining the XTS kernel.

XML Service Kernel

The XML Service kernel processes inbound XAPI messages. The XML Service kernel saves the XML document to disk, creates a unique handle, and then calls the callback business function that is provided in the DXAPIROUTE XAPI method ID element in the XML document. For specific information about the XML Service kernel, see the online API documentation.

Metadata Kernel

The Metadata kernel processes XML spec access requests. The way that BSFNs process on the server has changed with release 8.12 and Tools release 8.96 because of the change from Table Access Method (TAM) spec to XML spec files. The Metadata kernel changes XML into C structures that will be readable by the COK, which is the only kernel that uses the Metadata kernel. Other kernels contain an embedded JVM that performs the XML spec conversion.

Recommendations

The following recommendations and information apply to Metadata kernel tuning:

- For large implementations, it is a good practice to have one Metadata kernel for every 300 users. This generally keeps the metadata kernels down to under four.

- E1: KER: Metadata Kernel Performance and Tuning Guide (Doc ID 820367.1)

XML Publisher / BI Publisher Kernel

The XML Publisher / BI Publisher kernel handles XML publishing requests.

Recommendations

Turn to the following for more information about XML Publisher / BI Publisher kernel tuning:

- E1: XMLP: How to Obtain Jas Logs for the XML Publisher Kernel (Doc ID 782159.1)

- E1: XMLP: JDE.INI Kernel Settings for XMLP: Publisher (Doc ID 654237.1)

- E1: XMLP: Is There Specific Setup to Improve XML Publisher Performance? (Doc ID 761225.1)

- E1: XMLP: How to Encode Barcodes with BI Publisher for EnterpriseOne (Doc ID 782809.1)

Conclusion

This chapter covered various methods of troubleshooting issues. It also covered the inner workings of various technologies in Oracle JD Edwards EnterpriseOne. In addition some recommended settings have been discussed. The topics of this chapter include but are not limited to the following:

- Database connections

- SQL packages

- JDENET

- JD Edwards kernels

With the knowledge imparted in this chapter, you should be empowered to tune your system, troubleshoot issues, and understand how the technologies work. Reading the additional documents listed in this chapter will also help improve your knowledge. Using the tools explained in this chapter will help you the next time you have an issue to resolve.

CHAPTER

8

Tuning by Tier:
The Database Tier (Oracle)

This chapter on Oracle database tuning covers specific Oracle database configuration parameters, operating system (OS) tuning considerations such as interprocess communication (IPC) settings and disk configuration. This chapter also covers some of the Oracle SQL*Plus dynamic view commands that can be useful in performance tuning the Oracle database with EnterpriseOne.

This chapter covers the performance tuning of the Oracle database tier of the EnterpriseOne architecture. This chapter will also discuss the "large knobs" that have the biggest impact on the Oracle database in terms of changing its performance characteristics. Tuning these values is your first task in the tuning and review process. The chapter also discusses other Oracle database tuning settings that are more finely tuned "smaller knobs" with lesser impact to performance.

A large part of this chapter covers the Oracle database utilities such as Automatic Workload Repository (AWR) reports, specific Oracle dynamic performance views, and the use of Automatic Database Diagnostic Monitor (ADDM), Automatic Shared Memory Management (ASMM), baselines, and thresholds. SQL tuning and index and optimizer topics are also covered. Finally, issues related to tuning the instance, including memory components and initialization parameters, are covered as they relate to the EnterpriseOne application.

Database Tuning Overview

Before discussing Oracle database tuning and providing some of the areas in the database management that are common targets of modification from the default values for EnterpriseOne, a brief comment on a few basic principles will be introduced.

Principle 1: The Principle of Best Benefit

The tuning that provides the best benefit, and the business and technical requirements and that can be verified by easily identified metrics is better than tuning that do not exhibit such characteristics. A *metric* is simply the rate of change of a statistic measured over time. Of course, tuning that results in an efficient and optimized environment is preferred over a tuning method that is slower and less efficient.

Note three important aspects of the preceding statements:

- Most processes can have a number of definitions for "best benefit."

- Business and technical requirements are often not defined or are so nebulous in their definition that they leave too much room for interpretation.

- Many metrics can be evaluated to determine performance characteristics. It is important that you measure the correct metric for the correct problem definition to determine whether the goal is met when assessing the performance of a selected issue.

Although certain tuning can provide the "best benefit" in one circumstance, it may provide detrimental effects in other areas of the application. A good example of this is database tuning of indexes. Index tuning should be approached with great care, because tuning an index on a key table to optimize a specific batch process may adversely affect interactive user processes or other batch processing that use that same table. Whenever an index is added, the database optimizer might function differently with the same queries, making the process faster or slower.

Principle 2: Trust, but Verify Tuning Changes

Always follow the principle of "trust, but verify" when making any changes to the EnterpriseOne architecture, and specifically to the tuning and performance evaluation of the database. A common occurrence at customer sites when reviewing performance tuning changes is the practice of blindly following technical whitepaper recommendations, or the even more serious practice of "Google Search" tuning. Here, the Internet search engine is used to identify possible causes of a problem and the suggested solutions are implemented in a not so controlled fashion. The performance changes are never verified as to their benefit and furthermore are never restored to their original values when no benefit is observed, which can create adverse effects later on. Additionally, there can be changes made by a consultant that are never questioned or documented. These tuning changes, if left unchecked and unverified, can be the source of future performance issues.

Principle 3: Review Previous Tuning Changes When a New Change Is Introduced

Periodically, tuning values need to be reevaluated. Uptake of Electronic Software Updates (ESUs), or upgrading the versions of software (such as the database from Oracle Enterprise Edition 10gR2 to 11gR2), may result in the tuned value being deprecated or the value becoming a hindrance to performance. Documentation and review of all tuning made to the system in the past is recommended, and copies of the original and each modified version of configuration files should be kept when any change is made to the EnterpriseOne software or hardware architecture.

EnterpriseOne Load Profiles

The load profiles for JD Edwards EnterpriseOne presented here are for interactive users and batch processes. Other processes, such as Business Services (BSSV), Real Time Events (RTE), and third-party integrations, can use similar principle methodologies for tuning but will not be discussed specifically in this chapter.

To gain the greatest benefit for interactive and batch processes when tuning the JD Edwards EnterpriseOne application, you need to understand performance degradation as it relates to the Oracle database. A review of typical JD Edwards EnterpriseOne process profiles is helpful in approaching the Oracle database component tuning.

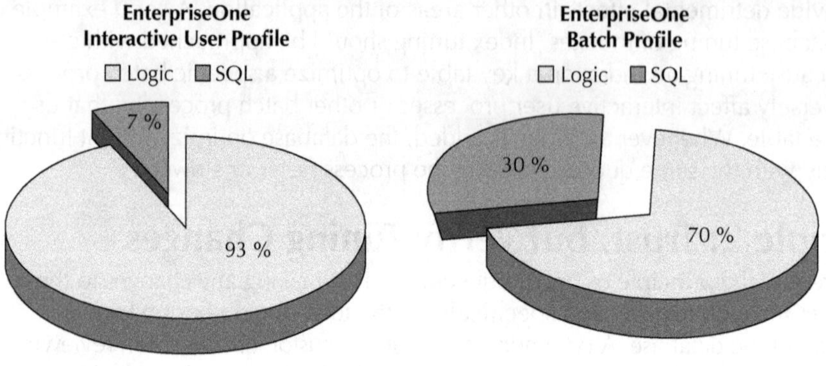

FIGURE 8-1. *EnterpriseOne interactive user and batch profiles*

The profiles in Figure 8-1 illustrate that the database component of the JD Edwards EnterpriseOne application typically consumes only 7 percent of the total processing for interactive users and up to 30 percent for batch processing. The remaining time is spent in business logic and Java processing. Thus, the greatest benefit to performance tuning opportunities for the database resides in batch processing when it comes to the EnterpriseOne architecture.

The profiles in Figure 8-1 should be intuitive to most EnterpriseOne users, because batch processes by their nature are a combined set of interactive actions and business logic calls that are processed together as a group using the process's processing options and data selection definitions. Furthermore, batch processes have no delay time, which is typical of an interactive user process. The delay time is the normal time spent by the user within the application when no request is made. The user may delay in their response, may be reviewing the information on the screen, or may be distracted by other activities. This delay time is also called think time.

Performance tuning the Oracle database for interactive users is useful for "Find," "OK," or "Submit" button clicks for processing, and the response time for retrieving information is considered slow or nonresponsive. This can often happen in open-ended queries to large tables in the database by end users asking for too much information in a grid query search, or if timeouts are occurring during query processing. As long as the interactive application responds in the typical 3 to 5 seconds, interactive users will not notice these minor improvements to the database.

Interactive Users

When is performance tuning required for the Oracle database for interactive users? Consider the following example condition:

■ Scaling of interactive users to large database request volumes within the application causes contention of similar interactive users on the same data and data tables, which can cause performance degradation.

■ When batch processes use some of the key tables and create locks on tables that are needed by the interactive users, the user experiences the application as sluggish and slow.

■ Larger volumes of users and contention with concurrently running batch processes can consume key Oracle database resources that might be constrained, such as connections, buffer pools, and temporary sort areas.

■ Applications are not returning the result set because of a timeout or because the result set returns in an unacceptable time frame. Increasing the configuration parameters of timeouts can resolve some of these issues and cover for the poorly performing database, but this approach to performance tuning is addressing the symptoms of the problem and not the root cause.

Batch Processes

Oracle database tuning for batch process is the most typical type of tuning for the EnterpriseOne application. The reasons for batch performance tuning may involve the following:

■ The need to have a batch process complete within a specific time period. Nightly batch processes, such as those in manufacturing used for generating morning pick slips, must be completed and generated at the production plant so that they may be filled and shipped to their destination.

■ Financial reports, payroll, and government-required batch processes also have time limitations for batch processes to be completed. Employees and anyone getting a check from the financial systems expect payments to be delivered predictably and on time. Government regulations also carry fines and late fees if financial obligations and deadlines are not met.

■ Synchronization processes may be occurring throughout the day, updating the EnterpriseOne tables from external third-party integrations. Also known as *bulk import* and *EDI processing*, this functionality can have a profound impact on all aspects of the EnterpriseOne architecture, because it can consume a large part of the Oracle database processing cycles.

■ As the company grows and the tables get larger, a batch process will have to process more and more records within a given time period. The metric of transactional records processed per minute will be a key factor in setting business expectations and planning for future growth and capacity.

Aspects of Database Performance Tuning

The most common methodology for tuning the Oracle database is the top-down method and is described in the *Oracle Database Performance Tuning Guide*. This approach is discussed in this chapter. The Oracle performance tuning steps involve identifying the scope of the problem and tuning the architecture appropriately to achieve the greatest benefit; then you evaluate whether the tuning goal has been achieved. In the top-down approach, you tune the design before tuning the application code, and tune the application code before the Oracle database instance.

The top-down approach for JD Edwards EnterpriseOne for an Oracle database involves three steps:

1. **Design**   Review the EnterpriseOne configuration, such as the number of Call Object kernel and metadata kernel processes, the queue size configuration, timeout values, and other base configurations. The goal is to make certain that the poorly performing processes identified in the Oracle database performance scope review are not directly responsible for bottlenecks in these configurations parameters. Configuring these options is the topic of other chapters in this book.

2. **Application code**   Apply current ESU fixes to the JD Edwards EnterpriseOne code, evaluating and correcting any improperly set processing options and data selection. Interactive user and batch process educational training can avoid the use of open-ended Find operations, resulting in Oracle database full table scans. Limit the application's use of reports that would create unnecessary load on the database. You should also periodically review the SQL initiated from the EnterpriseOne application and inspect the values in the WHERE clause that could cause Oracle database performance degradation. The Oracle database is capable of providing the same result set from differently formed SQL queries.

3. **Oracle database instance**   After the JD Edwards EnterpriseOne application has been installed and performance tuned, the last phase of the top-down approach would be the tuning of the Oracle database based on the scaling and load of interactive user, batch load, and other interfaces that are integrated with the EnterpriseOne architecture.

This is the basic approach to performance tuning, and like peeling an onion, it may require multiple layers of passes before you achieve the set goal and scope of the tuning effort. The goal and scope of the performance tuning effort should be well defined, specific, and measurable. Without a clear goal statement and a way to determine whether the goal is met, performance tuning will become nebulous and unattainable. Developers and managers are all familiar with the term "scope creep." Poor management and goal and scope settings are destined to result in scope creep, whereby any amount of effort cannot achieve tuning goals because the goals and metrics of success were never provided or well defined.

When in the consulting world, it is important that you fix the performance issues and train management and personnel in the methodologies of performance tuning. Although EnterpriseOne is filled with acronyms, the well-known business SMART goal approach is worth spending time to remember:

- **Specific** Create a written set of specific objectives, implementations, and back-out strategies.

- **Measurable** Define metrics that can quantify and measure the effects of changes made to the system.

- **Achievable** The goal must be practical in its scope definition and have a realistic expectation of being attained.

- **Realistic** Many goals cannot be achieved with the current architecture design, hardware, and software configurations. Realistic means that choices should be made based on technology and on the business end for the goal to be achieved.

- **Timely** Achieving the scope and goals should be time-limited. There are realistic costs to resources such as hardware, personnel, and business continuance in achieving any goal in a timely manner.

Following are a couple of examples of using the SMART principle for performance tuning efforts. For simplicity, well-defined, specific, and measurable parts of the SMART formula will be applied.

Example 1: Interactive User Problem

- **Well defined and specific** While in the P42101 ZJDE0001 interactive application, searching on the records for company 1 and branch plant 110, results are not returned for 20 seconds. This issue was experienced at 8:30 A.M., and consistently issuing the request yields the same result.

- **Measurable** Administrator reproduced the actions of the end user and achieved the same result. Additional metrics other than response time were measured, including generating an AWR database report during the time of the performance issue, and initiating the same activities at different times of the day to determine whether the issue occurred only at that time of day.

- **Results** Results showed that the end user was performing a full table scan. Specifying an additional parameter in the grid by the interactive user yielded a response of only a few seconds. The issue was considered resolved by end user training of proper data selection specification in the grid field.

Example 2: Batch Process Problem

- **Well defined and specific** Batch process R42800 ZJDE0001 was initiated at 11 P.M. as a nightly process through a normal scheduler. It did not complete until 2 A.M. the next day. The business manager is concerned that the EnterpriseOne batch process is taking too long. This process has been run before and never experienced this issue.

- **Measurable** The EnterpriseOne job master table was inspected and the process was found to take 2 hours, 35 minutes.

- **Results** Although the batch process definition could have been more specific as to the data selection and options used to run the process, it was found that the queue on which the query was submitted was full with other batch process submissions and did not start processing the query until 1 A.M. Corrections were made to move the process to another queue. The issue was one of an overloaded queue process and was considered resolved.

Example 3: Poor Problem Definition

- **Well defined and specific** The EnterpriseOne environment "feels slow."

- **Results** This problem definition is neither well defined nor specific. It will be difficult for an administrator to determine the source of the problem, whether it is specific to the Oracle database or systemic to the EnterpriseOne environment.

Tuning After the Design

A few basic questions to ask after completing the basic top-down approach are "What has changed recently?" and "Was the EnterpriseOne performing well at a certain point in time?" The "what has changed" answer can be increased load in the form of users, more batch load, a change in the scheduler that submits the batch processes, and a host of other factors. It is important that you qualify which process is slow and document the experience timeframe and conditions during which the problem occurs. Without these specifics, the performance administrator is limited as to where to find the metrics to identify the problem.

Using Metric Statistics

Before proceeding with the discussion on metrics, baselines, and analyzing the data for performance issues, let's discuss the difference between active and passive tuning approaches.

Active Approach

An active approach is characterized by collecting and monitoring metrics, comparing them against Oracle baselines, setting thresholds, and creating notifications. In an active approach, part of the normal duties of the administrator of the EnterpriseOne architecture is to view reports and notifications periodically, and react to fluctuations in a normally performing EnterpriseOne system. Before the administrator performs these tasks, two activities will have already been completed: the Oracle baselines will have been created, and the Oracle Database Threshold and Notifications will have been set.

Create Oracle Baselines   An Oracle database baseline is a collection of Oracle-defined metrics collected for a specific time period on a typical processing day. Setting a baseline allows you to compare Oracle database metrics against metrics gathered another day of similar time and activity. It helps you identify areas in the EnterpriseOne architecture in which performance and consumption of resources has changed. Baseline comparisons can be early detection tools for trends in processor and memory consumption increases, increasing size of Oracle resources of connections, increased occurrences of Oracle resources used in sorting and full table scanning, and in general consumption of Oracle SGA and PGA memory resources. In this regard, Oracle baseline comparisons help in capacity planning of the EnterpriseOne architecture for current and trending growth rates. The goal is to identify a potential EnterpriseOne database performance issue before the end users or management start to complain.

Set Oracle Database Threshold and Notifications   Oracle thresholds and notifications are normally upper limit boundaries on the Oracle resource metrics collected by the database that will be triggered when they are reached. When an Oracle resource boundary limit is reached, the Oracle Database will deny requests for the use of that resource. Thresholds and notifications are used to preempt this from occurring by giving the administrator a notification that the limit is being approached and action should be taken to avoid any Oracle resource denial of requests.

NOTE
Many Oracle database configurations, thresholds, notifications, and Oracle baselines are not implemented well, and thus their benefit is lost. In most circumstances, they are implemented appropriately only after a major event of downtime and loss of service has occurred. It is always an unpleasant experience to see the "ORA-01653: unable to extend table in tablespace" message in the EnterpriseOne server logs.

Passive Approach

In a passive approach, collected metrics and monitoring of the system are researched and analyzed only after a performance issue event has occurred. Unfortunately, this approach is the de facto reality for many companies. As a result, management is forced to make immediate decisions about whether to tune the system now or wait until it gets worse, which results in more customer complaints and possibly a crisis scenario.

NOTE
While I was performance tuning an EnterpriseOne application, a company CTO asked me, "What do you think is running through my company's EnterpriseOne server?" After I looked a little puzzled as to where he was going with this, he stated, "MONEY." A poorly performing EnterpriseOne application can cost the company money, and that is why an active approach is always encouraged.

Performance Tuning Diagnostic Checklist

Each area of the EnterpriseOne architecture should have a detailed checklist that is to be followed when you're going through the exercise of performance tuning. The following list outlines the basis of the remaining discussion in this chapter. As we go through the list, we will discuss a variety of commands and particulars of the application, database, and OS metrics that can be crucial in identifying changes necessary in the EnterpriseOne architecture. This is a short list of items that can include more; the information presented here includes important steps to help you avoid missing obvious performance problems.

1. View the Server Manager EnterpriseOne application metrics.

   a. Configure EnterpriseOne to log all long-running SQL queries into the jde.log files. This option can be changed manually through the Server Manager interface. Once enabled, SQL queries taking longer than the specified time will be automatically logged to the standard EnterpriseOne Logic Server logs.

   b. View the SQL connection information from each of the EnterpriseOne kernel processes. Server Manager provides an area of metrics analysis where the SQL connection information is listed. SQL connection information is an important metric in the Oracle Database connection requirements and is required for scaling and load analysis.

2. Use the Oracle Database utilities, including the following:

   a. View the information provided on the summary page of the Oracle Enterprise Manager interface for any alerts, recommendations, or warning messages issued to the Oracle Database.

   b. Generate and review Automatic Workload Repository (AWR) reports for specific time periods where EnterpriseOne performance is a concern.

   c. Use the optional Oracle Database Diagnosis and Tuning Packs, which provide additional automated features for tuning the Program Global Area (PGA) and System Global Area (SGA) of the database and other tuning utilities such as the SQL Tuning Advisor, which is not available on the Oracle Database Standard Edition version of the release.

   d. Use dynamic performance views to look at statistics and wait events, where the Oracle Database Enterprise Manager is not available or convenient to use.

   e. Review top wait events to determine SQL and processes initiated by the EnterpriseOne application with the highest Oracle Database wait times. An Oracle Database wait typically occurs on hardware resources (CPU, memory, disk), database locking events (table locking), or waiting on Oracle resources (temporary table space for sorting, database commits from other EnterpriseOne processes).

   f. Review the alert log and trace files for Oracle Database errors and warnings.

3. View the operating system metrics.

   a. Monitor the activity of the main metrics of processor, memory, and disk. Performance problems related to the load and scaling of the EnterpriseOne application in increased batch load, interactive users, or increased integrations is a common occurrence if the hardware was not sized properly for the anticipated load.

   b. If any one of the OS resources of processor, memory, or disk becomes constrained, then there will be a definite degradation in performance and will be noticed as a systemic issue to all interactive and batch processes.

   c. Systemic issues occur when performance problems are not isolated to a single process or business activity, but a system-wide slowing of process performance is experienced. In these situations, the culprit is normally a bottleneck in one of the OS resources.

Other performance tuning activities include the following:

- For EnterpriseOne, view JDEDEBUG reports and analyze them through Performance Workbench.

- Query your support staff for end user customer complaints.

- Measure execution times of batch processes and transaction rate completion; are they getting slower?

Performance Tuning Scope and Goals

Performance goals for the JD Edwards EnterpriseOne application fall into two main categories:

- **End user experience**   Specific application response times being slow, the performance tuning effort is to provide not only a consistent end user experience but to decrease the number of interactive user complaints reported to a call support center.

- **Batch performance**   The batch performance is slow, not completing within a specific business required window, impacts interactive users when run concurrently, and will not scale to expected levels at current performance levels.

The objective of performance tuning the EnterpriseOne system is to tune the Oracle Database component to achieve minimum end user response times, to be able to perform in an efficient manner to account for increased end user load and batch throughput, and to avoid reissued batch requests. The effort should result in a more consistent and predictable EnterpriseOne environment.

Analyzing the Metrics and Performance Issue Identification

This section will expand on the subject of performance tuning priorities. Once the metrics are collected through either the application, Oracle database (AWR and Oracle Enterprise Manager), or OS, you may have identified a significant number of problems. You cannot and should not fix everything at once, because you need to judge whether the changes you make have a positive impact on the total EnterpriseOne environment. The performance effort, in other words, should not fix one thing and break four others. Remember the SMART principle and that tuning should be specific, measurable, and the performance issue well defined. The tools (advisors) should also give you an indication of how much benefit the change will have on your EnterpriseOne environment.

When a required change is identified, your response should reflect the following priorities:

- Look for a change that is easy to implement.

- Look for a change that offers the greatest benefit (peeling the onion and the principle of greatest benefit).

- Limit the scope to what can be done on the application, instance, or OS level. Not all changes can be made dynamically and some will require a cycling of services, bouncing of the database, or entire reboots of the OS. Scope involves not only where to tune (operations system, database, or application) and when to tune (now, planned, tested), but how to tune (big changes to values versus small changes), the risk to implement, and back-out/recovery options.

- Evaluate concurrency issues: high throughput, multiple users performing the same tasks at the same time, unnecessary locking levels, and transaction boundaries.

- Evaluate disk I/O issues: slow disks, not enough space, faster disk or fast speed solid state disk (SSD) hardware components required, mounting options, and Automatic Storage Management (ASM) use.

- Determine whether processes are serialized and whether they could be put in parallel.

- Run reports and batch processes during off hours so that the impact is less felt by day-to-day processing.

- Determine whether the size and content of the report meet business needs, and whether the report can be smaller and thus consume fewer resources.

Tuning the Operating System

The operating system (Unix or Windows, for example) is one of the most neglected areas that is often missed in tuning the Oracle Database and identifying possible areas for a contention point or where the Oracle Database will encounter hard limits. It is the first place in the tuning exercise that an administrator should also review before initiating any direct tuning of the Oracle Database.

Unix has an extensive set of tools for tuning the OS for the Oracle database as compared to the other operating systems that will be presented in this chapter. Although Windows does not have the finer granularity in tuning options as its Unix counterpart, the sections that describe Windows tuning for the Oracle database will highlight those "knobs" that have been found to provide the largest benefit.

The majority of the Oracle database tuning values related to the OS will be general, in that they will affect all processes because they act to reserve more resources to the CPU, memory and disk I/O.

The most critical tuning of the OS will involve the resources of disk, memory, processor and process threads including IPC and user limit settings. Assuming that the Oracle Database and EnterpriseOne application are not resource limited by the OS resource, disk I/O contention is one of the main contention points that has to be addressed in performance tuning.

The following common tuning problems can be encountered with the OS:

- **Processes are CPU bound**   More CPU hardware resources are needed or you need to tune existing processes that are CPU bound.

- **Memory**   Not enough memory is allocated to the Oracle Database or available to be allocated to the Oracle Database, and thus the memory construct of the Oracle processes are constrained, causing memory-related performance degradation.

- **I/O issues**   I/O issues are the most common and are a single source area of performance bottlenecks. Faster disks, more disks, SSD technology, and disk caching are general solutions to performance issues related to disk activity.

- **Network**   Fast networks tend to result in better scaling and performance for the EnterpriseOne application. Increased network bandwidth allows faster movement of data from the EnterpriseOne application and database requests.

NOTE
Consult the Oracle documentation library hyperlinks for Oracle 10g and Oracle 11g for a complete listing and explanation of OS tuning and preinstallation guidelines:
www.oracle.com/pls/db102/homepage
www.oracle.com/pls/db111/homepage
www.oracle.com/pls/db112/homepage

The OS can provide many metrics; often, these metrics provide additional support in identifying and correcting performance issues. The main area in which the OS is configured is part of the top-down performance tuning methodology, and you should perform a careful review of I/O, swap, and OS parameter settings.

The key points when dealing with metrics and analysis is to make sure that there are sufficient numbers of metrics being collected to identify and tune the EnterpriseOne environment properly. You'll also need to strike a balance between the number of changes that are made, collecting new key metrics, and continuing this process until all planned changes have been made. Tuning is an iterative process, and you need to know when sufficient tuning has been accomplished and has achieved the initial goal of the performance tuning effort. The statement "stop tuning when the goal is achieved" is a good reminder to employ.

Tuning the EnterpriseOne Application

Performance tuning the Oracle database for the EnterpriseOne application is as much an art as a science. The science part is easy to interpret because it stems from the robust set of tools, commands, and reports that you can generate and use for performance tuning the Oracle database and the EnterpriseOne application. As for the art of performance tuning, this task is performed by individuals with different backgrounds and skills. Art, by definition, implies creativity, and the individual's creative skills help him or her form a well-tuned Oracle Database and EnterpriseOne application.

The following tuning problems are common with the EnterpriseOne application:

- **Inefficient or resource-intensive SQL statements**   Whether identified by Server Manager, the Oracle Enterprise Manager, or development, handling of inefficient and resource-intensive SQL statements is a common exercise. The result is normally an added index, change of a data selection, or training of end users to include parameters in their grid searches.

- **Oracle Database configuration issues**   The Oracle Database is under-configured for the resources it has for servicing the EnterpriseOne application. This means that more resources such as network and kernel processes can be defined to spread the load of the increased batch or user load. Increasing the number of network and kernel processes will increase the memory and processor needs of a server, but on under configured systems, this translates into increased performance.

- **Concurrency issues**   A process can complete with no issues and perform well when run in isolation, but when combined with other processes it may not fare so well. These issues can arise with user-to-user, batch-to-batch, or between interactive users and batch processes.

- **Performance degradation issues**   These issues may be caused by changes in business requirements, load, or use of the EnterpriseOne application. Business requirements can require that batch processes finish before certain times, such as the financial batch process of GL Post or the manufacturing process to print pick slips. Business requirements can also require that more users be added to the system or new divisions be brought online under the EnterpriseOne umbrella. An example of this would be the addition of the financial or human resource modules of EnterpriseOne; this can change the dynamics of the performance of the EnterpriseOne architecture, creating new performance tuning challenges.

Analysis Tools for the EnterpriseOne Application

Two primary tools are used for the analysis of the JD Edwards EnterpriseOne application Oracle database: the EnterpriseOne Server Manager and the EnterpriseOne Performance Workbench. The Server Manager and the utilities it provides is part of the normal installation of EnterpriseOne. Performance Workbench can be downloaded from the Oracle support web site (look for "Downloads and Patches" for the JD Edwards EnterpriseOne application).

The ability to use the Server Manager and enhanced logging options to monitor long-running SQL statements has been available since EnterpriseOne Tools release 8.98.3. Server Manager is the premier tool for looking at metrics and administration of EnterpriseOne. Server Manager can also help you collect connection information and provides a mechanism for enabling the logging of long-running SQL statements to the EnterpriseOne logs.

Performance Workbench can analyze SQL statements by parsing a JDEDEBUG log. The negative aspect of using Performance Workbench is that it must be used with the "debugging logging" option turned on, so it is not normally run in a production environment. Although Performance Workbench is a valuable tool, it is not covered in this chapter.

Business and Technical that Affect Performance

Following are some typical business requirements that affect the performance of an EnterpriseOne system:

- **Checkpointing** A checkpointing requirement is normally driven by the time-to-recovery after an Oracle Database instance has gone down. More frequent checkpointing translates to quicker recovery time if the database would go down in an unplanned fashion. The cost of this requirement is slightly slower application performance.

- **Performing archiving** Archiving has the benefit of point-in-time recovery, but there is a detriment to disk I/O performance (multiple write locations), as Oracle Database waits while the operations are in process.

- **Redundancy** Backups of data files, multiple control files, and multiple redo log members in a group can create redundancy. Redundancy translates into slower systems because of the duplicate effort that has to be achieved to provide for the feature of redundancy.

- **Security**   Security may involve activities such as auditing, encryption, and access control. The more auditing that occurs on the system, the more work will have to be done and the more overhead will be incurred. Security is normally a business-driven requirement, but protection of access to data and systems is also a technical requirement. Security in this context is the restriction of access through software and hardware resources.

- **Encryption**   Many systems need additional protection of sensitive data provided by encryption. The encryption and decryption operations do incur some overhead, but this can be insignificant.

- **Government regulations**   Sarbanes-Oxley, HIPAA, Department of Defense, and other regulations require that tables be audited. EnterpriseOne has the 21CFR11 module for this, and, in short, it creates separate view tables and logging to comply with these regulations. The Oracle Database can also be configured for auditing by using the Oracle Database auditing feature or by the addition of other manual triggers on specific tables. Government regulations often also require a robust archiving and retention policy, which can impact performance.

Tuning the EnterpriseOne Product Life Cycle

The life cycle for EnterpriseOne is the process flow the code goes through for development, the upgrades of tools and application code, the upgrade of hardware, integrations, and so on. The EnterpriseOne architecture should define baselines and metric sets that can show the impact of any changes made and to adjust the EnterpriseOne environment accordingly as it proceeds throughout its life cycle. The EnterpriseOne application must have sufficient overhead resources allocated to allow for changes to occur and the performance should not be severely impacted by changes.

EnterpriseOne Tuning Life Cycle Phases

Performance can be poor at the end of the year, end of the month, end of the quarter, and during nightly batch processing. Anticipate and plan for these performance-sensitive times. Focus on what is the performance today, what it was yesterday, and what it will be tomorrow. Tuning for day-to-day activities can be a main goal and activity of a database administrator, but tuning for only these short-term goals is a passive approach. An active approach involves tuning all of the EnterpriseOne life-cycle processes for typical and peak times, and this is a more comprehensive method of performance tuning.

Following are the typical phases of an EnterpriseOne life cycle and tuning requirements:

- **EnterpriseOne application design and development**   There is generally no initial considerations for performance in the initial design and development phase of the EnterpriseOne tuning life cycle.

- **EnterpriseOne testing**   The Oracle DB performance configuration is normally done at this stage, setting the initial values of memory, processes, and connections for optimal performance.

- **Deployment**   Deployment can be the first go-live event or the addition of new applications to the EnterpriseOne architecture that might impact the Oracle Database component. Oracle Database performance baselines and thresholds for notifications should be fully in place and set during deployment.

- **Production**   It is much more difficult to troubleshoot and tune a system once it is in production. Any changes to the Oracle Database must be evaluated, tested, and approved before they are implemented.

- **Migration, upgrade, and environment changes to the EnterpriseOne environment**   As with the production phase, it is very difficult to find cycles in the normal daily activities to evaluate performance impact of these events.

Showing the SQL in EnterpriseOne Server Logs

The following JDE.INI setting was introduced as part of the kernel resource management (KRM) initiative in Tools 8.98.3 and provides a methodology by which SQL statements can be logged to the JDE logs if they exceed a time threshold:

```
[DB SYSTEM SETTINGS]
QueryExecutionTimeThreshold=1
```

This functionality is turned OFF when set to zero and only positive integer values are valid for its usage. Set the `QueryExecutionTimeThreshold` to 1 second to track any SQL statements that take more than 1 second to complete. This setting is read by EnterpriseOne services at startup and will require a restart of services to use if implemented. In the case of batch processing, the value is picked up when the batch process is launched and must be set prior to launching the batch process to have an effect. (Reference: http://docs.oracle.com/cd/E17984_01/doc.898/e14718.pdf.)

EnterpriseOne SQL Statement Tuning

We can use a number of tools to determine whether the SQL is using excessive resources and where it is spending its time. This section of the chapter is a discussion of the tools and analysis to be performed to determine whether a SQL statement is using more resources than necessary.

The AWR report and other tools can show us the SQL statements that are consuming the resources, but how can we be sure that the amount of resources it is consuming is appropriate? One area in which we can look to see if there is longer than necessary times is the SQL overhead of parsing, binding, or fetching the data, by looking at the processing phase statistics of the SQL can help answer this question.

A common issue is found in disk I/O. Excessive physical reads and writes in the processing phase can slow down the overall time to execute the SQL statement. This shows up in the AWR report as excessive buffer gets. Bringing those buffers into the Oracle buffer cache is one way to alleviate this issue. Excessive buffer gets can lead to more processing cycles, causing performance degradation.

You can look in the following key areas in the AWR report to identify excessive resource activity:

- Look for SQL statements using the most CPU time. Focus on statements that not only use the most time but have large numbers of executions.

- Look at order by gets—What is reading the most number of blocks?

- Look for long parse time, excessive I/O, buffer gets, CPU time, and waits.

- Look at the top SQL reports, by time and by gets.

The same SQL statement may often appear in multiple key areas, and that is what we want to review first. You can create a SQL tuning set with the list of SQL statements you've identified and run it through the SQL Tuning Advisor.

SQL allows you to write statements in different ways to produce the same result, and each different statement can require different amounts of resources to complete. Poor SQL can correct but inefficient; it can result from bad design, poor coding, or from the optimizer choosing an inefficient execution plan. An interesting statistic in the Oracle documentation is that in a typical SQL profiling analysis, 20 percent of SQL consumes 80 percent of the resources, and 10 percent of SQL consumes 50 percent of the resources. Thus, if we use the AWR reports carefully, we should be able to identify those 20 percent or so of SQL commands that consume the majority of our Oracle resources within the EnterpriseOne application implementation.

NOTE
We have used this method of identifying poor SQL through AWR report analysis and found it to be a good source of identifying pain points for many companies with little effort or knowledge of their performance issues. This is another example of an active approach to performance tuning. We don't perform this activity to achieve the results of performance tuning, but we can use this analysis as a good data point when evaluating other metrics and analysis during the performance tuning exercise.

Tuning the Oracle Database Instance

Tuning the database will most likely occur early in the life cycle of the EnterpriseOne implementation and should not require much tuning unless events require it. EnterpriseOne events range from increased user loads, bringing online new EnterpriseOne modules, and processing more records because of the normal growth of the business. We'll review the techniques in tuning the database parameters that relate to these events.

The following common tuning problems can be encountered with the Oracle Database instance due to these EnterpriseOne events.

Undersized Memory Structures

Increased table record counts can create a greater need for Oracle process sorting space. Increased user counts on an Oracle Database dedicated connection configuration will also require more memory requirements for the EnterpriseOne application to function well. The Oracle memory structures will need to be increased in size to adjust for these increased loads.

Oracle DB Configuration Issues: Processes, Connections, and Cursors

Specifically with increased interactive user loads, the Oracle parameters of processes, memory requirements for larger numbers of connections, and cursors will be the large tuning knobs that will have to be adjusted.

Degradation of DB Performance over Time

EnterpriseOne database performance will normally degrade over time until events such as new table statistics are collected and normal cleanup processes are run. By default, the Oracle Database statistics are collected on a nightly basis or can be manually initiated. EnterpriseOne processes that clean up old and unnecessary records and archiving processes are necessary to provide a constant and efficient use of the Oracle Database.

Locking Issues

Locking or Oracle's use of enqueues normally occurs within the EnterpriseOne application because the Oracle processes such as table records, connections, and use of Oracle process resources are being shared among many of the components of the EnterpriseOne architecture. Locking is required for security and data integrity. Oracle normally handles locking well, but conditions can arise in which a particular Oracle resource is locked and creates a performance issue with EnterpriseOne. When two or more processes need to make changes to the same table record, the first process will acquire a lock and the other processes will wait for this process to finish before it in turn will require the lock. Even on the best tuned database, lock contention will occur, especially on an OLTP-based application such as EnterpriseOne. The EnterpriseOne administrators must ensure that locking is kept to a minimum.

The EnterpriseOne application code controls most of the transactional boundaries that create the locks. Efficient small boundaries will avoid unnecessary locks. One key metric that impacts the locking performance is application transaction rollbacks. If there are rollback messages in the Call Object kernel or JAS logs, locking contention should be a concern. Rollback messages are a result of application timeouts in which transaction boundaries are too large. Excessive locks and performance issues related to the locking of tables in the database can be determined either through the v$ dynamic views of the database or through the Performance tab in Oracle Enterprise Manager for session issues.

Checkpointing

Checkpointing is the Oracle background process of writing changed database blocks to disk. During normal EnterpriseOne operations, changes to table records are initially written to memory and then at the checkpoint event, to disk. The `FAST_START_MTTR_TARGET` Oracle initiation parameter controls the amount of checkpoint events.

More events benefit the Oracle instance recovery time in case of downtime, but large amount of checkpointing can affect EnterpriseOne application performance. Checkpointing also relies heavily on disk I/O performance, and checkpointing events are logged in the Oracle alert log. Although the default settings are sufficient for most EnterpriseOne implementations, if disk I/O is a concern with performance, more frequent checkpointing is not recommended.

Oracle Archive Log Mode

Oracle archive log mode is a high availability feature with the Oracle Database. When enabled, it allows the redo logs to be written to another location that is specified by the Oracle configuration parameters. More than one location can be specified. The performance impact of enabling this feature is that more write requests will be made to the disk I/O subsystem as a result. The following simple SQL*Plus command can be used to determine whether archive log mode is enabled:

```
SELECT LOG_MODE FROM SYS.V$DATABASE;
```

When the mode is enabled, performance will be impacted from the standpoint of interactive and batch processes. The degree of the impact will depend on the type of disk I/O subsystem that is configured for archive log mode and the number of archive logs. The tradeoff to this performance degradation is the business requirement of compliance to a redundant system architecture.

Redo Logs Members

Oracle redo logs store transactional information that has not yet been written to the Oracle data files. Evaluating the possible performance tuning of the redo log members is one of the easiest ways to improve overall performance of the Oracle Database. The following actions are well documented in the Oracle literature to improve redo log member performance:

- Place redo log files on SSDs.

- Optimize the log buffer Oracle parameter in the Oracle Database configuration by either measuring metrics or inspection of the Oracle tuning advisors.

- Make sure that sufficient numbers of redo logs are available and that they are large enough for the EnterpriseOne application not to encounter too frequent numbers of log switches. The log switch events are recorded when they occur in the Oracle Database alert log.

The Oracle Database Time Model

The Oracle Database time can be broken down into the Oracle Database time components and is documented in Oracle's tuning guides (see www.oracle.com/technetwork/oem/db-mgmt/s317294-db-perf-tuning-with-db-time-181631.pdf). Most of the metrics in the Oracle Database are presented in terms of each of these components.

Figure 8-2 illustrates that Oracle Database requests are composed of two variables: the database (DB) wait time and DB processing time:

- **DB wait time** The wait time is the cumulative statistic of all of the waits that a database request will encounter while completing the EnterpriseOne request. This includes waiting on lock releases for shared table records, disk I/O resources, and other Oracle resources such as Oracle process memory components.

- **DB processing time** The database processing time is the sum of the time the Oracle request is performing work on the Oracle Database server for the EnterpriseOne request. The request is normally initiated from the EnterpriseOne JAS Server application or the EnterpriseOne Logic Server, primarily from the Call Object kernel process.

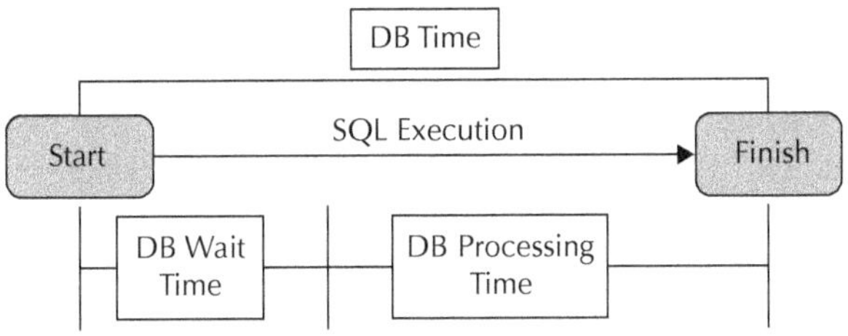

FIGURE 8-2. *Oracle Database time model*

The total DB time is normally measured on a user session level but could be broken down to the EnterpriseOne transaction level as well. DB time metrics collected by the Oracle Database equals the total time spent in the EnterpriseOne Database requests by user session.

The EnterpriseOne application requests that make up the total DB time for an EnterpriseOne transaction request to the database are a cumulative statistic of these interlaced combinations of DB wait time and DB processing time. The interlacing occurs because the business logic is driving these DB requests for a transaction, and execution flow will fluctuate between the DB requests and the EnterpriseOne business logic code (see Figure 8-3). Tuning the EnterpriseOne application is an effort both to decrease the DB wait time and decrease the need for CPU cycles processing these database requests.

DB Time and DB Processor Time Ratios

At a glance, it is easy to determine whether the EnterpriseOne implementation is busy and whether to target the resources for tuning by looking at the ratios of DB wait time and DB processor time. A very busy system will show more DB processor time. The DB processor time is found in the AWR reports, and Oracle Database statistics will be higher than the DB wait times. High DB wait times are early

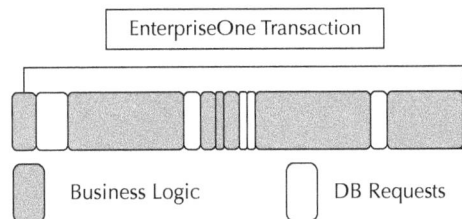

FIGURE 8-3. *Business logic and DB requests*

indicators of a system that is resource constrained. Resource constraints can occur at all levels including that of application, database, and OS.

- **High DB processing time**   Performance issues related to a database with high DB processing time are more likely to improve by adding more hardware resources such as memory, processor, and disk subsystems. High DB processor time needs less tuning and possibly more effort regarding the EnterpriseOne application level for tuning the Oracle Database request flow.

- **High DB wait times**   Depending on the source of the wait, the tuned Oracle Database instance will show significant impact along with tuning to the OS and EnterpriseOne application.

AWR reports will be examined in this chapter to illustrate DB wait time and DB processing time characteristics. Figure 8-4 shows an example of the SQL time spend for a typical EnterpriseOne application. For simplicity, the database request can be further broken into two main categories: SQL processing, which takes most of the request, and SQL overhead. The SQL overhead is the processing of the Oracle background processes including Java, parsing of the SQL, the time in establishing the SQL connection, and any PL/SQL execution. Normally, the majority of the time is spent executing the actual SQL statement, but a significant amount of time can also be spent in SQL initiation and other processes when the optimizer is preparing the SQL before execution.

In Figure 8-4, 40 percent of the time is depicted for these activities; this is an approximation of the overhead for a typical EnterpriseOne SQL request. The SQL time spent in initiation is also felt by interactive users the most when the first person using the application after a services restart has been completed. The first user in or the first time the batch process is run normally experiences the slowest performance.

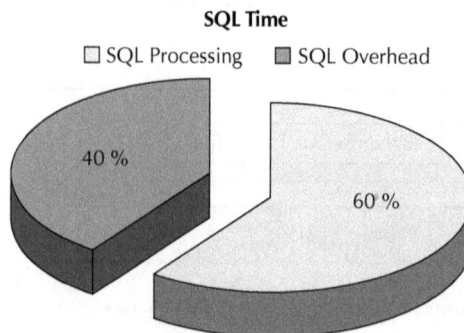

SQL Time

□ SQL Processing   ■ SQL Overhead

40 %

60 %

FIGURE 8-4.   *SQL time*

This is in part due to the overhead cost of the execution of the SQL statement as well as other caching activities. This overhead is normally incurred only once and future executions of the SQL statement will be in the Oracle cache and thus will have much greater SQL processing time.

Dynamic Performance Views

As mentioned, the Oracle Database has v$ views, which are also known as dynamic performance views. All the views are owned by the SYS Oracle user and reside in the SYSAUX tablespace. You can obtain a list of them using the following commands:

```
REM SQL To determine the dynamic performance views
select name from v$fixed_table where name like 'V$%';
select * from v$fixed_view_definition where view_name like 'V$%';
```

The Oracle dynamic views provide information on a variety of Oracle Database metrics including the following:

- Sessions

- Wait events

- Locks

- Memory usage and allocation

- System and session parameters

- SQL execution

Many SQL queries use these views. The v$ dynamic performance views differ from the DBA equivalent views in that the statistics reported from each are gathered at different time intervals and thus differ slightly in their reporting. The v$ dynamic views tend to be more real-time while the counter DBA views are a cumulative statistic and are reset whenever the Oracle Database processes are cycled. As a consultant, the real-time dynamic views are more useful when evaluating Oracle Database performance than the DBA equivalent view, although both have their specific benefits.

For these views to have significance, the statistics for them are populated only if the `TIMED_STATISTICS` initialization parameter is set to `TRUE`. The value for `STATISTICS_LEVEL` must also be set to `TYPICAL` or `ALL`. `TYPICAL` is the default setting for the Oracle Database. If the `STATISTIC_LEVEL` is set to `BASIC`, no statistics will be available for v$ performance views and will be unusable for assisting with the Oracle Database tuning for the EnterpriseOne application.

All the statistics that are gathered through the Oracle v$ and DBA views are based on the time model. That is why, by default, the statistics are gathered and refreshed during a nightly maintenance window by the Oracle Database. Gathering of statistics is necessary so that the Oracle optimizer has the latest and best statistics to form a proper explain plan, parse the SQL, and initiate the execution of the SQL statement. An Oracle explain plan is the internal utility that the Oracle optimizer uses to shows how it will be execute the SQL issued to the Oracle database. Stale statistics will result in a poorly formed explain plan and thus will limit the Oracle optimizer's ability to perform efficiently.

NOTE
The specific SQL queries of the dynamic views provided in this chapter were a combination of those found on the Oracle OTN web site and documents listed in the "Conclusion" section of this chapter.

Oracle WAIT Events

A listing of the possible reasons for a session to encounter a DB wait event in the EnterpriseOne application can be found in the AWR report in the "Top 5 Foreground Wait Events" section.

- **Free buffer waits** This wait can be attributed to waits for the buffer cache to become empty, or waiting on the DBWR process to write to disk before the process can write something into that buffer space.

- **Buffer busy waits** A current session is waiting on another session's processes before the buffer area can be used.

- **Latch free** Latches are a type of lock used for controlling process flows and ensure integrity in the database.

- **DB file sequential read** Related to disk I/O and a good candidate for SQL tuning.

- **DB file scattered read** Related to disk I/O and a good candidate for SQL tuning.

- **Log file sync** Possible tuning opportunity for the log buffer variable related to the DBWR Oracle background process needing to write information to disk after the completion of a transaction.

Figure 8-5 shows an example output of wait events for EnterpriseOne exercising a typical interactive user load.

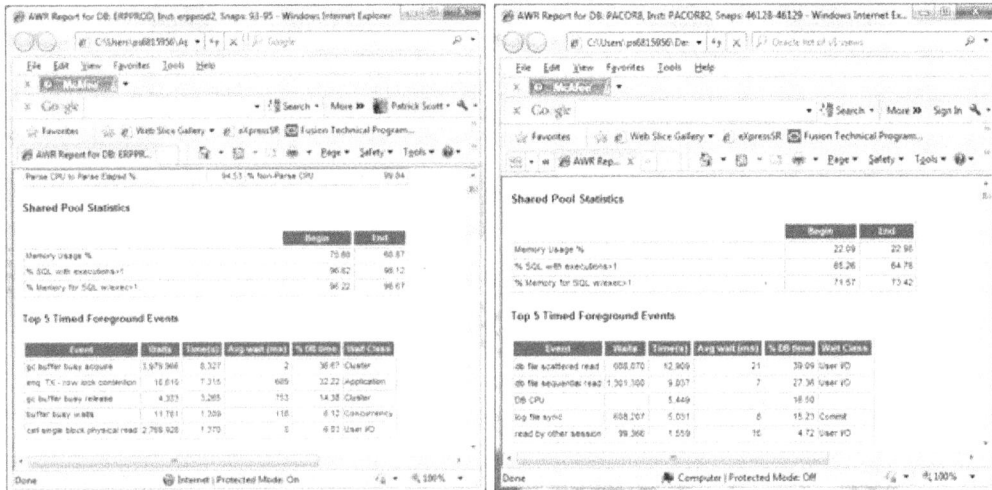

FIGURE 8-5. *AWR report wait events*

Figure 8-6 shows an example AWR report in which a log file sync DB wait event occurred.

All wait events are found in the V$EVENT_NAME dynamic view. The following SQL command will show these events from this view:

```
REM SQL to show all of the wait events in the Oracle database
column name format a20
column parameter1 format a20
column parameter2 format a20
column parameter3 format a20
select name, parameter1, parameter2, parameter3 from v$event_name;
```

The following shows the view:

```
NAME                     PARAMETER1         PARAMETER2                PARAMETER3
-----------------------  -----------------  ------------------------  ------------------------
...
Disk file operations I/O  FileOperation      fileno                    filetype
Disk file I/O Calibration count
Disk file Mirror Read     fileno             blkno                     filetype
Disk file Mirror/Media Re fileno             blkno                     filetype
...
```

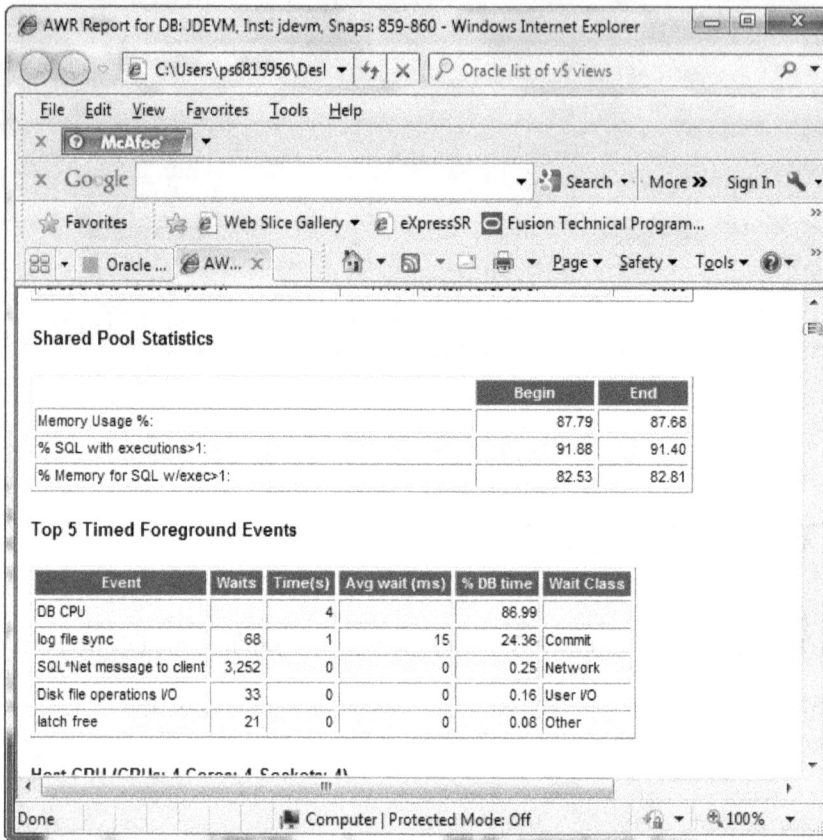

FIGURE 8-6. *AWR report of log_file_sync*

Oracle Alert Log

Another good source of information is the Oracle alert log. Information is recorded in chronological order, and selected event information is listed, including the following:

- Oracle database startup and shutdown, including the names of many of the Oracle background processes.

- Log switches, which occur when the Oracle background process log writer (LGWR) stops writing to one of the redo logs and switches to another. It shows the movement of completed transactions made to the tables in the Oracle Database to the Oracle DBF files on disk.

- Instance recovery start/complete times.

- Deadlock and timeout errors.

- Checkpoint information.

- Errors causing trace files to be generated.

- Create, alter, and drop DML SQL statements.

TIP
It is a good practice to archive and create new alert log files periodically when the database is recycled and to inspect the alert logs for errors and perform notifications if necessary based on key words in the log file.

User Trace Files

Trace files can be generated either automatically by one of the Oracle background processes (such as DBWR, LGWR, PMON, or SMON) or manually by turning on selected server process tracing at the session or instance level. Trace files are found in the same location as the alert log and contain the following information:

- SQL statements that are issued in that session or instance

- Statistics for the SQL statements processed

- Oracle background process errors

Oracle Database Monitoring and Tuning Tools

The following discussion is intended as a high-level overview of SQL statements that are normally used in evaluating some of the Oracle parameters for the EnterpriseOne application.

Tuning the Oracle Configuration: Processes

When the value of processes for Oracle Database dedicated connections has reached its limit, contention for these processes and connections to the database will begin to affect performance and functionality for the EnterpriseOne application. The following SQL command and output illustrate the minimum, maximum, and limits of the processes available for the Oracle Database. The output of this SQL shows a process limit value of 2500 processes and a current utilization of processes at 38. Since this snapshot was taken at JDE EnterpriseOne server startup, it shows the number of Oracle processes necessary to handle the startup of EnterpriseOne, with a total of 60 connections necessary at startup and 38 processes before any users access the system.

```
REM SQL To determine Oracle process utilization
select * from v$resource_limit where resource_name='processes';
```

```
SQL> select * from v$resource_limit where resource_name='processes';

RESOURCE_NAME              CURRENT_UTILIZATION MAX_UTILIZATION INITIAL_AL LIMIT_VALU
---------------------------  -------------------- --------------- ---------- ----------
processes                                    38              60       2500       2500
```

Using Oracle's AWR

AWR is the extension, not a replacement, of previous versions of Oracle's implementation of STATSPACK. AWR is managed by the Oracle background Manageability Monitor (MMON) process. AWR is an in-memory statistics collection facility that collects, stores, and provides a reporting method for Oracle performance analysis for current and historical information retrieval.

The AWR utility of the Oracle Database tool set collects the following:

- **Counters and value statistics**   Disk reads/writes per SQL statement

- **ASH data**   First to memory at 1 second intervals (ASH data is heavily used by the ADDM utility) by session, SQL, services, and so on

- **Advisor reports**   Normally part of the Oracle extended database tuning and analysis pack and are not included as part of the standard Oracle Standard Edition implementation of EnterpriseOne

- **In-memory statistics**   Cumulative statistics of activities such as wait events with time information in v$ views and persistent statistics on disk in DBA views

A single AWR report is a subset of the total amount of information collected in the statistics and presented to the user in an easy-to-read format. These reports list the top SQL statements for the time periods specified and may not include many of the lower priority SQL statements, events, or actions that take place in the EnterpriseOne application.

Reading AWR Reports

A snapshot is a set of Oracle statistics that are collected every 60 minutes at the top of the hour. An AWR report is generated from the statistics between two snapshots. This is by default, but the snapshots of Oracle statistics can be generated at any point in time. Snapshots also are retained by default for a period of eight days and consume approximately 2MB of space in the SYSAUX tablespace.

AWR reports should be specific to the performance of the time period of interest and not evaluated over a long period of time. Smaller AWR time periods will allow a more specified target area to view and allow a greater chance of a good analysis and identification of the potential performance issues.

The AWR reports can be run manually from a SQL*Plus session using the command-line interface from the rdbms/admin directory. Oracle provides two:

- @$ORACLE_HOME/rdbms/admin/awrrpt.sql

- @$ORACLE_HOME/rdbms/admin/awrrpti.sql

The goal is to show how we can quickly review these reports and check for an indication that a performance issue exists. We need to determine whether we are using too much resources, whether the problem is caused by the application or if it is OS related. A checklist of the areas of the AWR report to inspect is provided here:

- **Snapshot time**   Be sure that the time intervals of the report are in a reasonable time frame. The goal of performance tuning is to find metrics that are specific and measurable. A time period that's too long within the AWR report will not yield the specific metrics or target the time interval for the EnterpriseOne processes that are in question.

- **Top 5 timed foreground events**   It is recommended that the "Top 5 Timed Foreground Events" be the first area of the AWR report that is inspected. In this section, the DB wait time and DB processor time components can be most easily evaluated. The Top 5 events should not always require tuning; they are simply items of interest during that time period.

- **Memory usage**   A simple glance at the consumption of memory and validating that it is not a bottleneck in system performance is a good practice.

- **Load profile**   A set of statistic metrics that characterize the Oracle Database workload generated from the EnterpriseOne application.

- **Instance efficiency percentages**   This will be discussed later in the chapter but is related to tuning the memory parameters specifically of the Oracle database instance.

- **Shared pool statistics** These statistics are key in evaluating the `shared_pool` Oracle initialization parameter.

- **Operating system statistics** Operating system statistics are collected in an AWR report along with Oracle statistics. These metrics should match up and confirm any performance bottlenecks that are suspected at the OS level.

AWR Baselines, Thresholds, and Alerts

AWR baselines contain a set of AWR snapshots for an interesting or a referenced period of time. We can set thresholds with many of the metrics that are collected through the AWR report and set up alerts and notifications. These are important especially when some of the alerts warn of impending disaster or halting of processing. Notifications can include e-mail, pages, and launching of automated scripts. A full tablespace, errors on timeouts, or rollbacks within the EnterpriseOne application are good examples.

The use of permanently stored baseline snapshots on a well-tuned system is strongly encouraged. This saves a known state of statistics for comparison.

Using Active Server History (ASH) for EnterpriseOne

Either through the Oracle Enterprise Manager or by directly looking at the ASH session history, you can identify EnterpriseOne real-time SQL in several ways. It is sometimes impractical to have to generate an AWR report, but you need a general idea of what is going on in the system. A useful command for the ASH is to determine the most actively running SQL statements in the last minute:

```
REM SQL to determine actively running processes in the last minute
select sql_id, count(*), round(count(*)/sum(count(*)) over (), 2) pctload
from v$active_session_history
where sample_time > sysdate -1/24/60 and session_type <> 'BACKGROUND'
group by sql_id
order by count(*) desc;
```

SQL_ID	COUNT(*)	PCTLOAD
	48	.84
92b382ka0qgdt	4	.07
1h50ks4ncswfn	3	.05
c3zfy3qrwwdum	1	.02
92f47aa2q2rmd	1	.02

To determine the actual SQL statements that are in the ASH active session, issue the following command. In this example, the SQL_ID is 92b382ka0qgdt. For the purposes of EnterpriseOne performance tuning, concentrate on SQL specific to the application.

```
REM SQL to identify the potential E1 statement that is actively running
select sql_text from v$sqltext_with_newlines where sql_id='92b382ka0qgdt';
select sql_text from v$sqlarea where users_executing > 0;
```

```
SQL> select sql_text from v$sqlarea where users_executing > 0;

SQL_TEXT
-----------------------------------------------------------------------------
SELECT RPPST,RPNETTCID,RPDICJ,RPDDJ,RFVINV,RPCNTRTCD,RPWVID,RPNETST,RPKCO,RPHARP
ER,RPCRR,RPCO,RPCNTRTID,RPCRCD,RPPYIN,RPSFXE,RPHARSFX,RPICU,RPACR,RPPYE,RPDIVJ,R
PFAP,RPPO,RPCRRM,RPDCT,RPDCTA,RPICUT,RPADSC,RPPYWP,RPMCU,RPRP1,RPDRF,RPRF,RPPOST
,RPAN8,RPAAP,RPBCRC,RPBLSCD2,RPRP3,RPPWPG,RPNETDOC,RPDGJ,RPGLC,RPNETRC5,RPAG,RPP
KCO,RPSFX,RPPTC,RPCDS,RPDOC,RPPDCT FROM PRODDTA.F0411 WHERE (((((RPPST <> :1    A
ND RPPST <> :2  ) AND RPDCTA <> :3  ) AND RPAN8 = :4  ))) ORDER BY RPDOC ASC  ,
RPDCT ASC  , RPKCO ASC  , RPSFX ASC  , RPSFXE ASC
```

The results shown in the illustration reveal that the F0411 is currently in the ASH. The current Oracle Database activity provided in the output lists the JD Edwards EnterpriseOne financial module process that was initiated during this collection which is using the F0411 table, the Accounts Payable Ledger. This command is useful to view the category of EnterpriseOne tables that are actively being used by the Oracle Database. JD Edwards EnterpriseOne administrators familiar with the application and tables that they access should readily identify the potential processes responsible for a particular query appearing in the ASH active session list.

Given the actively running SQL statements as is found in the previous illustration, the administrator may want to know what explain plan the SQL statement is using; the following query can be useful:

```
REM SQL to view explain plan information for the E1 SQL statement
select sql_id, sql_child_number from v$active_session_history where sample_
time > sysdate -1/24/60 and session_type <> 'BACKGROUND';
select * from table(DBMS_XPLAN.DISPLAY_CURSOR('<sql_id>, <child_number>))
where <sql_id> ='9ks54zd0gu9zu' and <child_number> =0;
select * from table(DBMS_XPLAN.DISPLAY_CURSOR('92b382ka0qgdt',0));
```

The following SQL can be used to determine whether a session is progressing forward or the process is rolling back:

```
REM SQL to determine if process is progressing forward or rolling back
select sql_text from v$sqlarea
where address = (select sql_address from v$session where sid in (select SID
from v$transaction,dba_rollback_segs,v$session where SADDR=SES_ADDR
and XIDUSN=SEGMENT_ID and bitand(flag,power(2,7))<>0));
```

Note that the bit 7 of the `flag, power` variable is a flag for a transaction that is rolling back.

If things are progressing, the values in these v$ views should increase:

```
REM SQL to determine that a rollback of a process is taking place
select value rlbk from v$sysstat where name='user rollbacks';
select value cmt from v$sysstat where name='user commits';
```

Oracle Enterprise Manager (OEM)

Oracle Enterprise Manager (Figure 8-7) is a set of GUI tools provided by Oracle for controlling and managing the Oracle Database. Navigation within the OEM interface is simple, and you can dive into the performance of a running system quickly by using the many Oracle hyperlinks available in the interface.

The functionality of the OEM interface is enhanced with the Oracle Database Tuning Pack and addition of the Oracle Tuning Advisors.

Because of the limited space in this chapter to cover all of the material, the OEM interface will not be covered in this chapter; suffice it to say that the OEM interface can perform all of the manual tasks in this chapter and present information in graphs via its easy-to-use interface. You can learn more about Oracle Enterprise Manager at http://docs.oracle.com/cd/E11857_01/index.htm.

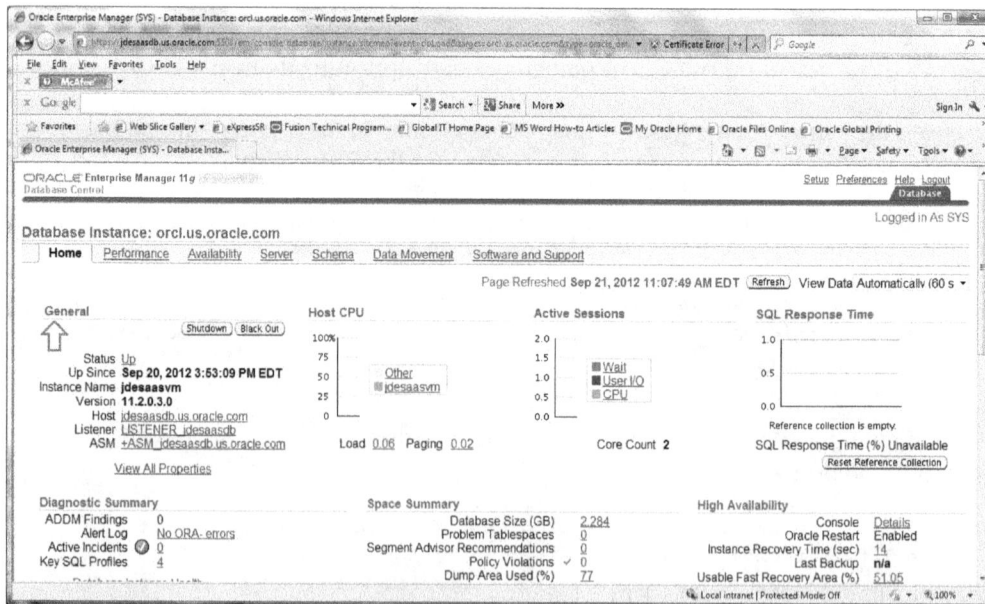

FIGURE 8-7.   *Oracle Enterprise Manager*

A good reason for including the v$ dynamic views in depth here is that at some levels, the OEM interface may not be available, and knowledge of these simple queries can assist you in determining performance issues when the OEM interface is not available.

Tuning Other Oracle Resources

This section will cover other aspects of the Oracle Database, including the optimizer, memory resources, and other parameters that are often topics of discussion on support calls with EnterpriseOne.

One of the common topics on customer questions concerning EnterpriseOne is this: Why does SQL perform differently between the different database types such as UDB and SQL Server? The most common answer to this question is in understanding how the Oracle optimizer works. Here's a quick overview of the Oracle optimizer to help you clarify SQL performance.

The role of the optimizer is a main factor in the performance of any SQL statement in EnterpriseOne. The optimizer's function is to do the following:

- Evaluate expressions and conditions

- Obtain object and system statistics

- Decide how to access the data

- Decide how to join tables

- Decide which access path is most efficient

Information needed by the optimizer includes

- Statistics for the system CPU, memory, and disk

- Schema object statistics (number of rows, indexes, and so on)

- The where clause qualifiers in the SQL statement

Two main aspects of the DB contribute to the performance of the optimizer when it chooses an execution plan: selectivity and cardinality.

- **Selectivity**   What am I selecting for? What are the expected results from that column or columns? What is the cost for doing that selection?

- **Cardinality**   Represents the number of rows and cost estimated to achieve the resulting data set from the SQL statement. It does not execute the query, but evaluates the cost of resources, doing full table scans, different index scans, and any sort or join operations.

Execution plans are used for the following:

- Determine current execution plan

- Identify affect of indexes

- Determine access paths

- Verify use of indexes

- Verify which plan may be used

Good statistics are necessary for the optimizer to perform its tasks. Thus the Oracle initialization parameters STATISTICS_LEVEL and TIMED_STATISTICS must be set in a properly tuned Oracle Database. When the statistics are not available, the Oracle optimizer is going to use the default value settings for the optimizer in Oracle, or it is going to have to use dynamic sampling.

Oracle Full Table Scans and SQL Joins

Full table scans read all rows from a table and filter out those that do not meet the selection criteria. This is the first access method considered by the optimizer. A full table scan is also one of the most expensive and inefficient costs in executing a SQL statement. A full table scan will be performed by the Oracle Database when there is a lack of index, a large amount of data is to be retrieved by the SQL query, and the query is on a small table. The following SQL command is useful in determining the tables that have performed a full table scan:

```
REM SQL to determine Full Table Scans
column sql_text format a50 heading 'Full Table Scans' wrap
break on sql_text skip 1
select executions,sorts,disk_reads,buffer_gets,cpu time,elapsed time,sql text
from v$sqlarea where (address, hash_value)
in (select address, hash_value from v$sql_plan
where options like '%FULL%' and operation like '%TABLE%')
order by Elapsed_Time
```

The resulting output file was inspected and the following line was identified:

```
EXECUTIONS    SORTS DISK_READS BUFFER_GETS   CPU_TIME ELAPSED_TIME Full Table Scans
---------- ---------- ---------- ----------- ---------- ------------ -----------------------------------------------------
    12796     12795     125705    55536353 3646976000   5.3859E+10 SELECT T1.IBBUYR,T1.IBSTDP,T0.MMMSGT,T0.MMTRQT,T0.
                                                                    MMHCLD,T1.IBMTF3,T0.MMITM,T0.MMOEDJ,T0.MMDSC1,T0.M
                                                                    MSFXO,T1.IBOT1Y,T0.MMLNID,T1.IBITM,T1.IBTIMB,T0.MM
                                                                    UKID,T0.MMKCOO,T1.IBSTKT,T0.MMDCTO,T0.MMDRQJ,T1.IB
                                                                    ANPL,T0.MMRRQJ,T1.IBLTLV,T1.IBPRP4,T0.MMMSGA,T1.IB
                                                                    MRPP,T0.MMMCU,T1.IBMCU,T1.IBLMFG,T0.MMVEND,T0.MMST
                                                                    RT,T0.MMMMCU,T0.MMSRDM,T1.IBMFST,T0.MMRSTJ,T0.MMDO
                                                                    CO,T0.MMPRJM,T1.IBLTPU,T0.MMREDJ FROM PRODDTA.F341
                                                                    1 T0,  PRODDTA.F4102 T1  WHERE ((((((T0.MMITM = :1
                                                                     AND T1.IBMCU = :2  ) AND T0.MMMCU = :3  ) AND T0
                                                                    .MMMSGT = :4  ) AND T0.MMDCTO = :5  ))) AND (T0.MM
```

NOTE
The presence of full table scans is not a bad thing, because they do occur in every implementation of EnterpriseOne. The question that should be asked when identifying full table scans is, what actions should be taken, if any?

SQL statements that are the source of full table scans are candidates for further indexing, pinning in cache, and impact analysis to the overall EnterpriseOne process in which it was identified. It is likely that no action will be taken when identifying full table scans, but when full table scans are a significant part of the EnterpriseOne execution time, the presence of full table scans can provide valuable performance tuning opportunity.

Oracle Automated Management Configurations

A number of Oracle features can be enabled to handle functions automatically. In general, for the EnterpriseOne application, all of the automated features of the Oracle 11gR2 Database should be enabled, which is the default on installation of the Oracle Database.

Automatic Segment Space Management (ASSM)

ASSM is used to manage the segments of an Oracle object via freelists, which maintain free space. Manual segment space management was cumbersome and inefficient; ASSM, introduced in Oracle 9i, automated this functionality with a self-tuning and scalable solution to this once cumbersome administration task. With Oracle 10gR2, ASSM is enabled by default whenever a new tablespace is created.

Automatic Shared Memory Management (ASMM)

ASMM is used to automate the management of the Shared Global Area (SGA). It is enabled when the Oracle initialization parameter SGA_TARGET is set to a non-zero value. ASMM dynamically adjusts the otherwise manual configuration of the database buffer cache, shared pool, Java pool, large pool, and streams pool.

EnterpriseOne functions mainly as an OLTP system, so the flexibility that Oracle provides to the database with this feature is more efficient and effective in the implementation of its architecture as it relates to how Oracle manages memory for its resources.

Operating System Caching   Operating system caching can be bypassed by using ASMM and direct I/O. If the file system is configured to bypass OS caching, then much of that file system cache memory can be reassigned to the Oracle buffer cache (or PGA and SGA in general). Oracle, in general, utilizes memory more efficiently for database activity than a general purpose file system cache and OS.

Automatic Database Diagnostic Monitor (ADDM)

ADDM is available if Oracle 11*g* Enterprise Edition is installed with the optional Tuning Packs. If Oracle 11*g* Standard Edition is available, AWR-based tools can be used. By default, the Oracle 11*g* Standard Edition is installed with EnterpriseOne. An uplift cost to the Enterprise Edition is normally required to use this feature.

Oracle Database and ASM

The storage generally available to the Oracle Database for the disk subsystems is hardware-based RAID technology from an assortment of devices such as a SAN, the NFS Server, a NAS appliance, a local disk, and the Oracle Automatic Storage Management (ASM).

Oracle's ASM solution is a stripe and mirror RAID implementation that creates a set of disk groups that can be used to create tablespaces for the Oracle Database's use. The stripe and mirror RAID is a good solution, because it allows the data protection offered by the fault-tolerant disk mirroring of the information and the entire data files share the same I/O bandwidth. ASM was introduced in Oracle 10*g* and was intended to remove the need for manual disk subsystem tuning.

EnterpriseOne will use the ASM in an Oracle RAC implementation and when ASM is used to configure disk groups to store EnterpriseOne database files and other Oracle resource files.

Shared Pool Performance Issues

The purpose of the shared pool is to store metadata information of the SQL statement in its cache for execution. Oracle uses cursors to perform the functions of moving SQL statement memory allocation to and from the shared pool.

EnterpriseOne use of the shared pool is efficient because of its use of bind variables, which avoids parsing costs and allows users to share SQL statements whenever possible. EnterpriseOne was also coded with repeatable SQL in mind and was designed to limit the amount of memory consumed by each SQL statement from EnterpriseOne.

The following dynamic views can offer an indication of the cursors that are shared in the EnterpriseOne application:

```
REM SQL to show objects in shared pool
select plan_hash_value, count(*) from v$sql
where parsing_schema_name not in ('SYS','DBSNMP','SYSMAN')
group by plan_hash_value order by 2;
```

```
PLAN_HASH_VALUE    COUNT(*)
---------------    ----------
      309400618           7
      189286166           8
     2602183296           8
     3264416173           8
     4060688636           9
     3920766470          10
     3361982155          11
     3177083396          12
     2390358070          12
     1546270724          13
     4289201150          32
```

To find the SQL related to the largest cursor sharing, run the following where <hash_value> is from the results of the first query.

```
REM SQL to show the SQL text of objects in Shared Pool
column sql_text format a50 heading 'SQL Text' wrap
select sql_text, executions from v$sqlarea
where plan_hash_value=<hash value>;
```

```
SQL Text                                              EXECUTIONS
--------------------------------------------------    ----------
 FROM PRODDTA.F4102  WHERE  ( IBMCU = :KEY1 AND IB
ITM = :KEY2 )


SELECT  *  FROM PRODDTA.F4102  WHERE  ( IBMCU = :K       941750
EY1 AND IBITM = :KEY2 )


SELECT IBITM, IBMCU, IBUSER, IBPID, IBJOBN, IBUPMJ        6839
, IBTDAY, IBLTCV FROM PRODDTA.F4102  WHERE  ( IBIT
M = :KEY1 AND IBMCU = :KEY2 )
```

Evaluating whether to set the Oracle initialization parameter of `cursor_sharing` to `EXACT` or `SIMILAR` has been an ongoing discussion within the EnterpriseOne DBA community. Typically, the default value of `EXACT` has sufficed in most customer implementations.

Shared pool memory is allocated in 1K or 4K blocks. A simple query to determine the blocks allocated by session numbers is shown here:

```
REM SQL to show shared pool allocation blocks
select * from v$sgastat where name='free memory' and pool='shared pool';
```

```
SQL> select * from v$sgastat where name='free memory' and pool='shared pool';

POOL          NAME                              BYTES
------------  --------------------------------  ----------
shared pool   free memory                       5125441752
```

Oracle Database Buffer Cache Performance Issues

The database buffer cache is a set of memory buffers in the SGA. Each buffer is sized to hold one database block. Oracle database writer processes (DBWn) are responsible for moving data resident in the memory database buffer cache that has changed out to the data files. Buffers have one of three states:

- **Free buffers** are empty or identical to the blocks on disk.
- **Dirty buffers** are holding data blocks that have changed.
- **Pinned blocks** are being accessed by a process.

Only one process at a time is allowed to access a database buffer to write. A pin "read" can share a database buffer in the cache. Pin is short operating and is not related to a lock. A buffer busy wait is recorded when another process tries to access a buffer that is pinned.

If ASMM is enabled, which is the typical configuration for an Oracle Database for EnterpriseOne, the database buffer cache memory is dynamically managed. However, the database buffer cache may exhibit some performance issues if not enough space is allocated to the SGA. It is advised that AWR reports be inspected for wait events if the EnterpriseOne Oracle Database configuration is not set for ASMM. Issues involved with the Oracle memory structure of database buffer cache in the AWR report include the following, along with the most likely performance issue generating that event:

- **Buffer busy waits**   EnterpriseOne application code issue; multiple EnterpriseOne processes are requesting same block at the same time. Evaluate the EnterpriseOne applications that are running and user and batch activity that might share common resources.

- **Read waits** OLTP applications such as EnterpriseOne are heavy in the read category. Read waits for EnterpriseOne are normally related to applications trying to access information that is currently being processed and in a transaction boundary or in the process of committing the transactions to the database.

- **Free buffer waits** Related to DBWn process efficiencies. Free buffer events are normally Oracle database tuning activities to the Oracle installation and configuration. Adjustment to this configuration is a typical action if consistently high and persistent free buffer waits are observed.

- **Cache hit ratio** Below 80 percent is another symptom of a small buffer cache and is affected by full table scans, repeated scans of the same table, or data and application contents and design. As consultants, we put a low priority at trying to tune the Oracle Database based solely on the cache hit ratio without further supporting performance degradation metrics pointing to a more significant issue.

Program Global Area Memory and Temporary Space

Sufficient Program Global Area (PGA) memory allocation is critical for performance. If there is not enough PGA memory, the Oracle database will use the temporary tablespace instead. Reading and writing to the temporary tablespace will slow down the execution of the EnterpriseOne application. The Oracle Database requests that use PGA include any activity involving sorts, ordering, or joins.

Optimal performance in these SQL operation activities will require the database to fit the data into the PGA working area cache. If the data cannot fit into the area, multiple passes to the cache area will be required.

The following two queries illustrate the SQL statements that require single and multiple passes to execute for some EnterpriseOne queries:

```
REM PGA Memory Utilization query
select sql_text, sum(onepass_executions) onepass_cnt,
sum(multipasses_executions) mpass_cnt
from v$sql s, v$sql_workarea wa
where s.address=wa.address
group by sql_text
having sum(onepass_executions+multipasses_executions)>0;
```

```
SQL_TEXT
--------------------------------------------------------------------------------------------------------------
ONEPASS_CNT  MPASS_CNT
-----------  ----------
SELECT  *  FROM PRODDTA.F1755  WHERE  ( ZASTAW = :KEY1 AND ZAITM = :KEY2 AND ZACLST >= :KEY3 AND ZADOCO <> :KEY4 )   ORDER BY
ZADOCO ASC,ZADCTO ASC,ZAKCOO ASC
     7226       1308

SELECT  COUNT(*)  FROM PRODDTA.F1755  WHERE  ( ZASTAW = :KEY1 AND ZAITM = :KEY2 AND ZACLST >= :KEY3 AND ZADOCO <> :KEY4 )
     5396          0
```

```
REM PGA multi pass query
select to_number(decode(sid,65535,null,sid)) sid,
operation_type operation,
trunc(expected_size/1024) esize,
trunc(actual_mem_used/1024) mem,
trunc(max_mem_used/1024) maxmem,
number_passes            pass,
trunc(tempseg_size/1024)  tsize
from v$sql_workarea_active
order by 1,2;
```

SID OPERATION	ESIZE	MEM	MAXMEM	PASS	TSIZE
70 SORT (v2)	7858	7858	7858	0	
1725 SORT (v2)	110	110	110	0	
16572 SORT (v2)	6598	6598	6598	0	
17554 SORT (v2)	7858	7858	7858	0	
19400 SORT (v2)	2944	2944	2944	0	
25153 SORT (v2)	6598	6598	6598	0	5396

Automatic PGA Memory Management

Automatic PGA memory management dynamically controls the SQL memory allocations based on the PGA memory available, the SQL operator needs, and the system workload.

Set PGA_AGGREGATE_TARGET to a non-zero value, which can be dynamically modified at the instance level. For OLTP systems like EnterpriseOne, set the PGA_AGGREGATE_TARGET to 20 percent of the size of the SGA. The WORKAREA_SIZE_POLICY will automatically default to AUTO. PGA_AGGREGATE_TARGET controls the work areas allocated for both shared and dedicated Oracle connections.

Temporary Tablespace Management Performance

Temporary tablespaces are used primarily to handle sorts, joins, temporary large objects (LOBs), and other similar data for a transaction or session. The data is, as the table implies, temporary, and will be lost after the session or transaction is completed. Oracle instance recovery of the temporary tablespace is not required because of the volatile nature of this Oracle object.

The v$tempseg_usage view is the dynamic query that shows what session information for EnterpriseOne is stored in the Oracle temporary tablespace:

```
REM Temporary Tablespace session query
select session_num,username,segtype,blocks,tablespace from v$tempseg_usage;
```

As shown in the illustration, primarily LOB temporary data is being stored in the temporary tablespace.

```
SESSION_NUM USERNAME                          SEGTYPE       BLOCKS TABLESPACE
----------- -------------------------------   --------- ---------- ------------------------------
        130 JDE                               LOB_DATA         128 TEMP
         73 JDE                               LOB_DATA         128 TEMP
        180 JDE                               LOB_DATA         128 TEMP
        976 JDE                               LOB_DATA         128 TEMP
        697 JDE                               LOB_DATA         128 TEMP
         91 JDE                               LOB_DATA         128 TEMP
```

The percentage usage of the temporary tablespace can be determined using this query:

```
REM Temporary Tablespace performance query
select (s.tot_used_blocks/f.total_blocks)*100 as pctused
from (select sum(used_blocks) tot_used_blocks
from v$sort_segment
where tablespace_name='TEMP') s,
(select sum(blocks) total_blocks
from dba_temp_files
where tablespace_name='TEMP') f;
```

```
SQL> select (s.tot_used_blocks/f.total_blocks)*100 as pctused
from (se   2  lect sum(used_blocks) tot_used_blocks
from   3  v$sort_segment
wher   4  e tablespace_name='TEMP') s,
(s   5  elect sum(blocks) total_blocks
from d   6  ba_temp_files
whe   7  re tablespace_name='TEMP') f;

   PCTUSED
----------
        10
```

The temporary tablespace performance is an issue only if the memory of the PGA has to spill over into its usage.

Oracle Database Performance and Disk Architecture

One of the most critical parts of the Oracle Database architecture that is tied to performance is the disk subsystem. This section will cover some indicators in the AWR reports that illustrate how disk subsystems need to be addressed for performance.

On a well-tuned system, the AWR report top events are CPU time and the DB file scattered and sequential reads, as depicted in Figure 8-8.

An example of an AWR report that might need some further performance analysis as it relates to disk I/O performance is shown in Figure 8-9.

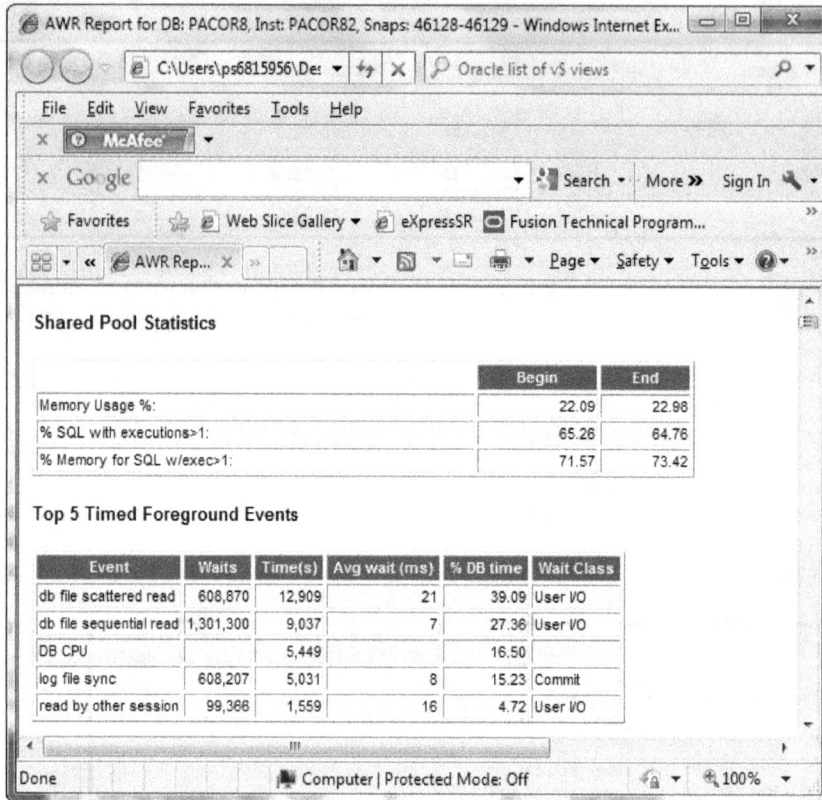

FIGURE 8-8.   *AWR Report: Top 5 Timed Foreground Events*

The following events in the AWR report should be a first indicator that the disk subsystem might be a potential bottleneck for the EnterpriseOne application:

- Buffer busy waits

- Write complete waits

- DB file parallel writes

- Enqueue waits

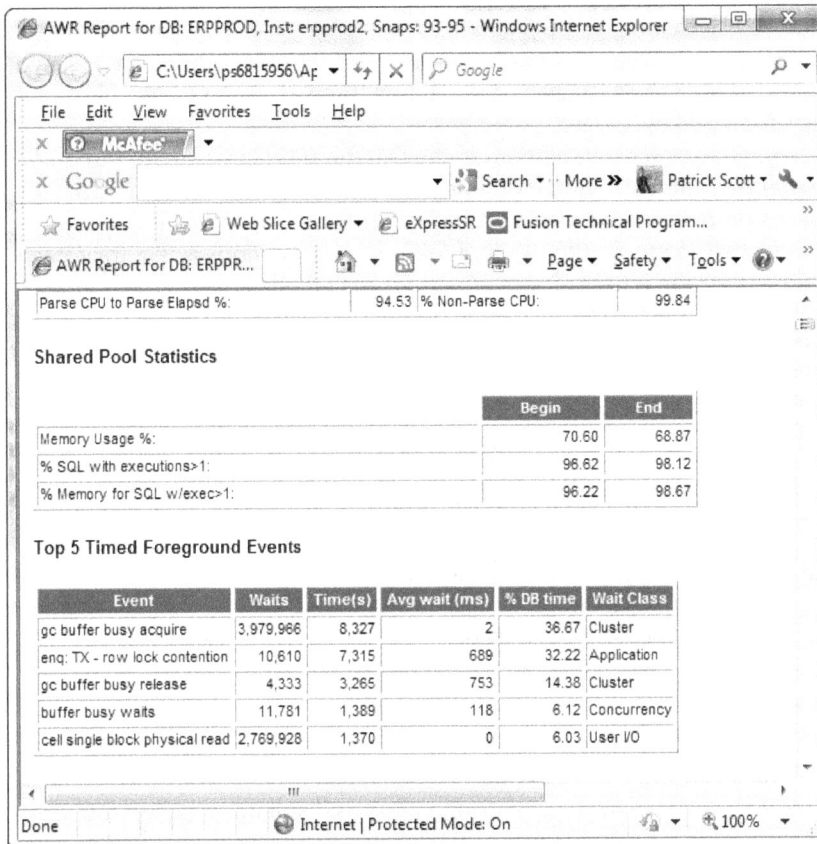

FIGURE 8-9. *AWR report showing slow disk performance*

Review the Logs

Review the Oracle installation log, EnterpriseOne Logic Server logs, EnterpriseOne Batch Server logs, and JAS Server logs periodically for Oracle error codes. The Oracle Database errors are of the format ORA-XXXX or TNS-XXXX. It is a simple task to perform and can have great benefits in identifying possible performance, memory, and process limitations as the Oracle Database is exercised and the load is increased on the Oracle Database server.

Sufficient Swap Space

"Swap space" is a term used on OS platforms to describe an area on the hard drive that is designated to be used when the amount of physical memory (RAM) is exhausted or in short supply. In short, swap space is disk memory used as part of the overall memory pool by the OS for process usage.

Insufficient swap space can hinder Oracle Database processes from responding, leading to process failures. "Out of Memory," "Not Enough Space," and "Unable to Fork a Process" errors in the Oracle Database alert log can also be attributed to a lack of sufficient swap space. The result of these error conditions is that the Oracle Database processes and other software functions making database query requests will lock up, go into a wait state, or fail. In addition, the EnterpriseOne software will become unusable. So as a general rule of thumb, allocate *at least* the recommended amount of swap space, and more if possible.

When the Oracle Database is installed, it will ensure that there is sufficient swap space configured on the system. The Oracle Database installer will provide information on the amount of swap space that it detects on the server on which it is being installed as well as what is minimally required. The minimum requirements of the Oracle installer can be overridden during installation so that it may proceed further, but this is a risky activity. When minimum requirements of an OS are not met during the Oracle installation, the installation should be stopped, requirements adjusted, and the installation reinitialized.

Unix

A general rule of 10 percent more than the recommended amount for the installation requirements for swap space is a good start for better performance for the EnterpriseOne software. Monitoring the swap space during peak and spiking usage of the EnterpriseOne software is a good time to evaluate the swap metrics on the OS.

Typical error messages that might indicate that not enough space has been allocated for swap include the following:

- TNS-12500, TNS-12540, TNS-12560, TNS-00510 Oracle errors

- Unable to fork a process

- Not enough space

Usually the server will lock up and hang shortly after these messages appear in the log files.

Windows

The Windows swap space is called the page file. The page file is an area on the hard drive that is used for additional memory to increase the performance of the applications initiated on the Windows Server platform. Page file management should be left to the Windows OS, and the size of the page file should be at least as large as the amount of RAM on the Windows Server.

Operating System Patches

Operating system patches for the Oracle Database are often ignored during the Oracle Database installation process and can impact performance if left unattended. The OS software packages include kernel and third-party library software that is needed by the Oracle Database to communicate and allow the functionality of all the Oracle Database features.

Often, the software is installed on the OS, but the version is one or two levels prior to the one required by the Oracle Database installation. Oracle Database features may in fact function, and they may even perform well, but there is a reason that the Oracle Database installation requires a later version. It may be a known bug in the functionality, but more often than not, the new version is required to improve performance in how the software functions in memory or CPU cycles. That is why it is crucial that you periodically review the specific Oracle Database requirements for OS patches.

Interprocess Communication Kernel Memory Settings

Interprocess communication (IPC) is a set of memory resources that allow the communication of information among process threads. These threads may be on the same server or between computers on a network. The three main categories of IPC resources are message queues, semaphores, and shared memory segments.

The EnterpriseOne application uses the mechanism available with IPC resources as a key way to manage its network and kernel processes. The Oracle Database also uses the functionality of IPCs to control its background processes and establish database connections. Performance degradation related to IPC resources is a real and common occurrence with customers.

Unix IPC Resources

Unix IPC resources are heavily used by the Oracle Database processes and EnterpriseOne application; thus a lack of these resources can be detrimental to the ability to install, startup, and initiate many of the key functions in the Oracle Database and EnterpriseOne application.

Unix user resources are normally included in the system or user settings `ulimit`. The `ulimit` variable controls how the OS controls certain functions within a starting or running process. It is important that the Unix shell limits be set properly for the Oracle Database. Many of the errors in the alert log when Oracle Database processes fail will be shown when the `ulimit` values are insufficient.

Of all the OS tuning variables, user resources, such as `ulimit` and max number of user processes, are the primary variables in performance degradation at the OS level for both the Oracle Database and EnterpriseOne application. Other IPC Unix resources that may have to be tuned are the SHMMAX (Shared Memory Segment) and SEMMNS (Maximum Number of Semaphores). Both of these settings require minimum configuration settings at Oracle database installation time, for they will be checked by the Oracle installer.

Windows IPC Resources

For Windows, IPC tuning is not required and is not allowed to be adjusted by the user. On Windows, few resources, including IPC shared memory and semaphores, are needed by the Oracle database.

Processor, Memory, and Disk Configuration

Access is the amount of time a request takes, and bandwidth is the transfer rate of information across the OS architecture. Table 8-1 illustrates the access time of the four types of storage that the Oracle database objects can reside in—registers, cache, main memory, and disk. The use of memory registers is the fastest and Oracle objects that are accessed on the disk is the slowest. Thus it is a great benefit to the EnterpriseOne application in performing SQL operations where the Oracle database objects will find its execution in the fastest medium possible. Performance tuning of the Oracle database objects to the fastest hardware resources requires both the knowledge of those resources and how to configure the Oracle database to use those resources.

Type	Access Time(ns)	Bandwidth(MB/sec)
Registers	0.25–0.5	50K–500K
Cache	0.5–2.5	5K–20K
Main Memory	50–250	2.5K–10K
Disk	5 Million	50–500

*Table Source: *Computer Architecture: A Quantitative Approach*, by John Hennessy and David Patterson (Morgan Kaufmann, 2011)

TABLE 8-1. *Access Time and Bandwidth for System Resources*

When physical memory cannot be used, disk subsystem components of a server become extremely important to the Oracle Database and EnterpriseOne application. Oracle recommends the use of the Oracle ASM feature of the database in Oracle 10*g* implementations or later or to use logical volumes from a SAN, NAS, or other RAID technology to mirror and stripe physical disks for the best performance and data integrity.

Conclusion

The important Oracle Database initialization parameters that affect performance are related to the size of SGA, PGA, and processes. Proper sizing of these alone and measuring the metrics that surround them will address the majority of the EnterpriseOne application performance issues related to the Oracle Database.

The most critical tuning of the OS will involve the resources of disk, memory, processor, and process threads, including IPC and user limit settings. Of the three resources on the OS, disk I/O contention is the one that should have a particular focus.

Many of the example SQL statements on the dynamic views were taken from the following documents and applied to the EnterpriseOne application:

- *Oracle Database Administrators Guide 11*g, part number E10595-06

- *Oracle Database 2 Day + Performance Tuning Guide 11*g, part number E10822-02

- *Oracle Database Performance Tuning Guide 11*g, part number E10821-04

- *Oracle Database Reference*, part number E10820-03

All of these documents can be found on the Oracle 11*g* portal: http://oracle.su/docs/11g/nav/portal_11.htm

CHAPTER
9

Tuning by Tier: The Database Tier (Microsoft SQL Server and IBM System i)

I n this chapter we will discuss processes you can utilize to tune your Microsoft
SQL Server and IBM System i databases. We will share some different strategies
involved, since there are differences regarding how the databases relate to their
operating systems. The Oracle database supported by EnterpriseOne can run on
multiple platforms, such as Unix, Linux, and Microsoft Windows. For EnterpriseOne,
Microsoft SQL Server operates only on the Microsoft Windows platform. IBM System
i is even more integrated where the DB2/400 database is included in the operating
system.

NOTE
*A number of the monitoring and metric procedures
discussed in this chapter are similar to those
provided in Chapter 8. To minimize duplication
of certain suggestions, please read Chapter 8 as
well as this chapter, even though you may not
be using an Oracle Database system. There are
definitely a number of common areas regarding the
EnterpriseOne databases, and we are attempting to
provide some of the key tuning elements for each of
those database systems.*

Tuning Microsoft SQL Server

With Microsoft SQL Server, it's important that you maintain patch levels, ensure that
you size and architect the database server appropriately, and perform a number of
tuning options, as described here. Microsoft SQL Server 64-bit addressing provides
great scalability and opportunities for JD Edwards EnterpriseOne; the 64 bit/x64
Microsoft SQL Server releases are the only supported levels now. Considering the
use of database and backup compression along with Read Committed Snapshot
Isolation (RCSI) can further enhance your system's capabilities and resource usage.

Reviewing the Logs

This is one of the obvious and sometimes neglected tuning tasks, but we often find a
number of clues in the various database, EnterpriseOne, and operating system logs.
If you are experiencing performance issues, you need to ensure that the various logs
have been reviewed. A number of general issues can occur due to application,
resource, network, and other areas, even when someone "thinks" it is a database
problem. We have often heard users blame "the network" or "the database" when
the root cause was entirely different. Generally, administrators have access to

SQL Server Support: 32-bit vs. 64-bit

JD Edwards OneWorld and EnterpriseOne have supported Microsoft SQL Server since the introduction of the software. Historically, Microsoft SQL Server was ideal for Windows-based customers with smaller installations due to the use of 32-bit operating systems. Enhancements over the years provided additional memory and scaling with the use of Physical Address Extension (PAE) memory and Address Windowing Extensions (AWE). Unfortunately, these settings were sometimes implemented incorrectly, and the memory above the 32-bit address line was not utilized correctly. In addition, some other memory settings for 32-bit Windows, such as the /3GB switch, are no longer needed in the newer operating system releases that operate in 64-bit mode. With the introduction of Microsoft SQL Server 2005, 2008, and 2012, the use of 64-bit database memory access is the preferred and recommended requirement for EnterpriseOne releases. You no longer have to be concerned with 32-bit memory address space limitations, and this helps reduce some of the performance and tuning challenges of the past. Our advanced tuning focus is on the 64-bit/x64 Microsoft SQL Server releases, even though a portion of these suggestions can apply to older releases as well.

behind-the-scenes logs of the processes, so we will focus on those. Error messages reported by the end user should generally be captured in a screenshot where possible and investigated to see if they can be linked to specific events in the various logs.

Microsoft SQL Server Logs

The Microsoft SQL Server logs can sometimes provide insights into the overall database activity if an error or warning occurs. A number of diagnostic tidbits can help you ascertain the release, patch level, configuration, and other information near the top of the log. If there are specific issues, such as a transaction log filling up, these are recorded here as well. This is an operational issue and not really tuning per se, but since all database activities that need to perform a data change halt until the log is cleared, it is a good first place to examine.

You can examine the SQL Server logs from the ERRORLOG text file, where the SQL Server instance is installed under the log folder. By default, for a 64-bit installation, this is C:\Program Files\Microsoft SQL Server\MSSQLxx.instancename\ MSSQL\Log folder. Or, if you have administrative access, use the Microsoft SQL

Server Management Studio application to view the log files. An example is shown in the following illustration.

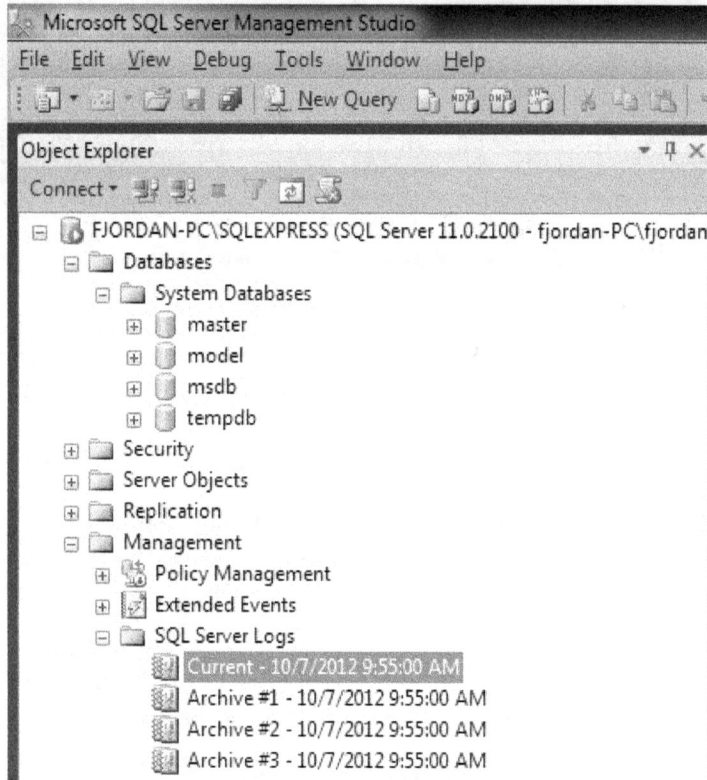

In the log, you can observe a number of informational items and the initial Microsoft SQL Server configuration. These can be very helpful in understanding the configuration of the system and what errors may be present.

Microsoft Windows Operating System Logs

The Microsoft Windows OS logs are used in a number of areas. The primary logs that we tend to investigate are the Windows Application, Security, and System Event logs. There are others depending how the server is configured, such as the Windows Firewall, file backup, or anti-virus logs.

Following are examples of what you may be searching for:

■ In the application event logs, any errors related to Microsoft SQL Server or JD Edwards applications

■ In the System event logs, any errors or warnings for Microsoft SQL Server services or related applications

■ In the Windows Firewall log, information about application ports being blocked—this is rare, but if present it will prevent a number of connection requests

■ In the file backup logs, information about resource/file locks occurring during the times being investigated; depending on how a backup is configured, it can consume significant processor, disk response, and possible network resources when running

JD Edwards EnterpriseOne Logs

Most JD Edwards EnterpriseOne Configurable Network Computing (CNC) administrators and developers are familiar with the various logs that are created by EnterpriseOne processes/services. In Chapter 8, we referred to a number of the areas to review, such as utilizing EnterpriseOne Server Manager as a launch point to obtain details about the various components that access the Microsoft SQL Server database.

Following are examples of what you may be searching for:

■ The WEB JAS logs, for database or other error messages that are initiated by the end users. Database errors such as duplicate keys, insert failures, or transaction rollbacks tend to affect the user application. The JD Edwards EnterpriseOne Server Manager application helps consolidate and provide access to certain logs.

■ The Enterprise server JDE and batch logs, for database messages that need to be reviewed. If you don't have the EnterpriseOne user set up correctly with an address book number, there can be work center failure messages that cannot be seen by the user for application-specific issues. Database errors typically are recorded in these logs for specific user processes or kernels.

■ Database performance metrics via the JAS and Enterprise Server Query Execution Time Threshold settings, for additional insights for longer running queries. You can also see these queries from database tools such as Microsoft SQL Server Dynamic Management View (DMV) reports, third-party monitoring, and SQL profiler traces.

Showing the SQL Statements in EnterpriseOne Server Logs

The following JDE.INI setting was introduced as part of the Kernel Resource Management (KRM) initiative in the Tools 8.98.3 release and provides a methodology by which SQL statements can be logged to the JDE logs if they exceed a time threshold. The JDE.INI setting is

```
[DB SYSTEM SETTINGS]
QueryExecutionTimeThreshold=1
```

This functionality is turned OFF when set to 0 and only positive integer values are valid for its usage. Set the `QueryExecutionTimeThreshold` to 1 second to track any SQL statements that take more than 1 second to complete. This setting is read by EnterpriseOne services at startup and will require a restart of services to use if implemented. In the case of batch processing, the value is picked up when the batch process is launched, so it must be set prior to launching the batch process to have an effect. (Reference: http://docs.oracle .com/cd/E17984_01/doc.898/e14718.pdf.)

Operating System/Database Patches

It is generally recommended that, where possible, you maintain the patch levels of your Windows OS and SQL Server. Different companies have various change management strategies, but we typically recommend that you attempt to keep the patch levels fairly current within 12 to 18 months if possible. This also applies to JD Edwards EnterpriseOne tools and software updates. If you allow the patch levels to become too out of date, it becomes more difficult to apply one-off or specific fixes over time due to increased dependency chains in the software. Also, from a support perspective, if your patches are out of date, it becomes more of a challenge for the software vendor to help resolve issues when the latest set of fixes that address known issues are not in place.

Every customer has different thresholds and philosophies regarding how they manage their patches. Very large customers with high levels of customization tend to apply patches at intervals of up to several years, while a number of smaller to midsize customers tend to be more current on their various patch levels. Another influencing factor can be government regulations and qualifications that limit the changes that can be introduced into the systems.

A general strategy employed during installations or upgrades is to attempt to update the software as frequently as possible before full integration tests occur. This helps to keep the patch levels more current and can indirectly influence the performance, since most patches are issued to correct functionality, memory, or performance issues. Once the various go-live phases are near the 30- to 90-day range, the patch levels tend to be stabilized and frozen until the next change window is reached that the business can tolerate. After the production environment goes live, we generally like to see security patches deployed monthly, database cumulative patches when needed, and Microsoft Windows/database service packs when certified by EnterpriseOne minimum technical requirements (MTRs) and your company is comfortable implementing them. Generally, this is a 12- to 24-month window and helps to reduce support challenges and apply corrections for known issues.

Keep in mind that the JD Edwards EnterpriseOne MTRs or certifications will also tend to influence the combination of Windows OS and SQL Server patch levels. If you update a Tools release level that is several years old, you typically need to examine newer Windows versions since the older releases most likely are near the end of their support life. For example, SQL Server releases typically occur every 3 to 5 years, so a newer JD Edwards EnterpriseOne tools release (9.1.x) may no longer be certified against a database level such as SQL Server 2005 x64 64-bit.

NOTE
A good Oracle Metalink document for EnterpriseOne Microsoft SQL Server customers is Document ID 1275500.1, "Tips for Running EnterpriseOne with SQL Server 2008 and SQL Server 2008 R2." This document contains several suggestions that can help an EnterpriseOne customer's architecture, which we also endorse and allude to in this guide. If we don't mention certain tips, that does not mean they are not recommended, but from the advanced tuning perspective, we assume those areas are or have been reviewed and addressed.

For the Windows OS, you should consider various strategies of patching. Examples are provided in Table 9-1.

Patch Type	Comment
Windows OS patches	Usually consolidated into service packs that most customers wait for
Microsoft hotfixes	Tend to be specific fixes with less regression testing than OS patches/service packs and are usually applied on an "as-needed" basis
Microsoft Security Updates	Tend to be critical updates that Microsoft has identified to minimize OS vulnerabilities and are usually applied in a scheduled timeframe, such as monthly

TABLE 9-1. *Windows OS Patch Types*

The SQL Server databases also utilize similar patching strategies, as shown in Table 9-2.

TIP
At the Windows OS level, the server admins will most likely need critical security updates to be applied, so these need to be considered. You can use those planned outage windows for other patch updates for the OS and database as well if desired. If at all possible, try to define a least a monthly maintenance window, depending on the architecture in place. The grid architectures discussed in other chapters would allow you to service a subset of servers in a planned fashion without observed outages until you fail-over the database cluster.

Always remember to review and operate within the JD Edwards EnterpriseOne MTRs/certifications for your Windows and SQL Server database configuration. Most customers adhere to the MTRs, which allows them to obtain support more readily. When the configuration becomes very old and back-leveled, it can become more of a challenge to tune or obtain patches since you may not receive support from the vendor. Since most vendors maintain their software for 5 years or longer, this may not be an issue, but we have observed some customers running software levels beyond 10 years, and it takes time to investigate and determine the best course of action when tuning or changing the configuration.

Patch Type	Comment
SQL Server patches	Usually consolidated into service packs that most customers wait for.
SQL Server hotfixes	Tend to be specific fixes with less regression testing than service packs and are usually applied on an "as-needed" basis.
SQL Server cumulative updates	Consolidated hotfixes that are subsets of a full service pack; released more frequently by Microsoft between full service packs. JD Edwards EnterpriseOne has in the past required certain minimum cumulative levels to meet the MTRs.

TABLE 9-2. *SQL Server Patch Types*

Microsoft SQL Server Service Account Privileges/Permissions

Most of the account policies and privileges for the SQL Server services are created during the database install into local user groups. This process began in SQL Server 2005 and later releases. (If you are still using SQL Server 2000, either upgrade or you will need to consult with older Microsoft Knowledge Base articles outside the scope of this book.) If you decide to use a domain or another user account, you simply add it to the appropriate local SQL Server group for that particular database instance. Some example privileges are SeBatchLogonRight, SeAssignPrimaryTokenPrivilege, and SeServiceLogonRight, among others.

The local user groups would have the format for SQL Server 2005, as shown here:

- **SQLServer2005MSSQLUser$ComputerName$MSSQLSERVER**   The default instance

- **SQLServer2005MSSQLUser$ComputerName$InstanceName**   Named instance you may create

You'll find a Microsoft Knowledge Base article listing the various SQL Server versions at http://msdn.microsoft.com/en-us/library/ms143504.aspx. You can select your database version and review the various permissions and account options available. Most EnterpriseOne customers that we have observed have a local account defined, and some utilize a domain user. There is no one-strategy-fits-all recommendation here; it is dependent on your infrastructure requirements.

Later, in the "Memory" section, we will discuss memory recommendations to consider such as using the Lock Pages in Memory (LPIM) and user rights on the SQL Server startup account. This recommendation is for *all* SQL Server releases, even though the memory management in Windows 2008 Server has improved substantially regarding hard trim working sets. Based on our consulting experience and observations, you can still have unintended performance issues with SQL Server being paged out at undesired rates. You can mitigate this by ensuring that the minimum and maximum SQL Server memory is set appropriately for your configuration.

SQL Server CPU, Memory, Network, and Disk Configuration

SQL Server performance is greatly influenced by the hardware configuration. The database is very scalable, with several editions from which the user can select. For JD Edwards EnterpriseOne Tools 9.1 and later, the SQL Server 2008/2008 R2 editions supported are the 64-bit x64 Standard, Enterprise, and Datacenter editions.

Most customers above 50–100 users tend to utilize the Enterprise edition for maximum flexibility and features. At the time of this writing, the SQL Server 2012 editions supported by JD Edwards EnterpriseOne have not been announced. The lighter SQL Server Express (SSE) that was previously an option for the JD Edwards EnterpriseOne Windows development client and deployment server is no longer supported, beginning with EnterpriseOne 9.1 applications release.

You should have a very good understanding of your projected business needs for the test and production environments using SQL Server databases. The use of 64-bit addressing provides a very scalable database architecture that can be used for dozens to thousands of JD EnterpriseOne users. As we have stated, if you can obtain a sizing from your hardware vendor with accurate information, your architecture should meet your business needs. It is strongly recommended that you conduct performance and scaling tests before a go-live to ensure your architecture does meet those objectives.

When procuring hardware for your SQL Server database, we typically recommend that you obtain the most robust configuration that your budget will allow. This may seem to be a bit obvious, but typically hardware and software investment tends to be a low percentage of the overall project/implementation budget. The infrastructure costs almost always tend to be much less than the costs and effort involved with upgrading and implementing your JD Edwards EnterpriseOne and associated components solution.

TIP
It is usually very beneficial to obtain a JD Edwards EnterpriseOne sizing from your hardware vendor. Then, once the majority of business processes have been configured, you can examine the sizing again to ensure that your system meets the requirements before moving to a production environment. Common sense, we know, but this seems to have been ignored by a number of customers we've worked with over the years. If this is ignored, it usually becomes a consulting opportunity that typically occurs near or shortly after a go-live, which creates some grief and frustration for the business. This is an obvious, but often neglected task, and we strongly suggest conducting performance and scaling exercises. This has been emphasized in other chapters as well to drive the point home.

The common items that have a relationship with and affect database tuning efforts are shown in Table 9-3. Generally, you will need to strike a balance between

Database Server Hardware/Infrastructure Element	Comments
LAN connections	Ensure that the fastest connections are configured as the database server is a consolidation point for all the SQL requests/clients. If local network connections are slow, you likely have a performance opportunity. Fundamental assumption is a fast network switch with redundant connections on the database server that are in the same virtual LAN (VLAN) or switch.
CPU or processors	The heart of the database server performs the actual operations/manipulations of the data. The robust capabilities of Intel/AMD chips provide multicore processors that scale well for EnterpriseOne customer workloads. Try to obtain as many processors as you can for the database server relative to the workload you expect. The hardware vendor can assist with the selection. Since Microsoft SQL Servers for EnterpriseOne Production environments typically have a single database instance, you'll tend to have more hardware on this server than your other EnterpriseOne servers such as the Web or Enterprise/logic servers. High availability needs will usually have the database within a Microsoft Cluster Service.
Memory (RAM)	The memory is critical since this is where data must reside to be read or changed by the processors. Obtain as much RAM as your budget permits to reduce the likelihood of being short of memory running the database. Rule of thumb if the overall JDE_PRODUCTION database size is known: Have a minimum of 10–20% of that size in RAM. For example, if you expect the database to be 1000GB, the memory estimate would be 128 to 256GB of RAM on the production database server. This provides a starting point. EnterpriseOne configurations can vary widely so you may need more or less memory to obtain the desired performance levels.

(Continued)

TABLE 9-3. *Hardware Elements of Database Server*

Database Server Hardware/Infrastructure Element	Comments
Disk	This is typically the area where the most bottlenecks and tuning occur. Accessing the disk takes longer than accessing memory or the network since the access times are usually in the millisecond range.
	The goal is for the database and log files to have the fastest read/write times you can obtain. Backup and files can be slightly slower.
	Many options and configurations are available for the disk systems such as RAID on local disk with cache controllers (direct attached storage), SAN or NAS attached storage, and solid state disks (SSDs)

TABLE 9-3.   *Hardware Elements of Database Server*

these elements, because if any of them are oversubscribed or saturated, this will affect the other areas. The basic goal we strive for is to ensure that each component is optimized on the server and using the various Microsoft performance tools such as Performance Data Collector, Performance Monitor, Task Manager, Resource Monitor, and DMVs, which allow you to observe the behavior of the components under the workload.

CPU or Processors

The SQL Server database depends on the processor being available to perform its work. As we stated, working with your hardware vendor on the machine sizing if you have good information of the workload characteristics will help greatly. With today's Intel/AMD processors, you get a lot of "bang for the buck" in the commodity hardware. Typically we see higher-end blade or larger servers for the SQL Server database. Production environment databases are generally not virtualized except in some customer configurations where the user counts are relatively small, such as under 200 users.

NOTE
We are not stating that you cannot virtualize a production database, but make sure that additional planning, testing, and review occurs since you will be adding another layer of potential complexity that could impact your performance levels.

When reviewing the processors from a tuning perspective, we examine the overall CPU usage of the machine from a high level using the various performance monitoring tools available in Windows and SQL Server. From a consulting perspective, if we start to observe average usage greater than 30- to 60-minute intervals above 70–80 percent, we need to investigate what is using the CPU time.

Most EnterpriseOne SQL Server databases tend to have sufficient processor capacity since more robust hardware is usually purchased for the database server. In one case, a customer was running SQL Server and observed very high processor usage especially during the month-end processes with heavy batch usage. They were using SQL Server 2000 SP3 Enterprise Edition, which had far fewer performance monitoring tools than we have today in Windows 2008 R2 and SQL Server 2008 R2. Using manual SQL scripts and Performance Monitor, we found thousands of queries that were performing full table scans (FTSs) and using full parallelism. Due to the parallelism settings and the high number of FTSs, they were consuming all the processor capacity for days at a time along with the buffer pool memory. They had gone through a couple of hardware upgrades over the years, increasing the processors and memory without purging the data to reduce the query response time or tune the FTS queries significantly. The system had in fact grown to a non-uniform memory access (NUMA) configuration with two physical servers merged to appear as one logical server. They were near a go-live to a newer EnterpriseOne release along with a database migration as well. The bulk of the effort went into the new EnterpriseOne release, and the needed indexes on several custom tables were identified and implemented. Query parallelism was also reduced along with eliminating the need for the more expensive NUMA hardware configuration. That tuning effort resulted in the processor usage being reduced significantly, and the month-end processes were reduced by more than 36 hours.

That example leads us into some database settings that can affect the processor usage for EnterpriseOne configurations. By default, SQL Server has the maximum degree of parallelism (MDOP) set to 0, which denotes that all available processors should be used. This setting is useful when your goal is to use all available resources to provide the fastest query response time. In an EnterpriseOne configuration, however, we want to reward the interactive transactions, and large queries that need to perform full table scans should not consume whatever resources are available. If you have a number of users and batch Universal Batch Engines (UBEs) along with external systems that may require performing an FTS on large tables with millions of rows, you may want to reduce the processor and resource consumption. The large throttle is the MDOP setting; by limiting the number of processors that a parallel query will consume, you will increase the execution time of the large query but reduce the processor usage so they are more likely available for the smaller OLTP queries in the system. Due to the large potential variations in EnterpriseOne workload characteristics, there is no hard-and-fast rule regarding the MDOP setting. For most customers, we recommend setting the MDOP either to 50 percent of your processors or, for large configurations with hundreds/thousands of users, to one or two processors. This reduces the potential for a small number of queries against millions of rows monopolizing your processors. Why reward the large user parallel queries with improved response time rather than the queries that are smaller and more efficient? For certain administration/operation tasks, you can normally set the MDOP higher if you need the resources.

For most EnterpriseOne configurations, we like to set the MDOP to 2 or 4 so that some parallelism is used by default to help the larger queries, but we still leave processor capacity available for other tasks. You need to develop a baseline of your configuration and determine the setting that works best for your business goals. There is no one best answer for all situations, but if you find that certain large queries affect the interactive transactions, this can be a very good option to consider. Table 9-4 provides a summary of our recommendations.

Generally, if you see high processor usage, you need to determine whether the issue is with SQL Server or perhaps other applications running on the server. For JD Edwards EnterpriseOne, we recommend that the database server be used only for the production instance and that other applications run on separate servers. Again, architecturally, you can combine multiple applications such as the enterprise services and database together, but you may not have the optimal configuration, especially if hundreds of users access the database.

Resource Governor

SQL Server 2008 also has a newer feature called the Resource Governor that can allow you to manage your resources between the online/OLTP users and various batch requests. Unfortunately, we have not observed or engaged any JD Edwards EnterpriseOne customers that are using this advanced feature. The Resource Governor could prove useful for larger configurations that want to reduce the priority and resource usage of larger or runaway queries. The Resource Governor can specify resource pools by a connection, which means that if you have a separate UBE or reporting server, it could be distinguished from the interactive workloads from the web and logic servers. This can then provide an avenue to prioritize your workloads between interactive and batch, if desired.

Potential MDOP Setting	Comment
50% of server processors	Example: I have a 4-processor, 4-core system for a total of 16 cores. The MDOP setting would be 8 for the default parallelism.
1	A setting of 1 basically disables default parallelism.
2 or 4	A setting of 2 or 4 breaks the query into 2 or 4 subsets, respectively.

TABLE 9-4. *Maximum Degree of Parallelism Setting*

Areas That May Cause High Processor Usage

Following are some areas you should review that may be causing high processor usage:

- Missing or out-of-date database statistics. We strongly recommend that SQL Server auto update statistics be present and that for any major database changes, such as a data refresh or upgrade, you manually execute the database statistics to ensure that current information exists. Some customers run these on the weekend before month-end processing, for example.

- Missing indexes or suboptimal queries being executed. If the production database server has business intelligence, data warehouse, or large reporting queries running against the OLTP transactions, you can see a significant increase in the processor usage. For larger and busier JD Edwards EnterpriseOne architectures, we recommend that a replicated database using tools such as log shipping and read-only copies on another server are used to offload this activity.

- Large numbers of FTSs consume the processors, especially with the MDOP default of 0 as stated earlier.

- Online virus scanning can sometimes be misconfigured and consume large amounts of processor demand, which requires investigation and resolution.

- Various backup and restore utilities at the file and database level can also influence the processor demands at certain times. Depending on your architecture, you may have options to offload this to other servers and drives or execute during off-peak hours whenever possible.

- The power management settings by default on most Windows 2008 servers are set to Balanced, which can dynamically adjust the processor clock frequency. You can sometimes experience slower response and widely fluctuating processor loads especially if large numbers of concurrent UBEs are executing. You may want to consider using the High Performance setting for the production database and enterprise servers. Note that this will most likely increase the energy consumption. On virtual machine configurations, these can be even more complex to review since several potential layers of the BIOS, virtual machine host, and guest settings must be reviewed.

Memory

SQL Server performs the database operations in the memory and reads/writes the changes to the disk system. One of the larger consumers of the memory is the buffer pool, where the data rows are referenced. The usage of the buffer pool can vary widely due to the large variety of queries JD Edwards EnterpriseOne business processes utilize. One of the main goals in the buffer pool use is to minimize the disk I/O and find the data in the cache/buffer pool. You cannot avoid all disk I/O, of course, but memory speeds are easily an order of magnitude faster or greater than going out to the disk subsystems. In a number of situations, the best disk I/O is the one that we don't have to perform.

There are many different opinions on how much memory is sufficient for the SQL Server database. In our experience, it seems that whatever amount of memory is available, the database will use it. (Unless the total database size can fit into the memory of the server, which is rare for most customers.) We provided a general sizing rule of thumb of 10 to 20 percent of the total database size as a decent starting point for the server memory. There is no hard-and-fast rule that states you must adhere to this suggestion, but it at least provides a beginning for performance and scaling tests. If you tend to have mainly large batch queries that must scan through millions of rows, you will usually require more memory to hold those tables in the buffer pool, versus a customer that is highly tuned with mainly OLTP transactions that are very small in nature. Most JD Edwards EnterpriseOne customers fall somewhere in between, which is why the testing is so important to determine how the business processes operate in your configuration. If you don't exercise the architecture with representative workloads you will most likely have several undesired surprises when you operate in production.

SQL Server dynamically manages the various memory areas it controls, unless you expressly override an area such as the Index Creation Memory or Minimum Memory Per Query database settings. For JD Edwards EnterpriseOne, the main memory setting that tends to be changed is the database Minimum Server Memory (in MB) and Maximum Server Memory (in MB). The default settings dynamically allocate/deallocate memory as needed and in cooperation with the Windows OS. This works well for test and workstation databases, but for a production level server, we recommend that the majority of resources be reserved for the database.

For production SQL Server databases, we suggest examining the Min/Max server memory settings along with the Lock Pages in Memory (LPIM) user on the SQL Server startup account. This is suggested for the latest Windows 2008 64-bit server configurations as well, even though this may be considered a bit controversial. (Some think that the latest SQL Server 2008 and Windows 2008 R2 no longer have this issue. Our experience is the occurrence is less frequent, but it still can occur.)

We suggest this configuration because we've noticed "unexpected" response swings that could not initially be explained after a system had been reviewed and tuned with application/index changes, and so on. Using Performance Monitor, we could see that during the slowdowns, the operating system was heavily paging and that the Memory/Available Mbytes counter was very low. In some customer configurations, we would see a warning in the Microsoft SQL Server error log about the working set being trimmed, and in other situations, no message was present. Some customers did have the Maximum server memory set to provide resources to the operating system, but did not have the pages locked. What we observed was significant paging when other applications were in contention with the SQL Server and the OS would page out large portions of the buffer pool. In a couple of situations, we did *not* observe memory pressure, and still the SQL Server working set was being trimmed back. Some examples that caused the issue were disk backups running from the operating system and large file copies of log files. So, as a general default rule, for production SQL Server, we tend to recommend LPIM.

Let's walk through an example configuration to setting the memory:

- Our production database server has 128GB of memory.

- The database size in total on disk is about 800GB.

- Since we have 128GB, let's reserve at least 20 percent for the OS and other processes, which would be about 28GB, leaving 100GB for Microsoft SQL Server. (We know this is not precisely 20 percent, but we did say at least 20 percent.)

- We set the minimum memory to 100GB (102,400MB) for the physical hardware server or 50GB (51,200MB) for a virtual machine with a guest reservation greater than the 50GB setting.

- The maximum memory is set to 100GB (102,400MB) to ensure that SQL Server does not consume all the pages and starve the OS or page out unexpectedly when other processes such as backups occur on the database server.

Generally, the SQL Server should utilize no more than 80 percent of the server memory to leave room for other processes such as the OS, backup software, monitoring, and so on. If you have monitored the server for several months and find that you do not use all the OS memory and the database could use more resources, consider adjusting the memory. We are providing starting points that tend to work well in the majority of JD Edwards EnterpriseOne configurations, but every customer configuration has differences/requirements that can influence these configurations.

The SQL Server service startup account of sqlserver has been granted the "lock pages in memory" user right. When you start the database instance, you should see in the SQL Server error log a startup message indicating it has locked the pages for the buffer pool near the CPU detection message.

TIP
Review the Microsoft SQL Server Knowledge Base articles about how to enable the locked pages in memory setting. The SQL Server Enterprise and Datacenter editions for x64 simply need the LPIM user right assigned and the database started. However, the SQL Server Standard edition that JD Edwards EnterpriseOne supports has additional tasks needed for the x64 version, such as the potential application of SQL hotfix KBA 970070 and enabling trace flag 845 for versions 2005/2008 and 2008 R2. It is our understanding that in SQL Server 2012, the x64 editions will change and the LPIM user right will be all that is needed.

If you decide that the LPIM is not an option for you, and you have multiple production database instances on the same machine, consider at least setting the min/max server memory settings to allow for dynamic allocation/deallocation of resources. If you do this, however, you may need to watch the Performance Monitor counters a little more closely and ensure that the paging levels are kept low for optimum response times. You can also use the LPIM for multiple database instances on the same server as well for each service account, but ensure that when you are locking the pages, each database instance's maximum memory settings are all added up and the total of those instances does not exceed 80 percent of the physical memory. (You may even want to use 75 percent for the database instance total instead, since you will have more overhead running multiple database instances for the Windows OS to manage.)

Disk Subsystem

Your disk system is a critical element of the SQL Server database configuration. Typically the I/O subsystem is the slowest component relative to the processor and memory speeds. The network does not usually factor as much into the disk performance unless network attached storage (NAS) is in use. Most of the JD Edwards EnterpriseOne customer configurations we have observed tend to have dedicated disk and/or some type of storage area network (SAN) with multiple I/O channels present. The disk system tends to have high availability and reliability features such as RAID to minimize outages due to a disk failure.

It is very important that you understand the physical versus logical configuration of your disk subsystem. For example, if you have a SAN-attached set of drives that are presented as one logical F: drive, you need to know what the disk response time characteristics will be. If the logical drive has only three physical drives allocated, this may not provide the ideal response times if all your transaction data is running there. Likewise, if the SAN administrator has a large logical pool with dozens to hundreds of disks, he or she may state that it will perform very well without needing to worry about the physical disks present. In some situations this may be true, but experience has shown that you need to monitor the actual logical disk response times (which consists of queue + service times) to ensure that your database receives the desired access times. If the SAN disks are being shared with other applications/ servers, you can sometimes have competing workloads or issues that affect your SQL Server database. We are not recommending that a SAN be totally dedicated for JD Edwards EnterpriseOne, even though some customers do that for the production architecture, but it is very important that you understand and monitor the servers on the SAN to ensure that they do not have a negative impact. The main thing is to communicate the disk response characteristics you want to use the database for in each of the major files. You may have to compromise for various reasons, but at least the potential impact to the JD Edwards EnterpriseOne database is documented.

Some SAN Examples

Following are a couple examples in which the logical presentation masks the physical complexity and interactions of the disk system.

First, in a client configuration, the SAN had the production JD Edwards EnterpriseOne database, enterprise servers, and a large data warehouse application. Overall, the JD Edwards EnterpriseOne system had very good response until the data warehouse extracts and reporting runs were initiated during the day. The overall disk response of reads/writes went above 400–500 ms and in a couple of situations caused the SAN controllers to reset due to the huge I/O requests from the data warehouse. The resolution was to separate the data warehouse to another SAN since they had reached the capacity of the present SAN. Once the workloads were separated, the contention was eliminated and the problem was resolved. The data warehouse requirements had pushed the SAN beyond its design limits, which impacted the response times.

Another example was a very large customer with hundreds of servers accessing multiple SAN devices with a fiber-based switch fabric. The production JD Edwards EnterpriseOne database had the logical disks separated, as recommended, between data, transaction log, and the TEMPDB. During the peak hours, the transaction log disk response would climb from 4–5 ms to more than 600–800 ms, which slowed down the entire database. No contention at the SAN disk level could be found, except for the slow disk response on certain servers accessing a particular set of SANs. Further investigation revealed that the SAN switch fabric had one Windows server that was not related to the EnterpriseOne architecture; this caused a "broadcast storm" of packets on the switch and affected a number of the servers accessing a particular SAN group. Once the fiber card on that Windows server was replaced, the intermittent issue was resolved.

For JD Edwards EnterpriseOne SQL Server disk and file layout considerations, we generally recommend the following for a production database, as noted in Table 9-5. Each of the major files has different disk response and I/O considerations. If possible, you want to separate these files to different logical drives for multiple reasons such as the following:

- Type of disk access such as random (data/TEMPDB) versus sequential (transaction logs)

- Potentially different I/O paths used

- Assists troubleshooting/diagnostics with separate drives in use

File Usage	Comments
Production data/indexes	Usually largest set of files 5–25 ms LogicalDisk avg. read/write/transfer recommended RAID 1, 10, or 5 suggested for reliability/performance
Transaction logs	Fastest write access; if possible 1–10 ms desired Use best performing drives where possible (SSD drives or large cache controllers can be of value) RAID 1 or 10 suggested
TEMPDB	Used more heavily in later SQL Server databases (online operations, RCSI, etc.) Similar operational characteristics to data/indexes 5–25 ms LogicalDisk avg. read/write/transfer speed recommended Use separate TEMPDB file per processor/core to minimize latch contention (Example 2 processor/4 cores would be 8 TEMPDB files) RAID 1 or 10 (RAID 5 is last preferred option)
Backup files	Backup of transaction logs and data/index files Can be a mirror copy or slightly slower disk Ideally separate drive letter with large storage SAN or NAS storage can be utilized here RAID 5 typically used

TABLE 9-5. *Database Disk/File Considerations*

TIP
If at all possible, at a minimum, separate your transaction log from the data/TEMPDB files. You want the transaction logs to be using the fastest performing drives as possible to ensure the best response times for the commits.

From the operational aspect, it is suggested that you attempt to minimize the auto growth of these files in production. You can have the auto growth feature available, but if possible let it be the exception instead of the rule for the files to grow. Planning and maintaining the growth during off-peak hours can reduce potential response pauses that may occur if your database file has to be extended. Later in this chapter, we discuss the recommendation to preallocate the TEMPDB files on a production JD Edwards EnterpriseOne database to minimize waits for extent allocations.

We discussed that the disk response (queue + service) time is the important area to monitor and review for your production database. Generally for JD Edwards EnterpriseOne, you need a balance between OLTP and batch workloads for the disk system. OLTP wants very fast response times, while batch such as UBEs favor throughput to get as much data as possible. There are multiple methods to monitor the disk response time from your SQL Server database. Windows performance counters provide a wealth of information about your OS and various applications such as the SQL Server database. For JD Edwards EnterpriseOne, the main counters we tend to review are the Physical/Logical Disk for the individual drives of the OS and database.

Within the Performance Monitor (perfmon.exe), you would add counters for the following items. These are by no means the only counters you can use, but these provide good indicators of the disk response times to the database files.

- PhysicalDisk or LogicalDisk: Avg Disk Sec/Read

- PhysicalDisk or LogicalDisk: Avg Disk Sec/Transfer

- PhysicalDisk or LogicalDisk: Avg Disk Sec/Write

These counters operate in the millisecond (ms) scale. Example: $0.005 = 5$ (ms)

You want to see the SQL Server disk response at or below a certain level to ensure that the database receives the data in a timely manner. If the response times are high, you can almost be certain that the users or your batch jobs will be affected with slower runtimes. One caveat to note is that heavy batch workloads will tend to increase your disk response times since you are typically processing much more data,

Understanding How the Logical Drives Map to the Physical

To determine which disk counter to use, you'll find it helpful to understand how the logical drives map to a physical disk. You may have a one-to-one mapping of logical to physical, or you could have several logical drives using the same physical partition/device. For example, a C: and D: logical drive could be on the same physical disk in a RAID-1 configuration. The physical disk would provide Avg Disk Sec/Read info for the *entire* disk, while the logical would show you the response for that particular drive. Most of the time, we use the LogicalDisk counters to determine the overall drives response and then focus on the physical drives to understand how they map to the logical. You have to know the underlying physical disk presentation because contention could be causing response issues. A quick example would be where you separate your data, TEMPDB, and transaction logs to different logical drive letters, but you put all these files on one large physical RAID-1 disk configuration. Any of the three sets of files could cause contention issues with certain usage levels. The Windows Resource Monitor could tell you specifically which files have the greatest read and/or write usage on the disk at a particular point in time.

where we tend to have higher throughput (MB/s) than response time I/Os per second. So depending on your business process goals, you may need to strike a balance between the interactive users' response and batch throughput. (This is one reason that heavy batch is executed during off-peak hours when possible to minimize disk response time concerns for the interactive users—that is, unless you have infrastructure that can allow concurrent interactive/batch processing.)

The disk response range that we like to observe is specified in Table 9-6.

Avg. Disk Sec./Read or Transfer or Write	Comments
0–10 ms	Desired disk response range Provides 100s to 1000s of I/Os per second
10–25 ms	Good disk response range that is acceptable
25–50 ms	A warning sign of contention or a busy system Users generally start to see a response change
50 ms and above	Investigation of the disk and I/O controller configuration is suggested

TABLE 9-6. *Disk Latency/Response Recommendations*

Note that the averages should be sampled for durations of at least 15 minutes or longer if possible. If you start/stop the monitor for a brief period of time, such as 1 to 5 minutes, you may be observing a very narrow sample or window of time that does not represent the overall response time. The sampling interval is usually somewhere between 15 seconds to 5 minutes, depending on how long the duration of monitoring is desired. So if you were going to monitor for, say, 8 to 24 hours, the sampling interval should be 5 minutes to reduce the data you have to analyze. If the monitoring duration was 1 hour, you could set the sampling interval to 15–60 seconds.

Network

The SQL Server network component for JD Edwards EnterpriseOne typically does not require much, if any, tuning. The capacity of 1-Gbs or 10-Gbs Ethernet on switched networks with additional bonding/aggregation options tends to minimize tuning opportunities. The general recommendation is to implement the best networking infrastructure you can put in place. We know that is a generalization, but most correctly implemented network configurations tend to be the areas with least concerns from a tuning perspective.

Here is an example in which tuning/configuration was needed. One customer was running SQL Server 2008 R2 and Windows Server 2008 R2, and we noticed some messages in the JDE and SQL error logs regarding timeouts. The queries, when reviewed, should have been subsecond, and they intermittently timed out and had very long durations. We reviewed for cumulative patches and found those current. Examining the Windows 2008 configuration, we issued the command shown in Listing 9-1 from an administrative command prompt.

Listing 9-1 *Check TCP interface settings*

```
Netsh int tcp show global
```

We searched for Chimney Offload state and found it enabled. In Windows 2003 Server this is enabled, and for Windows 2008 Server it is usually disabled by default. I suggested that we disable this setting on the database server since certain hardware vendor's network cards have not always implemented this feature in an optimal manner. Using the administrative command prompt shown in Listing 9-2, we issued a command that is dynamic.

Listing 9-2 *Globally disable TCP chimney*

```
Netsh int tcp set global chimney=disabled
```

The TCP chimney setting that offloads to the network hardware had high connection counts, which a SQL Server can have in some cases. We have run into this situation with a few customers using certain network hardware cards, and if we observe SQL timeout messages occurring or unexpected batch response times, we review this setting. For these customers, when we disabled the TCP chimney, we observed a 25 percent reduction in the batch runtimes for longer executing jobs. For the interactive users, the important item was no evidence of timeout errors in the logs and hence they observed more consistent response times.

For Windows and SQL Server, we normally do not have to change any of the network settings or buffer sizes. With other JD Edwards EnterpriseOne platforms such as Unix/Linux and IBM System I, you may want to investigate further, because send/receive buffer sizes along with potentially jumbo packets may be viable options to consider.

SQL Server Configuration Ideas

Earlier we examined some major operating system areas that SQL Server utilizes. Remember that most tuning principles apply to whatever database platform you are using, so examine Chapter 8 as well for more information. In the following sections, we will discuss specific areas of SQL Server that we have found to benefit the JD Edwards EnterpriseOne configurations. We don't cover every potential area, but we provide guidance for items that should give you the benefits that can influence JD Edwards EnterpriseOne implementations most frequently. Overall, SQL Server will perform very well if you have adequate hardware resources for the various workloads you may introduce. Tuning is almost always an option, but it may not be on the database side where changes need to occur. In effect, the main goal of a database server is to respond to the SQL requests presented with the lowest plan cost it can determine. Whether those requests are efficient or consume large portions of the configuration influences how well it can respond to those requests.

Database Configuration

Earlier we discussed the critical components of the SQL Server database configuration. Your main goal is to ensure that robust hardware components are in place to support the business processes and objectives for JD Edwards EnterpriseOne. You don't always know up front what those business processes will be, but at some point in the project the processes will be in place so that a performance/scaling exercise can occur to ensure the operational goals can be met. Failure to confirm that the infrastructure will meet your business and software requirements increases the risk for unexpected issues to occur when the production workloads are introduced.

Assuming that you have sized the database server and laid out the memory, disk, and network with some of the previous recommendations, you can consider some of the following areas as well.

SQL TEMPDB

The SQL TEMPDB should be allocated with multiple files that match the processors available, as recommended for EnterpriseOne configurations. The default TEMPDB will allocate disk space dynamically, which means it extends and grows during the database operations. For larger database configurations, it is recommended that TEMPDB be preallocated evenly with a percentage such as 10 percent for expansion. This ensures that the temp database I/O will be more evenly spread and that processor latch contention will be minimized. The Oracle Metalink document ID 1275500.1, "Tips for Running EnterpriseOne with SQL Server 2008 and SQL Server 2008 R2," has several good suggestions along with the appendix referencing a sample script to preallocate the TEMPDB files. It is strongly suggested that you consider this for production-level databases when using Read Committed Snapshot Isolation (RCSI), which we will discuss later in this chapter. The preallocated TEMPDB will improve overall efficiency and will assist the RCSI performance if implemented, since it utilizes TEMPDB heavily for the version store images. Even if RCSI is not used, we recommend using preallocated TEMPDB configurations.

Client and JDBC Drivers

A commonsense, but often missed, item is to ensure that all your client ODBC/ Microsoft SQL Server Native Client (SNAC) and JDBC drivers are at the same levels as your patched database. This is one of those areas where different client drivers can affect the stability and performance of your system. It is one of the very first areas we check when reviewing a configuration for tuning opportunities. As mentioned, this is one of those "trust, but verify" items that should be reviewed for each server that accesses the SQL Server.

Database Statistics

The database statistics are another configuration area that is very useful to have enabled. At the database level, you would usually want the "auto create statistics" and "auto update statistics" options in place. Without good statistics in place, you may encounter a number of intermittent and inconsistent performance issues, since the database cost-based optimizer uses these statistics to determine the best access plan to the data. It is strongly recommended that for optimal performance you consider manual full-scan statistic updates on at least a monthly or quarterly basis. A number of customer configurations achieved noticeable response improvements just by ensuring that the statistics were up to date. Consider the options in Table 9-7.

Statistics Option/Feature	Comment
Auto create statistics	Recommended for all JD Edwards EnterpriseOne tables
Auto update statistics	Helps maintain the statistics in *most* situations Sometimes can be disabled on small tables like F0002 if you run a manual stat, but this is not usually done by most customers
Manual/off peak full scan statistics	Generally recommended after * Any large table/environment refreshes * Database cumulative patches/upgrades * Monthly/quarterly full statistics maintenance

TABLE 9-7. *Statistic Options to Consider*

TIP
When you're considering running manual statistics, be sure to cover all your production databases, which include the JDE_PRODUCTION, JDE910 (system, object librarian, data dictionary), and JDE_PD910 (central objects, versions, serialized objects). With package builds and deployments, we have seen a number of configurations in which the central objects Java serialized objects tables F989998/F989999 did not have statistics present. The web response for that instance would load the applications slower initially as a symptom. With the later JD Edwards EnterpriseOne releases using XML specifications, the database is critical as well for both the web and Enterprise server to retrieve those specification records in a timely manner.

Database Recovery Level

Ensure that for production-level databases you enable the full recovery model instead of the simple recovery model. You want to back up the transaction logs so you can have a point-in-time recovery of the transactions. Most customers' test environments use the simple recovery model, but if you do that for production, you can only recover the database to the last backup point, which may be days or even a week old. There is increased operational maintenance in ensuring that the transaction logs are backed up, but if you do have some type of disk failure or data recovery for required tables, you have many more options if you can restore up to a certain point in time. A *very* small number of JD Edwards EnterpriseOne customers use the simple recovery model for production databases, and we have always made sure that their management understands and signs off on the recovery limitations present.

Other SQL Server Features

SQL Server also has a large number of features that we will not discuss in this chapter since the complexity and design are complete engagements that can takes weeks to months to fully design, architect, test, and implement. We discuss architectures and high availability in other chapters, but specific vendor implementations can vary widely.

Several viable options are available to increase availability and performance for various business requirements. Options such as log shipping and replication allow you to create a copy of the databases for disaster recovery, backups, and read only reporting/query activities. Database mirroring can increase high availability options. SQL Server 2012 using the AlwaysOn availability groups increases the flexibility you have while consolidating several of the features mentioned for easier administration of DR, backup, and reporting environments.

We suggested that if your business requires a large number of ad hoc–type SQL queries from users or reporting tools, you may benefit by moving those users to a replicated or mirrored database instance instead of running those queries on your production JD Edwards EnterpriseOne database. Each customer situation is different, since the architecture can have many influencing factors along with the business processes in use, and this means there is no one-size-fits-all recommendation.

Note that once JD Edwards EnterpriseOne certifies Windows Server 2012 and SQL Server 2012, additional options may be available at the OS and database levels that we cannot currently discuss in this book. You can, however, leverage a number of configuration areas in SQL Server 2005 and 2008/2008 R2 that are built upon in the 2012 editions, so it helps to watch those technologies as well. Basically, the majority of recommendations in this book should apply to the SQL Server 2012 release as well.

Production Parameter Settings

The following are some SQL Server parameter settings at the instance or database level that you should review. We discussed some of these settings earlier in this chapter, such as the min/max memory and MDOP, so they will be reinforced here.

EnterpriseOne Databases May Initially Be Set to 80 SQL 2000 Compatibility

It is generally recommended that once JD Edwards EnterpriseOne is installed, each database be changed to level 100 for SQL Server 2008/2008 R2 to enable that database functionality. (This assumes of course that you are running SQL Server 2008/2008 R2; adjust the setting to your appropriate database version.) See Table 9-8.

Microsoft SQL Server Version	Suggested Compatibility Level
2005	90
2008/2008 R2	100
2012	110

TABLE 9-8. *Suggested Compatibility Level for Each Database Version*

If you are running later releases of JD Edwards EnterpriseOne, you'll probably be using SQL Server 2008 or 2008 R2. If you leave the setting at the 80 level, you may restrict certain database capabilities/features available. This can sometimes create unexpected behaviors in the database, since you are limiting the functionality to an older release. You can find the settings at older levels when you first install, upgrade a database server, or restore a database. Compatibility level is mainly intended as a migration aid and not as a long-term solution, so you want JD Edwards EnterpriseOne to leverage the functionality available in the SQL Server database release you are using. Make sure you change this setting only when there are *no* active users attached to the database, or you can risk impacting active queries.

Server Memory Options at Instance Level

We discussed the minimum and maximum server memory options and the use of LPIM. The main goal here is to set a maximum server memory (in MB) that does not overcommit your memory resources. For test databases and virtual machines, you may consider using dynamic memory management without the LPIM, but for production databases on physical hardware, we recommend using LPIM and ensuring that you leave enough memory for the OS and other processes on the database server. The minimum server memory (in MB) is useful for test databases and virtual machines to ensure a certain amount of memory is reserved for the SQL Server database instance when dynamic memory management is in use. For production database instances using the LPIM setting, the minimum and maximum memory settings are the same to preallocate/reserve the memory. Virtual machines (VMs) have additional special considerations, where the minimum memory setting influences the amount you reserve for the guest VM to minimize the risk of ballooning the guests and causing large amounts of paging, which impacts response time in most situations.

Maximum Degree of Parallelism (MDOP)

The SQL Server database instance Advanced setting can be changed from 0 to 1 or 2 for multiple processor configurations if desired. More details were provided earlier in the chapter for potential settings you can consider. This can reduce database locks by limiting parallel queries to one or two processors instead of all of them. No or low parallelism effectively prevents a large SQL query from "taking over" several processors and affecting other SQL queries. The large SQL query can take slightly longer to complete, but it will not slow down other queries in the system. This setting requires a restart of the database server to take effect. Some customers like to utilize all the processors for large queries, while in busier customer configurations we have found that limiting the parallelism provides a more consistent response for the interactive users, without penalizing the large queries completely.

Performance Monitoring and Index Review

Microsoft provides a number of very good performance collection tools that can be used at the OS and database levels. Prior to SQL Server 2005, you would tend to use SQL profiler, scripts, and the Performance Monitor to obtain insights into the database and Windows OS. Third-party monitoring tools are also available that ease some of the data collection and evaluation tasks if you elect to utilize those products. Windows 2008 and SQL Server 2008 offer many additional features to collect and monitor the performance of the database server.

Some of the performance collection tools available in Windows 2008 Server and SQL Server 2008 are listed in Table 9-9.

These provide starting points that can benefit your staff and any consultants assisting with tuning/performance efforts. Using these tools helps identify potential opportunities or issues within your architecture, and each offers a number of features when you focus on a certain area of the database server. The various real-time monitors provide feedback as events occur in your system, while other tools can capture and store for historical purposes how your system is operating. The third-party tools such as Dell/Quest Spotlight for SQL Server, and Idera SQL diagnostic manager have dashboards and performance recommendation capabilities that can assist you in determining database events and potential corrective actions. Your comfort level, training, expertise, and time availability can influence the value the performance monitor tools can bring to your configuration. We have observed a wide spectrum of customers use a number of tools, and they have various degrees of knowledge, training, and experience to utilize them. Some implement the performance tools more completely than others.

The main point with any performance monitoring is if you don't track and baseline the events, it is difficult to measure/quantify any changes you make to the system. As stated in Chapter 8, you can make relatively simple changes that can have limited or very broad impacts to your configuration. Knowing where your system has been and how changes affect it are extremely important.

Tool	Comment
Windows Task Manager	Good for examining real-time processes, memory, network
Windows Resource Monitor	Can be invoked from Task Manager Provides more in-depth information regarding the OS main components of CPU, memory, disk, and network Good tool to observe specific real-time activity
Windows Performance Monitor (perfmon)	Large number of detailed counters from the OS and certain applications/services such as the database Can sample the data at specific intervals and log the information to a file for review/analysis Provides many insights into the details of your Windows server Performance counters can feed other tools as well
SQL Server Management Studio Dynamic Management View (DMV) reports	DMV reports allow you to review your database at the instance and database levels Provides relatively easy insights into your database that used to require several SQL scripts
SQL Server Profiler	Provides SQL event collection and monitoring Robust capabilities to create, watch, save, and review trace files/tables Ability to filter trace data to reduce overhead and analysis
SQL Server Performance Data Collector	Helps integrate the above tools for collection, analysis and troubleshooting Can maintain historical SQL Server diagnostic information Useful for larger configurations with multiple instances or to consolidate monitoring
Additional monitoring/ performance tool examples: * JD Edwards Server Manager * Oracle Enterprise Manager * Dell/Quest Software (Spotlight on SQL Server) * Idera (SQL diagnostic manager)	Good tools that can provide additional monitoring, collection, issue/configuration identification, and reporting capabilities This is by no means a comprehensive list, but some of the more popular tools observed at JD Edwards EnterpriseOne customers

TABLE 9-9. *Microsoft and Other Monitoring/Performance Tools*

Index Review

Once you have good performance monitoring baseline information in place to see how your system is performing, you can utilize performance tuning diagnostic checklists to identify potential areas to review. We always like to start at the application levels and work through the operating system and database. Remember that the database simply responds to the SQL requests presented to it. The more efficiently designed the application and user SQL queries are, the better the database typically is able to return the results in a timely manner. Assuming that most of the Windows OS and SQL Server configuration items are in place to provide adequate resources based on the workload presented, you invariably tend to get drawn down to creating indexes.

When examining a customer configuration, we typically go through the performance tuning diagnostics and ensure that the overall architecture and related components are working well together. Index review tends to be near the end of the list of items reviewed, since you want to ensure a firm foundation is in place before changing the database. There are many good reasons to add an index, but it is a balancing act to ensure that large numbers of indexes are not added that could possibly cause negative performance issues for the tables under review. Remember that each added index can increase the overhead to be maintained, stored, and scanned along with the other indexes on that table. If the table has millions of rows present, the maintenance to perform modifications can become significant.

JD Edwards EnterpriseOne delivers a number of indexes that are fairly comprehensive for the base applications delivered. This does *not* mean that every column for each table is indexed, which would be impractical, but for the majority of business processes, you will typically have a usable index for that table. However, there are a number of situations in which a business process or application is designed to use columns that may not have an efficient index available for that particular procedure. These can become opportunities for which it makes sense to consider an index. Some example situations are listed in Table 9-10, but these are by no means all the situations that may require an index. Typically, the situations most noticeable are for queries against large tables, but that is not always the case, since you could have thousands or millions of smaller SELECTs that take a few tenths of a second, and that would add up significantly.

In a number of situations, an index can be justified, as you can see from the examples in Table 9-10. When we are to the point in the performance checklist where you review index opportunities, we like to consider the following process to justify the creation of an index. Following the gears and cogs principle, we want to address the largest influencing areas first and then, if needed, focus on the smaller opportunities that have less impact.

In some customer engagements, we'd see the SQL Server administrator use the tuning index wizard/advisor and then attempt to create all the indexes that it recommended. In our opinion, this is a very general and blanket approach that does

Situation for Index Opportunity	Comment
Custom applications where a proper index was not created to access a table or business view	Programming design and performance standards can help mitigate and reduce the chance that improperly designed SQL queries get to production.
Custom modifications to an application or business function where SQL statements have been added or modified	Programming design and performance standards can help mitigate and reduce the chance that improperly designed SQL queries get to production.
UBE data selections and sequencing against large tables where a reference column may not be indexed	User education and awareness for those who create or modify data selections can help minimize these situations. The data selection affects the WHERE clause and sequencing the ORDER BY. The Work with Submitted Jobs execution details or a JDEDEBUG log provides a good method to review the data selection/sequencing and the actual SQL statement created. For frequently executed queries that cannot be changed, an index may be the best option.
EnterpriseOne row security applied to transaction tables	Row security added to data items that are not indexed can adversely affect the query performance. Any row security should be justified first and then if necessary indexes may be considered. Generally row security on specific tables is recommended vs. using *ALL for all tables to reduce the scope of the change. Row security using data items such as MCU and CO typically have indexes on those columns, but if data items such as category or reporting codes are used, these are typically *not* indexed based on their intended use. (Category and reporting codes are not usually indexed.)

TABLE 9-10. *Potential Areas That May Require Additional Indexes*

Situation for Index Opportunity	Comment
Query by Example (QBE) entries that do not use indexed columns on large tables, or performing "wide open" finds	User education of how the QBE line queries against large tables can help. In this case, user behavior changes or EnterpriseOne Application Query Security may be of benefit. Certain business processes can generate the requirement for an index. Example: F4211/F42119 and the use of the Vendor Reference (VR01) field that is normally not indexed. Some tables have a detail/history relationship such as the Sales order F4211/F42119, where a view is utilized. In some cases, there is not always a matching index in the F42119 to those present in the F4211 table. You may need to add a matching index since the F42119 history can become quite large.
Use of non-searchable arguments (NSARGs) such as *ABC* in QBE/forms	This can be used for relatively small tables, but against large tables with millions of rows it results in full table scans since every character in the column must be reviewed. User education to ensure this type of search is done on smaller tables such as address book and not on large transaction tables can help.
Use of external SQL statements outside JD Edwards EnterpriseOne Some customers use functions in the WHERE clause which typically are NSARGs unless properly addressed	Generally it is discouraged to perform any transaction data changes outside of EnterpriseOne due to several factors such as auditing, recoverability, and proper data integrity. Well-designed and efficient external SQL statements can be considered, but strong testing and controls should be present. If functions are used in the WHERE clause, you may observe full table scans. SQL Server has a computed columns feature that can allow an index to be created. (Similar in concept to function-based indexes on the Oracle database.)
User overrides (UO)/grid formats Saved Queries	JD Edwards EnterpriseOne–delivered UOs tend to utilize the primary key index for the sequence. Custom UOs may be placed over large transaction tables such as the Sales Order or Work with Submitted Jobs table. If columns that are not indexed are used the response can slow significantly. Education of users and testing/promoting efficient UOs and saved queries are recommended. Indexes can be considered if the business process is used frequently to provide justification.

TABLE 9-10.   *Potential Areas That May Require Additional Indexes*

not tend to be very successful. It is better to establish the baseline of how the system is operating, and identify the potential opportunities and how to address them, whether they are application and/or database tasks. If the change(s) do come down to index opportunities, we tend to take a very measured approach to introduce them in small groups at a time depending on the customer circumstances. If you start adding dozens or hundreds of indexes, how can you monitor/measure and evaluate all those changes effectively? We use the multiple pass method and address the indexes that can have the greatest impact, monitor them, perform another cycle of the monitoring, and measure and tune to evaluate the effect. Once those indexes are in place, we usually have new opportunities trickle to the top of the list and we continue the process over days, weeks, or months until we reach the business goals desired.

So how do you determine which index opportunities are the ones to address first? You can consider a number of factors to prioritize which index changes can have the most immediate impact. Table 9-11 lists some of the criteria that we have used during customer engagements to help prioritize which index changes can have the most immediate effect.

So to review index opportunities, we want to reduce the query response time, and this can be considered for queries that consume a high amount of I/O or CPU. The execution count is the main factor that can influence whether an index is justified, since if you execute a query only a few times per day versus a query that is executed hundreds or thousands of times, you will usually obtain more benefit reducing the resources consumed by the higher execution count. If there is a critical business process, such as the timing for a financial closing processes, it may justify the index. One of the key points is to utilize a measured and managed approach to indexes and not blindly introduce them to see what may work. The goal is to balance the resources available in the SQL Server as well as you can to provide consistent response to the application queries.

Dynamic Management View Reports

In the previous sections, we mentioned DMVs and that SQL Server 2005 introduced these views. From the SQL Server Management Studio you can access a large number of standard DMV reports at the database and instance level. You can also access the DMVs yourself if desired via SQL, but for JD Edwards EnterpriseOne tuning purposes, you can obtain most of the critical information using the standard reports delivered with the database. If you like to delve into the details, you'll find a large number of Microsoft documents and blogs available that provide examples of SQL queries using DMVs.

So what is the greatest benefit of using the DMV reports from the JD Edwards EnterpriseOne perspective? Well, in past consulting engagements using SQL Server 2000 and early 2005, we would need to rely on a combination of several performance methods to identify database and index opportunities. SQL Profiler, Performance Monitor, custom SQL scripts, JD Edwards EnterpriseOne debug logs/Performance Workbench, or third-party tools would be needed to identify suboptimal SQL or

Factor to Consider	Comments
Listen to the user community feedback for any application response concerns.	Determine the root cause for the response concerns, and if an index opportunity exists and the business justification is present, apply the index.
Review long running SQL over x second(s). (Example: x response time could be 1, 5, or 10 seconds depending on baselines).	Consider the response time AND the number of executions per day. If the query is executed only 1–50 times per day, it may not be a good candidate for an index. Factor in the business process and the requirements that might influence the eligibility.
Review SQLs with high execution counts and subsecond runs instead of millisecond or microsecond response times.	If a query executes thousands or millions of times per day and the average response is above 10 milliseconds, you may want to consider an index if possible. (Example: 1 million executions with 10 ms response is 10,000 seconds or 167 minutes of total time.) The individual response may not be apparent if your filtered response is greater than 1 second, but the aggregate total of the executions consumes hours. That is why it is important to review the execution counts as well.
Review queries with high average I/O counts.	If queries have a high number of executions (say > 100) and the average I/O counts are in the millions or billions, there's likely an index opportunity. The visual execution plan can help you determine what portion has the largest cost and how the query was performed. A full table scan for an infrequent query may be the best option since you are balancing the overhead of adding/maintaining an index. That's where the execution frequency and business justification influences the index creation.
Review queries with high average CPU.	Determine what portion of the query is consuming the CPU by reviewing the visual execution plan. You may have an inefficient business view or sorting that needs adjustment.

TABLE 9-11.   *Potential Index Criteria Factors to Consider*

resource bottlenecks. Now the standard reports using the DMVs in SQL Server 2005/2008 and beyond consolidate and provide this information. The other tools still have their benefits and place, but it is now easier to obtain the desired events you are attempting to measure/monitor.

The DMVs are not the complete solution to every tuning exercise, but they do provide some very good insights to identify what is occurring within the database that can lead you to other areas. We wanted to list some of the standard reports you may find useful when reviewing your JD Edwards EnterpriseOne database. Figures 9-1 and 9-2 show examples of accessing a standard Disk Usage by Table report from the SQL Server Management Studio application. This provides a quick list of the tables in that database along with details such as the number of records and space used for data/indexes. You can also print or export the report, which provides additional flexibility for review or scripting tasks. Another option is to take the DMV and create your own script to manipulate the data returned as desired, such as listing tables over a certain size or row count.

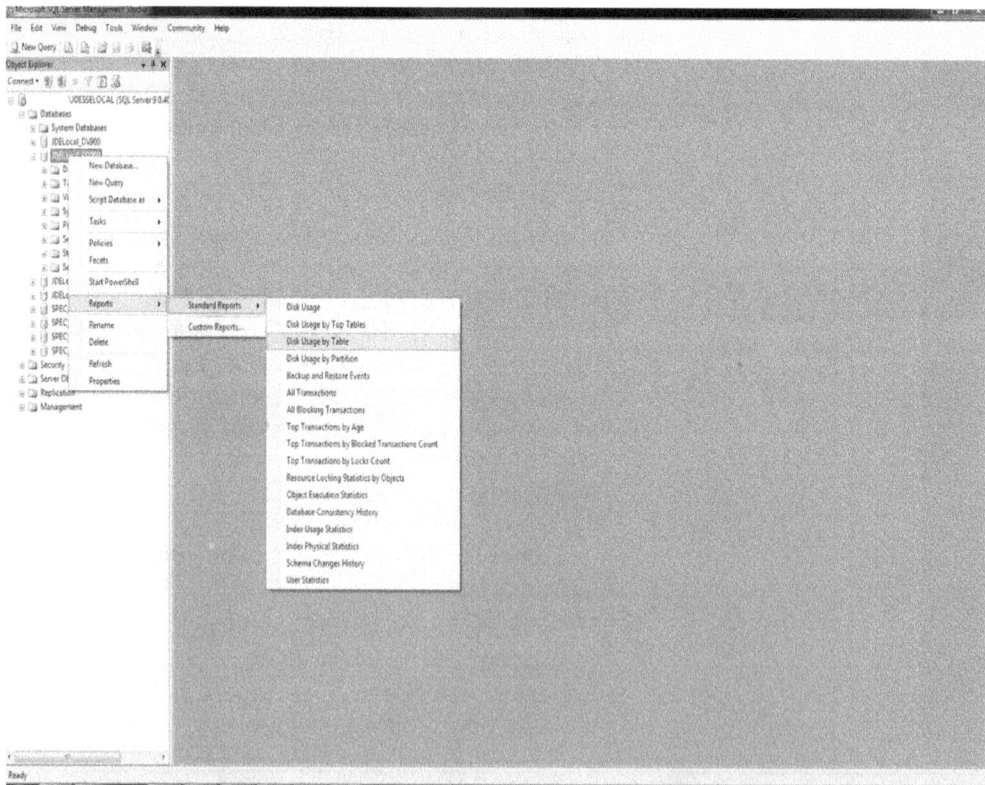

FIGURE 9-1. *Launching a database Disk Usage by Table report*

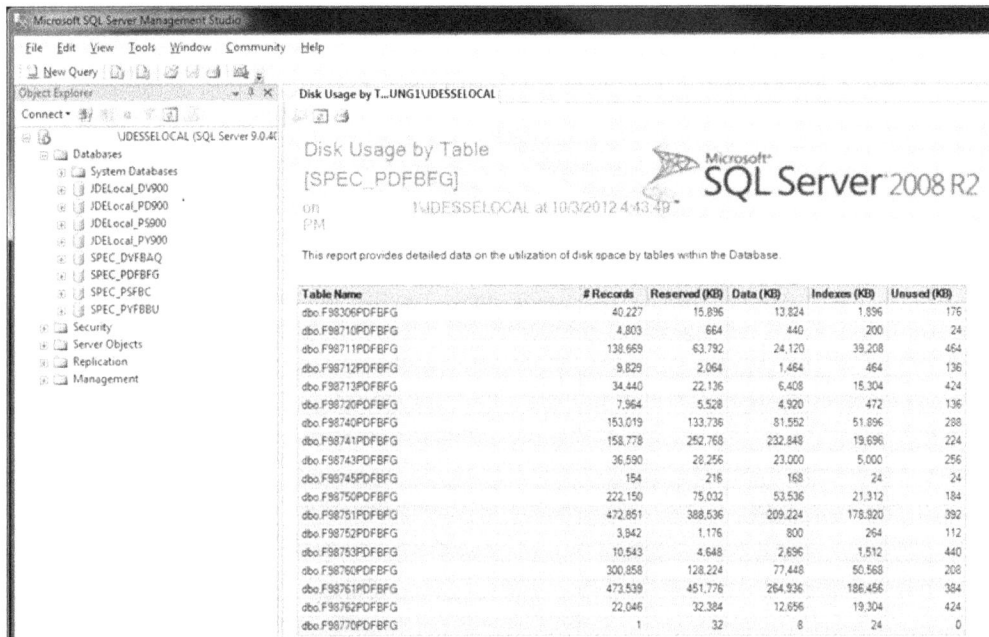

FIGURE 9-2.   *Disk Usage by Table*

Table 9-12 shows some of the standard reports that we utilize when reviewing a JD Edwards EnterpriseOne database for tuning opportunities. You may find others that apply to your situation as well, but these provide some real-time queries. We also provide some comments regarding how the report may be utilized.

DMV Report	Tip/Comments
Instance level/Server Dashboard	Useful for overall database perspective and configuration. Allows you to observe how the CPU and logical I/O overall is utilized.
Instance level/Configuration Changes History	Quick review of any parameter changes.

(Continued)

TABLE 9-12.   *Suggested DMV Standard Reports*

DMV Report	Tip/Comments
Instance level/Memory Consumption	Insights into what objects are consuming memory. Page life expectancy in seconds can provide insights into the buffer pool references. Generally this should stay above 300 sec. (5 min.) to increase the likelihood that data is present in the buffer. If it is consistently lower than this, investigate to determine what queries are flushing out the buffer pool and take steps to remedy (e.g. indexes, increase memory, compression, application changes, etc.).
Instance level/Activity – All blocking transactions	Useful to identify any databases that have blocked transactions. If blocks occur for several seconds or minutes, you need to investigate.
Instance level/Activity – Top sessions	Provides several categories of session activity such as oldest, top CPU, top memory, and top #reads/#writes. Provides good insights into the transactions that are within the database instance at that time.
Instance level/Top transactions by locks count	Insights into which transactions may be holding large numbers of locks. You may have custom code that holds locks for a transaction for long periods unintentionally or an incorrect transaction boundary design.
Instance level/Top queries (all of these reports)	Lists queries by average CPU, average I/O, total CPU, or total I/O along with number of executions. Good method to find potential index or inefficient application opportunities.
Database level/Disk usage by table	Allows you to see the row counts and data/index space usage patterns of your database.
Database level/All blocking transactions	Specific transactions blocking/holding locks within that database.
Database level/Index Usage Statistics	Provides good insights into your indexes and how they are being utilized/accessed.
Database level/Resource Locking Statistics by Objects	Allows you to see which objects (e.g., tables) may have significant locks or waiting transactions on them.

TABLE 9-12. *Suggested DMV Standard Reports*

More than 100 DMVs are available and can provide database information along with the ability to create custom reports if desired. As you can see, with the standard reports you can obtain a number of insights into your database without having to create SQL scripts. (You are welcome to create your own scripts as well, which many administrators do.) As field consultants, we have found most of the performance tools available provide very good information to monitor and measure how the database is performing.

Database and Backup Compression

With the introduction of SQL Server 2008 Enterprise and Datacenter editions, the ability to compress at the row or page level was introduced for several datatypes. In SQL Server 2008 R2, support for Unicode datatypes was also added, which covers the majority of data that JD Edwards EnterpriseOne utilizes.

One of the key elements of database compression is that you reduce the overall number of bytes stored on the disk and in the buffer pool if your data can be compressed. You essentially have more rows per 8K data page, which in turn reduces the number of disk I/Os needed to retrieve the data. As with most situations in life there is no free lunch, however, since there is additional processor overhead and time needed on the database to compress/decompress the data. However, if your database server is not CPU constrained (such as average CPU usage below 70 percent), you may be a good candidate to consider compressing the larger JD Edwards EnterpriseOne database tables. You have the option of using row- or page-based compression.

From our experience, we consider using the page compression for customer databases that are 1.5TB or smaller because it works very well with the type of data stored in JD Edwards EnterpriseOne. If your database size is greater than 1.5TB uncompressed, we typically consider using row compression due to the lower overhead involved. Row compression is used for very large tables, because page compression could take significantly longer for maintenance tasks such as index rebuilds. There is nothing to prevent you from considering row compression, but you tend to see better disk savings by using the page compression option. Also, you can use different compression options on a per-table basis, but most customers tend to gravitate toward either row or page without mixing them. The bottom line is that an analysis of your infrastructure and business needs should be conducted to determine which compression option may be best for your company.

You will need to ensure that your SQL Server 2008/2008 R2 edition is Enterprise or Datacenter, because this feature is not currently available in the Standard edition. To take full advantage of the compression option, you need to be running SQL Server 2008 R2 or later, where the Unicode compression is included as well. If you are using the earlier 2008 release, there are still advantages to compression, but it will depend on your JD Edwards EnterpriseOne installation data. If you are a new install, your database would be using Unicode data; if you upgraded from a previous release, you may still have your data in the non-Unicode format for business data/control tables. We have done database row or page compression for both configurations with very positive results. If you can leverage the maximum potential, however, it provides the most cost-effective benefit.

Several JD Edwards EnterpriseOne customers using SQL Server 2008/2008 R2 have implemented row or page compression. If you can use SQL Server 2008 R2 and a supported JD Edwards EnterpriseOne Tools level, the combination provides the maximum benefit currently available. One of the considerations for JD Edwards EnterpriseOne is that most of the data columns are populated with data, since null values are typically discouraged. This is a great benefit for database compression since a large number of columns, even if "empty," will either have zeros or spaces in them. This helps increase the ability to compress the tables and indexes. We have observed very good compression improvements (3 to 12 times better) for some tables, depending on the data in those tables. Overall disk savings can be double-digit percentages, which allow more database pages to be stored in the buffer pool, and which in turn can reduce I/Os needed to retrieve the data.

Generally, the approach we utilize is to run the sp_estimate_data_compression_savings stored procedure against the business data and control tables schemas (for example, CRPDTA and CRPCTL) to get a general estimate. You should perform the actual row or page compression on the data and indexes only when you have exclusive access to that database, such as during a planned outage. You can take the results from the stored procedure and then use that list to sort by the tables over a certain size, such as 100MB, or a particular row count. Mainly, you want to compress tables with data present and leave smaller tables uncompressed to minimize the overhead. We have used both T-SQL scripts to generate the statements for the compression and taken a list and created a copy/paste of the table/index names into the SQL statements.

Regarding the compression, note that you should utilize the parallelism (MDOP) option as much as possible. Table compression can require several hours, depending on the amount of data you have. For example, one customer on a relatively small configuration with a 400GB database took about 3 hours to compress all the selected tables to about 37GB. It is strongly recommended you test the compression on a copy of the data in prototype to determine an approximate runtime for the production compression. Listing 9-3 shows an example of using page compression on the JD Edwards EnterpriseOne F0911 table with two different approaches.

Listing 9-3 *Example page compression syntax for data/indexes*

```
Use JDE_PRODUCTION;
ALTER TABLE PRODDTA.F0911 REBUILD WITH (DATA_COMPRESSION=PAGE,
MAXDOP=4)
Note: Set MAXDOP parallelism to a number between 50-75% of your
processors for faster rebuild
--* Individual index compression. Can consider other option below
ALTER INDEX [F0911_1] ON [PRODDTA].[F0911] REBUILD WITH (DATA_
COMPRESSION = PAGE, MAXDOP=4)
```

```
ALTER INDEX [F0911_6] ON [PRODDTA].[F0911] REBUILD WITH (DATA_
COMPRESSION = PAGE, MAXDOP=4)
ALTER INDEX [F0911_8] ON [PRODDTA].[F0911] REBUILD WITH (DATA_
COMPRESSION = PAGE, MAXDOP=4)
ALTER INDEX [F0911_9] ON [PRODDTA].[F0911] REBUILD WITH (DATA_
COMPRESSION = PAGE, MAXDOP=4)
ALTER INDEX [F0911_10] ON [PRODDTA].[F0911] REBUILD WITH (DATA_
COMPRESSION = PAGE, MAXDOP=4)
ALTER INDEX [F0911_11] ON [PRODDTA].[F0911] REBUILD WITH (DATA_
COMPRESSION = PAGE, MAXDOP=4)
ALTER INDEX [F0911_12] ON [PRODDTA].[F0911] REBUILD WITH (DATA_
COMPRESSION = PAGE, MAXDOP=4)
ALTER INDEX [F0911_13] ON [PRODDTA].[F0911] REBUILD WITH (DATA_
COMPRESSION = PAGE, MAXDOP=4)
ALTER INDEX [F0911_15] ON [PRODDTA].[F0911] REBUILD WITH (DATA_
COMPRESSION = PAGE, MAXDOP=4)
ALTER INDEX [F0911_17] ON [PRODDTA].[F0911] REBUILD WITH (DATA_
COMPRESSION = PAGE, MAXDOP=4)
ALTER INDEX [F0911_18] ON [PRODDTA].[F0911] REBUILD WITH (DATA_
COMPRESSION = PAGE, MAXDOP=4)
ALTER INDEX [F0911_19] ON [PRODDTA].[F0911] REBUILD WITH (DATA_
COMPRESSION = PAGE, MAXDOP=4)
ALTER INDEX [F0911_23] ON [PRODDTA].[F0911] REBUILD WITH (DATA_
COMPRESSION = PAGE, MAXDOP=4)
ALTER INDEX [F0911_24] ON [PRODDTA].[F0911] REBUILD WITH (DATA_
COMPRESSION = PAGE, MAXDOP=4)
ALTER INDEX [F0911_25] ON [PRODDTA].[F0911] REBUILD WITH (DATA_
COMPRESSION = PAGE, MAXDOP=4)
ALTER INDEX [F0911_27] ON [PRODDTA].[F0911] REBUILD WITH (DATA_
COMPRESSION = PAGE, MAXDOP=4)
ALTER INDEX [F0911_28] ON [PRODDTA].[F0911] REBUILD WITH (DATA_
COMPRESSION = PAGE, MAXDOP=4)
ALTER INDEX [F0911_29] ON [PRODDTA].[F0911] REBUILD WITH (DATA_
COMPRESSION = PAGE, MAXDOP=4)
ALTER INDEX [F0911_30] ON [PRODDTA].[F0911] REBUILD WITH (DATA_
COMPRESSION = PAGE, MAXDOP=4)
ALTER INDEX [F0911_32] ON [PRODDTA].[F0911] REBUILD WITH (DATA_
COMPRESSION = PAGE, MAXDOP=4)
ALTER INDEX [F0911_33] ON [PRODDTA].[F0911] REBUILD WITH (DATA_
COMPRESSION = PAGE, MAXDOP=4)
ALTER INDEX [F0911_34] ON [PRODDTA].[F0911] REBUILD WITH (DATA_
COMPRESSION = PAGE, MAXDOP=4)
ALTER INDEX [F0911_35] ON [PRODDTA].[F0911] REBUILD WITH (DATA_
COMPRESSION = PAGE, MAXDOP=4)
ALTER INDEX [F0911_36] ON [PRODDTA].[F0911] REBUILD WITH (DATA_
COMPRESSION = PAGE, MAXDOP=4)
--* Alternative option for table/index compression instead of explicit
entries above
ALTER INDEX ALL ON [PRODDTA].[F0911] REBUILD WITH (DATA_COMPRESSION =
PAGE, MAXDOP=4)
```

You can use the database backup compression option to compress the backup file even further when you utilize database row/page compression. With compressed data and index tables you should observe a measureable reduction in the backup and restore times for your database. (Makes sense: with less data backed up there is less to restore saving time.) Even if you do not choose to use database row/page compression you should strongly consider using compression on your database backups to save disk space. It does utilize more processor capacity, but if you have it available you reap more benefits than negative consequences. We have observed some customer's database backups decrease from hours to minutes and the backup file size be 5–10 times smaller than the database when both database page and backup compression are in use. Just make sure you are not CPU-constrained before going down this path or it will cause additional resource and response issues.

There are many benefits to considering SQL Server database row/page and backup compression, and you should look into it if you have the edition that provides this feature. All of our JD Edwards EnterpriseOne customers that have implemented these compression strategies have seen significant reductions in the database disk storage, backup times, and incremental improvements in batch runtimes, since more data was available in the buffer pool.

Read Committed Snapshot Isolation (RCSI)

Since the early JD Edwards releases such as OneWorld Xe, there has been a little-known JDB database feature regarding SQL Server queries. The SQL Server database utilizes a pessimistic locking mechanism, where both read and write locks are present when a row is accessed. This is a very good database locking model for most situations, but for highly interactive applications such as JD Edwards EnterpriseOne, with both interactive and batch SQL requests against the same tables, you can observe increased locks and blocks. If you introduce ad hoc queries or reporting tools such as Microsoft Access ODBC, you increase the opportunity for locks to be held for long periods of time, which negatively affects web and batch applications.

JD Edwards introduced a query timeout and retry mechanism that would run a query for a few seconds and timeout/cancel that query if it exceeded the timer. It would retry several times and then modify the SQL query to use the NOLOCK option, which can be observed in JDEDEBUG logs when that situation occurs. By using the NOLOCK option, the query would read uncommitted data and allow it to complete. You might have a UBE or large user query against thousands of rows holding read/update locks that would prevent interactive applications from accessing the record. With the query timeout on JD Edwards operating under the covers, you would see a delay in your interactive users' query or UBE, but it would eventually process and not be blocked. We call these blockages caused by large numbers of user requests a "block party," since everyone attempting to access that table or resource waits together until the blocker releases its lock(s). Overall, this mechanism worked well for JD Edwards OneWorld and EnterpriseOne, but it did cause some response time fluctuations during heavy contention that most customers could not explain.

In SQL Server 2005 and later releases Read Committed Snapshot Isolation (RCSI) was introduced. This database setting uses row versioning to provide read-committed isolation levels and relies on creating an image of the committed records at the time of the SELECT queries in TEMPDB. This effectively prevents SELECT statements from holding read locks and blocking other read requests to the same tables. The largest effect for JD Edwards EnterpriseOne is that overall throughput improves for interactive and batch users due to reduced blocking. Update/delete lock isolation levels are still present by SQL Server, so your data integrity is maintained. This is sometimes called optimistic locking, which has been used by other database vendors over the years.

Here's an example in which this effect is most noticeable: A user with a third-party tool using ODBC access can hold a large number of locks if they access the transaction tables. These locks can block UBEs or web users from retrieving or updating the data in some situations. EnterpriseOne has specific code built into its tools for SQL Server that allows it to timeout queries and then eventually switch to a read uncommitted or NOLOCK option. This can help inquiry SQLs, but will not help a user that needs to delete or update certain rows. RCSI basically prevents reader threads from blocking writer threads in the database. This provides better response to the user when larger SQL queries are present. However, there is an observable increase in the TEMPDB database usage and size since the version store is present. The rows at the start of the SQL SELECT statement are saved in TEMPDB as a "version" to ensure a consistent read occurs. In later JD Edwards EnterpriseOne tools releases, we worked with development to enhance the query timeout settings so that we could utilize RCSI and correspondingly change our settings to disable the query retries and timeouts for SQL Server.

The method to change this requires the database to be in single user mode, and changes to the Enterprise server and Web server query timeouts are recommended to minimize the chance the NOLOCK option will be used. A Tools version of 8.97.2.x or higher is recommended to use these features properly. On the SQL Server databases such as JDE_PRODUCTION and JDE910, you can use the statements in Listings 9-4 and 9-5.

Listing 9-4   *Query to determine if RCSI is enabled*

```
SELECT sd.name, sd.is_read_committed_snapshot_on FROM sys.databases AS
sd
```

NOTE
Databases with RCSI enabled will have a value of 1 and others will be at 0 to indicated disabled or default pessimistic locking.

Listing 9-5 *Enable RCSI on database (ensure no active users in database)*

```
ALTER DATABASE <database name> SET READ_COMMITTED_SNAPSHOT ON
Example:
ALTER DATABASE JDE_PRODUCTION SET READ_COMMITTED_SNAPSHOT ON
```

Once you have the databases identified and changed to enable RCSI, you will also need to review the EnterpriseOne JAS.INI and Enterprise Server JDE.INI settings. In the JAS instance JDBJ.INI file under the [JDBj-RUNTIME PROPERTIES] stanza, you need to disable the JDBJ query timeout and retries. Note that you may have to add this manually if you can't locate it through Server Manager for the Web instance.

Here is a description of what these two settings do along with the default values:

```
msSQLQueryTimeout=10000
msSQLQueryAttempts=3
```

This indicates the maximum number of times a SQL Server query will be executed within the specified msSQLQueryTimeout period (see msSQLQueryTimeout details); then the last attempt of query execution will append the SQL statement with the NOLOCK syntax. This last attempt should retrieve data, but the data may be uncommitted or "dirty."

The retry attempts are made only when following SQL error conditions are detected:

- Timeout

- Timeout expired

- Serialization failure

- Deadlock

The JDBJ settings have a SQL Server query default of 10,000 ms, or 10 seconds, and will retry two times before switching to the NOLOCK option on the third attempt. This means that if it performs three retries, each one takes 10 seconds, so the entire query could be 30 seconds or longer.

On the Enterprise server JDE.INI file under the [DB System Settings] stanza, the SQL Server query default is 1 second with 17 retries before the NOLOCK option is used. That means a minimum delay of 17 seconds can occur if a query goes to the NOLOCK option. This was used mainly for the call object threads to reduce the wait time, but if you have a table with heavy locks it can significantly slow down the runtime of the queries for that application. This also affects the batch UBE queries that run on the Enterprise server.

The default settings apply to JD Edwards EnterpriseOne when running SQL Server and using the default record locking settings, which is pessimistic locking.

If Read Committed Snapshot Isolation (RCSI) is enabled at the database level, you should disable the JD Edwards EnterpriseOne SQL Server timeout/retry settings using the parameters shown in Table 9-13.

NOTE
These parameters became available in Server Manager starting in Tools 8.98.4.2 to review and have been present in earlier 8.97/8.98 Tools releases if you manually added them to the INI settings.

Generally, if RCSI is utilized, you want to change from the default settings so that you do *not* utilize the NOLOCK syntax or query retries since that can delay the SQL statement response or perform a dirty read. The query may actually take several seconds, just as it would with default locking, so you don't want extra retries present with RCSI in use.

Again this recommendation should be used *only* if the SQL Server database has implemented RCSI to eliminate contention between database readers and writers. If you simply want to adjust the timeouts and utilize the NOLOCK option, you can certainly consider that option as well, but we have found from customer engagements that the RCSI option works very well. Every customer for which we have implemented this feature on a JD Edwards EnterpriseOne database has provided very positive feedback, and the result has been improved response with timeouts reduced significantly. Once the INI settings are in place with coordination of the databases enabled with RCSI, no customers to date have requested to return to the default locking model. In most situations, the blocking and transaction timeout effects are significantly reduced or eliminated.

JDBJ.INI or Server Manager Web Instance JDBJ Database Configuration	Comment
msSQLQueryTimeout=0	Reflects no timeout on SQL Server query
msSQLQueryAttempts=2	Reflects no retries will be attempted
Enterprise Server JDE.INI [DB System Settings]	
SSQueryTimeout=0	No call object or UBE SQL query timeout
SSQueryTimeoutRetries=2	No query retries

TABLE 9-13. *JD Edwards SQL Server RCSI Query Timeout Settings*

Tuning IBM System i Database

The IBM System i (formerly known as IBM iSeries or AS/400) is a very robust integrated platform that includes the DB2/400 database integrated with the OS/400 operating system. The JD Edwards EnterpriseOne application roots sprang forth from the JD Edwards World Software functionality and it is a very viable platform with a wealth of robust features and capabilities. The current V6R1 and V7R1 OS releases with associated cumulative patches applied provide an excellent configuration that can automatically manage a large number of jobs. We ask our customers, "When was the last time you met an IBM System i database administrator?" We are not stating that there are no tuning opportunities available to maximize the performance of the IBM System i by any means, but the integrated nature of the architecture allows it to self-manage for a number of customer configurations.

The two most critical areas that are similar to what we have stressed for other platforms are performing an accurate hardware sizing with your vendor and ensuring that the IBM System i OS cumulative patches are relatively current. We understand that keeping the cumulative patches current is viewed by some as a disadvantage that can potentially affect the applications. It has been our experience, however, that if solid application testing processes are in place for the critical business applications and time/resources are made available to stay current, your system tends to have fewer issues and provides flexibility to adopt new changes in the JD Edwards EnterpriseOne application.

You can find a large number of very good documents regarding tuning the IBM System i. Overall we believe that these provide a very good foundation to tune your configuration and that the other databases did not have quite as much JD Edwards EnterpriseOne materials written about them.

In this section, we highlight certain areas to consider without the extensive detail. Some of these tuning recommendations are also contained in "IBM Power Systems with IBM i Performance and Tuning Tips for Oracle's JD Edwards EnterpriseOne 9.0" and certain elements from the IBM JD Edwards website referred to in the JD Edwards EnterpriseOne MTR documents (www-03.ibm.com/systems/i/advantages/oracle/). There are a number of IBM documents, Redbook and white papers available that provide additional tuning insights for the EnterpriseOne applications running on IBM System i. IBM has also published a good paper for smaller customer configurations since a number of these recommendations apply to most JD Edwards EnterpriseOne configurations. When you have a single processor with limited memory and disk you actually may need to tune a little bit more since fewer resources are available that need prioritization.

Following are some areas that affect the JD Edwards EnterpriseOne configuration performance. This is not a comprehensive discussion, but it provides some good areas for you to investigate and consider if you do not already have them in place. Ensuring that you have prestart allocations and shared memory pools properly configured can help significantly. Reviewing the large number of documents, guides, and papers, along with considering consulting assistance, can also be of great value. Experience and understanding your business processes can help in tuning the system. Properly sized hardware for your workload to obtain a balanced IBM System i database platform is the main goal.

Performance Collection

It is normally recommended that you enable the Collection Services and allow performance data to be available for review. System i Collection Services has a very low overhead for performance gathering and is strongly recommended. It allows you to review your system from a historical perspective for a certain window of time, such as seven days. Collection Services automatically purges the older data and tends to use a small amount of disk space. You can have this data sent to IBM support for assistance; or, if you want to perform a JD Edwards EnterpriseOne sizing, you can see where this data is utilized in the analysis.

In the IBM System i versions, such as V6R1 and V7R1, the System i Navigator is the preferred method for initially reviewing the performance data. More detailed performance tools, such as iDoctor and Performance Explorer (PEX), are also available. We are not going into detail regarding these tools; you should use the System i Navigator tool when possible for reviewing system performance. The historical and graphical information is easy to use and identifies potential bottlenecks such as high processor consumers or hot-disk issues.

Database Index Configuration

The System i has a very robust database (DB2/400) integrated into the OS. One of the advantages for JD Edwards EnterpriseOne configurations is that it will automatically create a temporary index for a query that can be reused by other applications. Some customers may notice that after an Initial Program Load (IPL), the system may appear a little slower in response, and over the course of a few days it will "speed up." Some of this may be due to temporary indexes being created.

You can utilize the IBM System i Navigator to review the SQL Cache and indexes that are present. At that time, you can decide whether you want to create a permanent index via the Navigator or from the JD Edwards EnterpriseOne OMW toolset. There are a number of opinions regarding where custom indexes should be created and maintained. We think that you should leverage the resources you are most comfortable using to document and maintain the custom indexes. If you have a System i administrator who documents and maintains the indexes, that is a good thing; or if you have strong change management and development resources for JD Edwards EnterpriseOne, you can maintain them there, where the index will be more readily visible to developers.

Index opportunities utilize criteria similar to what we discussed earlier in the SQL Server sections of this chapter: you assess the need for the index based on business requirements, executions, and what response time is desired. The Navigator provides a very easy method to monitor the queries in use and filter/review by many criteria such as most expensive time, executions (total times run), average processing time, and so on. In Figure 9-3, you can see an example of some SQL statements from the SQL Plan Cache.

Navigator makes it very easy to review the SQL statements, provide a visual explain plan, and generate a custom index if desired. You can also determine the temporary indexes that have been created and how many times they have been executed. This can allow you to decide whether you want to create the index permanently.

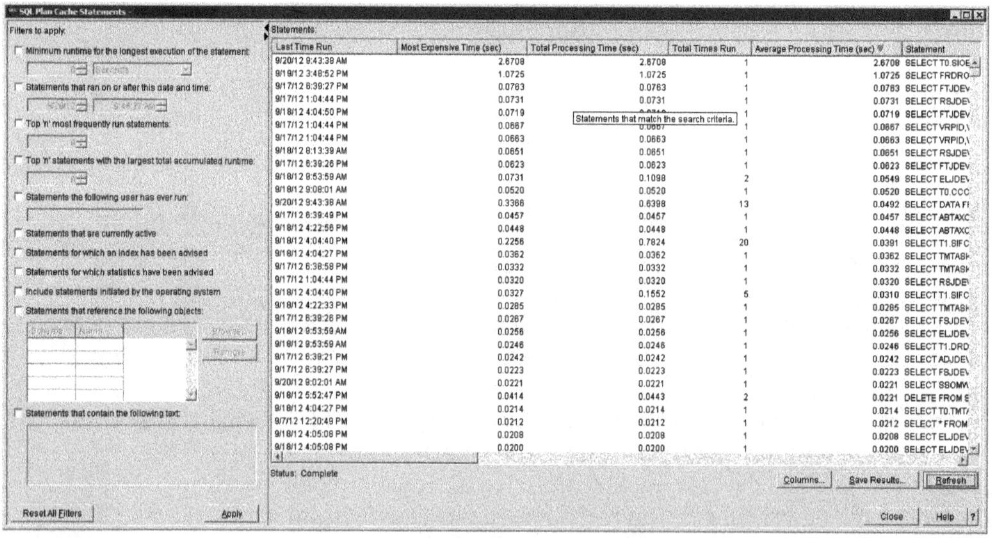

FIGURE 9-3. *SQL Plan Cache index review*

TIP
If you elect to create indexes via a script outside of JD Edwards EnterpriseOne, we would strongly suggest that you save all the custom index creation SQL in either a single text file or a folder with the names of each index. This will allow you to track and document the custom indexes added, and if you update or upgrade in the future it will allow you to easily reapply them after reviewing their validity. Use a naming convention to identify the indexes easily. (Sometimes an index is no longer needed when you make business process changes or implement new modules, so it helps to review whether an index is being used.)

JDE.INI and QAQQINI Settings

Every CNC administrator who installs or upgrades JD Edwards EnterpriseOne should review the installation/upgrade guide for JD Edwards EnterpriseOne. The latest JD Edwards EnterpriseOne 9.1 install/upgrade guide contains a large number of useful configuration settings that should be reviewed. We have found several customer configurations where simply implementing the recommendations in the JD Edwards EnterpriseOne installation/upgrade guide would save time and frustration. One small example is ensuring that the Enterprise server JDE.INI SQL Package Library=2 setting is changed to a 0 or 1 after the install/upgrade. We have seen this set to 2 at many customer sites, which increases UBE runtimes and SQLPKG entries significantly.

Every JD Edwards EnterpriseOne configuration on System i must create a QUSRSYS/QAQQINI in order to increase the LOB_LOCATOR_THRESHOLD to 10,000, or your package builds will be challenged. In addition to this user setting, you can consider where you want the SQL Query Engine (SQE) to have different optimization goals such as *FIRSTIO or *ALLIO. For the majority of customers, the default of *ALLIO works very well between web requests and batch jobs. However, some customers have primarily web-based users with very little batch requirements. Others with more diverse requirements may want the best of both options by setting *FIRSTIO as the default optimization_goal option in QUSRSYS/QAQQINI and have a custom library for the QAQQINI setting such as UBEBATCH/QAQQINI with the *ALLIO optimization_goal, where the batch subsystem jobs have a routing entry use the CHGQRYA command to use the UBEBATCH/QAQQINI settings instead.

Basically what the QAQQINI optimization_goal does is influence the SQE (we are assuming that all your queries are utilizing SQE and not the older Classic Query Engine [CQE], which can use this parameter as well) to favor using indexes to return initial data as quickly as possible for *FIRSTIO. The *ALLIO default setting for most connections is designed to return all the data, which works well for most customers except those that want to provide the interactive web users some better query response times where the data appears before the query completes. So if you want, you can consider one of the above options for your configuration and see how it benefits your system.

Use the IBM System i Navigator and review your ODBC/JDBC and batch job SQL plan cache in detail. The details of the query can tell which `optimization_goal` and SQE/CQE engine is in use. In the V6R1 and V7R1 OS releases, you may find that the desired `optimization_goals` are already in use. ODBC/JDBC typically utilizes *FIRSTIO, and batch jobs may be using *ALLIO, depending on your configuration.

TIP
One hardware change that can also improve I/O response rates is to investigate the option of using Solid State Drives (SSDs) for a portion of your IBM System i. IBM System i V7R1 and later releases utilize these drives with increased flexibility, and this typically improves your overall system response such as UBE runtimes. These drives may be beyond your budget, but if you can include them in your configuration with relatively current IBM System i hardware, you could be pleasantly surprised. You may also be able to obtain hardware sizing information from IBM to aid in the decision and potential benefit of using these drives.

Job Prestart Allocations

A very useful change that impacts JD Edwards EnterpriseOne significantly is ensuring that you allocate sufficient QSQSRVR and `QZDASOINIT` prestart jobs that are ready to accept database connections. Unfortunately, although the JD Edwards EnterpriseOne installation/upgrade guides recommend how to prestart the `QUSRWRK/QZDASOINIT`, for some reason the more heavily used `QSYSWRK/QSQSRVR` prestart settings are not documented. Some Oracle Metalink documents show how to do this, such as ID 841314.1 and the EnterpriseOne installation/upgrade guides. The method used for `QZDASOINIT` prestart jobs is the same for QSQSRVR jobs, so ensure that you have prestart levels configured for *both*. With the later releases of JD Edwards EnterpriseOne, the QSQSRVR jobs tend to be more heavily used for database operations than external connections via `QZDASOINIT`. External connections such as web servers, radio frequency bar code solutions, and Windows clients will utilize the QZDASOINIT database connections. JD Edwards EnterpriseOne kernels, Vertex, and UBEs typically use QSQSRVR unless you decide to disable UBE QSQSRVR connections using the Enterprise server JDE.INI sqlServerMode=0 setting. (Note that customers using Vertex will not be able to disable this option and must have QSQSRVR jobs enabled so *do not* consider this option or a number of Enterprise kernels may fail due to Vertex CLI usage.)

Generally you want the prestart jobs to be near the average number observed or slightly less, such as 10–20 percent. If the average is 285 jobs, for example, you want the prestart to be somewhere in the 230–300 range. If the peak number is used, you will consume more memory and resources, so you want your system to grow to the peaks and then gradually release them during lower activity.

Each user consumes three to six connections (jobs), so an average of five works well. You have to identify what type of applications are connecting, however, since you will tend to be on the higher side if the tax software Vertex is present, which uses additional connections. If you are not running Vertex software, you will gravitate toward the lower number of average connections per user. There will usually be four or five QZDASOINIT connections for the Web JDBC users and three to five QSQSRVR connections for the users' call object session that jdenet_k is using.

We are going to walk through an example for setting the prestart allocations, where a customer misunderstood the settings and *over*-allocated the prestart jobs, which used significantly more resources compared to the actual levels observed. This example illustrates that if you utilize the default prestart allocations delivered by IBM System i, you may be too low, but in this case if you go too high, you may adversely affect your system as well as unnecessarily consume memory. The goal is to monitor your usage and find the "Goldilocks zone," which is not too low and not high, but just right for your workload. Figure 9-4 shows the large prestart allocation screenshot.

DSPACTPJ SBS(QUSRWRK) PGM(QZDASOINIT) is issued to review the prestart levels. For QZDASOINIT, we can start 750 or 1000 jobs with a threshold of 50 and allocation of 50 new jobs. This setting matches the actual usage much better than the 2000 allocated jobs, which is significantly higher than the peak usage that wastes resources.

Figure 9-5 shows the prestart settings for QZDASOINIT using the WKRSBS QUSRWRK command and prestart job settings option for the QZDASOINIT entry. The threshold is very low to start additional jobs and could cause delays if more than one user logs in when the 2000 prestart jobs are used. Adding 200 at a time will also create significant delays as well instead of a smaller number like 50. Currently QZDASOINIT runs in shared pool identifier 1 as well, which is planned to change to an appropriate shared memory pool.

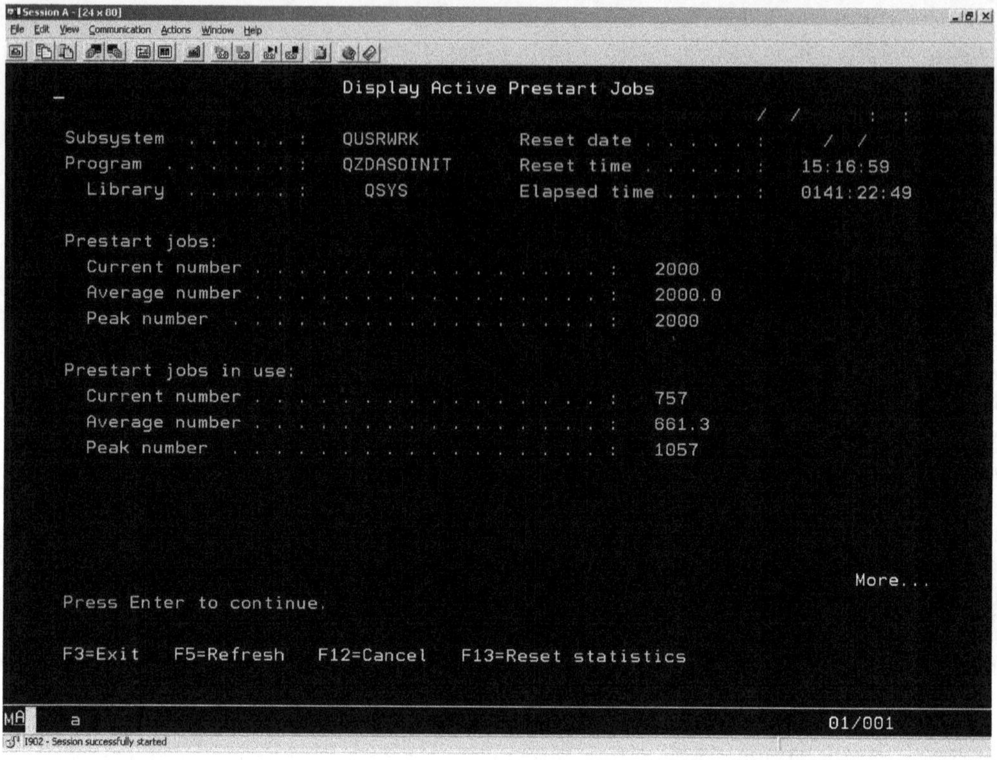

```
Session A - [24 x 80]
File  Edit  View  Communication  Actions  Window  Help

                       Display Active Prestart Jobs
                                                        /  /      :  :
    Subsystem  . . . . . :   QUSRWRK       Reset date . . . . . :    /  /
    Program  . . . . . . :   QZDASOINIT    Reset time . . . . . :   15:16:59
      Library  . . . . . :     QSYS        Elapsed time . . . . :   0141:22:49

    Prestart jobs:
      Current number . . . . . . . . . . . . . . . . . . . :   2000
      Average number . . . . . . . . . . . . . . . . . . . :   2000.0
      Peak number  . . . . . . . . . . . . . . . . . . . . :   2000

    Prestart jobs in use:
      Current number . . . . . . . . . . . . . . . . . . . :   757
      Average number . . . . . . . . . . . . . . . . . . . :   661.3
      Peak  number  . . . . . . . . . . . . . . . . . . . . :   1057

                                                                More...

    Press Enter to continue.

    F3=Exit    F5=Refresh    F12=Cancel    F13=Reset statistics

MA    a                                                         01/001
  1902 - Session successfully started
```

FIGURE 9-4. *QUSRWRK/QZDASOINIT prestart allocation usage levels*

In Figure 9-6, we issued the DSPACTPJ SBS(QSYSWRK) PGM(QSQSRVR) command to view the prestart jobs. We recommended 750 to 1000 prestart jobs with a threshold of 50 and allocation of 50 and MAXUSE of 200.

The MAXUSE parameter was set to 25 instead of the default 200, which causes the overhead of new jobs to be almost 10 times higher than desired. You would be starting a new QSQSRVR database job after 25 uses instead of 200, which for stable connections is much too frequent, increasing overhead unnecessarily.

In Figure 9-7, we have similar settings for the QSQSRVR prestart jobs using the using the WKRSBS QSYSWRK command and prestart job settings option for QSQSRVR entry. We provided similar recommendations in this customer situation due to call object and batch workload present.

The bottom line is to review your prestart settings in use by the JD Edwards EnterpriseOne configuration. You start out with an estimation of the number of users

```
Session A - [24 x 80]                                                      _|8|x|
File  Edit  View  Communication  Actions  Window  Help
[toolbar icons]
                         Display Prestart Job Entry Detail
    _                                                      System:
    Subsystem description:    QUSRWRK          Status:    ACTIVE

    Program  . . . . . . . . . . . . . . . . . . . :    QZDASOINIT
      Library  . . . . . . . . . . . . . . . . . . :      QSYS
    User profile . . . . . . . . . . . . . . . . . :    QUSER
    Job  . . . . . . . . . . . . . . . . . . . . . :    QZDASOINIT
    Job description  . . . . . . . . . . . . . . . :    *USRPRF
      Library  . . . . . . . . . . . . . . . . . . :
    Start jobs . . . . . . . . . . . . . . . . . . :    *YES
    Initial number of jobs . . . . . . . . . . . . :    2000
    Threshold  . . . . . . . . . . . . . . . . . . :    8
    Additional number of jobs  . . . . . . . . . . :    200
    Maximum number of jobs . . . . . . . . . . . . :    *NOMAX
    Maximum number of uses . . . . . . . . . . . . :    200
    Wait for job . . . . . . . . . . . . . . . . . :    *YES
    Pool identifier  . . . . . . . . . . . . . . . :    1

                                                              More...

    Press Enter to continue.

    F3=Exit    F12=Cancel    F14=Display previous entry

MA    a                                                          01/001
I902 - Session successfully started
```

FIGURE 9-5.   *QZDASOINIT prestart settings set by customer*

and connections. Over time as you have actual usage, you can adjust the settings to match your average and peak usage based on how the workloads behave. In most cases, once the workload is stable, you do not have to monitor these often, but don't forget to review them since business processes, code, and configuration changes can influence how many connections are used.

TCP/IP Buffer Size

One change that can benefit larger volume servers connecting to your IBM System i is to consider increasing the network TCP/IP send/receive buffer size. In V6R1 and below, the default buffer size is 8192 bytes, which was useful for slower networks, but not as relevant in the much faster and more reliable networks in use today.

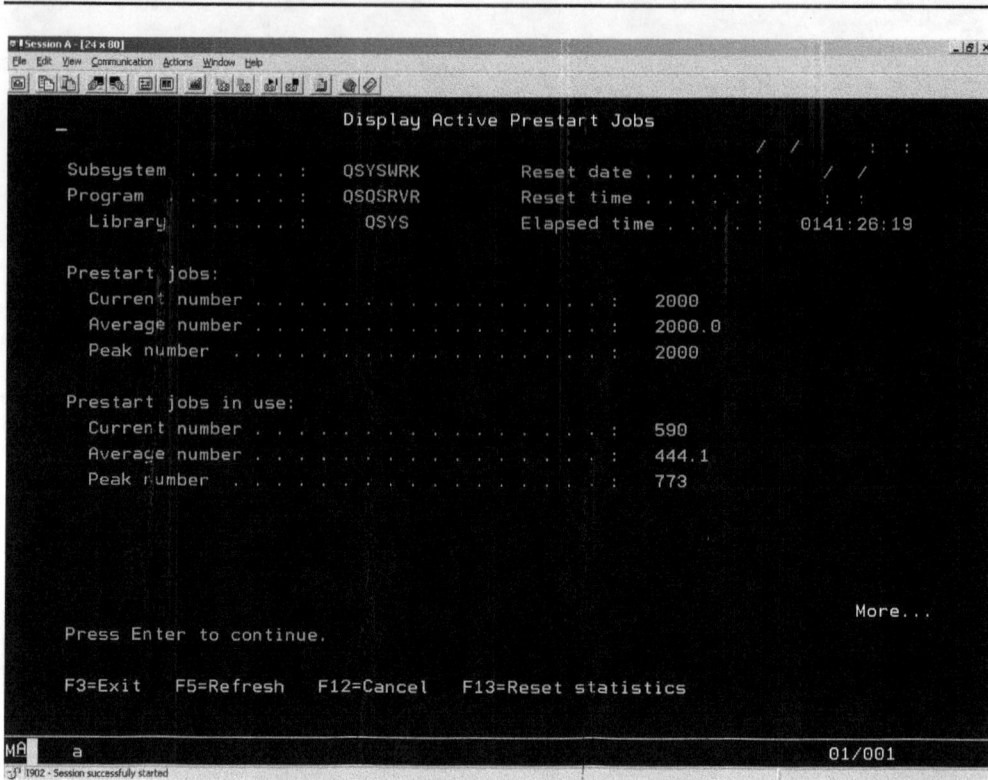

FIGURE 9-6. *QSYSWRK/QSQSRVR prestart allocation usage levels*

The default for V7R1 is 65,536 bytes, but this can also be too low, especially if you have other IBM System i, virtual three-tier or Windows servers connected in the local network to the IBM System i machine. Most customer System i machines utilize 1GB network cards, so changing the TCP/IP attribute can provide improved network throughput. The CHGTCPA command is dynamic, taking effect immediately, but we generally perform this during low activity levels to be conservative.

The command is

```
CHGTCPA TCPRCVBUF(1048576) TCPSNDBUF(1048576)
```

- For 100Mbs network cards the value is typically 65536.

- For 1000Mbs network cards the value is typically 1048576.

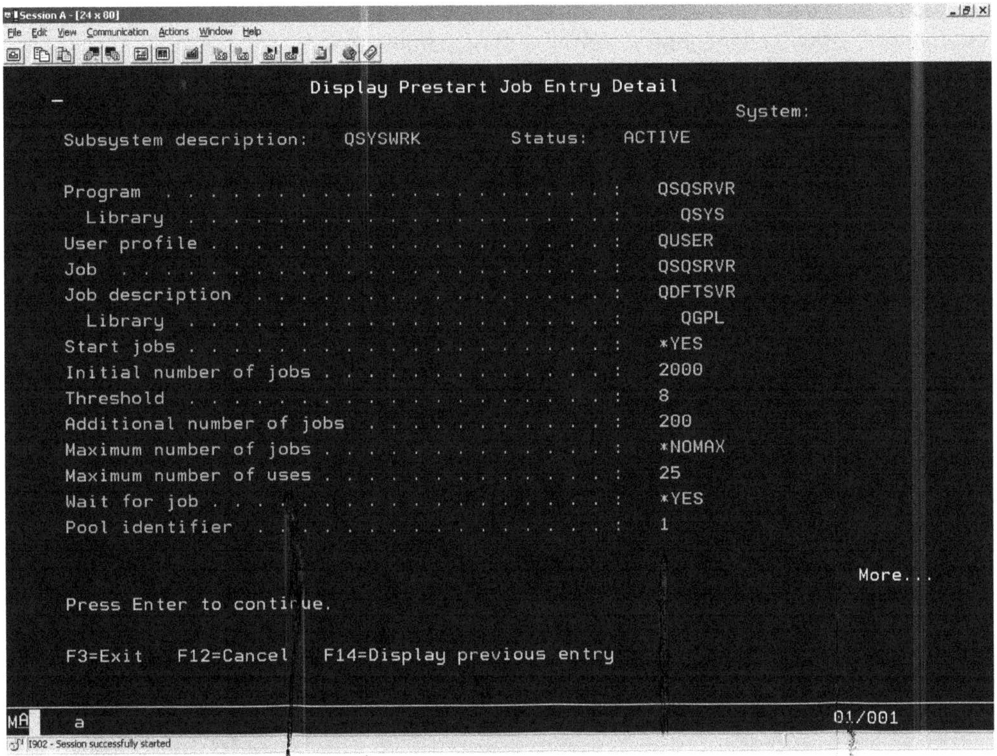

FIGURE 9-7. *QSQSRVR prestart settings set by customer*

Job Class Time Slices

The job class time slices were initially created back in the '70s and '80s and have not been adjusted for faster processors—in our opinion—over the years. Generally, after all the other performance tuning has been completed, we examine potentially reducing the time slices by at least a factor of 10 (hundreds instead of thousands) when a customer has thousands of active jobs present in the system. You can consider this for smaller configurations, but you may not observe as significant an improvement versus a system with a large number of active jobs. This allows faster jobs to go through and prevents larger jobs from holding the processor as long. Since you free up the processor time slice sooner, the other smaller eligible jobs get the processor sooner, which can become a cumulative effect. In most situations for busy systems, these changes will result in better performance for JD Edwards EnterpriseOne Web and the batch runtimes when many (thousands or more) active jobs are present.

If a class is already in the hundreds, it should *not* be changed, and we do not change the time slice values for system parameters that are protected. Basically, the system won't let you change the system job class parameters.

Use the command WRKCLS CLS (*ALL/*ALL) to view/edit the entries. An example is shown in Figure 9-8.

When changes are desired, use option 2 to change the entry. Not all system entries can be changed, and those will remain at defaults.

In Figure 9-9, you could change the time slice to 500 milliseconds. Note that these changes do *not* take effect until the system is recycled or a new job starts, so it is best to coordinate the changes near or within a maintenance window where you IPL the machine.

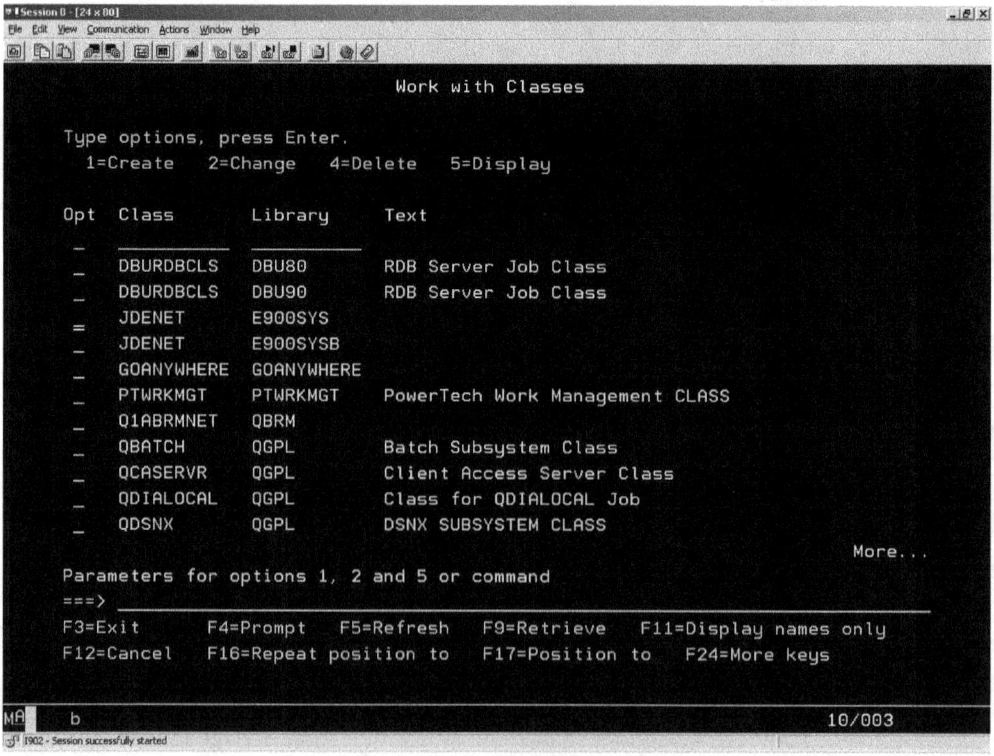

FIGURE 9-8. *WRKCLS class time slice review and change*

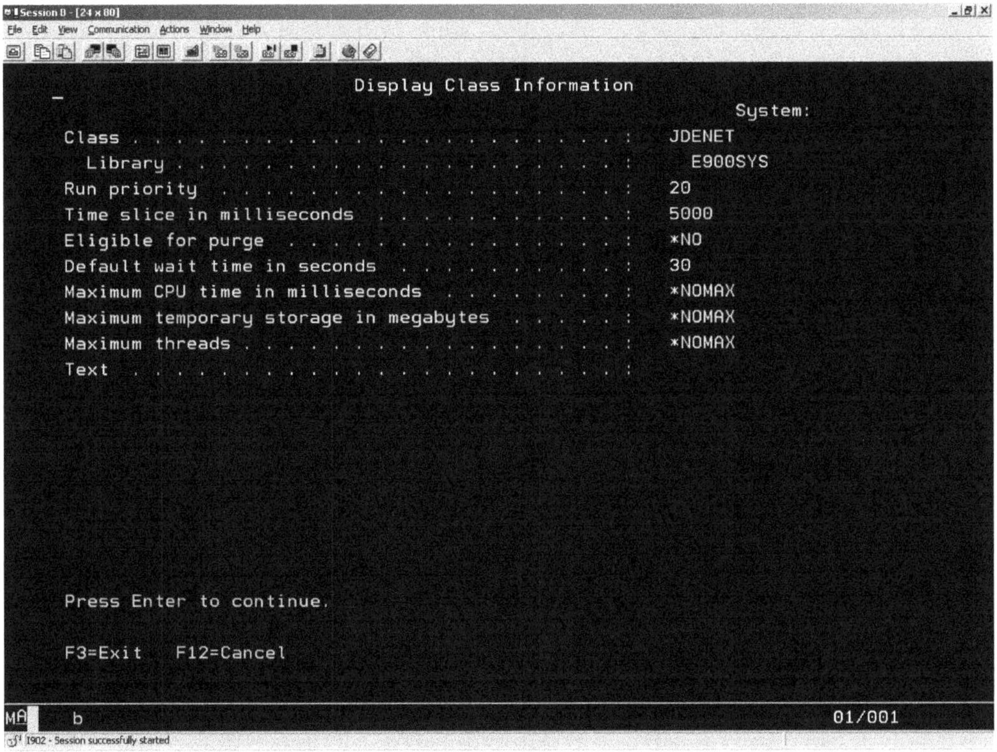

FIGURE 9-9. *Example of JDENET time slice at 5000 milliseconds*

There are several opinions regarding this type of change, but we have found that with the newer generations of IBM Power processors, you can observe incremental improvements when you have a high number of concurrent jobs running in your IBM System i. This change is typically one of the later ones that are considered after implementing other recommendations such as the QAQQINI Optimization_goal, prestart allocations for QZDASOINIT/QSQSRVR and memory pool settings. Changing the job class time slices for busier configurations does skew the configuration to favor shorter jobs such as the queries from web users, but it can also help short-running batch jobs since the longer running jobs do not hold the time slice as long as they previously could. This is a good option to consider once the other areas have been addressed. Do all your other tuning activities before considering this option.

Batch Subsystem Priorities

Another option is to divide your batch workloads into different IBM System i subsystems with priorities for the job and memory. You can, for example, use the QBATCH subsystem for most jobs submitted by users and create another batch subsystem such as JDEBATCH at a lower priority such as 60. The QBATCH subsystem typically operates at priority 50, and you could place longer running, more resource-intensive jobs into the JDEBATCH subsystem queues. You would need to modify the queue name in the UBE versions that you want to submit to the JDEBATCH subsystem to match your queue entries. By running at priority 60, these jobs would typically take a little longer than if running at priority 50, but they'd use only leftover resources once the higher priority jobs have their share. Consider this option for UBEs that take perhaps an hour or longer and would be good candidates for this type of batch subsystem configuration. This is a more complex configuration to implement, but it has proven useful when you have a lot of batch activity and want to prioritize certain batches above others.

Memory Pools

In general, there are two primary methods of tuning an IBM System i environment. One option or line of thinking is to allow the machine to manage the resources in a common memory pool. This is the default model used where the bulk of memory management occurs in the *BASE memory pool.

The second option is to allocate shared memory pools, enable the expert cache option, and set priorities as desired for the different jobs/applications. You can then allow the system to dynamically manage the various activity levels, memory, and priorities or you can disable these features and manually tune/monitor them. Our recommendation in the later IBM System i releases is to allocate shared memory pools and allow the system to manage itself with monitoring to ensure the workload goals are being met.

The newer releases of IBM System i have reduced the tuning needs significantly. The move from the Classic Query Engine (CQE) to SQL Query Engine (SQE) provides several advantages to SQL execution and optimizations. IBM System i's ability to manage the workload dynamically has improved over the years as well. You can use shared memory pools to refine the workload priorities to your business requirements or run generally well in the default *BASE configuration.

Sometimes a compromise exists in that memory can be allocated into several shared pools. A memory pool can be created for the following reasons:

- Different paging characteristics caused by batch and interactive/online jobs

- Different execution priorities

Based on the JD Edwards EnterpriseOne workload criteria, you can create the following suggested pools if you want to separate the workloads:

- **Machine pool**   Must have a low fault rate (below 10 pages or less per second) and operates at the highest memory priority (1).

- ***BASE pool**   For running the system and unassigned job transients at memory priority (2).

- **Shared pool**   For running all of the QZDASOINIT/QSQSRVR jobs that perform the EnterpriseOne ODBC and internal call object/UBE activity. The EnterpriseOne subsystem may also be placed here or in a separate shared pool. Generally the same shared pool as QZDASOINIT/QSQSRVR jobs.

- **Batch pool**   For running UBEs.

- **Shared pool for the Java resources**   If WebSphere is running on the system

- **Interactive shared pool**   For 5250 terminal usage where most EnterpriseOne customers generally have little to no interactive users present

- **Small pool**   For spooling

Under the WRKSHRPOOL command you can modify the shared pool sizes and characteristics and then at the subsystem definitions define which jobs go into the specific shared pools. Figure 9-10 shows a shared pool configuration.

Note the memory priority settings has the machine pool at 1 and the rest at 2, minimum size percentages are present, and for this configuration the maximum percentage for *INTERACT was set to limit the memory 5250 terminal users could obtain. In some cases, if you have a low priority batch subsystem, you might set the memory priority to 3.

Figure 9-11 shows the text descriptions of the shared pool purpose to help you understand what jobs/subsystem(s) are in that pool.

Figure 9-12 provides an example, where the system has run for a day the dynamic adjustments, and expert cache moves memory between the pools. The JD Edwards EnterpriseOne/QSQSRVR/QZDASOINIT tend to retain more memory for this particular configuration, and the *BASE and batch subsystems move memory back and forth as the workloads change.

Basically, for shared memory pools the key is to set some minimum memory levels for the EnterpriseOne/QSQSRVR/QZDASOINIT and batch subsystem to ensure that a certain level of response is maintained. The priority has been changed to 1 for *MACHINE and 2 for all other pools. Minimum memory percentages have been set to ensure a certain amount of memory in that pool is always reserved. You can adjust over time by monitoring the paging and response time of the jobs in that

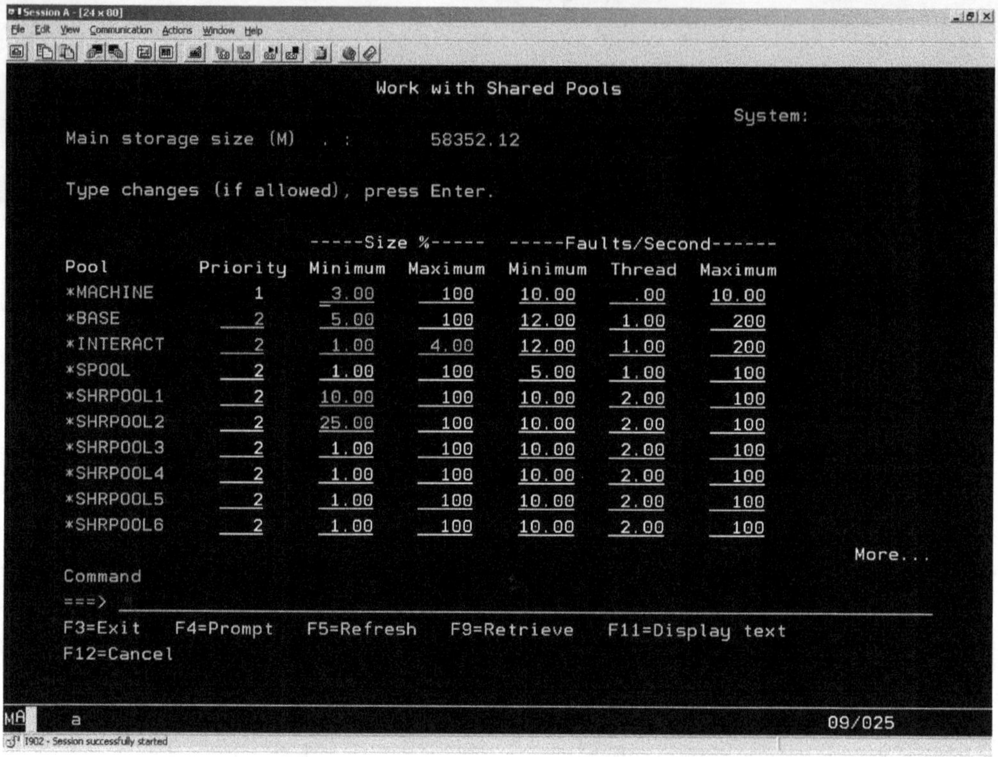

```
Session A - [24 x 80]
File   Edit   View   Communication   Actions   Window   Help

                        Work with Shared Pools
                                                        System:
       Main storage size (M)   . :        58352.12

       Type changes (if allowed), press Enter.


                          -----Size %-----   -----Faults/Second------
       Pool        Priority  Minimum  Maximum  Minimum  Thread  Maximum
       *MACHINE        1      3.00      100    10.00     .00    10.00
       *BASE           2      5.00      100    12.00    1.00     200
       *INTERACT       2      1.00     4.00    12.00    1.00     200
       *SPOOL          2      1.00      100     5.00    1.00     100
       *SHRPOOL1       2     10.00      100    10.00    2.00     100
       *SHRPOOL2       2     25.00      100    10.00    2.00     100
       *SHRPOOL3       2      1.00      100    10.00    2.00     100
       *SHRPOOL4       2      1.00      100    10.00    2.00     100
       *SHRPOOL5       2      1.00      100    10.00    2.00     100
       *SHRPOOL6       2      1.00      100    10.00    2.00     100
                                                                 More...
       Command
       ===>
       F3=Exit   F4=Prompt   F5=Refresh   F9=Retrieve   F11=Display text
       F12=Cancel

MA      a                                                 09/025
    1902 - Session successfully started
```

FIGURE 9-10. *WRKSHRPOOL definitions*

shared pool. The *CALC expert cache is enabled for all the shared pools to manage the pool if dynamic adjustments are allowed.

If too much memory is removed from the pool, it can increase the paging rates to bring back either data or programs. We generally start with a value of 5 or 10 percent and then monitor the general response and paging rates of that memory pool. We like to see relatively low paging rates for the EnterpriseOne/QSQSRVR/ QZDASOINIT pool, and for the batch you can usually endure higher paging rates. This does depend on the batch job mix and the turnaround time needed by the business. If you have some really high priority batch jobs that need quick turnaround along with large long-running batch, you may need to separate them into different subsystems and pools, but this is an exception rather than the rule. Note that if you are relatively low on memory, the use of shared pools becomes

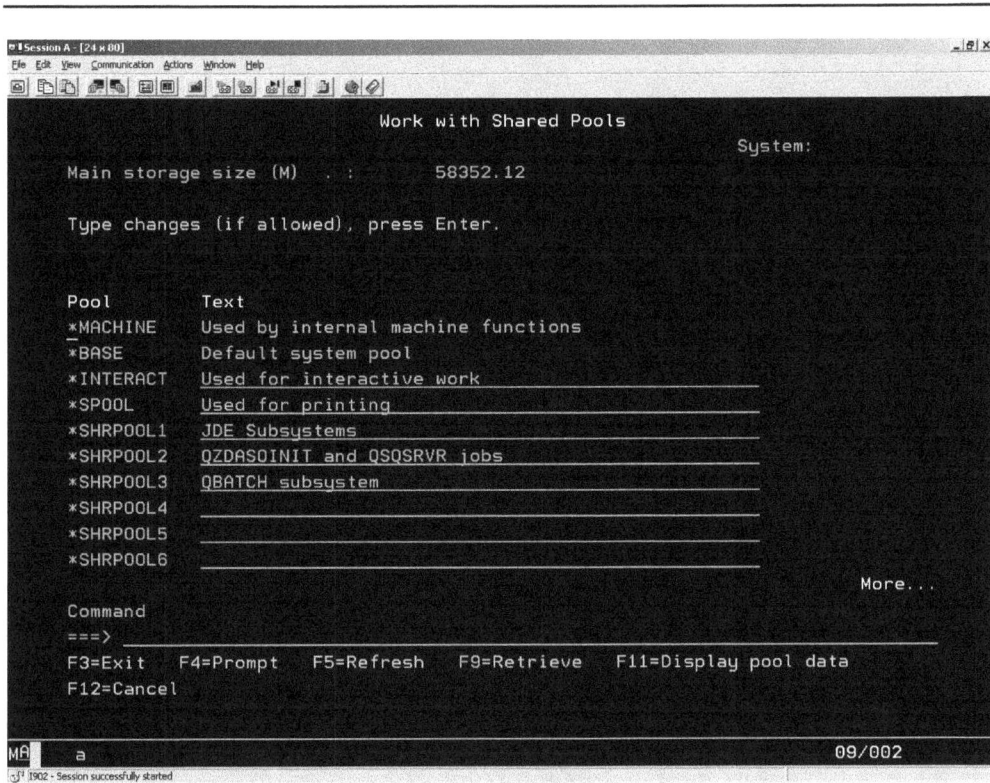

FIGURE 9-11.   *WRKSHRPOOL descriptions*

even more valuable, since you are prioritizing the workload pools and reserving certain resources in those pools.

The shared memory pool strategy is very flexible, and we only touched on it in this section. To set up the pools properly takes some initial time and monitoring, but it can allow the IBM System i to adjust itself when workload demands change. There is definitely no one strategy for all customers when it comes to workload management.

Table 9-14 lists some of the performance system parameters that should be reviewed and evaluated. The goal is to allow the IBM System i to manage the memory pools, priorities, and activity levels of the configuration. Each configuration is different in the business processing goals, but the capabilities of the IBM V6R1, V7R1, and later OS (with cumulative patches applied to be as current as possible) work very well. Older OS releases provided more opportunities to tune manually, and you have that option as well, but in our opinion for most JD Edwards

```
Session A - [24 x 80]
File  Edit  View  Communication  Actions  Window  Help

                        Work with Shared Pools
                                                        System:
    Main storage size (M)    . :       58352.12

    Type changes (if allowed), press Enter.

                 Defined    Max    Allocated   Pool  -Paging Option--
    Pool         Size (M)  Active  Size (M)     ID   Defined  Current
    *MACHINE      1838.08   +++++   1838.08      1   *FIXED   *FIXED
    *BASE         3020.01     756   3020.01      2   *CALC    *CALC
    *INTERACT      583.51     146    583.51      5   *CALC    *CALC
    *SPOOL         500.00      26    500.00      4   *CALC    *CALC
    *SHRPOOL1     5835.20     254   5835.20      7   *CALC    *CALC
    *SHRPOOL2    45239.35     100  45239.35      3   *CALC    *CALC
    *SHRPOOL3     1335.95      20   1335.95      6   *CALC    *CALC
    *SHRPOOL4         .00       0                    *FIXED
    *SHRPOOL5         .00       0                    *FIXED
    *SHRPOOL6         .00       0                    *FIXED
                                                              More...
    Command
    ===>
    F3=Exit   F4=Prompt   F5=Refresh   F9=Retrieve   F11=Display tuning data
    F12=Cancel

MA     a                                                    09/014
  1902 - Session successfuly started
```

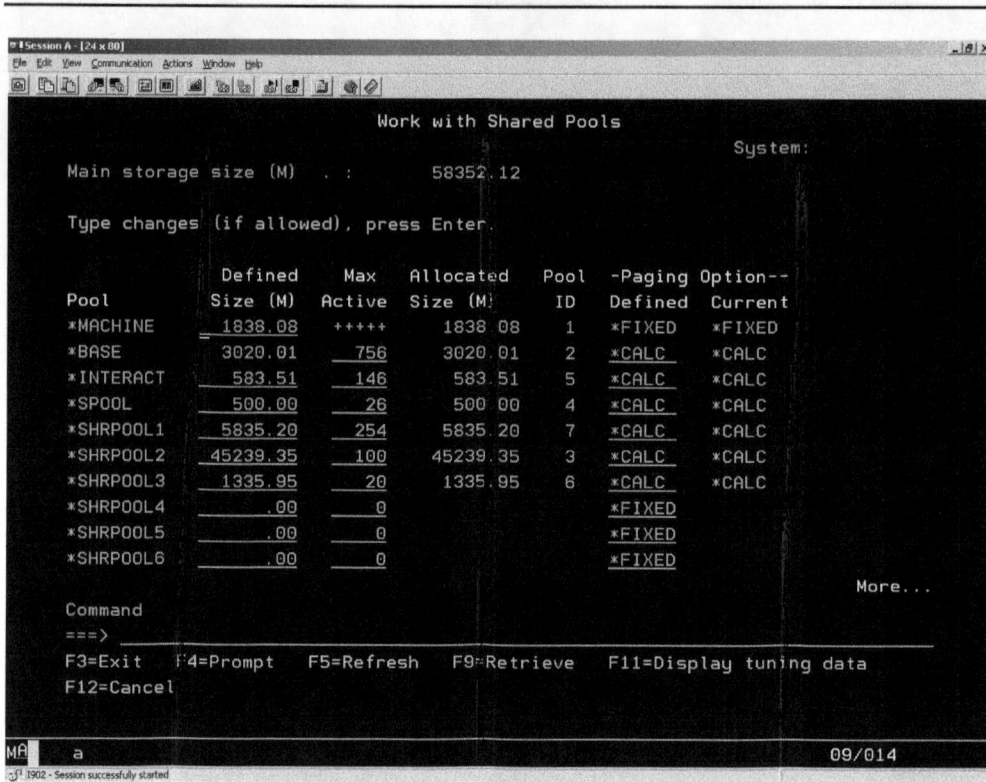

FIGURE 9-12. *WRKSHRPOOL example of memory allocations over time*

EnterpriseOne customers, one of the goals utilizing the IBM System i is to minimize
manual management and tuning tasks.

With a properly sized hardware configuration and well-defined business process
workload goals in place, the IBM System i is an excellent platform to operate. As
stated previously, you can set the configuration to be fairly static if desired, but that
strategy tends to work better in older releases of IBM System i and JD Edwards
OneWorld, where you would tend to have a larger number of interactive 5250
users, possibly coexisting with World on the older OS releases. With JD Edwards
EnterpriseOne, the workload is heavily skewed toward batch since Web and UBEs
are both batch requests with different priority levels. This is why using shared
memory pools with dynamic performance adjustments tends to be utilized more
often than in the past. Not everyone will agree with dynamic performance
adjustments, but our experience has demonstrated that for JD Edwards EnterpriseOne

System Value	Comment
DSPSYSVAL QPFRADJ	Performance Adjuster Suggested this be set at 3 to allow the system to manage the automatically adjust performance
DSPSYSVAL QDYNPTYADJ	Dynamic Priority Adjustment Recommend this be set at 1 or enabled Allows changing a longer running job priority to permit shorter running jobs to complete faster
DSPSYSVAL QDYNPTYSCD	Dynamic Priority Scheduler Recommend this be set at 1 or enabled
DSPSYSVAL QPRCMLTTSK	Processor Multi-tasking Recommend this be set at 2 at system controlled

TABLE 9-14.   *Performance System Parameters to Consider*

workloads this configuration can be very effective. As with all the tuning recommendations we have provided, you need to verify and evaluate in your particular environment.

CHAPTER
10

Tuning by Tier: The Interface Tier

I n this chapter, we'll cover the intricacies of tuning the interface tier. We'll look at clustering the Business Services Server and transaction server. Also, we'll check out some of the new functionality associated with mobile applications.

Business Services Server

The Business Services (BSSV) Server software solution provides clients with the ability to extend business applications into a Service-Oriented Architecture (SOA). BSSV Server allows customers to expose native EnterpriseOne BSSVs through web service standards, which deliver the ability to develop, publish, consume, and administer web services directly for JD Edwards EnterpriseOne tools.

These web services interfaces are built on the JD Edwards EnterpriseOne Business Services, Java-based business functions that perform discrete units of work and interact with systems external to EnterpriseOne. With BSSV, you can accept a business document based on XML standards and use that information to interact with other EnterpriseOne objects such as business functions or table I/O to complete transactions. As you can imagine, BSSV represents a powerful tool in a successful Enterprise Resource Planning (ERP) implementation and another component for the administrator to tune. In this section, we will address some of the larger performance items: Java Virtual Machine (JVM) parameters, clusters, and load balancing.

JVM Arguments and BSSV

JVM startup arguments determine how the JVM will act and can affect the overall performance of the BSSV solution. These startup arguments can be modified in both IBM WebSphere Application Server and Oracle WebLogic Server. One of the most common modifications is to increase the maximum amount of memory (heap size). However, other modifications can also be made to improve performance. Note that aside from increasing maximum memory, it is more effective to baseline your performance prior to making some of the other option changes (that is, determine where a bottleneck might be prior to making too many initial changes).

NOTE
As the startup arguments can change over time/ release levels, it is a good idea to verify the settings for your release prior to making any changes.

Increase Maximum Memory

The most common tuning option for the JVM is to increase the maximum memory (heap size) by setting the –Xmx parameter. When you perform a BSSV installation, Server Manager will set this parameter for an optimized value for a "standard" number of users (roughly 100–150 users).

However, both IBM WebSphere 7.0 and Oracle WebLogic 11*g* support 64-bit JDKs and 64-bit operating systems. (Check the Oracle JD Edwards Minimum Technical Requirements document for exact supported configurations.) This makes a system administrator salivate over the possibilities of memory allocation for JVMs. In reality, you will probably never increase the maximum memory for a single JVM to more than 2GB (and even this value won't be available on some platforms). As your system grows, you can achieve greater gains by spreading your load across your hardware effectively. To accomplish this, you can try clustering your JVMs as part of a vertical cluster and/or horizontal cluster.

Set Minimum and Maximum Memory to be Equal

Another possible tuning step to consider is setting the minimum and maximum memory to be the same (for example, `-Xms=1g -Xmx=1g`). For those of you who are familiar with the concepts of Java, this might seem a little odd. Wouldn't you want the memory to expand dynamically? Setting these memory parameters to the same values is an attempt to prevent a performance draw on the system from increasing the memory due to a large number of users signing on to the system at the same time. The JVM will start up already using the maximum amount of memory, so it will never need to increase the size. The downside is that making these parameters equal may increase the JVM startup time.

Setting the Maximum PermGen Parameter

The PermGen (permanent generation) size tuning parameter (`-XX:PermSize=`) is often modified for performance reasons. Java uses this area of memory to store information about classes that are loaded. This parameter often needs to be increased for the following reasons:

- An application uses a large number of classes that are not part of the standard Java library (this does apply to BSSV).

- A large number of users are accessing the system.

Determining whether your system needs to increase the PermGen parameter can take some doing. This most commonly happens if the BSSV application refuses to start through Server Manager. Then you need to review the logs for the pesky error `java.lang.OutOfMemoryError: PermGen space`. You can look for this error in a couple of places in the WebLogic Server logs:

- *<WL_HOME>*/user_projects/domain/*<domain_name>*/servers/AdminServer

- *<WL_HOME>*/user_projects/domain/*<domain_name>*/servers/*<server_name>*

Another set of logs to review are the BSSV instance logs. These can be checked through Server Manager by clicking the name of the BSSV instance and then clicking the logs. However, the PermGen space error is a very low-level logging message, so you might need to turn on debug logging to see the actual error.

Once you've decided that you need to increase your PermGen parameter, how do you determine the correct value? Well, three values are most commonly used:

- **128m** The most common value is 128 MB. This will give you enough PermGen space for most simple BSSVs that do not call many Java objects that go into the PermGen space (including most Oracle JD Edwards BSSVs to date).

- **256m** This works for many moderately complex BSSVs.

- **528m** This is the largest value that we've seen used (yes, 528, not 512). This is used for only the most complex BSSVs. However, there are drawbacks to using a value this high. The most obvious is that your maximum young generation memory should be set to something much higher than 528MB (such as 1.5GB). Also, it may take a little longer for your BSSVs to start.

Clustering

Clustering solutions with BSSV are supported with EnterpriseOne Tools Release 9.1. Although clustering is by no means a silver bullet, it can provide a number of tangible benefits to an implementation. When considering key items such as scalability, reliability, high availability, and of course performance, clustering and/or the ability to tune the JVM start parameters can provide many advantages to your system. These options can offer the ability to grow (scale) to meet your business requirements, redundancy to keep your system up in the event of a failure, and load distribution to allow users to utilize your system resources effectively.

This section of the chapter will discuss clustering BSSV for EnterpriseOne and denote some of the strengths and potential drawbacks to this type of solution.

NOTE
It is always a good industry practice to check the current MTR (Minimum Technical Requirements, Doc ID 747323.1) for the latest supported configurations.

Why Cluster?

Perhaps one of the most common questions asked is, "Why should I cluster?" There are numerous reasons for clustering, but we will address the three primary reasons:

- Scalability

- Reliability/high availability

- Performance

Each of these reasons can be addressed through vertical clustering, horizontal clustering, or a combination of each. Vertical clustering allows you spread your load across a server; horizontal clustering allows you to spread the load across multiple servers.

Clustering and Scalability   *Scalability* is essentially the ability to allow more users to access the application(s). Both types of clustering (vertical/horizontal) can provide scalability. Many additional users can be allowed to log onto a system by implementing clustering without necessarily having to modify the jde.ini JDBC file or any of the tuning parameters within Server Manager. This type of solution allows you to expand your implementation (due to new company acquisitions or growth due to business demand). Scalability allows you to stay ahead of this growth and manage your system effectively.

Clustering and Reliability/High Availability   *Reliability* is the ability to keep using the system if something goes wrong. Most often, a Java runtime instance or JVM crashes. In a vertical clustering solution, this involves starting multiple Java processes on the same machine. A setup such as this can provide a measure of reliability if a single Java instance fails, but it also offers a single point of failure since all processes are on one machine. If the entire physical machine goes down, the solution is no longer functional.

A horizontal clustering solution places Java instances on more than one physical machine as part of the cluster. This provides a more robust option for reliability: if one physical machine goes down, the remaining machines can still receive requests. Note that requests made at the time of the failure may need to be resent.

As you can see, leveraging a clustering solution (vertical, horizontal, or a combination of the two) can provide a highly available system to your user community and defuses the risks of outages due to single component failures.

Clustering and Performance   *Performance* is the ability to increase response times or make the software run faster (generally a good thing to the user community at large). Clustering along with load balancing can be used to increase response time.

Vertical clustering tends to work best for performance, since all Java processes are on the same machine so the messages do not have to travel a long physical distance. However, as mentioned, reliability considerations are associated with a vertical cluster.

Horizontal clustering is a valid performance solution, but it can be impacted if the machines in the cluster are separated by vast distances. This may be mitigated by implementing a weighted round-robin load balancing system. (This is not an issue if the machines are near each other or in the same data center.)

Both types of clustering can be tougher to troubleshoot, because you'll need to track down on which JVM the issue occurred. This often requires that you sift through all the log files for each JVM.

Horizontal clustering, in general, offers robust options for scalability and reliability, with some performance tradeoffs. Following are some of the strengths of implementing horizontal clustering with BSSV:

- Better scenario for failover and reliability

- More options for scalability

- Resource requirements spread across several machines

- Reduces chances of resource constraints

Following are some of the weaknesses of implementing horizontal clustering with BSSV:

- Reduced performance

- Additional machines to administer

- Increased cost due to possible additional hardware purchases

- Increased complexity

- Can be more difficult to track down or troubleshoot support/product issues

Load Balancing

Load balancing allows you to determine how Java resources are utilized across your technical architecture. This is generally accomplished by using algorithms that determine how best to split your load over your server resources. The most common algorithms are round-robin and weighted round-robin types. Random is an option with some other load balancers, but it is rarely used because it makes little sense in a production environment. Oracle JD Edwards supports the round-robin method of load balancing that ships with IBM WebSphere and Oracle WebLogic Server.

Round-Robin and BSSV

Round-robin is the most basic form of load balancing and is usually the easiest to implement. A list of servers is kept by WebSphere or WebLogic, and the load is distributed to each server in the order in which they appear. This method of load balancing can work for most architectures, especially if all machines have similar specifications and if they're in the same physical location. However, if horizontal clustering is implemented, round-robin can create a performance hit.

Law of the West: Weighted Round-Robin and BSSV

Before going into weighted round-robin, we need to offer a generic disclaimer. If you call the Oracle JD Edwards response line, you will probably not get any guidance on weighted round-robin. Nevertheless, using weighted round-robin could benefit your implementation.

Weighted round-robin is often implemented to improve the performance of a horizontal cluster. If you have a series of machines that are physically closer to the clients that are going to connect to them, you can set up weighted round-robin so that the clients connect to those servers more often. Also, if one or more of your servers are more powerful than others, you can increase the workload for the more powerful servers through weighted round-robin.

To set up weighted round-robin, you must assign each server a numeric value called a "weight." The maximum value of the weight depends on the load balancer being used, but in general, the higher the value, the more often the load will be distributed to the server. There is no hard-and-fast rule, but often the percentage change difference can be used as a guide. For example, if server 1 has a weight of 10 and server 2 has a weight of 20, then clients will connect to server 2 roughly twice as often as server 1. Weights should be assigned based both on how close the servers are to the clients that are connecting to them and the server specifications.

Forbidden Knowledge: Random Load Balancing and BSSV

Some load balancers allow a random form of load distribution. The server receiving the load is determined randomly. This is a very bad idea for production environments, especially with horizontal clusters, because there is no way to determine which server will receive the load.

Transaction Server (Real-Time Events)

You might have heard of a Transaction Server referred to by its old moniker, "real-time events." Transaction Server allows the processing of certain events in real time. The processing of these events is performed by code that is deployed to your application server (either WebLogic or WebSphere). Clustering of Transaction Server solutions was supported as of EnterpriseOne Tools Release 9.1.

Clustering Transaction Server

The solution for clustering Transaction Server is radically different from that of BSSV. Although some of the same terms and ideas apply, they are implemented in very different ways. In addition, some technologies apply to Transaction Server that are often misapplied to BSSV. This section will discuss those technologies and provide suggestions as to how to set the best tuning parameters for different scenarios.

You may decide to implement clustering as part of your architecture, to distribute load and add an extra layer of reliability. As an added bonus, the clustered Transaction Server solution delivered with Tools Release 9.1 provides an automated method that makes it easier to implement than other clustered typologies with EnterpriseOne.

Clustering offers several benefits:

- Scalability

- Reliability/high availability

- Ease of deployment

- Performance

Scalability   You can distribute the load across multiple JVMs on the same machine or across multiple machines.

Reliability/High Availability   Oracle JD Edwards delivers a clustered Transaction Server solution with Tools Release 9.1 that offers a unique "double reliability" feature. Not only does it incorporate the failover features that are shipped with WebLogic Server and WebSphere Application Server, but it includes its own failover feature that records failed events in a database.

Ease of Deployment   Transaction Server is one of the easier solutions to deploy to a clustered environment. Just create a cluster of two or more nodes and use Server Manager to deploy to the cluster.

For vertical clustering, very little manual effort is required after this step, because file stores are used to store persistent data. Server Manager will already create the file stores for you so you don't have to do any additional configuration.

Horizontal clustering requires additional configuration steps, because Oracle recommends using database data stores to store persistent data. The actual database is left to your discretion as long as it's supported—refer to the Oracle EnterpriseOne Minimum Technical Requirements document on support.oracle.com for more information. Because Server Manager allows you to choose your database, you must manually configure it to hold persistent data.

Performance   Performance is often not a primary consideration. You can take some steps (detailed later in the chapter) that can help reduce the performance hit that is sometimes associated with clustering.

Web and Transaction Server Technologies

The Transaction Server solution for EnterpriseOne Tools Release 9.1 incorporates several technologies: Web Client, BSSV Server, Transaction Server, and mobility applications. The differences among these are not always well understood. We'll cover some of the differences among these solutions and describe the web and Transaction Server technologies.

Web Technologies

The main impact on your system from a web interface perspective deals with how much logic is run on the JAS and how much the JVM needs to be tweaked to enhance system performance.

Web Client (HTML Web Client) Solution   The Web Client solution is what most people think of as the EnterpriseOne solutions for the Web. When you access owhtml or E1Menu.maf and see the EnterpriseOne menu, this is the Web Client deliverable. The Web Client is written largely in HTML. Much of the logic for the Web Client is still performed by processes that run on the enterprise server, so a good place to perform some tuning is on the back-end of the solution, with tuning of database servers and enterprise servers being critical.

BSSV Server Solution   BSSVs written for EnterpriseOne are compiled using the EnterpriseOne package build utility and deployed using the package deployment utility. BSSVs are written in Java, and because they are deployed to the appropriate JAS, most of their logic is executed within the JVM. Because of this, tuning the web server is more important for business services.

With Tools 9.1, clustering of BSSVs is supported so that it can be utilized for load balancing and failover options.

Transaction Server Solution The Transaction Server solution is written largely in Java with most of the logic residing in the web server. The clustering of the web server is supported with Tools 9.1 and is more important since the majority of the logic is run within the web server. The Transaction Server is a very specific solution that allows a real-time event to be generated and processed by EnterpriseOne. It is often used in manufacturing plants where high volumes of product are run across a conveyor belt and scanned into an inventory system.

Transaction Server Technologies

In addition to the "web offerings" provided by EnterpriseOne, several technologies are specifically associated with the Transaction Server offering. These allow for remote control of processes and for the handling and queuing of events in memory.

Java Management Extensions (JMX) Java Management Extensions (JMX) is a set of libraries used to remotely control and monitor services. It's actually not quite that simple, because a lot of under-the-covers programming goes into implementing this. You only need to know that when Server Manager connects to a managed instance, it is using JMX technologies. They allow you to start and stop your managed servers and monitor their performance.

It turns out that using JMX technologies has a low impact on your system, so you don't have to spend a lot of time tinkering with the JVM options. However, since it is a Java-based technology, certain configuration requirements apply—mainly, making sure the JDK release shipped with your web server is the same as the one Server Manager is using. If not, you may need to perform manual steps to switch the JDK that Server Manager is using.

The acronym for Java Management Extensions begins with "JM" but ends with an "X," so it shouldn't be confused with the technology described next.

Java Message Service (JMS) Java Message Service (JMS) is a Java API that involves creating, reading, sending, and receiving messages. Messages are stored in the following memory structures:

- **Queues** Structures used to pass messages from a single provider to a single consumer. Used most often in point-to-point (PTP) messaging.

- **Topics** Structures used to pass messages from a provider to multiple subscribers. Often referred to as the "publish/subscribe method" of messaging.

EnterpriseOne supports both methods of messaging, and whichever one you use will depend on which application you're using. Transaction Server clustering supports both, so you'll have access to failover and load balancing no matter what.

Important Transaction Server Tables   The Transaction Server solution uses a number of relational tables to store information. However, some are more important than others. The major tables are listed here:

- **F90710 – Event Transfer Table**   Although it's not first in numeric order, the F90710 table is described first because of its importance. The F90710 contains a list of all the events that pass through the Transaction Server solution. Each status has a specific meaning. Here are the major event statuses:

  - 3: The event is ready for processing.

  - 4: The event is being processed.

  - 5: The event is processed. The event is immediately marked for deletion from the table.

  - 6: The event failed to process.

NOTE
If you have an extremely quick system (capable of processing the events in real time), you will not often see the events go to status 4 or 5. They will simply appear in the F90710 table and then disappear. Server Manager will allow you to view the number of events processed. You can use several cool tricks regarding database scripts, the WebLogic Admin Server, and SIBexplorer utility that we will describe later in the chapter.

- **F90706 – Event Subscriber Table**   This table lists each subscriber that is listening for an event.

- **F90707 – Event Subscription Table**   This table lists each event that a subscriber is listening for.

- **F90712 – Event Transfer Failure Table**   If an event reaches a status of 6, it is transferred to this table. The Transaction Server solution will then periodically try to submit the event for processing again.

NOTE
With Transaction Server clustering, the number of events that go to a status of 6 should be reduced if failover is enabled. If one node fails, the messaging will flip to an operational node.

Monitoring Events Using the Database One way to monitor events is through database queries. In this way, you can see the events that are passing through the Transaction Server. A simple query to capture all events that are being processed when using an Oracle database would look something like this:

```
Select * from SY910.F90710;
```

Monitoring Events Using Administrative Tools

Many tools outside of databases can be used to monitor events. You can use the administrative console for either WebLogic Server or WebSphere. The Service Integration Bus Performance Tool is another option for WebSphere users. You can even use the Universal Table Browser (UTB) or databrowse utilities.

Administrative Console Event Monitoring

You can use the administrative console for both WebLogic Server and WebSphere to monitor real-time events. The events processed are not stored in a file, so they must be viewed in real time; this solution will work best when used on a system with a large number of events passing through it. To view the events, you must first start the Transaction Server. You cannot stop the Transaction Server and view the events.

NOTE
Although both the WebLogic Server and WebSphere administrative consoles can be used to monitor events, WebLogic Server will be used as an example throughout this book.

The monitor for events can be accessed through the Oracle WebLogic Server Administrative Console: *<domain>* | Services | Messaging | JMS Modules | *<Module Name>* | *<SubQueue Name>*. Each node of the cluster will have its own module name that includes the name of the clustered server. Within the module name, you will see a list of subqueues. EnterpriseOne requires that each user has a unique subqueue. Click the subqueue for a user and you'll see a list of events, as shown in Figure 10-1.

JMS messages are stored as in the persistent data store created when the Transaction Server is first deployed. Flat files are written as a .dat file, so it's difficult to view them. By default, they are written to the *<WL_HOME>*\user_projects\ domains*<domain_name>*\FileStore-*<node>* directory. See Figure 10-2.

JDBC data stores are a database that can be queried like any other. Use this persistent storage type if you want to be able to query which node processed which events. Since a JDBC data store is the easiest way to monitor event load and maintain persistent events, this section will go more deeply into how to set up a JDBC data source.

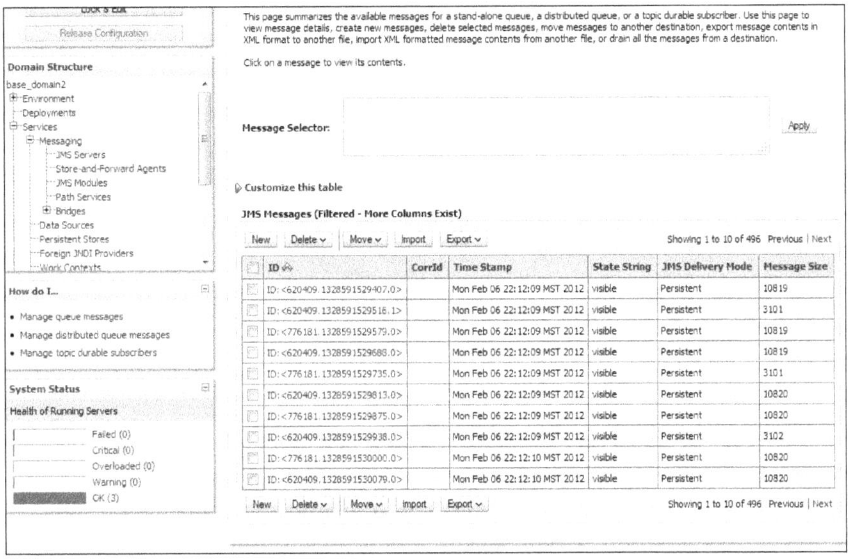

FIGURE 10-1. *List of events*

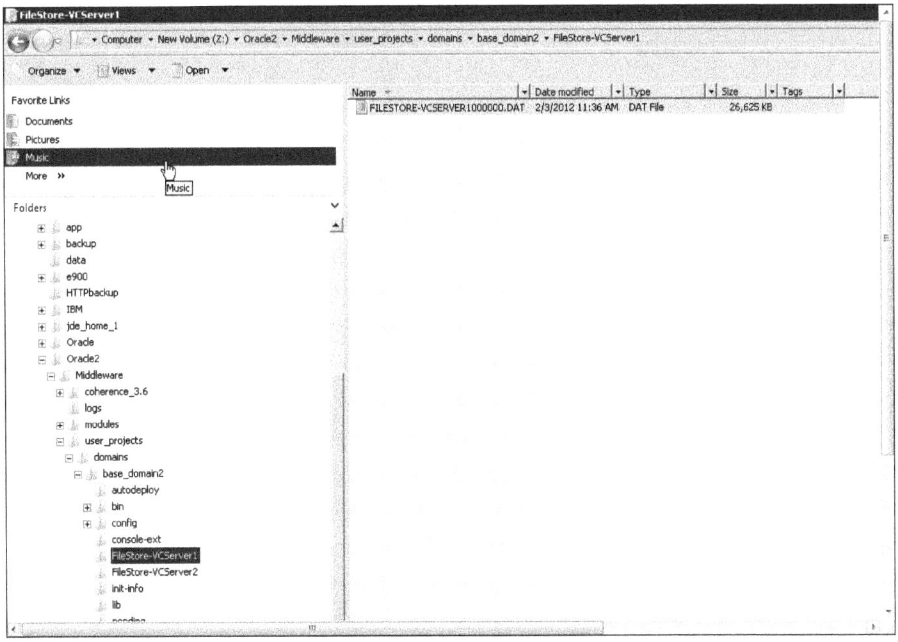

FIGURE 10-2. *Persistent data file location*

Configuring the Persistent Data Store   A persistent JDBC data source exists in a relational database. For an Oracle database, this means that the persistent tables must exist in unique schemas and tablespaces. In Oracle WebLogic Server, the data source must also be set up not to handle global transactions.

The location in which to install the persistent database files is always a concern. This book uses the example of installing the database files in the same location as the Oracle JD Edwards EnterpriseOne data. This is for ease of backup and because the data tables are probably already on a machine sized for databases.

1. In the Administration Console, set the persistent data tablespace to Automatically Extend Datafile When Full (AUTOEXTEND), as shown in Figure 10-3.

2. Set up the persistent data tablespace for Read Write options and set as permanent data storage, as shown in Figure 10-4.

3. Next, create a user to access the tablespace, as shown in Figure 10-5. Each JDBC persistent data source must have a unique tablespace and a unique user to access that tablespace.

4. You must set the authorities of the persistent data user correctly. When JMS migration is first initiated, the services create the database tables. Once load

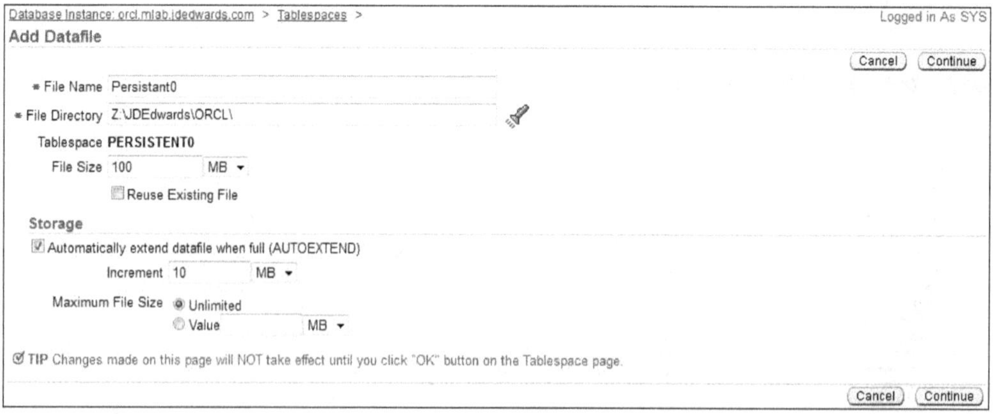

FIGURE 10-3.   *Persistent data tablespace Oracle attributes*

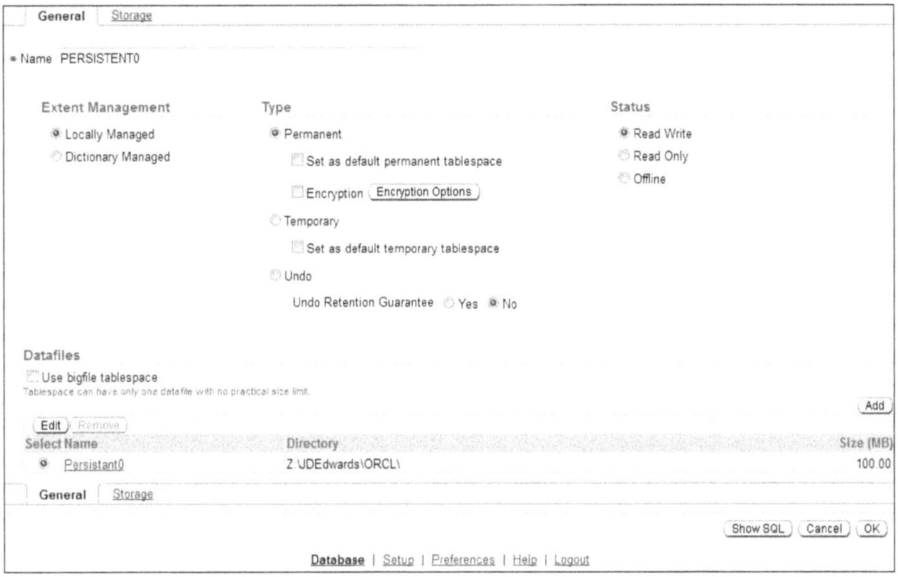

FIGURE 10-4. *Persistent data tablespace additional parameters*

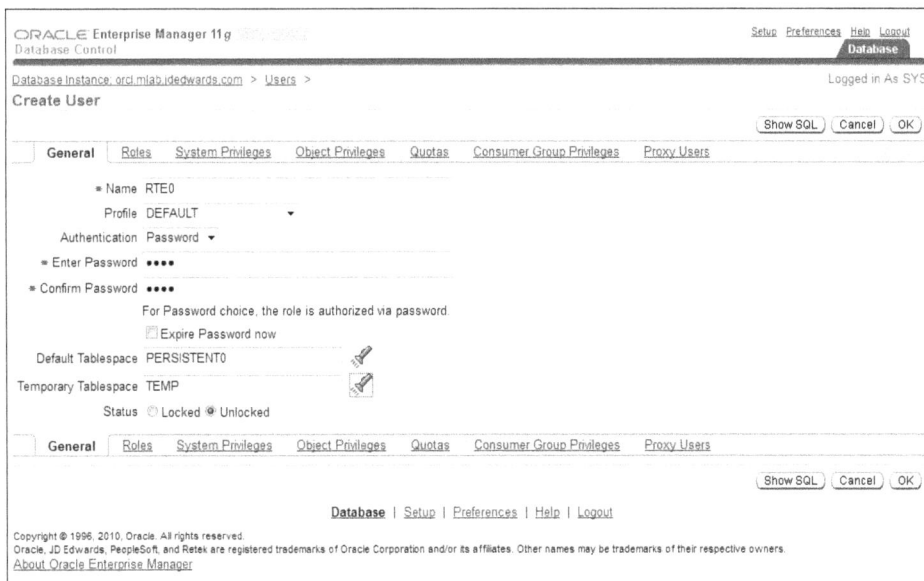

FIGURE 10-5. *Example persistent data user*

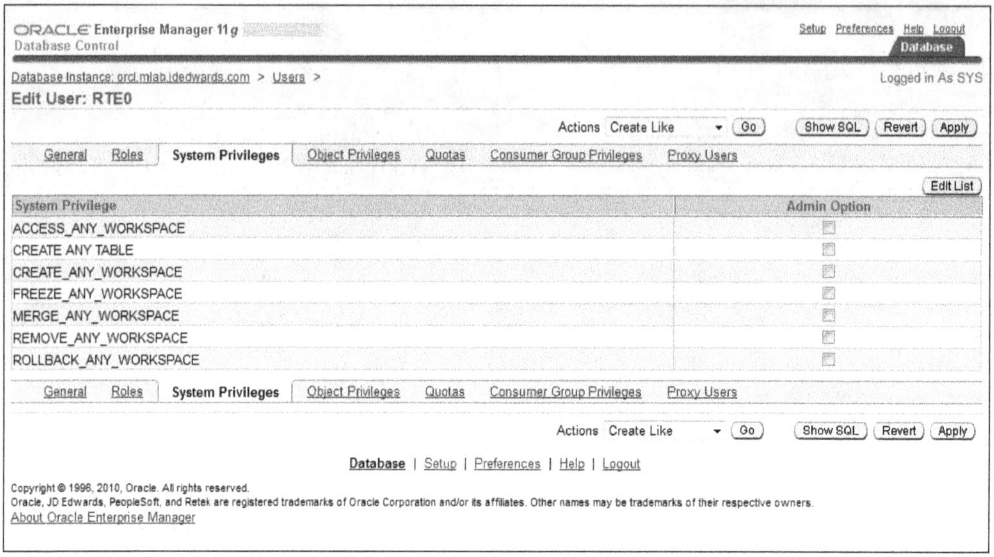

FIGURE 10-6. *Persistent data user authority*

balancing or failover occurs, the tables are populated with data. Figure 10-6 shows the minimum authorities needed by the users to access the data tables.

5. In addition, make sure the quotas for this tablespace are set to Unlimited, as shown in Figure 10-7.

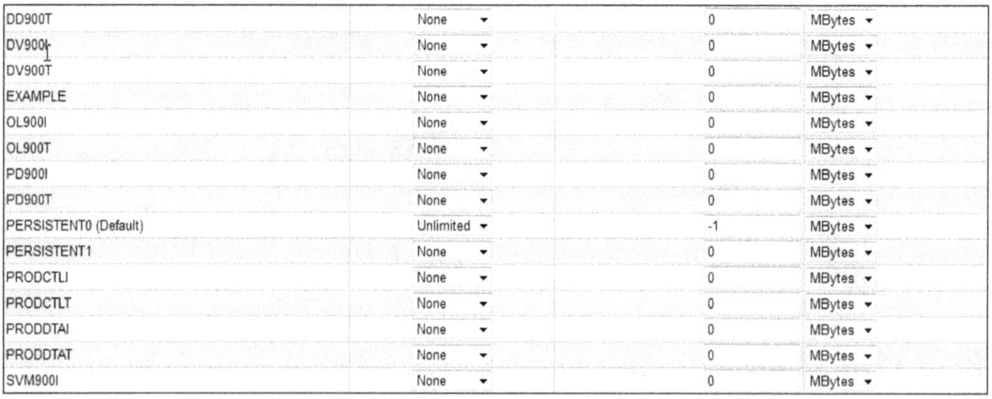

DD900T	None ▾	0	MBytes ▾
DV900I	None ▾	0	MBytes ▾
DV900T	None ▾	0	MBytes ▾
EXAMPLE	None ▾	0	MBytes ▾
OL900I	None ▾	0	MBytes ▾
OL900T	None ▾	0	MBytes ▾
PD900I	None ▾	0	MBytes ▾
PD900T	None ▾	0	MBytes ▾
PERSISTENT0 (Default)	Unlimited ▾	-1	MBytes ▾
PERSISTENT1	None ▾	0	MBytes ▾
PRODCTLI	None ▾	0	MBytes ▾
PRODCTLT	None ▾	0	MBytes ▾
PRODDTAI	None ▾	0	MBytes ▾
PRODDTAT	None ▾	0	MBytes ▾
SVM900I	None ▾	0	MBytes ▾

FIGURE 10-7. *Setting quotas for tablespaces*

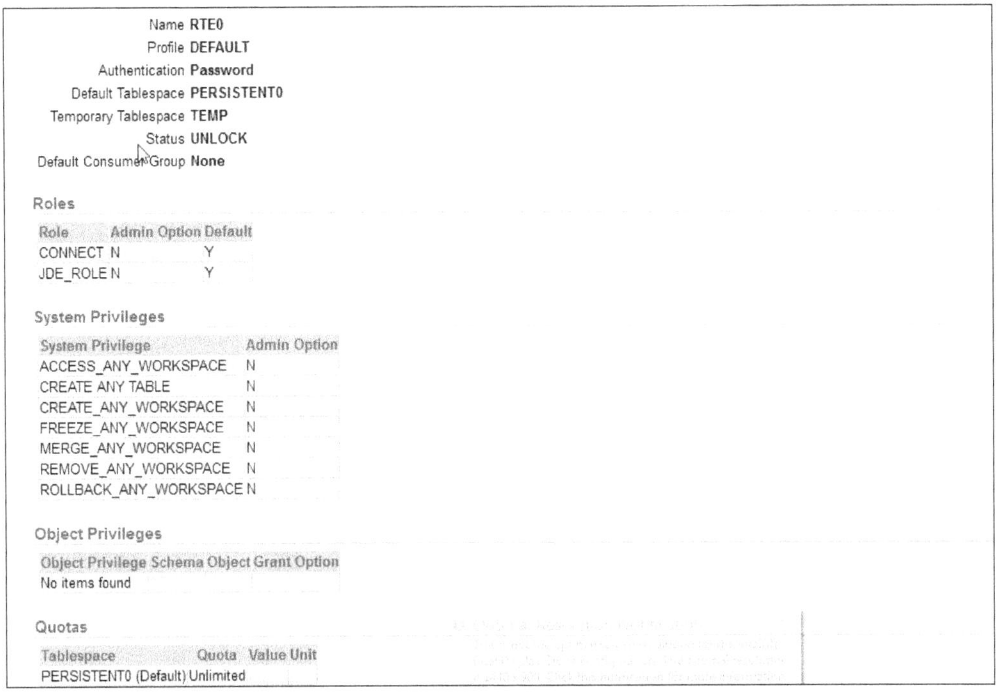

Name **RTE0**
Profile **DEFAULT**
Authentication **Password**
Default Tablespace **PERSISTENT0**
Temporary Tablespace **TEMP**
Status **UNLOCK**
Default Consumer Group **None**

Roles

Role	Admin Option	Default
CONNECT	N	Y
JDE_ROLE	N	Y

System Privileges

System Privilege	Admin Option
ACCESS_ANY_WORKSPACE	N
CREATE ANY TABLE	N
CREATE_ANY_WORKSPACE	N
FREEZE_ANY_WORKSPACE	N
MERGE_ANY_WORKSPACE	N
REMOVE_ANY_WORKSPACE	N
ROLLBACK_ANY_WORKSPACE	N

Object Privileges

Object Privilege	Schema	Object	Grant Option
No items found			

Quotas

Tablespace	Quota	Value	Unit
PERSISTENT0 (Default)	Unlimited		

FIGURE 10-8.   *User attributes*

The user attributes should look similar to those shown in Figure 10-8.

6. After you create the persistent database tablespaces and users, you need to create the data source in WebLogic Server or WebSphere. In WebLogic Server, the data source is first created and given a JNDI name, as shown in Figure 10-9.

7. If you're using the Oracle Database, select the thin driver as shown in Figure 10-10. No matter which database, from which vendor you are using, Oracle WebLogic Server will not recognize the data source if it supports global transactions.

8. On the next screen, shown in Figure 10-11, make sure that the Supports Global Transactions setting is not checked. This data source will not be visible as an option for a migratable data source if this option is active.

9. Fill in the database parameters (Figure 10-12) so that the data source can connect to the tables. The database user should be the schema that accesses

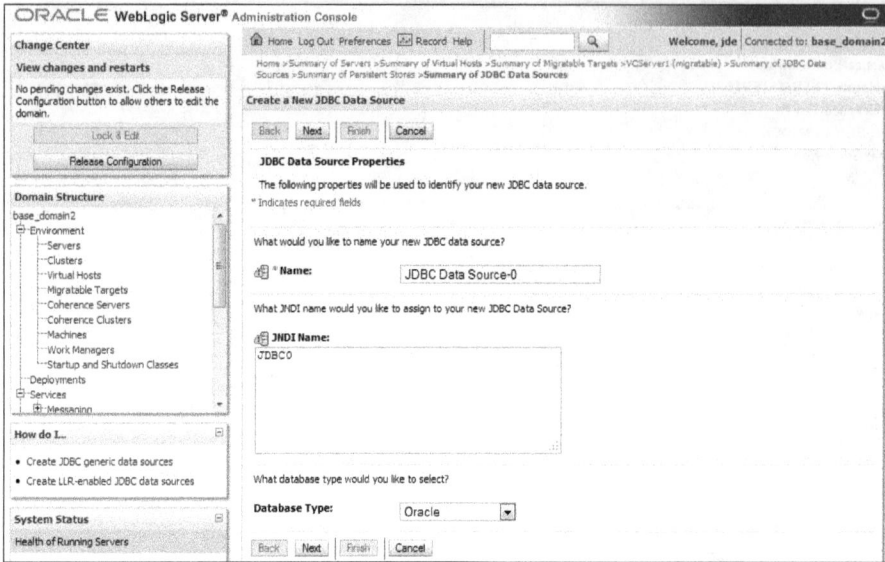

FIGURE 10-9. *Creating the JDBC data source*

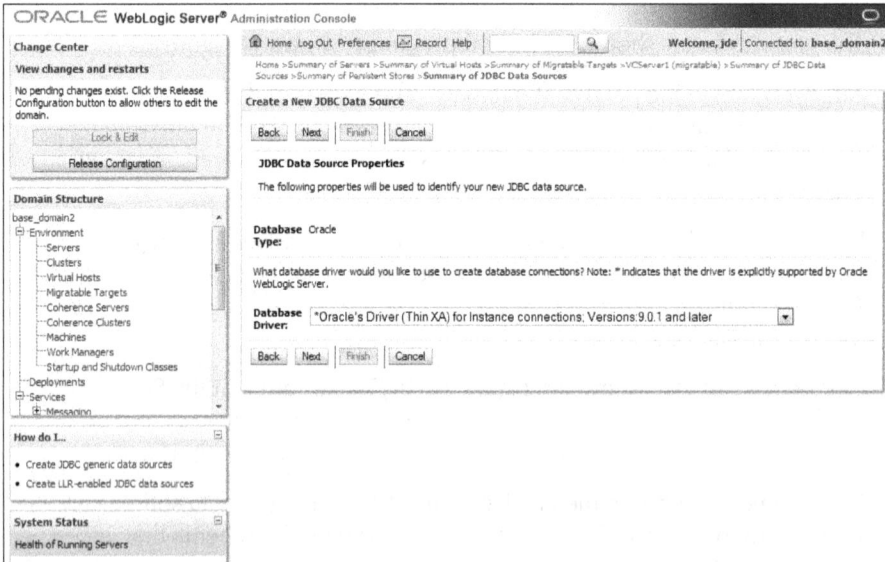

FIGURE 10-10. *Oracle database driver*

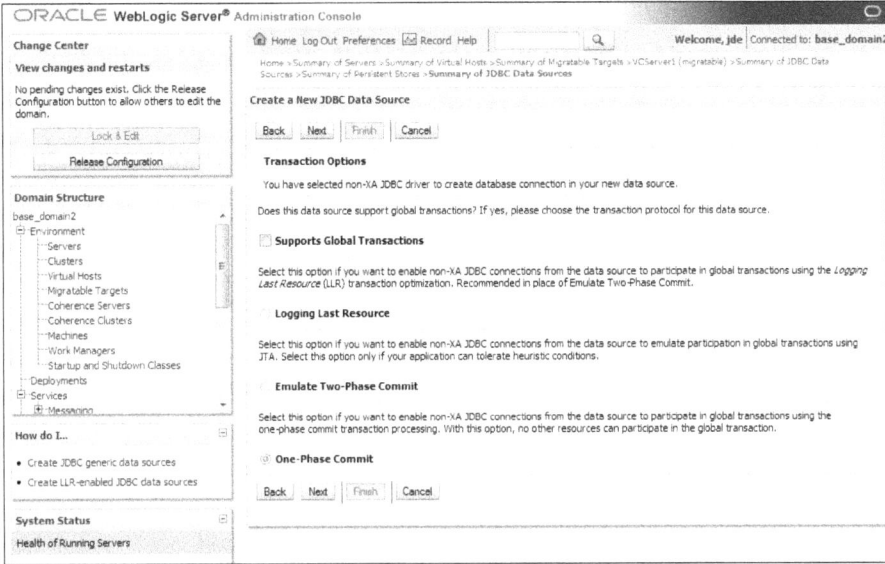

FIGURE 10-11.   *Global transactions settings*

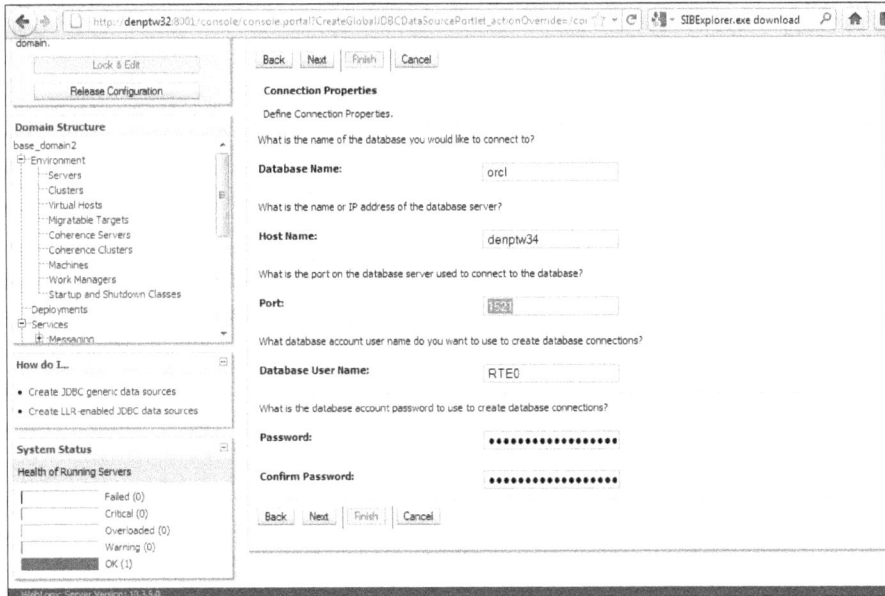

FIGURE 10-12.   *JDBC data source connection parameters*

the persistent tablespace. If your authorities are not set correctly for this user, you will receive an error when trying to test the connection.

10. Test your connection. The driver class name will automatically be filled in (Figure 10-13) based on the database driver you selected. The database URL field is populated based on the test connection parameters you filled in. You don't need to have the database set up and the connection pass in order to click on the Finish button, but it's a good idea.

11. Deploy the JDBC data source to the nodes in your cluster (Figure 10-14). There is no visible draw on a system by deploying a data source onto a node, so there is nothing wrong with deploying the data source to all nodes of the cluster, even if a specific node will not be accessing the data source.

12. Once the JDBC data source is created, a new JDBC store must be created. This is done by selecting the Services | Persistent Store option. Then click the Add button. In the next screen (Figure 10-15), give the data store a name (anything will do). When selecting the target, make sure you select the (migratable) version so that the persistent data will be copied to the next available node should the target node become incapacitated.

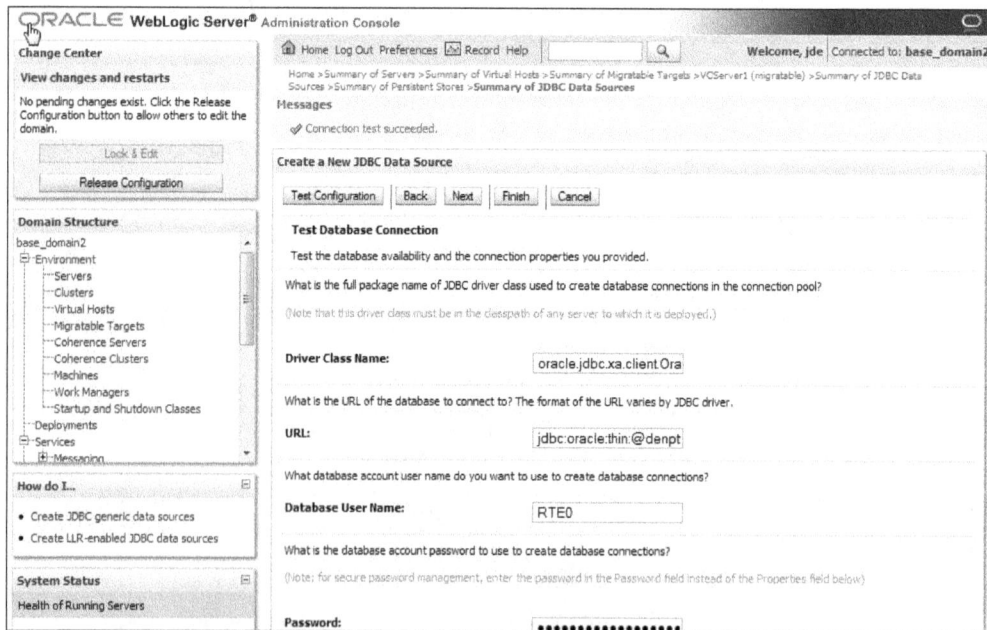

FIGURE 10-13. *Test the database connection*

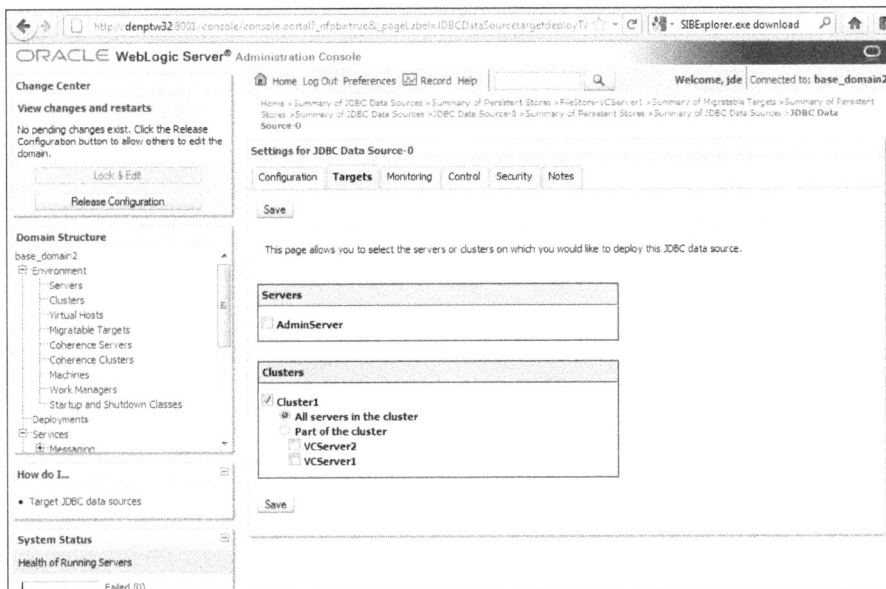

FIGURE 10-14.   *Deploy to cluster*

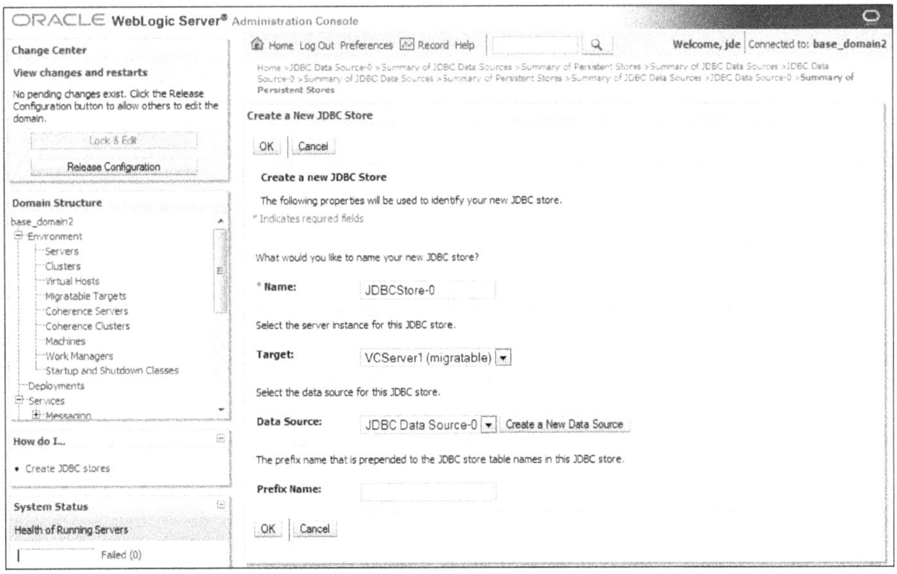

FIGURE 10-15.   *JDBC store parameters*

The next step is to change the JMS module to use the JDBC data source. Server Manager deploys the JMS modules with a file data source, so you will need to change them to database data sources.

Setting JDBC Stores for Migratable Targets   To set the JDBC stores for migratable targets, follow these steps:

1. On the console, select Environment | Migratable Targets.

2. On the next screen, click the JMSServer - *<node_name>* value, as shown in Figure 10-16.

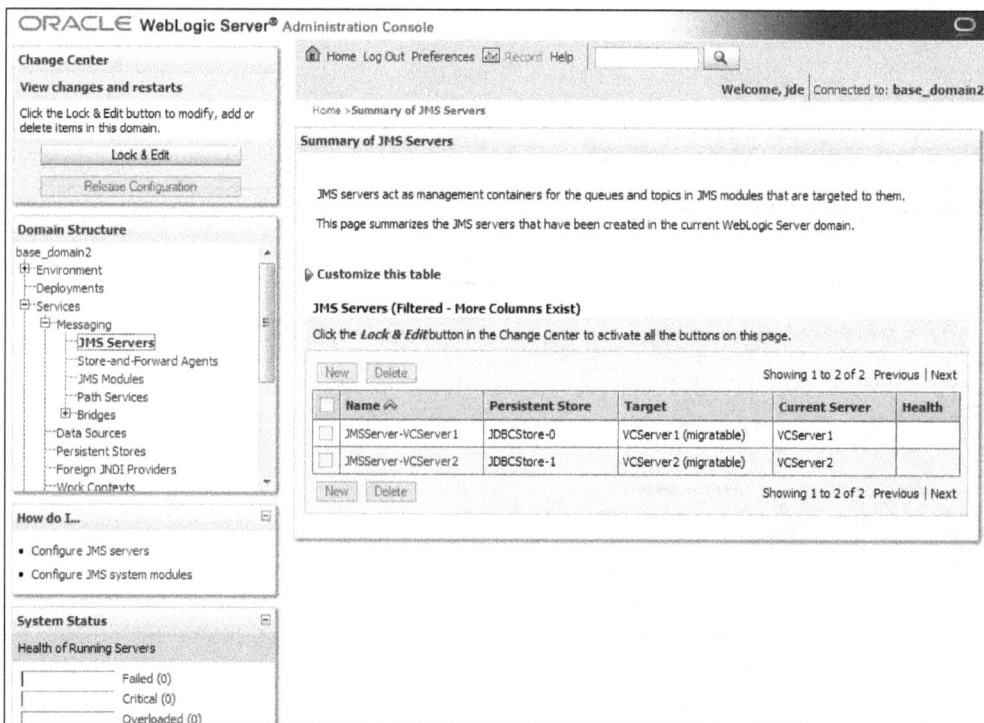

FIGURE 10-16.   *Selecting JMS servers*

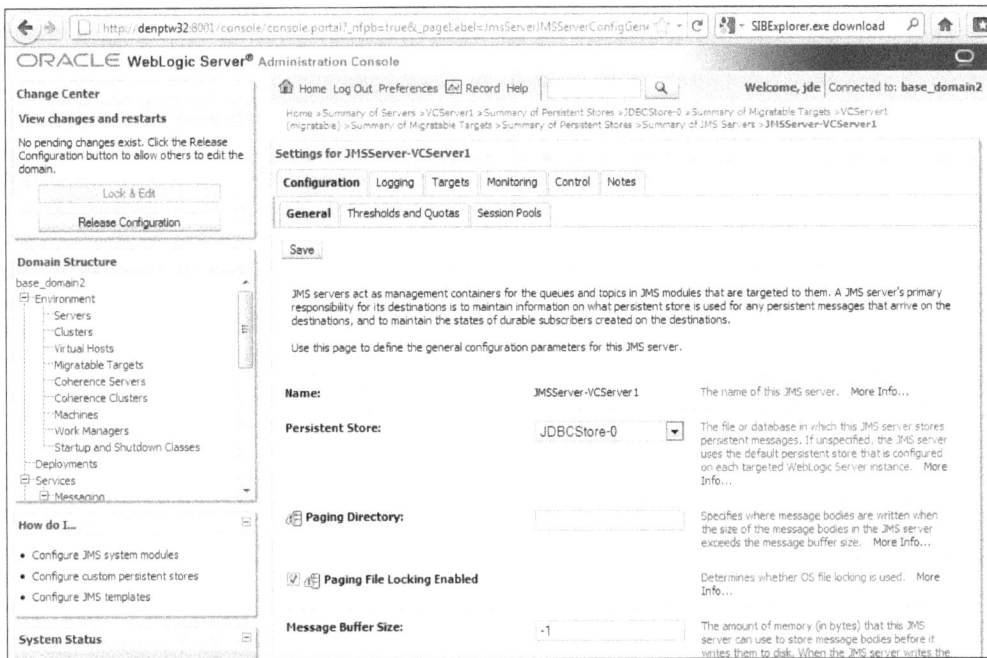

FIGURE 10-17. *Setting the persistent store*

3. Click the General tab.

4. For the Persistent Store field, select the JDBC store you created from the drop-down list, as shown in Figure 10-17.

Viewing the Data in Persistent Stores

After you've created the data store and associated it with the migratable target, the table for persistent data storage still does not exist. The services must be migrated at least once before the tables will be generated. To do this, you must either migrate the services manually or set the migration policy for one time only and manually kill processes for the nodes yourself.

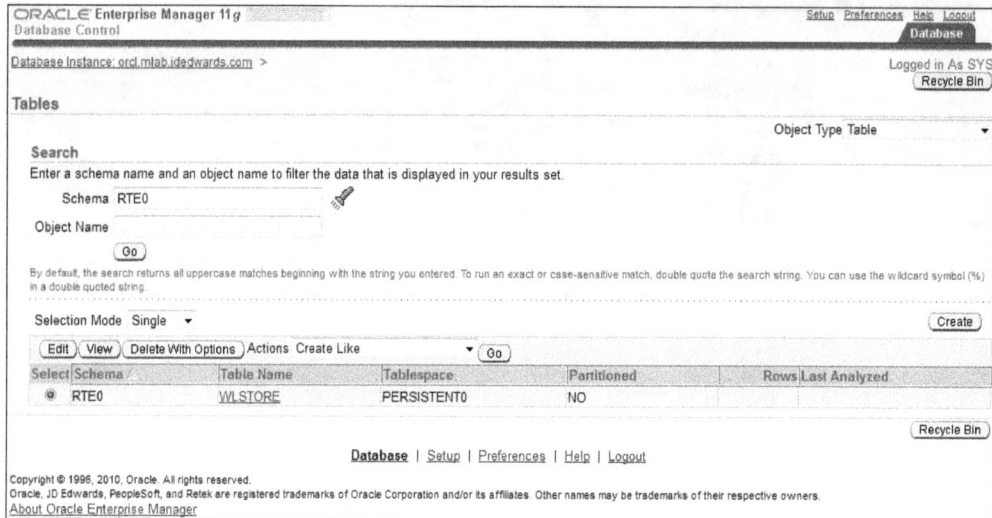

FIGURE 10-18. *Persistent table*

After the services are migrated, the table WLSTORE is created in the tablespace for the persistent data that you created, as shown in Figure 10-18.

If the RTE is still processing events, you can view them in the database table through a simple SQL query, as shown in Figure 10-19.

Viewing Events via the SIB Performance Tool   Events in WebSphere used to be viewed through the Service Integration Bus (SIB) Performance tool. With IBM WebSphere 8.0 this tool has superseded the old SIBexplorer tool. Evaluation versions of the new SIB Performance tool can be downloaded from the IBM alphaWorks web site.

The SIB Performance tool can be used for many things, but what we're most interested in is its ability to track events through the various subqueues. When the EnterpriseOne Transaction Server solution is deployed, it automatically creates 15 subqueues to which messages can be deployed. Each user expecting to receive a message must be subscribed to their own subqueue. At a minimum, one user must be subscribed to one subqueue and no users can share the same subqueue. For example, in this section the user JDE will be subscribed to SubQueue00.

The SIB Performance tool requires that the Transaction Server (RTE) solution be running in order for it to track events. The tool works best if it's run from the same machine as the RTE server, but keep in mind that SIB is an in-memory tool. To connect with the server, you need to provide the host name and the SOAP

```
View Data for Table: RTE0.WLSTORE
                                                          Refine Query    OK

Query  SELECT "ID", "TYPE", "HANDLE", "RECORD" FROM "RTE0"."WLSTORE"



Result
              ID TYPE HANDLE RECORD
        134217727   -3      0 00
        268435454   -3      0 00
        402653181   -3      0 00
        536870908   -3      0 00
        671088635   -3      0 00
        805306362   -3      0 00
        939524089   -3      0 00
       1073741816   -3      0 00
       1207959543   -3      0 00
       1342177270   -3      0 00
       1476394997   -3      0 00
       1610612724   -3      0 00
       1744830451   -3      0 00
       1879048178   -3      0 00
       2013265905   -3      0 00
       2147483632   -3      0 00
                1    0      1 ACED00057372003A7765626C6F6769632E73746F72652E696E7465726E616C2E50657273697374656E7453746F7265496D706C24436
                2    0      2 ACED00057372003A7765626C6F6769632E73746F72652E696E7465726E616C2E50657273697374656E7453746F7265496D706C24436
                3    0      3 ACED00057372003A7765626C6F6769632E73746F72652E696E7465726E616C2E50657273697374656E7453746F7265496D706C24436
                4    0      4 ACED00057372003A7765626C6F6769632E73746F72652E696E7465726E616C2E50657273697374656E7453746F7265496D706C24436
                5    0      5 ACED00057372003A7765626C6F6769632E73746F72652E696E7465726E616C2E50657273697374656E7453746F7265496D706C24436
                6    2      1 0008000000000000000001
```

FIGURE 10-19. *Database query for persistent table contents*

(Simple Object Access Protocol) port. To find the SOAP port in the IBM WebSphere Administration Console, select Servers | Server Types | WebSphere Application Servers | <Server_Name>. Then expand the Ports section. The SOAP port is the value listed for SOAP_CONNECTOR_ADDRESS, as shown in Figure 10-20.

After the SIB Performance tool is connected, you will be able to see the events pass through the queues in real time. In the example shown in Figure 10-21, user JDE is assigned to receive events in SubQueue00.

Real-Time Events Settings

The settings unique to the Transaction Server solution reside within the Real Time Events section of the Server Manager console. The Trigger Listener Kernel section is rarely changed and will not be covered in this chapter. However, you can realize some performance gains by modifying the Event Processor Configuration settings:

■ **Trigger Listener Delay** This value, in milliseconds, determines how often events are queried in the database. This value can be decreased if large

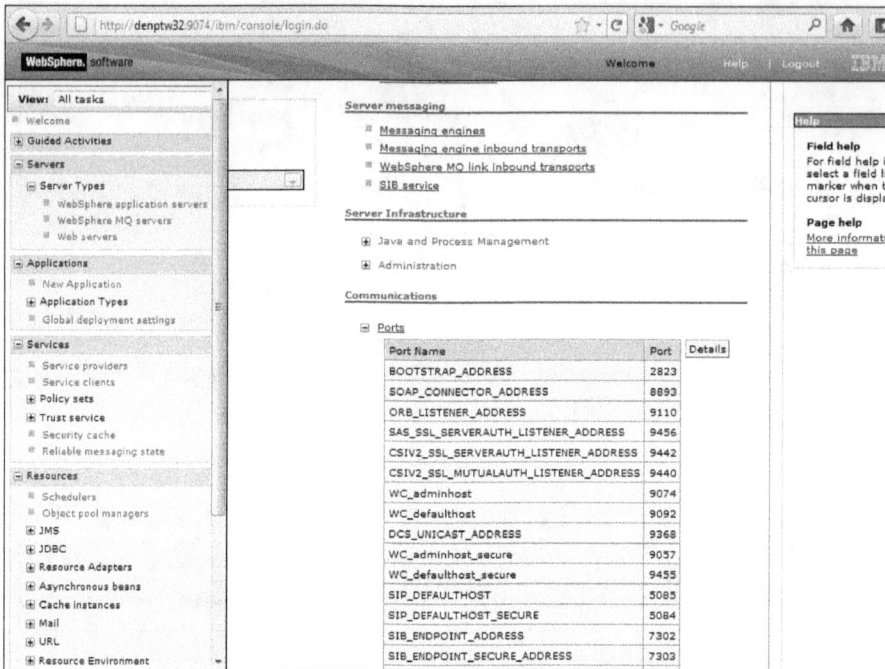

FIGURE 10-20. *SOAP connector port*

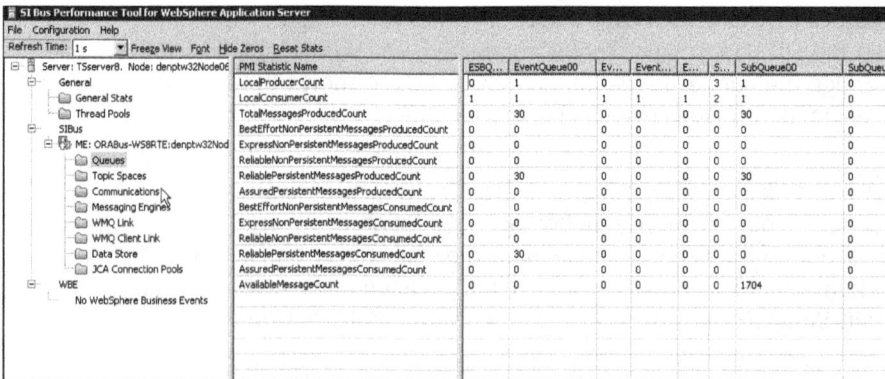

FIGURE 10-21. *Real-time events through the SIB Performance tool*

numbers of records are in the database but not being transferred into memory. This value can be increased if large numbers of events are going to a failed status, and memory issues are prevalent on the nodes in the cluster. The Max Transfer Session Size parameter is often modified before this one.

- **Max Transfer Session Size** This value, in milliseconds, determines how many records are queried at any given moment. It is often increased if a large number of records are in the database, but there are still enough resources to process events in memory. It is decreased if memory issues persist within each node.

- **Event Client Session Timeout** This parameter, in milliseconds, determines how long the client remains open to receive events. It is often increased if errors indicating Timer Closed are present throughout the log.

Mobility Applications

Oracle JD Edwards EnterpriseOne released mobile applications with Tools Releases 9.1 and 8.98.4.6. These applications will allow you to perform a variety of tasks from your supported mobile device. Plus, you can access the E1 Menu directly from your mobile device to perform any function that is not available as a mobile application. These apps can be accessed over an Internet connection from just about anywhere in the world. Just activate your mobile data or Wi-Fi connection and go.

New Technologies for Mobile

The mobile application solution introduces new technologies that have never before existed in an Oracle JD Edwards EnterpriseOne architecture. This section will offer descriptions of those terminologies and address their limitations of them. We'll also discuss how to implement these successfully within your architecture.

Application Developer Framework Mobile (ADF)

Oracle Application Developer Framework (ADF) is the Java-based set of extensions and libraries that are used to develop the display layer of Oracle JD Edwards EnterpriseOne mobile applications. The ADF layer is created through JDeveloper and contains a set of classes and methods that can help you create forms for applications. The BSSV Server offers the web services that are responsible for the logic and data access of the applications.

Mobile Devices

Forget the old term "pervasive device." That is so mid-2000's! The new term is "mobile device." But not all types or brands of mobile devices are supported by EnterpriseOne. As of this writing, one of the most common questions is, "Why is the iPad supported but not the iPhone?" Here is a list of the main reasons why these distinctions are made.

- **Screen size** This is the answer to the "Why isn't the iPhone supported?" question. For enterprise-wide applications, the more screen size the better, and tablets offer the most screen size of mobile devices. Although you'll probably see at least one person in your lifetime running the E1 Menu from a smart phone, the mobile applications themselves are meant for a device with more real estate. Trying to use these apps on a phone may result in buttons or columns misaligning or not appearing at all.

- **WebKit libraries** The Oracle JD Edwards EnterpriseOne Mobile Applications require some libraries that are delivered as part of the WebKit open source project. WebKit is the foundation upon which the mobile Safari and Google browsers are built. So most Apple and Google Android devices should be able (in theory) to run mobile applications. However, devices that allow only Internet Explorer are out of luck. As of this writing, Internet Explorer does not incorporate WebKit libraries, so any device that will run only the Internet Explorer browser will not be able to run EnterpriseOne mobile applications (but may be able to run the E1 Menu).

- **Testing** The final factor that determines whether a device is supported is whether Oracle JD Edwards EnterpriseOne has invested resources to test the solution. A device will not appear on the MTRs unless it has been tested through a formal process. Although some devices could possibly run the mobile client applications, they have not been tested, so they are not supported.

Data Download Rate

The hot topic issue with all mobile devices is the *data download rate*—the speed at which your wireless carrier guarantees information will be downloaded to your device. As of this writing, the two options are 3G and 4G. In addition, most mobile devices also support Wi-Fi. There is no minimum download rate for Oracle JD Edwards Mobile Applications, so they will work using either download rate.

Working hand-in-hand with the download rate is the data plan. Again, there is no minimum data plan required for the Mobile Application solution, but if you're using these applications often during the workday, you may want to invest in an unlimited data plan or use the Wi-Fi option.

Mobile Architecture

A "typical" architecture for supporting mobile applications contains the following servers:

- ADF Server
- Database Server
- Enterprise Server
- BSSV Server

ADF Server

The ADF server is a required part of the architecture. This should be a standalone server with WebLogic installed. This server contains the presentation layer for mobile presentations. The machine should be large with plenty of memory and high CPU speed.

Recommended tuning options: The `-Xms` and `-Xmx` parameters should be set to be the same and as high as possible for the JDK you are using (1.5–2.0GB for most 64-bit JDKs).

Database Server

This server contains the Oracle JD Edwards EnterpriseOne data installed by the platform pack. It conforms to the specifications listed in the "JD Edwards EnterpriseOne Tools 9.1.x Minimum Technical Requirements for Microsoft Database" document.

Recommended tuning options: Refer to other chapters in this book for guidance on tuning your JD Edwards EnterpriseOne database and database server.

Enterprise Server

The Enterprise Server processes the logic necessary to execute the EnterpriseOne software. It conforms to the specifications in the document titled "JD Edwards EnterpriseOne Tools 9.1.x Minimum Technical Requirements for Enterprise Servers."

Recommended tuning options: Refer to other chapters in this book for more information on how to tune the enterprise server.

BSSV Server

The BSSV Server contains the web services that perform the logic associated with the ADF mobile applications. It conforms to the specifications in "JD Edwards EnterpriseOne Tools 9.1.x Minimum Technical Requirements for Business Services Server with Oracle WebLogic" or "JD Edwards EnterpriseOne Tools 9.1.x Minimum Technical Requirements for Business Services Server with IBM WebSphere Application Server" depending on the application server used.

Recommended tuning options: Refer to the "Clustering" section earlier in this chapter as well as to previous chapters in this book for more information on how to tune the BSSV Server.

Security Considerations

Mobile devices are notoriously insecure. Introducing one onto your network can add quite a few new security questions into your environment. This section will try to address the security concerns.

Secure Sign-On

To help reduce the possibility of your data being hacked, and to provide the single sign-on (SSO) capability, Oracle JD Edwards provides a new authentication module as part of the Mobile Foundation deliverable. This can be downloaded from edelivery.oracle.com.

However, the E1 Menu is not delivered with the new module. To increase the security of data transfer between the EnterpriseOne HTML Server and the mobile device, you may want to implement Secure Socket Layer (SSL) connections. Also, most mobile devices allow you to require a passcode to be entered before the screen can be unlocked. For the iPad, this can be accessed under Settings | General | Passcode Lock.

Application-Level Security

As of this writing, the only way to secure users out of a mobile application is to completely secure them out of BSSV. However, this applies to *all* BSSVs. Also, application-level and row-level security is not recognized by mobile apps. Applying vocabulary overrides can cause unwanted results. If you want to secure people out of a mobile app, the best solution may be not to give them the URL to the application.

Memory Usage

As part of the iSeries operation system SDK, Apple provides many tools for monitoring the memory used by applications running on the mobile device. However, because the applications are written in Java/ADF as opposed to objective C, the majority of resources are used in the ADF server and BSSV Server. If applications are hanging or crashing when viewed on the iOS device, double-tap the home button and close any other applications (other than Safari) that are running. You can further test whether resource contention is local or remote by trying to run the mobile apps on a PC running a Safari browser.

ADF Tuning Tips

These tuning tips should be applied to the ADF server (some suggestions may also contain a notation to apply to the BSSV instance). Much of this information has been pulled from the 2011 Microsoft PowerPoint presentation "ADF–Real World Performance Tuning" created by Duncan Mills. Additional guidelines can be found in the *Fusion Middleware Performance and Tuning Guide*, "Section 8–Oracle ADF Performance Tuning."

- Turn on the ADF logger.

- Set the appropriate JVM options:

    - Run in server mode: `-server`

    - Enable HugePages: `-XlargePages:exitOnFailure=true`

    - Enable generational parallel garbage collection: `-Xgc:genpar` (apply this to the BSSV instance as well)

    - Set the heap size to as high as possible for the ADF managed server: `-Xms -Xmx` (apply this to the BSSV instance as well)

        Sample JVM argument line:

```
-server -XlargePages:exitOnFailure=true -Xgc:genpar -Xms 1.5G  -Xmx 1.5G
```

- Log into the WebLogic Console and set the logging level to SEVERE.

- Set the JVM option for the Administration Console to start with less memory (such as 512m).

CHAPTER
11

Virtualization

This chapter concentrates on full virtualization and paravirtualization. Full virtualization completely separates the operating system from the hardware layer, while paravirtualization is more hardware-dependent. Both solutions allow you to provide a standardized platform on which to deploy your architecture. Not all vendors support full virtualization, so refer to your provider for more information on which form of virtualization is supported.

Using virtualization, you can deploy a fully configured workstation or server within just a few hours. If you have a large external drive, you can even build a server image on your laptop—a configuration that can be used for demoing and proof of concept (but never production).

Administration of virtualized machines can often be much easier than administering nonvirtualized counterparts. Many virtualization offerings come with a suite of remote administration tools that allow you to monitor workload, revive failed servers, and deploy new images. These and other tasks that used to require a lot of manual labor can now be accomplished in just a few minutes or hours and with a few button clicks.

This chapter will cover the following topics:

- Benefits of virtualization

- Oracle VM

- JD Edwards VM templates

- Oracle VM VirtualBox

- VMware

- JD Edwards tuning for virtualization

Benefits of Virtualization

You can realize many benefits through the use of a virtualized solution. These vary from simple tasks, such as deploying a new server onto your network, to such mission-critical and complex tasks as disaster recovery.

Server Deployment   Suppose you want to deploy new servers to your network with frequency? If your servers do not have the same specifications, trying to install uniform software across the architecture can be difficult. With a virtualization solution, you can create a single image for servers independent of hardware differences. This can reduce your time for introducing a new server from days to hours. The server can be rolled into place, hooked up into the network, and the image deployed to the machine remotely.

Recovery Strategy   What if your office is destroyed by a fire or a flood? A virtualization solution can aid you in recovering from such a scenario. Once the new hardware comes in, you can deploy your old images onto the servers.

Hardware Independence   A virtualization solution lets you put the same image on servers or workstations despite hardware differences. This frees you from vendor lock and allows you to search for the best offer from multiple vendors. Also, you don't have to buy the servers at exactly the same time; you can buy them as your budget permits.

Integration   Many virtualization solutions integrate well with software from other vendors. Oracle VM integrates well with other Oracle products. VMware integrates with Microsoft and IBM products.

Oracle VM

Oracle VM is a virtualized solution that allows you to create a virtualized image securely and quickly. The following components make up Oracle VM:

- **Oracle VM Server**   The platform for creating the virtualized image

- **Oracle VM Manager**   The console for administering the virtualized environment

- **Oracle VM Agent**   The middleware that communicates between Oracle VM Server and Oracle VM Manager

Oracle VM is geared toward data centers and servers. It does not require a host operating system. Instead, it installs directly on the hardware. (Refer to the Oracle Certify system for information on supported configurations.)

Oracle VM Tools

Oracle VM provides a toolset you can use for monitoring your system. You can also change certain components of your configuration on the fly.

Oracle VM Manager

Using Oracle VM Manager, you can monitor your system resources and change how they are allocated. The default URL for the Oracle VM Manager is as follows: http://server.network.com:port/OVS

Once you log onto the Oracle VM Manager, you'll need to set up an initial Oracle server pool master, a utility server, and a virtual machine server. All three of these values can be mapped to the same physical machine. The first screen, shown in Figure 11-1, will ask you for the server pool name and the connection properties for the Oracle VM host.

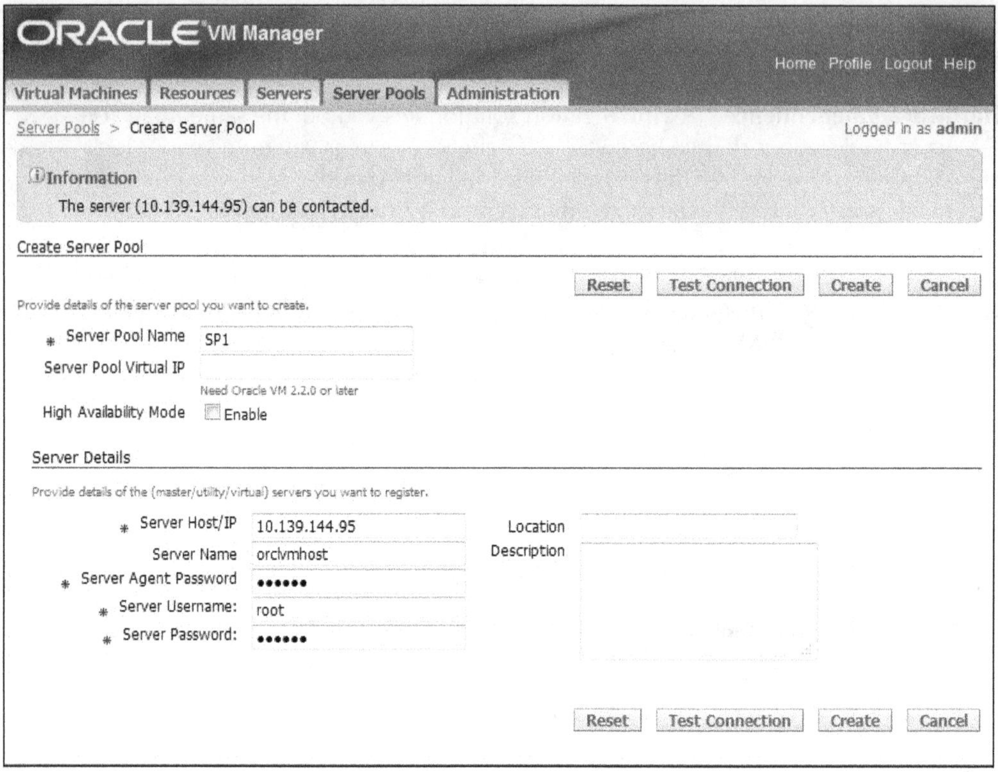

FIGURE 11-1. *Oracle VM Manager server pool setup*

The next screens will prompt you to define a utility server and a virtual machine server. For our example, one physical machine will be used for all three functions.

Eventually, you will see a screen showing the machines you've defined, as shown in Figure 11-2.

Next, you'll need to either create or import your VM templates. You can order VM templates specifically related to Oracle JD Edwards EnterpriseOne software; we will use these as examples. The Oracle JD Edwards EnterpriseOne VM solution uses three predefined servers:

- **orclvmdb**   The image for the shipped Oracle Database server

- **orclvmhtml**   The image for the shipped Oracle JD Edwards HTML Web Server

- **orclvment**   The image for the shipped Oracle JD Edwards Enterprise Server

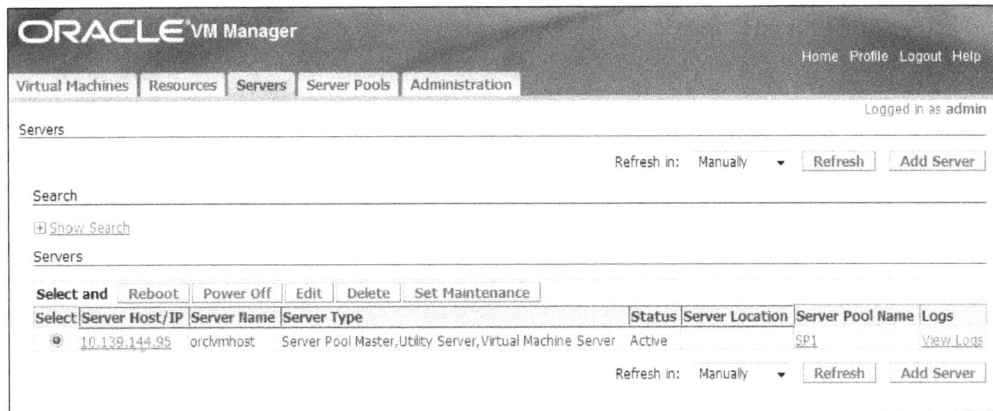

FIGURE 11-2. *Oracle VM servers*

NOTE
The Oracle JD Edwards deployment server is not included as an Oracle VM template. You must still install the deployment server the old-fashioned way on either a nonvirtualized box or an Oracle VM VirtualBox image.

Complete the following steps for the HTML Web Server and Enterprise Server template images. To import your Oracle template images, follow these steps:

1. Log into the Oracle VM Manager.

2. Select Resources | Virtual Machine Images.

3. On the source screen, click the option Select From Server Pool (Discover And Register), as shown in Figure 11-3. Then click Next.

4. On the General Information screen, fill in the details for the image you want to import. Then click Next. (Throughout this chapter, we will use the database server image in examples. Remember that the same steps need to be performed for both the HTML Web Server and Enterprise Server images.) General information for your server pool is displayed in Figure 11-4.

5. In the Import screen (Figure 11-5), review the information. Click Confirm to advance to the next step. You can elect to go back to the previous step or cancel the entire process by clicking the appropriate buttons.

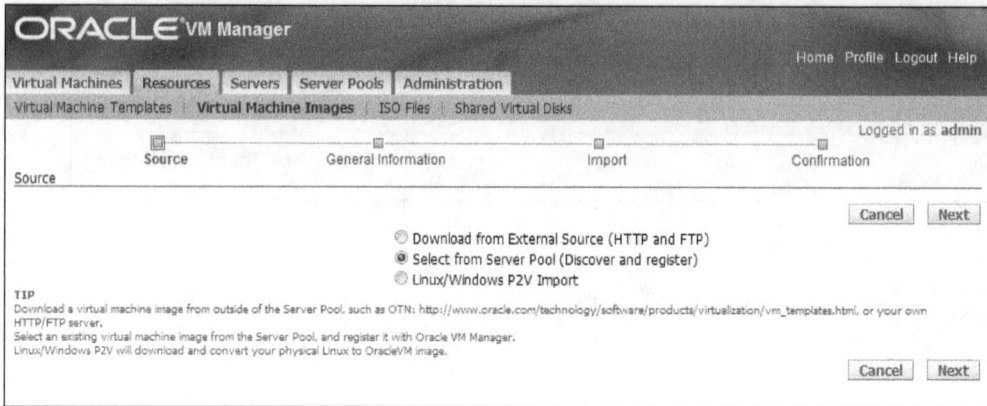

FIGURE 11-3. *Import virtual machine*

6. On the next screen, click the Import button, as shown in Figure 11-6. The status of the image will change to "Importing." This may take several minutes.

7. When the status of the image changes to "Pending," the process will never advance to the next stage until you select the radio button next to the image

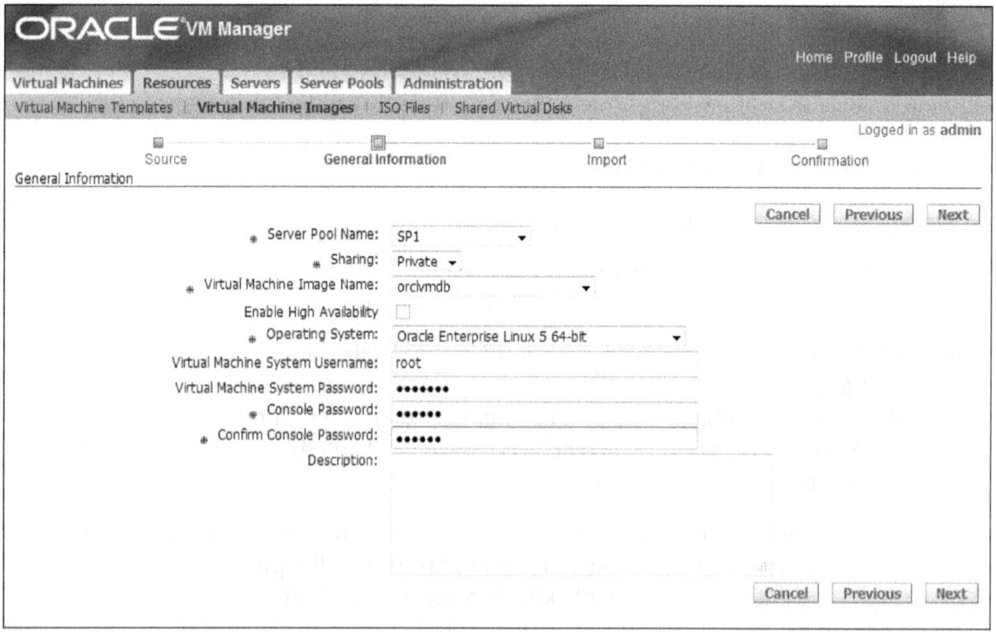

FIGURE 11-4. *General Information screen*

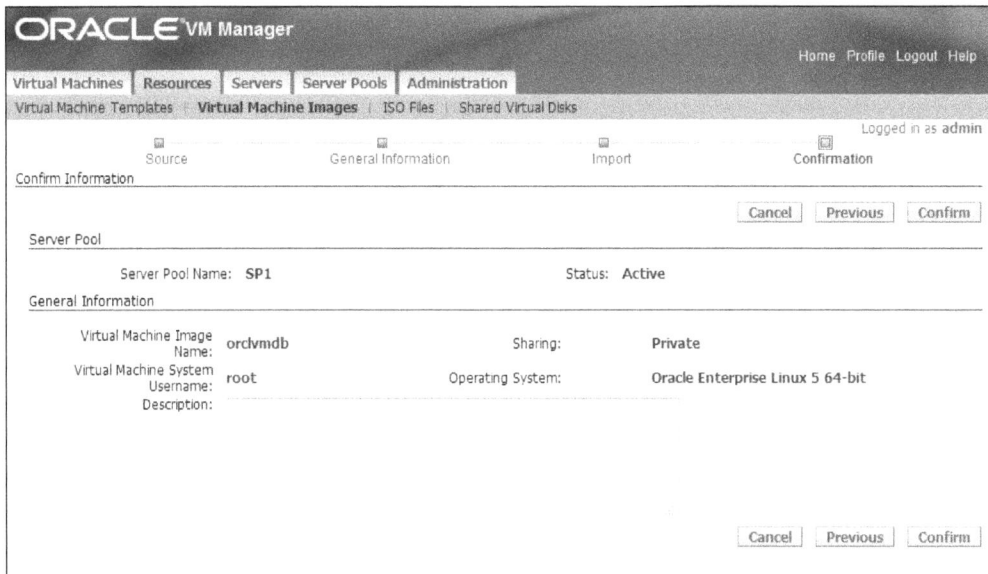

FIGURE 11-5. *Confirmation screen*

and click the Approve button. Do so to continue the image installation. As shown in Figure 11-7, make sure the radio button is selected and click Approve.

8. Review the image information on the next page. Click Approve to finish the importing process. If you click Cancel, you will exit the entire process. Figure 11-8 shows the screen necessary to finish the importing process.

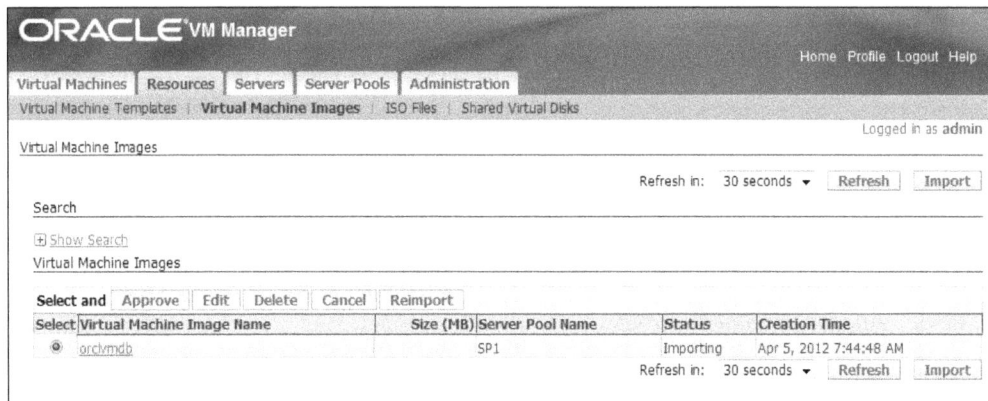

FIGURE 11-6. *Click Import to import the image.*

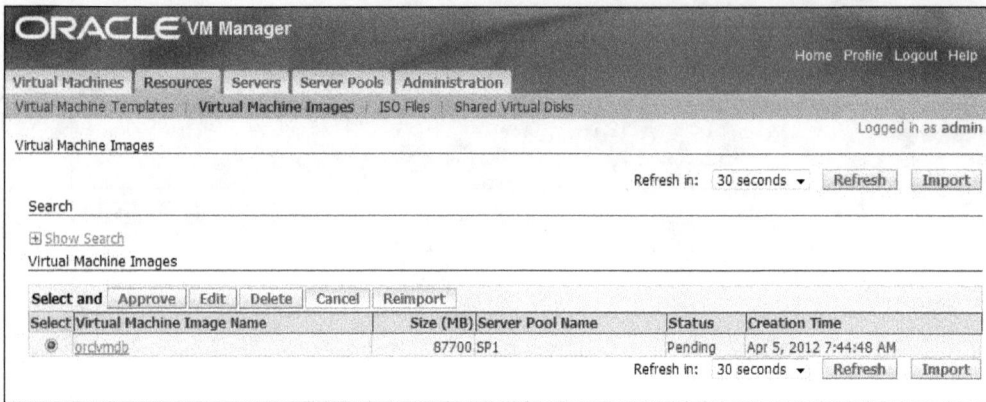

FIGURE 11-7. *Image import approval*

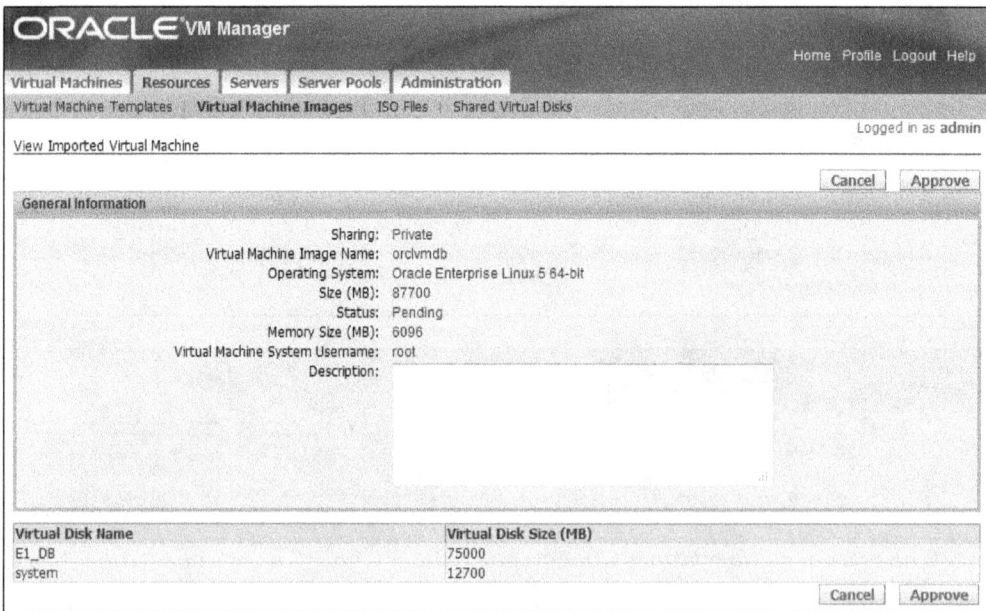

FIGURE 11-8. *Approval detail information*

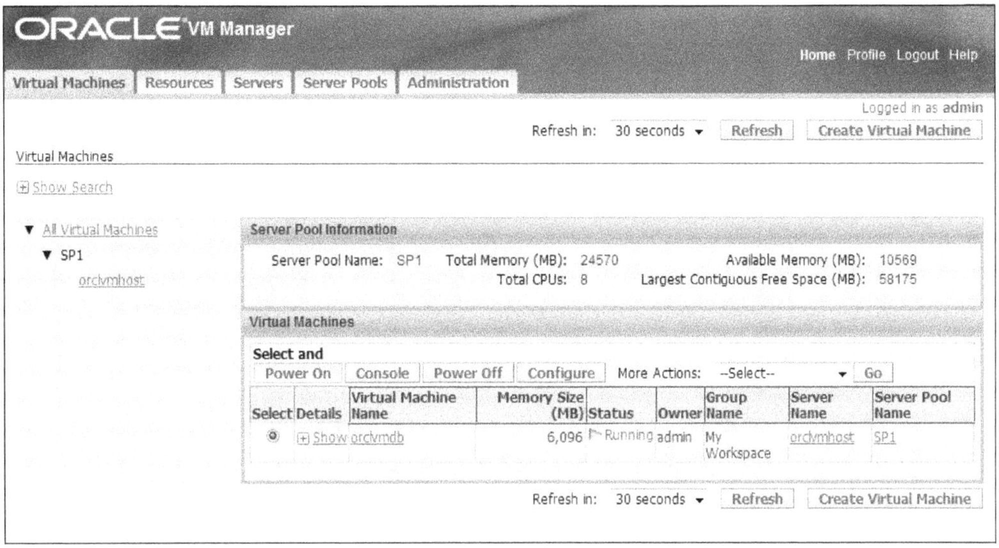

FIGURE 11-9. *Virtual Machines information*

9. Once the template import is completed, the Resource | Virtual Machine Images screen will refresh, showing no servers! Fear not, because the template has been imported; you just need to click on the Virtual Machines tab to see it (Figure 11-9).

After the three templates from the three servers have been imported, the full functionality of the Oracle VM Manager will be available.

Monitoring the Functions of Oracle VM Manager 2.2.0

As of this writing, the JD Edwards EnterpriseOne VM templates are meant to be used with Oracle VM Manager 2.2.0. This release of the Oracle VM Manager has a distinct look and feel. Other versions of Oracle VM Manager may appear differently.

Virtual Machines Information

On the Virtual Machines Information tab (Figure 11-10), you can view the status of each VM server. You can also see how much memory each server is using and what server pools they belong to, and you can remotely power on or power off the machines.

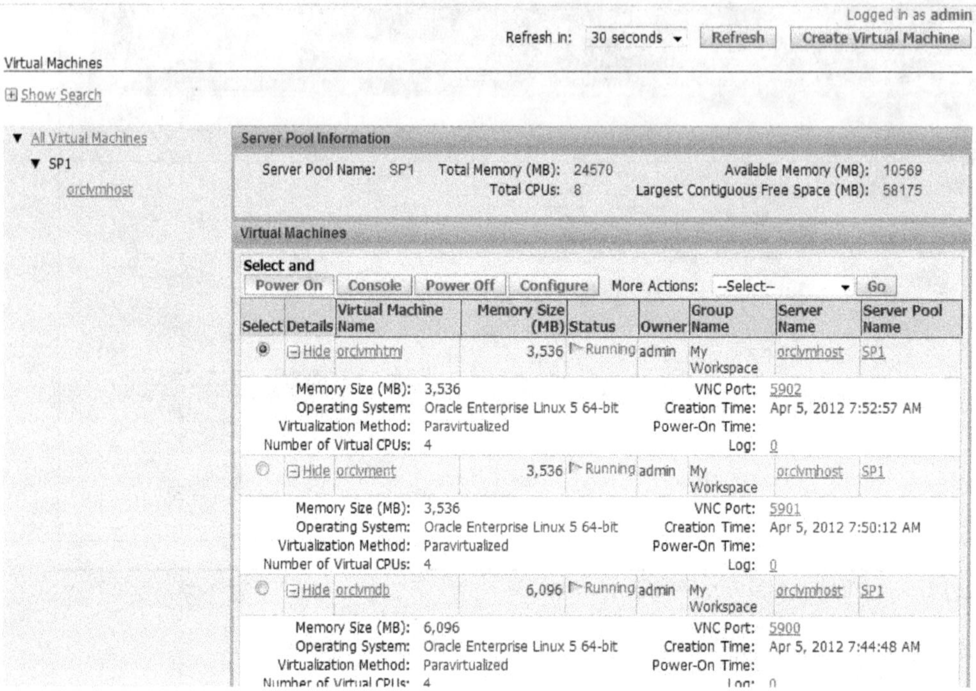

FIGURE 11-10.   *Virtual Machines Information tab*

NOTE
If the server name is not correct or appears as "unknown," wait a few minutes. It can take a while for this field to load with the correct information.

Servers

The Servers tab (shown earlier in Figure 11-2) shows the server pool master, utility server, and virtual machine server you defined. You can also view the logs of these machines.

Server Pools

The Server Pools tab offers another view of your server pool master, utility, and virtual machine servers. The Servers column refers to these machines, not the VM templates. You can also see the number of users logged in (click the Total: link for

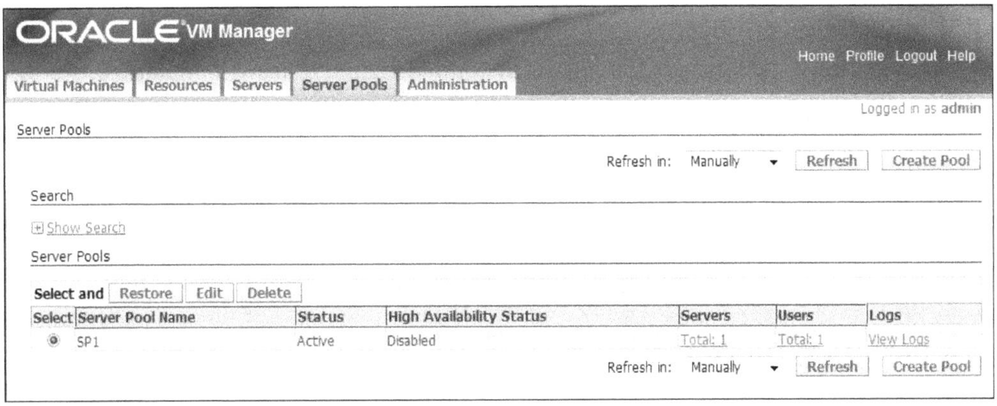

FIGURE 11-11. *Server Pools tab*

more information). The Logs column lets you view the logs of all three servers. Figure 11-11 shows the Server Pools tab.

Administration

On the Administration tab (Figure 11-12), you can add and modify users that are allowed to log into the Oracle VM Manager. This gives you a way to restrict users from using the VM console. It also displays a list of e-mail addresses that you can use to contact VM console users.

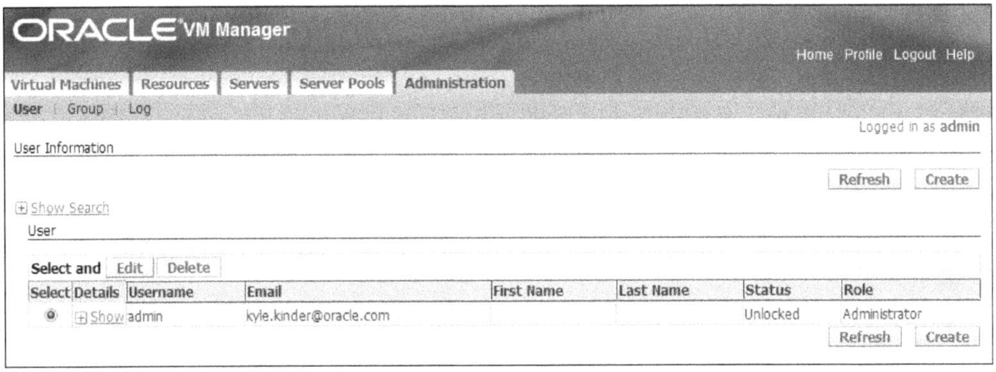

FIGURE 11-12. *Administration tab*

JD Edwards VM Templates with Oracle VM

As mentioned, Oracle JD Edwards ships with templates for Oracle VM that can be used to load Oracle JD Edwards EnterpriseOne onto a system quickly. Templates are provided for enterprise, database, and web servers. The deployment server, however, must be installed separately.

> **NOTE**
> *For more information on how to install the Oracle JD Edwards VM templates, refer to "JD Edwards EnterpriseOne Applications Release 9.0 Quick Installation Guide Using Oracle VM Templates for Oracle Database on Linux." For information on the components provided by the Oracle VM solution, refer to "JD Edwards EnterpriseOne Current MTR Index" (Document ID 747323.1) at mysupport .oracle.com.*

Tips for Using Oracle VM Templates

Following is a list of additional configuration tips for using Oracle VM templates:

Editions and Upgrades   The Oracle JD Edwards EnterpriseOne Database VM template is delivered with the Oracle Database Standard Edition. Install the Enterprise Edition for better performance or for production use. To upgrade, install a new Enterprise Edition of the Oracle database instance and then import the old data. Database users, schemas, and other artifacts must be duplicated in the new database.

Hot Disk Issues   The disk image for the database VM template is contained in a single .img file. Depending on how the disk is configured, this may cause *hot physical disks* (individual physical disk heads being overloaded while other physical disks sit idle). One way to address this issue is to create new .img files, attach them, and move hot tables into the new .img files. The location of the .img files can then be manipulated to avoid hot disks. The .img file for the database is sized as small as possible for single-user use. For production use, this .img file will quickly fill up. To mitigate this drawback, either the file should be enlarged or its tables should be moved onto new .img files before going into production.

Bottlenecks   Poor shared disk performance will greatly reduce Oracle VM performance. If the operating system is running out of space, system operations will be slowed down by any I/O bottlenecks. Assigning a large number of CPUs and large amounts of memory may not improve performance if the I/O bottleneck occurs first, before CPU or memory. The I/O bottleneck can happen well before the CPU or memory limits are reached. On the other hand, having too little memory and pushing the virtual machine (VM) into using swap too heavily can cause an I/O bottleneck. A local disk can be faster than networked or shared file systems, but a local disk limits hardware failover options and may not be appropriate for all configurations. RAID or mirroring can also slow performance, but it may be needed regardless of the performance impact to avoid physical disk failure.

Overloading CPU Allocations   Oracle JD Edwards EnterpriseOne works well with overloading CPU allocations, especially when the server is used to run long-running run-batch jobs during off hours and heavy interactive web loads in the day. The CPU can float from the Web Server for handling interactive jobs, to the Enterprise and Database servers for processing run-batch jobs.

Solaris "Sparse Zones"   Solaris "sparse zones" provide the smallest image size and are sufficient to run Oracle JD Edwards EnterpriseOne.

Incremental Backups   Backups in virtualized images should be done the same way they are done with a standard nonvirtualized system. Use incremental backups instead of whole backups. A good rule of thumb is to increase these allocations by 10 percent increments until a performance improvement is realized. Trying to create whole backup copies of a VM or zone image while it is running can result in corrupted backups. If a full backup copy of a VM or container must be done, the VM or container must first be shut down by stopping the Web Server, Enterprise Server, and Database Server before stopping the VM or container.

Resource Requirements   The CPU, memory, and disk space MTRs for VM templates listed in the MTRs and VM manifests/README files are the minimum requirements for a demonstration or single-user environment, but they are not the minimum requirements for a production environment. The web server includes only a single DV900 development environment by default and does not include any other environments. Additional web servers are likely to be required to run all four "standard" web environments (especially in production) and additional CPU, memory, and disks are required. Individual .img files generally will need to be expanded to fit production use. The Enterprise Server will need more space for multiple package builds, and the Database Server will need more space for customer data. The database internal memory settings are configured to require 4GB of memory. These internal database settings will have to be resized for production environments as they would be for a nonvirtualized installation. The swap space for all three images is configured for single-user use. The actual amount of memory assigned to each VM image should be used to determine the amount of swap space that is configured. One rule of thumb is to match the size of swap to be the same size as memory.

More Memory, More Disk   If all else fails, revert to the tried-and-true formula of "more memory, more disk." Performance issues within a virtualized environment can often be resolved by adding more disks and memory to the server that is experiencing the most significance performance hit.

TIP
System administrators should make enough resources available to be able to accommodate a failed server.

Oracle VM VirtualBox

Oracle provides another solution previously created by Sun Microsystems called Oracle VM VirtualBox. Oracle VM VirtualBox is available as open source software under the terms of the GNU General Public License (GPL) version 2. Oracle JD Edwards created a whitepaper on how to install a development client and deployment server on Oracle VM VirtualBox entitled, "Configuring JD Edwards Deployment Server and Development Client on Oracle VM VirtualBox." For more information on Oracle VM VirtualBox, refer to the web site www.virtualbox.org/.

VMware for Servers and Workstations

One of the most common virtualization solutions is VMware, which provides solutions for both servers and workstations. VMware integrates well with Microsoft and IBM products. Close association with both IBM and Microsoft allows VMware users to receive assistance from the vendors when they run into issues.

NOTE
For more information on the operating systems supported by VMware, refer to www.vmware.com.

You can realize several benefits by implementing a virtualization solution. One of our customers was able to realize some specific real-life gains by deploying a VMware solution onto their network in a live production environment with 200 users.

VMware Deployment Specifications

The following specifications are for a VMware deployment of Oracle JD Edwards EnterpriseOne.

- Four Enterprise Servers: each is an IBM HS22V blade in an IBM BladeCenter H chassis.

  - Two Quad-Core processors (each)

  - 148GB of memory (each)

  - 1G LAN connectivity (each)

  - 1G iSCSI connectivity (each); the iSeries serves as the SAN or "disk" for all virtual servers.

- Six Database Servers running IBM DB2 for the iSeries; total combined disk space is 5TB.

- Six Citrix servers: Four have Internet Explorer published for the users; two have the fat client published along with Internet Explorer for users. Each Citrix server is accessed by about 30–35 users per server.

- Six web servers with 200 total users supported

- VMware 4.1 Enterprise Plus

Example Benefits Realized

The introduction section discusses the benefits that can be realized by implementing a virtualization solution. This section covers some specific real-life gains a customer was able to realize by deploying a VMware solution onto their network.

Recovery Strategy   Suppose you planned on going to work one day, but couldn't because there was a hurricane? What if the hurricane destroyed your office including all of your servers? That's exactly what happened to the client that is the subject of this case study.

VMware aided them in recovering from such a scenario. Once the new hardware came in, they were able to deploy their old images onto the servers. In a matter of days they were up and running in a scenario that would have taken weeks, possibly months to recover from. It helped, of course, that they kept their backup media in a place closer inland than their destroyed office.

Microsoft and IBM Integration   VMware integrates well with Microsoft and IBM products. Our example client uses VMware in conjunction with both Microsoft

Windows and IBM System i servers. Close association with both IBM and Microsoft allows them to receive assistance from the vendors when they run into issues.

VMware Tools with Veeam Reporting

In this section, we'll cover some of the tools provided by VMware.

VMware Administrative Console

The VMware administrative console makes it easy to monitor and configure your virtualized environment. You can use it to obtain a high-level Summary view of your architecture (Figure 11-13) that includes statistics, such as the total number of hosts and processors.

Drill down further, and you can see a detailed list of your machine's specifications (Figure 11-14) including such information as CPU, memory utilization, and datastores being used. This information gives you a good idea of the machine's capabilities.

When you access the Resource Allocation screen (Figure 11-15), you can see how your machine is using current resources. You can also change the disk space and memory assigned to the node. Memory and disk can be assigned in real time

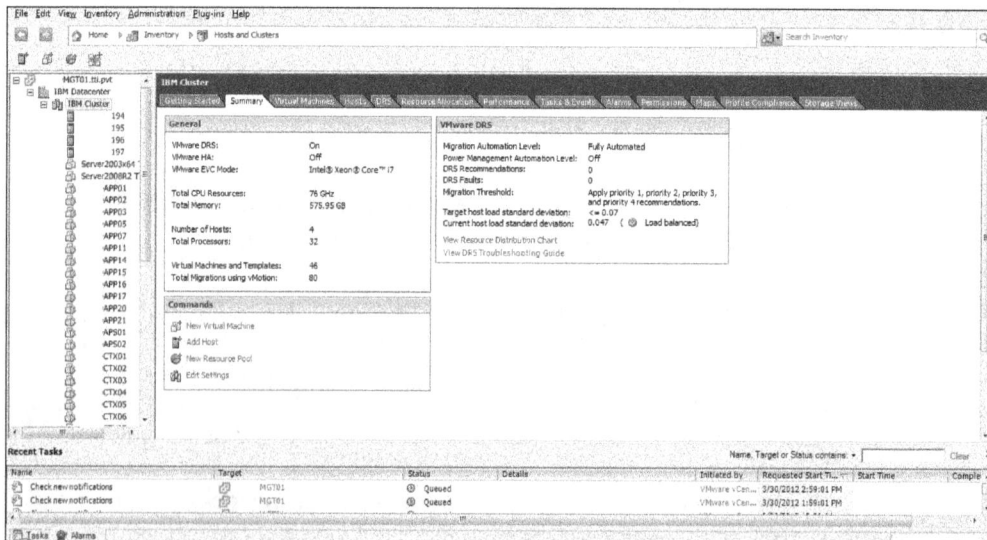

FIGURE 11-13. *Summary view*

VMware ESXi, 4.1.0, 260247										
Summary	Virtual Machines	Performance	Configuration	Tasks & Events	Alarms	Permissions	Maps	Storage Views	Hardware S

General

Manufacturer:	IBM
Model:	IBM System x -[7871AC1]-
CPU Cores:	8 CPUs x 2.4 GHz
Processor Type:	Intel(R) Xeon(R) CPU E5620 @ 2.40GHz
License:	vSphere 4 Enterprise Plus Licensed for 2 physical CPU…
Processor Sockets:	2
Cores per Socket:	4
Logical Processors:	16
Hyperthreading:	Active
Number of NICs:	7
State:	Connected
Virtual Machines and Templates:	13
vMotion Enabled:	No
VMware EVC Mode:	Intel® Xeon® Core™ i7
Host Configured for FT:	No
Active Tasks:	
Host Profile:	
Profile Compliance:	N/A

Commands

- New Virtual Machine
- Enter Maintenance Mode
- Reboot
- Shutdown
- Enter Standby Mode

Annotations

Edit

Resources

CPU usage: **4882 MHz**		Capacity	8 x 2.4 GHz
Memory usage: **46297.00 MB**		Capacity	147443.90 MB

Datastore	Status		Capacity	
IBM Datastore 1		Normal	499.75 GB	1
IBM Datastore 11 …		Normal	199.75 GB	
IBM Datastore 12		Normal	499.75 GB	
IBM Datastore 2		Normal	499.75 GB	1
IBM Datastore 3		Normal	499.75 GB	1
IBM Datastore 4		Normal	499.75 GB	3
IBM Datastore 5		Unknown	499.75 GB	
IBM Datastore 6		Unknown	499.75 GB	
IBM Datastore 7		Unknown	499.75 GB	
IBM Datastore 8		Unknown	499.75 GB	
IBM Datastore 9		Normal	499.75 GB	
IBM Datastore 10		Unknown	249.75 GB	

Network	Type	Sta
IBM Production N…	Uplink group	
IBM Production Po…	Distributed virtual port group	
IBM Migration Ne…	Uplink group	
IBM Migration Ne…	Distributed virtual port group	

Fault Tolerance

Fault Tolerance Version:	2.0.1-2.0.0-2.0.0
	Refresh Virtual Machine Counts
Total Primary VMs:	0
Powered On Primary VMs:	0
Total Secondary VMs:	0
Powered On Secondary VMs:	0

FIGURE 11-14. *Machine specifications summary*

without requiring that the system be rebooted. Memory can also be "reserved" for a node to allow it to access memory as it needs it up to a maximum amount.

NOTE
If additional CPUs are added to the machine, the virtual machine requires a reboot.

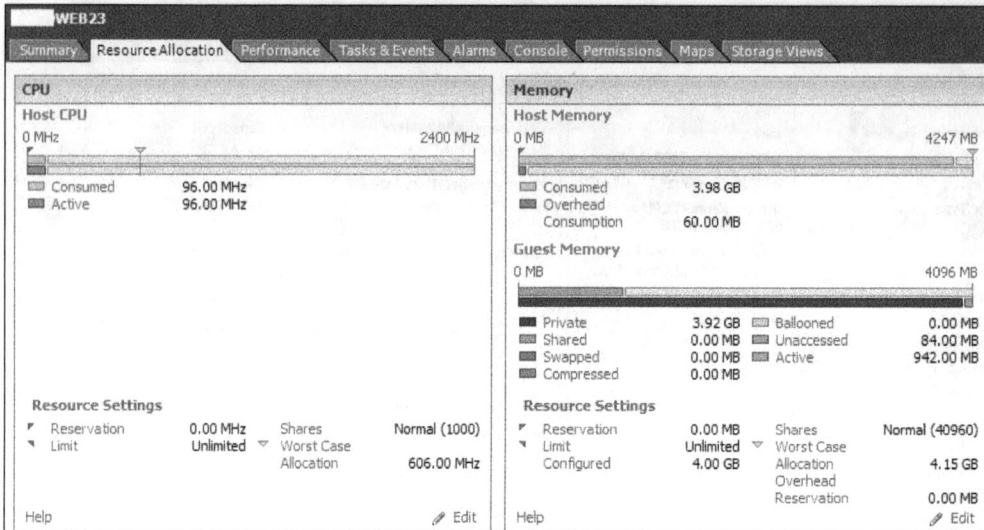

FIGURE 11-15. *Resource Allocation screen*

Click the Hosts tab to review all of the configured virtual hosts and see the percentage of CPU and memory being used by each host. In Figure 11-16, you can see that the hosts are using only a small percentage of the CPU and memory allocated, so these resources don't need to be adjusted upward (but could be adjusted downward if other hosts needed more resources).

To view all of your virtual machines, click the Virtual Machines tab. You can see several properties here, such as provisioned space, used space, and memory usage. This gives you a complete view of all the virtual machines being used. Figure 11-17 shows an example Virtual Hosts screen.

What good would an administration console be without giving you the ability to set alerts? Luckily, the VMware console lets you set alarm so that e-mails or text

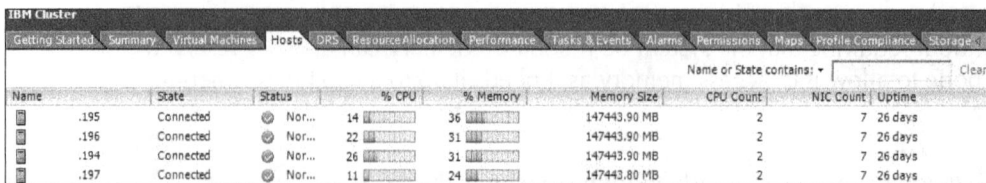

FIGURE 11-16. *Hosts screen*

IBM Cluster

Getting Started | Summary | Virtual Machines | Hosts | DRS | Resource Allocation | Performance | Tasks & Events | Alarms | Permissions | Maps | Profile Compliance | Storage

Name, State, Host or Guest OS contains: ▾ [   ] Cle

Name	State	Status	Provisioned Space	Used Space	Host CPU - MHz	Host Mem - MB	Guest Mem - %
DC01	Powered On	Normal	54.01 GB	54.01 GB	72	4130	5
DBS04	Powered On	Normal	124.01 GB	124.01 GB	24	4155	0
DBS04-Backup	Powered Off	Normal	124.00 GB	33.65 GB	0	0	0
CXPVS01	Powered On	Normal	126.01 GB	126.01 GB	0	6206	1
CTX02	Powered On	Normal	74.00 GB	74.00 GB	216	4160	15
CTX03	Powered On	Normal	15.00 GB	15.00 GB	1320	5190	20
CTX05	Powered On	Normal	15.00 GB	15.00 GB	768	5191	51
APP01	Powered On	Normal	78.26 GB	78.26 GB	120	4175	15
APP16	Powered On	Normal	144.00 GB	144.00 GB	0	4072	1
APP21	Powered On	Normal	89.01 GB	89.01 GB	24	3689	0
DC02	Powered On	Normal	44.00 GB	44.00 GB	240	4052	5
Template - 2008 R2	Powered Off	Normal	29.00 GB	25.00 GB	0	0	0
CXPVS02	Powered On	Normal	126.00 GB	126.00 GB	0	3549	1
CTX01	Powered On	Normal	144.03 GB	101.32 GB	192	4160	10
CTX00	Powered Off	Normal	14.00 GB	10.00 GB	0	0	0
CTX07	Powered On	Normal	15.00 GB	15.00 GB	1248	5188	35
APP05	Powered On	Normal	180.08 GB	180.08 GB	96	4155	3
APP02	Powered On	Normal	152.53 GB	137.83 GB	72	3167	3
DBS03	Powered On	Normal	140.07 GB	140.07 GB	216	4148	2
APS02	Powered On	Normal	90.05 GB	90.05 GB	2832	3500	10
APP11	Powered On	Normal	70.05 GB	70.05 GB	288	4151	5
APP15	Powered On	Normal	144.01 GB	144.01 GB	120	4155	15
WEB20	Powered On	Normal	84.02 GB	84.02 GB	24	4073	28
WEB22	Powered On	Normal	84.01 GB	84.01 GB	96	4071	38
WEB24	Powered On	Normal	84.00 GB	84.00 GB	24	4155	6
APP17	Powered On	Normal	144.01 GB	144.01 GB	24	4073	5
IT01	Powered On	Normal	448.00 GB	448.00 GB	408	8297	2
APP20	Powered On	Normal	171.00 GB	88.10 GB	24	1067	23
WGN01	Powered On	Normal	59.68 GB	59.68 GB	72	4162	9
APS01	Powered On	Normal	78.26 GB	78.26 GB	2592	3296	16
VC01	Powered On	Normal	44.00 GB	44.00 GB	48	2702	0
DBS02	Powered On	Normal	110.06 GB	110.06 GB	144	3339	5
DEP02	Powered On	Normal	184.03 GB	184.03 GB	48	4156	6
WEB21	Powered On	Normal	84.03 GB	84.03 GB	24	4156	6
WEB23	Powered On	Normal	84.00 GB	84.00 GB	48	4072	25
APP07	Powered On	Normal	104.00 GB	104.00 GB	24	4128	12
CXMST01	Powered On	Normal	15.00 GB	15.00 GB	24	5079	2
Unknown (inaccessible)	Powered Off	Unknown			0	0	
XAPP04 (inaccessible)	Powered Off	Unknown	0.00 B	0.00 B	0	0	
CTX04	Powered On	Normal	15.00 GB	15.00 GB	576	5192	15
CTX06	Powered On	Normal	15.00 GB	15.00 GB	1080	5191	21
Server2003x64 Template	Powered Off	Normal	26.00 GB	25.00 GB	0	0	0
Server2008R2 Template	Powered Off	Normal	44.00 GB	40.00 GB	0	0	0
APP03	Powered On	Normal	104.02 GB	104.02 GB	0	4158	2
APP14	Powered On	Normal	136.10 GB	75.66 GB	96	3140	3
DBS01	Powered On	Normal	190.07 GB	190.07 GB	72	4164	5
CX01	Powered On	Normal	70.06 GB	70.06 GB	240	4162	7

FIGURE 11-17. *Virtual Machines screen*

messages are sent to administrators when certain events happen. In the Alarms tab in Figure 11-18, alarms have been set for everything from datastore use, to migration problems, to spikes in voltage.

PlateSpin: Hosting on a Physical Drive

One of the most common concerns when you're thinking about adopting a virtualized solution is whether your application vendor will support the configuration. No one

FIGURE 11-18.   *Alarms tab*

wants to call customer support only to hear the phrase, "We don't support virtualized environments." The good news is that a viable option is available. The client in our case study used PlateSpin from Novell to move their virtualized images onto a physical drive. Once the issue was fixed, the image could be virtualized again. This process is often referred to as "V-to-P" (Virtual-to-Physical). The reverse, "P-to-V" is more common. You can find out more about PlateSpin at www.novell.com/solutions/virtualization-workload/.

SnapShot

VMware provides the SnapShot tool that lets you to make a quick image of your current configuration. Before performing upgrades, it is common to take a snapshot of your system. If something goes seriously wrong, the servers can be rolled back to the state when the snapshot was taken an all updates not applied.

Veeam Reporting

Veeam is a product produced by Veeam Software that integrates with VMware to provide better reporting options for a virtualized environment. These reports can easily be exported to Microsoft Excel. You can, for example, create a report covering memory and disk usage that incorporates pie, bar, and line graphs, making it easy to read and understand. For more information on Veeam, see www.veeam.com.

You can also use Veeam to create a high-level report that shows the resource usage of all clusters. Such Veeam reports can help you determine how best to allocate resources. VMware offers many ways to dynamically allocate resources, and you can often change the distribution with the click of a button. In the report shown in Figure 11-19, both the Testbed and IBM Cluster are well within the resource usage.

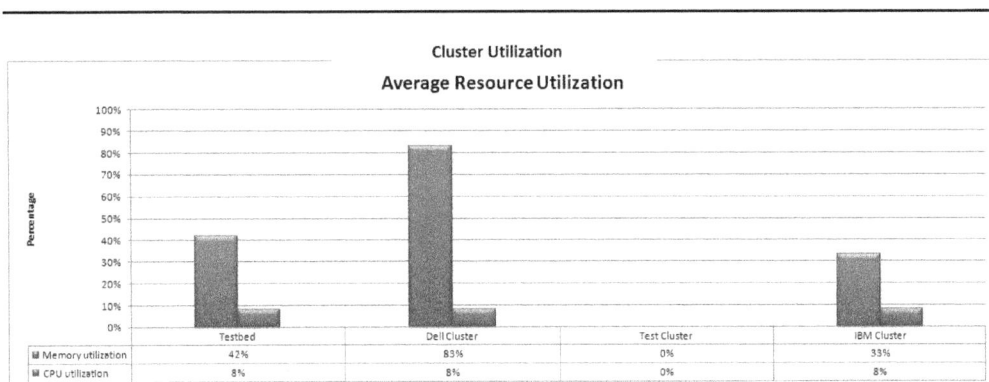

Cluster Utilization				
Average Resource Utilization	Testbed	Dell Cluster	Test Cluster	IBM Cluster
Memory utilization	42%	83%	0%	33%
CPU utilization	8%	8%	0%	8%

FIGURE 11-19. *Veeam Cluster Utilization report*

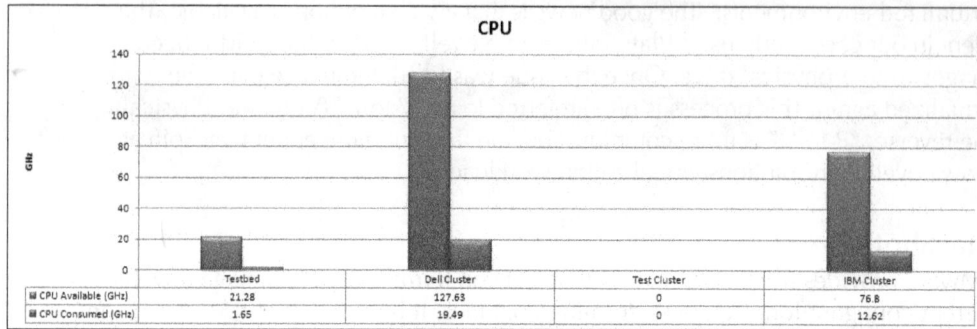

FIGURE 11-20. *Veeam CPU Summary report*

However, the use of memory by the Dell Cluster needs to be monitored closely and more memory allocated if usage stays consistently above 90 percent.

You can also drill down to see a more detailed CPU usage graph that shows the amount of CPU usage compared to the amount allocated. You can then change CPU allocations accordingly. In the report shown in Figure 11-20, all clusters are not using much of the CPU memory, so their allocations could even be adjusted downward if other nodes needed more CPU memory.

You can also see a report on your disk space utilization, which shows you the amount of disk space being used and the health of the disk drive. Another report, shown in Figure 11-21, indicates which VMs are using the most disk space.

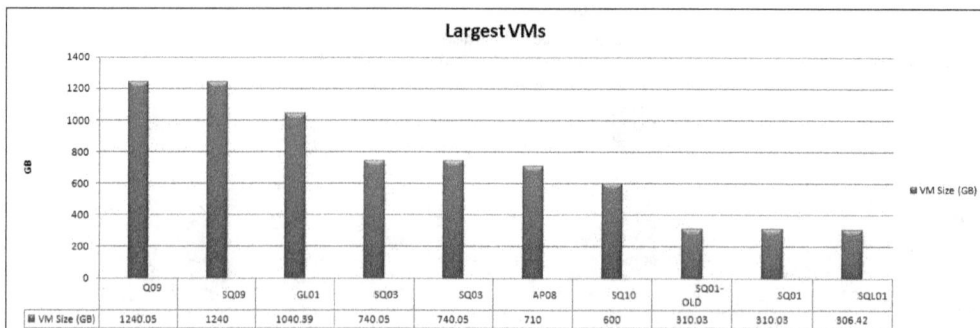

FIGURE 11-21. *Veeam Top 10 Storage Consuming VMs report*

Memory Allocation

	Testbed	Dell Cluster	Test Cluster	IBM Cluster
Physical Memory (GB)	32	575.95	0	575.95
Memory Allocated (GB)	35.86	531.76	0	199.25
Memory Consumed (GB)	15.57	480.09	0	190.95

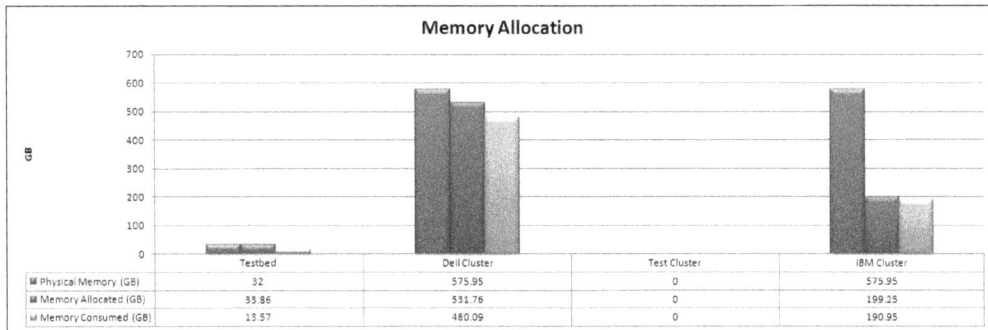

FIGURE 11-22. *Veeam Memory Allocation report*

And, of course, you can review the memory usage of each node, as shown in Figure 11-22. This information can help you make decisions on how to allocate memory properly across your architecture. You can change the memory month-by-month if necessary, depending on use.

Veeam also offers a power usage report. Since "green" is the latest buzzword these days, you want to know how much power is being used, right? This report can help you make sure that the rooms in which the machines are located have sufficient power; or it could be used to remind people to turn off the equipment when they're done using it. It could also be used the next time equipment is acquired, since many vendors now offer servers that use power more efficiently. Figure 11-23 shows a sample Veeam power usage report.

Datacenter	Host	Average Power Usage (kW·h)
Office	4	32.8
	.197	32.26
	.195	32.09
	.196	33.43
	.194	33.43
IBM Datacenter	4	23.77
	.195	25.03
	.196	23.35
	.194	23.35
	.197	23.35

FIGURE 11-23. *Veeam power usage report*

Health State

Error Count	Warning Count	Info Count
■ Testbed ■ Dell Cluster ▦ Test Cluster ▥ IBM Cluster	■ Testbed ■ Dell Cluster ▦ Test Cluster ▥ IBM Cluster	■ Testbed ■ Dell Cluster ▦ Test Cluster ▥ IBM Cluster

Cluster Utilization

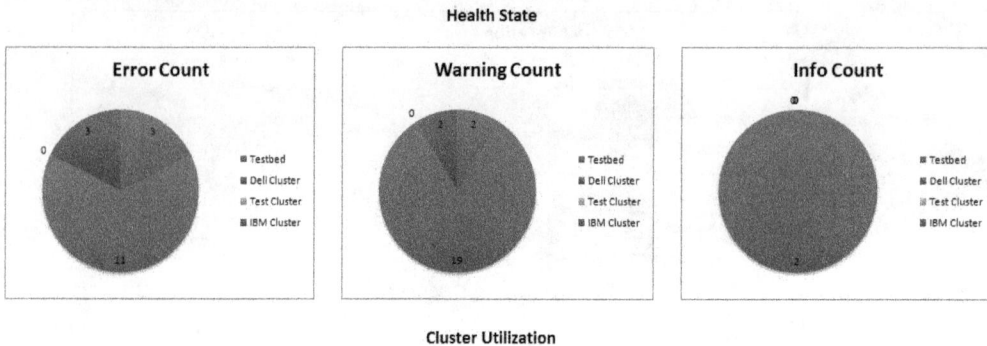

FIGURE 11-24. *Veeam Health State report*

The Health State report shows you at-a-glance which clusters are providing errors and warnings. Then you can spend your day tracking down what the actual errors and warnings are and fix them. Figure 11-24 shows an example Veeam Health State report.

You can also view the Top Datastores to see the total capacity versus the provisioned space. You can change your datastore allocation as appropriate. Figure 11-25 shows an example Veeam Top Datastores report.

Finally, you can create an overall resource usage report. The report shown in Figure 11-26 is a custom dashboard that shows CPU, memory, and storage. It makes it easy to see how efficiently your resources are being used.

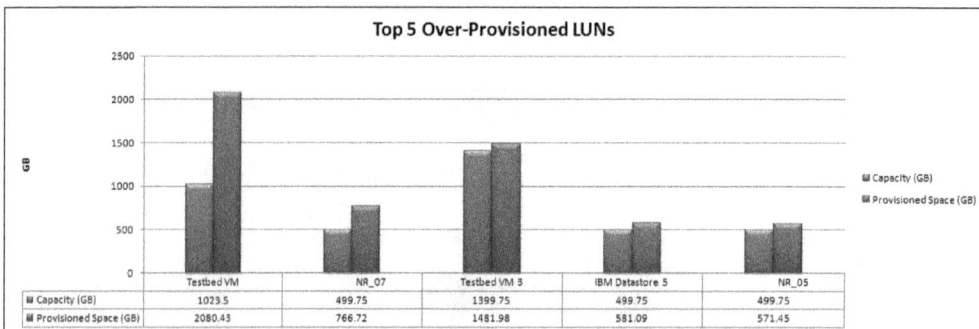

Top 5 Over-Provisioned LUNs

	Testbed VM	NR_07	Testbed VM 3	IBM Datastore 5	NR_05
▥ Capacity (GB)	1023.5	499.75	1399.75	499.75	499.75
▥ Provisioned Space (GB)	2080.43	766.72	1481.98	581.09	571.45

FIGURE 11-25. *Veeam Top Datastores report*

Infrastructure Summary

vCenter Servers	Datacenters	Clusters	Hosts	Virtual Machines Online	Virtual Disks	Datastores	Consolidation Ratio
vc02	1	2	5	107	217	33	21.40
MGT01	1	2	4	44	110	11	11.00
Total	2	4	9	151	327	44	16.78

Cluster Resource Usage

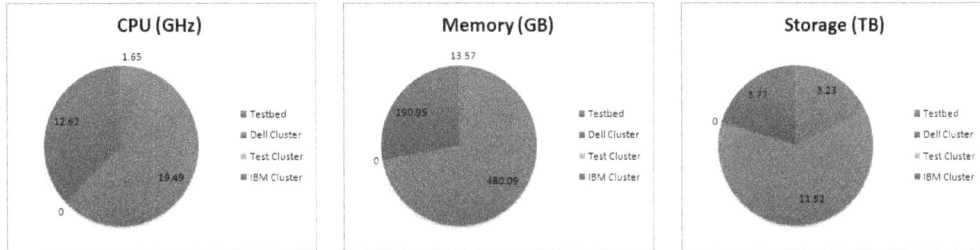

FIGURE 11-26. *Veeam Resource Usage report*

JD Edwards Tuning for Virtualization

The following configuration information comes from our client in the case study, who implemented a virtualization solution. This information applies to a configuration of up to 200 concurrent users that access Oracle JD Edwards EnterpriseOne from all over the world. Virtualization does not produce an extra load on the system; therefore, there are no modifications to these INIs that are specific to virtualization.

The following jas.ini settings are specific to running Business Services Server for up to 200 users on a virtualized environment.

BSSV JDBJ.INI

The following set of jdbj.ini settings are for a web client accessed by up to 200 users. The database data is stored in an IBM DB2 for i database.

```
[JDBj-CONNECTION POOL]
jdbcPooling=false
minConnection=0
maxConnection=50
poolGrowth=5
initialConnection=5
connectionTimeout=1800000
cleanPoolInterval=300000
maxSize=50
cachePurgeSize=5
```

```
[JDBj-CONNECTION POOL]
jdbcPooling=false
minConnection=0
maxConnection=50
poolGrowth=5
initialConnection=5
connectionTimeout=1800000
cleanPoolInterval=300000
maxSize=50
cachePurgeSize=5
```

Web Client JDBJ.INI

The following settings are from the jdbj.ini for the web client for 200 users while connecting to an IBM DB2 for i database:

```
[JDBj-CONNECTION POOL]
minConnection=0
maxConnection=50
poolGrowth=5
initialConnection=5
connectionTimeout=1800000
cleanPoolInterval=300000
maxSize=50
cachePurgeSize=5
[JDBj-RUNTIME PROPERTIES]
dataCacheEntrySizeThreshold=500
dataCacheEntryThreshold=100
resultSetTimeout=60000
retryInterval=0
retryMaximum=5
ocmCachePurge=3600000
securityCachePurge=3600000
serviceCachePurge=600000
specCachePurge=3600000
e1MenuCachePurge=3600000
transactionTimeout=120000
triggerAutoFetch=none
usageExecutionThreshold=20000
usageFetchSizeThreshold=500
usageResultSetOpenThreshold=60000
usageTracking=false
usageTrackingOutput=log
usageTransactionActiveThreshold=120000
parallelAppGens=10
as400NativeJDBCDriver=true
msSQLQueryTimeout=10000
msSQLQueryAttempts=3
```

Enterprise Server JDE.INI

The following is a listing of the important tuning parameters of a JDE.INI running on an IBM i for Power Systems that is accessed by about 200 users:

```
[JDENET]
maxNetProcesses=4
maxNetConnections=800
netShutdownInterval=15
maxKernelProcesses=143
maxKernelRanges=34
enterpriseServerTimeout=60000
statsUpdateInterval=30
maxNumSocketMsgQueue=200
maxIPCQueueMsgs=100
[JDENET_KERNEL_DEF2]
krnlName=UBE KERNEL
dispatchDLLName=JDEKRNL
dispatchDLLFunction=JDEK_DispatchUBEMessage
maxNumberOfProcesses=5
numberOfAutoStartProcesses=3
```

Tips for Additional Virtualization Tuning

Companies often utilize less hardware to support more application and batch servers. With many JD Edwards instances, heavy batch process occur at night and most interactive sessions occur during the day. The Oracle JD Edwards EnterpriseOne batch and application servers can "share" CPUs and RAM. During the day, the batch server will use little of the resources of the host server, allowing the application server to have access to most of the CPU and RAM. At night, when batch jobs kick in, the batch server will have access to the host resources it needs because few users are accessing the system. This might appear to over-allocate the host resources, but if this is done correctly, it can result in a huge cost savings. This is, however, a slippery slope, because if over-allocation does occur, the servers will experience major performance issues. If this resource sharing is implemented, you can run reports for the virtual solutions that show the resource consumption over the past certain number of hours or days. They should be examined closely. Also, you might prefer to allocate only as much CPU and RAM to the virtual servers as there is available on the host.

Another item of concern for virtual servers is the disk that is being utilized. Keep in mind that only so many disk arms exist. If all of your virtual servers are using the same disk, this can cause a bottleneck.

CHAPTER
12

Oracle Exadata Database Machine and Exalogic Elastic Cloud

According to computer history books, the first mechanized computer, the Difference Engine, was developed and partially built by Charles Babbage in the mid-nineteenth century. It was a simple computing machine, but because of various circumstances, it was never completed. Jump to the year 1991 in London, where a group of computer scientists found and resurrected Babbage's original design; it functioned properly, just as the inventor designed it. Although Babbage never realized the future importance of his machine, he and others like him spawned the concept of computing devices, capable of performing calculations and providing accurate results. Technology has come a long way since those days, and the concepts of computing are continuing to change and evolve. The newest of these innovations are those of Oracle Corporation, cloud computing, and the introduction of the "Exa" line of Oracle engineered systems.

This chapter will cover the following:

- The "Exa" revolution

- Basic concepts of the Oracle Exadata Database machine and the Exalogic Elastic Cloud including architecture, configuration, and usage of Oracle engineered systems utilities

- Fabric-based technologies

- Implementing Exadata and Exalogic for EnterpriseOne

- Enhanced Linux operating system configurations for Exalogic

- Exadata and Exalogic performance tuning for EnterpriseOne

- Implementing JD Edwards EnterpriseOne on the Exalogic Elastic Cloud

JD Edwards EnterpriseOne and the "Exa" Revolution

The "Exa" revolution describes a set of engineering solutions that couples software enhancements with hardware to achieve a more integrated architecture. The Exa solution is more than simply adding software to a hardware platform and optimizing it. With Exa, hardware and software engineers take advantage of the hardware design and architecture delivered with Oracle engineered systems by coding specific instructions from the Oracle Database and other Oracle software packages such as WebLogic to provide an optimized and integrated solution architecture. This solution lets you take advantage of the hardware components of disk, memory, and specific CPU models and optimize them to work with Oracle software achieving better performance, increased scalability, and creating a more stable and predictable environment for both Oracle and non-Oracle software implementations.

Oracle calls these solutions "engineered systems." The engineered system targeted for Oracle Database is the *Oracle Database Machine* (aka *Exadata*). The engineered system that addresses the software application realm is the *Oracle Exalogic Elastic Cloud*. The solutions are currently available for both the Linux and Solaris operating systems.

The first engineered system from Oracle was introduced during the annual OpenWorld conference in 2008 by Larry Ellison, with the announcement of a prebuilt, preconfigured, and optimized Oracle Database Machine, dubbed the Exadata (Figure 12-1). At this conference, Oracle launched a new company direction in technology, merging its most notable product, its database, and integrating it in a new way to deliver a single integrated software and hardware solution. Initially, Exadata worked on HP servers, but since Oracle's acquisition of Sun Microsystems in 2010, the Exadata engineered system became available on Sun hardware and the Solaris operating system.

According to Oracle, its engineered systems are "pre-integrated to reduce the cost and complexity of IT infrastructures while increasing productivity and performance." In short, Oracle has integrated the hardware and software components of its certified applications to work together. JD Edwards EnterpriseOne is only one of the many software applications that integrate with the engineered system, and more applications are being added continually.

Integrated systems of all types are the trend in the IT industry, and Oracle expects that by the end of 2015, 35 percent of its systems shipped will be as integrated systems.

FIGURE 12-1. *Oracle engineered systems*

Fabric-based Technologies

Why the need for engineered systems? To answer this question, you must first understand the concepts of *fabric-based computing*. A *fabric* is simply a consolidated network of components that brings together the hardware elements of storage (disk), memory (solid state disk and RAM), and computer processing power (CPU with inline cache). Fabric-based infrastructure concepts have brought about a shift in the architectural design of data centers. Interesting enough, this shift was not entirely a product of the advances in IT technology, but has been driven by cost, manageability, the need for integration, and other concerned deliverables of a business.

Business and technical drivers include the following:

- Ability to take advantage of market advances in software, hardware, or business opportunities.

- Reduce IT infrastructure costs associated with space, cooling, and power. Newer technologies have made great advances in savings in these areas.

- Reduce management overhead costs of support of disparate systems. Integrated systems design and virtualization technologies have accelerated this process.

- Need to increase current performance of applications. Applications are continuing to increase in their delivered functionality; the challenge is to add this functionality without the cost to current performance.

- Upgrade of software and hardware seamlessly. Concepts of rolling upgrades, with enough redundant components in the architecture to provide a path of upgrading software with little to no service downtime.

- Meet customer Service Level Agreements (SLAs). Availability is becoming the normal operations within the business. Customers have an insatiable desire for fast and immediate access to their applications without interruption.

- React to scalability, availability, and serviceability (RAS) concerns. RAS is often used at the business level to describe an architecture that is redundant and highly available, and that provides good SLAs to customers as the business grows.

NOTE
In 2010, Gartner published an article, "Clearing the Confusion About Fabric-based Infrastructure: A Taxonomy" that discusses the IT computer architecture trends to a more fabric-based data center (see www.gartner.com/id=1430729).

The fabric technology places all the hardware components in the network in a horizontal fashion to help achieve maximum connectivity, usability, and efficiency among these components. Figure 12-2 illustrates this concept of interconnection of components.

Following are the basic component elements of a fabric-based infrastructure that are illustrated in the figure:

- **Blade servers**   In most cases, this is a server class computer that has been stripped down to its components of processors, memory, and minimal disk. For Exadata and Exalogic machines, solid state disk (SSD) storage is used for the boot partitions to increase efficiency and performance of the base operating system.

- **Storage**   Storage includes solid state disks, storage arrays (SAS disks for Exadata), and network attached storage (NAS for Exalogic). There is no extended use of the solid state disk on the Exalogic, which is strictly used for the boot partition.

- **Memory**   Memory includes the physical RAM on the box, disk RAM, onboard CPU memory, and the PCI-based Smart Flash Cache Memory available on the Exadata.

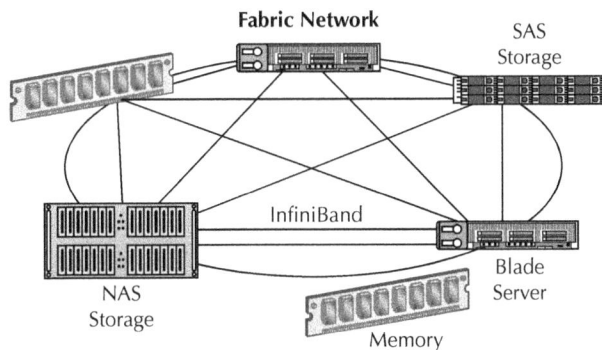

FIGURE 12-2.   *Fabric technology network*

■ **Network connectivity** The network connectivity is the glue that holds the fabric-based infrastructure together. Both Exadata and Exalogic technologies employ the InfiniBand network technology when connected together. External network connectivity is through the available 1Gbps and 10Gbps network interfaces available in each Exa rack switch.

Fabric-based Technologies: Advantages and Disadvantages

Fabric-based technologies offer definite advantages and disadvantages. Figure 12-3 shows how the advantages and disadvantages can shift from a traditional data center approach to that of fabric-based data centers.

Following are some advantages of fabric-based technologies:

■ **Integration** Standardized hardware components are integrated to work together; therefore, they tend to be less labor-intensive in maintenance and support. Traditional hardware architecture technologies have disparate systems that must be tested and maintained to work together with their operating system releases, hardware release levels, and hardware and software drivers. It is in the fabric-based technology of integration where the issues revolving around integration are avoided.

■ **Flexibility** Fabric technologies offer flexibility to reconfigure any of the fabric components dynamically. Many of the components are designed to be hot-pluggable, meaning they can be added or swapped out and replaced without the need to bring the entire hardware system down for maintenance.

■ **Centralized management** You can view the entire set of hardware components as a single unit. The Exadata and Exalogic components have centralized management software that allows a desktop view of the entire set of components and its architecture.

■ **Resource administration** You can assign, move, or reconfigure fabric element resources as needed based on IT, business, or workload needs.

Traditional Data Center ⟵⟶ Fabric-Based Data Center

FIGURE 12-3. *Traditional and fabric-based data centers*

■ **Efficiency**   Space, power consumption, and heat specifications on fabric-based hardware are, in general, more efficient than those for traditional data center machines, because newer hardware was designed with this in mind.

The disadvantages of fabric-based technologies include the following:

■ **Adding resources**   Adding more storage, memory, and blade servers can be limited by physical resource limitations of the fabric network that supports it and by fabric-only hardware component vendors.

■ **Customizable**   You may be limited in the choices of hardware that you can include in a fabric-based infrastructure. Specific versions of software, and even the way that the system must be configured, are often well defined in a fabric-based technology

■ **Connectivity to external fabric components**   Connectivity to external fabric components is normally through slower network segments and can create a significant bottleneck in the IT infrastructure. The bottleneck of connectivity to external sources of data, processes, and integrations has shown to be a major concern when implementing a fabric-based technology in an already complex and heterogeneous company.

■ **Network protocols**   Fabric networks can take advantage of other, faster network protocols and thus additional configuration may be required to use these protocols and take advantage of the faster network speeds. Some software applications may not support these protocols.

Fabric-based Technology for Exadata and Exalogic

Employing Exadata and Exalogic with JD Edwards EnterpriseOne offers many advantages. Because the components of Exadata and Exalogic are already proven, tested, and certified, the EnterpriseOne software is also deemed certified. This was demonstrated in many of the early adoptions and testing of EnterpriseOne with the engineered systems. The engineered systems eliminate the hardware and software integration risks associated with disparate hardware systems and software providing a more uniform and consistent installation experience.

In addition, the benefits of EnterpriseOne on an engineered system are predictability and business continuity as the load is increased, interactive user growth, and greater batch load were demonstrated with the EnterpriseOne benchmark testing on the engineered systems. The large numbers of Exalogic nodes and VM instances also provide the ability for consolidation of other EnterpriseOne instances to the engineering system architecture. Finally, Exadata and Exalogic offer the ability to manage the components of the software and hardware from a central location.

Several specific fabric-based technologies are employed with Exadata and Exalogic, including the components listed next.

- **InfiniBand network**   The InfiniBand network and Sockets Direct Protocol (SDP) within the engineered systems communicate at a speed of 40Gbps, thus allowing a much higher network throughput, lower network latency than the traditional 1Gbps standard, and enhanced 10Gbps network speeds. The EnterpriseOne code base does not currently support the SDP protocol but is aware of the advantages of using the thinner protocol of SDP.

- **External network capable**   1Gbps and 10Gbps traditional network links are available to the Oracle engineered systems.

- **High-capacity SAS disks (Exadata)**   The storage subsystem components are optimized for the Oracle Database and allow for greater disk I/O and database request performance.

- **High-capacity network attached storage (NAS) disks (Exalogic)**   NAS storage is not optimal for database activity but can be an ideal match for many software applications, including JD Edwards EnterpriseOne. NAS disks are the delivered storage solution framework on the Exalogic Elastic Cloud. The NAS disk storage infrastructure is the primary reason that Oracle Database is not recommended to be configured on any of the Exalogic VM partitions or nodes if delivered in a strict node server architecture.

  - **Exadata Smart Flash Cache**   Exadata uses PCI-based flash cards; Exadata Smart Flash is an automated software algorithm for smart caching that also includes the capability for manual user manageability. Exadata Smart Flash Cache is not to be confused with the Oracle feature of flash cache. The Exadata Smart Flash Cache resides on the Exadata Storage Cells and is configured and used apart from the Oracle Database flash cache feature.

NOTE
Disk I/O is a primary concern with the creation of reports (PrintQueue) directory and logging in the JD EnterpriseOne foundation software. The Exalogic Elastic Cloud version 3 is the default NFS protocol; version 4 is now available and can be implemented on older models of Exalogic and should be the default version on newer models. The NFS version 4 protocol addresses many of the performance and disk I/O concerns found on the earlier models with software application performance for NAS storage.

InfiniBand Network

The InfiniBand network is one of the major engineered system components that enhance the performance of the Exa architecture. The InfiniBand network architecture communicates at a dual 20Gbps (40Gbps effective rate) as opposed to the standing fabric channel network speed, a full 40-times improvement in performance compared to older and slower 1Gbps networks and four times better on faster 10Gbps networks, the current standard for fast network speeds.

When implementing Exadata and Exalogic together, the Oracle engineered system has the added benefit of being able to communicate between the Exadata and Exalogic rack systems at the higher 40Gbps speed through InfiniBand network fabric connection. The InfiniBand network fabric allows a scalable daisy chain of any Exa rack system for greater scalability and interoperability.

Exadata Smart Flash Cache and Exadata Smart Read Functionality

The integrated hardware technology on Exadata, together with the storage server software that drives it, allows for the automatic caching of tables. Some features of the Exadata Smart Flash Cache are offered here:

- Expandable to 1.1TB flash for quarter rack Oracle Exadata configuration

- Exadata card is preconfigured for high performance for the Oracle database

- Exadata Smart Flash Cache coupled with the Exadata storage software allows automatic caching of database tables that can be manually configured to force caching of selected tables

When evaluating the performance of Exadata, both the Flash Cache and Smart Scan technologies contribute to its speed. The Exadata PCI Flash Cache will reduce the I/O efficiency to disk, but the major performance gains in the Exadata are due to the Smart Scan technology. Smart Scan Technology has the following key features:

- **Predicate Filtering** Ability for the operators in the where clause that contain full table scans and the operators such as =, >, to utilize the storage cell memory directly.

- **Storage Indexes** Exadata storage cell's in-memory structures that store information about where specific data exists on the disk. Like an index on a table, the storage index allows for fast retrieval of information on disk without having to scan the disk for the information, reducing the I/O for faster processing.

Much of the published statistics regarding the enormous amounts of operations (1 million operations per second) that can be achieved with Oracle Database on Exadata is attributed specifically to the Smart Flash Cache technology. Here again is an example showing that engineered systems offer advantages over traditional technologies. Traditional technologies of using flash cache and solid state disk technologies on a database have been implemented in the past, but in an engineered

FIGURE 12-4. *Exadata Smart Flash Cache card*

solution, the added database table caching automation and ability to control the use of the cache offers additional value.

You can manually alter the automated algorithm of caching database tables to force certain database tables to be entered into the Smart Flash Cache at any time. This enhances the granular control the IT staff can have in tuning applications more efficiently on the Exadata machine.

Figure 12-4 shows the Exadata Smart Flash Cache card.

Exadata Database Machine

The Exadata Database Machine solution provides performance enhancements for both data warehouse online analytical processing (OLAP) and online transaction processing (OLTP) solutions. EnterpriseOne is more reflective with the online transaction processing model. Current detailed specifications for the Exadata Database Machine are available on the Oracle web site: www.oracle.com/technetwork/database/exadata/dbmachine-x2-2-datasheet-175280.pdf

The configurations included are full, half, and quarter racks. Each node on the Exadata Database Machine is equivalent to a node on the Oracle Database configured as Real Application Clusters (RAC). An Oracle database configured for RAC is an option in the Oracle Database Enterprise Edition and can provide a high availability database solution within a single Oracle engineered fabric-based solution.

Exalogic Elastic Cloud

The Oracle Exalogic Elastic Cloud is a little more granular in its configuration and scalability. The smallest Exalogic configuration that is available on Exalogic X2-2 is an eighth rack capable of supporting four nodes and up to 60TB of NAS storage, as shown in Figure 12-5. EnterpriseOne also supports through its templates an Exalogic VM configuration if more discrete machines are required for the implementation of the EnterpriseOne architecture.

The EnterpriseOne Customer Challenge

A number of key challenges face all business customers using Enterprise Resource Planning (ERP) software and JD Edwards EnterpriseOne in particular. EnterpriseOne and the engineered systems provide answers to these challenges for customers as follows:

- Solutions are preintegrated, tested, and certified to provide an increased level of assurance and confidence that these solutions will meet technical and business challenges.

- The number of interactive and batch processes that must be supported by the EnterpriseOne software in a single instance has grown. Consolidation of EnterpriseOne implementations to a single instance capable of supporting a more global architecture is made possible by technology and the advances in the feature set of EnterpriseOne.

- A business volume for customers can grow at an enormous rate; in fact, doubling every year is not an unrealistic assumption for the planning of an EnterpriseOne implementation or upgrade strategy. The engineered systems provide a mechanism of increasing storage capacity and the handling of large data sets.

- Integration of current software into new and existing technologies is a key business challenge as company acquisitions, mergers, and collaborations are becoming commonplace in the IT industry.

- JD Edwards alone can be the central solution for supporting all of the divisions of the company through a consolidation software implementation effort when more than one software vendor supports the different divisions of the company.

- Support for new technologies including mobile device support and other features are included in the EnterpriseOne feature set.

- The EnterpriseOne feature set provides interactive users and batch processes with a consistent and reliable performance profile (end user response time and time to process batch reports).

- EnterpriseOne ease of manageability is now more seamless since the introduction of the EnterpriseOne Server Manager and the integration of the Oracle Enterprise Manager. The Enterprise Manager is the manageability tool for the engineered systems.

- Analysis of bottlenecks and risks to the business is easier through the dynamic nature of the EnterpriseOne application through Server Manager.

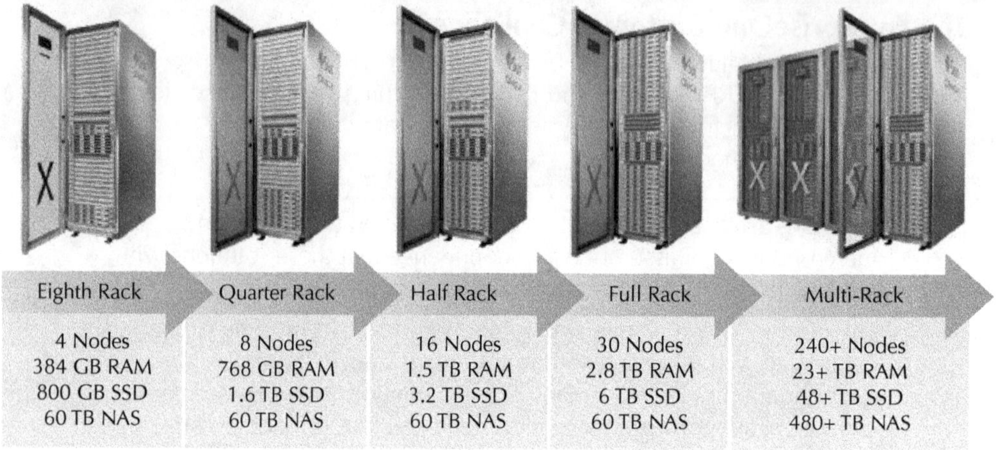

FIGURE 12-5. *Exalogic X2-2 rack scalability*

Each node is a representation of a blade server machine capable of supporting any one of the many JD Edwards EnterpriseOne architecture components. Since Exalogic Elastic Cloud is built on a fabric-based infrastructure, memory, and storage (NAS) can be assigned to any one of the node machines. The SSD available on the Exalogic servers is used for the boot partition and not available for general use by any application.

Exalogic Elastic Cloud Application Stack

Figure 12-6 depicts the Exalogic Elastic Cloud application stack. Each of the Exalogic nodes has access to the full range of components in the Oracle stack, including applications, middleware, database, operating system, virtual machine, servers, and storage.

For the purpose of this discussion, only the key components of the EnterpriseOne application on the Exalogic Elastic Cloud application stack will be discussed.

Applications Applications associated with the Exalogic compute nodes that have a potential for installation include the following:

■ JD Edwards EnterpriseOne Logic and Batch Server

■ JAS Server, most notably WebLogic Server

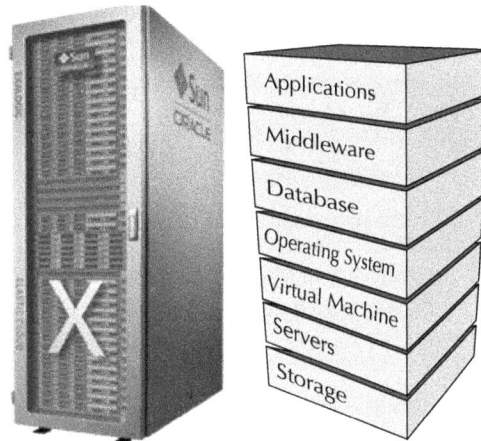

FIGURE 12-6. *Application stack on the Exalogic Elastic Cloud*

■ Web HTTP Server, commonly Oracle HTTP Server (OHS), replacing the WebLogic internal HTTP server for greater scalability, reliability, and performance

■ JD Edwards EnterpriseOne BSSV Server

■ JD Edwards EnterpriseOne BI Publisher Server

■ WebCenter and Portal

Middleware   This includes any of the additional components added to the JD Edwards EnterpriseOne architecture that are needed to support the EnterpriseOne application. These include the following:

■ Oracle HTTP Server (OHS)

■ Journaled File System (JFS) support software for WebLogic Server

Database   Oracle does not recommend installing an Oracle database on any of the Exalogic nodes for use in production. The engineered system design was intended for high performance applications.

Operating System   The Oracle engineered systems support the Oracle Linux operating system with the Linux unbreakable kernel version and Solaris operating systems.

Virtual Machines   Oracle supports its version of Oracle VM; coupled with EnterpriseOne, Oracle VM's use of templates provides a quick methodology of installing and deploying EnterpriseOne on the Exalogic Elastic Cloud. The Oracle VM template technologies also allow the creation of many more discrete servers in the EnterpriseOne architecture, and thus extend the possible configuration and uses of the Exalogic Elastic Cloud within an EnterpriseOne implementation.

Servers   The X2-2 release of Oracle Exadata and Exalogic contains two Intel Xeon processors with multiple cores. (Refer to the specific specifications for the number of cores that are available on the machines.) Servers use their internal SSDs, available on each individual node, for booting up and initiating the operating system. This technology on the blade servers for Exalogic makes it extremely easy to rebuild node configurations quickly.

The deployment server, a required Windows-based machine, is still needed in the EnterpriseOne architecture and is a separate server outside of the normal fabric-based infrastructure of the Exalogic Elastic Cloud. With the deployment server on an external network means communication will be slower, the deployment server cannot fully benefit from the InfiniBand network.

Storage   All disk subsystem storage is available through the fabric-based infrastructure, providing high-speed interconnection over InfiniBand. Although creation of the Automatic Storage Management (ASM) and partitions for installing EnterpriseOne software on Exadata is not part of this chapter, a discussion of some of the problems encountered with the storage arrays is provided.

NOTE
The purpose of this chapter is not to configure and install all of the components of the Exalogic Elastic Cloud. The Exalogic utilities that are available for configuration are described in detail on the Oracle web site and are summarized in the Oracle whitepaper, "Oracle Exalogic Elastic Cloud: System Overview."

Implementing Exadata and Exalogic for EnterpriseOne

Implementing the Exadata and Exalogic EnterpriseOne solution makes the most sense at certain opportunistic times during the development lifecycle.

For example, if a new customer is considering implementing the Oracle JD Edwards EnterpriseOne software for their business and they anticipate large amounts of users and batch loads, they require high availability, and they are interested in exploring the Oracle engineering solution, they should consider incorporating the Exadata Database Machine and Exalogic Elastic Cloud into their architecture.

During platform hardware upgrades/replacements, incorporating Exadata Database Machine and Exalogic Elastic Cloud into the architecture may make sense. IT infrastructure hardware improvements occur at a very rapid pace, approximately every 3 to 6 months. Trends in fabric-based technologies, virtualization, and other factors can contribute to a reevaluation of platform hardware.

Or suppose the business is growing rapidly and requires a change in the enterprise architecture because of the following:

- Additional software functionality is required.

- New software integrations have been added.

- More batch and interactive users are accessing the system.

- More departments in the company are using the software.

All of these factors can contribute to your reevaluating the initial design and implementation of the architecture to include Exadata and Exalogic.

EnterpriseOne Certified with Oracle Engineered Systems

At the Oracle OpenWorld conference in 2011, the JD Edwards EnterpriseOne ERP solution software announced certification on the Oracle Exadata Database Machine and Oracle Exalogic Elastic Cloud. The following illustration shows the certification of JD Edwards EnterpriseOne flows from the logic that the components of the engineered solution are certified.

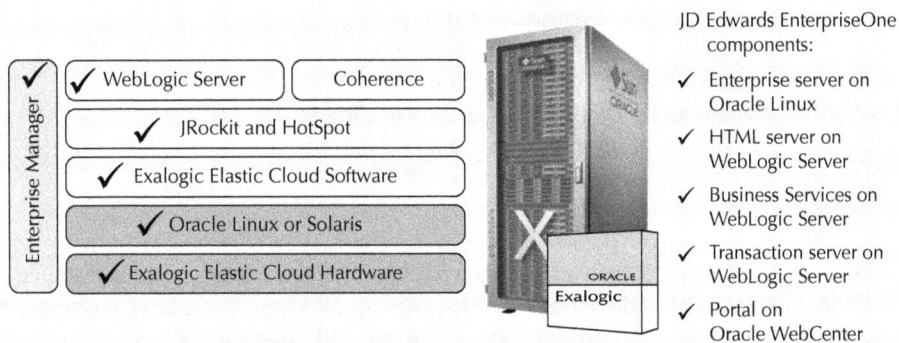

Implementing EnterpriseOne on Exalogic

Implementing EnterpriseOne on any hardware platform is a complex and cumbersome task. This section will discuss the various aspects of the Exa architecture as it relates to EnterpriseOne installation. The topics in this section will include

- EnterpriseOne on Exalogic Elastic Cloud

- Exalogic enhanced performance for WebLogic JAS Server

- Common user profiles and directories

- Size of disk storage for EnterpriseOne installations

EnterpriseOne on Exalogic Elastic Cloud

Each node server on the Exalogic Elastic Cloud has its own operating system, disk, and memory allocations from the fabric infrastructure. Each node can be configured for any of the components of the JD Edwards EnterpriseOne architecture, including these most common components. This is not an all-inclusive list.

- JD Edwards EnterpriseOne Logic Server

- JD Edwards EnterpriseOne Batch Server

- BI Publisher Server

- Primavera Server

- Java Application Server (WebLogic) and the web server (Oracle HTTP Server)

NOTE
The EnterpriseOne component of an Oracle Database Server can reside on one of the Exalogic nodes, but this is not a recommended configuration for a production level of support, because NAS storage is not an optimal storage solution for OLTP database implementations. Implementing the Oracle Database on another server or on the Oracle Exadata Database Machine is a more acceptable architecture configuration when performance is a major concern.

Exalogic ships with the operating systems for each of the Exalogic nodes installed or the ability to create VM nodes from the EnterpriseOne VM templates. For the purpose of the following discussion, the pristine Exalogic nodes with no software installed on them are covered in some detail. The implementation of JD Edwards EnterpriseOne on the

Exalogic nodes, configured with the Linux operating system, for the components of JD Edwards EnterpriseOne Logic, JD Edwards EnterpriseOne Batch Server, JAS and Web HTTP, is the same as the implementation on a standalone Linux server machine.

The installation of the JD Edwards EnterpriseOne software can proceed almost immediately after a basic setup of the engineered system. These additional steps are required:

1. Set up the operating system users, permissions, and directory structures for installation. This step is no different from that of a standalone JD Edwards EnterpriseOne installation process.

2. Configure additional disk space partitions and mount points. This is accomplished through the interface of the Exalogic storage appliance. The Exalogic Storage appliance provides an easy-to-use GUI interface allows IT staff to control disk resource allocation to any of the nodes in the Exalogic Elastic Cloud.

Figure 12-7 illustrates a three-Exalogic node configuration. Each of the Exalogic nodes is connected through the InfiniBand switch and each node has a specific EnterpriseOne server function. The first Exalogic node serves as the EnterpriseOne Logic Server. This is where the majority of the business logic for the EnterpriseOne application will be performed. The second and the third nodes are designated for the EnterpriseOne JAS Server and BSSV Server. EnterpriseOne JAS and BSSV Servers both require the WebLogic Server software to be installed to support those application functions. The remaining nodes in Figure 12-7 can be used for other components in the EnterpriseOne architecture.

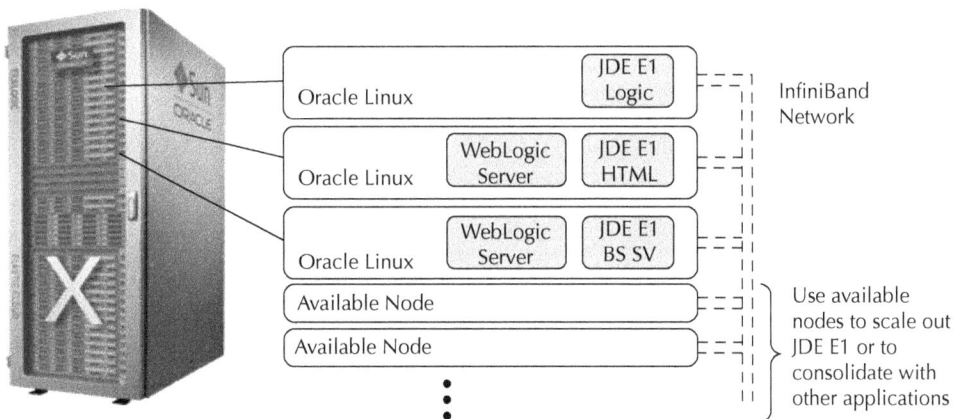

FIGURE 12-7. *EnterpriseOne on the Exadata Elastic Cloud*

Published results of JD Edwards EnterpriseOne testing on Exalogic have provided the following:

- EnterpriseOne can be implemented on Exalogic with no changes to the application. No specific patches, code fixes, or versions of EnterpriseOne need to be used on the Oracle engineered Exalogic system.

- No changes were necessary for the WebLogic 10.3.5 JAS Server, although an additional optimization and performance-enabled Exalogic feature is available for optimal performance configuration.

- Oracle HTTP Server was implemented instead of the internal Web HTTP Server for WebLogic Server–managed instances for greater scalability and reliability of performance.

- Modifications were made to the WebLogic data sources to take advantage of the 40Gbps InfiniBand high-speed network for all database activities made from the JAS Server and JD Edwards EnterpriseOne Logic and Batch Servers.

- Testing on Exalogic with EnterpriseOne was performed with the recommended EnterpriseOne Application 9.0 Update 2 and Tools 8.98.4.2. The Tools versions 8.98.4.5 and 9.1.2 were also tested on the Exalogic infrastructure.

- EnterpriseOne benchmark testing has showed scaling of concurrent interactive users of up to 16,000 on a quarter rack, and 8000 users were achieved on an eighth rack.

- The engineered systems provide excellent batch processing throughput.

- The engineered systems provide excellent concurrency of batch and interactive processing.

Exalogic Enhanced Performance for WebLogic JAS Server

Exalogic provides a more enhanced solution for applications. Exalogic optimizes Java and, more specifically, the WebLogic software. Starting with Oracle's WebLogic 10.3.5, the integrated solution of hardware also includes some performance enhancements specific to the Exalogic architecture. Figure 12-8 shows the Exalogic performance checkbox that must be enabled to utilize this enhanced feature. Without checking the box, the WebLogic Server will not use these enhanced features. The checkbox is located under the base domain general configuration tab. In this example, the base domain name is "base_domain."

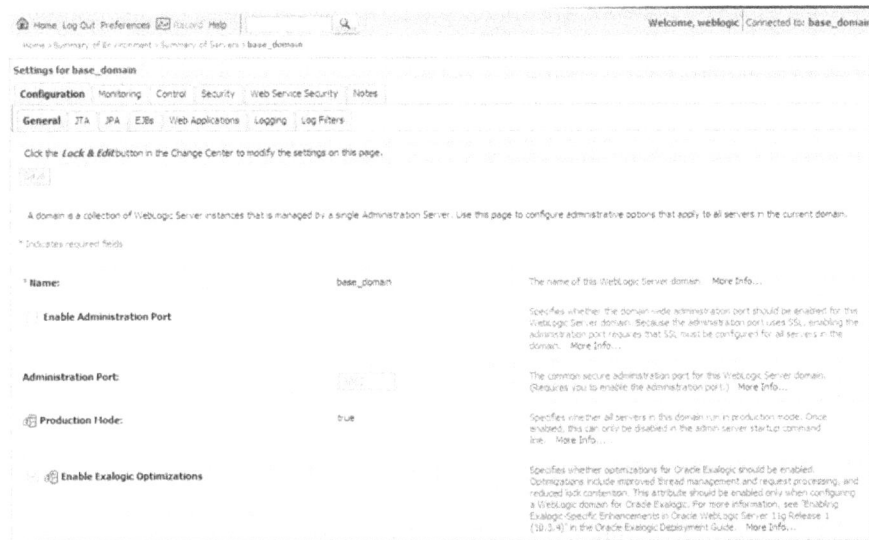

FIGURE 12-8. *WebLogic Server Exalogic performance checkbox*

Exalogic WebLogic Data Source Configuration   To take advantage of the InfiniBand network speed and more efficient SDP to replace Transmission Control Protocol (TCP) in its configuration, the WebLogic data source for communication must be modified and applied to all managed server instances supported by the Exalogic Elastic Cloud.

Refer to the guide for configuring the WebLogic JAS Server specifically for use on the Exalogic. The document "Oracle Fusion Middleware Exalogic Enterprise Deployment Guide EL X2-2 Part Number E18479-08" describes setting up a new GridLink data source and the required changes necessary for generating the correct JDBC URL for Exalogic X2-2 for use with JD Edwards EnterpriseOne.

Exalogic WebLogic Configuration Use Case   This section will describe the specific entries that were configured on an Exalogic X2-2 EnterpriseOne configuration. With the WebLogic data sources section and following the reference document above, the configuration was completed. The next set of points will help in the understanding of the configuration by defining the Exadata configuration parameters.

The Oracle database is on an Exadata Oracle Database Machine configured for RAC. The smallest implementation available is the Oracle database RAC 2-node configuration. The cluster node names used in the following example is `exa1-ib` and, the InfiniBand network name addresses are used so that the traffic will go across the higher speed network. The Oracle database RAC-configured SID port on which the database communicates is on the defined port 1522. The Oracle database configured RAC global instance name is EXADB.

Here is the initial automated JDBC URL that will be generated:

```
jdbc:oracle:thin:@(DESCRIPTION=(ADDRESS_LIST=(ADDRESS=(PROTOCOL=TCP)
(HOST=exa1-ib)(PORT=1522)) (CONNECT_DATA=(SERVICE_NAME=EXDB)))
```

Modifying this JDBC to use SDP and the InfiniBand network already specified by the host names of the Exadata Oracle RAC database would result in the following:

```
jdbc:oracle:thin:@(DESCRIPTION=(ADDRESS_LIST=(ADDRESS=(PROTOCOL=SDP)
(HOST=exa1-ib)(PORT=1522)) (CONNECT_DATA=(SERVICE_NAME=EXDB)))
```

To finish the configuration, the tnsnames.ora file will have to be modified in a similar fashion to specify using SDP instead of TCP and the InfiniBand network on the WebLogic Server through the JD Edwards EnterpriseOne Server Manager.

Oracle HTTP Server (OHS) Tuning Considerations   Oracle OHS is used in place of the internal HTTP server for WebLogic when clustering WebLogic-managed instances that require access to WebLogic-managed server instances through a single defined port or a more robust Web HTTP server for scalability. There is no specific Oracle Exalogic considerations for Oracle OHS; however, high load and user testing has prompted the use of OHS over the internal WebLogic HTTP server for its configurability and ease of use.

Installing the Oracle HTTP Server requires that the Developmental Web Tier Application Developer package be installed. It is downloadable from the Oracle Fusion Middleware web site. The Web Tier code is a required software package that should precede the installation of Oracle OHS. The Web Tier code, installed in the oracle_common directory of the WebLogic directory structure by default, will then need to be applied to the WebLogic domain by using the WebLogic QuickStart utility to extend the current WebLogic domain. By choosing the Oracle JRF (Java Required Files) module to be extended, the foundational code required by the Oracle OHS software is installed.

There are no configuration considerations with the httpd.conf Web HTTP configuration file with the default settings for nonproduction environments. Production environments should consider the following performance tuning values:

■ For Oracle OHS configuration, comment out the line in the httpd.conf file that logs access requests; you can experience a 5 to 10 percent performance improvement if access logging is removed:

```
# Access logs are set in logging.xml by default. If you want to
# use the CustomLog directive
# instead then uncomment the line below
### CustomLog "|${ORACLE_HOME}/ohs/bin/odl_rotatelogs ${ORACLE_
INSTANCE}/diagnostics/logs/${COMPONENT_TYPE}/${COMPONENT_NAME}/
access_log 43200" common
```

■ Set the MaxKeepAliveRequests to unlimited:

```
#
# MaxKeepAliveRequests: The maximum number of requests to allow
# during a persistent connection. Set to 0 to allow an unlimited
# amount.
# We recommend you leave this number high, for maximum
# performance.
#
MaxKeepAliveRequests 0
```

■ Set the Server-Pool ServerLimit:

```
##
## Server-Pool Size Regulation (MPM specific)
##
## Upper limit on the number of server(child) processes
# that can exist or be created. Overrides StartServers value if
# that value is
# greater then ServerLimit value.
ServerLimit 1024
```

■ Set the MaxClients and set the MaxRequestsPerChild to unlimited:

```
# prefork MPM
# StartServers: number of server processes to start
# MinSpareServers: minimum number of server processes which are
# kept spare
# MaxSpareServers: maximum number of server processes which are
# kept spare
# MaxClients: maximum number of server processes allowed to
# start
# MaxRequestsPerChild: maximum number of requests a server
# process serves
<IfModule mpm_prefork_module>
StartServers          5
MinSpareServers      25
MaxSpareServers     100
```

```
# Default MaxClients          150
MaxClients          8192
MaxRequestsPerChild  0

# worker MPM
# StartServers: initial number of server processes to start
# MaxClients: maximum number of simultaneous client connections
# MinSpareThreads: minimum number of worker threads which are
# kept spare
# MaxSpareThreads: maximum number of worker threads which are
# kept spare
# ThreadsPerChild: constant number of worker threads in each
# server process
# MaxRequestsPerChild: maximum number of requests a server
# process serves
<IfModule mpm_worker_module>
StartServers          2
### Default MaxClients          150
MaxClients          8192
```

Common User Profiles and Directories

Fabric-based computing and initial Exalogic directories allow the sharing and mounting of not only the disk subsystem across multiple nodes on the Exalogic Elastic Cloud, but the sharing of operating system users and operating system profiles.

This means that only a single operating system user is required to initiate the following:

- All JD Edwards EnterpriseOne startup processes such as RunOneWorld.sh for JD Edwards EnterpriseOne Logic and Batch server on the UNIX platform, providing service to the same environment and pathcode.

- WebLogic processes such as Node Manager and the managed server instances would all be controlled on that Exalogic node by the same operating system user ID, eliminating possible confusion by having multiple operating system user naming conventions on the different Exalogic nodes.

- Common installed binaries could be shared between nodes that support similar functions such as the EnterpriseOne Logic and Batch Servers.

- Common directories are extremely useful because they provide a central location on all of the Exalogic nodes for storing shared information, such as the following:

  - Software for installation

  - Location of log information

  - Shared third-party software necessary for EnterpriseOne functionality, such as Verity (search engine) and Vertex (Tax Software), that could be implemented only once and shared across all of the nodes on the Exalogic Elastic Cloud that utilize them.

- Information can be configured on each node to be isolated for that node or allowed to be mounted as a partition on other nodes for information sharing.

Implementing Common Users and Profiles   To implement common operating system users and profiles, some manual scripts would be handy in separating unique areas of the JD Edwards EnterpriseOne directory structure such as configuration file, log locations, and the setting of such variables as the $EVRHOME and $SYSTEM Linux variables.

The line in the operating system user startup profile for a common JD Edwards EnterpriseOne Batch and Logic Server is

.   `/u01/E1/jdedwards /e900/SharedScripts/enterpriseone.sh`

Within this file is the definition of the UNIX variables for JD Edwards EnterpriseOne. If two Exalogic nodes are implemented, two distinct startup files must exist:

.   `/u01/E1/jdedwards-node1 /e900/SharedScripts/enterpriseone.sh`
.   `/u01/E1/jdedwards-node2 /e900/SharedScripts/enterpriseone.sh`

When initiating, stopping, or managing a common operating system user, the appropriate node configuration file must be used.

Assume that the /u01/E1 is the common shared directory among all EnterpriseOne Logic and Batch Servers. Each node for EnterpriseOne has a separate directory below this specified by the jdedwards-node<X> stanza, where X is the number of the node in Exalogic providing specific EnterpriseOne Logic or Batch services. This line must be unique for each node instance of EnterpriseOne installed on the Exalogic Elastic Cloud in a shared storage configuration. The location of the individual node directory structures and configured startup files would be located in each respective directory.

Size of Disk Storage for EnterpriseOne Installations

There is a limitation in the size of a partition that can be configured on the Exalogic Storage Manager interface for use on Exalogic nodes supporting JD Edwards EnterpriseOne Logic or Batch processes. The partitions must be configured to be less than 1TB. The EnterpriseOne software installation is based on a 32-bit concept. Therefore, any partition larger than 1TB in size will exceed its detection of "available space." In fact, partitions larger than 1TB will be listed as having negative amounts of space. The installation of the EnterpriseOne Logic, Batch, or WebLogic software will not be allowed to continue.

Enhanced Linux Operating System Configurations for Exalogic

The following lines are added by the default Exalogic configuration utility and additional documentation instructions for the Oracle database nodes in the /etc/sysctl.conf file that are specific for Exalogic:

```
########## BEGIN DO NOT REMOVE Added by Oracle Exadata ##########
kernel.shmmni = 4096
kernel.sem = 250 32000 100 128
# Exadata correction for file-max and aio-max-nr
fs.file-max = 6815744
# DB install guide says the above
fs.aio-max-nr = 1048576
# Exadata correction
net.ipv4.neigh.bond0.locktime=0
net.ipv4.ip_local_port_range = 9000 65500
# DB install guide says the above
net.core.rmem_default = 4194304
net.core.wmem_default = 262144
net.core.rmem_max = 4194304
net.core.wmem_max = 2097152
# The original DB deployment was net.core.wmem_max = 1048586 but IB works
# best for Exadata at the above net.core settings
# Exadata correction remove vm.nr_hugepages = 2048
# Exadata correction system reboots after 60 sec on panic
kernel.panic=60
########## END DO NOT REMOVE Added by Oracle Exadata ##########
```

Implementing EnterpriseOne on an Exadata Database Machine

The software implementation of the EnterpriseOne Database Server on the Exadata Database machine is performed through the standard Oracle installation wizard for EnterpriseOne application code 9.0 and later.

Figure 12-9 illustrates a full implementation of EnterpriseOne on both the Exadata Database Machine and Exalogic Elastic Cloud. This illustrates a ¼ Exadata rack, 2-node configuration where the Oracle RAC configuration is supporting a ¼ Exalogic 8-node bare metal configuration. Within the ¼ Exalogic 8-nodes, there are two sets of EnterpriseOne configurations of EnterpriseOne Logic Servers—WebLogic Server and EnterpriseOne Batch Server configuration. In this example the sets of EnterpriseOne configurations were to support the production and development environments on their own hardware, sharing the ¼ Exadata database as the central repository for the EnterpriseOne data. A ¼ Exalogic rack configuration includes 8 nodes; in this example, these nodes are unused but could function as additional Web, EnterpriseOne Logic, or EnterpriseOne Batch servers.

The Exadata Oracle Database Machine is configured for RAC; disk storage is to be configured through Automatic Storage Management (ASM). Oracle database ASM, introduced in Oracle 10g, provides an alternative to the storage of data files, control, and log files on the operating system and the management of this resource through Oracle Enterprise Manager. Oracle ASM is required for use with Exadata and all Oracle database RAC–configured implementations.

For EnterpriseOne Oracle RAC database implementations, the EnterpriseOne database schemas can be created on the Exadata ASM before the EnterpriseOne database installation wizard (aka EnterpriseOne Platform Pack Installer) is initiated. The screen shown in Figure 12-10 is presented during the install.

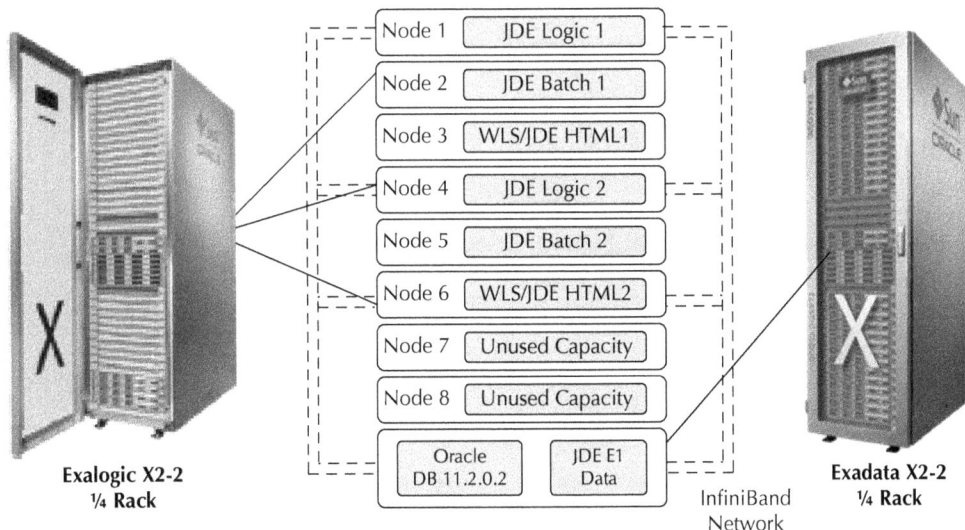

FIGURE 12-9. *JD Edwards EnterpriseOne on Oracle-engineered systems*

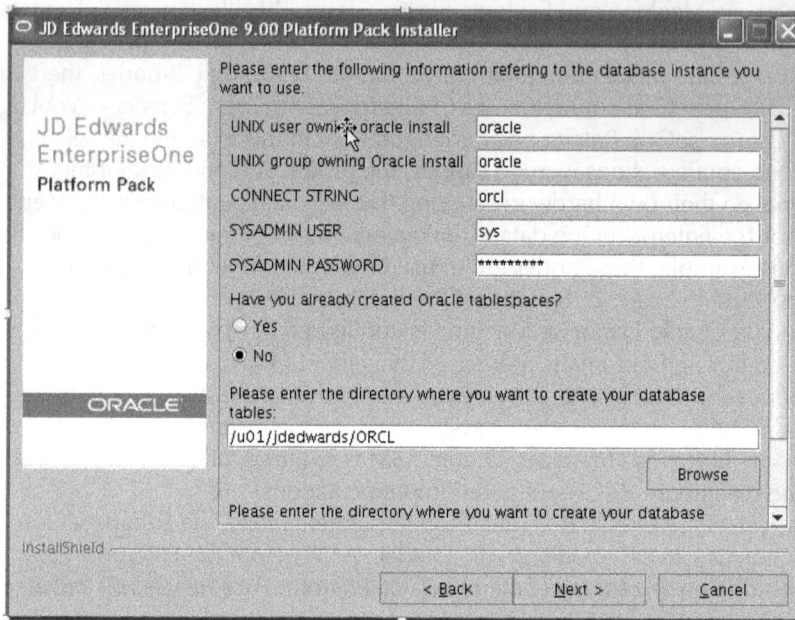

FIGURE 12-10. *JD Edwards EnterpriseOne installation on Exadata*

For the question, Have You Already Created Oracle Tablespaces?, select the No radio button. The EnterpriseOne database machine installer will then do the following:

- Install all the JD Edwards EnterpriseOne required dump files.

- Install the JD Edwards EnterpriseOne database installation scripts.

- Configure the JD Edwards EnterpriseOne configuration scripts ORCL_set.sh and InstallOracleDatabse.sh with the information specified through the installation wizard.

The following sections describe manually creating the JD Edwards EnterpriseOne schemas on ASM and manually running the JD Edwards EnterpriseOne database installation scripts.

Creating the EnterpriseOne Schemas on ASM

Creating the JD Enterprise JD Edwards EnterpriseOne database schemas required by the installation can be performed either through the Oracle Database Enterprise

Manager or by running a simple SQL script. All of the required schemas must be created before the EnterpriseOne Database installation may occur.

Example SQL request creation commands for the JD Edwards EnterpriseOne specific tablespaces are shown in the following code examples. The predefined ASM disk group on the Oracle Exadata Database Machine in this example is exadb.

First, define the base EnterpriseOne Schemas of System (SY900), Object Librarian (OL900), Data Dictionary (DD900), and Server Map (SVM900).

```
create smallfile tablespace "SY900T" datafile '+exadb(datafile)' size 2g
logging extent management local segment space management auto;
create smallfile tablespace "SY900I" datafile '+exadb(datafile)' size 2g
logging extent management local segment space management auto;

create smallfile tablespace "OL900T" datafile '+exadb(datafile)' size 2g
logging extent management local segment space management auto;
create smallfile tablespace "OL900I" datafile '+exadb(datafile)' size 2g
logging extent management local segment space management auto;

create smallfile tablespace "DD900T" datafile '+exadb(datafile)' size 3g
logging extent management local segment space management auto;
create smallfile tablespace "DD900I" datafile '+exadb(datafile)' size 2g
logging extent management local segment space management auto;

create smallfile tablespace "SVM900T" datafile '+exadb(datafile)' size 2g
logging extent management local segment space management auto;
create smallfile tablespace "SVM900I" datafile '+exadb(datafile)' size 2g
logging extent management local segment space management auto;
```

Define each of the environment database schemas. Only Development (DV900) and Pristine (PS900) environment schemas are shown here; other schema definitions can be added for Production, CRP, and Prototype.

```
create bigfile tablespace "DV900T" datafile '+exadb(datafile)' size 4g log-
ging extent management local segment space management auto;
create smallfile tablespace "DV900I" datafile '+exadb(datafile)' size 2g
logging extent management local segment space management auto;

create bigfile tablespace "TESTCTLT" datafile '+exadb(datafile)' size 4g
logging extent management local segment space management auto;
create bigfile tablespace "TESTCTLI" datafile '+exadb(datafile)' size 4g
logging extent management local segment space management auto;

create bigfile tablespace "TESTDTAT" datafile '+exadb(datafile)' size 700g
logging extent management local segment space management auto;
create bigfile tablespace "TESTDTAI" datafile '+exadb(datafile)' size 300g
logging extent management local segment space management auto;

create bigfile tablespace "PS900T" datafile '+exadb(datafile)' size 4g log-
ging extent management local segment space management auto;
```

```
create smallfile tablespace "PS900i" datafile '+exadb(datafile)' size 2g
logging extent management local segment space management auto;

create smallfile tablespace "PS900CTLT" datafile '+exadb(datafile)' size 3g
logging extent management local segment space management auto;
create smallfile tablespace "PS900CTLI" datafile '+exadb(datafile)' size 2g
logging extent management local segment space management auto;

create smallfile tablespace "PS900DTAT" datafile '+exadb(datafile)' size 3g
logging extent management local segment space management auto;
create smallfile tablespace "PS900DTAI" datafile '+exadb(datafile)' size 2g
logging extent management local segment space management auto;
```

Manually Initiating EnterpriseOne Database Creation Scripts

The first step before running the creation scripts manually is to inspect and correct any JD Edwards EnterpriseOne installation directory root path. In Figure 12-10, the directory that specifies where the database files will be installed is /u01/jdedwards/ ORCL. Because we selected the "No" radio button where it asks if we have created the Oracle tablespaces, this is the root location of the log files, Oracle DMP files for import, and manual configuration scripts for Oracle RAC.

Instructions in later Oracle JD Edwards Install and Upgrade Guides describe how to run the script manually in an Oracle RAC configuration on ASM:

1. Change the ORCL_set.sh script and set the RUN_MODE=INSTALL stanza.

2. Initiate the EnterpriseOne database creation manually with the now configured ASM and EnterpriseOne schema tablespaces by starting the InstallOracleDatabase shell script, passing it the option specifying the installation directory: /u01/app/oracle/jdedwards/e900/ORCL.

   ```
   ./InstallOracleDatabase.sh /u01/app/oracle/jdedwards/e900/ORCL
   ```

3. Verify that the installation of the EnterpriseOne database schema records was successful and properly populated the Oracle database by reviewing the logs of the manual initiation of the script located under the same base root installation directory.

Tuning Guidelines for Oracle Database for EnterpriseOne

Oracle database tuning for the Exadata Oracle Database Machine varies only slightly from that of tuning a normal Oracle database configured for RAC with regard to the EnterpriseOne application. EnterpriseOne tuning of the Oracle database is covered in Chapter 8.

You can find general information regarding configuring of specific Exadata features by reviewing the Oracle Exadata Database Machine web site: www.oracle.com/us/products/database/exadata/resources/index.html

The specific tuning for JD Edwards EnterpriseOne includes

- Using Oracle shared connections as discussed in the Oracle Database tuning section

- Query the database for additional tables that perform full table scans and might benefit from being manually pinned in the Exadata Smart Flash Cache

Exadata Smart Flash Cache for EnterpriseOne

The query in this section was used to determine whether the Oracle Database included tables that were performing full table scans, and whether they could benefit by manually pinning these EnterpriseOne tables onto the Exadata Smart Flash Cache for better performance.

In the following example, two tables are identified and pinned into memory; although performance impact was minimal, it proved to be a useful technique and powerful use of the Exadata Smart Flash Cache feature for an additional control to the Exadata Smart Flash Cache algorithm.

Here's the Oracle SQL query to determine high "buffer gets" and "full table scans":

```
Script: SQL script fulltablescan.sql
-- Full Table Scan SQL Query
set pagesize 999;
set lines 150;

-- Set spool file
spool full_table_scans.out

-- Set Output Format
column sql_text format a60 Heading 'Full Table Scans'
-- Use break on to make the output more readable
break on sql_text skip 1

-- Query the v$sqlarea and v$sql_plan for information
select sql_text,cpu_time,buffer_gets, fetches,executions ,disk_reads,sorts
from v$sqlarea
where (address, hash_value) in (select address, hash_value from v$sql_plan
where options  like '%FULL%') order by executions;
/
spool off
```

The resulting output file was inspected and the following SQL was identified:

```
SELECT T0.WBJPO,T0.WBUID,T0.WBOID,T0.WBLNGPREF,T0.WBJVER FROM DV900.
F989999 T0, DV900.F989998 T1  WHERE ((T1.WBJOBID = :1  AND T0.WBUID =
:2 )) AND (T0.WBOID = T1.WBOID)
```

The large number of disk reads, executions, and buffer gets indicate that these tables are excellent candidates for caching.

Manually Pinning Table into Smart Flash Cache Memory   The process of manually pinning tables into the Exadata Smart Flash Cache memory is a simple Oracle database SQL query:

```
alter table dv900.f989999 storage (cell_flash_cache keep);
alter table dv900.f989998 storage (cell_flash_cache keep);
```

Dedicated vs. Shared Connection for EnterpriseOne   The Oracle Database has increasingly been improved with regard to its database software technologies and connectivity. Although dedicated connections are the most beneficial from a performance standpoint, Oracle connectivity for database requests consumes a large portion of the memory on the EnterpriseOne Database Server. To mitigate this consumption and to control the size of the memory footprint on the EnterpriseOne Database Server, Oracle has been increasingly stressing the use of Oracle shared connections.

Dedicated and shared connections are configured by the tnsnames.ora configuration, and these configuration files are located on the Oracle Database Machine and all of the database clients that initiate database requests to the Oracle database server.

Specific testing on the Exalogic and Exadata machines with EnterpriseOne with shared connection configuration showed minimal impact to performance:

- Less than 5 percent increase in key EnterpriseOne performance metrics was found to be incurred with dedicated connections over shared connections on the Exadata Database Machine.

- Oracle dedicated connection metrics showed efficient and good performance of the threads used in EnterpriseOne connections from both the WebLogic and EnterpriseOne Batch and Logic Server database requests.

This small overhead comes at a small cost to the immense profitability of using dedicated connections in terms of operating system memory management and ability to scale the EnterpriseOne application to thousands of interactive users and large batch process loads.

In part, this could be attributed to the fast request-response turnaround of the Exalogic Database Machine, the quick transmission of large database packets on the InfiniBand network, or a combination of this and other variables inherent in the Oracle engineered solution. An example of tnsnames.ora entry is shown below. In this example, the SDP protocol is specified and the cluster Oracle RAC name is used to direct traffic to the Exadata Database Machine.

```
EXADB =
   (DESCRIPTION =
        (LOAD_BALANCE=off) /*Oracle recommends */
        (ADDRESS = (PROTOCOL = SDP)(HOST = exa1-ib)(PORT = 1522))
        (CONNECT_DATA =
        (SERVER = SHARED)
        (SERVICE_NAME = EXADB)
     )
   )
```

The LOAD_BALANCE stanza is included in the tnsnames.ora file to illustrate that Oracle recommends that the load balancer not be used. In an Oracle RAC configuration, this setting will result in a greater number of connection requests than is necessary. Note that the normal PROTOCOL of TCP has been changed to SDP.

Configuration of the Oracle database for RAC on Exadata regarding dedicated and shared connections is no different from that of a normal Oracle database RAC configuration, with the exception of some of the Exadata utilities used for configuring storage, disk groups for ASM assignment, and additional utilities for monitoring and management.

Exadata and Exalogic Performance Tuning for EnterpriseOne

Several concepts of interactive user and batch processes must be made clear to help you understand the benefits of integrating the Exadata Database Machine and Exalogic Elastic Cloud into an EnterpriseOne architecture implementation. In this section, the following topics are considered:

■ Interactive user processing profile

■ Batch processing profile

Interactive User Processing Profile

Interactive user processes are the online end users that access the EnterpriseOne application through the JAS Server URL. Interactive user processes' database requests can be initiated by the EnterpriseOne application through either the JAS Server or the EnterpriseOne Logic Server.

On an average, less than 7 percent of the processing of requests, in even the most intensive interactive applications, are spent in database activities. Therefore, implementing an Exadata Database Machine specifically for end user applications might not be a realistic business argument. Even if fulfilling database requests is instantaneous, only a 7 percent benefit is going to be experienced by the business for an interactive-only implementation of EnterpriseOne.

Integrating an Exadata Database Machine–only solution into the EnterpriseOne architecture is beneficial in the following areas.

Scaling of Concurrent Users　The Exadata Machine has excellent scalability properties when it comes to concurrent interactive users. As mentioned, only 7 percent of interactive users' time is spent in database requests; however, this statistic is from conditions in which end user concurrency is low (less than 500 users) and the user activity is spread across multiple EnterpriseOne modules.

The profile changes significantly when the following conditions occur:

- Large numbers of database requests occur on the same tables.

- Interactive user queries result in database requests that require more processing time due to full table scans, large database request result sets, and sorting of data for presentation in the EnterpriseOne grid.

Times of Day and High Spikes in Business Activities　The Exadata Database Machine provides excellent performance during peak times of day, interactive user activity, and spiking database activity because of increased business activities. The Exadata Database Machine implementation in an EnterpriseOne architecture provides a more scalable and consistent end user experience that was not subject to conditions of amount of concurrent users or spikes in the number of requests due to times of day or periods of high business activity.

Batch Processing Profile

An average of 25 to 30 percent of processing time is spent in database requests. A large performance benefit can be achieved in batch processing for many of the more frequently used batch processes. The most common high-percentage database request UBEs are shown in Table 12-1.

Figures 12-11 and 12-12 are from the Exadata performance characterization that was performed by the JD Edwards EnterpriseOne PSR development team (Oracle Support web site, Document ID 1188240.1).

Batch Process	Description	Comments
R07200	Payroll	Long running
R09801	General Ledger Post	Long running
R31410	Work Order Processing	Long running
R42800	Sales Order Update	Long running
R42520	Print Pick Slips	Long running and short running
R42565	Sales Order Invoicing	Long running
R43500	Purchase Order Print	Long running

TABLE 12-1. *High Database Batch Request Processes*

Exadata provided an increase of 33 percent in batch transaction rates, as shown in Figure 12-11. The comparison was between a standard Oracle and EnterpriseOne–configured Oracle VM environment and an environment built with only the Oracle Database Machine residing on the Exadata Database Machine.

Exadata also decreased the amount of time spent in database requests by 52 percent. These results were obtained in a similar fashion as the transaction rates, in which a lower user load of concurrent batch processes were profiled together to form an average UBE processing profile, as shown in Figure 12-12.

To the JD Edwards EnterpriseOne application, in cases of both interactive users and batch performance, Exadata can provide stability (a more consistent end user experience), scalability (increased load of concurrent users), and reliability (increased performance).

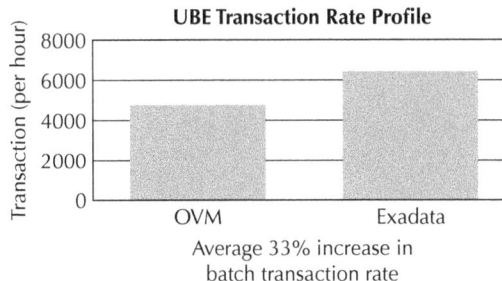

FIGURE 12-11. *UBE transaction rate profile*

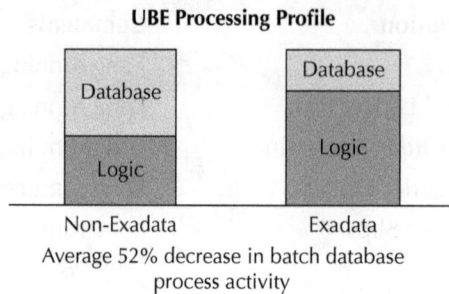

FIGURE 12-12. *UBE processing profile*

Summary

It is not an easy thing as a developer to admit that good engineering resulting in good performance makes for a good business argument. Exadata Database Machine and the Exalogic Elastic Cloud integrate hardware and software technologies together with EnterpriseOne and demonstrate what good scaling and performance can look like if many of the traditional limitations in IT technology are removed.

Testing on the Exadata and Exalogic machines has produced some of the fastest interactive user number and batch processing statistics to date. In short, the Exadata Database Machine and the Exalogic Elastic Cloud with EnterpriseOne is

- JD Edwards EnterpriseOne certified

- Found to be an excellent solution for scaling large amounts of interactive and batch users

- Easily implemented with minimal changes to current installation methodologies

CHAPTER
13

Load Balancing/Scalability Opportunities for EnterpriseOne

O racle JD Edwards EnterpriseOne supports a wide range of database and hardware platforms that can scale both horizontally and vertically. Scaling horizontally typically means you are dividing the users or processes across several discrete servers or logical machines. When scaling vertically, you tend to use one large machine within which the users and processes operate.

When you scale for larger workloads with either configuration, you typically use one or more load-balancing strategies (even if you don't realize it). A number of areas within EnterpriseOne utilize a variety of load-balancing methods. The EnterpriseOne kernel processes, for example, use a simple round-robin load-balancing method for many of the kernel types, such as the call object kernels when multiple processes are present. By adjusting the maximum number of processes for a particular kernel, you can spread the load across multiple processes to optimize the performance and scalability of that particular service/function.

We will examine various common load-balancing solutions in this chapter. In general, as your system availability, performance, and scalability requirements increase, the need for load balancing becomes more justified. No single requirement determines when it's best to use a load-balancing solution. Load balancers are used by some customers, for example, with only 30 users who want high availability and redundancy. Other customers with hundreds of users with large servers choose not to utilize load balancing for their web clients—the thinking being that if the machine goes down, all the services are unavailable anyway.

The following topics are covered in this chapter:

- Software solutions such as EnterpriseOne virtual servers, kernel processes, and cluster configurations

- Hardware/software network solutions such as content switches/network appliances

- Load-balancing examples of various components within an EnterpriseOne architecture

TIP
It is usually beneficial to consider a hardware network load balancer when you have more than 100 web users and you desire high availability in case of a system failure. The hardware devices typically offer the best performance and integrate into your network infrastructure well. Software network load balancers can also be considered, but you should test them extensively to ensure that they can handle the traffic levels you need to support. Test all the configurations described here thoroughly, because it seems each EnterpriseOne architecture has its own nuances that need to be discovered.

Load-balancing solutions are often influenced by the availability and throughput requirements of your business. Identifying and planning for these requirements will impact the cost, complexity, and versatility of the configuration.

Following are a couple of questions regarding your high availability and throughput requirements:

- What are your enterprise business requirements? Table 13-1 lists some examples.

- If your system experiences a large volume of batch activity or reporting, what is the desired time frame in which to complete those tasks? For example, a 3-hour batch window may require much more hardware/load balancing than a 9-hour window for the same workload.

Establishing requirements will help you do the following:

- Determine what solutions to implement

- Determine what priority to place on each solution

- Determine what level and amount of hardware/software you will need

- Determine what the costs will be to support and administer the configuration

Goal	Comment
5 days × 8–16 hours or 7 days × 24 hours operations availability	Typically online web, but can also include batch and/or interfaces
98%, 99.7%, 99.999% system uptime	High levels of system uptime generally require additional redundancy, complexity, IT expertise, features, and cost
50%, 75%, 100% capacity during failures	Affects response and throughput levels

TABLE 13-1. *Business Goals and Requirements*

Use Experienced Consultants and Test, Test, Test

The ideas and strategies presented here assume that strong network expertise is available to configure a hardware/software network load balancer in your EnterpriseOne system. Because this is an advanced tuning guide, the EnterpriseOne configuration examples such as adding a virtual server, Object Management Workbench (OMW) changes, and Object Configuration Manager (OCM) modifications require that you have or will contract an expert to perform those activities. Most of these activities have been performed by experienced EnterpriseOne Configurable Network Computing (CNC) consultants over the years and are considered field consulting engagements. Some organizations have very experienced CNC, network, and server infrastructure teams that implement these solutions.

Whatever experts you consult and elements you choose for your EnterpriseOne architecture, remember to *test, test,* and then have others *test* the configuration to ensure that it meets all your identified goals. Ensure that you fully test the architecture and the subtle interactions that are involved; this is one of the largest considerations to address when you implement your EnterpriseOne load-balanced configuration.

Some of the reasons for which you might consider a load-balancing solution are discussed in the following sections.

To create a structure for testing, maintenance, and package deployments   Your company needs high availability to avoid a single point of failure interrupting your business. A solution can occur at both a software and hardware level, such as separate servers and network paths. For the web, application, batch, business services, and on some databases, you can create a grid architecture that allows you to take down portions of your infrastructure gracefully for testing, maintenance, package deployments, and so on. The complexity and overhead is greater with this setup, but you have the ability to operate with very high levels of availability and scalability with minimal outages to the end users.

To determine capacity and scaling   Predictable scalability is usually required so that you can incrementally increase system capacity due to business requirements or workload changes. You can set your web servers to handle 100 to 200 users per server; this lets you pretty easily determine capacity and scaling for the presentation layer.

To change performance levels of your servers or business processes   Sometimes it is an advantage to break up the users or a batch workload into more manageable pieces so you can either reduce the overall time for a batch process or provide additional concurrent capabilities. The key to this, however, is that other areas of your infrastructure must be configured to handle the increased workload and concurrency. For example, the database server(s) may be sized to handle only a certain level of concurrent transactions. If you exceed those limits, the overall system response in those areas can suffer greatly without load balancing.

To split a long-running batch job into concurrent jobs   You'd like to split a long-running batch job (Universal Batch Engine, or UBE) into concurrent jobs to reduce the overall processing time. You can use a couple of different strategies for the majority of UBEs. Some UBEs, by the nature of their processing, cannot be split up, such as the R03B16A Statistics Refresh. (On Metalink, look for Doc ID 1301768.1, "List of UBEs that must be run through a single-threaded job queue in EnterpriseOne," for a good reference of batch jobs that you *cannot* run concurrently. This is a very small list compared to the thousands of UBEs provided in EnterpriseOne.)

To use virtualization to separate servers   The need or desire to use virtual host names can lead to virtualization—logically grouping computer resources separately from their physical definitions. This can be used to provide a very flexible and robust configuration when needed. We consider virtualization a component of load balancing, because you are adding a layer (the virtual host/server name) to separate the underlying physical servers. Using virtualization in a general sense can lead to the need for some type of load balancing, depending on your requirements—it may just be the virtual host/server name or virtualized operating systems.

Hardware- vs. Software-based Network Load Balancers

Although hardware-based solutions tend to be more often implemented at the EnterpriseOne customers we've visited over the years, both hardware and software network load balancers can be effective. To decide which is best for you, you'll need to weigh the various advantages and disadvantages for your company's configuration and the costs associated with that decision.

Hardware-based Network Load Balancing

Hardware-based network appliances such as the Cisco Application Control Engine (ACE), Citrix NetScaler, or F5 BIG-IP families can be considered and are in use by EnterpriseOne customers. These network appliances tend to be part of a large family of products with a wide range of capabilities. They offer a large feature set and a variety of flexible options. Hardware-based solutions are usually at the appliance level and offer full support from the vendor. This can be an advantage in setup and testing, when compared to going with software-based or open-source load balancers, which may require additional time and expertise to configure.

NOTE
Cisco in late 2012 appears to have ended development on the ACE so you may need to examine other vendor's options at some point in time.

Here are some examples of hardware load-balancing features:

- **HTTP compression**   Reduces the data packet size between the client and server. Server Manager in EnterpriseOne Tools 8.97 and later includes a setting for HTTP compression that can perform this from software if hardware compression is not available. Generally, you perform compression at one level only, so you do not "compress a compressed file."

- **SSL (Secure Sockets Layer) offloading/acceleration**   Significantly reduces the web server's HTTP processor demand for encryption and authentication requirements when HTTPS is used.

- **TCP offloading and buffering**   Consolidates HTTP 1.1 connections to the web server to gain efficiencies. Buffering can help offload slower web client connections to allow the web server to service other requests.

- **HTTP caching**   Allows the static content such as .jpg files to be cached so they are not retrieved as frequently from the server. Server Manager in EnterpriseOne Tools 8.97 and above includes a setting that allows certain static content to be cached on the local browser, which helps performance. Caching can also occur at the network appliance so it does not have to retrieve the file repeatedly from the HTTP server.

- **Firewalls**   Integrates a number of the appliances with firewalls.

Software-based Network Load Balancers

Software-based network load balancers can perform many if not all of the hardware-based functions listed in the preceding section. The key difference is that software-based network appliances are usually running under a host operating system such as Linux or Windows or they are a virtualized appliance. You may observe reduced throughput on software-based load balancers, but this greatly depends on the hardware configuration on which it is running.

In addition, with certain software-based network load-balancer solutions, you may not have as much vendor support as you would from a hardware-based appliance vendor. Open-source load balancers, which tend to be "build-and-support-it-yourself," may be a viable option for certain customers; however, most companies require full vendor support and documentation. Customers purchase the appliance type solutions since they tend to be turn-key to implement and support. Nevertheless, vendor-based software load balancers, such as the Citrix NetScaler, are available with full support from the company.

Software Solutions

NOTE
The software solutions discussed here involve users or workloads that are distributed to provide high availability, scalability, and/or performance. Another section in this chapter will discuss network load balancers.

You know that EnterpriseOne architectures can comprise various levels of complexity, depending on your business requirements. Production and quality assurance environments are typically the most complex environments in which to provide an architecture that fully supports the business requirements. These environments usually have load-balancing solutions in place, although load balancing can be a part of less complex environments in some configurations.

Ideally, at least two architectures exist in your configuration: production, where the real work takes place, and nonproduction, where you can evaluate, support, and test new software and other configurations. For example, you could implement a quality assurance architecture that has similar properties to the production architecture, but on a lesser scale, such as a smaller number of servers. Without creating a testing architecture, you severely limit your ability to ensure that any changes to the infrastructure, such as updated servers, operating systems, patch levels, or firmware, can be thoroughly tested before being introduced to production.

Web/HTTP Virtual Server Names

With EnterpriseOne virtual servers, multiple virtual names can exist at the web layer and potentially for EnterpriseOne Enterprise servers as well. From an EnterpriseOne presentation layer perspective, we can use a virtual name and/or virtual IP (VIP) that represents an EnterpriseOne web server; the VIP typically is a network address name that may or may not be the same as the virtual server name.

A VIP is typically defined within a network load balancer and is available to users via a domain name service (DNS). For example, multiple web servers may support your company workload. Usually, most companies do not want individual users to access the physical server name since it can be confusing and you run the risk of too many users accessing one server and possibly overloading it.

In Listing 13-1, you can see that if we use a VIP, we can define an alias type name, such as JDEPROD, that is easy for the users to relate to and remember. This alias is used by a network load balancer, which could be hardware or software; the load balancer then directs the user's session to one of the web or HTTP servers. You can even perform multiple load-balancing tiers by using a hardware network load balancer for the client-side web, and it routes the request to an HTTP server, such as the Oracle or IBM HTTP server, which directs requests to one of the JVMs within the HTTPd.conf file. The HTTPd.conf configuration file can contain named virtual hosts that it matches against the URL sent from the browser. Listing 13-1 shows an OAS virtual host definition example that uses the name jdeprod on port 80 and another listener on port 8080 across all IP addresses on the local server jdepdweb. This gives you a direct port of 8080 to the individual server, and port 80 is for the load balancer to use. (Later, in the section "Network Load Balancer Solutions," we will provide some examples regarding the presentation layer.)

Listing 13-1   *Oracle Application Server HTTPd.conf virtual host example*

```
Listen 80
#    PD instance listening on port 8080
NameVirtualHost *:8080
Listen 8080

<VirtualHost *:8080>
    ServerName jdepdweb
    Oc4jMount /jde PDOC4J
    Oc4jMount /jde/* PDOC4J
    Port 8080
    ServerAlias jdepdweb.company.com
</VirtualHost>

<VirtualHost *:80>
    ServerName jdeprod
    Oc4jMount /jde PDOC4J
    Oc4jMount /jde/* PDOC4J
    ServerAlias jdeprod.company.com

    Port 80
</VirtualHost>
```

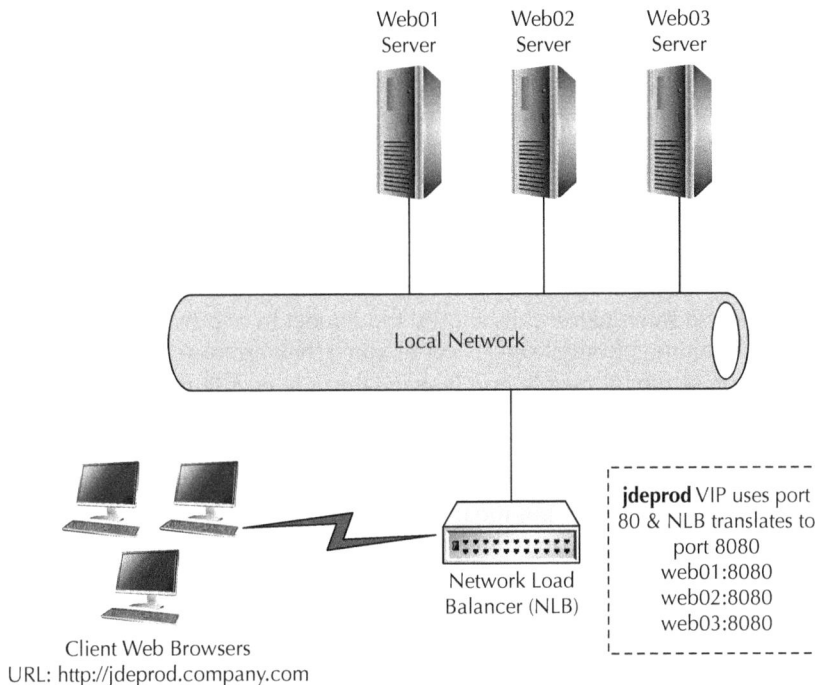

FIGURE 13-1. *Example VIP for web server*

Figure 13-1 shows an example of a VIP name that is used for multiple HTTP web servers, where the network load balancer has the VIP of jdeprod that a user types in the browser. The network load balancer then redirects the request to one of the web servers and maintains the web session to the server to ensure that the state information is retained. (This session persistence is required to prevent you from losing your HTML session to a particular server.)

TIP
Oracle WebLogic has an embedded HTTP server that can be used. However, if you plan to scale beyond 50 users, it is suggested that you consider a separate HTTP server to handle the requests. The Oracle HTTP server (OHS) would be the recommended software in this situation. You can adjust the httpd .conf file to handle the combined user workload for one or several application JVMs that you define for a certain virtual host.

Most customers are familiar with network load balancers for this type of activity using the web servers. It allows the system to scale, provide high availability when multiple servers are present, and take various servers in and out of service for the VIP. The VIP using a network load balancer gives you a lot of flexibility to manage the operation of your web presentation tier.

EnterpriseOne Virtual Server Names

EnterpriseOne virtual server names are usually created by customers and/or field consultants to provide a generic network name for the database, logic, and/or batch servers. Because a network load balancer or an /etc/host file override can reference this virtual name, the same name can be used to connect to one or more physical servers. You maintain the physical server names since they are needed to provide a unique network presence to operate and manage that server. The virtual name defined in EnterpriseOne is *generally* used from the network reference perspective and would normally *not* be used for Configurable Network Computing (CNC) tasks such as a package build or deployment. This is because a generic virtual server does not reference a particular server, but the physical name does. So in the case of the package build or deployment, you would not know on which server the package was going to be placed. Having an inconsistent package deployment occur would not be a good situation because the users tend to notice unexpected behaviors like this. Figure 13-2 shows an example of both web server VIP jdeprod and an EnterpriseOne Enterprise server virtual name of VAPPPD being network load-balanced to three physical servers, JDE01 through JDE03.

There is, however, an exception to this architecture for the latest EnterpriseOne 9.1.x Tools release. If you decide to implement the time zone support that is referenced in Metalink (Doc ID 1379886.1, "Time Zone Support for Oracle JD Edwards EnterpriseOne"), that particular configuration utilizes a special architecture of virtual servers with dedicated copies of foundation and path codes. This is a more complex extension of the virtual server implementation for active/active load balancing. In fact, an appendix in the Metalink document references how to implement the time zone support within the active/active configurations by using an additional virtual server name for deployments. Basically, you use a virtual name for the time zone support and load balancing, and because multiple virtual servers exist on *one* physical server, you need an additional virtual name for each time zone defined to allow you to deploy packages. Time zone configurations are not part of our advanced tuning discussions, but a large number of the elements we discuss are utilized in this type of configuration, depending on the architecture you implement. The Metalink document can provide you with some ideas of how to utilize virtual server names.

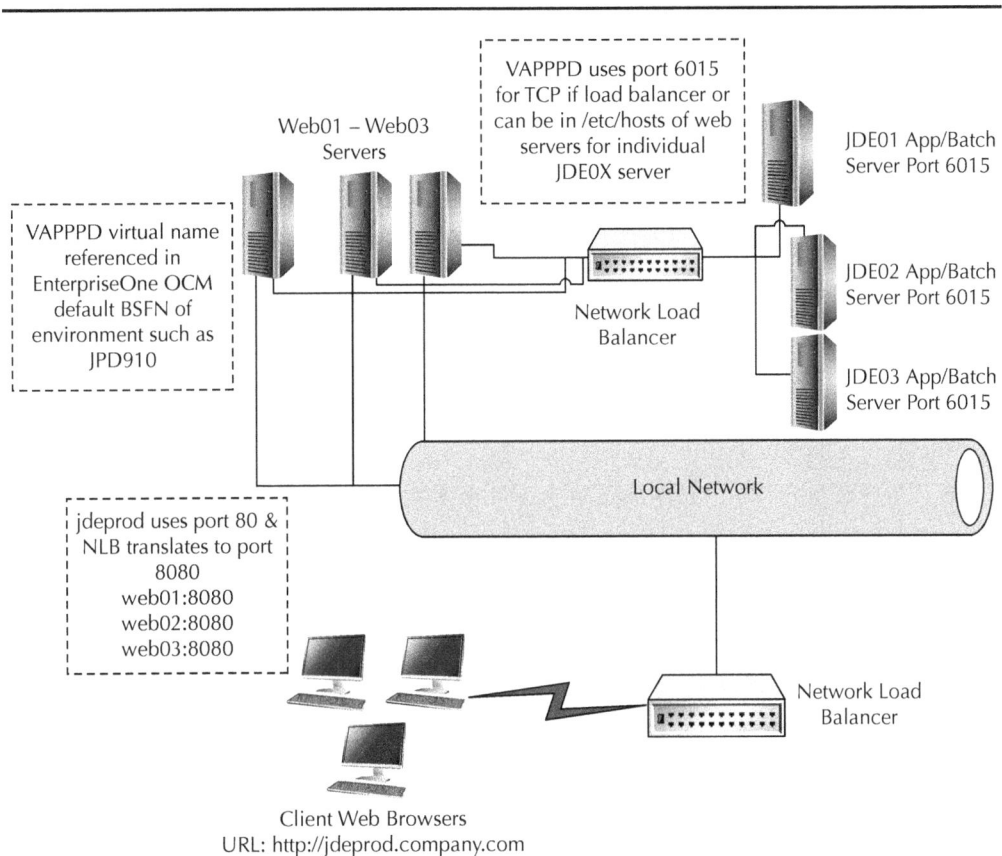

FIGURE 13-2. *Example virtual server name*

Active/Passive Cluster Virtual Name

A JDE.INI setting that is used for active/passive EnterpriseOne Enterprise servers in a cluster configuration is the `PrimaryNode` setting listed in Listing 13-2. Basically, this is used to bind the JDENet processes to the operating system cluster network package IP name. Typically, two physical servers would use a shared disk that can be mounted at one time to one of the servers. This type of configuration can be used in System i, Unix/Linux, and Windows architectures, where you can tolerate a short outage if a server fails, but you want to prevent an outage of hours or days to wait for parts to be replaced. Operating system clusters are tested, certified, and supported by Oracle with a number of installation documents available. The "EnterpriseOne Server and Workstation Administration Guides" offer several OS cluster examples for review.

Listing 13-2   *JDE.INI PrimaryNode example*

```
[CLUSTER]
PrimaryNode=JDECLUSTER
```

We generally see OS cluster configurations used for EnterpriseOne and/or database servers since the presentation layer typically is load balanced, and it is *very* rare to see it in an active/passive cluster configuration. To see the EnterpriseOne perspective, you can read the Metalink document "Minimum Technical Requirements (MTR) for EnterpriseOne Clusters (Doc ID 705395.1)."

The following list of OS cluster software is supported for EnterpriseOne servers; you can also review the Oracle Metalink minimum technical requirements (MTR) for database servers or Certifications section for this information.

- MC/ServiceGuard from HP for HP/UX

- IBM PowerHA (formerly HACMP) for IBM AIX

- High Availability Cluster from SUN Microsystems for Solaris

- IBM System i solutions:

    - iCluster from Data Mirror

    - MIMIX Cluster Server from Lakeview Technology

    - Vision Suite from Vision Solutions

- Microsoft Cluster Service for Windows

- Red Hat Cluster Manager from Red Hat Enterprise Linux or Oracle Enterprise Linux

- Clusterware from Oracle Enterprise Linux

Most EnterpriseOne database configurations use one or more of the following three options:

- Single database server, which is usually nonproduction

- OS cluster database, which is usually QA and production architectures

- Oracle Real Application Clusters (RAC) for Oracle databases

Production systems that require high availability will generally use option 2 or 3, depending on the database software in use. Planned maintenance windows for system outages and package deployments usually occur during the outage windows. All the EnterpriseOne databases can use option 1 or 2. The Oracle database from an

EnterpriseOne perspective can span all three options, where the use of RAC and Transparent Application Failover (TAF), when properly implemented, can minimize database outages even more.

Starting with EnterpriseOne Tools release 8.98.3.x, the ability to failover actively on an Oracle RAC database can allow active SQL SELECT's to move to another database node if a failure using TAF occurs. (Oracle Metalink document "JD Edwards EnterpriseOne Oracle 11g Database Real Application Cluster" [Doc ID 1277362.1] provides good information regarding how EnterpriseOne operates when Oracle RAC and TAF are implemented.) If you need an architecture in which a database node failure will automatically move the EnterpriseOne database sessions over to another node, consider this option.

Maximum available architectures (MAAs) include disaster recovery scenarios and are usually very complex configurations that require a large amount of time, discipline, planning, and testing to configure and implement. All database vendors have suggested strategies of how to implement disaster recovery and MAAs: IBM System i utilizes the cluster replication technologies, Microsoft has transaction log/data mirror strategies, and Oracle databases generally use Data Guard as the tools for a standby/DR site.

Other options can include hardware storage area network (SAN) solutions that replicate various databases and files instead of software solutions. A number of documents on disaster recovery configuration and one example on Metalink from an EnterpriseOne perspective is "JD Edwards EnterpriseOne Oracle 11gR2 Database Data Guard with RAC" (Doc ID 1315368.1).

NOTE
Each customer's business requirements and IT infrastructure have many demands they must meet, so no "one size fits all" strategy is available. Most customers use consulting expertise from the vendors or third-party firms to assist in planning, designing, and implementing these types of configurations, and this is strongly encouraged if your business has these requirements.

Getting back to the EnterpriseOne side of cluster solutions, a *cluster stanza* tells the JD Edwards processes whether the enterprise server is within an OS cluster; this setting is in the enterprise server's JDE.INI. The PrimaryNode setting shown in Listing 13-2 causes EnterpriseOne services to answer on the network and gethostname calls to use the cluster name specified instead of the physical server node on which the services are running.

Let's assume, for example, that you have two OS clustered nodes of JDESRV1 and JDESRV2. Without the PrimaryNode statement in use, the EnterpriseOne services will perform a `gethostname` lookup and use the short name of the physical server on which it is running, such as JDESRV2. Enabling the `PrimaryNode` statement causes the UBEs executed to use the cluster name (JDECLUSTER) when they record the execution host in the server map tables F986110/F986114 instead of the physical host name.

Assume that the services are running on JDESRV1, so the JDENet processes bind to the name JDESRV1. However, if you implement the `PrimaryNode=JDECLUSTER` statement when the services are brought up, it will respond as `JDECLUSTER` on the network and the `gethostname` lookup for EnterpriseOne processes will return `JDECLUSTER`. This means that in areas that use the server name, such as server package builds or UBE jobs, the EnterpriseOne processes will see JDECLUSTER instead of JDESRV1 or JDESRV2.

The main caveat with OS clusters is that you define a "package" of services such as the network, EnterpriseOne, and possibly the database. On at least two nodes, the defined service runs on only one of the nodes at a time and can fail-over to another node if a portion of the active server fails for some reason. It takes seconds to minutes for a failover to occur, depending on the cluster package defined, so the users may observe an outage or need to resubmit a transaction or batch job. Again, if you do not have high availability criteria that require active/active architectures, this can be a very viable option that is more robust than a single server that may fail.

Figures 13-3 and 13-4 show some examples of an active/passive cluster and how a failover might look when a node becomes unavailable.

Referring to the figures, if a network or hardware failure occurs on JDESRV1, the cluster package would move over to JDESRV2, depending on how you configure failure scenarios. Some customers use a hot-standby server that has few processes running, while others prefer a "mutual takeover configuration," in which the

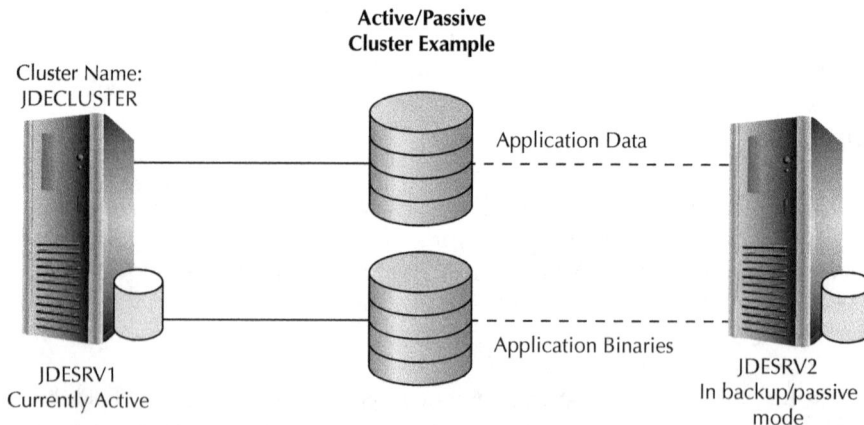

FIGURE 13-3. *Active/passive cluster example*

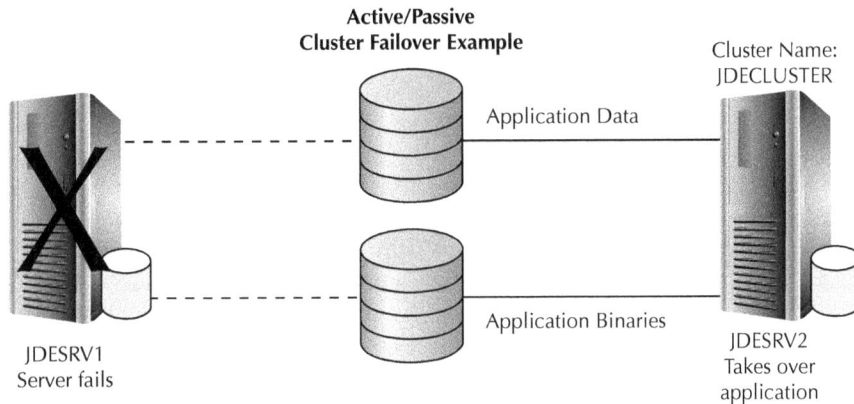

FIGURE 13-4. *Cluster failover example from one node to another node*

database is on one node and the enterprise services are on the other node. With either of these configurations you must ensure that you do not oversubscribe the capacity of the server. For the mutual takeover, ensure that you don't exceed 40–45 percent of the capacity when both nodes are running to guarantee during a failure that you can run both packages on one server. If you do oversubscribe, you run a very high risk of reduced response times unless you mitigate/control the workloads.

Active/passive clusters have been used for decades and offer a viable and cost-effective method of providing high availability, as long as the business requirements allow for relatively short outages when a failover occurs. Active/passive clusters are used by enterprises of various sizes today. Active/active clusters, such as the load balancing and Oracle RAC database configuration, can provide even higher availability and shorter outage timeframes if that is needed.

Taking the EnterpriseOne PrimaryNode Configuration a Little Too Far

Some customers have attempted to use the `PrimaryNode` statement in active/active configurations, which in our opinion is beyond what it was designed for in the EnterpriseOne Tools releases. The assumption of this statement is that you have only *one* active node running on the network with the cluster name defined. If you place this on multiple Enterprise servers to get the cluster name to match your virtual server name, you could have issues with batch submission data selections. Remember that the cluster name becomes the network name to which the JDENet processes bind, so if multiple servers use that name, intermittent "confusion" can result when a user submits a batch version and it creates the runtime cache and UBE override folders.

(continued)

We have observed a customer that used this strategy, and during higher volumes, the users' data selection would disappear and run wide open. Once the `PrimaryNode` statement was commented out in their active/active Enterprise servers, the user-submitted batch data selections were rock solid again.

In Tools 9.1.x, a new feature for time zone support was added, which in combination you use `listenOnSpecificIP=1` and `PrimaryNode` on the Enterprise Server JDE.INI. The key point, however, is that this configuration assumes there is *one* unique time zone virtual host defined for each foundation, and you don't duplicate the name in multiple JDE.INI files. We've also seen consultants share the path code's runtimeCache and UBEOverrides folder across servers, which appear to work, but as we stated about testing, you need to review this type of configuration, because you may experience unexpected results. With multiple EnterpriseOne foundations reading/writing to the same files, the usual IPC sharing mechanism is not in action, so be aware that it may work, but you could experience intermittent issues.

The following example shows `listenOnSpecificIP` and `PrimaryNode` statements in JDE.INI:

```
[JDENET]
; Intended for time zone virtual hosting to bind jdenet to
specific IP address virtual name
; jdenet normally binds to ALL physical/virtual IP addresses on
the local machine
listenOnSpecificIP=1


[Cluster]
; Time zone virtual host name instead of a cluster name
PrimaryNode=JDETZN5N
```

Active/Active Virtual Name Web Solution Examples

A good Metalink document, "E1: PKG: Questions about Package Management in a Cluster Configuration (Clustered Server Configurations)" (Doc ID 1325593.1), helps explain the field consulting implementation for an active/active web configuration. In addition, the Oracle Metalink red paper (ID 1325593.1) called JDE_Package_ Deploy_24_7.PDF shows an example for earlier table access management (TAM) file-based specs of EnterpriseOne 8.11 SP1 and below along with another set of examples using EnterpriseOne 8.12 and above, which use XML Metadata specification tables.

An enhancement under Bug 10970611 that development implemented provides the ability for active/active configurations within EnterpriseOne to continue operating, similar to what occurred in prior releases. It became available in Tools 8.97.1.x, with the [Package Build] stanza in Listing 13-3 added to the JAS server JAS.INI. By default

PackageDomainServer and PackageDomainPort are disabled so that the package discovery will utilize the OCM default business function (BSFN) logic server mapping for the JAS server when the package "auto discovery" feature reads from the system F96511 machine table. This tells the JAS server where the logic is running and what XML package it should use to generate its serialized objects to the associated F989998/F989999 tables.

If the auto discovery feature was not available and in OCM you mapped your default BSFN to a virtual server name such as Virtual Enterprise Server (VENT), and because packages are built against physical server names, a package would not exist for the VENT server and the auto discovery feature would not find the XML package specs it should use. Some customers use a manual SQL statement to add/update the VENT server to the SY900.F96511 table for every package; however, doing this prevents you from using the active/active load-balancing architecture since *all* JAS servers would be using the same XML package when the table was updated. If this was done during higher workload periods, you could interrupt the web users with a new package midstream during the day.

To utilize the active/active solution fully, you'd need to configure two areas on JAS servers:

- The PackageDomainServer and PackageDomainPort to point the auto discovery to a physical Enterprise server to retrieve XML package specs.

- A JDBJ.INI spec data source override for separate F989998/F989999 tables so that serialized objects from different package builds do not mix inappropriately. We have an example of those statements in Listing 13-4 below. Usually you don't override the spec data source, but for active/active configurations it can be an advantage to do so for flexibility and stability.

Listing 13-3 *[Package Build] stanza example: JAS.INI or JDEINTEROP.INI*

```
[PACKAGE BUILD]
PackageDomainServer=physicalentserver
PackageDomainPort=entjdenetport
; Default settings below
;PackageDomainServer=DEFAULT
;PackageDomainPort=0
```

Listing 13-4 *[Package Build] stanza example: JDBJ.INI*

```
[JDBj-SPEC DATA SOURCE]
...
name=JASSO-SVRA1
database=
server=JDEDB
physicalDatabase=JASSOSVRA1
```

NOTE
The [Package Build] stanza was recently added to the Server Manager list in tools 8.98.4.x and above for HTML/JAS servers. It is not yet listed for BSSV, Data Access Descriptor (DAD), or Transaction/ RTE servers from the Server Manager configuration screens, but you can add it manually. For JAS, Transaction/RTE, and DAD servers that have a JAS.INI, you can manually add the statements there. For BSSV, which uses jdeinterop.ini instead of the JAS.INI, you can place the stanza in that file. Similar strategies apply for all these services from the package auto discovery process perspective. The parameters are getting into Server Manager, but depending on what tools release you use, they may not be obvious.

To help you see all the elements we described above, Figure 13-5 provides you an example of the active/active load-balanced configuration. We have three sets of servers using a virtual name of VPDAPP for the enterprise servers. The web browsers are using a network load balancer access the web servers via the VIP name of jdeprod. To provide independent package deployments we also have three sets of serialized objects tables, SerObj_01 through SerObj_03. Using the network load balancer to direct the web sessions we can take any set of servers offline for maintenance or package deployments, and insert them back when desired.

EnterpriseOne JDE Kernel Process Load Balancing

We've covered the JDE kernel processes in depth; however, we would be remiss if we did not mention the load balancing that occurs when having multiple kernel processes for a specific kernel type.

EnterpriseOne Enterprise Services uses a basic round-robin type of load balancing that may not be obvious at first. From earlier discussions about the various JDE kernels such as the call objects, you know that you can scale an individual server by allocating additional kernel processes. (Just make sure you have sufficient processor and memory available for the increased resource usage.) The services a particular EnterpriseOne server is providing will influence the kernels that are running on that server. Here are some examples:

- An enterprise server would have a variety of kernels running, such as security, call object, metadata, UBE, workflow, and so on.

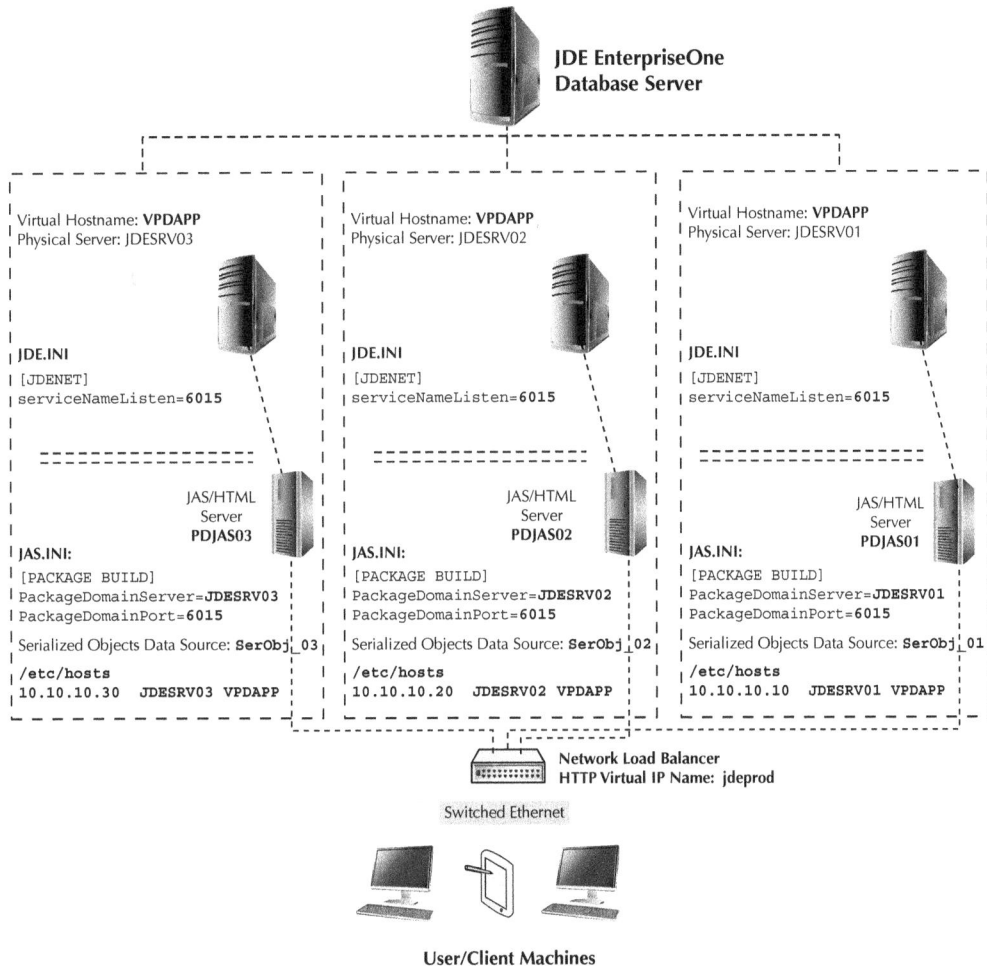

FIGURE 13-5. *Example virtual name server configuration for E812 and above*

- Application/logic servers might have mainly security and call object kernels running, since it would most likely have little batch present.

- Batch or integration type servers might have fewer security and call object kernels and more UBE kernels since most of the processes are batch in nature. An additional Metadata kernel in this scenario might handle the increased XML specification translations to cached files and user-submitted versions.

Round-robin load balancing behaves a little differently, depending on the kernel type in use. A call object kernel, for example, will start a new kernel for each new user request until the `maxNumberOfProcesses` is reached under the `[JDENET_KERNEL_DEF6]` stanza of the JDE.INI. So if you have 50 `maxNumberofProcesses` defined and the `numberOfAutoStartProcesses=10`, it would use the first 10 kernels, and as each new user logs in, another call object kernel would start until 50 were started. You would observe more users being added to the call objects started. What you would *not* observe, for example, is 100 users running on just the 10 call objects you autostarted—which would be 10 users per call object kernel. Instead, you should see 2 users per call object kernel since you have 100 users/50 call object kernels running.

From a tuning perspective, this is one reason we like to autostart *all* the call object kernels to minimize the startup delay for the kernel being attached to the user. Some good Metalink documents, such as "E1: KER: Explanation of JDE.INI Kernel, IPC Settings and JDENET" (Doc ID 656040.1) and "Information Center: Kernels in the JD Edwards EnterpriseOne Tools and Technology Product" (Doc ID 1322388.1), can provide additional background information and tuning suggestions for your consideration.

Generally, the following kernels are the only ones you need to autostart *if* you are using them. (Meaning: Do *not* start a kernel unless you are actually using it to minimize memory and resources in use.)

- **Scheduler kernel** Only one per foundation allowed if using the EnterpriseOne scheduler.

- **Call object kernels** Mainly autostarted for performance reasons

- **Management kernel** Use by Server Manager for runtime metrics

- **Metadata kernel** Needed to convert XML specs for other kernels

- **Security kernel** Optional for performance if you have large numbers of users log in concurrently, such as in the morning

Other kernels, however, are not allocated automatically on each request with respect to the `MaxNumberofProcesses`, such as the security, UBE, workflow, and SAW kernels. The JDENET_N (or jdesnet.exe for Windows) master network process routes the user request to the matching kernel type. Using the message identifier the JDESNET/JDENET_N will decide which kernel will handle the message, and if the kernel is busy or not available, it will start a new process automatically up to the `MaxNumberofProcesses` limit for that particular kernel definition. You may have the `MaxNumberofProcesses` limit for security set at 5, but if only two or three security kernels are running, that may handle your peak loads and the remaining two are never started. This is the key to ensuring that you match the number of processes for a certain kernel to the workload being presented. If you do not size correctly in Server Manager, you may observe a large number of outstanding requests, which can indicate a bottleneck or that you do not have enough kernel processes for the workload. One nice feature in Server Manager for the Enterprise servers is the Kernel Ranges page that allows you to increase the maximum processes for a certain kernel. You cannot decrease them once they are allocated, but it can help when monitoring and tuning a workload on the server.

In earlier chapters, we provided a number of suggested guidelines for specific kernel processes regarding how to size them for your configuration. The settings vary greatly based on the business processes and operating requirements of the EnterpriseOne system you are using. The need for performance and scaling load testing is critical to identify and remove potential bottlenecks in your configuration. If you don't perform some type of load testing, you will almost certainly observe issues when you get to production-level workloads, unless the production system has been well established. Without load testing, it can be challenging at best to ensure that all the various EnterpriseOne configuration settings are working well together for your particular environment.

Network Load Balancer Solutions

As stated, both hardware and software network load balancers are available for EnterpriseOne and other services in your network. The hardware-based network load balancers such as the F5 BIG-IP, Cisco ACE, and Citrix NetScaler are popular and used by EnterpriseOne customers. In addition, specific network WAN optimization devices such as those from Riverbed Technology may aid the traffic utilization. On the software side for network load balancers, a large number of options are also available. Citrix NetScaler offers a software-based product, and several open-source network load balancers such as Zen Load Balancer by Zeus Technology and Linux Virtual Server (LVS) are just a few of the choices available. Even when using a network load balancer, you will most likely use some software load-balancing capabilities, which are available in the various application server products for vertical clustering, such as IBM WebSphere Application Server Network Deployment and Oracle WebLogic Enterprise Edition when clusters are used, and Oracle Application Server.

NOTE
We won't recommend a network load balancer because each customer configuration requirements and budgets are different. For most EnterpriseOne customer installations, from a consulting perspective, the hardware-based products far outnumber the software solutions. There is no right or wrong solution, but we recommend that during the evaluation process, you thoroughly test and vet each solution to ensure that it meets your business/IT requirements.

From the tuning perspective, you should consider several major areas when implementing a network load balancer within your EnterpriseOne configuration. The network load balancer can be used in one or several layers of your infrastructure, depending on the level of availability that you need. As mentioned, we recommend that you involve in-house network expertise or a contractor who is well versed on the network load-balancing solution that you implement. Extensive testing is usually needed to tweak and tune the behavior of the various servers' interactions. You'll also likely need network, server, and Configurable Network Computing (CNC) team members working together to ensure that the expected workloads and planned/unplanned situations are tested.

Network Hardware and Software Load Balancer Considerations

Because there are many different network load-balancing solutions available, we'll focus on the main considerations they should address to provide a solution for EnterpriseOne. These suggestions are not the only method that can be used, but they are procedures that the majority of configurations have in common. By using these features, you can help ensure that you have the network load balancer working in a way that suits your requirements.

We typically discuss the following topics with the network team and architects.

Has the network load balancer been configured with a redundant network appliance? If you have only one network load balancer appliance and it fails, your business/applications could halt since there is no method to direct the client or server requests appropriately. Most customers implement two load balancers, which splits the load between the two appliances so they back each other up. This is similar to the mutual takeover cluster concept we discussed earlier. You can place some VIPs on one load balancer and other distinct VIPs on the second unit. If one fails, the sessions are moved or redirected to the other appliance.

Some customers ask whether session replication should occur, which increases the resource and network overhead. But how often does a load balancer fail, and if you needed only a minute or two to switch to the backup, is that worth the overhead and complexity? Most of these devices are very reliable and the mean time between failures is measured in years. Most customers that implement redundant network appliances generally do not enable session replication, since it is usually a very limited outage window for a rare event. The key point is that if you desire full high availability, it requires redundant components to prevent a single point of failure.

What protocol type for the virtual IP (VIP) is needed? If the VIP is web browser clients, it typically uses HTTP or HTTPS. If the VIP is for a web server going to an enterprise server, the communication is via JDENet and uses TCP. The behavior and configuration of these protocols are different depending on how the client machine interacts with the destination server.

Is session persistence needed for the VIP in use? Web clients using HTTP/HTTPS typically need to maintain a persistent session to the same web server for EnterpriseOne. (Otherwise, users would observe an application timeout message since they would be directed to a different web server each time they posted a new web page.) You can use several methods to maintain persistence. Most of the time, a session cookie on the client web browser is used to direct to a particular web server. Work with your load balancer network engineer/consultant to determine what they recommend given your particular environment.

An enterprise server uses TCP for JDENet, and for the majority of sessions, such as call object kernels, you *must* maintain persistence since the processes use cache for the users' session. If the VIP is used only for batch UBE submissions, you can test with or without persistence in place. Usually, using persistence or "sticky IP" is the preferred method and it reduces lost connection messages in the JDENet logs. Also note that a TCP session is one source IP to a destination server, so *all* the connections from that source will go to one destination server. Some people generalize how HTTP connections operate—these are web clients with different IP addresses that can balance pretty evenly to several servers.

A web server that uses a VIP to an enterprise server will *not* have JDENet connections to all the enterprise servers, because it is *one* source IP going to a destination server. You can observe this behavior from the network perspective by using a `netstat -a` command or via Server Manager by examining an HTML instance for JDENet Stats to see the connections. Ensure that each web server directs its requests to a different enterprise server if multiple servers are in use. This can be done using /etc/host overrides and/or creating multiple load balancer VIPs with different preferred/primary servers in each service list. Using this strategy helps you balance the load more consistently, since other methods may not direct the requests as you intend.

What type of load-balancing algorithm will be used? Most of the network load balancers have many options to choose from. Generally, round-robin or least connections are the prevalent choices that customers use for EnterpriseOne configurations. Note that load balanced connections may not always be perfectly balanced, especially if you have lower volumes of users. This sometimes confuses customers when they see more users accessing one server than the others when a round-robin algorithm is used. We have observed that using least connections for web HTTP and round-robin for TCP sessions tends to work well. Your configuration and mileage may vary, however.

Other Questions In addition to the preceding questions, ask these as well:

- How will you monitor the destination server defined for the VIP to ensure that it directs traffic only when the node is active and running properly?

■ What should the timeout be (generally 30–300 seconds) if a probe does not respond to take the node out of the VIP service?

Tables 13-2 and 13-3 provide some example network load balancer probe monitors and methods to consider using. The web server monitor probes in Table 13-2 are slight different than the monitor probes for enterprise servers in Table 13-3 due to the services involved.

The monitoring probes are very useful to automate various failure conditions and alert the network/operations teams. It does require some time to test and evaluate the best set of probes/monitors for your particular configuration.

Monitor	Method	Comments
Web server address Servers jdepdweb1, jdepdweb2	ICMP	Ensure that server OS is responding. If not, server should be taken out of load balance.
HTTP probe	HTTP://jdepdweb1:8080/jde/ HTTP://jdepdweb2:8080/jde/	Should receive an HTTP 200 response (301/302 responses are acceptable as well). Need to monitor port (8080) on server; if port is unavailable, the server should be removed from load balance until the port responds again.
Enterprise services probe Servers jdeent1, jdeent2	TCP port 6015	Ensures that the application services are running. If no response, the server should be removed from load balance. Optional probe, but if enterprise server is down, web clients will not operate.

TABLE 13-2. *Web HTTP VIP Example Probes*

Monitor	Method	Comments
Enterprise server address Servers jdeent1, jdeent2	ICMP	Ensure that server OS is responding. If not, server should be taken out of load balance.
Enterprise services probe Servers jdeent1, jdeent2	TCP port 6015	Ensures the EnterpriseOne services are running. If no response, the server should be removed from load balance.

TABLE 13-3.   *Enterprise Server VIP Example Probes*

An Enterprise Server Setting That Can Help Network Load Balancers

If you are creating a VIP that uses TCP connections, you may find it balances the connections better if you enable a setting in the enterprise server JDE.INI called enablePredefinedPorts=1 under the [JDENET] stanza. This setting is normally used to allow the EnterpriseOne ports to be defined within a range so they can pass through a firewall. The default JDENet connections negotiate a port automatically, which you can observe using netstat –a or Server Manager JDENet stats, or even the netwm command.

Suppose, for example, that the enterprise server is listening on port 6015 and the web server negotiates a JDENet connection. The web server will start the connection to port 6015 and the return port may be something like 42198 (sometimes labeled a foreign port). If you set enablePredefinedPorts=1 on the receiving enterprise server, you would see the ports on 6015 or within a range such as 6015–6024 if you have ten JDENet processes defined. It uses the parameters under the [JDENET] section of serviceNameListen=6015 and maxNetProcesses=10 to define the range of ports. So 6015 + 10 maxNetProcesses defines the range 6015–6024 (hence the label predefined ports). The point here is that a load balancer can behave similarly to a firewall in that it may perform Network Address Translation (NAT) or port remapping. Using the predefined ports option gives you better control of the JDENet ports in use. You may not have to consider using this feature, but it helps some load-balancing algorithms operate more consistently.

Examples of Load Balancing an EnterpriseOne Configuration

In this chapter, we've attempted to provide the framework and options you may want to consider for a load-balanced EnterpriseOne configuration. Now we'll provide several typical examples of what you will be evaluating. The examples are by no means all the combinations that you can put together, but they do represent some of the more common architectures that EnterpriseOne customers are using. Once you determine your availability goals, it can help lead you to the architecture that is needed to support your objectives.

The examples here are from a number of different customer configurations that we have worked with over the years. The involvement of your network, server, and infrastructure teams can assist you in making sure the solution works within the framework of your company. There is definitely no "one-size-fits-all" architecture, and you may find the configuration changes as the business requirements evolve over time.

If your company decides to outsource and use a hosting service or operate using software as a service (SaaS, or cloud computing), these examples can still be applicable to you. Be sure that you understand and can provide the requirements to the hosting/cloud vendor; this is extremely important. The vendor is most likely performing the actual tasks and work to support you, but it helps to be aware of what the vendor will be implementing if you are managing the requirements/operations. Generally, what occurs with outsourcing is that you reduce your IT staff levels, but you must still maintain knowledgeable people within your organization who manage, coordinate, and review the day-to-day operations.

Strategic planning is also beneficial to ensure that the business concerns and metrics are well documented and voiced to the vendor/partner—you need to have some fundamental understandings of the various elements of operation and maintenance. Knowing and defining what you can maintain and where you need professional assistance allows you to leverage your time and resources appropriately. There is usually a balance that may change over time based on your business needs.

However you choose to implement your EnterpriseOne architecture, you should understand the options available to you. Every customer has different needs and resources available to meet their requirements. You may start out with less complex load-balanced configurations and grow into them as the business changes. The business may have very high availability and maximum available architecture (MAA) needs that dictate implementing a large number of the suggestions in this book. Whatever your architecture may become, try to utilize the best people, skills, and resources available whenever possible. Typically, the hardware/software architecture of an EnterpriseOne configuration is a relatively small percentage of the overall project cost, so it pays to invest in your infrastructure to be as reliable and solid as possible.

HTML/JAS: Presentation Layer

The presentation layer where your HTTP server and HTML/JAS server operate is the most common area where we see load-balancing occur, because we want to optimize availability, capacity, performance, and scalability for users. Since the release of EnterpriseOne 8.11, the only supported client is the HTML web browser running on a JAS server. In prior releases with the Windows client, we would predominately see a Citrix/Terminal server solution in place, which has software load balancing in use.

TIP

If you have one or more of the following criteria, a Citrix/Terminal server solution may have merit: older or undersized desktop machines (such as Windows XP or Linux); a data center in one region of the world and users located across the globe where high latency is present; satellite network links to certain locations; the need to manage/maintain the web browser from a server instead of the desktop.

Running Internet Explorer (IE) or another supported web browser using Citrix/ Terminal server is a viable option. This can add cost/complexity to the configuration, but it can provide cost savings if you run older desktop machines and improve manageability. The desktop browsers may not perform as well running the IE browser with the various software combinations that user desktops tend to have and network latency in certain regions of the world. Anti-virus scanning can also contribute to HTTP browser response concerns that you would not usually observe with a Citrix/Terminal server solution.

We sometimes remind customers that you cannot break the laws of physics such as the speed of light. If you have network packets going across a satellite link, you have a minimum round-trip time that can easily be 500 milliseconds or longer where most terrestrial latency is 50–250 ms, which is 2 to 10 times faster. Basically, this means that if you needed 10 network turns for an HTML page, with satellite it could take 5 seconds to render; with 100 ms latency it would be 1 second.

Remember that your presentation layer does not have to be an all-or-nothing strategy. You can have some locations or users on the Citrix/Terminal server and others that meet the technical requirements using a supported web browser. Evaluate and test your particular configuration to ensure that it meets the business goals and response. The HTTP web browser works very well in the majority of situations with the proper desktop configuration in place, but not all user desktops or networks are optimal in certain businesses.

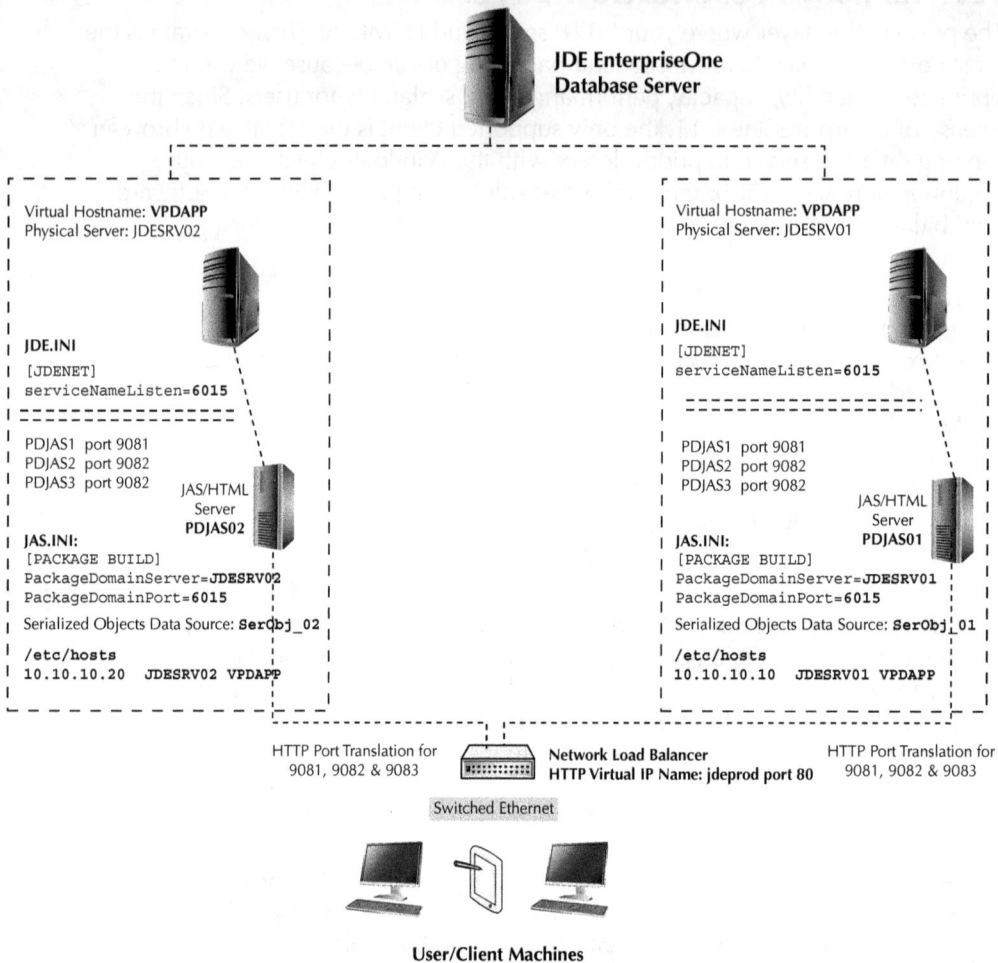

FIGURE 13-6. *Network load-balanced web configuration*

Figure 13-6 shows a network load-balanced configuration of web servers. The network load balancer VIP such as jdeprod is published to the client machines. It then directs the web session to an available server and creates session persistence to ensure that the data and cache for that user is consistent. Since each user typically has a different IP address, the load balancing works well. This may behave a bit differently if you are using Citrix/Terminal server, since there is usually just a single IP address for that server, but using multiple servers helps balance the load. The benefit of this type of configuration is that all the service availability is controlled via the network load balancer. So if you design the web servers into groups, you can bring up/down a silo/group of servers at a time for maintenance/deployment. The Metalink document (ID 1325593.1) JDE_Package_Deploy_24_7.PDF dealing with 24/7 package deployment mentioned earlier in the chapter offers details on splitting out the virtual enterprise server using the package domain setting, JAS serialized objects, and different full packages.

Another commonly used configuration is software balancing via Oracle WebLogic cluster, OAS clustering (as of EnterpriseOne Tools 9.1 no longer supported), and WebSphere Application Server Network Deployment (WebSphere ND). Using application server clustering has the advantage of letting you make the JAS configuration changes in Server Manager in one place, and then propagating it to all the instances/nodes defined in that cluster. Server Manager started supporting WebSphere and WebLogic clusters in Tools 8.98.3.x. This type of configuration can work well, but in some situations a network load balancer may still be a choice.

We have occasionally found that in some customer configurations, the WebSphere ND or WLS cluster is running on several servers, but only one HTTP server is processing the requests that are directed to the application servers. This essentially can become a single point of failure. If you add two or more HTTP servers to spread the load, you then need some type of network load balancer sitting in front to provide the VIP. Again, HTTP servers are very reliable, similar to network load balancers, but machines and software do fail on occasion. This is a point to consider for your architecture if your requirements do not allow for a single point of failure. Figure 13-7 shows a WebSphere ND/WLS cluster example.

Another point when using WebSphere ND and WLS clusters is that vertical nodes in the cluster work well for JAS logs, but once you go across to horizontal servers/nodes, you may have challenges viewing the JAS logs from Server Manager. This means you would have to go to that particular server and view the log files there. Oracle has said that this concern will be addressed in an EnterpriseOne Tools release and may be in place by the time this book is published, but you should investigate based on your Tools release level.

Application Logic

The enterprise server, if being used for security and call object logic, can be load balanced for several web servers. If you decide to go this direction, the TCP sessions using JDENet must be persistent or using "sticky IP" to ensure that the cache and session data are maintained. If you don't ensure that persistence is used, the web applications will fail since the business function requests could be routed to several enterprise/logic servers instead of the one initially used. If you fail to make the sessions persistent, it won't take long to recognize that there is a problem.

You may also want to consider using a common set of server map tables to reduce your maintenance from the CNC perspective. By default, when a server plan is created, you may get a different set of server map tables if you do not ensure that

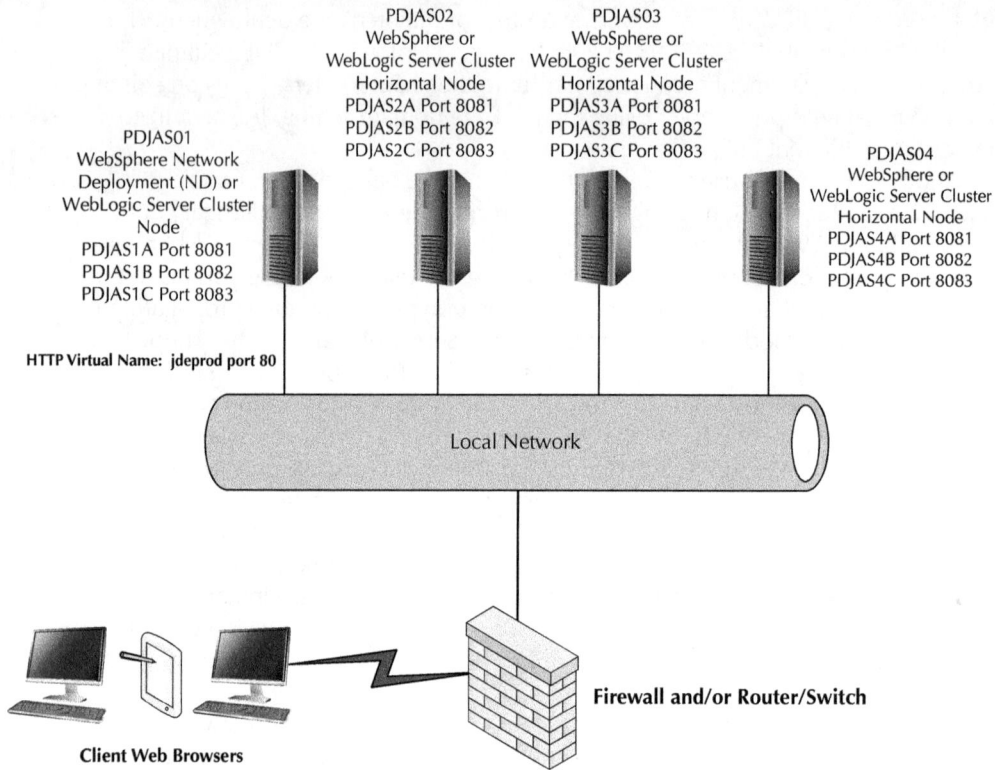

FIGURE 13-7. *WebSphere ND/WLS cluster example*

the data source is pointing to a common schema or library such as SVM900. The advantage of a common server map is that all data source and OCM maintenance occurs for the servers using that set of tables. If you have separate sets of tables, you will have to maintain each set, which can be more error prone. The only caveat is that each set of server map tables assumes a specific platform such as Linux or Windows. You can't mix and match different platforms within the same set of server map tables since there are machine-specific settings in the EnterpriseOne data source definitions.

The example configuration shown in Figure 13-8 is similar to the 24/7 package deployment document configuration, with groups/silos of logic servers and a predefined set of web servers pointing to a particular application/logic server. This lets you take a group down, recycle the server, and deploy a new package. You can then make the servers available again and repeat the cycle for the other group(s) for the maintenance event.

**JDE EnterpriseOne
Database Server**

Virtual Hostname: **VPDAPP**
Physical Server: JDESRV 03

JDE.INI
[JDENET]
serviceNameListen=**6015**

PDJAS1 port 9081
PDJAS2 port 9082
PDJAS3 port 9082
                        JAS/HTML
                        Server
JAS.INI: **PDJAS03**
[PACKAGE BUILD]
PackageDomainServer=**JDESRV03**
PackageDomainPort=**6015**

Serialized Objects Data Source: **SerObj_03**

/etc/hosts
10.10.10.30 JDESRV03 VPDAPP

Virtual Hostname: **VPDAPP**
Physical Server: JDESRV02

JDE.INI
[JDENET]
serviceNameListen=**6015**

PDJAS1 port 9081
PDJAS2 port 9082
PDJAS3 port 9082
                        JAS/HTML
                        Server
JAS.INI: **PDJAS02**
[PACKAGE BUILD]
PackageDomainServer=**JDESRV02**
PackageDomainPort=**6015**

Serialized Objects Data Source: **SerObj_02**

/etc/hosts
10.10.10.20 JDESRV02 VPDAPP

Virtual Hostname: **VPDAPP**
Physical Server: JDESRV01

JDE.INI
[JDENET]
serviceNameListen=**6015**

PDJAS1 port 9081
PDJAS2 port 9082
PDJAS3 port 9082
                        JAS/HTML
                        Server
                        PDJAS01
JAS.INI:
[PACKAGE BUILD]
PackageDomainServer=**JDESRV01**
PackageDomainPort=**6015**

Serialized Objects Data Source: **SerObj_01**

/etc/hosts
10.10.10.10 JDESRV01 VPDAPP

HTTP port translation for
9081, 9082 & 9083   **Network Load Balancer**   HTTP port translation for
                          HTTP Virtual IP Name: jdeprod port 80   9081, 9082 & 9083

Switched Ethernet

User/Client Machines

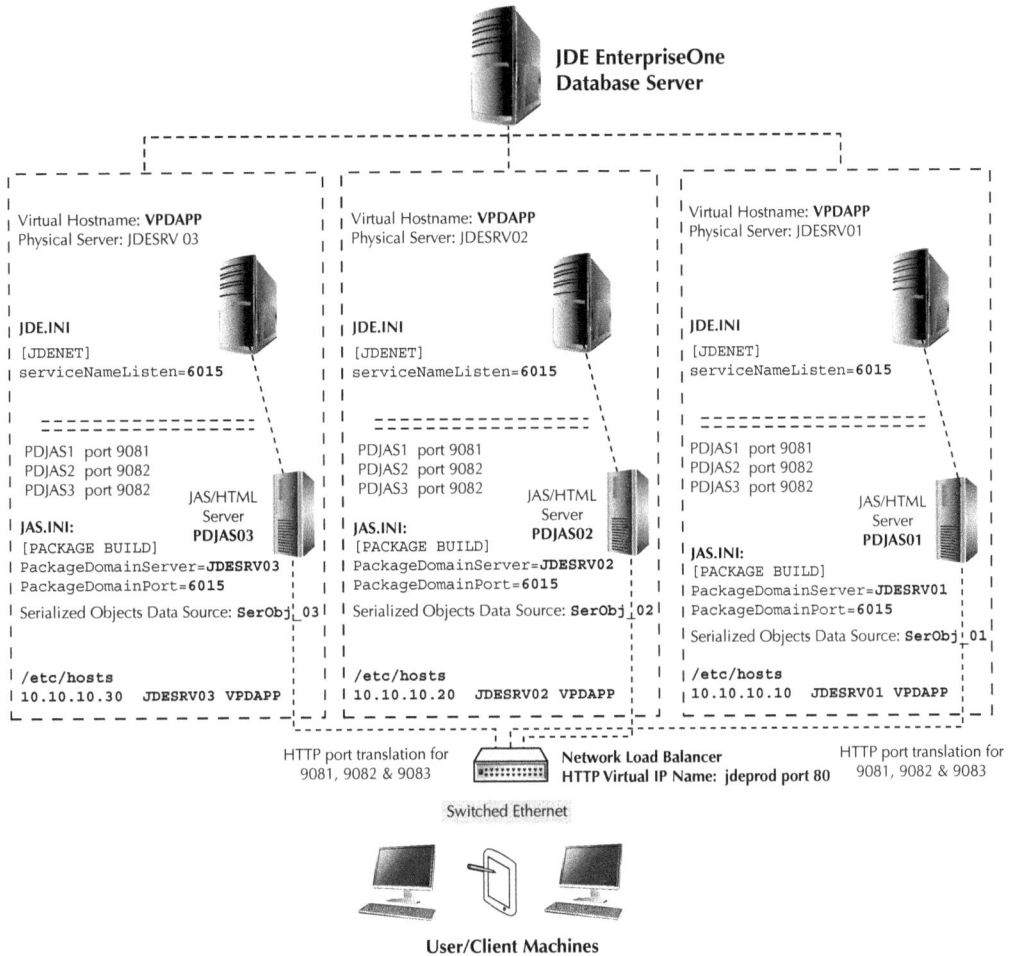

FIGURE 13-8. *Load-balanced application server example*

The example shown in Figure 13-9 is a bit different: it doesn't use a VIP for the application server, but uses the web/app server combination instead. You load balance the web requests, but the application server is on the same physical machine using a /etc/host override for the EnterpriseOne logic server virtual name of that server. You have an implied load-balanced application server since it is part of the web server that is being load balanced. This effectively works similar to older architectures when Citrix/Terminal server Windows machines were used and the logic ran on the same server. With the advent of 64-bit Linux and Windows servers, you can easily scale these servers between 50 to 300 users per server, depending on how many you want to group together.

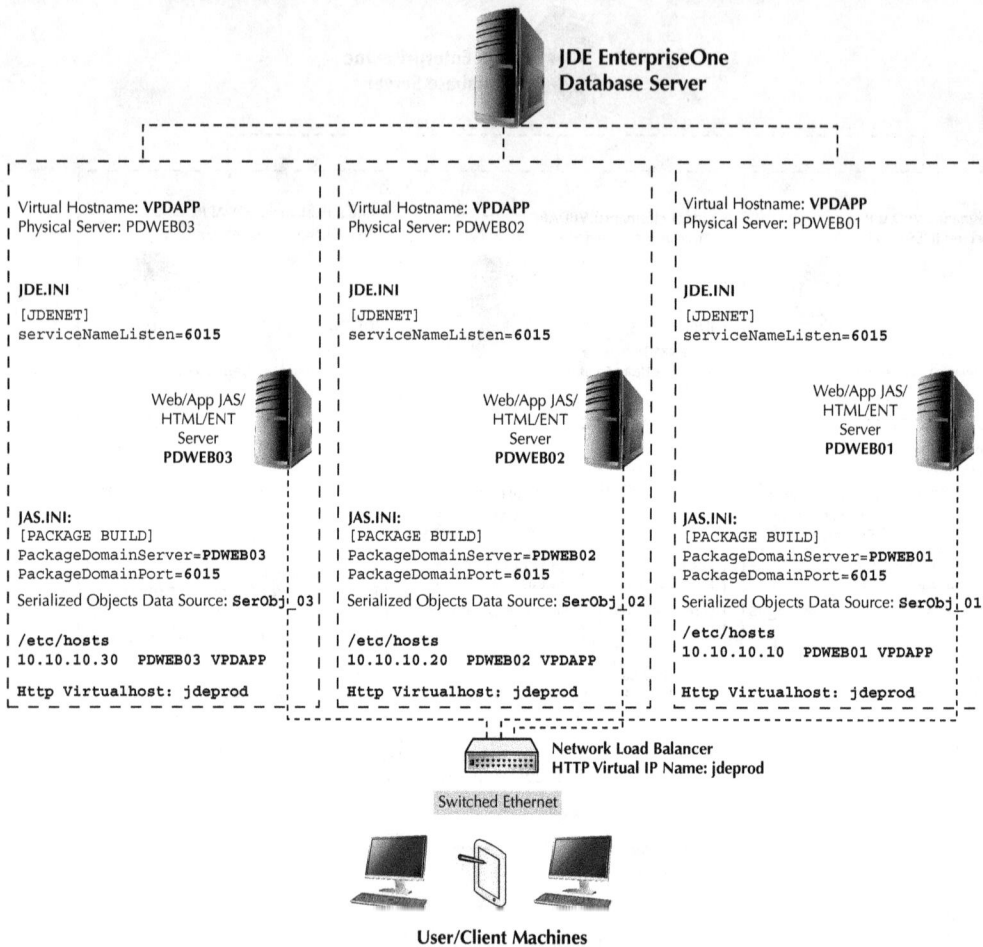

FIGURE 13-9. *Web/application server example*

We typically see between 75 and 200 users per server with this configuration. If you use it, you should limit the number of users so you don't have too many affected in case of a failure. Every customer is different regarding what that number should be, but if you do group them in the 75 to 200 user range you can estimate capacity and scalability pretty easily and allow for failures of a server as well. This option can help simplify your architecture by reducing the number of servers you have to maintain, whether it's in a physical or a virtualized configuration.

NOTE
We have heard some enterprise architects state that this is not a "pure" design, because the presentation layer is not separated from the application logic. But we maintain that this is not the case, since the web application server is running Java code, which does a number of application logic events and database lookups. Granted, the heavier database and calculation type of code is done in the C business function logic, but we are running application logic.

UBE/Batch

A UBE batch server that uses a network load balancer can operate similarly to the application/logic server examples in the preceding section. One difference if they are separate is that the VIP definition may be able to use either persistence/sticky IP or it may spray the connections without persistence. Since a UBE submission is generally a request that is transmitted once, you don't normally need to maintain persistence. However, it is definitely best to test this in your configuration, because you may find that some persistence is needed. The batch server can receive requests from web servers and/or other parent UBE servers that launch child jobs asynchronously.

The JDENet communication tends to keep a communication channel open once it is started and does not add JDENet connections unless the others are busy. You can see this behavior from Server Manager when you examine an HTML instance for the JDENet status and observe the number of JDENet socket connections. The first connection tends to have the most messages read/written and the counts are lower progressively down the list, since this is an indirect measure of concurrent activity.

Figure 13-10 shows an example of a set of batch servers that handle web requests and use a parent/child group of servers for UBE load balancing as well.

To make it easier to view batch reports in this configuration, you can share the server map tables for the batch servers, assuming they are all on the same OS platform. By using the same set of server map tables, you can view all the reports across those servers.

Custom Modification

They can be viewed individually by host name or via a custom modification to P986110B. The Work Submitted jobs application can allow you to see all the jobs submitted and view their PDFs or logs. This modification assumes that you have a virtual server name defined and the change simply replaces the server name with an * to allow searching for all entries in the server map F986110 table. Using this modification allows you to keep the original functionality and it searches all hosts only if the default OCM UBE or virtual server name is used. It should work for even

Example Web & UBE Virtual Server Names with Hardware Load Balancers

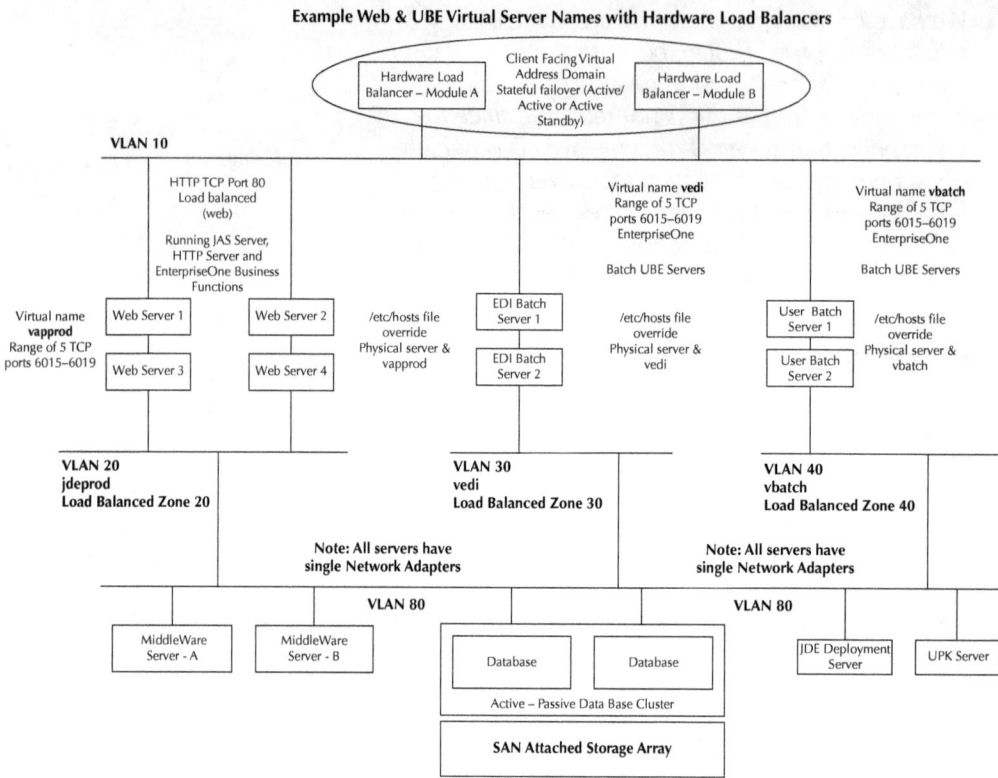

FIGURE 13-10. *UBE/batch example*

the current EnterpriseOne 9.1 code since it simply changes a form variable. In fact, if you examine the latest P986110B in EnterpriseOne 9.1, you may find that it already performs this type of function by default.

The custom modification changes the execution host name when it is passed a virtual server name such as VAPPPD or VBATCHPD to an * to allow viewing multiple servers within the same server map set of tables (F986110). If a server is manually selected or the default UBE OCM mapping has a non-load-balanced server set, it will use that server name instead. (We assume that you have JD Edwards development experience to make this type of modification.)

Here are the general steps for making this custom modification:

1. Go into OMW to modify the base object.

2. Add P986110B to a custom project.

3. Check out P986110B and go into Form Design Aid.

4. Highlight the Submitted Job Search Section and right-click and choose Edit ER.

5. Add the following code in event rule to the + Dialog is Initialized section. Change the comments to your name and virtual host(s) as well and review this code. (This code example is for a slightly older applications release so it may look different depending on the release you are using.)

```
Added the following lines to this section before the SAR 2760919
comment
// 06072007 FJordan Set Host to * instead of server name when a
load balanced
// virtual server name
If FC Execution Host Name is equal to "VAPPPD,VBATCHPD"
      FC Execution Host Name = "*"
End If
// 06072007 FJordan End of Changes
```

6. Save, test, and check in your code.

In Figure 13-11 you can see the code change in the EnterpriseOne Form Design Aid (FDA) Event Rules editor as a reference point to help a CNC relate to where the code is being modified.

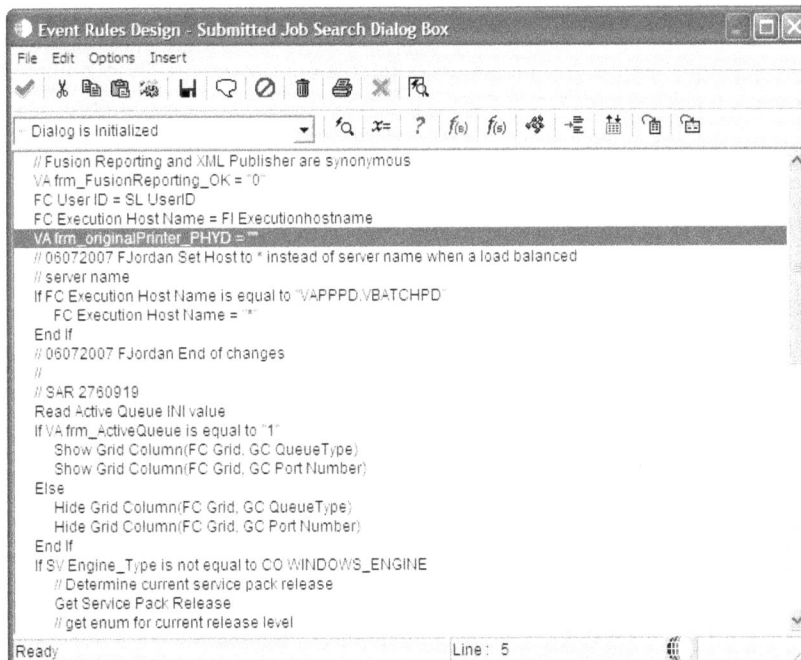

FIGURE 13-11.   *Example code snippet for virtual load balancer*

NOTE
Some customers have used a custom database trigger on the F986110 to change the server name to the virtual name, but we don't recommend this strategy, because you lose the history of which server the UBE was running on. This also requires that you ensure that the PrintQueue folder under the [Network Queue Settings] *stanza for* OutputDirectory= *on all the batch servers' JDE .INI goes to a common shared folder to access the PDF/log files. This is again not one of those "right or wrong" choices, but an option. We avoid database triggers when possible since it is another layer we have to maintain and is not always evident to the CNC support.*

UBE Load Balancing

Another form of load balancing that can utilize network appliances is to create a custom UBE parent that can pass a data selection to child UBEs to split the workload to multiple jobs and perhaps servers. This leverages the power of multiple batch servers and jobs to divide a large amount of work, such as invoices, into concurrent streams to be processed. As long as a unit of work is maintained for data integrity, you can consider this approach. One method that functional users utilize for UBEs is to split the job into multiple batch versions. This works well if the changes are fairly static and you don't have hundreds or even thousands of versions to maintain. In fact, this is one of the primary methods used to divide a larger business process into smaller, more manageable segments.

If you have a set of batch jobs with hundreds of versions that you need to change each month for a processing option, for example, you may want to examine a more customized and automated approach. Also, if you have hundreds of thousands to millions of invoice lines to process in a certain batch window, you may not be able to achieve this with 10 or 15 batch versions running concurrently. If your architecture is designed for large concurrent batch activity, you may be able to leverage UBE load balancers.

Most UBE load balancers are custom-developed processes, but you'll find a good example within EnterpriseOne that you can examine as a template for other situations. Starting with EnterpriseOne 8.10, there is a Sales order update load balancer called R42820. Its purpose is to evaluate the processed invoices, and based on processing option directives, it will launch multiple R42800 Sales update versions to run concurrently. R42820 will append to the R42800 batch version specifying a data selection with an invoice number range, so the unit of work is just a subset of the total number of invoices to process. This helps reduce and minimize the potential for record locks and blocks in most situations. A good Metalink document that provides background information regarding this UBE is "E1: 42: Load Balancer (R42820) UBE (R42800)" (Doc ID 659060.1). Another example for MRP processing is the parallel subsystem procedure referenced in Metalink "E1: 34: Parallel Processing for MRP R3482/R3483" (Doc ID 626115.1).

Your data can greatly influence how efficient and effective a UBE load balancer will be. The R42820/R42800 example works very well when a broad range of customers have been invoiced. However, if your invoices are mainly for one or two customers, you may find (depending on your processing configuration) that the database locking and blocking increases.

Here's an example in this particular scenario: Suppose you have 100,000 invoices, and 75,000 are going to the same customer. If the customer master record is the same in all the invoices and you have ten R42800 jobs running, you may observe blocking on the F03012 customer master table since each job might need to update the same customer master record.

This is another reason that we stress the need for performance and scaling testing using actual data where possible. You may have to perform several tests/ executions to determine the best concurrent job levels, which are heavily influenced by your server infrastructure and data. In some cases, you may even observe some deadlocks since R42800 utilizes transaction processing extensively. The strategy there is to run a "sweeper" R42800 UBE that would process any rolled back transactions after all the child R42800 jobs have completed. This procedure also gives you an indirect measure of how much contention is present if there are pages of invoices remaining in the sweeper job (that is, if no contention, there are no invoices in the sweeper PDF report). If you had more variation in the customer numbers, the likelihood for this particular situation would be reduced considerably. A number of strategies can be employed to optimize the concurrent UBEs once you identify the characteristics of the data and how the processing options influence the business logic.

One method to create a custom load-balancer UBE is to segregate the data into manageable chunks, or batches, and use multiple asynchronous calls to an update UBE using these data selections. The calls must be made asynchronously, meaning multiple calls to submit the update UBE can be made while the load-balancer UBE is still running. You can obtain a number of ideas by examining how the R42820 and R42800 work together.

Within the following definitions, the term *Parent UBE* will refer to the custom load-balancer UBE and *Child UBE* will refer to the called update UBE being executed concurrently. To accomplish this goal, the following UBE objects need to be created or modified:

■ A custom batch application (*Parent UBE*) that counts the records required for the update UBE. This processing identifies the range of records to be asynchronously submitted for each execution of an update UBE (*Child UBE*). The *Parent UBE* will make successive calls to the *Child UBE*. The call to the *Child UBE* will utilize a range of records based on From/To values (Example: From/To Order Number, Shipment Number, and so on).

■ A batch application (*Child UBE*) that uses values in a report interconnect to run the Data Selections provided by the *Parent*. This UBE can be a copy of an existing UBE or an updated production UBE, with modifications specific to the calling requirements.

High-level overview

■ The *Parent UBE* will count and break by some value, such as an order or shipment number. Each call to the *Child UBE* involves passing a From and To value using a Report Interconnect Data Structure. This helps keep the process simplified when coding is performed

■ Data Selection should be assigned to the *Parent UBE* version. Data selection for a called *Child UBE* is internally set to match the data selection from the *Parent UBE* version. The *Child UBE* will ignore the parent's data selection if it is overridden at runtime. To avoid this situation, different versions of the *Parent* UBE should be created and run as-is. Security can be placed on the versions to prevent runtime overrides of the data selection.

■ If the *Child UBE* is called from the *Parent UBE*, which is the standard for this process, the *Child UBE* data selection defaults from the *Parent UBE,* so you won't need multiple child versions to be created. You typically will want a matching parent-to-child set of versions to track the names a bit easier. Example: R55LB001/SCH0010 parent and R554981/SCH0010 for child UBE.

■ *Child UBEs* can also be executed directly but this is not recommended in this customized process. If you run the *Child UBE* directly, any data selection assigned to the *Child UBE* version or overrides at runtime would be used because user specs remain from the last execution and since an asynchronous submission does *not* override the version specs. This is similar to what occurs for scheduled batch versions as no user override specifications are submitted.

■ If multiple *Parent UBE* versions are created with different data selection, caution must be exercised to prevent data selection overlap of the records. If not addressed, this can result in multiple updates of the same records by the *Child UBEs,* causing unexpected or undesired updates to the data.

Figure 13-12 illustrates a high-level overview of the interaction between the Parent UBE and the children it submits asynchronously. Here's what happens:

1. The load-balancer UBE (*Parent*) reads the input table based on data selection and counts the number of records to be processed.

2. A calculation is made to determine the number of submissions of update UBE (*Child*) to be performed. This calculation is based on the number of records to process and the number of threads/jobs requested in Processing Option.

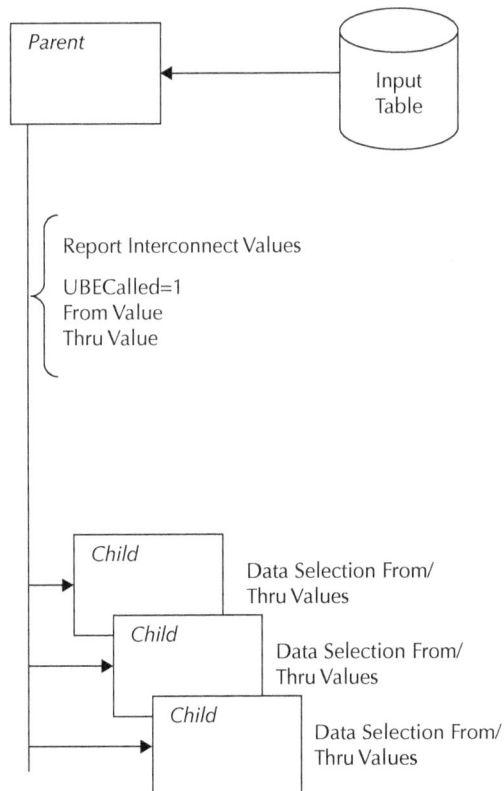

FIGURE 13-12. *High-level overview of custom UBE load balancer*

The actual number of submissions may not match the number of threads due to the number of records selected to process. This determination is based on a "Minimum Records to Process per Thread" value entered in Processing Option.

3. The input table is read again, based on the original data selection, in proper sequence, based on the count requirement (that is, by Order Number, Shipment Number, and so on). When a proper break is encountered, based on the record count, *Child* is called asynchronously, which starts to process immediately. The beginning and ending values to process are passed with the report interconnect call.

4. *Child* selects records from the input table based on the initial data selection, which is copied from *Parent* and passed in number range (that is, From/Thru Order Number, Shipment Number, and so on).

5. Standard update processing is performed on selected records.

One additional reason for the asynchronous submission is that it allows you to direct the Child UBEs to a load-balanced VIP using an OCM UBE mapping in the server map table. (You need the entry in the server map because the Parent UBE is running on a server.) If the Parent UBE server has a /etc/hosts definition for the Child UBE VIP or it is defined in the DNS, you can use this configuration.

TIP
If you are using a VIP load-balanced set of batch servers, you should run the Parent UBE on a batch server that is not in the children's VIP load-balanced group. If you submit enough Child UBEs to the same server as the Parent, you run the risk of the same JDENet port being used. Essentially, the Parent UBE is submitting on the same JDENet port for the Child that is in use. Depending on how many children you submit and the number of JDENet network processes, you may see this occur intermittently. If you have ten JDENet network processes, you would have to submit at least ten Child UBEs on the same server to observe the potential concern. Utilizing separate servers between the Parent and Child UBEs eliminates this potential issue.

Business Services

Business Services (BSSV) can operate similarly to HTTP web clients regarding the incoming HTTP side. You can cluster and/or use a network load balancer to distribute the HTTP requests, and since they are usually single requests, you may not need to use session persistence. Always test for your particular situation, of course, to ensure that the requests are balanced and working as desired.

A Metalink document, "JD Edwards EnterpriseOne BSSV Cluster Project Result Analysis" (Doc ID 1296931.1) provides some good background information regarding an example WebLogic-clustered configuration. If you have a network load balancer, you could use separate JVMs and ports defined for the VIP to direct the requests to in case you are not using Oracle WebLogic server clustering or IBM WAS Network deployment. You might also want separate HTTP servers for high availability and redundancy.

NOTE
If you use a virtual logic server definition, the Package Domain settings for business services are in the jdeinterop.ini since there is no JAS.INI file. The stanza works similarly to the JAS HTML definition to allow you to specify the physical server for the XML specifications that should be loaded.

If you have UBEs that access BSSVs, they use the JDENet communication, which is TCP. If you ensure that one JVM is running a BSSV instance per server, you can consider using a network load balancer for the TCP sessions, because if you attempt two or more JVMs on the same server, you will receive an incoming JDENet "port in use" message on the BSSV instances that start after the first one grabs the port. They have to use the same JDENet incoming port unless you want to direct certain users to a BSSV server via OCM. You might be able to utilize a network load balancer's port

Additional Custom UBE Load Balancer Considerations

Some other areas to note when using a UBE load balancer is that the increased number of UBE version executions can increase the number of PDFs and work center messages created. This can become a management challenge if you need to see a consolidated view of the PDFs since you may now have 20 or more created. Also checking work center messages, if needed, can take more time since there are additional executions to review. These potential challenges will depend on whether you need a consolidated PDF to view, since most customers use some type of additional printing. Examples are Oracle BI Publisher or other third-party printing tools that would direct the output to the desired destination(s). Consolidating work center messages, if they are used, might require a custom application and/or UBE to aggregate certain messages. If the messages are directed to an e-mail account, you may utilize different EnterpriseOne user IDs with a dedicated address book number associated for specific UBEs.

translation, but we have not seen this configuration used for JDENet communications. Since this type of activity is used much less often, you may not have to consider whether it needs to be load balanced. A Metalink document with some additional information to consider is "E1: BSSV: Is it possible to have more than one BSSV server for a single environment to load balance?" (Doc ID 871505.1).

The example in Figure 13-13 illustrates using a network load balancer between two BSSV servers, where the Web Services Description Language (WSDL) would have the VIP name and port for the URL it is accessing. The servers have different JDENet incoming ports defined since the TCP side is not load balanced.

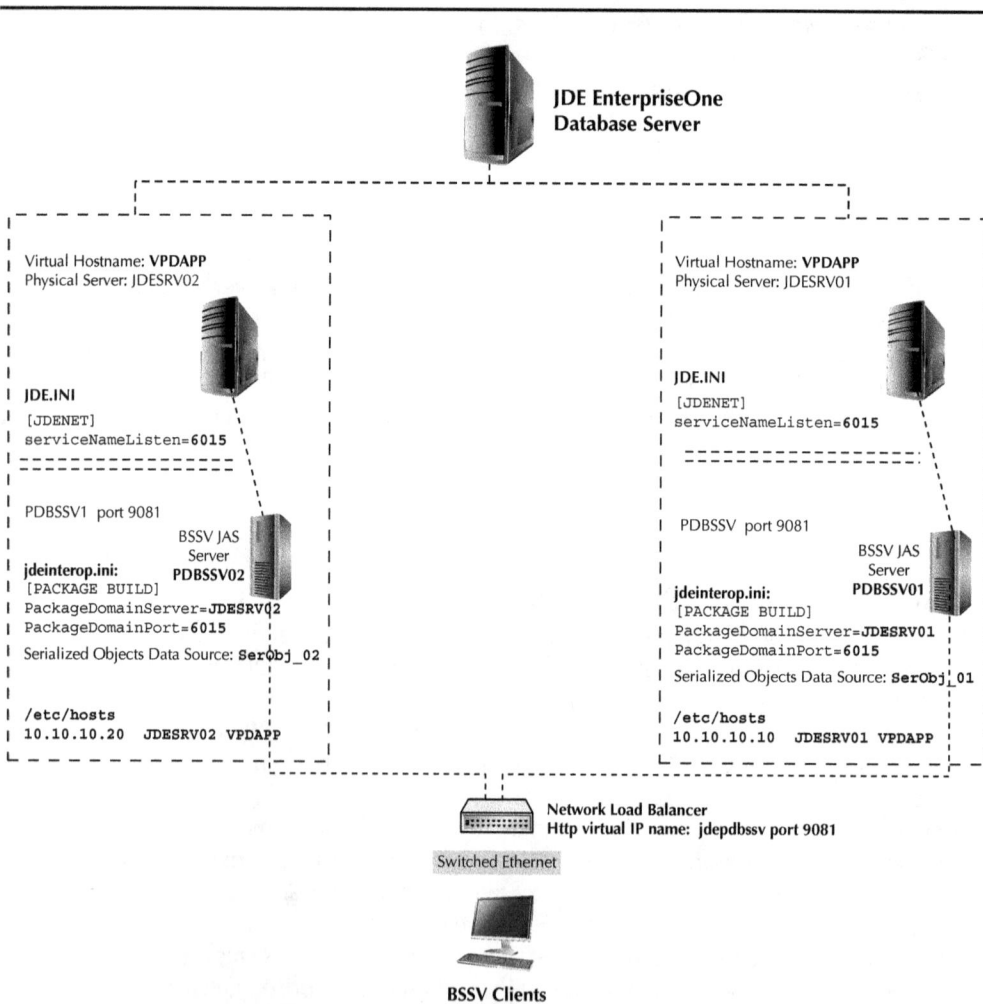

FIGURE 13-13. *BSSV HTTP network load-balanced example*

Summary

Hopefully you have found some ideas for your load-balanced architecture that can help you meet the availability goals of the business. We reviewed several different types of load-balancing configurations that are observed in many EnterpriseOne systems:

- Software solutions such as EnterpriseOne virtual servers, kernel processes, and cluster configurations

- Hardware/software network solutions such as content switches/network appliances

- Load-balancing examples of the various components within your EnterpriseOne architecture

You can see that a number of choices are available, along with quite a bit of flexibility. If you can keep the architecture as clean and straightforward as possible, you'll tend to have the fewest problems. One of the observations we have about JD Edwards CNC architectures is that the advantage of CNC is the flexibility it brings to the table, but that can also be a downfall since you can make it very complex if you take it too far! The old IT acronym of KISS (Keep It Simple Stupid) definitely applies to architecture and code design.

Index

Numbers

128 MB value, PermGen parameter for BSSV, 376
256 MB value, PermGen parameter for BSSV, 376
32-bit and 64-bit versions, of SQL Server, 310–311
528 MB value, PermGen parameter for BSSV, 376

A

access logging, tuning HTTP Server, 155, 385
account privileges/permissions, SQL Server, 317
active/active clusters, 481
active/active virtual name web solution, 482–484
active approach, to database metrics, 267
active/passive cluster virtual name, 477–482
active redundancy, 115
ADDM (Automatic Database Diagnostic Monitor), 295–296
Address Windowing Extensions (AWE), 311
ADF (Application Developer Framework) Server, 399, 401, 403
Administration Console, WebLogic Server, 167–168
Administration tab, Oracle VM Manager 2.2.0, 415–416
Administrative Console, event monitoring
    configuring persistent data store, 386–394
    JDBC stores for migratable targets, 394–395
    overview of, 384–385
    Real-Time Events, 397–399
    viewing data in persistent stores, 395–397
Advanced Mode, JADE, 238–241
AIX operating system, IBM's R/S 6000, 15
AJAX (Asynchronous JavaScript and XML), tuning Internet Explorer, 190
Alarms tab, VMware administrative console, 422, 425
alerts
    AWR (Automatic Workload Repository), 290
    performance information in alert logs, 286–287

alias type names, VIPs, 474–475
Allocate Area, IBM JVM, 179
ALLOCATION_THRESHOLD, tuning WebSphere Server, 173
analysis tools, EnterpriseOne applications, 273–274
API (Application Programming Interface), 100
application code, in top-down performance tuning, 264
Application Developer Framework (ADF) Server, 399, 401, 403
Application ER loops, tuning JAS layer, 157
Application Programming Interface (API), 100
application servers
    enabling verbose garbage collection, 181–183
    in EnterpriseOne Foundation pillar, 94
    horizontal scaling, 128–129
    load balancing, 485, 495–499
application stack, Exalogic Elastic Cloud, 444–446
application tier, tuning, 34–35
applications
    analysis tools, 273–274
    design and development, 276
    Exalogic Elastic Cloud application stack, 444–445
    mobile device security, 402
    tuning user interface pillar, 92–93
architecture
    complexity level examples, 117–120
    components, 120–123
    configuring/validating installation, 135–136
    customizing, 136–137
    defining size of, 126–131
    designing, 132–133
    directing traffic with switches, 138
    in EnterpriseOne environments, 109–110
    extending nodes/resources, 137–138
    implementation types, 109–117
    installing components, 133–135
    mobile, 401–402

511

T

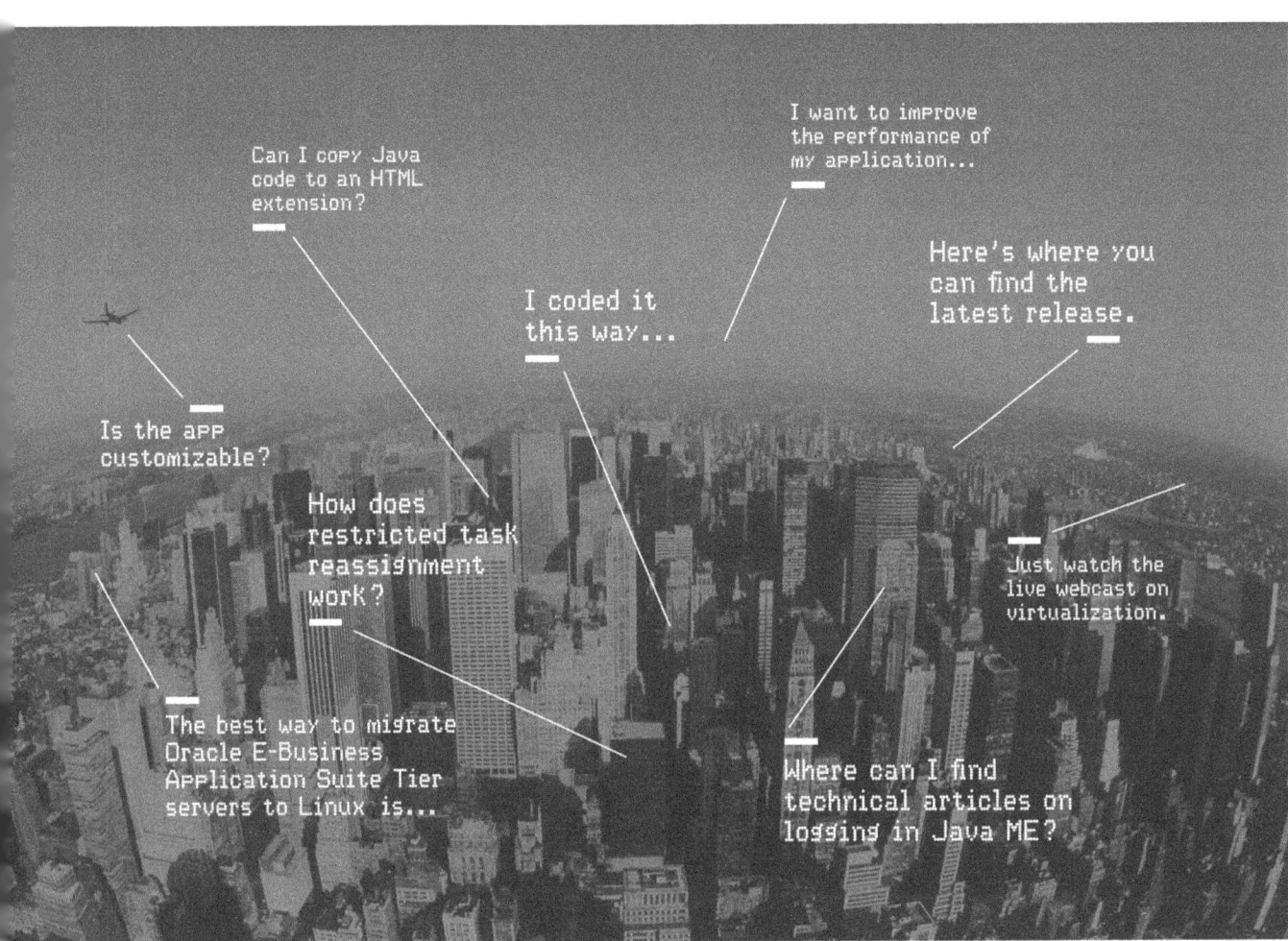

Reach More than 700,000 Oracle Customers with Oracle Publishing Group

Connect with the Audience
that Matters Most to Your Business

Oracle Magazine
The Largest IT Publication in the World
Circulation: 550,000
Audience: IT Managers, DBAs, Programmers, and Developers

Profit
Business Insight for Enterprise-Class Business Leaders to
Help Them Build a Better Business Using Oracle Technology
Circulation: 100,000
Audience: Top Executives and Line of Business Managers

Java Magazine
The Essential Source on Java Technology, the Java
Programming Language, and Java-Based Applications
Circulation: 125,000 and Growing Steady
Audience: Corporate and Independent Java Developers,
Programmers, and Architects

For more information
or to sign up for a FREE
subscription:
Scan the QR code to visit
Oracle Publishing online.